How Big is your GOD?

The Spiritual Legacy of
SAM PATTERSON, EVANGELIST

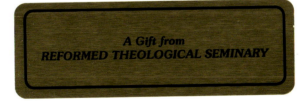

How Big is your GOD?

The Spiritual Legacy of
SAM PATTERSON, EVANGELIST

REBECCA BARNES HOBBS

RTSFCA PUBLISHERS
FRENCH CAMP, MISSISSIPPI

TABLE OF CONTENTS

DEDICATION

This book is prayerfully and humbly dedicated to two individuals who knew Sam Patterson intimately and without whose help the book would never have been written.

Rebecca Patterson Rogers

Becky Rogers is Sam Patterson's only child who has lived in the small community of French Camp, MS for most of her life. Becky attended French Camp Academy and later served on its staff, as well as serving as a teacher and principal of the French Camp Public School for many years. Becky and her husband, Jimmy, have been of immeasurable help in the research and publication of this book.

Lewis A. Graeber, Jr.

Lewis Graeber's father was a long-term chairman of French Camp Academy's Board of Trustees. With the able help of his son Lewis, Jr. (Marks, MS), he was instrumental in Sam Patterson becoming president of French Camp Academy back in 1950. Lewis Graeber, Jr. was a strong member of French Camp's board for over thirty-seven years and was not only responsible for helping keep the school fiscally sound, but also made the initial motion to have *How Big Is Your God?* written. It is unfortunate that this dear Christian leader did not live to see the book finished.

TESTIMONIALS

I always felt that I was just a preacher, just a sinner saved by grace and called to preach the unsearchable riches of Christ I once blasphemed. I did not know that an evangelist and shepherd could be the leader of such a great seminary. However, Sam Patterson has become God's word of "Yes!" to me. But more importantly, and of interest to all of us, his life was used of God to become a catalytic leader of Gospel works that endure not as institutions, but as movements of the Lord. RTS is one of them. That is the greatest tribute I can think of when I think of Sam Patterson; his ministry did not die when he did, for it was of the Spirit.

—Michael A. Milton
Chancellor and CEO-Elect of Reformed Theological Seminary

Above all, Sam Patterson was an evangelist. He was not an academician. He loved the Lord, and he loved the Gospel. More than anything else, he wanted to honor Christ and to make him known to the ends of the world.

—Luder Whitlock
Former President, Reformed Theological Seminary

Norman and I always appreciated the genuineness of Sam's friendship to our family ... never pretentious, but always filled with a Christlikeness that demonstrated a sweet and humble spirit. Norman was a graduate of French Camp Academy and later taught for Sam there, as well as at Reformed Theological Seminary. Norman's love and admiration for Sam increased every year!

—Mary Ida Harper, Widow of
Dr. Norman E. Harper

Mr. Pat's life was the greatest lesson I learned in seminary. His simple, yet profound, ideas; his fervor and love for Christ; his heart filled with ardor and passion for the Savior ... all were a breath of fresh air in an academic setting. He loved the Lord Jesus Christ, and it flowed out of him every time he preached.

—Larry W. Wanaselja (RTS '78)
PCA Pastor Rehoboth, DE

Of all the great preachers we were able to hear as seminary students, no one preached with more authority "and not as the scribes" than did Mr. Pat. You knew he had unshakeable faith in the way he talked.

—Dana W. Casey (RTS '80)
Former PCA Pastor

The time was back in the late 1940s and early 1950s when I was a young high school teenager and a member of First Presbyterian of Jackson, MS. It seemed that every time our church needed a fill-in preacher, the elders would invite Sam Patterson of French Camp Academy. Mr. Patterson had been active on French Camp's Board of Trustees before becoming its president in 1950.

Like most folks who heard Sam Patterson preach and relate heart-warming and exciting stories about French Camp students, I, as a youngster, was spellbound by his preaching and, in my heart, began praying that I might one day become a part of French Camp, working with Sam Patterson and his young people!

That prayer began to be answered in later years. In 1971, I ended up by God's grace as the first business administrator at Reformed Theological Seminary, serving directly under Rev. Sam C. Patterson, founder of RTS and former long-term president of French Camp Academy.

After I'd been blessed through serving under Mr. Pat for ten years (with never a cross word), he retired from RTS early and moved back to French Camp, where his only child, Becky, lived. A year or so after Mr. Pat left RTS, I received a brief long-hand note from Rich Cannon, then president of French Camp, asking if I'd be interested in joining the staff at FCA!

That was the beginning of a twenty-three-year, glorious career in development work with French Camp Academy. During my first four years with FCA, my wife and I did not move to French Camp, but waited until our youngest child was in college. During those four years, I spent many wonderful days with Mr. Pat and/or Rich Cannon, visiting prospective donors about supporting French Camp. After our daughter finally went to college, we moved to French Camp in February 1987 and saw Mr. Pat day in and day out, even attending his small church out in the country on Sundays. After hearing him preach for the second time soon after we'd moved to French Camp, I commented to Sallie, "This is just too good to be true—being here with Mr. Pat and having the rich privilege of attending his church."

Unfortunately, my words proved to be prophetic. We moved to French Camp on January 17, 1987, and Mr. Pat died of a heart attack on March 12, 1987, just two months later!

However, I had had the great blessing of working closely with and for him during those foundational years at RTS, and then similar blessings of working closely with him and in his shadows at French Camp during the next wonderful twenty-three years. During this time French Camp Academy grew tremendously under Rich Cannon's able leadership, clearly into the broad, strong, effective and well-funded institution that Mr. Pat had been dreaming and praying about for so long.

The details of Sam Patterson's influence and ministry during these two sets of years (RTS and FCA) are effectively recorded in this book through the comments, tales, stories and experiences of many, many men, women, and young people who knew and loved Mr. Pat. All of them were interviewed, corresponded with, or researched in an exceptionally able fashion by author Rebecca Barnes Hobbs.

The original idea for this biography came from Lewis A. Graeber, Jr. of Marks, Mississippi, now deceased. He was a long-term friend of Sam Patterson's, as well as a long-term French Camp board member and generous supporter. Mr. Graeber initially thought the book would simply be a rather short and concise history of Mr. Pat's exciting and productive life in building French Camp Academy and founding and building Reformed Seminary—and that the book could be written over a rather short period of time!

The FCA board appointed a three-man committee of Lewis Graeber (Chairman), Ewing Carruthers (Memphis) and Ed Williford to get this unique book written and distributed. In seeking a writer and editor for the book, Mr. Graeber contacted Dr. Luder Whitlock, then president of Reformed Seminary, who recommended the editor of RTS's *Reformed Quarterly*, Rebecca Hobbs. She seemed just right to the committee.

When Rebecca began her research and interviews for the book her basic outlook and plans changed. This would be no short, quickly written book! Once she had interviewed numerous French Camp faculty and graduates, Reformed Seminary faculty and graduates, and numerous older Christian men and women who had known Mr. Pat, Rebecca slowly came to realize the uniqueness and the size of the giant Christian character about whom she was writing.

The deeper she dug, the more she found herself challenged to more interviews, more research, and more time in recording for posterity the depth and breadth of how God had used this dedicated spiritual leader in building His Kingdom here on earth. Unfortunately, Mr. Graeber did not live to see his idea, and Becky's excellent work, become a reality.

I hope that no one reading this foreword will put this book down until having read it in full. What a blessing! You will both weep with joy and laugh in fun!

Ed H. Williford

─────── ACKNOWLEDGMENTS

Some say raising a child requires a village. I don't believe it. However, I do believe with all my heart that writing a book demands a small city. A simple "thank you" seems a paltry offering for all the valuable help I have received, but I give it with deep gratitude.

We are all indebted to Lewis Graeber, Jr., who had the original idea for a biography of Sam Patterson. I owe profound thanks to Sam's daughter, Becky, and her husband, Jimmy, who provided me with a wealth of information and let me keep it for years. Becky even traveled to Arkansas with me to visit with Sam's few living relatives and see his boyhood haunts in Morrilton.

Many thanks to those who wrote, called, or emailed comments and stories to me, as well as those who endured personal interviews (sometimes multiple ones). I called on scores of people for help in almost every conceivable fashion, and many went far beyond the call of duty. Special thanks to Marjorie Adams, Bill Barnes, Pons Bautista, Bruce Broomfield, Brother Ron Linkins, Ralph Buchanan, Bill Bynum, Bill Caruso, Bess Corbitt and her son Arthur, Tommy Covington, Philip Feltis, Caroline Franck, Bill Garrett, David Gill, Jerome Gutierrez, Ben Hailey, Bert Henry, Becky Keith, Erma Lawson, Frances Leavitt, Melissa McCoy-Bell, Ken McMullen, Otis Millenbine, Carolyn Mounce, Bill Parker, Guy Richardson, Jim Robertson, Charlie Rodriguez, Bill Short, Paula Skreslet, Jim Stegall, Lane Stephenson, Billy Stevens, Pat Tillery, David and Ann Vincent, Luder Whitlock, and Patricia Wingler.

The chapter on Sam's war experiences would have been about three pages long were it not for the gallantry of several Marines. James "Rip" Collins provided invaluable help on Zamboanga, and Jack Mimnaugh loaned me extensive material on the China years. Thanks also to Harold Stephens for kind permission to use several thrilling excerpts from *Take China: The Last of the China Marines* (Garberville, California: Wolfenden Publishers, 2002, www. wolfendenpublishing.com.). I can see why the Marine motto is Semper Fidelis— Always Faithful.

Similarly, the Martinsville years would be dull indeed were it not for Buck Powell, a delightful, energetic octogenarian who helped me immensely. Meeting you, sir, was one of the highlights of this project!

The trustees of both Reformed Theological Seminary and French Camp Academy deserve praise for their patience and farsightedness in allowing me the time to follow my vision for the book. Particular thanks to RTS Chancellor Ric Cannada for reading the manuscript and making timely suggestions. French Camp provided me with a Gulf Coast cottage in which to write, and RTS gave me an office in the library for many months. Special appreciation goes to RTS Library Director Ken Elliott and his assistant, Mac McCarty, for meeting my every need. Ken, thank you also for valuable historical perspective in our many conversations. RTS archivists John Crabb and David Ponter were longsuffering and will surely be glad my incessant knocks on their doors have ceased; thank you both for all the research (and microfilm) help you gave this novice historian.

I worked closely with five genuinely special people to get this book published, and every minute of the journey was a delight. Ed Williford kept us all superbly on track, always believed in my approach to this project, and convinced others to believe. Ed, you truly went as far as you could in the right direction. Sam would be proud.

Mary Courtney Sorensen proofed copy endlessly and spent hundreds of hours getting the manuscript ready to print. Your eagle eye, Mary, is unmatched, as is your kind and pleasant personality.

Hannah O'Brien did a masterful job graphically, designing a beautiful cover and pleasing layout. What a joy to work with!

Dr. Richard de Witt carefully read the manuscript and offered valuable perspective and editorial help. Thank you for your godly wisdom and for saving me from much embarrassment!

Sandi Tucker Kooistra is one of the best transcriptionists I have ever had. Sandi, thank you for your attention to detail, your passion for this material, and your sweet nature. You made my job so much easier!

Most importantly, I appreciate my family for sharing me with this book for all these years. To my children, Caroline, Turner, Kirby, and Mitchell, I offer deep thanks for your blessing on this work and for living patiently in its shadow for a decade. Finally, to my faithful and loving husband, Van, goes the most gratitude for all the ways you helped me get this project done. What would I do without you? For over thirty years, you have stood by me stalwartly through every circumstance, encouraging me to fly free and follow God's leading. You always see a "better me" in me, and for that I am profoundly grateful to God.

The first time I saw Sam Patterson, I was a young seminary student at RTS in 1976. There he was, in the middle of the Student Center, down on one knee, head bowed and ear pressed to a telephone receiver, praying earnestly with someone. He seemed oblivious to the students busily passing to and fro, some even brushing against him. They, too, seemed not to think his posture odd at all. Even though I had been brought up in the church, I had never seen someone pray with such immediacy, such boldness, such passion. Come to think of it, I haven't since then either.

As the years rolled by, I marveled at this unusual seminary president—a kind, humble man who lived in a camper in the RTS parking lot and prayed with people anywhere, any time. Surely he was very different from anyone I had ever encountered.

I didn't know him personally, but I wish heartily that I had because I owe him a great deal. RTS and those connected with it have been a major part of my life for over a quarter of a century. I was a student there, met my husband there, was married by Dr. Wallace Carr in Grace Chapel, and worked for the seminary for almost twenty years.

I always wanted to know more about this singular individual. My curiosity was especially piqued when, as editor of RTS's *Reformed Quarterly*, I had to write accounts of the seminary's beginnings. However, I could find only the most general sort of information, even from Sam himself, about his involvement in RTS's genesis. I now know that Sam intentionally hid his leadership during those early years and urged others writing about the seminary to do the same.

One of my missions in writing this book was to discover, once and for all, what happened during those pivotal years. After much research, I pieced together seminal events occurring from 1963-1966, the three years prior to RTS's opening. With this, I wrote the chapter on RTS, even though I knew a great deal was missing. Then, as if God said, "Enough is enough," Sam's personal scrapbook of letters and documents from 1963-1966 providentially surfaced about three years ago. It contained so much heretofore unpublished material concerning Sam's involvement that the entire RTS chapter had to be rewritten.

Similarly, writing about Sam's early life was far from easy. Although Sam's daughter, Becky Rogers, was extremely helpful with a wealth of information, many relatives and friends were dead or unable to communicate with me. Imagine my joy when Becky showed me Sam's childhood diary, much of which

I have preserved for you in its original form. Finally, had God not provided a lovely gentleman named Buck Powell in Martinsville and a helpful group of Marines all over the country, we would know next to nothing about Sam's years in Virginia and his war experiences.

Early on, I discovered that Sam's sermons across the years are replete with personal experiences from his very earliest memories. I was able through several sources and kind individuals to dig up about one hundred of his messages. I listened to them all, some several times. Many of the most interesting passages in the book are from those sermons. I didn't realize that, in addition to providing critical information, they would change my life.

Happily, that dear Arkansas twang still rings out today. Compelling and alive, Sam's sermons reverberate with God's jealous love for the souls of man and His tender call to repentance. You can listen to or download a number of them free of charge at www.sermonaudio.com and www.thirdmill.org.

Even though tracking down information about Sam has been a challenge, God has kept my enthusiasm for the project high through the years. Always, just as I felt I had reached a dead end, He unearthed a new find and gave me fresh hope. I still feel that much of what we'd like to know went to heaven with Sam, and it was merely God's grace that allowed us to discover what we did. You can ask Sam any unanswered questions when you get to Glory!

While writing the book, I constantly had two groups of people in mind—those who knew Sam well and those who didn't know him at all. In my heart, I dedicate this book to both groups. If you knew Sam, you already realize you were blessed beyond measure. The book is a sacred offering to help you remember and savor the beauty of his life and his relationship with you. For those of you who didn't know Sam, I tried to paint him vividly so that in some way you might comprehend the tremendous power and faith of this unusual individual. I hope I succeeded in some small way. However, describing Sam Patterson on paper is much like trying to paint a sunset in black and white—you lose a lot. Sam often rued his inability to speak of Christ as effectively as he wanted; in the same way, I lament my often inadequate attempt to draw the larger-than-life person Sam was.

More than any other material with which I have worked, this had a life of its own. It virtually pulsated with tremendous spiritual energy that crept into my very soul. I am not the same person I was when I began working on this book. Even though I have been a Christian for thirty-four years, Sam has helped me to know God's love and care in a much deeper, more beautiful way. He has convinced me that I am indeed a new creature with the limitless power of the Holy Spirit to conform to Christ's image. He taught me that God does own the cattle on a thousand hills (Psalm 50:10) and that I can live my life with an open, generous hand to channel His unending bounty. All of this from a man I never knew and who has been dead these twenty-three years. Indeed, "He being dead yet speaketh."

Sam's ministry lives on in so many other ways. Month after month at French Camp, deserving youngsters continue to enjoy life-changing Christian love and guidance. The French Camp Singers performed at my church recently, and I realized yet another generation of children have been saved because of Sam's faith in God back in the 1950s. As RTS graduates move out into the world each year, thousands of people across the globe continue to be influenced for Christ.

Anytime a person spends his life living so consistently in Christ's image, his story deserves to be told if for no other reason than to help the rest of us get it right. Sam would be the first to object that his life was any such thing. While he would not be in favor of a work singing his praises, I think he could stomach some of that if the book sought to lift up His Savior. This I have tried to do. If anything in this volume brings Christians the least bit closer to Christ or ushers someone out of darkness into a saving knowledge of Him, Sam would say the time and effort to write it was worth it. I would, too. When we meet in heaven, I believe he will still shake my hand.

Rebecca Hobbs
Madison, Mississippi
August, 2010

The silhouettes of a few Joshua trees caught my attention. They looked lonely on the horizon of the Arizona desert. If there had been many of them, I might have missed the artistry and impact of the one that stood out because of its magnificent, up-reaching arms.

Legend says that the Joshua tree is so named because it resembles arms stretched upward in prayer. It has been described as a sullen tree that moves only slightly and rather awkwardly when the wind grabs it, somewhat like a stubborn man in adverse circumstances.

Much like the Joshua tree, Reverend Sam Patterson was strong and unyielding in the winds of world pressures, and he was truly a giant in the power of the Holy Spirit. We are surrounded by run-of-the-mill, sagebrush Christians, but only a few Joshua trees stand erect with their faith in almighty God.

How blessed is the one who meets a Joshua tree in the course of his walk through this life! How blessed, indeed, am I to have had Reverend Sam Patterson as my friend and mentor.

Ladell "Dell" Flint
French Camp Academy ('52)

CHAPTER ONE

THE EARLY YEARS
1916–1934

I can hear the bullfrog callin' me,
Wonder if my rope's still hangin' to the tree.
Love to kick my feet 'way down in shallow water...
Shoofly, dragonfly, get back to mother.
Pick up a flat rock, skip it across Green River...

"Green River"
Creedence Clearwater Revival

I bet I have to stand in the corner more than any kid in school.
Sammy Patterson, 1929

Thirteen-year-old Sammy Patterson slammed into his room and threw his schoolbooks on the bed. Today had definitely not been a red-letter day for him, even though the unruly shock of hair he sported was indeed deep crimson. It had really started yesterday when he got an F in science by not bringing his paper to class. Doggone that old Miss Coleman! How he hated school!

Reaching for the diary he had started just a few days before, he began pouring out his frustration:

Nov. 19, 1929—brite and fair and cold as time. My science teacher is Miss Coleman. I got an F yesterday for not bringing my paper to class. Today she threatened to lick me for lagheing at a joke I read in class. No fites today. I had to sit up strait in a chair in English for laughing and I wasn't the only one laughing eather. Miss Coleman has it in for me ever since I stepped on her toe and didn't say 'Excuse me.' I didn't no I stepped on her old toe. After supper I'm going down to the corner to see the state cops pinch folks whos cars have no tail lights.

Sammy read over his entry, satisfied that he had intentionally misspelled a sufficient number of words. He had also noted that the weather was "brite and fair and cold," just as Mr. Henry Shute had given the weather report in every entry in *The Real Diary of a Real Boy* and its sequel *Bright and Fair*. Those were bully books!

The more he thought about it, the more he liked the idea of keeping a diary. He and Ralph Hellums had read the books together, and Ralph had asked his dad for the beautiful 5x7 green leather USF&G yearbooks. With Hellums Insurance Agency and the year 1928 embossed in gold, they couldn't be smarter diaries!

Turning to the title page, he was a little sorry that it looked so messy with all that erasing. He'd spelled Diary first as "diry" then "dairy" before he finally got it right. But he was proud of the second page. There, in his finest boyish scrawl he had written: "This diary is affectionately detecated to God's greatest gift to me—Mother and Dad. Signed Samuel Coleman Patterson."

And then, there was his first entry just three days ago. Sammy scrutinized it carefully. Too wordy? No, he thought, it contained some bully information:

> *Nov. 16—I am Sam Patterson. I am redhedded. I am 13 years old. My chums are Al Merritt, Doc Bruce, and Dizzy Byname. I am center on the 8th grade football team. We went to Atkins to play there team, but they forfited the game to us. When I got back I went to the scaiting rink and scaited a hour. When I got done I felt sort or dizzy and sick, and Doc ast me if I could come to his house and eat some cake. I wasn't sick any more.*

Sammy lay back on his bed and let his mind drift. I wonder, he thought, if I'll be writing in this diary in ten years—in twenty years? If I do, I wonder what I'll be writing about. Maybe I'll be a famous football or baseball player. Will anyone ever want to read what I've written? Naw, what a crazy notion!

Samuel Coleman Patterson would probably find it highly comical that anyone cares what he wrote half a century ago in this small, tattered volume with the yellow, brittle pages, now in the possession of his daughter, Becky Patterson Rogers. He would likely be embarrassed, too, since throughout his adult life he was an extremely private person and studiously avoided ever calling any attention to himself, desiring always to fade into the background as he pointed others to Christ. In that divine endeavor, he wore many hats across the years— beloved pastor, evangelist, teacher, administrator, mentor, benefactor, and friend. Thousands grew to love and admire him, counting their relationships with him among their most cherished.

Yet, even those who felt the closest to Sam admit they knew virtually nothing about his life history or his childhood. Most seemed mildly surprised when asked, as if Sam's earlier life had nothing to do with their relationships with him. And, quite likely, that was exactly the case. Sam's friendships during his adult life ultimately revolved around two things: either fellowshipping with other Christians for mutual edification or sharing Christ with an unbeliever, seeking to deepen that person's commitment. Almost never did he afford anyone even a glimpse of his personal life, because doing so would have taken the focus off of Christ and put it on Sam Patterson. This he strove mightily to avoid. About ten years before his death, Sam said, "I don't think it's right for men to write an autobiography unless it's put under lock and key until their death to let some one else write the last chapter. If I were Billy Graham, I'd want all of 'em burned up. We don't know what the last chapter on Billy Graham or you or me will be. We haven't gone all the way yet."[1]

Well, Sam has gone all the way now, and we've had over two score years to think about his sojourn on this earth. It's high time to pull back the shroud and examine the life of a man to whom hundreds owe their entrance into God's Kingdom. Our first glimpse is a little tow-headed tyke named Sammy almost a century ago in a small town in Colorado.

FORT MORGAN, COLORADO

Sam began life out West, born in 1916 in the shadow of the Rocky Mountains. A year earlier his parents, Samuel Jasper and Lily Patterson, had moved their family to Fort Morgan, Colorado, where Samuel Jasper ("S. J.") had accepted a pastoral call to First United Presbyterian Church (United Presbyterian Church in North America). It was his third pastorate, the first outside the Associate Reformed Presbyterian (ARP) denomination.[2] Delivered by a midwife at home, Sam was born at 11:55 p.m. on July 8, 1916, the youngest of seven children and "a red-headed Westerner in every sense of the word, who was destined to be a source of joy and happiness to his parents when their older children left home."[3] He inherited his father's red hair and was named for him, even though an older brother had already been named Samuel, too. The family solved the problem by calling the oldest son "Jap" and nicknaming the youngest "Sammy." In between were Grier, Foster, Lois, and Hugh Morris.

The country was at war, but the thundering guns seemed not to reach this tiny hamlet nestled on the banks of the Platte River, some seventy-five miles east of Denver and tucked into the heart of the heavy-yielding sugar beet country. We don't know much about Sam's life during these years, but we do know the family enjoyed their time there. They went with some misgivings, especially about the weather. S. J. had been reared in Mississippi and Lily in Arkansas, and all their pastorates had been in the South, so they had seldom seen snow or felt the chilling blasts of subzero weather. Instead, they were accustomed to rolling hillsides covered with dense forests and fields of white cotton. Yet, we can imagine Sammy and his siblings reveling in the winter sports that abound in such climates.

S. J. and Lily also wondered how they would fit in with northern and western people, but their fears proved groundless. His congregation grew and prospered, for the westerners liked to hear a minister who spoke with a southern drawl. Samuel Jasper, in his autobiography, *One Man's Family*, said:

> *We were never received more graciously or treated more kindly anywhere. We came to like the ways of northern and western people. On the surface they seem more blunt and abrupt than southern folks, but they are more sincere and democratic. They do not wear the 'front' nor indulge in the blarney that we of the South deal in so much. Being the only southern family in the town gave us a unique position that carried quite a bit of prestige.[4]*

The year of Sam's birth was also the year the Patterson family bought its first car, a Ford. The church burned in 1919, and the family had to move from 224 Kiowa Avenue, where Sam was born, to another manse closer to the location of the new church. No other real records have survived about Sam's first years in this Colorado town, except a few scattered comments in his diary later in his life about friends from Ft. Morgan coming to visit them in Morrilton. One of his favorite visitors was Aunt Hattie Bell Jackson, his mother's sister, for whom he developed a lifelong love. From other records we know that she spent much time in the homes of her siblings and lived with the Pattersons at least a year while teaching school in Ft. Morgan.

Although the Pattersons loved living on these fertile plains, in the fall of 1921 Lily had to undergo major surgery and was in the hospital for six weeks. The bout of sickness weakened her heart and doctors advised S. J. to get her to a lower altitude at once. Had it not been for her illness, five-year-old Sammy would probably have spent his boyhood days in Colorado, not Arkansas.

Samuel Jasper resigned the next Sunday and almost immediately was called to a Presbyterian church in West Point, Mississippi. Coming home to the South of his boyhood seemed natural. S. J. agreed to become stated supply for the congregation but declined to accept a permanent call because it was a federated church composed of Northern, Southern and Cumberland Presbyterians. The family remained in West Point for only a year, but Sam did begin first grade here. The Pattersons occupied a fine new manse. A family scrapbook shows little Sammy with Aunt Mehaley, "Sammy's Boss"; another picture shows Sam and brother Hugh with "Spot," indicating Sam's lifelong love of dogs had already begun.

From West Point, S. J. answered a call in March 1923 from an ARP church in Fayetteville, Tennessee, primarily so his older children could attend the newly established Bryson College. S. J. had been made chairman of the college's board of directors. However, he soon realized that stabilizing the school financially would take a long time; some feared it might not even survive. To stay would be unfair to everyone; his children couldn't attend a school whose credits might not be recognized, and he couldn't live in the city and not patronize the college.

Therefore, in December he accepted a call to First Presbyterian Church (Presbyterian Church in the United States) in Morrilton, Arkansas, and began his pastorate there on January 18, 1924. At seven and a half, little did Sammy know that this small village on the banks of the winding Arkansas River, in the shadow of another mountain—Petit Jean—would offer him the childhood of a young boy's dreams.

MORRILTON, ARKANSAS

Morrilton, Arkansas, is scenic paradise at its best. Locals boast, "The Lord made Morrilton, then, seeing what a great work He had done, built the South around it." Nestled in the foothills of the Ozark and Ouachita Mountains in the northwest part of the state, the town rubs shoulders with the Ozark National Forest to the north and Ouachita National Forest to the south. Hundreds of acres of fine hunting grounds surround the town, while numbers of creeks and streams are brimming with bass and trout. Camping, boating, picnicking, and swimming all vie for attention, especially to a nature-loving young boy like Sammy.

The Arkansas River beckons invitingly, too, as it winds around the south edge of town, nearing the end of its 1,450 mile trek from high in the Rockies to join the Mississippi River. Dotting the river's cool, clear water are numerous long, wide sandbars where Sam and his friends spent many lazy summer days fishing and camping. Yet, they also knew and respected the river's wrath; raging floods such as the ones in 1927, 1935, and 1943 devastated thousands of acres of valuable land, leaving large numbers homeless and causing farmers to lose crops. There are an abundant variety of crops to lose, since the village lies right in the middle of the fertile Arkansas River Valley. Peaches, strawberries, apples, grapes, and watermelons abound.

Although Morrilton is the busy county seat of Conway County, the town's population of 6,000 hasn't changed much since Sam was a boy. At the turn of the century, the dirt streets of downtown Morrilton provided a broad, smooth thoroughfare for travel on foot, on horseback, by horse and buggy, and later by auto—except when seasonal rains turned the streets to hub-deep mud. Paving of the streets began in 1919, just five years before Sam and his family arrived.

Samuel Jasper and Lily settled in at First Presbyterian, located at 105 West Church Street in downtown Morrilton. The couple soon won their way into the hearts of the people of Morrilton, as they had in their other pastorates. They were known and loved by every class of citizens in the community. People felt very at home with the Pattersons' winsome ways and sense of humor; once, S. J. even dressed up as Red Riding Hood at one of Sam's scout banquets. Because of their selfless ministry, the pastorate was quite successful. The church almost doubled in membership and became the most organized and efficient church in the Synod of Arkansas.

We know very little about Sam's early school years in Morrilton, since none of his teachers are still alive, and no records exist. However, it's safe to say they didn't set the town on fire! He entered the second grade at Morrilton Elementary School. At the time, Victor Boren, husband of Sam's first cousin Louise Boren,[5] was superintendent of schools. This couple became precious friends of Sam later in life.

We do have some indication of Sam's irrepressible personality even at that young age. "There probably never was a youngster who attracted as much attention from other people as he, with his red hair, freckled face, and 100 percent American boyhood," wrote his brother Foster.[6] S. J. confessed that little Sammy was hard to keep up with:

> *Sam was inclined to range too far from home when he was a little fellow. One day his mother could not locate him in the neighborhood and became disturbed, lest he might have strayed off and fallen into an irrigation ditch. But I told her that I had an idea where he was. So I drove down to the business section of town and looked in the Busy Bee, an ice-cream confectionery, and there he was sitting on a high stool eating ice cream at the expense of Paul Jones, the proprietor.[7]*

Originally, the manse was right next door to the church, where the public library stands today. However, for unknown reasons, the Pattersons later moved from that location to 300 Southwest Street, right around the corner just south of the church. Sammy surely didn't mind, since it put him a block closer to the woods, creeks, and river just south of town, an area he grew to love. Morrilton is bounded on the south by a hill; beyond or "over" it are the woods, the waterworks, Point Remove Creek, and the Arkansas River. "Going over the hill" either by himself or with friends (and everyone's hunting dog in tow) was a continual pastime, and the hundreds of hours spent in this lush wilderness encouraged a love of nature and the outdoors that lasted throughout Sam's life.

Not until junior high do we learn a lot about Sam as a teenager, and, fortunately for us, it's from his own mouth! In the pages of his small green diary, Sam's teenage years unfold in vivid detail as it paints in bold strokes the man who eventually changed so many lives. Begun on a lark in November 1929, the diary almost vanished as soon as it was begun because of youthful fickleness. We have Sam's mother to thank for its existence:

> *Dec. 25— ... I thought I would quit riting in my diry but mother found it out so here goes ...*

After that first sputter, however, Sam wrote faithfully in it off and on for nearly fifty years, recording all the major moments of a lifetime—births, deaths, marriages, joys, sorrows, hopes. The little volume seemed to become more and more precious to him as the years went by. Sam was quite the artist, and throughout the diary he sprinkled hilarious pen and ink drawings of Buffalo Bill, bodybuilders, cartoon characters, football and baseball players, hunters, and lawmen. Often he tells us where he is as he writes—lying on his bed or on the floor, lounging in the living room listening to hymns on the radio. It's as if he wanted to remember in great detail the small happenings of his life. Curious about the weather in Morrilton at that time? Just consult Sam's diary, at least from 1929 to 1934. Almost every entry records the weather and the exact day and time he wrote in it. During the first year, 1929–1930, the weather might be brite and fair, cold as time, cloudy as Job's terky, clear as crystal, or raining pitch forks. In succeeding years he became more mature and spoke of the weather in less colorful terms.

At times he must have used the diary as a spelling primer. "Woal" and "wuo" scribbled across the page finally emerges as "would." In a postscript written in the diary August 3, 1947, thirty-one-year-old Sam writes:

> *As I recall, my reading of* Brite and Fair *and another printed edition of a boy's diary gave the inspiration that started this diary. All the misspelling is not, therefore, due to my ignorance (though most of it probably is!) but can be credited, especially in the early entries, to my copying the two above-mentioned diaries in their 'funny' phrasing and misspelling. Almost eighteen years have passed since the first entry. Already I have no memory of many of the incidents here recorded. Hence, this poor book has a growing value to me.*

1929

During his childhood, Sam lived through some of the worst times our country has seen. The late 1920s were tumultuous years for the United States. World War I had just ended, and by the fall of that year, the entire U.S. economic structure had crumbled. Sam began his diary just one month after Black Thursday (October 24), when stock prices plummeted, ushering in the Great Depression. The next decade ranked as the longest and worst period of high unemployment and low business activity in modern times and was the first of its kind in the industrialized world. Banks, stores, and factories were closed and left millions of Americans jobless, homeless, and penniless.

People suffered worst during the '30s. The average wage was sixteen dollars a week, and folks did everything they could to earn extra money. Prices dropped dramatically—a dime bought a dozen eggs or a pound of butter, and a dollar bought a chicken.

In Arkansas, bad times had come calling even before 1929. The 1927 flood had wiped out thousands of acres, followed by the 1930 drought, a major factor in the fall of cotton prices to eight cents a pound. Thousands of farms failed.

An auto dealer in northeast Arkansas recalls, "If you didn't live through it, you can't understand how hard it was. We sold a car in September of 1930 and never sold another until spring."[8] Sam probably heard the following ditty often:

> *Put your car in the garage,*
> *Put your seed in the ground,*
> *Put your trust in God, and*
> *Work from sunup to after sundown.*[9]

Some people were even driven to violence because of the hardships. One man was electrocuted for stealing ten gallons of gas.

But God protected Sam's family during the hard times, even if they had few frills. "Daddy's family always lived in manses, and people 'pounded' the preacher, providing them with plenty of food and clothes," explains Becky Rogers. "Anyway, my grandparents and my parents were never concerned with material things. Hard times were hard for everyone, but they were familiar to Dad's family. Daddy was surrounded by devout Christians who worked for God here on earth with no thought of rewards." Ironically, with the world virtually in shambles around him, Sam's biggest problem was how to stay out of the corner at school. Poor Sam! He vented his frustration more than once in the eighth grade:

> *Nov. 20— ...I got sent out of history class this morning for talking by Miss Gordon ...*
> *Nov. 22—partly cloudy cold as time. Had to stand in the corner for talking today.*
> *Nov. 24— ...I bet I have to stand in the corner more than any kid in school. I hope I don't have to tomorrow. Al does nearly as much as me and they never do anything to him.*
> *Dec. 4—I had to stay in till 15 minutes to 6 today by Miss Coleman.*

His enthusiastic spirit always seemed to get him in trouble in school. Marie Jones, a member of First Presbyterian in Morrilton, remembers having him in junior high math. "Mischievous, that's what he was! Smart, but boy did he have a temper! Bless his heart, he knew he had to keep up his part as a member of a minister's family and not get into too much trouble, but you can't blame him for wanting to be a normal child."

Combine Huck Finn, Tom Sawyer, Dennis the Menace, and Calvin (of Calvin and Hobbes fame) and you'd have a faithful portrait of youthful Sam Patterson. A lovable, freckled red-head, he was all boy and a real scrapper. The high point of his day was a fight at school:

Nov. 18—brite and fair and cold as time. There was a bully fite between J. C. somebody and Hat Siers. J. C. said he could make Hat go throguh the belt line and Hat said 'Your a liar!' and J. C. tried it and got licked. Miss Gordon broke it up and then she laught and told them to go play. She's that way, she don't git mad at the least thing, but she sure can use a paddle.

"He was mean as a striped snake and would fight a circular saw—one tough little knot!" recalls his daughter Becky Patterson Rogers, laughing. Uncle Jim, a faithful servant of the family, agreed heartily, once calling Sammy a "minute man," ready to fight in an instant.

And then there were his perennial bad grades, a constant thorn in the flesh. With such a fascinating world to explore, and with hundreds of ducks to be shot, rabbits to be trapped, and fish to be caught, why oh why did he have to be stuck in this boring classroom? By first semester's end in the eighth grade, he reported these discouraging marks:

Dec. 4—I got my report card today. This is it:

	Scolarship	*Deportment*
Math	*D*	*B*
Spelling	*B*	*B*
History	*C*	*B*
Sience	*D*	*C-*
English	*D-*	*C*

"Daddy was smart, but he never applied himself until college," reveals daughter Becky. "Schoolwork wasn't important to him because he was busy with other things. I'll never forget when I first saw one of his report cards with all those Ds! And here was Mother who had to have straight As. He said he made poor grades in grammar and high school before he realized the importance of learning. Later, when he gained a purpose in life, his grades at Southwestern and Union were wonderful."

For someone who did not make good grades early on, Sam certainly became a fine writer and communicator, proving that often grades are not an adequate gauge of talent. Older brothers Grier and Foster were quite studious and may have influenced him eventually. Although his grades were questionable, Sam was always quite popular. He was president of his class in the eighth grade, an office he held several more times in later grades. He also became a favorite pick for school plays, even though he had a hate-love relationship with acting. Perhaps he hated practicing (too much like work), but liked being on stage:

Nov. 20—Tomorrow nit theys going to be a play at the high school. I am in it. Whew. School turned out at 2:45 this evening but I had to practice on that blamed play. I'll be glad when its over.

However, life was glorious when he could escape to his sanctuary, over the hill south of town into the dark woods, the river bank, and creek bottoms beyond. Here he could be Daniel Boone, taking shots at the teeming wildlife, or Hernando Desoto charting new routes through the wilderness. The games were endless:

> *Nov. 23—no school today. Went camping today with Doc and Al. I organized a club named the Doves. Our call is oo oo ooeoo like the doves call. When we do things and leave notes we express ourselves as 'The 3–3s.'*
> *Nov. 29—Doc, Al, and me went hunting with our 22 rifles, only Doc ain't got one. We took our dinner too.*
> *Dec. 30— ...Al and me caught a possum.*

Virtually all of Sam's friends played sports, liked to hunt, enjoyed Boy Scouts, or all three. It's safe to say Sam wasn't a close friend of the class valedictorian. His best friend and constant companion became Allan Merritt, one whom Sam prayed for and kept up with for the rest of his life. In Sam's papers today are notes he and Allan wrote to each other in high school. Attached at the hip, they did everything together, and Allan is on literally every page of Sam's diary. Sam later discovered that "Allan and me is 5th cousins."

A year older than Sam, Allan was not as talented at sports as Sam ("Al ain't much in athletics but a bully kid"). They had their spats, but they didn't last long:

> *Nov. 29, 1929—Al and me had a argument and we ain't ever going to make up.*
> *Nov. 30, 1929—Me and Al has made up.*

In Sam's own words, Allan was always closer to him than any of his four brothers, probably because Sam was so much younger than his siblings. At Sam's birth, his oldest brother, Jap, was graduating from high school; Grier, the next in line, was sixteen; Foster was eleven, sister Lois nine, and Hugh Morris, seven. By the time Sam was ten, he was almost an only child, since Hugh Morris graduated from high school that year and the others were either in college or grown.[10]

Vicki Knapp, Victor and Louise Boren's daughter, says, "Sam was so fine and gentle. He was not like his brothers, who were mostly successful business and career men. Sam's goals were not about money and success. He didn't care about a dime; he'd give you anything he had."

What he lost in sibling relationships, however, he made up for in a special relationship with his parents, to whom he always felt very close. He wanted to be humble and meek like his father. In fact, this closeness to his father was, by Sam's own admission later, one of the main influences pulling him to the ministry.

Looking back on parenthood, however, S. J. was rather hard on himself as a father:

> As I look back over the days when the children were growing up ... my only regret ... is that I have not been a better father ... I did not make sufficient allowance for childhood's immaturity and lack of experience. Consequently, I expected and required too much of my children ... having myself been brought up under the old system of parental discipline, I now see that I was at times too rigid and exacting. I was inclined to resort too readily to the rod, when milder measures would have secured as good, if not much better, results. I wish now I had been more blind to their childhood faults ... It requires so little to make a child happy that often a little indulgence where neither right nor wrong are involved would bring a thrill of joy to a child's heart. And it requires so little to hurt and disappoint a child; often a slight rebuff or repression thoughtlessly given will wound a child's spirit.[11]

Because Sam was the youngest, he also had a special place in the heart of his maternal grandmother, Allie Coleman Davis:

> Sammy had just cause twice for claiming first place with Grandmother Davis. Besides having her maiden name and red hair, he was _her_ baby. She put his first clothes on him.
> She always said spoiling would not hurt a baby—just look at Sammy. And if she could see him now, that very special favorite of hers, one who performs marriages of her grandchildren and baptizes her great-grandchildren.[12]

Sam loved and respected Grandma Allie very much. At her death in 1931, he penned this poignant entry:

> Feb. 5, 1931—Grandma died. The best woman in the world received her reward from her maker today at 11:15 o'clock. Though the hours, days, and years roll on, the sweet memory of this kind, Christian old lady will hold in the hearts of all who new and loved her. My Grandma, Mrs. Allie Davis.

Sam's entire extended family was close and, especially on Lily's side, had numerous family reunions. Every two years all the Davis houses congregated at a state park—the House of Lily, House of Oma, House of Guy, House of Annie, etc. Sam was still going to those reunions in the 1980s.

By the close of 1929, Sam and Allan were both delivering the _Morrilton Democrat_ twice a week. Often Sam's little rat terrier, Speck, went along. From the time he had gotten Speck in March 1926, they had been inseparable.

Kids today would find it hard to be satisfied with Sam's Christmas gifts that year, but he was elated over "a dandy Christmas." His diary reveals he received two ties, a Polo shirt, $2.75, bedroom slippers, gloves, handkerchief, and a haversack.[13]

1930

Hunting "over the hill" and camping on the river claimed most of Sam's time in the early months of 1930. Increasingly, he began to hunt with his brother Jap and in January killed his first quail. He and Allan had plenty of memorable times, sleeping outdoors and in the woods:

> *Jan. 17, 1930—It snowed like the dickins today and Al and I went rabbit hunting and nearly froze. We found a old house where we took off our boots and stuck our feet in our coats to keep them warm, but that didn't do no good. So we ran around the room till we got hot then lit out for home …Al going to stay all night with me so Doc got jealous.*

Years later in a sermon about David and Psalm 23 entitled "The World's Most Famous Teenager," Sam happily recalled his communion with God's world in those camping experiences:

> *David often spent the night with his flock out in the open. He'd do what I used to do in Arkansas when I spent so many nights out in the hills. He'd try to count the stars in the sky as he went to sleep. God only knows how many times I tried to do that as I went to sleep—never got 'em counted because I always went to sleep first.*

And, in that same sermon, he recalled some not so happy experiences with nature. When a large bear attacked him in Yellowstone once, he confessed, "I ran as hard as I could to the car, jumped in, and locked the door just in time."

Scouting was a major emphasis in Sam's young life. We don't know when his scouting career began, but by this time, it had become a consuming passion. In February, he attended the annual Father/Son Scout Banquet held at the Presbyterian Educational Building. Sammy apparently stole the show before nearly one hundred people. A *Morrilton Democrat* article on February 18, 1930, reported:

> *Scout Sammy Patterson proved to be a keen listener when Mr. Roberts lined up a stack of chairs and announced he would give 50 cents to the first scout who would come out, take off his shoes, and jump over them. All the Scouts with the exception of young Patterson … seemed to be under the impression that Roberts wanted them to jump over the stack of chairs, so they refused to enter the contest. Whereupon young*

Patterson stepped up, took off his boots, and jumped over them (the boots, not the chairs), and received the prize!

In June he and Allan attended Camp Quapaw, an area Boy Scout camp on the Saline River seven miles south of Benton, Arkansas. The camp was one of Sam's all-time favorite places in the world. He fairly salivates in his diary anticipating his annual visits there. Cabin 1, "The Flying Eagles," seemed to be the gathering place to scare the pants off campers:

> *June 13—We have been gathering in our cabin and telling ghost stories. Doc Bruce was down the other nite and he wouldn't go back to the Pioneer cabin where he stays because of the scarey tales we told. He slept with me.*

By early September he had become a Star Scout with twelve merit badges, well on his way to earning the precious Eagle Scout award. He also entered the ninth grade and continued to hate school:

> *Nov. 18—I played football after 'school' today. That word makes a kid want to cuss.*

Later in life, Sam relished telling on himself and his poor grades with the story of Mr. King, his ninth grade algebra teacher. It became one of his favorite sermon illustrations about God's holiness:

> *Mr. King was a great man of God, a humble and loving man whom all the kids respected. All my life I have been thankful for the privilege of sitting under such a godly man. He preached in a little Baptist church out in the country on Sunday, but he ministered to the students during the week. I belonged to a little boys' club he sponsored, and I had been on campouts with him. Those were depression years and Mr. King always wore tennis shoes because he barely had enough money to take care of his family. He was one of the highlights of my boyhood.*
>
> *We had a boy in our class who did very poorly in his work, and the year was pretty far gone. Mr. King called him in toward the end of the year and said, 'It's just barely possible that you might pass, but here is what you must do. Prepare every daily assignment diligently, and do well on your weekly tests and the final examination. You will have to work hard every day. I will be praying for you all the way.'*
>
> *Friends, when I went out of that class, I thought I had an 'A'! I knew I was Mr. King's pet and closer to him than any boy in the class. I knew he loved me. He was a man of limitless good will. I knew if Mr. King was praying for me, I didn't have anything to worry about!*
>
> *Through the rest of the year I didn't take him seriously. I couldn't believe Mr. King would fail me. When I got the report card, that was the*

*first grade I wanted to look at. But when I looked at the grade, it was an
'F.' He had failed me!*

*My respect for him skyrocketed. I really had thought that he would
subjugate his love of holiness to his love for me. But I had read him
wrong. He was a man of great love and didn't like to fail students, but it
would not have been right for him to give me a passing grade because I
did not earn it. I have recalled that lesson my entire life.*[14]

However, studies that year certainly did not keep him off the river. He and
Al camped out and hunted constantly during the fall. Both had 22 rifles, Sam's a
Stevens crack shot long rifle. Sam also owned a single barrel "Special," an extra
long 12 gauge shot gun. He was proud of both. When he and Al weren't hunting
and camping, a group of boys just "messed around" on the river:

*Sun., Nov. 16—Went over on the river with Jim Cunningham, Fussy
Hilman, Beardon, Al, and Gipy (Robert) Gibson. Me and Al got in a
argument over whether his old dog had a longer tail than mine. I think
I won. I usually do. But I git mad. I reckon that's due to my red hair. As
usual, I had to take a bath tonite.*

By year's end, the economic woes of the nation had come to roost in Morrilton:

*Nov. 17—I'll be doggone. Both banks in Morrilton closed. We only
had too. The schools might close. Everbody is cussing and are mad. I
wonder what'll happen?*
Nov. 18—Brite and perty. The bank might open up.

Between 1929 and 1930, forty-two percent of Arkansas's private banks
closed their doors,[15] and at least one of the banks in Morrilton never reopened.
We don't know much more about how Sam's life was affected by the depression
except from a few diary comments in later years. He mentions, "We talked to a
feller who came to the back door for some food. Mother gave him some. He had
blood poison in his left arm."

1931

The second semester of Sam's freshman year began ominously when Allan's
house burned down. Notice Sam's comical take on the situation:

*Jan. 2—Allan moved. His house burnt that nite. Looks suspiscius.
But they didn't own the house, so they didn't set it.*

This year marked the beginning of Sam's lifelong love affair with Petit Jean
Mountain, about fifteen miles southwest of Morrilton across the Arkansas River.

At 2,600 feet, it is one of the tallest mountains in the state. In correspondence much later in his life, Sam wrote, "Since boyhood days Petit Jean Mountain has been the picture conjured up in my mind when I read Psalm 121:1–2. It has always been holy ground to me." [16]

January 30, 1931, is the first recorded instance of his camping on the horseshoe-shaped mountain. His companions on the trip were his algebra teacher, Mr. King, and Allan. Over the years, he and Allan enjoyed the mountain together many more times. In September he writes:

> *Sept. 6—Me and Allan and others went up on the mountain a week ago on a camp till Friday. We had a big time.*

And two years later:

> *June 19, 1933—Me and Allan hitchhiked to the mountain today and carried our lunch. We had pretty good luck [getting there] but had to walk all the way up. We got a ride all the way home.*

"He loved Petit Jean Mountain," remembers Becky. "He started going up there as soon as his mother and daddy thought he was old enough. He and Allan Merritt and other boys frequently camped out there on Friday nights. It was primitive camping, very rough, but they loved it. Most of the time he hiked the fifteen miles over there going by the road, although I think he had some shortcuts through the woods."

The park encompasses nearly 3,500 acres of rare natural beauty guaranteed to enthrall young campers then and now. An abundance of unmarred woods, ravines, streams, springs, spectacular views, and interesting geological formations remain almost as the French explorers found them three hundred years ago. Fossilized giant tropical ferns hide in the mountain rock, while hundreds of Indian artifacts lurk in the soil, and ancient aboriginal pictographs, painted in red ochre, adorn cave walls. [17]

Sam and his friends could spot golden eagles flying over the valley or wildcats and foxes roaming the hills. They could see black and turkey vultures roost on the windy bluffs and sheer canyon walls of Cedar Creek Canyon, with the Petit Jean River in the distance. Sam's diary tells us that he loved to camp at Cedar Creek Canyon, and he even took dates there in high school. They might have watched the water plummet from Cedar Creek Falls or might have walked across the seventy-foot-high Natural Bridge at Seven Hollows, a vast and intricate labyrinth of sandstone canyons. Perhaps at Palisades Overlook he and his buddies sat around a campfire watching the sun set over the Arkansas River as it snaked through the beautiful, fertile valley blanketed with crops. Or perhaps they explored Bear Cave, where a mountain resident shot a bear in the 1920s. Or did they marvel at the amazing sandstone formations found near Nelson's Point

(Stout's Point today), one of his favorite spots in the park? Almost certainly they fished in the excellently stocked Lake Roosevelt and Bailey, both of which contain some of the purest water known.

However, getting to the mountain was not easy, even if one had a car, which Sam did not. When he was old enough, he probably hitchhiked across the Highway 9 bridge to a parkway leading to the mountain. However, when he was younger he and his friends probably enjoyed the adventure of hiking two rural roads winding through the wilderness south of town. They could take The Lower Road, down Moose St. to Sayle's (or old St. Anthony's) Hill, then on to the Lewisburg Ferry to cross the river. But during floods, much of the Lower Road washed away. That left The Upper Road, which Sam could access by going "over the hill" a little further north, crossing Point Remove Creek on the old steel bridge, going through Willow Bend, and crossing the river by ferry at the foot of Petit Jean Mountain.

But if he were going to hunt rabbits along the way and had brought Speck along, crossing that bridge was mighty time-consuming. Sam later shared:

> *As long as he lived, Speck never trusted that bridge. Getting him across it was always an ordeal. I'd walk across with my gun, stand on the other side and wait. Although he weighed only twelve pounds, he'd tip-toe very slowly across that bridge with its huge steel beams and giant oak timbers, obviously afraid he was going to cause it to collapse.[18]*

Arriving at the foot of Petit Jean, most of the time Sam and his friends probably hiked up the new mountain road built in the 1920s. However, at times they may have enjoyed the thrill of a dangerous old 1890s trail on the north face. A very narrow and steep slope, in some places a thirty-degree incline, it was perilous in ice and snow. In earlier days, wagons often had to have logs tied to the back to slow their descent.

The peak itself was shrouded with mystery, a sure way to a boy's heart. Legends abounded, including the fact that Jesse James once lived on the mountain and buried some of his loot in the vicinity. Some are based in fact, but one of the most popular is pure legend and recounts the tragic love story of a French boy and his fiancé:

The Legend of Petit Jean

A young French nobleman named Chavet lived in the period of the French exploration of the New World and was said to be a kinsman of the king of France. He asked the king for permission to explore a part of the Louisiana Territory, and for a grant to whatever part of it he might find to his liking. The king agreed to his request.

Chavet was engaged to be married to a young girl in Paris who, when told of this plan, asked that they be married before he left France so that she might accompany him. Thinking of the hardship and danger that would probably be encountered, Chavet refused the girl's request and told her that on his return, if he found the country good, they would be married and go to the New World to spend their lives.

The girl, however, refused to accept his denial. She disguised herself as a boy and applied to the captain of Chavet's ship for a place as a cabin boy, calling herself Jean. The girl must have been incredibly clever in disguise, for it is said that not even Chavet recognized her or suspected that she was not a boy. The sailors called her Petit Jean [Little John]. They crossed the ocean in early spring and ascended first the Mississippi, then the Arkansas River to the foot of this mountain, which must have looked to the voyagers as they approached it like the prow of a great ship. The Indians who lived on the mountain, seeing a ship for the first time, came down to the river and gave Chavet and his sailors a friendly and hospitable greeting and invited them to the summit. They accepted and found life with the Indians so pleasant that they spent the entire summer there. Petit Jean fished the streams and hunted the forests of the region with Chavet, the sailors, and the Indians until fall approached, when Chavet began preparations for the voyage back to France. When the ship was ready, supplied with food from the forest and water from the springs of the mountain … Chavet, his sailors, and Petit Jean went aboard on the evening before the departure. Chavet told the Indians that he would return the next year. However, that night Petit Jean became ill with a malady strange to Chavet and his sailors. It was marked with fever, convulsions, delirium, and finally, coma. The condition of the patient was so grave at daylight that the departure was postponed.

During her delirium and coma, Petit Jean's identity was, of course, discovered. After two days, during which her strength ebbed fast, she had a lucid interval and confessed her deception to Chavet. She begged to be carried back to the mountaintop to spend her last days. The Indians made a stretcher of deerskins and bore her up the trail to their camp near the point of the mountain, on the brow overlooking the mountains and valley to the south. At sundown that day she died.

Many years later, residents found a low mound of earth in a cove on the east point of the mountain, with rocks that fitted so perfectly they could not have been there by accident. The grave had to be very old and is believed to be the grave of Petit Jean.[19]

Today, a small wrought iron fence surrounds the grave. Sam spent countless hours at this point, perhaps his favorite spot in the park, both as a child and an adult. We can imagine this legend captivating his boyish imagination, as he and his friends gazed out over the valley, in their mind's eye seeing Chavet's ship plying the waters of the Arkansas yet again. As a man, Sam would later claim this part of the mountain for the Lord Jesus Christ, hoping to make it a Christian conference ground.

If he could have, Sam would probably have stayed up on that mountain constantly. But life always conspired to drag him home, back to chores, back to church, back to school. Ah, school was always such a trial! In the spring of 1931, his high school transcript shows final semester grades for his freshman year were: Ds in English I and Algebra I (failed the other half), two C minuses in Latin I (failed the other half) and Occupations, and a C in Civics.

However, Scouts and other extracurricular activities were another story. Allan earned his Eagle Scout award that February, a great incentive to Sam to continue working hard for his. In April he and Allan were in *The Kid's Awakening*, a four-act play put on by the Boy Scouts in Morrilton. Either they didn't have enough people for the parts, or Sam was very talented. In the first act he was a gang member, in the fourth a juror! Sandwiched between ten-mile hikes to Lower Island on the Arkansas River, Sam attended debate tournaments, even placing third in one.

A pastor's salary doesn't go far, so Sam's possessions were few. But he snapped up bargains when he could, and his parents helped:

> *March 5—I bought a bicycle from Carl Crowell today and have rode the thing to death. Dad paid 6 and I paid 6…*

By the beginning of tenth grade in the fall of 1931 he had become, in daughter Becky's words, "a football fool." His diary is replete from now on with details of almost every Morrilton Devil Dog event in which he played or scored. Sometimes he gave a play by play of games he merely attended. An all-round athlete, he would eventually play several sports, including basketball, baseball, football, and track. It was an odd day that did not have a sports entry, usually at the very beginning, except on Sunday when he noted first that he had gone to Sunday School and church. In the fall of each year he listed the entire season schedule. He came by his love of sports naturally. Jap and Hugh were big sports nuts, and both played football. His father loved baseball and would not miss a game except to marry or bury someone!

In September Sam, Allan, and several other friends went out for football. Although small, Sam made up for it in spirit and usually got to play:

> *Oct. 9—We played Paris. Me and Allan got to play. I played tackle. I only weigh 112 lbs. and I played against a big guy that weighed about 185 lbs. Score: Us 43, Paris 6.*

But sports did not keep him from enjoying the outdoors:

Nov. 17— ...I saw 2 big flocks of ducks today. Oh, boy, just wait till Saturday and I'll make them buggers fly!

Nov. 22— ...went over on the river. I took my duck caller and called a duck from a quarter of a mile down the river up to 10 ft. from me.

Another year ends with a splendid Christmas, even with meager gifts and the Great Depression still raging. Sam was overjoyed with a scout ax, two sweaters, a pair of pajamas, a pair of underwear, and twenty-five cents.

1932

The spring semester of Sam's sophomore year was quiet in his diary. He joined the Glee Club, while he and Allan continued to be inseparable. Gordy Houston joined them much of that spring tent-camping in Sam's backyard. In March Sam had to go to the dentist:

March 4—I didn't do anything much but get my teeth worked on. About 4 years ago I got my tooth busted nearly half in two on a old galvanized tank. I had it pulled about 3 weeks ago and he put me a false tooth in its place today. It sure feels funny....

Scouts kept him busy. When Troop 40 entertained the Kiwanis Club, Sam led the song service, while Allan presided. The Boy Scouts ruled the city of Morrilton "with an iron hand" one Saturday that spring and replaced the city's leaders. Groups gathered at every corner to see how Special Patrolmen Sammy Patterson and Allan Merritt handled the traffic. They must have shined, since they collected $38.50 in fines!

Final grades for the year were a little better, but Sam was still not honor roll material:

English II—D
Latin I—C-
World History—C
Algebra I—C (brought up from a D)
Plane Geometry—B-

Yet, who cared about school when summer beckoned? And Sam packed it as full as he could! Young people today bore easily, but apparently Sam and his friends were rarely hard up for activities. They made their fun from simple things—a creek, a swimming hole, marbles, a football, a book. Even with nothing special to do, they "monkeyed" or fooled around and played with the dogs. Whiling away time could be exciting!

Many times Sam spent part of the day just lounging:

> *June 20—teusday noon—I am lying on the lounge in the parlor*
> *listening to the radio. Some woman is singing 'That's What Heaven*
> *Means to Me.' My dog Speck is lying on the floor here beside me…*

Throughout his diary Sam always seemed to be reading something. And a pleasant afternoon with a friend often involved a book:

> *July 2—I read this morning on the book* Jenny Todd *and the*
> Whispering Mummy. *It is a dadgum good book.*
> *July 8— …Bob Bentley came over this p.m. and we went into the*
> *parlor and read.*

Sam also read *Robinson Crusoe, The Boy's King Arthur, Tom Sawyer, Call of the Wild, Oliver Twist, Twenty Thousand Leagues Under the Sea, The Beloved Vagabond*, and several biographies of Abraham Lincoln.

That summer his diary was strangely quiet about going "over the hill," so attractions in town must have kept him busy. The city pool, south of town near the river, was not far from his house, and he visited it as much as he could:

> *July 2—Al and me went swimming. The pool is about 2 and a half*
> *miles from town and we had to walk all the way in the boiling sun. We*
> *got a ride back on a truck.*

Cousin Hugh Baskin visited Morrilton often with his family and has fond memories of swimming with Sam. "Sam was a great swimmer and diver. One time he did a flip off the board and was a little too close and bumped his head pretty hard on the board, but it did not disfigure him."

Sports still claimed much of his attention. While playing catcher on a baseball team, he began getting in shape for fall football. As Sam grew older he spent more and more time at the movies. Favorite stars of the day were Laurel and Hardy, Will Rogers, Spencer Tracey, and Norma Shearer. At the Rialto Theatre downtown he saw movies such as *Pack Up Your Troubles, Dr. Jekyll and Mr. Hyde*, and *Me and My Gal*.

Politics enthralled Sam from an early age, and, as he grew older, he liked to hear the candidates' speeches:

> *July 26— …I think I will go and hear Mr. Jacaway speak. He is*
> *running for congressman from Ark.*
> *August 14—[Sam gave the complete results for the state and county*
> *elections and even saved the sample ballots from the newspaper.]*

On July 6, Sam had his tonsils taken out. But he had plenty of time to recover before leaving with his family for their annual two-week vacation in Hot Springs. When they returned, however, Sam had to go to the eye doctor:

August 29—Last Friday I went to the eye doctor to see what was wrong with my eyes. They have been hurting me. The doc said I have astigmatism—that means that both of your eyes don't focus together I think. Well, doc ordered me some glasses and I got them today. I have to wear them nearly all the time for about a month. Then I don't have to wear them unless I'm studying or reading.

The summer was over all too quickly and school loomed ahead. As he began his junior year, he seemed resigned to his fate:

Sept. 25— … Well, old school starts tomorrow. I don't care so much though….

By the middle of the semester, things were running true to form. Notice in the following editorial by Sam on grades, As didn't even appear on his radar screen:

Nov. 10—I got my report card yesterday.
Math III—D-
English III—C
History III—B-
Latin II—D
Science II—C
B- means pretty good, C means average, D means dumb (punk),
D- means awful dumb.

As usual, so many things kept him from studying, not the least of which was sports. Almost every fall diary entry talks of football, with hopes that he will get to play. Actually he must have showed promise, since he subbed at right-end substitute while Allan subbed at quarterback. A clipping from the *Morrilton Democrat* on September 15, 1932, reads:

At end … Sammy Patterson, who weighs 125 pounds, every ounce of which is real football stuff, will be a worthy substitute …

Each diary entry told whether Sam played, how well he played, the final score, and his weight. In November he gave the complete MHS line and backfield lineup for 1932, including the substitutes, with weights for everyone. At season's end he included the complete win-loss schedule.

Yet, even while playing he had one eye on the sky, searching for wildlife:

Nov. 9—while we were practicing football yesterday we saw one grove of ducks and one single duck go over. Duck season starts Wednesday, a week from today. Hot dog!

And every chance he got, he went hunting, usually with friends:

Nov. 19—I went duck hunting with Robert Bentley Thursday morning early. We killed none. Robert and me went rabbit hunting today and Robert's dogs got up about 12 rabbits. I killed one and Robert killed none. We saw some duck on the creek.

Dec. 11—Me and Bob Bentley is trapping together. We have caught 3 rabbits and 2 possum altogether. We have 5 rabbit traps out. I run them early every morning. Allan has one rabbit trap out. Not long till Christmas. Hot dog!

When he wasn't hunting, the lure of the woods and river still called to him. Usually he and Allan, always accompanied by Speck and Stag, went over the hill countless times. Thrills were cheap; every piece of wildlife he saw was a precious addition to the diary:

Sept. 24—Me and Al went over the hill today and went over to the creek and ate possum grapes and persimmons. Stag and Speck went.

Oct. 29—Allan and I went over the hill on the creek to the river … We saw: 1 grove of geese, 3 single geese, 4 single ducks, 3 groves of ducks. Speck jumped a rabbit.

Hunting was an interest he shared with his brother Jap, and one of the high lights of Sam's young life was going to Batesville to visit Jap and his wife Peg. Peg's father, "Boss" Yetter, became a huge influence in Sam's life. Originally from Lincoln, Nebraska, he lived with Jap and Peg.

Dec. 26—came to Batesville with Jap, Peg and Boss today. Me and Jap and Boss went quail hunting this p.m. I got 1. We had quail for supper. Boss played us some tunes on a fiddle tonight.

Dec. 27—I went hunting with Jap and Boss today. All four of us got more than 36. I got 3. Me and Boss cleaned them tonight. We took dinner and ate by a creek.

Dec. 28—I played checkers with Boss tonight. He beat me every time.

"Daddy followed Boss everywhere," recalls Becky Rogers. "Boss could build anything; we still have some furniture that he made. Daddy loved that creativity and ingenuity. He also admired Boss because he was a quiet, common man who worked with his hands."

And then came Election Day, probably one of Sam's favorite times of all. In later years, he said:

When I was a kid growing up in Arkansas there was no day like Election Day. Armistice Day, the Fourth of July, none of them could hold a light to the popularity of Election Day. Every other year were state and county elections. Everyone came to town to see how the election was coming along. From all around everyone gathered at the county seat to vote and watch the returns. Just about every Election Day was thought to be the most important in the state and even in the nation. Each new Election Day seemed to involve the greatest issues.[20]

Four years before, in 1928, Arkansas temperance leaders had championed Republican Herbert Hoover over Al Smith, who favored ending Prohibition. However, Hoover's devotion to Prohibition failed to sustain his re-election bid in 1932 against Franklin Roosevelt in the gloom of the Great Depression. Now, as the fourth winter of the depression approached, voters rejected Hoover and turned to Roosevelt in 1932. In the landslide that buried Hoover, FDR carried every southern state. Sam jubilantly wrote:

Nov. 8— ...today is the presidential election of the U.S. Whoopee!! [He lists the contenders and draws pictures of them.] Roosevelt is ahead so far. We are listening in on our radio. Dad and Mother are for Roosevelt, so I suppose I am too...

Nov. 9—Wensday—Hooray for the Democrats! Roosevelt won by a large majority. Poor Hoover. Poor Republican. They say beer will be brought back now. I hope not...

Roosevelt's New Deal reforms helped ease the depression by giving people jobs and helping them acquire skills, for which the citizens of Arkansas were grateful. Through the Works Progress Administration (WPA), local people worked on construction projects; young men of the Civilian Conservation Corps built wildlife reservations, planted trees, and ensured soil conservation. In fact, the CCC vastly improved Petit Jean Mountain, building cabins, overlooks, bridges, lodges, and two lakes to make the area even more inviting for Sam and his friends. In 1933, Petit Jean became the first state park in Arkansas.[21]

The year ended, as usual, with a wonderful Christmas:

Dec. 25—Oh boy today is Christmas! I got 2 pair of pajamas, 1 tie, a fountain pen and 'ever sharp' pencils, a watch, and a scarf.

1933

This year saw more entries in his diary than any other year. During the spring of his junior year Sam kicked sports up a notch by branching out from football, beginning to play baseball, basketball, and running track. He started off running the 880 yard dash, but in April he gave no explanation for quitting. Late in April he began working on hurdles, aiming to run the high hurdle during his senior year, but his diary never reveals that he did.

His thespian endeavors continued, and he was chosen for two plays:

> *Jan. 4— …I am Trout the overgrown lanky dumb country boy in the play* The Wild Oats Boy*—MHS Dramatic Club annual play.*
> *Feb. 20—Practiced the play* The Man in the Green Suit.

Final grades for his junior year are better, even with all the emphasis on sports—all Cs except one D in Business Arithmetic. As usual, school and sports didn't keep him from going over the hill:

> *Jan. 7—Me and Al (Stag and Speck) with our 22 rifles went over the hill this a.m. We shot at a duck but missed …I found a dime and Allan had a dime so we bought 2 hotdogs and some candy to pass away time.*
> *Jan. 18—Bob Bentley, Allan Merritt, and me went hunting with our 22 rifles. We had our dogs Speck and Stag and Ranger (Bob's dog). We got up about 4 rabbits but we killed none.*
> *Feb. 19—Allan and I went over the hill this p.m. Speck got up a rabbit and the rabbit ran right up to where Stag was standing and the dadgum rabbit jumped right over Stag's head. I bet that rabbit jumped 10 to 15 ft. away before it landed and it lit on its back, but it got away.*
> *Jan. 1—I went over the hill with Bob Bentley. We had a rabbit in our trap.*
> *April 1—Al and I went over the hill this a.m. and took our dinner. We didn't come in till this evening. Speck, Stag and the Pup went too. It was so hot today that Al and I blistered our arms. My neck blistered too. I gotta go take my 'bawth.'*

Apparently, this was the year Sam started dating. A "steady girl" never appears in his diary, but he did have several favorite dates, including Maxine Bassett and Ruby Farish:

> *Jan 14— …I went to a party at Mary K. Harrison's tonite. aIa aissedka ackiema assettba ota itena. [Translation: I kissed Mackie (Maxine) Bessett tonite.]*
> *Jan. 23—Me and Jim Cunningham dated Maxine Bessett and Ruby Farish tonite.*

That spring Sam became the proud owner of a boat:

> *March 4—Bob Bentley gave me a boat the other day so Allan and I went after it a few days ago. Bob and myself soldered a few holes in the boat yesterday (the boat is made of tin) and after we finished we took it over to the water works on the river. I took it from the water works up the river to the creek [Point Remove Creek] and set out some lines then*

came home. I went back about 4:30 p.m. but I had caught nothing so I took in the lines...

In March, Allan gave Sam a very unwelcome gift. This is one of the few times Sam speaks of being sick:

March 7—Cripes, I got the measels (roseola) from Allan! Sunday morning when I woke up, I was broke out thick. I got to stay in all week I suppose.

State and national issues continued to fascinate him, and he took every opportunity to hear them debated. One of these was the temperance issue, which, from earlier entries, we know he favored:

April 9— ...I went to the 'temperance' meeting at the Baptist church tonite. The people of the U.S. are trying to repeal the 18th Amendment (bring back beer) and the temperance meetings are against repealing it.

The battle between the "wets" and the "dries" raged in every Arkansas county and community. "John Barleycorn must die" rang out everywhere across the state. No doubt Sam heard about the minister in nearby Faulkner County who was thrown in jail for distributing temperance tracts at one emotional "dry" revival. Three months later on July 18, 1933, the voters of Arkansas supported repeal of the 18th Amendment by a 3–2 margin.

That year Sam was again president of his class and was the toastmaster for the Junior-Senior Banquet in April. Again he visited Jap in Batesville and stayed on the river fishing:

May 16—Boss, Jap, and me went fishing. The creeks were too high though. The White River is awful high.
May 17—Boss, Jap, and me went fishing on Briar Creek. Got 3 bass. I didn't catch anything.
May 27—Went fishing with ... Jap and Boss ... they caught 29 bass ... we had a fish fry.

Summer came, and to Sam's delight, Allan's dad formed a baseball team and asked Sam to pitch:

June 24— ... Mr. Merritt says I can pitch the ball over homeplate better than any of the other teams' pitchers.

Apparently it was a great match because by July 20 the team was leading the league at 5–1. Sam had pitched all the games, walking only three men. To Sam's delight, friend Gordy Houston joined the team:

July 24—Gordy has made our softball team. He catches, I pitch. Hot dog! We got beat today by 1 point but it got too dark so we had to stop. We might have won. We got more hits off of them than they did off of me. Gordy batted good.

Even as Sam and his friends grew older, they still didn't need sophisticated amusements. Having fun was easy; they either "monkeyed" around, went to softball games, played mumblety-peg, romped with the dogs, or wonder of wonders, read books, either individually or together. This summer, he and Allan had fun going to the Barnum and Bailey Circus, building a "humdinger" pool table, and making homemade root beer:

June 12—Al and me put up 1 gal. of root beer this a.m. and 1 gal this p.m.
June 14—Opened root beer. Awful good.
June 15—Put up more root beer (me and Al).

That summer Sam helped a great deal around the house and said nothing about getting paid for it:

June 7—I painted on a baby bed and froze some ice cream this morning…
June 20—I painted on 2 chairs and played softball this a.m. … I painted the floor of the kitchen that the linoleum didn't cover late this afternoon.
June 21—Painted 2 chairs and bottom of swing this a.m. and read some.
June 22—Painted a rocker this a.m. Played catch with Ben and Allan this p.m.
June 23—I painted on that rocker and a table and froze some sherbet.

Summer always meant Camp Quapaw, and this summer Sam said, "I had about the best time of my life at Quapaw!" The camp was small that year, with only fifty boys. Sammy and Allan went as patrol leaders. Both were assigned to the Hog-Caller Patrol. Each day the staff chose honor campers; if chosen three times the scout could get an Honor Badge at week's end. Although Sammy made the list at least once, he must have fallen prey to misconduct because he didn't get an Honor Badge, but Allan did!

However, Sam did earn certificates in lifesaving and reptile study that summer at camp. His probable notes for the reptile study have survived in a small three by five lined booklet simply labeled "SAMMY'S NATURE BOOK." Filled with drawings of birds, animals, leaves, and trees, it is splendid testimony of Sammy's love for the outdoors. It is brim full of things boys treasure—various animal tracks, bird tracks, Morse Code interpretation, semaphore code, and how to spot a mallard duck from close and from afar.

In July he supplied the ever-present weight and height check:

July 28—I weigh 140 lbs. now and 5 ft 10 and one fourth inches.
July 31—I have been working out in the little house, getting in shape
for football. I weigh 140 lbs. I weighed 122 lbs. this time last year. That's
18 lbs. I have gained in a year. Hot dog.

With each passing year Sam seems to love family vacations at Hot Springs more and more. There he spent lazy days with extended family members swimming at Fountain Lake Center and going to the movies. Some years he was even able to take Speck. As he counted down the days until the family's departure, comments such as these sprang off the page exuberantly:

Just 10 more days.
Oh Boy! Just 9 more days.
The days are flying by! Won't be long now.
Merrily we roll along.
Whoopee! Oh boy! Tomorrow!

The fall of his senior year begins with this less than enthusiastic entry:

Sept. 18—School starts next Monday. I don't care.

The only grades we know about for Sam's senior year are his mid-term exams, which he said he passed. Morrilton High burned some years later, and the records were likely lost in the fire.

He landed his first job at J. C. Penney as a salesman, but it doesn't seem that he was able to work a great deal. He probably didn't have time since sports kept him very busy. His brothers helped him buy his sports equipment:

Sept. 6—Hugh and Jap have both given me a pair of football shoes,
and both have hard rubber cleats. Hugh's are brand new.

Sam was a regular on the football team this year and played much of the time. His diary records every single move he made:

Nov. 24—Searcy won 26–0. I played my best game. In the writeup in
the Arkansas Gazette *it listed me with several others as playing the best*
game. [Brother Hugh coached the Searcy team.]

Having fun that fall meant going over the hill with Allan, Bob Bentley, and others to see ducks or a covey of quail. Or going over the hill with Alexander Hamilton to pass off the cooking merit badge. Or going to the circus with Boss. Or just picking pecans:

Sept. 30—Me and Al and Boss went over on the Stallings farm and got a lot of pecans. I got pecan stain all on my hands.

Christmas holidays came, and Gordy Houston came for a visit. He and Sam monkeyed around and went riding with Ruby and Maxine. Gordy left all too soon:

Dec. 29—Gordy left today. We matched to see which of us would write the other first and I lost so I have to write him first. I might date Ruby tonight. If I don't I hope she comes so I can take her home.[22]

1934

In January and February of Sam's senior year, he moved up in the job market by landing a position at the *Morrilton Democrat*. He doesn't say what he did, but he even managed to bring sports to the workplace:

Jan. 1— …I don't know whether my job will be regular or not. Allan is working there too. He started before I did. I think his is a regular job.
Feb. 3—Al and myself worked at the Democrat *today. We are start-ing boxing and gymnastics in a room above the* Democrat *office. It is a great big room and there is a basketball goal in it (a basketball too). Al and I went to the wrestling match last night. It was good. Mr. Hurley, the owner of the* Democrat, *is about the best man I know except Dad.*

Sam met one of the highest goals in his young life when he became an Eagle Scout in February 1934, a year after Allan received his award. In that era, making Eagle was a huge honor. Of the almost 1,263,000 Scouts in America in 1932, less than one percent made Eagle Scout.

The last semester of Sam's senior year he added basketball and track to his sports schedule. And it was time for another height and weight check:

March 8—I have grown quite a bit since football season. Now I am over 5 ft 11 inches tall and I weigh 150 lbs. These figures might not be specific but they are about right.

March was an auspicious month for Sam. He had done something NONE of his brothers had accomplished!

March 14—We got our football sweaters with the 'M' on them a week or so ago. I got one, of course, because I lettered as left end. I am the first of all five boys to letter in football in high school.

He played "Jimsy" in the March senior comedy *Zippy*. He was senior class president and was voted Sweetest Boy, Most Bashful Boy, and Wittiest Boy in the Latin I Who's Who contest that year. The class even honored him by adding a verse about him in their senior class song:

> *There's a class in Morrilton High School*
> *Has a president tried and true.*
> *He's a red head and a grand head*
> *He's a leader for you, too.*

Sam continued to date several girls, including Ruby and Maxine:

> *Jan. 20—Ruby Farish and I and Jim Cunningham and Maxine Bessett went riding tonight. I broke a date with Ruby last week so I could go to a wrestling match, and Ruby found out. Boy, she told me about it last nite, too! I fixed it up though.*
> *Jan. 12—I went to Conway to a wrestling match tonight. Allan and others went with me.*
> *Jan. 25—had a date with Ruby and James Johnston dated Maxine— went to a basketball game.*
> *Feb. 8—Dated Ruby and doubled with Maxine.*

Sam graduated in a class of sixty from Morrilton High School on Friday, May 18, 1934. As president of his senior class, he presented a set of books to the school library as a class memorial. His father gave the invocation. Allen Merritt received the $5 *Morrilton Democrat* award as an outstanding student at MHS. Is it a surprise that Sam did not receive any awards?

Later, in remarks to the fiftieth class reunion in 1984, Sam reminded everyone that they had received "no frills" diplomas during the Great Depression, with no class ring, school annual, or senior trip.[23] However, with Sam's grades, he was probably completely satisfied just to get the diploma!

A STRONG SPIRITUAL HERITAGE

Probably the most important experience Sam carried from his childhood years was his introduction to and training in the things of God. Just about every Sunday without fail he went to church and in the middle of the week, prayer meeting. Sam told congregations later:

> *I had the privilege of being reared in a fine Christian home. I was at church every Sunday, as soon as I was barely old enough to be taken. I don't remember, like many of you, when I first heard the name of Jesus or who I first heard speak that name. I don't remember when I first began to recognize the Bible as the symbol of our faith.[24]*

He seemed to have an affinity for the things of God at an early age. As a teenager, he began to attend many meetings and revivals in other towns and even began rating his father's sermons:

> *Sept. 11, 1932—I got a new tweed suit last nite…. I will go to the Baptist church tonite I think. They are starting a meeting there.*
> *Sept. 20, 1932— …I think I will go to church tonite at the Baptist revival meeting.*
> *July 26, 1933—I went to a meeting at the Methodist church tonight.*
> *Feb. 28, 1934—We are having a revival meeting at our church now …may God grant it success.*
> *June 18—Dad is the best preacher in town and I believe most people believe it. He preaches a doggone good sermon.*

He later told congregations that Psalm 23 was the first passage in the Bible of which he had any conscious memory and the first he memorized. "My only sister in quite a large family of boys worked faithfully to teach me this passage. I've preached on this psalm many times but almost never have been able to get out of verse one."[25]

Sam's mother was a crucial spiritual influence in his life. The first prayer he learned was at his mother's knee: "Now I lay me down to sleep…," and later in life he still prayed it every night.[26] He readily admitted that God called him first through his mother:

> *Remarkably, one of the first things that an unsaved man wishes to tell you is that his mother was a Christian, read the Bible, and prayed. That sticks and holds a warm spot in his heart; it is the call of Christ to him through his mother. I am sure God called me first this way. One of my fondest, dearest memories is my mother at bedtime. Night after night I can recall seeing her bedroom light go off, but she did not get into bed for many minutes. I peeped in the door once and saw her praying. In her life of faith, He called me![27]*

In later years he enjoyed recalling early spiritual influences. In a 1953 diary entry, he fondly recalled an old Sunday School teacher:

> *How refreshing Mrs. Poindexter is! Her spiritual impression made on me as a boy in her Sunday School class has been permanent. Along with Mother she is one of the blessed 'Bible women' who walked with the Lord in the Gospels.*

Later, in the sermon series *Revolutionary Aspects of the Lord's Prayer*, Sam spoke of his early instruction in Bible study. Apparently it stuck with him all of his life. "Whenever you study a verse, try to find out whether it's a promise, a warning, a precept, or a commandment—a warning to heed, a promise to keep, a precept to obey." [28] Sam's diary gives us more glimpses into his growing spiritual awareness as a junior in high school in 1932:

> *Jan. 25— ...Dad left this morning for Malvern at 7 o'clock ... Me and Mother is by ourselves, but what has a person to fear with God on his side?*
>
> *June 23— ...me and Gordy Houston are going to sleep in my tent out in the backyard tonite I think. It has been kinda stormy lately. The best thing to do when you get scared is to remember this little verse: 'Fear not for it shall bring a snare, But trust in the Lord and ye shall be safe.' This verse goes for everybody who keeps the Ten Commandments and believes in the Lord God, and Christ his Son who is Holy.*
>
> *Aug. 1—Tomorrow we leave for Hot Springs. You know, God is so good to me, and us all, that I just don't know what to do to show my appreciation. I don't deserve it.*
>
> *Nov. 22—Day after tomorrow is Thanksgiving. Heck, it would take all our lives and forever more to be thankful for all God has given us.*
>
> *July 30—I must go wash my feet, say my prayers and go to bed.*

During the fall of his senior year in 1933 he recorded in his diary two serious New Year's Resolutions:

> *1. To try to live a better life.*
> *2. To throw aside all cowardice and show 'guts' in everything I do.*

Yet, as with all of us, Sam had to work out his own salvation. Although he exhibited signs of growing spiritual awareness, the world was ever near, especially in his teen years, beckoning him to question, to try worldly pleasures, to doubt God. He chafed under his father's diligent spiritual training:

> *I grew up in a home with a father who accepted his responsibility as priest of the home. He had a practice of family worship, the Scottish family altar. He would read a long passage (it seems always from the Old Testament) after breakfast every day. We were not allowed to leave the table until the devotion and prayers were finished. Afterward, we all knelt by our chairs and Dad interceded—for his family, for the church, for the community, for our country, for people in trouble, for the world. It just ran me crazy as a boy! I thought he read and prayed too long. But it didn't take too much reading and praying to be too long for a boy my age. It irritated me especially when I had people visiting for the night or weekend.[29]*

A turning point in Sam's spiritual life occurred, by his own admission, in his late teens. He and his friends were drinking and making fun of religion and Jesus

Christ. At one point he fell over a chair, convulsed with laughter. He looked up at the others, and the Holy Spirit convicted him of his sacrilege in ridiculing the salvation of a soul. It was the first of many divine appointments over the next few years that would eventually bring him to the feet of Jesus.

High school was fast drawing to a close, and college was looming. The time had come to grow up and determine what he would do with his life. Sam certainly respected his father and wanted to be like him, so he thought some aspect of the ministry might work. By graduation he had made a decision. His father writes:

> *I had always indulged the secret hope that one of my sons would choose the ministry and follow me in that work, but the older boys all seemed inclined otherwise. So, when Sam came into my study one day just before graduating from high school and told me that he had definitely decided to enter the ministry, I was greatly rejoiced. He never wavered from that decision.* [30]

Unfortunately, the decision at this point was more a career choice than a call from God. But there it was. Soon Sam would leave the protected village of Morrilton to venture into the world. His first stop would be Southwestern College (now Rhodes College) in Memphis, Tennessee, then seminary somewhere. However, the road would not be smooth. In fact, in a few years Sam would discover that he wasn't even saved!

CHAPTER TWO

COLLEGE, THE CALL, AND CONVERSION

1934–1941

The fear of the Lord is the beginning of wisdom, and the knowledge of the Holy One is understanding.

Proverbs 9:10 (NKJV)

It's what we learn after we think we know it all that counts.

Frank M. Hubbard

Why Sam chose Southwestern College is a question lost in time. The fact that it was Presbyterian probably weighed heavily in his decision. A football team that regularly made the headlines didn't hurt.

He probably hoped for an athletic scholarship, but college records do not show that he received one. However, tradition in Sam's family called for older siblings or extended family to help with the education of younger children. Certainly, it was the reason that S. J., Sam's father, received any education at all, much less graduated from seminary. (For more on Sam's parents' history, see Appendix F.) By the time Sam was in college, older brothers Grier and Hugh were successful lawyers and could help.

We don't really know much about Sam's college years. His diary entries are sparse and short, and most of his classmates and professors are gone. He must have been tempted to quit writing in his diary; after all, he was a grown man now! Fortunately for us, however, he compromised:

Dec. 20, 1934—I did not take my diary with me and never will take it to school, I suppose, but I intend to write in it when I come home.

Sam helped with college expenses by continuing to work. Immediately after graduation from high school in 1934, he joined the staff of the new Ferncliff Conference and Retreat Center near Little Rock, Arkansas, where S. J.'s brother Hugh was site manager.[1] Hugh was one of Sam's favorite uncles, and throughout college Sam spent a portion of several summers there, mainly lifeguarding. He always enjoyed it immensely. He also sweated many summer days in the hot Arkansas sun building county roads. During the school year, he worked his way through Southwestern, primarily waiting tables in the dining hall. He hadn't lost his love of a good joke because classmate Lewis Graeber, Jr. recalls, "After ringing the bell to ask the blessing, he sometimes pulled a prank and poured soup down my neck!"

He and Allan went to different colleges but got together as often as possible during breaks. Ironically, college gave Sam the opportunity to grow closer to first cousins Harold and Erskine Falls from Wynne, Arkansas. Although they had lived only minutes away, they had been a part of his life only on family visits. Redheaded Harold had been center on the nearby Russellville team, and Erskine had been halfback. Harold and Sam had wrestled, boxed, and camped on Petit Jean Mountain. Sam and Erskine were the same age and not only roomed together, but also pledged the same fraternity, Alpha Tau Omega. Now a college man, Sam traded the diminutive "Sammy" for "Pat," and on the football bench he was simply "Red."

Lifelong traits began to emerge at Southwestern. Harold remembers buying clothes in Memphis with Sam and witnessing his cousin's utter lack of concern for material goods. "We went to this haberdashery to get Sam three shirts. After measuring him, the clerk asked what colors he liked. Sam replied, 'Oh, the top three on the stack will be fine.'"

Having chosen the road to Christian ministry, Sam joined the Ministerial Club and remained a member all four years. Designed for students interested in discussing religion, the club supported all religious work on the campus and at least once a month held a devotional service at one of the city's charitable or penal institutions.

Classmates took notice of this morally upright, industrious young man who was also an outstanding athlete. "Even in college I was impressed with Sam Patterson," relates Frank England. "He was several years ahead of me and was one of the few people extremely active both in the Ministerial Club and athletics. I never heard him curse, and I never remember him saying anything ugly about anyone."

"Sam stood out on the football team because he was such a straight arrow," says classmate Lewis Donelson, "while some of the other athletes were a little on the rough side. He was also serious about school, whereas many of them were just there to play football."

Henry Watson remembers that Sam never missed church. "I never heard him give a testimony, but he didn't have to. He was a walking testimony."

Yet, Sam's behavior did not spring from deep wells of spiritual maturity:

> *When I went to Southwestern, I knew nothing of real Christianity. Paganism and worldliness ran rampant on campus, but everyone, including me, accepted the moral standards of the Bible. We didn't live by them most of the time, but when we broke them we believed we were doing wrong.[2]*

As in high school, Sam had no trouble making friends. Students liked the friendly, low-key boy with small-town charm. He got along with everyone and had interesting methods of settling disputes. "I've always described Sam as a big, old, ruffled Arkansas boy," notes Ewing Carruthers mirthfully. "But he was a terrible fellow to disagree with. If we ever argued, he wouldn't give up his position. He'd finally pick me up, put me over his shoulder, and twirl me around, laughing heartily. I weighed 164 pounds, and he was a hulking football player. How can you argue with a man like that?"

Sam might have been heading toward the ministry, but football, not Jesus, remained the supreme love of his life. He wrote confidently:

> *Dec. 20, 1934—I lettered on the Southwestern Frosh Team. I played regular center. I am sure of lettering on the varsity next year.*

Nevertheless, that was not to be. A diary entry on April 19, 1935, states that he broke his left foot in spring football training and was on crutches for four weeks. Yet, the injury apparently did not keep him from hunting and fishing with old friends during April. Nor did it deny him several summer activities—a tough stint working on the county roads, a camp at Petit Jean, and Camp Quapaw with Allan.

Injuries, however, continued to dog him. During the autumn of his sophomore year, a photo in the *Memphis Commercial Appeal* on October 17, 1935, lists "Red" Patterson on the injured bench with this cutline:

> *From the bench, Southwestern's hospital squad sadly views the remainder of the Lynx in practice sessions for the game tomorrow with the Mississippi College Choctaws of Jackson.*

An entry on December 21 explains why that football season would be his last:

> *I got my foot broken again in football and so I didn't letter. I would have lettered otherwise.*

Academically, Sam gives us detailed information on only one course taken at Southwestern:

> *I took only one year of science at Southwestern—chemistry during my freshman year. On the first lab day, the professor gave me a manual to perform this simple experiment. It told me what product should be precipitated in the test tube if I combined these elements correctly. I was right excited to see this work, since I'd never performed this experiment before. I put the elements in, and then had a great disappointment. After I'd done what the book said to do, I didn't get what it said I should get. I'll never forget it; I just stood there for a little bit looking at that book and thought, 'Isn't this a fine thing! Here I am in my first year of college, in my first lab, with a book the college has given me, and I've found a mistake almost on the first page!'*
>
> *Then I decided to give the book the benefit of the doubt. Maybe there was something that I didn't do just right. So I tried again, and it still didn't work. Now I KNEW I'd found an error in that book. Then I read it over carefully again and got the best lesson I've ever gotten in science. I had failed to do one step exactly as the book said, but it was so little it hadn't seemed important at all. I corrected that, and it made all the difference. I got exactly what the book said I should. After that I performed many experiments. Sometimes I didn't get what the book said, but I always knew who was wrong.[3]*

Through his junior year Sam's coursework leaned heavily to history and Greek. His grades were lackluster—mostly Cs, with a couple of Ds. He took several philosophy courses his senior year, and his grades greatly improved—mostly Bs, with even an A in the philosophy of Kant.

The rise in grades could have been influenced by a Southwestern philosophy professor named Dr. Alexander Peebles Kelso—"Kel" to his friends—whom Sam had come to admire as a "fine scholar and Christian." Through him Sam developed a deep love for philosophy. The son of Presbyterian missionaries in India, Kelso had a master's degree from Oxford and was one of a select group of Rhodes Scholars brought together in 1925 to teach at the college. Records show that Kelso was one of the most colorful and influential professors in Southwestern's history.

It's easy to see why Sam loved him. Tall and imposing, clad always in professorial tweeds and sporting his omnipresent pipe, Kelso looked like the legend he was. Although affable and friendly, he could be shocking, constantly daring students to challenge orthodoxy. He loved the Greeks, and it was said he believed that everything important had already been said—by them.

Lectures were never boring, and students delighted in Kelso's personality. The Kelsonian method of instruction involved quiet reflective questioning shattered periodically (and unpredictably) by eruptions of thunderous rhetoric. Often after a blizzard of his own queries, he humbly confessed, "I don't know." He cared about each and every student; on the first day of class he knew every student's name and hometown. As the year wore on, he proved to have a marvelous knack for eliciting a correct response even if the student had no idea what to say.

One never quite knew where Kelso's lectures might lead. On one occasion, in the midst of a discussion on ethics, he suddenly froze, stared fixedly out the window and hissed, "I see a face!" The class turned as one to the window. It later developed he had decided to move into aesthetics and was quoting a line about Helen of Troy's beauty.[4]

Very soon after his ordination, Kelso had become a philosophy teacher. As Sam became more and more influenced by his mentor, he could see himself as a professor or teacher. But to accomplish this he'd first need postgraduate work at a seminary. Could this be the direction in which he needed to go?

The spring and summer of 1936 flew by, marked by numerous fishing trips with Jap and Boss, plenty of hunting with Allan and Bob Bentley, and trips to Petit Jean during school breaks. With no work that summer, he spent most of his time camping out with Bob or making lawn furniture for his father. A June 2 entry notes:

> *I am growing steadily. I am a little over six feet tall and have been weighing over 170 lbs.*

The summer before his senior year, a diary entry on July 5, 1936, reveals he had definitely decided to enter the ministry but was still at a loss to say why:

> *Possibly I have mentioned it before in this very terse and scribbled book that it is my intention to enter the ministry. After reading this diary and recalling other of my many episodes that I dared not set down here [ha ha], I often wonder (so do Bob and Allan) how I choose the ministry, but I have.*

In March 1937, a rather poignant entry heralds Sam's coming of age just short of his twenty-first birthday:

> *March 2—I am home for Easter holidays and am certainly enjoying myself. It has been a very long time since I have written in this diary and the time will probably come when I shall stop writing in it altogether, but I would not sell this ramshackle old book for any amount of money. There are things herein recorded that doubtlessly will pass from my mind but these writings will always be a source of forgotten and past days.*
>
> *I am a junior at Southwestern College now—at least I have reached an age which brings the realization that childhood is over. I regret it—I*

sincerely do! I believe that I have had more than my share of pleasure and fun in these past 21 years and am thankful to God for them.

As a senior, his activities became more ministerial than athletic. In 1938, he became president of the Men's Bible Class and a member of the Christian Union Cabinet, which sponsored and directed student religious activities on campus. No diary entries appear during his senior year except a bittersweet note in September 1937:

Sept. 4—I suppose that this will be the last time I shall write in this diary. It's been mostly a record of the things that Allan and I have done. Ever since we were in knee pants we have practically lived together, and even since we have been in college—during the summer months. We were always together. Allan has now become the Associated Press correspondent at Fort Smith and I am about to begin my last year in college. Al left this morning, and I leave next week. This virtually breaks up our old relation and likewise this diary.

Yet, we will see that Sam comes back to this old book time after time through the years, covering spans of years as if catching up with an old neglected friend. It seemed to be the first thing he reached for at crucial times of his life.

Sam graduated from Southwestern on June 7, 1938, with a Bachelor of Arts Degree. Records do not show his major area of study. He spent the summer lifeguarding at Ferncliff and came under care of Arkansas Presbytery as a candidate for the ministry in August 1938.[5] After spending a few days with Allan in September, he left for Union Seminary in Richmond, Virginia, on September 16. He does not divulge how he chose Union, and there are no notes in his diary while there. If he was clueless about why he chose the ministry, he was even more clueless about why he was going to seminary:

By the summer after I graduated from college I had confirmed in my mind that I really did want to go to seminary, though I didn't have any interest in a conventional pastoral ministry. I really didn't know what I was going for.[6]

The next year and a half proved to be the hardest and most confusing time in Sam's young life. He became a renegade, scrutinizing and rejecting most of the sacred beliefs he had held from childhood. Yet, as shocking as this may sound, Sam had to come to the end of himself so God could set the stage for a personal encounter with Jesus Christ.

THE UNION YEARS

Later in life, Sam told folks he didn't know how a person could enter seminary and not know Jesus Christ, but he knew it was possible because he had done it! That first year he continued to have no idea why he was at Union:

> *I remember in one of my first letters from Union to a Southwestern professor, I expressed my confusion at the time. I told him, 'I don't know what in the world I'm doing here.'[7]*

While he was certainly at sea about his direction in life, he had somehow acquired a new motivation to study. His grades were better than at Southwestern; in fact, he was an A-B student during his entire three years at Union. Only one professor at Union surfaced in Sam's papers as influential. According to Sam, he was "not very handsome but a very godly man." That professor most likely was Dr. James Edwin Bear, Jr., well-loved by students and known as "Beaky Bear" because of his beak-like, large Roman nose. A former Presbyterian missionary to China in the 1920s, he was associate professor of New Testament exegesis and biblical interpretation when Sam was there.

Sam continued to work to pay his way through school and became one of four managers of the campus bookstore. Lessons learned in that job became fodder later for a sermon to his first congregation:

> *I once ran a little store. I was bookkeeper, proprietor, and manager. I held more offices than ever before. It had every reason for success. There was plenty of business, yet it was failing. I was going in debt. My prayer to God [one] morning was, 'Tell me what is wrong. What must I do?' I opened the Bible and my eye fell on this verse: 'Be not slothful or negligent in business.' I checked in my mind. Neglect WAS my trouble. So much to do, and I was neglecting a number of things. I thanked God and got down to work. Things immediately got better in business![8]*

Just as at Southwestern, Sam impressed his fellow students favorably. Four classmates all remember him fondly. "Sam was well-liked by everyone—an energetic, enthusiastic, and dedicated Christian man," recalls ninety-four-year-old Ralph Buchanan. "A splendid, capable man," agrees classmate Maurice Warren. "A charming, redheaded fellow, one of the most admired students at Union!" remembers ninety-two-year-old James Richardson. "Quite a fine fellow and outstanding in his class," notes eighty-nine-year-old William Manson.

But the picture Sam paints of himself at Union is not nearly so appealing. We can envision a brash, headstrong young man who knew virtually nothing but thought he knew it all. He had begun smoking and was definitely feeling his oats.

He had also acquired a boatload of questions and "hellacious ideas" about his faith since going to Union and was ready to argue about them at the drop of a hat:

> *I was so mixed up. I went to seminary with very little theology and that not Reformed. I wanted answers, but not 'because the Bible says so.' I wanted to know if it was true. During that first year I argued that the atonement of Jesus was just a demonstration of God's love. Jesus' substitution on my behalf had no validity. The Trinity? I didn't believe it. Hell? No such thing. Personal devil? Nope, just a hangover of superstitious language in the Bible.*[9]

The first time Sam went home from Union, he decided to shock his elderly, Bible-believing father by vowing that he no longer believed in a personal devil or hell. Sam waited for his father to come up out of his chair in horror so the young seminarian could dazzle him with the arguments he had constructed from all his reading. However, his father simply gazed at him and remarked, "Is that right?" Sam was stunned:

> *That's all he ever said! At the time, I thought it was a cop-out. Yet, that was the smartest comeback he could have made.*[10]

Adding to Sam's theological confusion was the extracurricular Christian service that he and his twenty-seven classmates were required to perform. Sam simply had no heart for evangelizing groups of factory workers. How does one share Christ's love for the lost when one has not experienced it oneself? Then he made a horrifying discovery:

> *It finally dawned on me that I was not a Christian. Before that, I hadn't even thought too much about what being a Christian meant ... It was a terrible burden, and I simply dreaded any call that came to me. I wanted to dodge everyone I could in that first year because I really was not in any way spiritually prepared to serve Christ.*[11]

Daughter Becky Rogers feels he went into the ministry for a noble reason, if not the right one. "I think Daddy decided to go to seminary because he loved and respected his father and wanted to do what he was doing. Daddy was the only one of his father's seven children to follow him into the ministry. I don't think Daddy knew he wasn't saved. He grew up in a Christian home and never knew anything else. He knew all the language; it was the way his family lived. He patterned himself after his father and was outwardly a Christian, but he didn't have a personal relationship with the Lord."

Sam echoed these thoughts in a talk given at French Camp in 1983:

Looking back on it, I've often thought that I was really called to the ministry before I ever came to make a personal commitment to Christ. I was reared in a wonderful Christian home with excellent Christian parents, for whom I'll always be grateful. I was exposed all through my life to the truths of the Gospel, but it just didn't 'take' in a personal way. I had a clear consciousness of the existence of God, although it was more in terms of an Old Testament fear, I guess. I feared having to stand before God someday because I knew He was a God of judgment. These general boys' concepts shaped my thinking. I had to go to church and Sunday School, but I went because I was in that kind of family and had to do it.[12]

"The inner struggle for him at Union was exquisitely painful," says Becky. "Although he had been raised in a Christian home and knew how to act like a Christian, he had never been saved! It must have been humbling to know that, despite the excellent academic preparation for seminary at Southwestern, he needed to be ministered to before he could minister! He was trying to learn how to preach and minister to people with his head and not with his heart and soul. He discovered that if he stayed at Union, he and the Lord were going to have to be on the same page."

Buck Mosal, who was later converted under Sam's ministry, remembers Sam telling of the struggle to admit his sin and need for a Savior. "Sam was on a train leaving Arkansas sometime during that dark period at Union, and a man confronted him. He wondered if Sam were really a Christian. The man's questions enraged Sam because he (Sam) definitely wasn't a Christian at the time! Sam told me he could never get away from that encounter; it had come back again and again to haunt him. He saw it later as one of the primary tools the Lord used to turn him around."

The pain continued during the summer after his first year when Sam and his classmates spread out to serve churches. Sam returned to Morrilton to intern in his home church but was miserable. He was like a hose unattached to its spigot; nothing came out:

I guess that was the most hellish experience I've had. I had to lead people [in worship] and preach, but I couldn't get messages; I was just empty. I don't know how men who don't really know Christ can carry on a ministry. It looks to me like it would drive them to insanity. I made it through most of the summer, but I quit the work about two weeks before I was supposed to and left.

I went back to the seminary, and almost upon my arrival one of the faculty members asked, 'What kind of summer did you have?' I don't remember what I said to him, but I recall thinking afterwards, 'I wonder what he'd think if I told him the truth?'[13]

Through the fall of 1939 Sam continued to spar with God and anybody else who would listen. But one day in October a lithe, pretty little brunette walked into his life and turned him on his ear. Three years Sam's junior, Estelle O'Berry Sellers was a student at the PCUS Assembly Training School (ATS) across the street from Union, preparing to be a Director of Christian Education. From Darlington, South Carolina, this diminutive southern belle was Sam's polar opposite. Where he was flighty, nervous, and impetuous, "Stelle" was disciplined and level-headed. She had been valedictorian of her class, the kind of person with whom Sam had *never* fraternized. And if Sam had a million questions about the validity of the Bible, Stelle had none.

"Stelle could get along with all of us without compromising her convictions, for she was a staunch Bible-believer," reminisces eighty-nine-year-old Ellen Bridewell Elliott, Stelle's classmate at both Montreat Anderson College and ATS. "She kept us laughing all the time. I never heard her say a cross or unkind word. I believe she could have found some good traits in the devil! She was an excellent student, but studying was not her main focus. People were her primary interest."

That fall, the most important person in her life became Sam Patterson. They met on a blind date to a skating party, but skating that night didn't hold much appeal for either of them. In fact, they ended up sitting under a tree and talking the evening away. Their second date came a little over a week later—to a possum hunt. If that doesn't sound very romantic, you just aren't up on the social scene in the 1930s.

"Possum hunts were fun social gatherings," explains Elliott. "Students found an area with a lot of possums and set up a party. Fellows could take dates. We'd build a huge fire, cook out, and fellowship. When the dogs found a possum, whoever wanted could chase it and try to shake it out of the tree. However, usually that possum had no intention of coming down!"

On their dates, Sam shared his theological questions with Stelle. While concerned about his difficulties, she refused to argue or debate with him. If it was in the Bible, she simply believed it. Stelle had never known a time when she didn't know and love Jesus. The two young people mystified each other; she was astounded that he had any biblical questions at all, while he was amazed that she had absolutely none.

The impact on Sam was tremendous, far greater than if Stelle had set out to argue him out of his beliefs:

> She never tried to straighten me out. She also never let my odd ideas disturb her faith; she simply made her beliefs clear. I marveled at her sweet and simple faith; the Bible just settled things for her. God used that eventually to precipitate faith in me and lead me to the experience that I finally did have with Jesus Christ.[14]

Stelle's grounding in scripture was ironic, for her upbringing was far from Sam's sheltered childhood in a Presbyterian manse. She came from rough people; her father was a coarse tobacco trader. However, her mother and grandmother had taken her to church, and she had given her heart to the Lord at an early age.

Sam knew a good thing when he saw it, and the two were engaged a few days after that possum hunt. They continued to talk about theological issues through the waning months of that year, Stelle holding her ground and remaining confident that Sam would come to the right answers before God.

SAM'S CONVERSION

In February 1940, just five months later, the Lord broke into Sam's world in a special way. As often happens with divine appointments, he was caught unawares. He regularly gathered with other students at noon at the bookstore in Watts Hall to sing Gospel songs. Reverent worship was not their aim, but, by Sam's own admission, more a "make-fun time jazzing up hillbilly songs." On Thursday, February 29 (Leap Year), about ten or twelve students had gathered there for their usual banter when suddenly someone began singing quite a different song, "Calling the Prodigal,"[15] and the mood grew serious:

> *Why we were singing that, I don't know. Ten minutes before, I'd have never had any idea that a special spiritual perception would ever come to me. What happened is so odd; I still don't know how to explain it exactly. But while we were singing that hymn, some strange kind of movement took place in my own heart. Of course, I was a prodigal in a way; I was certainly away from the Lord.*
>
> *As soon as we finished that song I left, taking another student with me, and went into one of the dormitory rooms on the fourth floor of that building. I got down on my knees by a cane-bottomed chair. I have not the faintest idea what I said to the Lord; all I know is that when I got up, I knew that a change had come in my heart that would last forever. I remember telling that student, 'It'll be different from now on.' It certainly has been.[16]*

The student who witnessed Sam's conversion was probably his close friend Ralph Buchanan. Apparently Ralph thought they were simply praying about a mission trip they had just conceived moments before and has never known he watched as God ushered Sam into His Kingdom.

"After we sang 'God Is Calling the Prodigal,' I asked Sam if he wanted to go out the next summer and do evangelism, and he was enthusiastic about it," recalled Ralph. "There we were, committed to going out somewhere, but not knowing where or how. So we went upstairs to our room to pray about it; we decided to continue praying until we received an answer."

A letter Sam wrote to his siblings on February 28, 1962, the twenty-second anniversary of his conversion, gives us more insight into the event he called "the beginning of the greatest thing in my life":

> *Some things even parents can't do for a child. Some things a person must do for himself.*
>
> *For reasons that were more vague and confused for me than they were for anyone who knew me, I entered seminary in 1939.*
>
> *The next year and a half provided a bad experience. This was because I was morally and spiritually negative, and in the field of faith, confused. It had always been like this for me, I guess. I didn't have the natural strength of character to be either very bad or very good. In seminary the inconsistency became intolerable, at least to the Lord.*
>
> *In a direct and good way, typical of God, on the last day of February 1940, for me faith became first-hand. There was nothing spectacular outwardly or emotionally, but that day in my own heart I came to a new and personal relationship with Jesus Christ as Savior and Lord. Life, and even I, have been better since. I'm still no prize for the Lord and have a long way to go.[17]*

In 1973, Sam gave listeners a brief glimpse of that intimate moment with God. "In my second year at Union, God opened my heart to see myself as I really was and opened my heart to Christ, enabling me to embrace Him in faith."[18]

And in 1977 he shared a bit more about his conversion:

> *It was not the work of the seminary that brought me to Jesus Christ, but His marvelous grace after several years of deep conviction. Christ penetrated … in grace the dark, filthy life of a boy kneeling down in the fourth floor of a boys' dorm. He stepped right in. Christ is now in me, helping me as I strive against sin and resist Satan.[19]*

Later in life Sam frequently said, "I became an evangelist the moment I got off my knees." Yet, on that February day he became more than that. He became a slave, a bondservant to Christ, sold out to Him lock, stock, and barrel for the rest of his life. He is a stunning example of repentance—a total one-hundred-eighty-degree turn in the opposite direction. The hymn writer must have meant someone like Sam when he or she wrote, "I have decided to follow Jesus … Though none go with me … No turning back, no turning back."

Apparently one of the first things Sam did after his conversion was to begin tithing, and he never stopped. In 1980 he told a congregation:

> *What am I able to give? God says His people can live on nine tenths, give Him one tenth. I know I have been able to do it. Of course, I think*

it's easy when you get started early. I began right when I was converted. It's hard after that. If you don't have much, it's easy to get started.[20]

After his conversion, Sam immediately experienced a great yearning to know what the Bible teaches about Christ. Of course he was familiar with the Bible's teachings, but he now hungered for details about Christ.

I began to be a Bible student, and to this day I've been searching back and forth through the scriptures with one primary objective—to learn about Jesus Christ. While I have found great profit in the entire Bible and see it all as God's true, inerrant Word, certain passages arose that fascinated, captured, and blessed me above all others.[21]

The first was 2 Corinthians 5:17, discovered just a week after his conversion. He wanted to write Allan, Erskine Falls (his cousin and college roommate), and one of his brothers to let them know what had happened to him, but he couldn't find the words. It all sounded too "Holy Joe." A few days later he read 2 Corinthians 5:17: "Therefore, if anyone is in Christ, he is a new creation; old things have passed away; behold all things have become new" (NKJV). He knew instantly that such a new birth had happened to him and that all he had to do was relate what had occurred in his life, quote that verse, and sign it "Sam Patterson." Over the years, Sam revealed he had preached more times from 2 Corinthians 5:17 and its surrounding text than any other passage.[22]

Philippians 4 also quickly became a refuge to him. As he bumped into those problems that plague most new Christians, he realized he needed the four promises either implied or explicitly stated in that passage. In a 1975 RTS chapel message, Sam confessed:

I saw certain things I had never seen; though they had always been in the Bible … it was as if God was giving me my first entrance into the Garden of Eden. I had a stubborn heart, making it difficult to adjust to a lot of things, so I needed the lessons here.[23]

He later admitted that he had done more Bible studies on Philippians 4 than any other passage.

Next, he began to discover the beauty and depth of the Gospel of John. Nurtured by it, he said later that he turned more frequently to this Gospel than any other for evangelistic preaching and personal edification.

Then came Ephesians 1 and 2. It was here that he really learned about the amazing grace he'd sung about since childhood. These chapters—not Calvin's *Institutes*, Reformed theologians, or the Westminster Confession of Faith—caused him to embrace the Reformed faith and the mighty concepts of salvation introduced in Ephesians.[24]

As a new Christian, Sam was eager to learn as much as possible from as many Christians as possible. Apparently one person who influenced him greatly during those early months after his conversion was Dr. John Blanton Belk, the well-known, yet controversial, pastor of Grace Covenant, one of Richmond's largest Presbyterian churches. Sam probably knew of him through Belk's popular radio ministry. Belk was also a charismatic leader, and Sam likely was impressed by his tender heart for the lost and his desire to follow Christ's commands at all costs. Belk was an outspoken advocate of the Oxford Group Movement, an association that had caused a messy split in his church in 1937.[25]

The Oxford Group, at its zenith in popularity during Sam's Union years, was the brainchild of the controversial humanitarian-turned-evangelist Frank Buchman. After his conversion in 1908, Buchman's goal was to convert to Christ as many world leaders as possible. To that end he traveled continuously, even attempting unsuccessfully to speak with Adolf Hitler. Stamping out communism as a temptation to university intellectuals also became an obsession.

Soon, he became convinced that the disease eroding the moral fabric of society was sin in the human heart, and the only cure was Christ. He determined that personal encounters could be the key to evangelizing. At Oxford University about 1915 he formed an evangelical group of student leaders and athletes, first known as A First Century Christian Fellowship and later as The Oxford Group. They practiced absolute surrender, guidance by the Holy Spirit, true fellowship, life-changing faith, and prayer.

The group spread all over the world and became known for university house parties, where fun and fellowship combined with open confession of sin. Buchman also hoped for Christian commitment from those attending and saw his efforts as an alternative to the attractions of communism to intellectuals. Essentially he believed that personal enrichment of faith through the Oxford Group could lead to lasting social change, with the emphasis on experience rather than doctrine.

Soon after his conversion, Sam enjoyed the fellowship and teaching of a Thursday night house party led by Belk. Oxford Group tenets taught at the group resonated with him both then and later in life:

1. *A daily quiet time to receive guidance from God*
2. *Public and private confession of sin*
3. *Restitution for harm done to others in the past*
4. *Evangelism of these principles to others*[26]

He found it a blessing to meet a broad cross-section of people, many of them led to Christ by Belk. One of his favorite acquaintances was a man he identifies only as McDowell. Twice Sam's age, he was a cheerful fellow—but an outspoken Communist. Sam recounts McDowell's conversion as a testimony to Belk's unorthodox style:

McDowell was always stirring up trouble in the newspapers. He knew the Bible and used it to his advantage. Belk, a man with a great heart for people, kept reading about McDowell. He didn't think of him as a Communist he'd like to kill, but a Communist he wanted to win.

One day he called McDowell and said, 'Let's agree to spend the day together. I'll give you an opportunity to tell me why I ought to give up Christianity and become a Communist. I'll listen with an open mind. Then you've got to give me your word that you will listen with an open mind as I tell you why you ought to give up communism and become a Christian.' McDowell snapped up the offer instantly. They met, talked for quite a while, and sometime that evening McDowell knelt and accepted Jesus Christ as his Savior.[27]

The Lord also used people in that group to teach Sam lessons he treasured for the rest of his life. George was a Presbyterian minister's son who had come to Christ about the same time as Sam. Once one of Richmond's leading attorneys, he had lost his law practice, his family, and his self-respect to alcohol and had become a bum, living in the streets. Some months before, Belk had scooped George out of the gutter, brought him to his home, and stayed with him night and day for six weeks until George began to experience victory over alcohol. During that time George had also met Christ and now worked as a salesman.

At one meeting, George shared one of his secrets of success with Sam. He vowed, "I'll lose my job if I have to, Sam, but I'll never ever leave my room in the morning until I've gotten on my knees and settled it with God again that He's the Lord of my life that day."

Sam took that with him for the rest of his life:

That's one of the most helpful teachings God ever gave me. I don't know how I would have made it through all these years without that. Every morning, just as if I'd never come to Him the first time, I come back to Him as a poor sinner, throwing myself on His mercy and claiming victory for that day. This is the fabric of the new life! I am going to live out Christ's character and compassionate concern. I'll do a poor job of it, but I'll try.[28]

The Oxford Group's attraction to a young Christian such as Sam is obvious. They were sincere in their intense desire to bring people to Christ—a growing passion in Sam's heart. Buchman himself was a compelling figure and his spirituality contagious. He was a man of prayer and rose early every morning to receive counsel from God. During his entire life he was an itinerant evangelist, living in celibacy and virtual poverty, depending only on freewill donations for his livelihood. He believed the way to reach those crippled by sin is not to demonstrate the superiority of our wisdom, but to expose the lie that hides the human condition by speaking the truth in love.[29]

However, apparently Sam distanced himself from the Oxford Group as he matured in Christ during his last year in seminary. One reason may have been the group's growing tendency to place more emphasis on man and his abilities to help himself than on Christ's atoning work. In the late 1930s the group changed its name to Moral Rearmament, and the experience of personal conversion was even more disassociated from the objective work of Christ's atoning work on the cross. A humanistic emphasis began to supplant the evangelical basis central to the group's earlier teaching.[30]

Moreover, as Sam's spiritual discernment became sharper, he realized that he had been depending too much on other humans' interpretation of scripture instead of the Bible itself:

> *Early on, I tended to adopt positions of people that I admired. Therefore, much of my Christian faith was not what came to me as I studied the Bible, but from Christians who I felt knew more about the Bible than I did. I trusted them to be right. Later, I began asking a lot of questions and didn't think those people were answering them very well. At first I didn't know how to deal with that, but after a bit I began doing what the Reformers had done—going back to the Bible to think through things afresh and discover what I really believed.[31]*

Yet, Sam treasured some of the Oxford Group principles and made them his own throughout his life. In his papers is a yellowed, stained, taped-together Oxford Group paperback entitled *Soul Surgery*; Sam apparently read it ragged as he digested the principles and importance of personal evangelism. Moreover, Sam's later devotion to a life of prayer, simplicity, and humility could have begun through his admiration for the life of Frank Buchman.

LEARNING TO SPEAK UP FOR JESUS

Meanwhile, that semester in 1940 wore on as Sam and Ralph busily prepared for their upcoming summer mission trip. They cleared it through the school's missions department and recruited classmate John D. Smith to lead the singing. The three began praying daily for God to oversee the trip in all aspects. Especially they begged Him to tell them where they were going and how to pay for it!

Soon invitations rolled in from three presbyteries asking them to hold summer-long revivals and vacation Bible schools. They chose Winston-Salem Presbytery, hidden deep in the mountains of North Carolina, since it seemed to be the neediest. Presbytery leadership had been encouraging churches to hold evangelistic crusades, but many of the rural, mountainous churches could not do so during the rugged winters. Sam and his friends felt they could really make a difference there.

The Men's Bible Class at Ginter Park Presbyterian in Richmond volunteered to underwrite the trip financially, and the PCUS Board of Education stepped up to provide all the VBS materials and hymnbooks. Union President Dr. Ben Lacey heard of the trip and donated a maroon Graham Page auto that had been given to the school. A few faded spots marred the finish, so the trio dubbed it "The Great Speckled Bird."

Why they chose that name is not totally clear, but we can guess. They had no doubt sung the old gospel song "The Great Speckled Bird," also a 1936 hit by Roy Acuff. The hymn likens the great speckled bird to the church, full of blemished sinners who are marching forward in Christ's name and power in the midst of enemies. It is based on Jeremiah 12:9: "Has not mine inheritance become to me like a speckled bird of prey that other birds of prey surround and attack…?" (NIV). Surviving in Sam's papers is a yellowed, brittle copy of the hymn, with Jeremiah 12:9 penned across the top. As the three headed out to win souls, they surely saw themselves in this great hymn.[32]

The three tirelessly crisscrossed the North Carolina mountains during the entire summer, holding eight ten-day revivals in church after church. The services were scattered over hundreds of miles, and the men traveled in all kinds of weather over all kinds of roads. They alternated responsibilities, with two teaching Vacation Bible School in the morning and one preaching a revival service at night, then switching duties at the next church. Members of each congregation gladly gave them food and lodging. Over the summer they taught 1,500 children and saw ninety professions of faith. One of the little boys in VBS later ended up at Union and became a pastor.

"We were amazed and overwhelmed by our great success over the summer and how God worked the details out," relates Ralph. "We knew it had nothing to do with our efficiency or preaching and teaching. We decided it was prayer because we had met every day since our decision to go out in February. The night before we left, we went over to Ginter Park and prayed all night."

Now that Sam had something to say, no one could shut him up. Back at school in the fall, he was on fire for the Lord, but the fire was burning out of control. Said Sam, "I began to be a problem in the seminary. I think they thought I was a nut."[33] Even though the Lord had blessed his preaching and teaching during the summer, his personal evangelism style needed much work, mainly in the area of attitude. Proud that he was a Christian, Sam's witness focused more on himself than the other person's spiritual condition.

About a month after his conversion, Sam was standing at the punchbowl at a party with a fellow he knew before he was saved. Full of his recent experience with the Lord, Sam wanted to talk to anybody he could. Looking back later, he realized he was probably irritating, since he believed hardly any other Christians existed in the world but himself.

The fellow asked Sam, "Do you really believe you are saved and have eternal life?"

Sam replied, "I really do."

"How do you know?" his classmate asked skeptically.

"The Bible says if you believe in Jesus you have eternal life, and I believe in Jesus," said Sam, rather proudly.

"Well, if I could watch you night and day for about two weeks, I think I could tell if you were really a Christian," the young man shot back.

Sam was speechless. He went home that night, got on his knees, and prayed, "Oh God, I'm so glad he can't watch me for those two weeks! I know You lovingly put him there to chastise me gently and reveal my arrogance to me."[34]

The first time Sam humbly tried to share Christ, he considered it an utter failure, but God taught him something about evangelism in the process. He stepped out of a drugstore one cold night, and a man met him at the door asking for fifty cents. The stranger smelled like a whiskey still. The request hit Sam pretty hard because that was the exact amount he had—just enough for streetcar fare back to the school. He was loath to give it up to a drunk. Sam had never in his life tried to talk to anyone about Jesus, but he made up his mind that, if this fellow were going to get his fifty cents, he was going to hear about Christ!

Sam remarked, "I can smell enough to know why you want this money."

"Oh, no," said the man. "I promise I just want to get something to eat."

Knowing that was a lie, Sam made his first feeble attempt to share with him a Person who could come in and really meet his need. Yet, as he shared the Gospel, Sam knew the fellow was listening only to get the money. Discouraged, Sam employed his last strategy. "I want you to do something for me."

The man said, "Yeah, you want to pray with me."

Sam replied, "No, I want *you* to pray. Walk on down the street and stop somewhere and ask God to help you."

The fellow agreed, and, even though Sam didn't really see any work of grace in him, he gave the man fifty cents and walked off. After going down the street a few yards, Sam reached into his pocket for a cigarette but suddenly stopped as his conscience was struck. Feeling uneasy, he decided not to smoke since he knew the fellow was probably still watching him.

As he walked back to school, Sam was more confused than ever. Why didn't I smoke that cigarette? Nothing's ever bothered me before about smoking in front of others. As he pondered the question, he realized if he had pulled that cigarette out, the fellow might have thought, "Who are you to tell me that a higher power can break the bonds of my alcoholism when He can't even handle your smoking habit?"

Reflecting on that experience years later, Sam was grateful he had begun to speak up for Jesus, but he marveled at his self-centeredness. "Witnessing had made me zealous to be sanctified in the eyes of others. It was years before it occurred to me to wonder what *God* thought about my shortcomings." [35]

His heavy smoking was hard to get under control, and, according to late RTS Professor Albert Freundt, Sam was quite rebellious about it at Union. One day in chapel the speaker was eloquently discussing sins of both seminarians and professors, including tobacco. Sam, on the front row, defiantly took his pack of cigarettes from his coat pocket and placed it prominently on his knee where the speaker could see it.

Stelle influenced him to quit smoking, but we don't know when. However, he struggled with the desire for tobacco the rest of his life. Those closest to him knew how much he loved an occasional chew of tobacco. He was careful, however, not to mar his witness for the Lord and indulged only in private or with close friends.

"Sam told me he had given up tobacco and vowed never to touch it again," revealed Freundt years later at Reformed Seminary. "But he still had a craving for it. So as I smoked my pipe, he'd join me by smoking either dried tea or lettuce leaves in a pipe."

A CHANGE OF DIRECTION

As Sam grew in the Lord during his senior year in 1941, God changed the direction of his life drastically, giving him a heart for the pastorate and a zeal for evangelism. One of the reasons for the change of focus might have been the influence of the legendary missionary Charles Thomas (C. T.) Studd (1860–1931), a compelling 19th century evangelist whom Sam came to admire greatly. Throughout his life Sam held Studd as a model for selfless service to Christ and quoted from his writings frequently. He was first introduced to Studd through the book *C. T. Studd: Cricketer and Pioneer* by Studd's son-in-law Norman Grubb:

> *During my college days I was given this book as a gift. At that time, I didn't personally know Jesus Christ as my Lord and Savior. I didn't read the book, but I kept it in my possession. Later, when Christ had become my Savior, I read this book and have re-read it many times in the years that followed. I would assume that no other book has so affected my life as this one, except the Bible itself.* [36]

Sam identified with the fiery, unconventional evangelist in many ways. Both had been inconsistent before their conversions, but after accepting Christ, neither looked back and both set out to find God's will for their lives.

Studd's life was indeed captivating and inspiring, likely giving Sam an exciting vision for reaching the lost. Born in England in 1860, he was one of the famous Cambridge Seven who offered themselves to Hudson Taylor for missionary service with the China Inland Mission in 1885. Before going, Studd gave away almost all of his 29,000 pound inheritance. While in China he met and married fellow missionary Priscilla Stewart. When he presented the remainder of his inheritance (3,400 pounds) to her at their wedding, she proved she could match his faith.

"Charlie," she said, "what did the Lord tell the rich young man to do? Sell all. We will start clear with the Lord at our wedding."[37]

After ten years in China, they returned to England in 1894, their health completely broken. Both had nearly died several times while there. C. T. gradually recovered, but Priscilla didn't, so a return to China was out of the question. Instead, in 1900 they took their family to India, where C. T. spent six fruitful years as a church pastor, even while fighting crippling asthma.[38]

Returning to England in 1906, C. T. saw a sign reading "Cannibals want missionaries" and began to feel God calling him to Africa. In 1910, against the advice of doctors, family, and friends, he sailed for Africa after establishing Heart of Africa Mission. Priscilla stayed in England to man the headquarters. Except for one brief visit to England, C. T. stayed in the depths of Africa until he died in 1931. Priscilla Studd died in 1929, and during the last thirteen years of her life saw her husband for only a scant two-week period.[39]

After a steady diet of Studd's complete commitment, it's no surprise that in the spring of 1941, Sam accepted the call to organize a tiny mission church in the cotton mill district of Martinsville, Virginia. Other choices would definitely have been much easier for a rookie—perhaps assistant pastor at a large church or the sole pastor of a safe, established smaller church. But not a cotton mill district.

Mention Martinsville today and a NASCAR fan will likely tell you the speedway in this small southeastern Virginia town is one of his or her favorite short tracks. But in Sam's day, it had become the Sweatshirt Capital of the world. After the Civil War, northern mill owners greedily eyed the cheap labor and lack of unions in the South and raced to build hundreds of mills in the Piedmont, a region stretching from southern Virginia, through the central Carolinas, and into northern Georgia and Alabama. Nestled in its gentle hills were many towns like Martinsville, whose workers literally rebuilt the postwar South with whirring spindles and giant looms.

But the cost of progress was dear to thousands of rural folk who, attracted by a steady wage and the promise of a better life, flocked to the villages built around the mills. This vast society became known as "cotton mill people," a distinct new culture in American history. Living in abysmal conditions and enslaved to the mill's inhuman demands, these hapless souls found themselves locked generation after generation into poverty much worse than what they had experienced on the farm.[40]

Cotton mill villages were rough and dangerous places, notorious for wild drinking and brawling as workers sought to escape the sheer desolation within its bounds. If Sam wanted a challenge, he certainly would have it. Cotton mill people cared little about the church. They wanted to know where the next meal was coming from and how to find clothes for their families.

But Sam was excited beyond measure about the possibilities of such a ministry, probably hearing Studd's clarion call to missions ringing in his head:

> Some want to hide within the sound of church or chapel bell.
> I want to run a rescue shop within a yard of hell. [41]

Virtually nothing could describe Sam's sentiments better as he headed to his own rescue shop in Martinsville. This would become the pattern of Sam's ministry for the rest of his life—going after those whom everyone else has forgotten, pulling for the underdog. Sam said later:

> It was a thrilling opportunity for a young minister who had the heartbeat of evangelism in his soul. Practically everyone in the church worked in the cotton mill. Many of them were rough and mean; most of them were unsaved and unchurched when I went there—when I left there, too! The Lord used us with some of them, though. They were the dearest people, and I loved them. [42]

But how long he would stay in Martinsville was anyone's guess. The guns of war were roaring again in 1941, this time across Europe and the South Pacific, as World War II escalated. The Holocaust was in full progress, and everyone seemed to be waiting for the inevitable involvement of the United States. Some of Sam's classmates had already joined the chaplaincy. No doubt he had considered joining as well, but with his upcoming marriage, he had Stelle to think about. Possibly, too, the wonderful evangelistic opportunity in Martinsville was something he just couldn't turn down. For now, he prayerfully decided that God could use him best in this small chapel in the midst of a sea of evil, unbelief, and squalor.

So, armed with his Bachelor of Divinity Degree received on May 13, 1941, he headed for Kate Anderson Chapel in Martinsville, while Stelle, her ATS degree in hand, headed for Marietta, Georgia, to become Director of Christian Education at First Presbyterian Church. God willing, they would be married in November.

Doubts filled Sam's heart as he looked toward his first pastorate. It would be a tough situation. Could he actually lead a church in such a godless area? He was only a little over a year old in the Lord. Rash and impatient, he knew he really hadn't a clue how to share his faith effectively. Soon Stelle would be in Martinsville with him. Was a foul cotton mill village any place to bring a new bride? God would certainly have to go before both of them to make this work.

CHAPTER THREE

THE WAR YEARS
1941–1946

I'm a natural leader. The problem is, nobody wants to go where I want to lead them.

Bill Watterson, Calvin and Hobbes

I am the vine, and you are the branches. If a man remains in me and I in him, he will bear much fruit; apart from me you can do nothing.

Jesus Christ, John 15:5 (NIV)

Someone once said, "All the world's a stage, and most of us need more rehearsals." That's exactly how Sam felt just shy of his twenty-fifth birthday as he faced his first pastorate at Kate Anderson Chapel. He was green, and he knew it:

> *I guess I've never known a time in my life when I felt so inadequate, useless, and limited as I did when I measured myself for the job I must fill in Martinsville.[1]*

He had set himself a lofty goal, probably after reading words such as the following from his hero, C. T. Studd:

> *Christ's call is ... not to build and furnish comfortable chapels, churches, and cathedrals at home in which to rock Christian professors to sleep by means of clever essays, stereotyped prayers, and artistic musical performances. [It is] to raise living churches of souls among the destitute, to capture men from the devil's clutches and snatch them from the very jaws of hell, to enlist and train them for Jesus, and make them into an almighty Army of God.[2]*

The one thing Sam did know was that God was going before him, and God—not the preacher—gave the power to the Gospel. Encouraged by this, Sam came to understand that he had the potential to be very useful in God's kingdom:

> *I soon realized that, even though I had no confidence in Sam Patterson, I had great confidence in the Gospel of Jesus Christ.... I had the 'true truth' that could transform any life and change the world!* [3]

Sam had every reason to be afraid, for God had burdened his heart for a literal hell on earth. Leading these people would be difficult. The words "mercy" and "salvation" had no meaning for them. For most of them, nothing had ever been strong enough to break their slavery to the mill and give them hope. The Gospel of Jesus Christ would not buy shoes for their children or food for their bellies. Liquor and gambling were much quicker fixes for the bleak, leaden deadness of their days. Sam had so much to learn—about God, about preaching, about pastoring, about these people and how on earth they came to be in this squalid place.

THE LURE OF THE FACTORY

Sam quickly learned what a tough life his parishioners had endured. Most of them had once been farmers and had known searing disappointment in life. Caught in the vice-grip of changing economic times, their ancestors had watched in despair as their way of life fell apart. They had fled to the only solution they could see—the city and its factories. Here, the promise of a steady wage instilled hope that they could give their families decent lives and escape a poverty-ridden future. They had no idea the cruel price that they, and their descendants, would pay.

Like most of the South during the 1800s, the economy of Henry County and its county seat of Martinsville was agricultural. Pre-Civil War Martinsville had nearly five hundred tobacco plantations, making it the Plug Tobacco Capital of the world in the nineteenth century. Most farmers worked small pieces of land, raising just enough to feed their families.

However, by the latter half of the nineteenth century, many factors made farming in the Piedmont unprofitable, not the least of which was worn-out land from years of tobacco production. Rural folk became locked in a never-ending cycle of poverty. In the late 1800s, furniture companies began coming to Martinsville, and farmers saw factory jobs as a good steady wage. Subsequently, textile manufacturers in the Northeast were drawn to the area by a ready-made work force—the wives of the men who worked in the furniture factories. [4] By the mid-1920s, railroad tracks crisscrossed this land of farms and farmers, and mill villages dotted the landscape. The Piedmont had finally eclipsed New England as the world's leading producer of yarn and cloth. [5]

Most of Sam's congregation worked in the Martinsville Cotton Mill, organized in 1909 by Robert Walker in a former tobacco warehouse on the corner of Fontaine and Franklin Streets. The entire area around the mill became known as Milltown or Cotton Mill Hill. Walker built many small homes around the mill on Fontaine, Franklin, and Dillard Streets to house the workers. Soon the community filled with families, and the population ballooned to four thousand.[6]

From all over the Piedmont, people streamed from the mountains and farms seeking work:

> Many paths led from the farm to the cotton mill. The move might come when a widow suddenly found herself the head of a large family of young children. Or a small farm owner ... might calculate that prospects for his maturing children were brighter in the mills, which offered ready cash and steady employment. The move could come when a labor recruiter visited the farm and persuaded them to come or when relatives sent back word that one could make more money in the mill.[7]

Frequently, workers were totally untrained and had limited education. Yet, they were quick to learn and became quite efficient at their jobs because they came from an area where hard work was a tradition. Endless quilting and sewing had bred manual dexterity and infinite patience in the women; besides, the machines were just needles set up "new-fangled." Contributing to the family income gave the women a sense of dignity and pride. They also enjoyed the sociability of their co-workers in the knitting and sewing rooms.[8]

Moreover, factory work meant escape from harsh farm labor for women; the fewer males in a family, the harder the females had to work. The blast of the factory whistles reached Ila Rice in her family's fields. Finally at the age of seventeen, she answered their call and ran away "to keep from plowing."[9] Diane Gauldin went "... to get out of milking cows and chopping tobacco."[10] Clay Frazier was only seventeen when she landed her first job at a cotton mill in Martinsville. "I went to work for twelve cents an hour. I got to work ten hours a day and five hours on Saturday morning. I got $6.75 a week, but I had to pay $3.50 of that for room, board, and laundry."[11]

Many in Sam's new church had the same stories. "Dad came up hard in the mountains of Grayson County in Virginia," relates Erma Lawson. "Farming gave out, and he knew others were getting jobs at the mill, so he followed. I was born on Cotton Mill Hill."

"My father was born and raised on a farm in Axton, nine miles down the road," says eighty-three-year-old Gideon "Buck" Powell, who grew up on Cotton Mill Hill and attended Sam's church for many years. A delightful and kind soul, Buck loves to reminisce about his days on Cotton Mill Hill and holds no bitterness about his upbringing. "My grandfather brought his family to work at the Martinsville Mill, boosting his age up a year so he'd be allowed to work."

"Me and my sister came over here to get work in the cotton mill," recalls Mrs. Sam Harris.[12] "We lived way out in the country where you could not buy a job since the employers usually gave them to family members. We had to walk about four miles to elementary school. I quit school after the seventh grade; I couldn't go to high school because I had to walk several miles just to catch the bus. I worked five years in the mill before I had my first child. After a short break I went back and continued to do that for each child."

SLAVES TO THE WHISTLE

Unfortunately, new mill workers discovered that life was not better in a mill village; in many ways it was worse. While they once had been slaves to the exhausted soil, now they were prisoners of the ever-present mill whistle. On the farm they had ordered their tasks according to their needs and the demands of their crops. Now they drove themselves to the continuous pace of a machine, rising early in the morning while still tired from the day before.[13]

The Martinsville Mill was not unionized (and would not be until the 1950s), leaving the workers terribly vulnerable to the greedy, ruthless mill owners. The Fair Labor Standards Act was passed in 1938, and by the end of World War II textile unionism had made a beachhead in some areas, but not the unorganized South. At that time, it remained a mecca for runaway shops and a constant source of cheap labor. Thus, in Martinsville mill owners could treat their workers any way they wanted without fear of reprisal.[14]

The mill ran twenty-four hours a day, seven days a week if it had orders to fill. Mill hands usually worked six twelve-hour days each week, but with a large order they were at the mill's mercy any time management called. Lint settled over their hair and skin, while choking cotton dust silently entered their lungs. Since most of the women dipped snuff and the men chewed tobacco, the floor was slippery with spit. The noise was deafening and the heat and humidity overwhelming.

"It was over one hundred degrees in the mill, and the lint was oppressive," recalls Buck. "They said they pumped humidity into the mill to make the machinery run well, but they really did it to weave moisture into the cloth to make it heavier since it was sold by the pound."

Children grew up in homes regulated by the mills' schedules. Mothers brought nursing infants to work or adjusted feeding schedules around breaks in the factory day.[15] "When Mama had a baby she'd be out for about a month, then right back," said Buck. "She paid Aunt Ginny Alcorn, an old black lady, three dollars a week—close to half her paycheck—to look after us when we were really small."

Families usually began millwork together, since employers paid adults poor wages and offered jobs to children to help make ends meet, thus luring them to millwork. Most children entered full-time work in the mill by age twelve, dropping out of school or moving between school and work as necessity dictated.[16]

"All of my brothers and sisters worked in the mill," remembers Buck. "I was twelve and in the sixth grade when I started working in the mill as a high-speed warper. I went to school until three in the afternoon, and then worked at the mill until nine. I quit school after the seventh grade and went to work full-time in the mill until I entered the military in 1943. When I left I was making a little over thirty-seven cents an hour, most of which I gave to my Dad. He said I had to pay board."

Most people never escaped the mill cycle, remaining in low-paying jobs, marrying other mill workers, having families, and watching their children become mill workers. But a few were able to flee and see success in life.

"After the war, I tried to come back to the mill, but I hated it," noted Buck. "I didn't like being cooped up inside day after day; I wanted to see the sun. I ended up getting a good job delivering milk and had a good life, even buying a nice modern house for my family."

New workers often labored for up to six weeks without pay while learning their jobs. The spinning room was usually predominantly female, with wages hovering near the bottom of the scale. Adult white men tended to get the best-paying jobs, followed by white women, black men, and finally children. Black women were excluded from millwork altogether.[17]

"My father made less than ten dollars a week as foreman of the spinning room," said Buck, "and my mother was a spinner so she made even less."

A small consolation to exhausted workers was the fact that mill owners allowed the atmosphere within the mill to remain social and family-oriented. Workers often had time to socialize on the job, gathering to sing or talk on lunch breaks or when production slowed or stopped due to machine failures.[18]

The consolation was indeed miniscule when compared with the significant health risks of millwork. Employees suffer severe injury or death when fingers, limbs, or clothing became entangled in the rapidly moving machinery. The deafening noise caused early hearing loss. If workers were sick or injured, the mill provided no insurance or workers' compensation to aid them in their recovery.

By far the worst risk of millwork was constantly breathing in cotton dust and lint, which contributed to conditions such as brown lung disease.[19] "A continuous fog of dust hung in the carding department at all times," recalls Grover Hardin. "When I'd hit the mill on Monday morning, I'd cough, sneeze, and fill my mouth full of tobacco or anything else to keep the dust from strangling me."

Grover discovered later that this "Monday morning sickness" was the first stage of brown lung disease, caused by irritation of the air passages. As workers adjusted to the dust over the week, symptoms disappeared. Yet, the coughing returned every Monday because a day or two away from the mill increased susceptibility.

After ten years, Grover's coughing became more persistent. Rather than pay doctor's fees, he asked the advice of other workers who "was able to go to the doctor." Most had been told they had a little touch of asthma, so Grover used home remedies for that. Like many workers with brown lung, Hardin gradually began having difficulty doing his job and started missing work. "I couldn't get no air in my lungs, and I slowed up. When I'd get a spare minute I'd go over and lay in the windows and get all the air I could." Finally, he had to quit.[20]

LIFE ON COTTON MILL HILL

Survival was the name of the game for Sam's congregation. The mill might wring almost all enjoyment of life out of these hardworking people, but they fought tooth and nail to make some sort of existence for themselves:

> ... in the muddy streets and cramped cottages, cotton mill people managed to shape a way of life beyond their employers' grasp.... Mill hands' habits and beliefs ... were instruments of power and protection, survival and self-respect, molded into a distinctive mill village culture.[21]

Buck Powell's family was typical of those in Sam's spiritual care. He was born in 1926 on Old Cotton Mill Hill, the small community of houses built for mill workers by Robert Walker at the turn of the century. Later owners built forty-nine new houses for mill workers, and Buck's family moved to Dillard Street on New Cotton Mill Hill, just two houses down from Kate Anderson Chapel. By the time Sam arrived, Dillard was paved with an asphalt/gravel mix and was the only street on the Hill maintained by the city, probably because private homes lined one side of it. The rest of the streets in Milltown were maintained by the mill and were only gravel (still a distinct upgrade from dirt).

The Powells lived in a bare-bones typical mill home, shaped like a box with a long front porch and a dirt front yard. Four dollars a month rented four fourteen by fourteen rooms with fourteen-foot ceilings. Since Buck's family had six children, they had to use all the rooms as bedrooms except the kitchen. Some families with fewer children even shared the four-room houses. The only amenity in each room was a worn linoleum rug; two small closets comprised the only storage in the house. The family owned no furniture except some iron beds, a table, and some straight chairs.

"Mom and Dad had a room of their own; the girls slept in another room, and my brothers and I shared an iron bedstead in yet another room. With two little brothers in bed with me, I slept in a water bed long before it was fashionable!"

The kitchen consisted of bare necessities—a coal stove and icebox, a big table with a long bench and two chairs. If the family had the money, they could buy small chunks of ice two or three times a week; they bought coal on credit, and the mill deducted the cost from the paycheck.

Although Martinsville workers didn't have a union to protect them, they were better off than most mill villagers without union protection. Water piped into the houses cost twenty-five cents a month, with a commode that connected to the Martinsville sewer lines. Most mill villages of that time offered no plumbing in the houses; they had outhouses, and the children brought water from central pumps or wells. Even houses with plumbing often had simply a spigot on the back porch, and sewage ran into a central septic tank, emptied periodically by "honey wagons."

Escaping hunger was a never-ending battle on Cotton Mill Hill. Even after World War II, the best wage in union shops was a meager twelve dollars a week, hardly enough to feed and clothe a family. Therefore, virtually everyone in Milltown had a garden.

"We got food from the welfare office when we ran low, but most of the time we tried to eat out of the garden," said Buck. "In the backyard my father raised green beans, tomatoes, cucumbers, squash, and potatoes. Our garden was huge because we lived on a large lot. If anything was left after feeding the family, Mama canned as much as she could for the winter."

Mill folk were a close-knit family. Neighbors helped each other keep the wolf from the door. Mr. Warren across the street plowed the garden for the Powell family each year for two or three dollars. Mr. Powell gave his next-door neighbor and close drinking buddy, Mr. Rakes, tomatoes and green beans because Rakes didn't have a garden.

Mrs. Powell fed her family mostly pinto beans, potatoes, and vegetables, following a time-honored pioneer tradition to save money. For lunch, she cooked the meal on top of the stove, and then baked the same meal in the oven for supper. Occasionally, cornbread was a real treat, but dessert was out of the question.

"On a real special occasion we'd have chicken," said Buck. "I can't ever remember having beef. Mama fried one chicken to feed eight people, so she cooked everything, including the neck and the feet. Yes, the feet do have a little skin on them!"

The greatest extravagance of all was salted fish out of the big barrel at Mr. Hatfield's store up the street. Hatfield ran an account for mill people, and Mr. Powell settled with him on payday.

Clothes came from the welfare office, except for the beginning of school and Christmas. "We hated the welfare overalls because they had buttons instead of metal galluses," confesses Buck. "We were embarrassed and tried to hide the buttons with our hands because they screamed that we were poor. People in other parts of Martinsville looked down on us, calling us 'cotton mill trash.'"

Christmas might have been inadequate by anyone else's standards, but for Buck and his siblings it was thrilling. The mill brought around gift bags, each filled with one orange, one apple, some dried grapes and a little hard candy. Mrs. Powell carefully put the treasures aside to give the children on Christmas morning.

"I usually got a new shirt and a little toy of some kind," recalled Buck. "I remember a small truck with headlights that turned on and off. But the most wonderful luxury was a pair of overalls with metal galluses from J. C. Penney. We felt rich and showed them things off!"

Very few people had cars in Milltown (Sam and Stelle didn't), but the ones who did gave rides to those who didn't. One of the mill workers cut hair on the weekends, and Mrs. Powell paid him with a pie for cutting her children's hair.

"If someone was sick," said Buck, "didn't nobody have to go tell the neighbors. Somehow or another they just sensed it, and they'd all pitch in and help. Someone had to be mighty sick for the doctor to come to the house. I didn't go to a dentist until I went to the military. A midwife delivered almost all the kids on Cotton Mill Hill."

Although life was hard, mill folk knew how to have a good time with no money. They often gathered for music and dancing or a watermelon cutting. Even simply relaxing under the old oak tree was fun. Although Buck and his siblings had chores—bringing in the wood and coal, weeding the garden—they had a lot of fun, too, with very little money. Witnessing that probably reminded Sam pleasantly of his own childhood.

"We thought we was living tough, but we was having a good time. We'd find two long sticks, nail something for our feet to stand on, and then we'd walk around on those 'Tom Walkers.' Or we'd make a wagon out of wheels from the mill. We played marbles. We'd roll tires, sometimes putting someone in it and rolling it down the street. We didn't have to mow the grass because we wore it out playing in the front yard."

MISS KATE ANDERSON: GOD'S MESSENGER

Contrary to most cotton mill villages, Milltown had no organized church at the turn of the century. Most mills owned the churches, as they did the schools and the company store. They also paid the preacher to bring messages they controlled. Religion kept the workers in line and cut down on absenteeism from drinking and carousing. But Martinsville was unique. Although the mill helped greatly in the beginnings of Kate Anderson Chapel, it never owned the church and there is no evidence whatever that mill owners influenced Sam's preaching in any way.

Around 1915, Kate Virginia Anderson (1857–1922) saw the critical need to bring the Gospel to this needy area. She was the daughter of Rev. Robert Campbell Anderson, the pioneer of Presbyterianism in Henry County and pastor of Anderson Memorial Presbyterian Church in Martinsville.[22] A well-bred gentlewoman, and from a child an artist, she never married, seeking instead to devote her life to helping people in the name of the Lord. Very evangelistic, she focused her attention on Milltown, sensing a spiritual hunger among the cotton mill workers and knowing they were embarrassed to go to the downtown churches. Her heart especially went out to the children, who needed a Sunday School.[23]

At age fifty-eight, she began holding afternoon Sunday School classes anywhere she could find a room in Milltown, either in homes or a vacant mill house. The mill management smiled warmly on her efforts and was helpful in many ways, especially in housing the Sunday School. She went door-to-door looking for children to teach. Sometimes she had help, and sometimes she worked alone. She visited homes, prayed with the sick, ministered to the needy, and everywhere taught the children the Bible. The work continued to grow, supported by Anderson Memorial, and her Sunday School flourished with the money given by Anderson members.[24]

Kate dreamed that one day Milltown could have its own church. She worked to secure funds for it but never lived to see it. Although land was donated on Dillard Street, she died in March 1922 at age sixty-five before construction began. The chapel was completed in 1923 at a cost of $1,800.00 and for years housed chapel services, Sunday School, community activities, and even an elementary school.[25]

However, in 1931 Anderson Memorial pastor Charles W. Reed noticed that the church had neglected the chapel, and the work seemed to be dying. Sunday School classes had disappeared, and the condition of the building was "shameful." The pastor's concern was contagious. Mrs. E. L. "Nannie" Williamson, Rev. Anderson's oldest daughter and Kate's sister, was first in line to take up the cause. She had helped her sister teach Sunday School in the chapel. Although seventy-two, she was energetic, and she and her husband had significant financial resources. Others joined with her in the chapel effort.[26]

In a matter of months, church members resurrected the chapel. Yet, with the depression in full gear, no money remained for pews, forcing the chapel to remain empty for months. Rev. Reed then discovered a bank account left by Kate specifically for the chapel. It contained eighty-six dollars, exactly the amount needed for the pews! The incident inspired a rebirth of Kate Anderson Chapel, which flourished daringly in the middle of the Great Depression.[27]

The year 1937 saw a small sanctuary added to the front of the building at a cost of five thousand dollars, with furnishings costing $250. Nannie Williamson donated three thousand dollars to the cause.[28] The work continued to grow so fast that a ministerial student had to help the church volunteers. From 1923 until Sam's arrival in 1941, a variety of people kept the work going, primarily Nannie Williamson.

A NEW CHURCH AND A NEW PASTOR

In 1941, Rev. Reed and thirty-six faithful members of Anderson Memorial felt the time had come to petition Roanoke Presbytery (PCUS) to declare Kate Anderson Chapel a church. For twenty years, the Anderson flock had poured money, materials, and prayer into the mission. Now they were giving blood—thirty-six warm bodies.[29]

Exactly when the committee first approached Sam about pastoring the church is difficult to determine, but Nannie Williamson was probably very instrumental in finding him. She frequently entertained young seminary students and "... scarcely a weekend passed without one of the students from Union paying her a visit."[30] Conceivably, Sam often drove the 180 miles from Richmond to Martinsville. Records show that he preached at Kate Anderson as early as June 26, 1940, and at least one other time before becoming a pastor.[31]

In April 1941, presbytery granted Reed's petition, and the Synod of Virginia and the PCUS General Assembly each appropriated six hundred dollars for Sam's salary. Presbytery gave permission to the Home Mission Committee to extend a call to Sam to become an evangelist in this field until the church could be organized and extend him a call to become its pastor.[32]

On Thursday, June 5, a month after his graduation, Sam was examined before presbytery in South Boston and "heartily recommended for approval." That afternoon he preached a sermon on Romans 1:16. The Home Missions Committee then called Sam as evangelist to Kate Anderson, and he accepted.[33]

In a highly unusual service three days later on the evening of Sunday, June 8, Sam was ordained and installed and the church organized all on the same day! The Rev. P. W. Hodge preached a sermon on Revelation 3:9, "A Church Jesus Loved" [the church at Philadelphia]. The presbytery commission posed questions to the thirty-six charter members and subsequently declared the church organized. Elders and deacons were elected, ordained, and installed. The congregation extended a call for Sam's pastoral services, which he accepted. The Commission then ordained and installed him as pastor of Kate Anderson Chapel. Rev. P. W. Hodge delivered the charge to the pastor, and Rev. Charles W. Reed gave the charge to the congregation.[34]

Earlier that day, Sam had preached his inaugural sermon at Kate Anderson, making promises to the congregation and asking for prayer:

> Today we are church conscious. This is a red-letter day for all of us, red-letter because today a new church is to be born. Some of you have watched it grow from the beginning and loved it. Many of you have placed your names on the birth certificate and are charter members. I have put mine there as the first pastor called by God. I thank God with

*all my heart that He called me to you. Long ago I had to be willing to
say, 'I'll go where you want me to go, dear Lord.'*

*But I wanted to come to you, and I am thankful that you were kind
enough to want me, to call me. In prayer, in your call, in circumstances,
in the advice of friends, in my heart I seemed to hear God calling us here.*

*I promise I come to you and this church with no other thought than
this—to give a short part, a great part, or all of my life to this work as
God shall require. I also promise I come to you with one message, one
Lord and one way—as Paul said in 1 Corinthians 2:2, 'I am determined
to know nothing among you save Jesus Christ and Him crucified.'[35]*

The ministry would be anything but glamorous. Sam's salary was $1,200
a year with no manse or car. His diary notes that he "boarded for a time at
a hotel on Broad Street managed by Miss Kate Winn." However, Sam was
probably supremely happy that he could identify so readily with the poverty of
his congregation.

We don't know much about Sam's thoughts and reflections during those years
in Martinsville except from later sermon illustrations. While his diary is silent
about the Kate Anderson years and the little correspondence from that period
does not divulge much, Sam did keep meticulous records of his church work in
a small five by eight green ledger. It gives us an excellent idea of his work there.

He kept up with both members and nonmembers visited (and the dates he
visited). He recorded the organization of the church, the charter members, and
the first elders and deacons. He listed every single sermon he preached in his
three years at Kate Anderson by title, text, and date. If he had to be gone, he
noted where and who preached in his stead. He kept lists of every new member,
every profession of faith, and every baptism, even recording whether he dipped,
sprinkled, or immersed them. He didn't care how he got them into the kingdom![36]

From the beginning, Sam hit the ground running and seemed never to rest. He
visited his congregation almost every day of the week and began immediately
to preach evangelistically, fervently hoping to start revival among the people.
His sermons were probably quite effective, since he took the time to visit the
cotton mill and cleverly used it to get his points across. Scarcely two weeks after
he arrived, Sam used the following illustration, urging his flock to go to God in
prayer for everything:

*I went through the cotton mill for the first time the other day with
Garland. I don't know much about it yet, but right after that I read about
a woman who worked in a cotton mill. On the wall of the workroom was
a card that warned, 'If your threads get tangled, send for the foreman.'
The first day on the job this woman let her threads get tangled, and she
took it upon herself to untangle them. You know better than I do the mess
she made.*

In a minute she had everything in a real tangle. When the foreman came in, he said, 'You been doing it yourself? Why didn't you send for me?' The woman replied, 'Well, I did my best!' The foreman said, 'Doing your best is sending for me!' A lot of people excuse their loose living with 'I'm doing my best.' They are not. No one is doing his best until he has sent for the great Foreman, Jesus Christ, to untangle the threads of his life and give him a life that is like His.[37]

Sam's innate humility began to endear him to his congregation, as it would for the rest of his life. Members regularly heard him admit failure and frustration in trying to present the Gospel, as in this September 1941 sermon on John 14:

I have never preached on heaven without a sense of failure. The first time I did, it seemed as if God must be laughing at me as I tried in my feeble way to describe what Paul, with more common sense, said: 'Eye hath not seen, nor ear heard…' The second time, I worked, prayed, studied, but still felt complete failure. I asked a friend to preach for me, but he wouldn't. I found the Lord that night in my sermon, and I said in my heart after the service, 'Surely those words were not of man but of God.' But I have learned my lesson since that time. My message on heaven tonight won't be very descriptive. I simply go to the Bible and lay before you the truths that God says in His own language, simple and plain.[38]

He also did not hesitate to upbraid his people kindly when he sensed they were not studying God's Word seriously, as in the following 1941 sermon:

A preacher used to have to know the Bible well because church people knew when he was preaching heresy. People knew the Bible then, but today they neglect it. That is why so much tomfoolery is preached from the pulpit. A preacher can just about say anything and get away with it because people don't know when he is speaking the truth and when he isn't.[39]

Throughout his ministry Sam hated to preach on tithing and rarely did. The first time he preached on the subject was at Kate Anderson, probably on March 22, 1942, in a sermon entitled "The Tithe" (Luke 20:25). He told the congregation that God is just and would not command tithing of His people if it were not possible to do it.[40] Garland Whisonant, one of the recently installed elders, caught Sam after the sermon and said, "I want to tithe, but I've got eight children and just can't! I'll make a deal with you, though. I'll honestly try to tithe for three months, but that's all I'll commit to."

Sam felt bad. He knew Garland worked in the mill and made very poor wages. Finances were always tight for cotton mill people. They lived from hand to mouth and still had not a cent left over. Yet, Sam decided not to try to talk him out of it; he was glad to hear Garland say he'd try to tithe. Privately, however, Sam wasn't any too sure that Garland could do it either.

In the course of the three months, Sam forgot about it. One day he saw Garland approaching him on the street, grinning widely. "You remember that proposition I made you?" he asked. "For the first time since I've been married, I've got a little money in the bank. We realized we were going to have to figure out how to live on one tenth less than we had been. So we took a look at all of our expenses to see what we could do without. And we did find some things! We are living as well as we ever were, I think. But now we're using our money with more wisdom and have more to give."[41]

Such willingness to obey God endeared Garland even more to Sam. He had found a true brother in the Lord. Sam grew to love him, and the feeling was mutual; Garland named his youngest child Taylor Patterson Whisonant. Even though Garland moved to Alabama in September 1942, Sam kept up a lively correspondence with him for the rest of his life.

Sam wasn't stingy with his pulpit and often invited others to preach; his good friend and classmate Ralph Buchanan filled the pulpit often, as did Rev. Reed.[42] Sam frequently preached for his friends, too.[43] When he did, he took the whole congregation with him if the church was within walking distance.

Sam was ahead of his time in realizing the value of radio in evangelism. Likely he was influenced by his Richmond mentor John Belk and well-known Bible teacher Charles Fuller, whose *Old-Fashioned Revival Hour* was by then heard across the country.[44] From November 1941 to March 1944 Sam did about seventy-five radio sermons on WMVA in Martinsville. Sometimes the programs stopped for several weeks or months, possibly for lack of funds to buy the time. Characteristically, he listed the date and title of each one in his small journal.[45]

At Kate Anderson, Sam also began setting the pattern for his ministry for the rest of his life. He saw himself primarily as an evangelist, and wherever he happened to be employed, he wanted the freedom to hold revivals regularly in other churches. No doubt he accepted the call to Martinsville with the understanding that he could be absent a reasonable amount of time for that purpose. While at Kate Anderson, he held at least twelve revivals in other southern cities and towns.

The Holy Spirit began to work immediately in the hearts of Sam's people, especially among the young. On June 22, 1941, during Sam's first month there, twelve-year-old Henry Bocock and ten-year-old Jack Whisonant (Garland's son) professed faith and were baptized.[46] Buck Powell's sixteen-year-old sister Dorotha was also one of Sam's first converts in July of that year.[47]

Although Buck did not accept Christ until much later (not under Sam's ministry), he attended Kate Anderson until he left for the military in 1943 and believes the church's ministry had a great effect on his life.

"Sam was the first pastor I ever knew. He was tall and lanky and so very nice. My family didn't go to church, but I went occasionally on Sunday because they gave out candy." Buck pauses as emotion overflows, and he cries quietly. "We were very, very poor, and a piece of candy was a jewel because we never got treats. My Sunday School teacher, Mrs. Easley, told me that God loved me and she did, too. I was in several bad situations in Germany during the war, including the Battle of the Bulge, and I remembered what she told me. I believe it helped me through."

SAM TAKES A WIFE

In November 1941, Sam actually took some time off to get married! His records show that he took two Sundays off from the pulpit for his wedding and honeymoon.[48] The ceremony was on Wednesday, November 12 at 5:00 p.m. at First Presbyterian Church in Marietta, Georgia, where Stelle had been working. Sam's good friend Ralph Buchanan attended and remembers the day held a bit of drama.

"Estelle was very upset that morning because of a telegram from her father ordering her not to get married. I don't know why, but he was very opposed to the marriage and had refused to come to the wedding. She was a nervous wreck, and we were worried that she could not go through with it. But she got herself together and did splendidly."

The Rev. M. O. Sommers, pastor of the church, read the marriage service in the presence of a large number of friends and family. The service was simple but marked by beauty and dignity. Sam and Stelle had no attendants and entered the church together. Stelle wore a street-length, sapphire velvet gown, with a matching blue veiled turban and a shoulder corsage of pink roses.[49]

Palms and ferns filled the interior of the church and formed a background to masses of chrysanthemums and myriad wax candles. In addition to other special music, the church's junior and intermediate choirs sang Lohengrin's "Bridal Chorus" as a processional and Mendelssohn's "Wedding March" as the bride and groom left the church.

After a wedding trip to Florida and Myrtle Beach, South Carolina, the two returned to Martinsville and roomed at Mrs. Nancy Shumate's home for a time.[50] Not even one month later, the Japanese bombed Pearl Harbor and the United States went to war.

Again Sam faced an excruciating decision—stay or go into the chaplaincy?

All of us began to study the scriptures. We were drawn to those doleful scriptures that tell about the power of Satan and his forces. How I thank God for the Reformed faith that began to bring perspective to me, showing how realistic the Bible is and how we should focus on what GOD is doing.[51]

For the time being, Sam determined that God wanted him to stay in his new pastorate with his new bride.

Shortly after they married, the manager of the Martinsville Cotton Mill offered the couple a vacant mill house on Dillard Street just six houses down the street from the church. Sam could have it rent-free if he wanted. On one hand, Sam was elated. He wanted and needed to live among his congregation. The location of this house was ideal, and the price was surely right. On the other hand, he was skeptical. Was it a fit home for Stelle? He'd been visiting in those houses and knew that, without a union to protect employees' rights, these people had to live in some rough conditions.[52]

However, he wasn't prepared for how rough it actually was. One day he went to take a look at it himself and was revolted. It was filthy. It had four rooms—a kitchen and three other rooms. The kitchen was bare except for a coal stove and a big sink—no hot water, no cabinets, no countertops. Another room contained a coal stove, while the other two had only dirty fireplaces. A lone electric bulb hung from a grimy cord in the center of each room. Sam saw no wall outlets. Paint was peeling off the dingy walls, and a layer of encrusted dirt seemed to cover every surface. On the back porch he found the bathroom—simply a commode in a closet. He should be grateful, he supposed, that at least the house had indoor plumbing.

Shaking his head in disbelief, he thought proudly, "I'll never let my wife live in a house like this!" Later he told a Christian friend, "I'm not even going to tell Stelle they have offered the house to us because I don't want to put her in the position of saying no." To Sam's surprise his friend disagreed and cautioned him not to make Stelle's decision for her. "She has a right to decide for herself what house she wants to live in."

Sam reconsidered and decided to take Stelle to look at the house. In his heart he wanted her to object strongly to it; he didn't want his wife living in such poor conditions. Yet, he was soon to find out what a godly woman the Lord had given him. They entered, and after Stelle had looked around a bit, Sam was stunned speechless when she said, "You know, we could paint this room green and that one blue ..."

Sam began to know right then what a wonderful wife he had in Stelle:

> *Stelle's selfless acceptance of my calling in the mill village was a true blessing. She knew that the best place for me to live was not across town, but right there in the midst of my people. It was a tough situation, but she never once complained. And I think she was about as happy there as anywhere else we lived. In fact, all through our married life, Stelle was a reservoir of peace, of simple and quiet trust to me. The*

*longer I lived with her, the more I began to see the impact of her sweet,
uncomplicated faith—the simplicity with which she took whatever the
Bible said and rested on it, the peace that pervaded her heart because
she trusted God's word.*[53]

"Daddy gave himself up to the Lord as a vessel, and Mother devoted herself
to helping him," says daughter Becky. "Daddy and her faith were the most
important things in her life."

Erma Lawson, Alva's daughter, remembers Sam and Stelle fondly today,
even though she was just a little girl when they were there. The couple stayed
with her family several days on Old Cotton Mill Hill while renovating their new
home. Erma's mother, Mae, wrote Sam regularly for the rest of her life.

Sam and Stelle quickly found they had more to deal with than a dirty house.
God couldn't have picked a rougher location. On one side were the Cooks and on
the other the Lawsons, some *tough* people! Sam and Stelle never got much sleep
on the weekend. Both Lawson and Cook were strong drinking men, raving from
Friday night until Sunday morning. Every Saturday night the police had to come
to one, if not both, houses to stop the upheavals.[54]

Cotton mill men were worked to the bone, paid little, and looked out on
a lifetime of grueling poverty for themselves and their children. Discouraged,
downhearted, and not able to see a way out, they drowned the hopelessness in
alcohol and gambling.

"Dusty Cook was an alcoholic," recalled Buck Powell, who lived several
houses away. "Men like Dusty worked like slaves all week, then drank whiskey,
brawled, and beat their wives on the weekend.

"The cotton mill paid in cash, and many men spent it all on liquor and cards
instead of providing for their families. On Friday night after work, my father
went down to a little house in the pasture behind the mill to drink and play cards.
Sometimes he'd stay there all weekend and lose all his money. That meant less
food, less clothing, less support for the family. My mom was a hard worker, doing
the best she could, and Dad's drinking caused huge problems between them. He
never got any help with his drinking, but my mother was a brave woman and
stayed with him."

Characteristically, Sam looked for the good in both the Lawsons and Cooks,
and, where others might have shunned them, Sam embraced them, saying later:

*Those two families became the dearest neighbors, even though only
one or two of them were converted during my pastorate. I'm still sorry
about that. The mayhem continued all the time we lived there; they didn't
cut down any because the preacher lived right there between them! They
just accepted us as neighbors, and never was anybody better to us than
the Cooks and the Lawsons.*[55]

But Sam was not silent in the pulpit about alcohol abuse, as evidenced in a sermon preached just two weeks after he came to Kate Anderson. He met the problem head on, anxious to show people that they were substituting alcohol for Christ:

> *That man who drinks—you call him just plain mean and no good. We Christians need to get Jesus' idea of the mean man, then maybe we would love him rather than abuse him. If you looked closely you might find the secret pain that causes him to drink. He is lost. He drinks because he doesn't know what else to do. What he needs is Jesus.*[56]

Not long after they moved into the cotton mill house, Stelle's father died. Sam and Stelle convinced her mother, Margaret, to sell her home in Darlington and move in with them. She lived with them the rest of their married life.

"The gesture was very selfless and generous," relates Becky, "but I think they all lived long enough to know it was a mistake. My grandmother was a stout, strong woman, only in her fifties when my grandfather died. She was one of thirteen children; she could have kept house in Darlington and been around all her relatives."

THE SLOUGH OF DESPOND

In the spring of 1942, Sam became quite discouraged. He had poured himself out in an effort to win the community to Christ. Preaching his heart out, he had held all the services he could, while visiting and knocking on hundreds of doors. Whatever he knew to do, he had done, but very little had happened even though it was a fertile field. He was trying to lead, but no one wanted to follow!

"I really was energetically active," confessed Sam later. "I thought that I was going to set the world on fire, that I would be used by God in a great way to move people tremendously. However, I discovered that I could move hardly anyone."[57]

Most of the professions of faith were coming from young people. Sam was tremendously disappointed that older people were not responding to the Gospel. While he was overjoyed to see youth coming to Christ, he had thought it would be just the other way around:

> *I had always thought winning older people to Christ would be easier than winning young people because the elderly are thinking about death; their lives are just about over. But I was dead wrong. How much easier it is to attract youth! Everything gets harder with age—harder to walk, hear and see—and far harder to come to Christ. An overwhelming number come to Christ in their youth, but precious few in old age.*[58]

Sam knew he had gaps in leadership skills and admitted as much to the congregation in his inaugural sermon:

> I request your patience because I am young. So many things I do not know. So many experiences in life I have not encountered. Because of this I know I will make mistakes. Be patient. I have a pastor friend whose impulsiveness and zeal result in mistakes. But someone said of him, 'He does make mistakes, but one thing I know. His head may be wrong, but his heart never is.'
>
> Youth is good, else God would not start us all out young. I take comfort in the words of Paul to a young preacher of his day in 1 Timothy 4:12: 'Let no man despise thy youth, but be thou an example of believers in word, in walk of life, in love, in spirit, in faith, in purity.'
>
> I need your prayers. I intend to pray for you and you do that for me. I need your work. This is your church. You make it all you can in every way you can to continue to grow. Be faithful, bring others, witness. Let's let this be known as a live church, a friendly church, a Gospel church, a light of Christ in this city.[59]

Sam admitted later that his immaturity had indeed raised the ire of at least one person in the congregation. "Several members criticized his brash impetuosity," noted RTS Professor Richard de Witt, "but one elder apparently took Sam's plea for patience to heart and stood up for him, saying, 'Don't give him so much grief. He'll turn out all right; just leave the young man alone.'" That elder could have been either Garland Whisonant or Alva Williams.

Realizing his inadequacies, in August 1942, Sam brought in Leslie Patterson (no relation), a rather well known pastor/evangelist in Virginia at the time, to hold revival services. He preached evangelistic messages to the congregation in the evenings and during the day visited with Sam in personal evangelism. He had been there only a day or two when Sam realized Patterson was performing another service—helping a young, fledgling preacher learn what he was supposed to be doing.

During that time God used an unorthodox method to give Sam guidance in trust. One sweltering day he had stopped in a church in Winston-Salem to pass the time and get cool when he spied a sign tacked to a Sunday School classroom wall. It read: "The greatest peril in the path of any Christian worker is to be energetically active and spiritually ineffective." Sam knew that described him perfectly:

> I had been active and didn't have to apologize to God or man for my activity. I'd been as busy as I could be. With all of my energies I had been trying to serve Christ. But I had been spiritually ineffective because of a lack of spiritual growth.[60]

REVIVAL!

As usual, God employed an unlikely person to further Sam's spiritual growth, humble him, and teach him the importance of both prayer and dependence on Christ's power, not human activity, for church growth.

One Sunday morning Sam came up to the church a little early and heard loud talking in the back. He investigated and discovered old Alva Williams, an elder and charter member, in one of the Sunday School rooms with the door shut. He was praying passionately for Sam and the church.

Sam was astounded. Alva was a very sweet, timid man who had never gone to school and didn't know how to read or write. He had one of the lowest jobs at the cotton mill—a sweeper, day after day cleaning up the never-ending lint and dust. He was also the church's janitor. Sam couldn't believe Alva was praying so boldly. Sam listened but didn't let Alva know he was there. How long had he been doing this?

The next Sunday Sam came early again, and, sure enough, Alva was already there. This went on for several more Sundays. Within two months, Alva had six or seven other men praying with him. About that time, Sam began to notice a change in the church. Hardly a week went by without a conversion that seemed genuine to Sam. Then the men began to meet in the afternoon before the evening service. It was the beginning of a two-year revival at Kate Anderson, a "constant coming to Christ" in that community. Sam knew for a fact that *his* efforts had not brought it about:

> *I had not changed. I was doing what I had always done, so I knew it wasn't because of a seminary-trained preacher. I had had my shot at it for a year and had accomplished virtually nothing. But an uneducated, Spirit-filled, godly janitor's prayers and the group he got started turned that church around.* [61]

By October 1942, Sam was on numerous presbytery committees,[62] and by April 1943, he received commendation for his work.

> *Rev. Sam Patterson of the Kate Anderson Church has done outstanding work the past year. This is an important work since it is the only one in a strictly industrial area … more than thirty members were added to the church during the year.* [63]

In addition to a $132 pay raise, presbytery appropriated $1,300 and General Assembly gave six hundred dollars to purchase a manse for Sam and Stelle at 560 Dillard Street, directly across the street from the church. A privately-owned residence, it was much nicer than a mill house.[64] Virtually all the houses on that side of the street have been torn down, including Sam's home. Only the concrete steps on the hillside remain.

Sam was also gaining some notoriety as an evangelist, holding his first evangelistic services in Zuni, Virginia:

> ... In September, Rev. Sam Patterson assisted the pastor in a very helpful meeting. Eighteen new members were added to the church, sixteen by profession of faith and two by restatement.[65]

Sam not only preached revivals in churches but also had contact with schools such as French Camp long before he came to Mississippi. Seventy-eight-year-old Byron Bray of New York City recalls the time in March 1942 when Sam came to hold a weeklong revival at Glade Valley School in Allegheny County, North Carolina. The Presbyterian boarding school served mountain children snowed in during the winter and unable to attend school more than about four months a year. Students paid very little tuition at Glade Valley; every student worked four hours a day for room and board. Donors from nearby churches made up the difference for any shortfall in school expenses.

Byron had left home at thirteen, fleeing "unbearable" circumstances. His mother had been in a mental institution since he was three, and he had lived with relatives in extreme poverty, without even electricity. When he visited his father and new stepmother, he realized he was living in a brothel. He showed up at Glade Valley with the clothes on his back.

"I met with Sam only once," recalls Byron, "but I vividly remember his compassion. Sam had such charisma and inspired such trust that he instantly gained the confidence of the students."

A couple of times that year Sam sent Byron a check for two dollars (a great deal of money back then). When school was out for the summer, Byron showed up on Sam's doorstep at 560 Dillard Street. He felt so welcome he stayed for two or three weeks, and Sam made a lasting impression.

"I remember Sam always prayed before we ate, and we had morning prayers. He prayed on his knees and included my name. I went to church with them while I was there. That fall I joined the Navy, and we kept in touch for a while, but I never saw him again. However, I have always remembered his kindness to me."

In May 1943, Sam began a long and fruitful relationship with evangelist Jimmie Johnson by bringing him to Kate Anderson for services. Twenty members were added to the church rolls. He would enjoy Jimmie countless times in years to come at French Camp Academy Chautauquas.

By September 1943, Sam had become a denominational leader, serving as chairman of several presbytery committees and as a member of a number of synod committees.[66] In October 1943, he was elected a commissioner to the General Assembly to be held May 25, 1944.[67]

December 20, 1943, brought the birth of a beautiful daughter, Becky (Margaret Rebekah). While Sam was excited beyond measure, the glorious event made even harder a decision he had been wrestling with for months. The United States had been at war now for two years, and Sam had seen many men his age leave to serve. A good many of his seminary classmates had already become chaplains, and Sam's heart was pulled harder and harder in that direction. He wanted to serve God and his country, and he felt he could do both in the chaplaincy.

Yet, becoming a chaplain meant going to war—going overseas. He knew his leaving would ultimately cost Stelle more than him. She would be concerned for his safety and have to care for the home front alone. This would be the first major decision of their marriage. Finally, he shared his dilemma with her, promising to pray through it and find the wisest counsel he could.

Stelle adopted the policy then that she maintained on every other issue that would ever arise in their marriage. She didn't tell Sam about it; he simply watched it operate. She became his silent prayer partner in all decisions. She never volunteered any ideas or suggestions about what he ought to do. Never. When he asked her for counsel, she always gave only a minimum amount, sharing any ideas that she might find helpful, but never imposing her will on the information. She was careful not to show any kind of emphasis that might sway him in any way. He knew she was praying fervently and earnestly, but she believed God would show Sam what to do. She didn't pray that God would show *her* what Sam ought to do; she prayed that He would show *Sam*. She waited for Sam to tell her what answer God had given to her prayers:

> *I knew I always had Stelle's silent support as I sought guidance. Finding God's will was a lot easier because I didn't have her pulling me in one direction. Every decision I had to make, I really made it! I had to because she would have no part of making it. And every one, she accepted. I don't even know what her personal feelings were sometimes on these decisions. I believe it was really easier for her. There was never any contest of wills, of her possibly getting some guidance that I didn't get. She honestly believed that the guidance God gave me was right. It made for a basic unity in our marriage for which I am thankful.[68]*

In April 1944, Sam was elected moderator of Roanoke Presbytery by acclamation.[69] Why he accepted the post is difficult to understand because he probably carried out few duties. On April 27 he applied for a chaplain commission with the Naval Reserve and scarcely a month later, on May 12, was given the rank of Lt. Junior Grade. He was appointed to the Naval Reserve chaplaincy on June 13 and sworn in on June 28.[70]

In June he resigned as pastor of Kate Anderson. His records show that he had seen eighty-seven professions of faith, many of them baptized for the first time, and nearly forty reprofessions.[71]

Kate Anderson historical records show that the people loved Sam:

> *We are persuaded that the young minister led the young church gently and firmly through the disturbing distresses of the times. After a three-year pastorate, he resigned, put on the uniform of a chaplain, and went out to the battle lines of the war to serve. The record shows that beginning with thirty-six charter members, he closed his work here with 122 members and 156 in Sunday School. He did a good work.*[72]

During the next decade, Sam came back to hold several revivals. He maintained correspondence with some members for the rest of his life. After he left, the little church continued to grow, and hopes were high for a self-supporting body. Yet, in the early 1950s, a great blow fell that spelled doom for the little chapel. Workers voted the union in, and the New York owners closed the mill, saying it was not making enough money to pay union demands.[73] Many families moved away as the mill sold their homes. The chapel closed in April 1967, but, happily, its remaining members were absorbed into the new Collinsville Presbyterian Church near Martinsville.[74]

Though numerous buildings have been torn down on Cotton Mill Hill, Kate Anderson Chapel still stands today. For years, it served as a Salvation Army Center, but recently that ministry shut down. Though vacant, the chapel stands as mute evidence to the mighty power of God to bring life-giving change to a place of evil and to the heart of a spiritually immature young pastor.

OFF TO WAR

For the rest of his life, Sam was extremely proud of his two-year stint with the Marines in World War II, first serving in the Philippine Liberation Campaign, then in China. Except for a couple of very brief entries, Sam's diary is silent about his war experiences, and no letters from him during that period have survived. Letters to him from Stelle and his parents, a few scanty chaplain reports from Sam, and later sermon illustrations are our only glimpses of his life during those war years. Fortunately, Marines who served with him survived the war and were quite happy to share reminisces.

On July 4, 1944, just four days shy of his twenty-eighth birthday, United States military records show that Sam reported to the Naval Chaplain's Training School in Williamsburg, Virginia. While he trained for two months, Stelle, Becky and Mrs. Sellers spent the summer with Sam's parents in Morrilton.

In September 1944, he was assigned to the Marine Corps and took up his duties as Assistant to the Base Chaplain at Marine Base in San Diego. His work also included acting as Protestant chaplain at the Recruit Depot. In November, Stelle and the others joined him.

By February 1945, he had been promoted to full Lieutenant and by March had been transferred to Marine Air at Camp Miramar to await transport overseas. For two months he and his family had an apartment at 1412 Tenth Street in beautiful Coronado, California, close enough to work for Sam to return from camp each night.

HEADING OUT

Nevertheless, the time came too quickly for Sam to leave. On May 9, 1945, he shipped out to Zamboanga, Philippines aboard the U.S. carrier *Hugh S. Scott*, traveling by way of Pearl Harbor, Admiralty Islands, and New Guinea. His new assignment was Protestant Chaplain to the Marine Aircraft Group 32 (MAG) of the First Marine Air Wing. Commanded by Colonel Jerome Clayton, the unit consisted mostly of Marine bomber squadrons—with names like Wild Horses, Flying Goldbricks, and Bombing Banshees—and had been fighting in Zamboanga since March.[75]

Parting with Sam was exquisitely painful for Stelle since they had been married only three and a half years. An excerpt from a May 10 letter shows her emotion:

> *I came home last night after you left and read Psalm 91. It comforted me so. I will meet you at eight every evening with those words in my heart.[76]*

At first Stelle wrote Sam every day. On May 19, 1945, she began signing her letters with an enigmatic "3/0," never explaining its meaning. While Stelle was a great influence on Sam's life, a June 1 letter shows how greatly he impacted hers:

> *You can never know how much your influence and example have meant to me…. You have made me see what Paul meant when he said '… for me to live is Christ.' …One of my most cherished hopes is that I might come nearer the goal that you reached and thereby be the helpmate you deserve.[77]*

The family stayed in the Coronado apartment for several months after Sam left and might have lived there until he returned had it not been for his mother's worsening heart condition. During the summer of 1945, the elder Pattersons sold their home in Morrilton and moved closer to relatives in Wynne, Arkansas. Shortly thereafter, Stelle, her mother, and Becky moved back to Wynne for the duration of the war to help care for them.

Thankfully, the voyage to Zamboanga was uneventful as Sam began to minister to his men. In an annual chaplain report to his superiors he wrote:

The trip over was certainly interesting. We had several thousand
men aboard and only five passenger chaplains, plus the ship's chaplain,
to care for their spiritual needs. Three of the six were Catholic and three
Protestant. Chaplain R. E. Carroll, who attended Union a few years
ahead of me, was among the number, and we had a lot of good fellowship
together. Besides regular Sunday services, we held a number of week-
day vesper services on the ship's deck. A submarine contact alert and a
couple of aircraft contact alerts added some excitement to the trip, but
we never did actually engage any enemy aircraft.[78]

Nevertheless, the trip was probably a bit more dangerous than Sam let on. By
January 1945, the Japanese Kamikaze Corps had become a real problem for the
United States Navy. Reports showed that one in four did some damage and one
in thirty-three sank a ship. Military officials warned all personnel returning to the
U.S. not to mention the kamikazes, and they carefully censored mail for any hint
of such attacks to prevent the enemy from knowing their effectiveness. Not until
April 1945 did the world become aware of this new form of warfare.[79] By God's
grace, Sam's transport was not one of their targets.

ZAMBOANGA

If you've never heard of the Zamboanga Peninsula, you aren't alone.[80] It is
one of those remote Pacific battle zones familiar to only the most diligent of
World War II students. Once known as Western Mindanao, it is the southernmost
part of the 3,600-square-mile island of Mindanao, the second largest in the
Philippine chain. This peninsula and places like it were the battlefields of
MacArthur's Army in the Allied effort to retake the Philippines. Japan had
wrested the islands from the Allies in 1942, setting up a defense headquarters
on Zamboanga. MacArthur had escaped, but vowed to return. The Filipinos had
fought on against the Japanese, providing him with intelligence and receiving
American supplies. MacArthur did indeed return two years later, invading
Leyte on October 20, 1944, and issuing his famous "I have returned" speech.
The Philippine Campaign became one of the largest operations of World War II,
involving nearly 280,000 American troops.

Since Zamboanga was where the Allies lost the Philippines, it was fitting that
this should be the place that ended the campaign to take it back. On March 10,
1945, while Sam waited to be shipped out, U.S. forces landed at Zamboanga
City, taking control of it and two nearby airfields. MAG 32 was one of several
squadrons providing excellent close air support for the assault as the U.S. Army
pushed the Japanese back. American forces took the city after a week, but more
encounters followed as MacArthur's men pursued pockets of resistance in
Mindanao.

MAG 32 flew out of Moret Field, a few miles north of Zamboanga City near the village of Santa Maria. The unit performed a variety of tasks, among them strafing, bombing, firing rockets, and patrolling Japanese troops and placements.

"We flew from the strip made by the Japanese at first, but it was fairly hard and had been torn up by bombs prior to our landing," recalled James "Rip" Collins, a Marine bomber radio operator assigned to MAG 32. "American engineers, with Filipino help, converted it into a longer, wider, and more solid all-weather airdrome. When they finished, it was a fine airfield."

Indeed, as the tempo of air operations on Mindanao rose, so did the use of Moret Field. Before long it housed over three hundred widely varying types of aircraft. Being so close to the front lines was a new concept for Marine pilots; fierce combat was now minutes, not hours, away. [81]

The men of MAG 32 saw much fighting and performed valiantly. They subsequently received a Naval Commendation for their outstanding performance:

> *[MAG 32 is commended] for exceptionally meritorious service and outstanding heroism … in flights made extremely hazardous by dense jungles; precipitous, cloud-obscured mountains; and adverse weather … [also for] relentless attacks to reduce vital enemy targets and destroy ammunition and fuel dumps despite intense anti-aircraft fire….* [82]

By the time Sam arrived in Zamboanga on June 5, 1945, most of the heavy fighting had ended, and the bombing had become "a rather routine daily maneuver that was relatively safe." [83] Yet, the men still desperately needed a chaplain. The week before Sam arrived, a MAG 32 commanding officer and three of his crew were killed on a bombing mission. Scarcely two weeks after his arrival, another commanding officer and his five crew members were burned badly when their plane went down in flames in dense jungle. Under enemy fire, all managed to escape. Conceivably, Sam provided solace for the victims and counsel to fellow soldiers in their sadness.

Apparently he was successful in sharing the Gospel because Stelle wrote on June 25, "I'm so thrilled to hear about your work, and I was so happy about the officer convert. I know the Lord will wonderfully use you …"

Surely another of Sam's duties was to deal with the men's frustration with tropical living conditions. Torturous heat, constant rain, and uncomfortable humidity conspired to make tempers short. The unit's camp in the middle of a coconut plantation next to the airfield gave some respite from the heat, but not much.

"The palms provided considerable shade," said Rip Collins, who helped lay out the camp upon arrival. "However, when the wind picked up we were peppered with coconuts! We tied the tent flaps to the adjacent tent, drooping them a bit to let the rain run off and to keep the sun from heating the area between the tents.

"The heat in the tents was almost unbearable during the day, unless we stretched out on our bunks to be low to the ground. Standing up was like sticking your head into a heated oven! But we did have good onshore breezes that cooled the area down nicely for sleeping."

Tropical animal antics weren't amusing either. "Monkeys regularly got into the tent and caused havoc," said Burt Henry, a MAG 12 pilot. "More than once they stole toothpaste and made a general mess inside. With tent flaps up to keep air circulating, keeping the monkeys out was almost impossible."

The camp was a tent city laid out in quadrants with rows of tents in neat orderly lines. With a mess hall, a medical facility, offices, and a theater, the men had all the comforts of home, so to speak. However, Burt Henry grew extremely tired of dehydrated eggs, black coffee, and potatoes. Rip Collins does recall a small PX on the flight line at the airdrome, but "the only candy they had was ZagNut Bars—by the thousands!"

With the Japanese army no longer a threat, life was much less dangerous but more boring and monotonous, making the heat, humidity, and constant tropical rain harder to endure. "I would have gone nuts if I hadn't thought up things to do with my time," said Burt Henry. "At night I'd lie in my bed and watch the lizards eat bugs on the ceiling.

"We had an O Club with lots of iced beer, and I still wonder where they got the ice. The only record we had was Bunny Berigan's 'I Can't Get Started,' and then the volume control on the phonograph went bad. So we cut the wires, put them in a glass of water, and sprinkled salt in it until we got the right volume."

The camp's "movie theater" was an open air semicircle with coconut logs for seats. Lana Turner and Betty Grable were certain to bring a full house under the stars!

Sam saw the variety of ministry opportunities as a challenge and felt his job was much more fulfilling than duty in the States:

> *In Zamboanga I got my first taste of real overseas duty. My experience indicates that, overseas, the chaplain is busier and more in demand than in a stateside post; to that extent, it is a happier and more satisfying duty. He is really needed by the men, who are attempting to adjust to unusual conditions and to the problems and strains that separation from home and loved ones brings.*[84]

Yet, Sam himself was separated from loved ones and apparently receiving no support from home because of the poor mail service. Even though Stelle wrote him every day and his parents wrote frequently, Stelle's letters show that by June 23, 1945, Sam had not received a single piece of mail. He must have received a truckload when he finally did hear his name at mail call!

Perhaps one of the things that kept him occupied was his delight in Zamboanga's culture and surroundings. Others might have been bored, but Sam, with his perennial optimism, found something to be thankful for in any situation. He told Union Seminary President Ben Lacey:

> *The work is interesting, the outfit a dandy one, and of course the tropics and its natives are most fascinating.*[85]

Indeed, Sam must have felt as if he had been dropped into an exotic version of his "over the hill" days along the Arkansas River in Morrilton. The peninsula was and still is a nature lover's paradise, with parks sporting tropical fruit trees interspersed with richly-hued, fascinating blooms. Mango and citrus plantations dot the plains, giving way to lush tropical rain forests, especially in the south around Zamboanga City where Sam was stationed. In the vast mountain wilderness rose formidable extinct volcanoes, with stunning waterfalls cascading from craggy cliffs. Sam probably loved exploring the verdant mountains and dense forests, even reveling in the fact that the swamps were crocodile-infested.

The island's cave system, a marvel of divine engineering, must have tempted him. In some places, from sunrise to sunset a spelunker can move from cave to cave without surfacing. Nearby Santa Cruz Island beckoned, with its beaches flushed pink by bits of coral washed up from the reefs. The crystal clear, sky-blue waters support a vast array of tropical fish.

Sam also must have found the natives fascinating. Numerous tribes inhabit the peninsula. Some are farmers, and others are "sea gypsies" who, until recently, spent their lives on their small boats; in fact, some of their villages are floating flotillas. Still other tribes are artisans and weavers whose unique colorful tapestries command high prices the world over.

The Badjeos are seafarers known for their colorful vintas (boats of ancient design), and their thatched homes perched precariously on stilts at the water's edge. Sam met the Badjeo tribe as his ship steamed into the harbor. He wrote in his diary later:

> *The natives meet incoming vessels, begging the GIs to throw coins in the water so they can dive and catch them. They succeed almost every time.*

Rip Collins loved his duty in Zamboanga, too. "It was the nicest place I spent time in during the war. The Christian Filipinos were wonderful people, and we were in no way restricted in our dealings with them, except that they could not come into the tents. We enjoyed sitting around the cooking fire at night listening to stories of the occupation. The beaches were expansive and beautiful, and we were able to swim, fish and even do a bit of boating in life rafts."

All was not idyllic, however, and surely Sam saw the horrors the Filipino people had suffered. Perhaps he worked alongside men like Collins, who tried to help the natives put their lives back together.

"Santa Maria was a lovely little village before the war," revealed Rip, "but the Japanese had trashed all the homes and destroyed what little the people had, including the electric plant. The city of Zamboanga had no electricity or waterworks when we came. Dried fish and fresh fruit were the staple foods. The Marines worked to open roads and even helped natives build a simple chapel. All materials came from the forest, except for a few nails and canvas windows. The seats were logs and the floors packed dirt, as in most of the homes."

Sam's tour in Zamboanga was very short, since the Philippine Campaign ended July 5, 1945. By August 14, Truman announced that the war had ended, and on September 2 the Japanese formally surrendered. In a perfect world, Sam would have been home by Christmas. However, even before the surrender ceremonies took place on the deck of the battleship Missouri in Tokyo Harbor, plans were in place for the occupation of North China by U.S. Marines. The World War had ended, but China now was on the verge of civil war.[86]

The rise of the Communist guerilla movement in China severely threatened Chiang Kai-shek's Nationalist regime, much to Washington's dismay. The Marines' job was two-fold: guard Nationalist holdings to prevent Communist takeover and assist in repatriating over six hundred thousand Japanese military personnel and civilians until the Nationalists could do it alone. However, repatriation would be slow; ironically, the Nationalists needed the help of the Japanese to guard key areas from the Communists until Chiang Kai-shek's forces could gain control of the interior. No one knew how long this would take.[87]

The news of North China duty was not pleasant to many men who had been fighting for years and simply wanted to go home. Conversely, Sam was like countless others and did not have enough service points to be discharged.

Said one Marine on his way to North China:

> When the war ended, we could imagine the destroyers escorting our troops as we steamed back into San Francisco under the Golden Gate. Victory was ours! But victory, we were about to discover, was not ours … only wishful thinking on our parts. We would not be returning to America to a cheering, waving population. We would be long forgotten by the time we returned.[88]

Even today most Americans don't realize that World War II continued for thousands of Marines until 1949—a distasteful fact for some soldiers. Whether Washington conspired to keep the Marines' policing role in North China under wraps is hard to say:

> Hardly a word about these incidents was published in American newspapers after the war. Other than the Marines themselves and their immediate families, I doubt if one hundred thousand Americans living at the time ever heard a word about what was happening in China. Marines

would be in North China for four more long years until they gradually phased out.[89]

HEADING TO CHINA

The last week of September 1945, Sam's MAG 32 squadron left in a convoy of LSTs (Landing Ship Troop) for the three-week journey to Tsingtao (now Qingdao) via Okinawa. Located on the Yellow Sea, it had begun as a small fishing village until the Germans took it over in 1897 and turned it into a strategically important port. Today, it is one of China's largest seaports and has the best natural harbor in the country. The Germans also made the town famous with the Tsingtao Brewery, known worldwide for its beer. In 2008, the city hosted several Olympic events, including the sailing competitions along its complicated shoreline.

The trip to North China was dangerous because the Japanese had heavily mined the waters during the war. Gunners in high turrets were on the alert, spotting mines to set them off before the ship reached them. However, on this trip they soon encountered a far worse danger than mines in the form of deadly Typhoon Louise on the China Sea.

In an annual chaplain report, Sam said:

> *We caught part of that awful October typhoon and had a very rough and dangerous time of it for several days. I thought of Acts 27:20 at times: 'Now when neither sun nor stars appeared for many days, and no small tempest beat on us, all hope that we would be saved was finally given up.' But a worthy ship, competent ship's officers and crew, and Divine Assistance brought us through safely.*[90]

As usual, Sam was a master of understatement. Typhoon Louise would become one of the worst in history, almost wiping out military operations on Okinawa. Sam and his fellow servicemen actually experienced several terror-filled days aboard their LST, which could have been the USS Napa. In his fascinating *Take China: The Last of the China Marines*, Marine Harold Stephens tells the riveting tale of those dreadful days:

> *I noticed the sky had turned an ominous black ... and the sea was flat, with an oily calm.... I could not believe it possible for the wind to blow as it did ... I felt ridiculous, standing in my turret, holding a tiny rifle and looking out at the raging sea. This was no time to be on the lookout for mines bobbing in a tossing sea. But it was less scary than being below ... Soon the ship began to pitch and list [tilt] violently ... and the wind grew even more frightening.*

There's no describing it. How can one describe a nightmare? It tore at my clothes, threatening to rip the buttons from my jacket. I felt the flesh on my face distort with each blast of wind, and I had to turn away to breathe.

It was a monstrous thing, ever increasing by the minute. The sea, which had risen at first, was beaten down by the wind. It seemed as if the whole ocean might be sucked up into another sphere, another world. No force could control this hellish thing other than, perhaps, the sea itself. The storm reached a point where the driving wind actually flattened the sea, but it did not reduce the swell. How high were the waves? The masts on an LST were at least forty feet above water and the one traveling with us would vanish for minutes at a time in the trough of two mighty waves. I had to get away for a spell and went down five sets of ladders to the bow where my bunk was located. Here the ship tossed and heaved at its worst, dropping so violently it took one's breath away. Vomit was everywhere and made walking nearly impossible. Men lost their balance and came down the aisle headfirst, feet first, sideways, rolling over and over, twisting and squirming. Now and again a man caught a grip on a bunk, but the weight of the bodies behind tore his grasp loose. It was chaos, a melee. A heavy cooking range broke away from its fastening and crashed from one side of the galley to the other, taking out all the tables. It had to be lassoed like a wild steer before it could be stopped.

I knew at once, no matter how terrifying the sea might be, I would be much better off topside. I went back to my turret. What happened next I will never forget. My turret was fifty feet above water, but when the first sea—there were three that I remember—broke over the entire deck, it flooded the turret. I was swept from my feet but managed to grab on to the railing. The second sea sent the LST to our port [left] so far over in a roll that her whole underside became exposed. I was certain she would continue to roll and not right herself, but she miraculously rose again. The third and worst sea was yet to come ...

... during a lull, we caught our breath, glad of a respite from the biting wind. But in the absence of wind and pressure, the sea rose. It jumped! It leaped! It soared straight up! It sprang from every point of the compass. We had passed through the eye ... but leaving the eye of a storm is far worse than entering. We were about to meet the full onslaught of wind and wave.

Just at that moment the third sea hit us. It struck, it slammed, it bombarded all at once, in one powerful, mighty blow.

It came so violently, so shockingly, that it felt as if the earth might have fallen from its axis. The waves had no system now, no stability. They were hollow, maniacal seas, higher than forty, fifty, a hundred feet.

What did it matter? They were not seas at all but mountains of tumbling water.

The tragedy was that there was no avoiding it. The helmsman could only steam ahead no matter what. We were flooded with a mighty sea that rose up from nowhere. No one saw it. It just came and fell everywhere. It was the sea gone mad! For sixteen endless hours the storm continued, and when we were about ready to give up, no longer caring, it ended as abruptly as it began. The next morning I looked out on a shocking, abominable sight. As far as the eye could see, the China Sea was littered with … wrecked junks. The poor boats had literally been ripped wide open, smashed into kindling wood—a fleet of demolished junks, all devoid of life. The convoy had slowed down to half speed, and all morning we searched for signs of life; yet, there were none. As we slowly churned forward, we glided through a sea of death. Bodies were everywhere, floating and some tied to the masts and rigging.[91]

"Sam thought they were going to sink," revealed James "Aubrey" Dendy, to whom Sam told the story in later years. "He had an officer's cabin and could have stayed there through the worst of it during the nights, but he went up on deck where most of the men were sleeping anywhere they could find a spot. They didn't want to be below if it sank. Sam walked among the men, comforting them. When it was all over, they wanted to give him a medal for taking care of his men in rough weather and risking his life, but he wouldn't have it. He said, 'I was just as scared as they were; I didn't want to be in that hole either if we sank!'"

"We lost our rudder and couldn't steer the ship," said Donald Arp (MAG 32), who could have been on Sam's LST. "That was scary, but most frightening of all was when the engineers came through checking the rivets on the side of the ship to make sure they weren't popping loose."

The typhoon devastated Okinawa, sinking twelve ships and other craft and grounding 222 more. It also destroyed from fifty to ninety-five percent of the tent camps and Quonset huts. Thirty-six were killed, one hundred seriously wounded, and forty-seven were missing. If the war had not ended on September 2, this damage would likely have seriously impacted the planned invasion of Japan.[92]

The Marines' first glimpse of the Chinese coastland left a lot to be desired:

… It was dismal, mountainous, and barren … no sign of life, not a tree, not even a shrub … and no color. It was gray and hard. Even when dawn turned into day, it was bleak. That first view was disappointing, but what came next was far worse. The smell. Far out at sea we could smell China. It was a musty, unforgiving smell, nauseating to the senses … It was the unwashed bodies, the human waste gathered to fertilize

*their crops, the garlic they ate to sustain their lives. The smell would
never escape us.*[93]

However, the soldiers may have been slightly encouraged when they first
sighted Tsingtao, since its modern name means "Green Island." As the city
sprawled across the craggy hillside above the harbor, the numerous cypress trees
and stunning beaches provided a break in the monotony of China's eastern coast.
Located on the tip of the Shandong (now Shantung) Peninsula, the area had
long been a popular summer resort for wealthy Chinese and foreigners. Beautiful
winding pathways with small shrines and pagodas led to lavish homes nestled far
back in the hills, some belonging to affluent locals. Visitors could also stay at the
lovely Edgewater Beach Hotel near the shore. A meal at the hotel was a treat for
soldiers, so Sam may have eaten here.

Whatever the men thought of China's scenery and smells, they couldn't argue
with the fact that the Chinese people in this area were overjoyed to see American
forces. Tsingtao was a Nationalist island in a Communist sea; Tsangkou Airfield,
where Sam's unit would be stationed, was in a neutral area, but more often than
not, the Communist and Nationalist armies chose to shell each other over MAG
32's heads.[94]

Steaming into Tsingtao's harbor about the end of October, the Marine convoys
received a welcome fit for kings and emperors:

> *By the hundreds junks were rafted together, their masts appearing
> like a forest of trees. One could easily have leaped from one vessel to the
> other for a mile or two without touching water ... masses of humanity
> had begun gathering on the docks to welcome us ... before our anchors
> had hit the bottom, hundreds and hundreds of Chinese vessels besieged
> us, their oarsmen waving American flags, shouting joyously ... Chinese
> hawkers, many dressed in rags, begged us to buy their wares.*[95]

Disembarking and actually driving to the quarters was difficult because of the
welcoming crowds:

> *No ticker tape parade in New York City could have been more
> grand than our reception in. The streets were one continuous mass of
> humanity, a carpet of happy, smiling, waving people.... There wasn't a
> telephone pole or signpost or tree that didn't have people clinging to it.
> Each and everyone there, without exception, held small American flags,
> which they waved frantically.*[96]

Tsangkou Airfield was about ten miles from downtown Tsingtao, and Sam
wrote home that the unit "moved into the buildings of a former Japanese
bomber school and after two or three months had the base in condition for fairly
comfortable living."[97]

"At first we had no second floor in the barracks," revealed Philip Feltis (MAG 32), "because the Japanese needed the vertical space from ceiling to floor to train the bombers. Carpenters put in a second floor so the building could house several hundred men. We found it pretty filthy, so we had a lot of cleaning to do, too."

Personal hygiene was a challenge in the camp, mainly because of Japanese customs. Latrines were enamel and tile but had no toilets, only enamel basins at floor level. By October 19, 1945, ingenious carpenters had converted crates into seats for these latrines until more customary outhouses could be built. Keeping clean was also interesting. Traditionally, Japanese bathe as a family in a large pool. The bathhouse contained a large, circular pool with waist-deep water heated by a coal-fired boiler. Early bathers got the clean water. Some Marines flatly refused this method, preferring simply to soap up while standing at the pool's edge and then pour bucketfuls of water over themselves to rinse.[98]

Soldiers even had their own convenience store of sorts in camp. Dubbed "The Wall," it was a ten-foot high brick wall flanking the main gate to the camp. Marines sat atop the wall and bargained with Chinese peddlers below. At this open-air flea market, a soldier could buy eggs, chickens, wristwatches, postcards, trinkets, and Tsingtao beer. "I bought the best peanuts in the shell I've ever had," said MAG 32 pilot Jack Mimnaugh. It was a popular place to shop during October and November but lost some of its charm by December when soldiers received liberty assignments.[99]

By the end of October 1945, the airfield had become the wing's busiest and most important base in China.[100] MAG 32 stayed busy flying "show of force" maneuvers in Shantung Province in support of the Nationalist Army and doing reconnaissance on Communist troop movements. A large part of their job was guarding Nationalist supplies from Communist sabotage or theft:

> We guarded our headquarters, supply buildings, coal dumps, ammunition dumps, airfields…. We even had guards to guard the guardhouses. Everything in China needed guarding at all times.[101]

The trains especially needed guarding, and Marines thought this duty was certainly the most dangerous. Coal shipments were vital to the Chinese people; one hundred thousand tons of coal must reach Shanghai every month for the Nationalist Army's survival, and Marines had to ensure the shipment's arrival. The Red Chinese regularly sabotaged rail lines, firing on and ambushing Marine-guarded trains, derailing trains, and tearing up track.[102]

Part of Sam's job surely included dealing with the men's job frustration. The situation was explosive and dangerous; the scout and torpedo bombers of MAG 32 often landed with bullet holes in their fuselages, but Marines were strongly discouraged from shooting back. Often, their guns and cannons were disabled so they could not return enemy fire. Marines had to avoid open warfare at all costs, so they remained discreet. But the average Marine did not understand the reasons why:

> *On both political and moral grounds, it was impossible for the United States to take a decisive military role in another nation's civil war, and the average Marine on postwar duty in China found himself an uneasy spectator or sometimes an unwilling participant in a war which he little understood and could not prevent.* [103]

Yet, all was not work for the men of MAG 32. The pilots had hired a local Chinese young man to cook for them on the flight line. Nicknamed Louie, he took them rabbit hunting regularly in the hills around Tsingtao, and Sam could have tagged along on many of the hunts. They didn't bag many, but a good time was had by all most of the time. One rabbit hunt didn't end so well. On the way home the group found themselves in a rough part of Tsingtao when fifteen to twenty rough-looking Chinese surrounded them, holding rifles to their throats. The Marines' Chinese was poor so they could not communicate that they were simply rabbit hunting and not trying to open fire. Thankfully, a Russian came along and rescued them from the Chinese ruffians, but not from the chewing out they received back at the base. [104]

Liberty in town was always enjoyable, along with plenty of sexual temptations, drinking, and riotous brawls. Certainly part of Sam's job was to warn against such indulgences.

A good meal could be had for less than a dollar at the EM Club. However, soldiers had to be careful where they ate, since dog meat was popular. Some Marines frequented a small steak shop until they discovered the "steak" was dog meat; other men saw Japanese soldiers roasting a dog, hair and all, over a campfire. [105]

"What really took my appetite was the sight of a side of beef being peddled into town and tenderized by a horde of flies," recalled Jack Mimnaugh. "Doctors cautioned us not to eat any of the vegetables grown below ground because the Chinese used human waste as fertilizer. Our doctors also inspected some of the Tsingtao restaurants to make sure conditions were sanitary so servicemen would not get sick."

"Even after getting sick from meals served in homes there, Daddy loved Chinese food," revealed Becky Rogers. "Nevertheless, he learned a trick to protect himself from questionable food. Once he was invited to a Chinese home where they served dog, which he definitely wasn't going to eat. He surreptitiously hid the food in a napkin and put it in his pocket. He perfected this maneuver and employed it for the rest of his life when he ate at others' homes, since he would rather die than offend a host or hostess. If the napkin was paper, he'd fold it up and put it in his coat pocket. If it was cloth, he would somehow transfer the items into his pocket before getting up."

China had to be unlike anything Sam had ever experienced, even in Martinsville. In fact, Tsingtao made Cotton Mill Hill look like Bel Air. He probably had the same reaction as Harold Stephens and fellow Marines:

> We were awed by the Chinese, the confusion of traffic, the vehicles, the noise, the filth, the dilapidation, the smell. Charcoal burning trucks bounced over torn pavements, so heavily loaded that some axles broke, causing a devil of a snafu in traffic. Battered buses with people hanging on the outside like flies on flypaper rolled past, their exhausts kicking out evil black smoke. Nationalist troops in columns of two marched through the streets ... stalls with dirty, sagging canvas awnings overhead lined the sidewalks ... motorcars with doors falling off and some tied with twine to keep the doors on, rumbled past.
>
> The saddest thing we witnessed were the heavy, overloaded carts—the backbone of the transportation system—pulled not by animals but by men. The coolies who worked these clumsy carts did so with backbreaking effort. They slid and often fell to the pavement, bloodying their knees and elbows, but not giving up ...
>
> Among all this traffic, rickshaws shot in and out, darting away from oncoming trucks and avoiding crashing into other rickshaws.... Now and then an immaculate rickshaw ...ambled past, carrying well-dressed Chinese men and women. They sat back smug and arrogant and looked upon the world around them condescendingly. The masses moved along the sidewalks and out into the streets as recklessly as the traffic. Many, mostly school children, had their faces covered with white surgical masks. Every fifth person had a pockmarked face.
>
> As we looked over the scene, there was no color ... all either black or brown. The pedestrians seemed oblivious to the beggars, who were as numerous as the shoppers. Lepers, the blind holding on to sticks following young children, men with missing limbs, young girls hardly old enough to be mothers cradling infants ... and there were some souls we saw—we couldn't call them beggars because they didn't beg—who appeared to have never washed in their lives. Their skin was black, black as coal miners coming from the pit, their hair uncut, matted and tangled, and their clothing tattered rags as filthy as their bodies.[106]

The weather also took them by surprise. For Sam and his men, China proved a far cry from the steaming jungles of the South Pacific. Although the October of their arrival was beautiful, winter soon roared in with a vengeance. The cold was even more penetrating because of the dampness of the seashore. The men had to adapt quickly. That was made more difficult when cold weather clothing didn't arrive until December, even then inadequate for the viciously cold temperatures. Pipes froze often, so the men were issued two canteens, which they kept full at all times. Electricity in the barracks was unreliable during December, and any night activity had to be done by candle or lantern.[107]

"We used four fifty-five-gallon oil barrels to heat the building," said Philip Feltis. "On the back of each was a five-gallon jeep can with tubing and a valve welded to it. We'd put paper in the barrel as a starter, then open the valve and drip fuel oil into the barrel. It dripped steadily and burned as long as there was fuel in the can. Unfortunately, if your bed was far away from the drum, you'd get very cold."

Yet, MAG 32 was much better off than the Chinese civilians in the outlying areas. As temperatures dropped, the poor tried to find shelter in Tsingtao, but, even there, winter spelled a gruesome death for many:

> *As more and more refugees pushed into the city, starvation was inevitable … Most pathetic were the child beggars, hordes of them dressed in filthy rags…. When winter finally came, they along with the lepers, were found frozen in doorways. Trucks drove through the streets each morning picking up frozen corpses in alleys and doorways … some of the victims of the cold didn't even make it to the city to die … on hikes we would see their bodies half buried in the snow.[108]*

However, on December 8, 1945, the cruel force of winter struck savagely at MAG 32 when six of twelve planes flew into a mountain in a blinding snowstorm near Tientsin. Only two of twelve flyers survived, and rescuers recovered only eight bodies. Sam later reported holding five funerals while in North China, so he likely had a part in this tragic event.[109]

While Sam probably wanted to go home very much at the end of the war, he seemed to enjoy his tour in North China, ministering, sharing the Gospel, and learning about the Chinese culture. He reported:

> *Here religious and recreational activities have kept me busier than I have ever been in my life, I believe. Of course it is an interesting place to have duty. The odd and ancient customs and ways of the Chinese are a constant source of interest.[110]*

Often, those Chinese customs that so fascinated him would become fodder for later sermon illustrations:

> *While we were still on the LST going to China they began to teach us how to conduct ourselves in China. They told us that Americans are big-hearted, but this is one place you can't afford to be that way. If you see a fellow sick or even dying, don't help him. If you do, you are expected to go the whole way and finance his recovery, much like the Good Samaritan. A missionary in China told me that until a few years*

ago, if you really wanted to get even with an enemy, commit suicide on his property. Then he was obligated to bury you.[111]

Sam preached only once to a congregation in Chinese through an interpreter ("That was an experience!"), but he must have preached many times in English. He reported that there were ninety-one professions of faith and 137 reprofessions in the services in which he took part. Some of those professions came from long and hard evangelistic work on Sam's part.[112]

One day he looked up from his desk in the cramped chaplain's office and saw the largest man in uniform he had ever seen. He knew he had seen him before; two giants such as this man couldn't exist! He recalled that months ago in Zamboanga he had seen this man walk down the dirt trail by MAG 32 and sit down in the open-air tin building the Catholic men used for worship. Sam had wondered why he was in their area, since he wasn't in their unit. He had seen him sit down with a prayerful attitude so he had assumed the man wanted to pray.

However, the man now confessed, "I wasn't Catholic, and I wasn't going in there to pray. But I was in trouble and that's the reason I'm here now talking to you."

His name was George Brazen, originally from Chicago. He'd never been to church or Sunday School. In fact, Sam had never met a human being brought up in America as ignorant about God and the Bible as this man, nor anyone under as much conviction. George poured out his heart to Sam, admitting he'd been a wicked man; he didn't even know if God existed. Sam asked if he would be willing to come in two or three times a week to learn about Christianity, and George agreed.

Sam taught him about God, beginning with the simplest concepts, and George was eager to learn. Week after week he came, heartily responding to the teaching, and Sam was encouraged. Then came the day that Sam said to him, " George, I have taught you everything about the Lord that I know. Now is the time for you to come on to him. Today I want you to believe on Jesus Christ and be saved."

Sam thought George would say immediately, "Chaplain, let's pray right now!" But a look of crushed disappointment came across his face as if Sam had slapped him. The soldier was offended, and Sam didn't know why. George shook his head and said in despair, "Chaplain, you can't tell a man who's been as wicked as I am that all he has to do is just believe and be saved. It's absurd. I can't do it." Suddenly Sam saw the problem. He had taught George nothing about faith!

Anybody who can say 'just believe' does not know what faith is. Faith in Christ is the most life-changing experience a human ever has. So I had to teach him that day. It took only one lesson before he knelt down right there and as best as I can tell opened his heart to Christ. The next Sunday he got down on his knees so I could reach him, and I baptized him in front of all his fellow Marines. I discovered much later that George ended up on the police force of a California city and was still an earnest Christian. [113]

But sometimes the going was a little rougher in witnessing to his men. Yet, Sam met unbelievers head-on just as he always had, making them prove their statements. One young marine officer had been an intelligent young lawyer before the war, but had, in Sam's words, "taken a very unintelligent approach to his unbelief."

He told Sam one day, "I have given up my religious convictions." He then proceeded vehemently to blaspheme God's character in the Old Testament.

Sam asked, "Are you sure about that? I regularly study the Old Testament and have never found a God such as you describe."

The soldier averred, "Well, it's there."

Sam countered immediately, "Could you cite me a passage to support your view? We can easily get a Bible."

The man then paused shamefacedly, admitting he couldn't give one example from scripture to prove his comments; in fact, he had read very little of the Bible. "I just always thought this was true," he said. Sam doesn't say whether the young man ever came to a saving knowledge of Christ. [114]

As usual, Sam didn't confine his ministry to the men of MAG 32 but talked about Jesus with anyone who would listen. However, Oriental thinking often prevented the Chinese from grasping the Gospel. One of the Chinese interpreters for the First Marine Air Wing had an unpronounceable name, so the men called him Willie. Sam grew to love Willie, and they became good friends. A brilliant university graduate, he had given up on all religions. Yet, he asked Sam one day to teach him about Christianity. So they began meeting twice a week for about an hour and a half. After a time, Sam was thrilled at Willie's progress in responding to the truth.

Then Willie missed a session, then two, then missed two whole weeks. Sam didn't see him on the base, so he knew Willie was avoiding him because they often ran into each other. Nevertheless, he did happen upon Willie one day in a store in a nearby village.

"What's wrong?" Sam asked. "Don't you want to know more about Christianity?"

"No," he said flatly.

"Why?" Sam asked, mystified.

"Wasn't your silk stolen a couple of weeks ago?" he asked Sam.

"Yes," Sam admitted. He had bought some silk for Stelle and put it in the jeep. When he had returned from shopping in another store, it was gone.

"Two days later, didn't someone steal your jeep?"

Again Sam nodded. Unfortunately, he had gone back to the same area and lost the jeep.

Willie was indignant. "Well, if God is good, and you're God's, nobody should be able to steal your silk or your jeep."

"That's not just Oriental thinking," Sam would tell congregations later. "We Westerners think that if we are Christians, nothing bad should happen to us either. But that is not true. The Heidelberg Catechism tells us that, ' … He protects me so well that, without the will of my Father in heaven, not a hair can fall from my head, indeed, that everything must fit His purpose for my salvation.'" [115]

Sam reported that he had performed thirty-two baptisms while there, and one of them was "a highlight of my experiences in China." Sam had become acquainted with Mr. John Lu, a young Chinese man who had attended a Christian school and professed faith in Christ but had never received Christian baptism. Upon his request, Sam baptized him at one of the base services.

"He also wanted me to give him another Christian name," said Sam, "so I added 'Paul" and baptized him as John Paul Lu." [116]

By December 1945 thousands of men had enough points of service to return to the States. Unfortunately, Sam was not one of them. He loved everything about the Christmas season, so it must have been painful for him to be so far away from home. On November 25, he took the time to record a Christmas message to Stelle and Becky:

> *Hello, Honey, and a mighty happy Christmas to you. This is the first Christmas we have spent apart since we started spending them together forever way back yonder. Anyway, it's not our birthday but His, and I know we are both together today in thanking our Father for our common Savior.*
>
> *And Little Becky, my, how I'd like to be with you today and a very Merry Christmas to you. I've got a notion that your little stocking is full to the brim this morning from the same Santa who used to fill mine every Christmas morning. Watch Granddad and don't let him play with your toys too much. And then, Mother, the happiest of all Christmases to you. I want to reserve some hugs from you at home next Christmas.*
>
> *Mother Sellers, Merry Christmas to you, too. I hope both of your boys will be with you next Christmas.*
>
> *I don't know just how long we'll be out here. I hope we'll be back before very long. But I want you to know that I'm well and having a lot of fun. I've seen some grand things as I travel around just a bit and see this part of China. I hope I'll have some interesting stories to tell you when I come home. I want you to believe everything I tell you, too. Let me tell you again: I wish you all a very, very happy Christmas and Stelle, just this last word to you: You already know it, but I want to tell you again. I love you with all my heart.*

On the other side was a birthday message to the two most important girls in his life:

> *Happy Birthday, Stelle and Becky! December is a red-letter month for me. Three people who mean so much to me were born then. Honey, this is the fellow who has shared the past four years of your life, and I'm looking forward to so many more. I hope with all my heart that I will be with you at home on your next birthday.*
>
> *I'm sending some birthday presents for you and Becky. They aren't much and may be a little late, but I hope you like them. The little doll for Becky was made by some Chinese girls in a school in Tsingtao. If Becky is close by, bring her up and hold her still and let her hear how her Daddy sings: 'Happy Birthday to you, Happy Birthday to you, God bless you, Stelle and Becky, Happy Birthday to you.'*

He also busied himself in helping his men find Christmas gifts. For months he had been trying to come up with a memento of China that his men could send home. He finally decided to print a leaflet with John 3:16 in English on one side and Chinese on the other. An American missionary helped him write the Chinese characters,[117] and he began looking for a printer in a nearby city. Finding one was difficult since he couldn't read the signs. Even when he finally found a print shop, the printer could not speak English.

At last he found one where a young man spoke a little English. Sam handed the small leaflet to him, and the boy's lips moved as he silently read the Chinese side. Then he turned it over and appeared to be trying to read the English. Three times he did this before he handed it back to Sam, saying, "This is very good!" He dipped a brush in some ink and proceeded to make himself a copy on a square of wrinkled, brown paper. Folding it carefully, he put it in his robe.

"It was quite some time until it dawned on me what I had experienced," said Sam later. "For the first time in my life, I had witnessed another human being, for the first time in his life, hear about the greatest single thing that has ever been said. What would it be like to see this statement for the first time in your whole life?"[118]

GOING HOME!

By April 1946, Sam was happily among that number standing in line for discharge. Public pressure in the States had been enormous to release combat veterans and other men eligible for discharge:

> *12/8/45 to 3/17/46—High point men begin leaving for the States. Chaplain Pat Patterson will soon leave and be replaced by D. D. Wilkinson [a Union Seminary classmate and friend].*[119]

But other men had to stay. The last Marine did not leave Tsingtao until June 1, 1949, almost three years later, when the Chinese civil war made it too dangerous for them to stay. The Marines' departure spelled death for many Chinese citizens, as Sam revealed later:

> *After our units pulled out, the Communists moved right into that territory and took it over. When we left, the Christian church was strong in populated coastal areas. But we were told later that a great number of Christians were put to death. How many Christians actually survived we don't know.* [120]

Sam returned to the States in the *Cape Bon* (Merchant Marine) via Japan, Honolulu, and San Francisco, where, after two years and thirteen days of service, he was honorably discharged from the Naval Reserve on July 10, 1946. He had served admirably and received several honors, including two bronze stars for participation in the Asiatic-Pacific Theater and the Philippine Liberation Campaign. He also received the American Campaign Ribbon and the World War II Victory Medal and Ribbon. [121]

Upon his discharge, he joyfully reunited with Stelle and Becky in Wynne. The family moved briefly to Virginia as Sam and Stelle considered where the Lord wanted them to serve next. They likely heard about possible pastorates through the PCUS's Defense Service Council, the agency overseeing all chaplain activity. Beginning in 1946, Central Mississippi Presbytery records show an ongoing effort by the Council to recruit discharged chaplains for vacant PCUS churches:

> *The Defense Service Council has endeavored to assist in the relocation of returned chaplains. A list of those available for work has been issued monthly. The speed with which these ministers have been located is remarkable. The entire church has seemed anxious to aid in their settlement.* [122]

In 1946, Sam accepted a call to Leland Presbyterian Church, a prosperous congregation in the fertile Mississippi Delta. The growing flock was filled with warm and friendly people, many of whom had cotton plantations. The tranquility of the setting promised just what the young couple needed—peace—after a new life together filled with five years of drama. Life stressors had been stacking up—marriage, ministry in a tough cotton mill town, the addition of an aging parent and a new baby to the home, and overseas war duty. Hard times were not over; in the coming months, Sam would especially need the consoling love of fellow Christians.

CHAPTER FOUR

THE LELAND YEARS
1946–1950

A minister should be a man among men, touching elbows with all in the community and identifying himself with every worthwhile movement for the neighborhood uplift. His byword should be 'Service Above Self,' and he should hold the lamp of God's word so close to the path of life that each traveler from time to eternity might see clearly the way to home and heaven.

Rev. Samuel J. Patterson
Sam's father

Sam not only ministered to us, but to all denominations and the community at large—the poor, the rich, the drunks, the sober, the young, and the old. He loved people and wanted all of us to love the Lord.

Margaret Dean
Leland Presbyterian Member

God could not have chosen a more restorative pastorate for Sam and Stelle. The Mississippi Delta is one of the last vestiges of the old South. Gracious living, warm hearts, slow talk, delicious food, and loyal friends abound there. Life moves slowly in the little towns scattered across the endless cotton fields. The soothing peace of Delta sunsets, the soft, plaintive cooing of mourning doves, row after row of manicured, lush green crops, all are a balm for the soul. Now, for the first time, Sam's family had a lovely home at 203 Willeroy Street and an adequate salary.

"They took our family to their hearts, and the future seemed good and secure," wrote Sam later in his diary. "It was a good place to be during those rather hard years following the war."

Sam began his duties in Leland in August 1946 and had been there less than three months when his mother died in Wynne on October 27. The loss was huge, especially for S. J. They had been married for forty-eight years. S. J. stayed for a short time with daughter Lois, but then Sam insisted he come to Leland, where he remained until his death four years later. Sam must have treasured that time, gaining strength from his father's robust faith as he had for years:

> *Seldom did I see my father pass a day without suffering. Yet, he bore it with such calm serenity. One day when he was at his lowest, he said, 'Sam, I know the Lord has a reason for my suffering, but I don't know what it is.' I said, 'Dad, over the years I have watched you suffer with patience and still trust in God. You have given me a faith that one can get nowhere else. If your suffering was only for this, it would be enough.'*[1]

Sam was installed as pastor on November 18, with Rev. Russell Nunan presiding. Nunan and Sam would become fast friends for the rest of Sam's life. Nunan had been in Mississippi a few months longer than Sam and in May had been installed as pastor of First Presbyterian Church in Greenville, only ten miles away. Given the unusual similarity of the men's lives, their close friendship seems no surprise. With Allan Merritt in another state now and Sam's connection with him by necessity a long-distance one, God seems to have given Sam another "soul mate" with whom he had more in common even than Allan.

Almost ten years older, Nunan had been president of his senior class and played football in high school and college. Much like Sam, athletics had been Nunan's life, and God's call on their hearts to the ministry was the only reason each became studious. Both had come from humble circumstances and had worked in the college dining hall. Nunan had also graduated from Union Seminary and had a heart for the poor, working in several inner city ministries, including Hell's Bottom, a Richmond mission to African Americans.

Nunan's first pastorate was also a small cotton mill church in Porterdale, Georgia, where he was ordained in 1938. The day after Pearl Harbor, he also volunteered as a Navy chaplain and served in the South Pacific, although apparently he and Sam didn't run into one another. Nunan, too, had deep empathy for those with alcohol problems and, over the years, established numerous Alcoholics Anonymous chapters. Although Nunan didn't reach Eagle Scout rank as Sam had, he was very active in Boy Scout work during his pastorates. In only one way did they seem to be polar opposites. In his youth, Russell had tended to be shy and lack self-confidence. Sam, of course, never knew a shy day in his life.[2]

In Leland, Sam realized his boyhood dream of becoming a carbon copy of his father. He and Stelle were loved beyond all measure by the congregation. At one point, they even gave him a new Chevrolet in appreciation for his work.

"There is no way in the world I can tell you all the little things that made me love him," confides Lawrence Jacobs. "I was probably closer to him than any minister I've ever known. I never saw him down a single day, and I was with him a lot. They were both so encouraging, a joy to be around all the time. Sam was obviously fully dedicated to the Lord's work."

"Sam was and still is a guiding force in my life," says Jim Arnold, who was a teenager when Sam came to the church. "He was a true man of God, a saint in my eyes, but certainly not in his. That's what made him a saint—the fact that he did not think he was."

"Sam is probably the most meaningful person in my spiritual life because he taught my communicants' class when I was eleven years old," revealed longtime member Mary Boteler. "He told us to write in the front of our Bibles the day we professed our faith in Christ. From that day forward, he emphasized, we were different people, children of God. He asked us to write down the plan of salvation and relevant scriptures in our Bibles. When I encounter Christians now who are unsure of their salvation, I can quote these verses and say, 'Yes, you really are saved.'"

A humble, unassuming man, Sam used 1 Corinthians 15:9–10 to describe himself, giving God all the praise:

> *For I am the least of the apostles, who am not worthy to be called an apostle because I persecuted the church. But by the grace of God I am what I am, and His grace toward me was not in vain, but I labored more abundantly than they all, yet not I, but the grace of God which was with me (NKJV).*

AN OUTSTANDING PREACHER

By the time he reached Leland, Sam was becoming an accomplished communicator. His father had been an excellent preacher, but Sam's ability already far surpassed S. J.'s. He was on his way to being outstanding. His father's sermons had been eloquent, holding much doctrinal purity and biblical truth. Yet, Sam's folksy talks from the heart were compelling, electrifying, and inspiring. They held an urgency and passion born of a commitment to living on the edge with Christ. As a result, this small town church began to be packed every Sunday.

"He was down to earth, but he read the scriptures with such authority," related Jim Arnold. "He opened God's Word up for me as no one else ever has. Even if he spoke at a club meeting and never mentioned religion, I felt as if I'd heard a sermon."

"I was in high school when Brother Sam first came to Leland," recalled Don Wilson, now pastor of First Presbyterian PC(USA) in Byhalia, Mississippi. "He was still in his Navy uniform. He was very sincere and interesting, and his sermons were practical and biblical. They were powerful because they were not flowery, but simple and clearly applicable to our lives."

"When he first came," says Margaret Dean, "I thought we'd never keep up with what he was saying because he talked so fast. I don't think he ever had any sermon notes because he never looked at them."

Actually, when Sam first started out in Martinsville, he wrote out word-for-word every sermon he preached (and kept every one of them). By the time he reached Leland, however, he had become comfortable in the pulpit and had long ago shed the tether of a handwritten manuscript. He carried into the pulpit only a small index card with a sermon outline printed in such infinitesimally small letters that no human could read it without a magnifying glass. Perhaps it was a "safety blanket," since Sam never looked at it!

Sam instituted children's sermons during worship, a most unusual step in 1950s Mississippi. Calling the children down front, he'd give them a special message. The sermons became a legendary hallmark of his ministry in Leland, with titles such as "The Cure for Cold Feet," "Spiritual Arithmetic," and "A Canned Voice." He called them "object lessons" because, well, he always used some common object to illustrate the principle. Members in their eighties still recall every detail of some of them.

One that really stood out taught God's promise, "I will be with you in trouble and deliver you"; Sam used only a candle, a glass, and a clear container of water. He lit the candle and held it up, saying that the candle represented man, while the flame represented happiness and joy. The water represented trouble, sorrow, and adversity. He then put the candle in the water, and the flame went out. "That does happen, doesn't it?" he observed. "Then we are unhappy."

He continued, "If we could get rid of all the trouble in the world, we could always be joyful, right? However, we can't. God nowhere promises us that we will not have trouble in this world. Wouldn't it be wonderful if somehow a person could go into trouble and retain joy? The Bible says there is a way!"

He then placed a glass over the candle as he lowered it into the water. The air in the glass displaced the water, and the candle continued to burn. The children's jaws always dropped at this apparent miracle. Sam branded the lesson indelibly on their tender hearts with these final words: "God is with and over us in trouble, so even there the fire of joy and peace can burn. Always remember that God will keep you if you trust in Him. Then you can have peace and joy in times of trouble."[3]

"Those children's sermons were awesome," says Kathleen Mulcahy. "He spoke so the young people could understand, but they helped a lot of older people, too!"

One can see why Sam often claimed that more people had begun reading their Bibles through his children's sermons than any other message he delivered.

THE ULTIMATE FRIEND

Carole King must have had someone similar to Sam in mind when she wrote the tune "You've Got a Friend" because Sam spoke those words with his entire life. Sixty years before the cell phone industry ushered in the ubiquitous "Best Friend Forever," he literally defined the sentiment. In season and out, he showed up when people needed him, often without being called.

"I never heard him talk about himself," said Lawrence Jacobs. "He was always doing something for somebody else. I had triple-bypass surgery and was at St. Dominic's Hospital in Jackson, Mississippi. He walked in one day with that big smile on his face and spent half an hour with me. I couldn't tell him how much I appreciated that, but he told me I could pay him back one day. Years later when he had the same surgery, I was able to repay him."

Even when members left the church, Sam was still there for them. "He always followed me through my life," recalls Mary Boteler. "When I was at Belhaven College, he never failed to look me up for a visit if presbytery met there."

When tragedy struck, one often knew that Sam had dropped whatever he was doing either to come or write a note of encouragement. Mary recalls that a few days after her first husband, Sammy Schaffer, was killed in 1970, she received a note on Holiday Inn stationary from Sam:

Dear Mary,

Immediately upon hearing of Sammy's sudden home going, my thoughts and love went out to you. And my prayers began going up to Him on your behalf. I know that His grace and your faith in Him will well sustain you…. The verse that came to my mind after hearing of Sammy's death was Romans 8:28…. Even though we don't understand this fact, we can as Paul said, know … and believe, trust, that God does work all for a good purpose for His own. His Son died what appeared to be a tragic, sudden, early death, but He turned it for the greatest good, our salvation. So while we can't understand Sammy's death, we can believe that neither his life nor death are meaningless…. I pray Christ will sweeten this bitter time by filling you anew with His love and presence.

Your friend in Christ,
Sam Patterson

"As a pastor, he influenced my life as no other person has," revealed Margaret Dean. "He was also a wonderful friend. Our church was without a minister when my husband died. When Sam was called upon to conduct the funeral, he immediately left French Camp to do it. There will never be another like Sam Patterson. What a legacy he left!"

"My husband and I were very young when Brother Sam came, and we became very close to him," said Mary Edith Walker. "He was the kind of minister with whom we could talk over problems because he was so down to earth. He saw people's needs and tried to meet them."

"Sam and my husband Gus roomed together for a time at Southwestern and remained friends through the years," said Ann Aldridge. "Gus's illness brought Sam to our home many times during those last months. What a comfort he was to us both! On one of his visits, I eavesdropped at the bedroom door and could hear Sam saying, 'Gus, we've been friends a long time, and it's good to know as Christians, we'll always be together. I've had a heart attack and may go home before you do, but it's good to know we'll always be together.' They sounded as if they were preparing to go on a wonderful trip, and I didn't want to be left behind!"

HE LOVED THE WHOLE TOWN

Sam and Stelle were loved not just by his congregation, but by the whole town. Shortly after his arrival, a *Leland Progress* columnist exuded:

> *He has the reddest hair and the nicest smile we have seen in a long time.*[4]

Sam didn't care what denomination one called home, or even if one attended church. He cared about everyone, taking his father's maxim "Service Above Self" to heart. In that small town of 4,000, he became an inspiration to the entire community.

"He couldn't do enough good," says Kathleen Mulcahy. "Thanks to Sam, we now have a ministerial association. He encouraged the preachers of all denominations to fellowship with each other instead of segregating themselves. The preachers met regularly to share, encouraging more relationship among the churches."

Thirty years later Sam would strongly warn seminary students about the critical importance of reaching out to the community:

> *God wants us to be united in love. When you get out in your ministry, make it a point to know those other pastors in your town. Knit yourself into associations with those of different denominations and faiths. We can be kidnapped by systems of thought in Christianity, and our loyalty*

to Christ becomes secondary to a system that human logic has fabricated out of scriptural truth. If we ever become owned by a system of thought, be it Reformed, dispensational, or whatever, fellowship and evangelism are ruined. We are too busy convincing someone to believe as we do to focus on Christ.

The most self-mutilating organism on the face of the earth is the Christian church. We attack one another because of our differences in views, and the world is not impressed. We should all together belong only to Jesus Christ. We can do that without sacrificing any of the doctrines we feel are nearer to the truth.[5]

"My parents had been going to the Greek Orthodox church in Vicksburg, but Leland did not have one," explains Kathleen Mulcahy. "So they started going to the Baptist church. One time Mother was sick, and Sam Patterson came knocking on the door to check on her even though we had never been to Leland Presbyterian. She thought that was wonderful, so she started attending! Later, our whole family ended up joining."

"When I left for the war, my family was going to the Baptist church, but when I came back home, they were Presbyterians!" says Lawrence Jacobs, laughing heartily. "Our families became very close; Mother and Stelle became wonderful friends. Stelle baked rolls and bread for Mother, and Mother took her homegrown flowers."

In 1949, Sam realized that Leland needed a wholesome activity for youth on weekends. He led the church to reach out to all the teens in town with Saturday Night Jubilee. Weekends saw the local Garden Club House come alive with youngsters having good, clean fun. It was an instant hit.

"He called on people from all the churches to help chaperone," says Mary Edith Walker. "Sometimes it was a dance, sometimes not. Usually it began with a short devotion, then someone spun records. Different churches provided refreshments each time."

Scouting in Leland also received an enormous boost upon Sam's arrival. Leland apparently had only one troop, and it had not been very active previously. Elected Scout Master shortly after he came, Sam soon had a citywide Scout Committee formed. Scouts began speaking to local civic clubs about scouting, and on Scout Day, the boys held city offices for a day. Sam himself was a frequent speaker on scouting at any organization who would have him. He worked to bring scouts in all churches together, having special services celebrating Scout Week for the Protestant and Roman Catholic denominations.

Columnist Jim Roberts observed, "If a person is to make a good scoutmaster he must really be interested in his work and have time to spend in carrying out his plans. With such a good one in Sam Patterson, Leland should have a good troop."[6]

A SCHOOL IN TROUBLE

Sam loved the gracious people of Leland and had the pastorate of his dreams. Yet, he was disturbed by the plight of a small synod-controlled school about 100 miles away called French Camp Academy. In 1949, rumors were rife that the Synod of Mississippi (PCUS) was about to close the beloved school and sell the property. The news upset Sam's church members, many of whom had long loved and supported the Academy. In fact, some of their parents had even attended the school in better times.

The school's rich history reached all the way back to the late 1800s when far-sighted Scotch-Irish Christians had established the Central Mississippi Institute for Girls (1885) and, later, French Camp Academy Military School (1886) to educate children in the strong convictions of the Presbyterian heritage.[7]

These schools and others like them, controlled by Central Mississippi Presbytery (PCUS), had ably filled a critical void in education during the late nineteenth century in the South, still suffering from the economic and cultural devastation of the Civil War. Public school systems had been established in all southern states after the war, but standards remained low and popular support non-existent until after the turn of the century. In sparsely settled areas, children had no access to good schools. What little education they received came from the King James Bible, the *Farmer's Almanac*, and an occasional *McGuffey Reader*. Fortunate youngsters had a father who survived the war and at least one parent with enough education to help with lessons. Even more fortunate children had parents with means to send them to private boarding academies, such as CMI and FCA, where they received the equivalent of a modern junior college education.

However, from their very beginnings, both schools struggled with painfully cramped quarters, poor and outdated equipment, extremely low teacher salaries, and perennial debt. Such conditions made it difficult to attract and keep teachers and presidents. John Frierson left FCA in 1900 after only one year as president, saying, "There was no help from any other sources, church contributions or otherwise. I had become personally responsible. I paid Mr. Tate his salary... and I had to leave."[8]

The schools' futures seemed brighter when, around 1900, the General Assembly of the Presbyterian Church in the United States began to emphasize Christian education, encouraging synods to take control of and regulate schools within their bounds.[9] Following the Assembly's lead, the Synod of Mississippi began concerted efforts to form a statewide "correlated" educational system. By 1913 it had acquired six schools, including French Camp Academy and Central Mississippi Institute.[10]

However, none of the schools was better off under synod's leadership. The idealistic plan was laudable, but executing it became a nightmare. Gaining total control of the six schools meant acquiring all their debts, and raising money became almost impossible during the depression-ridden years of World War I. Thus, FCA, CMI, and their sister schools continued to struggle financially. In years to come, synod's plan ultimately failed for lack of funds, but its death throes lasted for decades as synod looked hopefully to the future, ever expecting a change in social and economic circumstances, as well as better financial support for Christian education from Mississippi Presbyterians. Neither ever came.[11]

Much of French Camp Academy's history is bound up in synod's ambitious project and the efforts to make it work during the first half of the twentieth century. By the mid-1930s, three major crises had already occurred at FCA, any of which could have easily closed the school were it not for God's protecting hand. For a detailed look at these crises, see Appendix A, "French Camp Academy and Mississippi Synod's Grand Experiment in Christian Education."

The trials of the previous years, coupled with events occurring in the early part of the 1940s, would now conspire to create "the perfect storm," posing the most formidable threat to FCA's survival in its history. It was into that storm that Sam Patterson sailed when he came to Mississippi in 1946.

THE PERFECT STORM

At the midpoint of the twentieth century, French Camp Academy's most pressing problem lay in the fact that people no longer seemed to need its services. The advent of good public schools had for years been steadily diminishing the need for preparatory schools; students could now get a high school education near their homes. French Camp was a lingering relic of that bygone era, and students were getting harder and harder to find. As the number of boarding students dwindled, FCA began taking more and more children from problem situations simply to keep the school open. However, such children often could not pay full tuition and required synod support, which was not forthcoming.

Other serious problems continued to challenge the school as the decade of the '40s began. FCA's buildings and equipment needed repair and could not compete with those of the public schools. Finding and keeping faculty had been difficult; seasoned teachers could make more at the public schools, often forcing FCA to hire those with much less experience. Moreover, by 1941 the country was at war again; each year saw faculty members head overseas. Finally, a rapid succession of presidents during the 1940s contributed to a lack of leadership.

These facts were not lost on the Mississippi Synod, and they underscored what the PCUS had been realizing for years—the church could not provide quality education at the low cost of state schools. Church school attendance and financial support were declining. PCUS members resented paying taxes for state schools, while also supporting church schools doing the same job, but not as well.[12]

The matter of closure had come up more than once since Sam's arrival in Mississippi. His good friend Russell Nunan was on the French Camp Board of Trustees and had told him of synod's plan to close the school due to severe financial problems and lack of students. The threat was real, since synod had been downsizing its educational efforts for years. It had first merged Central Mississippi Institute and French Camp Academy (1915), then Mississippi Synodical and Belhaven College (1939), and closed Chickasaw College in 1932.[13]

Other signs confirmed that synod was ready to get out of the education business. For years, synod-controlled schools had been clamoring for greater autonomy. They wanted to develop their own budgets, be responsible for their own debts, and run their own fundraising campaigns without interference from synod. In 1940, synod gave the schools what they wanted[14], but it would prove to be a mixed blessing. Ironically, it would eventually serve as the genesis of FCA's fourth, and worst, crisis.

Initially, however, the ability to raise funds independently was promising. In 1943, Rev. O. C. Wardlaw led FCA's first campaign. It was successful, and the school paid off its remaining debt of eight thousand dollars in full.[15] In 1944, FCA began another quiet campaign to raise twenty-five thousand dollars for improvements, including a new water system. Again, Wardlaw was at the helm,[16] and by 1945, more than thirty thousand dollars had been garnered for the projects.[17]

Emboldened by their success, in 1946 the FCA board, with Rev. W. H. McAtee as president, approved a third campaign to enlarge facilities and increase teachers' salaries.[18] This time they erred by beginning the projects before collecting the pledges, which came in more slowly than usual. Because of the board's impatience and poor planning, McAtee had to report a deficit to synod in 1947; he was forced to recall the teacher raises, rescind other increased spending, and raise tuition.[19] He was frank with synod about the problems FCA faced and the need for synod support:

> *The cost of operating an accredited school is constantly increasing. FCA has for years operated on a limited budget without sufficient margin for needed repairs and with no reserve for unexpected costs. In spite of this it has done a work of tremendous importance. Dealing with students who can't pay usual boarding school fees, we need increased help to enable us to offer our advantages for those who most need them. We hope that we will eventually receive the financial support now so sorely lacking.[20]*

FCA's fragile circumstances received a one-two punch in 1948 when President Edward Boyce resigned and O. C. Wardlaw, the school's top fundraiser, resigned from the board to pursue other callings. He had contacted over two thousand people and raised some sixty thousand dollars for the school.[21] According to Margaret Kimball (FCA '28), then Boyce's executive secretary, the school's leadership simply gave up. At the end of the 1948 academic year, the board cashed in an endowment, paid the teachers, locked the buildings, and shut down the campus, leaving Sam Edwards, a hired man, in charge of the cattle. "The place was grown up in weeds, and the buildings were in serious disrepair. It was so desolate," says Kimball.[22]

The citizens of French Camp proved to be a formidable ally for the little school. Several of them immediately began searching for a new president, and, almost miraculously, the Rev. J. H. Laster finally agreed to accept the awesome task. He had refused several times, but when French Camp Presbyterian elder J. Y. Downing begged him to come, he couldn't say no:

> *I told [Downing] that we just could not take that kind of responsibility and started to leave. I will never forget the look of disappointment and despair on that man's face when he said, 'Mr. Laster, unless you come, French Camp is gone!'*[23]

Laster arrived in July 1948 and, against all odds, managed to gather a faculty to open classes in September. Since the school had no bookkeeper, he asked Margaret Kimball to take the job. Kimball remembers they had only three thousand dollars in the checking account to clean the school up that summer.[24] Laster began crisscrossing the state, challenging people to support the school. The job was daunting—back debts, little money for operating expenses, poor condition of the buildings, small enrollment.[25] Mrs. Laster worked just as hard, even washing the football team's uniforms in her personal washer. However, the overload of work and worry would eventually bring her to the brink of mental and physical breakdown.[26]

Laster inaugurated the *Academy News* to let people know the school's needs, and money finally began to trickle in. J. B. Davis from Itta Bena sent the first memorial contribution of five dollars. Then board member L. A. "Pop" Graeber, Sr. had a brainstorm.

"What if we suggest that, instead of flowers, a memorial gift for a deceased relative or friend be sent to the school?" he asked. "We can then print the names in the *Academy News*." It was a stroke of genius that soon would have money flowing into FCA. Today, memorials remain one of the school's important sources of income.

Even so, Laster reported, "…there was never enough. The needs were so many, the opportunities so great, and the funds so small!"[27] When support from synod still remained stalled, apparently FCA Board President McAtee became as pessimistic as Laster. At the September 1949 synod meeting in Memphis, McAtee shocked FCA supporters by moving that the school be closed. He emphasized that his motion was not an action of the FCA board but a personal desire for discussion.[28] Calls for closure had come before, but never from an FCA board president!

Much discussion followed McAtee's address. As they had numerous times in the past, the Presbyterian women came forward in FCA's defense. R. A. Bolling, Chairman of Women's Work, reminded the synod:

> *The current members of synod can hardly know the arduous struggle French Camp has made for existence nor the great contribution she has made to the culture and character of the South. The women of this synod have given ninety-nine thousand dollars over thirty-three years to keep this school alive.[29]*

Sam and Russell Nunan, among others, urged the synod to keep the school open and study the situation.[30] For some time, Sam had not been able to rid himself of the notion that the school could possibly be saved, especially when it had such enthusiastic support from Presbyterians all over the state. He knew that the type of student FCA was taking had changed, but the board had stopped short of declaring a change in purpose. Sam felt that their waffling could be the reason they were losing their vision and throwing in the towel.[31] Instead of closing the school, he could see new possibilities that could open vast areas of service to needy children and give the school new life. Why not officially move in this direction? In later writings, Sam outlined the extensive research in which he and others had been engaged:

> *We contacted welfare departments, churches, schools, judges, juvenile officers, everyone who had an interest in ministering to youth. The data indicated that there was a great need for an institution that would serve as a home and a school for kids who were not problems themselves, but who faced a social problem usually rooted in the home or the dissolution of the home and who were financially handicapped.[32]*

Their arguments won the day, and McAtee's motion was defeated. Several substitute motions were discussed, and, in the end, Dr. S. E. McFadden's carried. Synod authorized FCA to borrow money to operate during the current scholastic year and appointed a committee to work with the FCA board to study the entire matter of the school's present condition and future development. The committee would report to a later meeting of synod.[33]

The fifteen-member committee elected Sam as secretary and Russell Nunan as chairman.[34] The body met with the FCA Board of Trustees, Laster, and Kimball at French Camp on November 15, 1949. Although Sam had been in Mississippi for three years and lived less than two hours away, this was the first time he had set foot on the campus.[35]

Figures revealed first that the school was going into the red $152.09 every week or an average of $21.72 a day. Yet, the good news was that gifts to the school had almost doubled over the previous year. Later that day, the committee turned its attention to FCA curriculum. The committee viewed a film on the School of the Ozarks, an Arkansas institution with a practical program preparing students for life. Could it possibly serve as a model for FCA?[36]

"We cooked dinner for synod that day," recalls Mary Ida Harper, FCA dietician then. "When the meeting was over, Sam stayed for quite a while and looked the school over thoroughly."

Sam also served on a subcommittee appointed to study the purpose for FCA. Meeting at State College, Mississippi, on December 1, 1949, they came to the unanimous conclusion that a great need existed in Mississippi for a Christian school giving students training in Christian character and developing habits of initiative and work as in the School of the Ozarks. The group decided that FCA should focus on five areas:

1. *Development of Christian men and women*
2. *Vocational training (agriculture, carpentry, domestic science)*
3. *Mandatory work program*
4. *Service to needy boys and girls*
5. *FCA as community center of the school district*[37]

Just as the school's crisis seemed to be easing, FCA suffered another frustrating setback when, at the end of December 1949, Laster was forced to resign because of his wife's extreme illness. Doctors had ordered her to leave the stresses at FCA.[38] How would the school survive without a president? Margaret Kimball saved the day, stepping in and holding the office together until the spring. She went three months without a paycheck. Sam was later grateful:

> *Margaret's work had a great deal to do with FCA being able to sustain life until a final decision could be made. After I got here, her bookkeeping help and her knowledge of the school were invaluable. She never did get recognition from anyone except the board, who were deeply grateful because she alone carried the administrative load for almost a year.*[39]

The ad hoc committee met again on January 31, 1950, to hear the subcommittee findings. They subsequently reported to synod at a called meeting on March 7, 1950, advocating that French Camp Academy be continued as a uniquely Christian vocational school—with one caveat. The indispensable prerequisite for success was securing a man with vision, ability, and consecration to lead the institution. If in eighteen months the trustees could not find this man, the committee recommended that FCA be closed.[40]

Laster, however, would later object that "getting the right man" was not going to be enough. In a farewell letter published in the May 1950 issue of *French Camp Academy News*, he took synod to task for its lack of support of French Camp:

> *Synod must officially get behind FCA and ask others to do the same. The necessary energy must be supplied to offset or overcome the erosion and loss caused by years of neglect. No amount of pious praying, wishful thinking, or vain hopes of getting 'the right man between the plow handles' will substitute for the basic slag and plant food that is necessary to get that production going. Any procedure at French Camp Academy that ignores the above is, to put it mildly, erratic, exotic, and tommyrotic.*[41]

THE LEGENDARY JONES BOYS

Much discussion followed the study committee's report. Added to the pleas of Sam and Russell Nunan this time was the voice of a woman, Erin Lail of Lexington, Mississippi. She recounted to the listening churchmen the story of five little boys within Mississippi's borders who were in desperate straits. In the annals of French Camp history, they have become The Jones Boys. When she finished, the most skeptical heart in the room had reason to ponder—perhaps we do need French Camp.[42]

In February, Erin and her husband, Tommy, had heard about the little boys through a welfare worker in their Sunday School class at First Presbyterian Church in Lexington. "She told us she had come across the saddest, most tragic need she had ever seen in this area," said Erin. "A partially blind sharecropper with seven boys had recently moved near Lexington from Yazoo City. His wife had died of cancer three years before. The family had very few clothes, and she wanted us to get them some warm outfits."

Everyone gave generously, and that could have been the end of it. Yet, in the middle of the afternoon, Erin's husband said, "That story about those children haunts me. I think we should go see for ourselves about them."

They finally found them near the small rural community of Coxburg, buried in the hills about seventeen miles from Lexington. One look was enough. Erin and Tommy knew that charity was not the answer; these children needed a whole new world.

The entire family was living in an uninsulated, one-room hut with only a fireplace for heat. All the children were sleeping on an ancient mattress stuffed with corn shucks. The oldest son had joined the Navy and was sending home thirty dollars a month, the family's main source of income. The six boys at home ranged in age from five to sixteen. Teachers had noticed the children never brought any lunches or money, so the entire school had been bringing extra food each day for them.

Erin and Tommy looked at each other and both said simultaneously, "These kids need to be at French Camp." Erin assured the family that she would return the next day. She came straight home and called Laster at French Camp. "I knew they were about to close the school and Laster had resigned, but that was the only place I knew to turn. I figured even if the school closed in the near future, they could live there now. God would open another door if necessary."

Laster told her to bring them on, and somehow the school would care for them. On February 22, two days after they found them, five of the Jones boys— Matt, Garnett, Steinreed, Oscar, and Lewis—entered French Camp. Sam, the baby, was not old enough and would have to wait. There was never any question about taking them all. Their mother's main wish had been that they not be split up.

Erin shared with the synod the notes she had received from the boys. In scrawled, childish script, one of the boys had written, "Just a few lines to say hello and to let you know that we like it very much. You will have to excuse this writing, because I'm in a hurry since Coach said to turn off the lights. Everybody is so friendly. I have gained a lots of friends since I have been up here and doing fine in school." And that first night Matt had written, "Me and Garnett sleeps on a single bed each!" Another wrote, "Pray for us tonight, for we pray for you every night and for French Camp, too."

Such appeals for French Camp won the day. Synod voted to continue FCA operation along the lines of the committee recommendations and asked for another report at the Fall, 1950 synod meeting.[43]

Said Sam, "It was Erin Lail's appearance that persuaded the synod of the school's importance, and it was not by coincidence that she appeared at precisely that time. It was the work of the Lord."[44]

IF I DON'T GO, WHO WILL?

Surely Sam's heart went out to these children as Erin Lail detailed their poor quality of life. French Camp was her only option; if its doors had been closed, where would she have gone for help? If Sam did not take the job, would they be able to find anyone else? His heart told him no.

He had asked himself why he felt so strongly about that school. Could it be that his own father was an orphan? He had heard his father recount the heartbreaking details of his childhood. (See Appendix F.) Sam had once told the Kate Anderson congregation that he loved his father so much for providing a warm home for him even though S. J. had never known one.[45] Also, Sam loved children, and time had shown, especially here in Leland, that he had a true gift in dealing with them.

Sam came home from that synod meeting and asked his congregation to begin praying hard for a new president for French Camp, a person who could help forge a new purpose for its existence in the twentieth century. What the congregation did not know was that Sam himself had been standing before God for a long time now, continually asking, "Could I be that man?"

"Prayers were going up constantly for God to lead the right one to guide the school," says Becky Patterson Rogers. "All during the deliberations, my father had been carrying on his own private deliberations, praying and searching for God's will. He felt that God wanted him to have some definite part in this work. However, Christian education and administration were foreign to him, since he had experience only in preaching the Gospel. But, in the end, Daddy was always a vessel. Whatever God laid on his heart became what he did."

The late Mary Kathryn Stanton Broadfoot, longtime Leland Presbyterian member, used to say that the women of the church prayed Sam Patterson to French Camp. "Our little ladies were so concerned because French Camp was going to have to close its doors. They prayed and prayed in many special prayer meetings that French Camp would find a leader. The next thing they knew, Sam Patterson—their preacher, no less—had accepted the call! Sam was right when he told us to watch what we pray for!"

As a French Camp board member, Russell Nunan hoped Sam would take the presidency. "Sam was very honest about the experience of Christ in his life," said Nunan. "He had a unique ability to interest people in a school such as French Camp. I had spoken to him about it, and he seemed intrigued about what the school could become." [46]

Because of his leadership on the FCA study committee and obvious heart for the school, the committee members voted unanimously for him to be president. Two or three members drove to Leland to tell him. Still unconvinced, Sam said that he needed thirty days to pray about it. [47]

Perhaps the one who finally influenced Sam the most (besides the Holy Spirit) was L. A. Graeber. He and his wife had always had a tender spot in their hearts for French Camp Academy. Mrs. Graeber had gone to Central Mississippi Institute at the same time that the famous Dr. Robert Goode, president of School of the Ozarks, was at FCA Military School. L. A. was also the father of Lewis Graeber, Jr. and his brother Jim, both classmates of Sam's at Southwestern.

Lewis, a longtime FCA board member himself, recalled vividly that his father saw the great need of the under-privileged children at French Camp and came home from synod meeting in 1950 determined to find someone to take over the school's leadership.

"Who in the world can we get to go out there and take over French Camp?" he asked his sons.

The young men thought a bit and finally answered, "We don't know a soul who could do it but Sam Patterson, a pastor over in Leland."

"Well, get him on the phone quick!" ordered L. A.

Sam drove to Marks, Mississippi the next day and spent the night with the Graebers. The next day he and L. A. went to French Camp to look it over. Getting there was a challenge, with no paved roads. After a thorough inspection, Sam said carefully, "Mr. Graeber, I think I want to take it, but I need to pray about this with my wife."

Graeber agreed, and Sam went home. However, not long after, Sam called to say, "Mr. Graeber, I'll go out there."

A letter from the FCA board on April 21, 1950, extended the call of president to Sam:

> ... we would present to you what we believe to be the call of God to you to be the new president of French Camp Academy... We pledge ourselves to pay the annual salary of $4,200 to you as president in monthly checks, ... to pay the entire M.A.F. dues ... to compensate you for all travel expenses in carrying forward the work ... to put in good order the home originally built as the principal's home and to build a new president's home as soon as possible ... All of us are praying that, under God, you may feel a call in faith to this work. We would not minimize the greatness of the task. It is a tremendous job. We are optimistic about your ability and consecration to make French Camp what God and the Synod of Mississippi believe it should be.[48]

The board asked Erskine Jackson to serve as acting president until Sam could take over. Jackson began to change the entire direction of the school, making it less a college preparatory school and more of a vocational school. Sam was very grateful for his colleague's fine job.

"Erskine had some knotty problems to work out in the community and the school," revealed Sam. "He did it without complaint and in such a fine fashion that much of the resentment over the change of direction had dissipated by the time I arrived."[49]

The peaceful sojourn in an established church with an adequate salary and lovely home was over. Stelle and Sam had caught their collective breath and were ready for new challenges. A new job, a new town, new people to meet. Time for a name change, too. He'd been Sammy first, then Pat, then Brother Sam. Now to generations of future youngsters and adults he would become simply Mr. Pat, a gentle but piercing light shining in the darkness.

The people of Leland Presbyterian—in fact, the entire town—were saddened to learn that Sam was leaving. However, they knew they were losing him to a good cause. What they could not fathom then was that he was not gone for good. He would continue to pop up frequently, huffing and puffing into their homes and offices to update them on FCA and accept help if the Lord so moved them. In fact, some members didn't begin supporting the school until after Sam left.

"I had never heard of the school until Sam went there," confessed Lawrence Jacobs. "I'd look up from my desk, and there was Sam, pitching another project. 'Lawrence,' he'd say, 'here's what it costs to operate French Camp. I want you to pledge enough money to run the school for one day.'

"My Sunday School class began adopting a student every year," continued Lawrence. "We took up a French Camp collection for our student, then took up the regular collection. We sponsored students from freshman year all the way to graduation. The church also took up a French Camp collection separate from the regular church collection. Everybody gave double. To this day, I send memorials to French Camp."

"After he went to FCA, Sam came back and asked if we would help," remembers Mary Edith Walker. "I made a pledge and spread it out over a three or four year period."

"What else can I say about him except that he lived his faith?" asked Mary Boteler. "He gave a testimony to Christ every time he opened his mouth. He had always told us to trust God, but I was worried that he wouldn't be able to find the money to keep French Camp going. I asked him how he would do it. You know what he said? 'Mary, I'll just open my mailbox and see what's there.' I didn't worry anymore."

However, Sam knew in his heart that the job would be overwhelming. This was definitely his toughest challenge yet. Martinsville had been difficult, yet he had had the financial and moral support of an established, wealthy church, as well as presbytery and synod. French Camp Academy was virtually bankrupt, and the synod had given up. Moreover, Kate Anderson had not been a school; now he would be responsible for the physical, emotional, spiritual, and educational needs of many children. And the Lord knew that Sam was no educator. In fact, he laughed heartily at the irony that he of all people would be the president of a school!

Add to all that his youth—at thirty-three, he was younger than most of the faculty he would shortly hire—and the situation looked almost hopeless. Yet, thought Sam, that's just the kind of problem God loves to solve!

CHAPTER FIVE

THE FRENCH CAMP YEARS
1950-1967

French Camp Academy exists for youth and for Christ. Its mission is to bring the two together.

Sam Patterson

And my God shall supply all your needs, according to His riches in glory in Christ Jesus.

Philippians 4:19 (NASV)
FCA's Endowment

"Lazarus is the patron saint of French Camp Academy," Sam Patterson loved to quip. Actually, Sam himself blew new life into the school in its final death throes. God can accomplish anything, but history now shows that if Sam had not taken the job, French Camp Academy probably would not have survived.

Yet, Sam knew when he went to French Camp that God alone would have to resurrect the school. Even though he was a tireless worker, this project was doomed to failure unless the Lord was in it. He wasn't going to make the same mistake he had made in Martinsville. This time he would remember old, saintly Alva's prayers for the church and how God had blessed. This time he would begin on his knees and encourage everyone around him to do the same as they waited for God to work.

Of one thing Sam was convinced—the school could no longer look to the Synod of Mississippi for funding. Up to now, synod had been convinced that funding church schools was its responsibility:

> *The imperative need … is for an education that is positively Chris-*
> *tian. The church must supply this need or it will be unmet. There are only*
> *two sources of income for the church school, the one from tuition and the*
> *other from endowment. If the income from tuition is adequate it will be*
> *prohibitive to the child of moderate means. Hence, if the church is to do*
> *her full part, the endowment of schools becomes imperative.[1]*

Yet, consistently synod had failed to provide such funding.[2] Sam rejected the notion of human endowment, choosing to look to God for FCA's "Endowment." Undoubtedly, for inspiration he turned once again to giants of the faith such as George Mueller and C. T. Studd. Indeed, during Studd's lifetime his Heart of Africa Mission was never once in debt, even though no appeal for funds was ever made or collections taken.[3] Studd had absolute trust in the faithfulness of God:

> *No, not one penny will we take but what He sends, and be sure He*
> *will send.… We have a multimillionaire to back us up, out and away the*
> *wealthiest person in the world. I had an interview with Him. He gave me*
> *a checkbook free and urged me to draw upon Him. He assured me His*
> *Firm clothes the grass of the field, preserves the sparrows, counts the*
> *hairs of the children's heads. He said the Head of the Firm promised to*
> *supply all our need.…[4]*

As Sam leafed through his Bible, he spied Philippians 4:19: "My God shall supply all your needs, according to His riches in glory in Christ Jesus" (NASV). How much comfort that verse had always brought him! Let the Lord know about it, and He'd supply the money. Sam had always thought of it as the "accelerator text" of the Bible—the harder you press down on it, the more it gives. Since finding the money to run French Camp was such a conundrum, why not let God figure it out? Other schools might depend on endowments from humans to stay in business; wouldn't it be a radical concept to depend on the One who owned the cattle on a thousand hills? That's what he'd call Philippians 4:19—FCA's Endowment.

Immediately, Sam led the board in embracing the school's new financial policy. He told them what he would tell countless others:

> *In Philippians 4:19, God promises to supply our needs. That means*
> *that He is going to let us have needs. Allowing us to recognize and face*
> *genuine needs, He will in His own way and time meet them. While we*
> *wait for Him to show His hand in how He is going to meet them, we*
> *need to keep wide open to Him to find out what other lessons He wants*
> *to teach us and what traits He wants to cultivate in us as we 'wait on*
> *the Lord.'[5]*

The board determined never to ask for money or go into debt, but to make the school's needs known and depend on God to provide. They knew they would spend a great deal of time on their knees, and they would soon encourage supporters and even students to do the same.

Especially would the school not look to synod for support. The synod study committee that had reorganized FCA was united in the belief that the school needed a broader base of support than simply Presbyterians. The committee made it clear to synod that FCA was not going to look for official commitments by the presbyteries. The synod was already struggling to support its three institutions; in addition to French Camp, the synod was responsible for Chamberlain-Hunt Academy, Belhaven College, and was officially related to Palmer Home. This was an unusual number of educational institutions for a synod as small as Mississippi.[6]

Over the next decade, Sam slowly led FCA in becoming independent from synod. In Sam's first FCA report to synod on September 26, 1950, the FCA board requested that three of its members be from three Protestant denominations other than Presbyterian.[7] Sam explained:

> *We wanted to sell the job the school was doing, and we intended to raise our own funding. Therefore, we needed every advantage we could get. Since FCA had children and faculty members from other denominations, it made sense to have representatives from other denominations on the board.[8]*

By 1961, four of the sixteen FCA board members (or twenty-five percent) were not Presbyterians, but synod still had to approve their election.[9] Normally, this was not a problem; yet, one year, FCA trustees eagerly wanted a man on the board who had been a great benefactor to the school, and he was not approved by synod.[10] Sam observed:

> *We were given a good man, but we could foresee that from this point on, the board would not be able to pick its successors. We wanted men that the board members had cultivated and knew were highly dedicated to the Academy.[11]*

In 1965, the FCA board petitioned synod to change the school's charter to allow the board to elect its own successors, thereby precluding synod from overruling the board's choices. The motion sparked much debate, but it passed with the stipulation that the election would be nullified if three-fourths of synod members disagreed.[12] In 1973, the FCA Board again petitioned the synod to amend the school's charter, this time to delete the three-quarter vote to nullify the board's successors. The motion passed, and FCA was finally completely out of synod control.[13]

"That was a wise move," reflected Sam, "and that's the way it is now. The school is church-related but independent." [14]

Sam and the board realized that he knew nothing about directing an institution. Sam had often joked, "I was only a student and not a very good one!" Before he began his duties, he and several board members traveled to the School of the Ozarks in Hollister, Missouri, to counsel with its founder and longtime president, Dr. Robert Goode. The school was similar to Glade Valley School in North Carolina, where poor children worked for tuition and board. Sam wanted to model FCA after such a school.

"Dr. Goode," asked Sam, "please teach me how to operate a school such as this. What lessons have you learned?"

Goode gazed at Sam for a long moment. "The most important thing I've learned is how to say thank-you. We respond personally and quickly to every gift. We show as much gratitude for one dollar as we do for $10,000." [15]

Goode's words made a tremendous impression on Sam, and gratitude would become one of the hallmarks of his presidency at FCA, opening the floodgates of support for the school. Sam revealed later:

> *I could see the genuineness and rightness of that precept and determined that would be our policy at FCA. It's not that donors especially want to be thanked for what they do, but if they do give to a school like this, those in charge ought to have a sense of appreciation for the help God gives them.*
>
> *An expression of thanks should be given just because it's right. It all comes from people whose hearts have been touched by God. It is in this way that we have seen the fulfillment day by day of the special endowment [Philippians 4:19] on which this school has always depended.[16]*

Dr. Goode also had some unexpected, hard advice for the men. "Go home and get rid of all but two of the preachers on your board, one to open the meeting with prayer and one to close it. Replace them with some hard–headed businessmen, and your school will go." It was a tall order, for the board was filled with preachers. Yet, they returned and did just that. Many years later, Sam could say proudly, "God has blessed the Academy down through the years with strong boards of trustees." [17]

One experienced educator advised the board to move the school, since it was so isolated and lacked any paved road access. At the time, the Natchez Trace Parkway was only a sand bed. Sam disagreed, believing the setting was perfect for a school. "Even though the nearest paved road was six miles away, it seemed to me a benefit to be tucked away in this beautiful, rolling country near a fine, church-oriented community." [18]

Ann Angle, widow of late FCA President Stuart Angle, remembers with mirth her first introduction to the tiny village. "When we came over for an interview in

1956, we rode into French Camp, and we rode on out. At that time the Natchez Trace stopped right there, leaving us nowhere else to go. We looked around, and I asked, 'Stuart, where's the town?' Finally, we doubled back and found French Camp as it looked in 1956!"

Of course, time proved Sam right. Very rapidly in the 1950s, paved roads reached the hamlet. The Natchez Trace was completed, and now French Camp Academy sits on one of the loveliest national parkways in the United States. Millions of people pass by within eyesight of the school yearly.

Sam's presidency also benefited from improved communication between FCA and the outside world. Until 1950, telephone service in French Camp was nearly nonexistent; Sam's predecessors had to function with a makeshift, unreliable party line to the village of Weir, a few miles away. In April 1950, French Camp citizens rejoiced when Southern Bell connected FCA with the switchboard in Kosciusko. [19]

Sam, Stelle, Becky, and Stelle's mother, Mrs. Sellers, moved to French Camp in June 1950. The transition was hard on everyone, especially Sam, since his beloved father died on June 14, and Sam's duties at FCA began on June 15.[20] Stelle again had to overcome less than adequate housing. The president's home had been destroyed by fire sometime before, and Sam's family had to move into a home originally built for the principal.

"He moved into a very meek, old house, nowhere near adequate for his family," related the late Lewis Graeber, Jr. "However, the next year we built a new home for him, funded by my father.[21] Daddy also arranged with the local Ford dealer to give FCA a brand new two-door Ford coupe at cost."

Sam's salary was very modest, but as student Bill Rogers (FCA '65) put it, "Mr. Pat didn't come to French Camp for money. He came for love. That makes him one of the greatest people I've ever known."

Why would Sam leave a comfortable, secure pastorate for the overwhelming tasks awaiting him at French Camp? As usual, Sam gives us insight with an illustration:

> *A successful and gifted businessman in Canada determined to leave his position and go to India as a missionary. His firm tried four times to entice him to stay, each time upping his salary generously. He refused them all. His boss was puzzled. Enough money ought to buy anything. 'What's the matter?' he asked. 'Isn't the pay large enough?' 'The pay is large enough,' the man replied. 'The job isn't.'[22]*

FIND MONEY!

The job at French Camp was huge, and those first years were hand to mouth. Yet, Sam loved to boast, "It's God's hand to our mouths!" He spent almost every waking minute either on his knees asking God to provide the funds or out telling people of the school's needs—money, teachers, students, and building repair. At first, just finding the money for operating expenses was a daily chore.[23] Could they survive?

Sam had been at FCA only several days when the school received a ten or twenty dollar check from a man in Money, Mississippi. Sam rejoiced, "That was the first money to come in the mail, and I took it as a God-given sign that our needs were going to be met."[24]

Sam didn't ask anybody but the Lord for money, and he never begged. After four years in Leland, he had numerous contacts in the presbytery and synod, in addition to those made at his regular evangelistic services. He combined what he loved best—preaching and telling people about French Camp. He also asked others who were interested in FCA to visit churches and prospects for the school. Leaving no stone unturned, he found names of businessmen and did not hesitate to walk in, announcing, "I'm Sam Patterson, president of French Camp Academy. We've got a bunch of kids, and here's a list of needs for you to pray about."

Sam didn't carry on a conversation long before bringing up the subject of FCA support. At lunch with Jackson resident Sam McAllister one day, Sam abruptly changed the subject and asked, "Have you spent all your tithe this month?"

Surprised, McAllister replied, "Well, I don't know how much my tithe is going to be, but I doubt that I have."

Sam shot back, "Well, ask the Lord how much He wants you to give to French Camp!"

"Mr. Pat prayed for the school's needs, went out to see people about them, and the Lord brought the money in," recalled the late Sam Allen. "He never failed to get what we needed. One time we were in Memphis visiting one of Mr. Pat's business friends. When he asked about FCA's needs, Mr. Pat brought out a list, and many of them were met right in that meeting. If friends could not contribute, more than likely they knew someone who could."

Sam wasn't at French Camp one week when he made his first trip to raise money. He was nervous; what experience did he have in talking to people about FCA? Someone had given him Stuart C. Irby's name in Jackson, Mississippi. After being received graciously by the dignified, white-haired gentleman, Sam confessed that he couldn't give Irby any track record for the school because they hadn't even begun the new program. However, he briefly outlined the board's plans, then sat quietly. Irby was not a very talkative man, and the silence was unsettling. After what seemed an eternity, the philanthropist said, "Well, I'll give you $500."[25] Sam's faith soared:

> *That gift helped me to become more confident that God really did do what I'd preached. He does respond to His people's needs! The giving continued throughout my seventeen years at FCA.*[26]

However, more times than not in those early days, Sam came to the end of his financial rope. According to Lewis Graeber, Jr., that's when he'd call Lewis's father, board member L. A. "Pop" Graeber, saying, "I'm out of money, Mr. Graeber. What should we do?" L. A. proved to be God's man of the hour to help Sam put the needs of French Camp before people. As Sam recalls, Graeber had only one condition:

> *While still in Leland, I got a phone call from L. A. Graeber. He said, 'I'll do anything and go anywhere to support French Camp, but if you run that school into debt, I'm gone!' I told him that I was going to count on the Lord to keep us out of debt. Mr. Graeber kept his word. He'd take off several days at a time with me, and we'd go meet people—some we knew and some we didn't. He had his own way of telling a story, and he raised a lot of money for the Academy.*[27]

"When Sam called," noted Lewis, "Daddy always replied, 'Come on up here, son, and we'll go to Memphis tomorrow.' They'd hit the road, first visiting all the bank executives in Memphis, then moving down to Tunica and Clarksdale, calling on Daddy's business friends along the way. Bill and Willis Connell, both in the cotton business in Clarksdale, said every time they saw Daddy coming up the steps they'd go get the checkbook. Greenville and Greenwood were next, and by the time the two got home, they'd have about $5,000, enough money to keep the school going another month or two.

"One day Daddy visited John W. Caperton, who owned a John Deere dealership in Tunica, and declared, 'I want to get some money out of you for French Camp.' Caperton retorted, 'Graeber, I can't give you any money. French Camp is Presbyterian, and I'm a Baptist.' Daddy retorted, 'We've got more Baptist kids out there than all the rest of 'em put together.' Caperton gave up and wrote him a check."

Observers universally agree that Sam also had the gift of persuasion; one simply could not say no to him! His vision, coupled with his winsome personality and his unquestionable integrity, sold people immediately on the objectives of French Camp.

"Mr. Pat was the biggest hustler I have ever known, in the best sense of the word," remembers Pete Franks (FCA '51). "He was always going off in many directions to drum up any kind of contribution to the school—money, equipment, animals, you name it. When he was onto something, he'd jump into his 1951 green Ford and tear out of the school like a hound dog after a rabbit. As a senior in 1950-1951, I was frequently called on to pick up something he had persuaded somebody to donate. Every time I saw him speed off, I'd say, 'Well, boys, one of us had better get ready to take a trip 'cause he's not coming back empty-handed!'"

Ben Hollis (FCA '52), dubbed Big 'Un for his massive physical size, knew firsthand about that. A few weeks after he arrived at FCA, Sam asked him and several other boys to go with him to see someone about a donation in Kilmichael. The road was nothing more than a rutty, gravel washboard.

"Mr. Pat was driving with one hand the only way he knew how to drive—fast! As he skittered around those curves, talking a mile a minute, I offered my first foxhole prayer. I vowed never to get in a car with him again! Later, I realized that God wasn't going to let anything happen to Sam Patterson, so I concluded I'd be safe with him in a vehicle. He probably put 200,000 miles on that car raising money for FCA."

As word spread, contributions began coming in. Sam had forged a formidable network of support in the Mississippi Delta during his years at Leland. If he was behind something, often people needed to know nothing else. Leland Presbyterian had long supported French Camp, and after their beloved Sam became president, a steady stream of money and goods found their way to FCA. On any given Sunday afternoon, one might see a whole caravan of folks with odds and ends—cows, tractors, horses, corn pickers—heading for the hills with their gifts for Sam and his children.

Ann Aldridge, longtime member of Leland Presbyterian Church, always chuckles at a tale told by Gritter Mabry, one of the Aldridge's hired men, about the time he and Mr. Aldridge took a cow over to French Camp in the back of a pickup truck. Gritter thought it might be his last road trip on earth. On the bumpy road, the cow staggered from one side of the truck to the other with every jolt, causing the vehicle to rock violently; the two men were sure the truck would turn over any minute. They finally arrived safely amid the cheers of those who had gathered to witness the triumphal entry. They both were sure that a guardian angel had been riding in the truck that day.

Almost immediately after his arrival, Sam began speaking wherever he could, sharing the French Camp story:

> *I had inherited an institution with a huge deficit. Seems we owed everybody. I knew nothing else to do except set out to present our story to friends across the state. We went into churches and homes telling about French Camp's children, sometimes letting the children themselves help tell the story.*[28]

Since the Jones boys had received so much publicity, Sam gave groups regular updates on their progress. He quickly realized that a picture is worth a thousand words and began taking them with him as often as he could that first summer. They didn't have to say a word; as Sam told their story across the Southeast, they served as an apt vehicle to inform people about FCA's ministry. Sam loved them:

They always had strong appeal. They were cute, fine, bright kids with good, unique personalities. They never made talks, but after church people came up to speak to them. Every one of them knew how to handle himself. They weren't coached. God had put them here and used them greatly.[29]

"We were Mrs. Lail's kids!" exclaimed Steinreed Jones (FCA '58). "We went with Mr. Pat everywhere to show that he was not blowing hot air about helping kids. We were hard evidence that FCA was making a difference in the lives of children in tough circumstances."

People from all over the country sent money and clothes to French Camp for the Jones boys. Not only was there enough money to keep them there, but the Lails also had to convert a room in their home into a clothes closet for the boys. They received so many clothes that they finally had to ask people to send the clothes directly to French Camp, allowing many more students to benefit from friends' generosity.

Besides traveling, Sam worked overtime inventing new ideas to raise support, as bookkeeper Margaret Kimball looked on in wonder. "He took former president Laster's idea about memorial giving to a new level. We were already putting the names of donors in the FCA newspaper. One day Mr. Pat cried out, 'That could save French Camp if everyone knew about it!' Subsequently, everywhere he went he began advertising FCA's donor program. Like a snowball barreling downhill, more and more money came rolling in. It was truly amazing."[30]

Not long after that, Sam had another brainstorm. Why not give a loaf of homemade bread, baked by French Camp students and staff, to every donor? He began taking several boxes with him when he traveled, and later, during Stuart Angle's presidency, the school began mailing them. In 1983, long after Sam's time, FCA sent out 1,500 loaves and in 2006, over 15,000! Each loaf bears the verses Philippians 4:19 and John 6:35: "And Jesus said unto them I am the bread of life; he that cometh unto me shall never hunger" (KJV). Sam's brainstorm continues to be one of the main sources of donations at FCA today.

A note of thanks went with each of those loaves, specifically quoting Philippians 4:19 as the school's Endowment. Sam loved to tell the story about the students who once mistakenly wrote "French Camp's Endowment is Philippians 3:19" instead of 4:19. Unfortunately, 3:19 says "…whose god is their belly!"

In the midst of finding enough money to survive, Sam was faced with a horribly deteriorated campus. When he arrived, the campus consisted of only three dilapidated dorms, two humble cottages, and a decrepit gym.[31] Where in the world to start? Another person might have begun by painting the fronts of the buildings and fixing the "showy" items, but not down-to-earth Sam:

Our remote location and bad roads offered poor visibility and accessibility for the campus in 1950. Even when we did attract a visitor, the first two questions were, 'Where can we get coffee?' and 'Where's the restroom?' Since our bathrooms were all in terrible shape, I set out to fix them, beginning with the ones in the basement of Old McBride. I thought that was a major contribution to public relations for FCA![32]

The buildings were not only rundown and unsightly, but also dangerous. One night Sam awoke frightened, thinking about the three-story girls' dormitory with its ancient, overloaded wiring. He realized for the first time that it was a fire hazard. That night he prayed, "Lord, if you'll keep that building from catching fire tonight, I'll get right on it in the morning." The Lord protected the girls, and the next morning Sam called for estimates to fix the wiring. He began working to raise the funds that day, and almost immediately God provided just the amount needed to rewire the entire building.[33]

What set Sam apart was his utter certainty that God would provide. He never doubted that whatever God led him to begin, God would complete. He also never made the mistake of thinking he was doing it; he knew it was all of God. Most of the FCA staff had never seen such faith in action. Sam wrote checks, and Margaret Kimball would blanch, protesting, "Mr. Pat, we don't have any money in the bank!" Sam would soothe her, saying, "The Lord will provide."

"What faith he had! I just couldn't understand it!" she marveled.[34]

Even Sam's staunch new friends, such as the late French Camp Presbyterian deacon Talmage Branning, had trouble with Sam's attitude. "If a saint ever walked this earth other than Jesus Christ, Sam had to be one of them," said Talmage. "The only argument I ever had with him was over money. He wanted to get rid of it, and I thought the church needed a little to operate on!"

FCA history teacher Charles Rich recalls with awe Sam's abundant faith. "Shortly after his arrival, Mr. Pat encouraged the board to enlarge the student body by accepting elementary youngsters. Yet, FCA didn't have a dorm in which to put them. He accepted eight elementary boys and commissioned a Starkville architect to design a dorm that would cost $5,000. We certainly didn't have that kind of money.

"As the school year approached, we still had no money and no dorm. Mr. Pat went to bed praying, 'Lord, I've got eight boys coming and no place to put them. You have got to provide.' In the early morning hours, the phone rang, and a stranger in the Mississippi Delta said God had awakened him and told him to give $5,000 to FCA. The result was Moriah Dorm."

Sam himself could have coined the old saying, "The difficult we do immediately; the impossible will take a little longer." By Christmas, just six months after he came, FCA's deficit had evaporated. The school paid all the bills and even had a surplus, the first in many, many years. God had been more than faithful; enough was left for a fifty-dollar bonus for each staff member!

"Everybody helped," rejoiced Sam. "Staff members were patient, even though it looked at times as if paychecks might not come. People began to respond to the needs of FCA. Staff and students were interested in rebuilding. God did supply our need." [35]

Lewis Ward (FCA '38), longtime French Camp resident who returned as a staff member, speaks for countless people when he gives Sam unstinting praise. "You can look around here and see where that man has been. He picked this thing up and went with it. When he came here, this school was like a shoe without a tongue. Son, he made this place!"

The outpouring of love was so great towards FCA that Sam was able to report the following good news to the Fall 1950 Mississippi Synod:

> *...God has directed to the school this summer in miraculous manner contributions from people of all stations of life and many denominations. Many local churches and classes have risen to our support. This wonderful inflow of funds made it possible for us to accomplish the summer objectives and still not go into debt.*
>
> *Our new LeFleur Football Field is typical of the work of God and the method of doing things at the Academy. On August 1, we had a pasture with horses, calves, stumps, trees, and unlevel ground. On September 15, we played our first football game on that same piece of ground, now converted to a level field, covered with green grass, lighted with equipment purchased by French Camp citizens, and supported on poles cut, dragged, and peeled by the football players themselves.[36]*

He also reminded synod that FCA would be looking to God, not man, for financial stability. The school would not be asking for funds or conducting any fundraising campaigns. Thus began a tradition of yearly reports to synod of God's faithful generosity:

> *The financial policy of the school is one of faith and good sense. We have resolved to stay out of debt by spending only what we have at hand. We will put on no endeavor to provide the funds necessary, except by faith, prayer, and winning the support of individuals, organizations, and local congregations.... We have a real heart appeal. We believe God will provide through current and future friends.*
>
> *We ended last year in the 'black' ... and begin this year with only enough to meet immediate needs, but we did have that in such amount as to indicate that our need as it arose was to be fully supplied. Thus God will continue to work.[37]*

"If we had a need, we'd pray for it," says Peggy Cockrell. "We prayed for that old blue school bus, 'The Blue Goose,' and were thrilled to get it in 1959. The kids brought in dimes and nickels that we kept in a jar until we had enough. We wore that bus out!"

Indeed, Sam always reminded the staff, "There is no substitute for prayer, no provider as able and active as God, and no force as fruitful as faith." [38]

Such dependence on God was a powerful witness. It prompted admiration from a skeptical Kosciusko columnist:

> *The Academy lives, breathes, moves and has its being on a day-to-day basis with the cash gifts sent in by friends and supporters from here, there, and yonder. This must seem like precarious business to those realists among us who are also on the skeptical side. But it works, and so do all the staffers at FCA, and so do all the kids that go there. All power to Sam Patterson and his associates as he walks with his hand in God's hand and teaches Christian philosophy and fortitude by example rather than talk.* [39]

"The job was demanding beyond all expectations," declares Becky Patterson Rogers (FCA '61). "From the beginning Daddy gave wholeheartedly of his time and energy. Often he went until both were exhausted, and still he kept going. There seemed to be no end to the problems and situations that had to be faced and overcome. A typical day for Daddy started at his desk around 4:30 a.m. and ended around midnight, usually after long hours of counseling with students and faculty. Many days he was away from the school speaking and contacting people both individually and in groups to gain support for the work. We all prayed, and God met the needs. It was not easy work, but Daddy always felt the rewards far outweighed the efforts."

Many wonder how Sam did not become jaded and weary as he labored night and day for FCA. However, he understood the danger and guarded against it with scripture and warned his staff to do the same:

> *Satan takes all kinds of advantages in weariness, which is not just being tired. It is being tired to the point of being discouraged and disheartened. Our victory over weariness is promised in the Bible: 'But they that wait upon the Lord shall renew their strength...' (Isa. 40:31 KJV).* [40]

Good old-fashioned humor, Sam believed, helped everyone through those lean years in the early 1950s. Everyone can remember his quips and stories that still tickle the funny bone, such as, "I don't understand why God didn't put eyes on the end of our fingers, because then we could stick our fingers in our pockets and see what's in there."

Sam would be the first to tell you that French Camp Academy is not a monument to his efforts. It is a tribute to what can happen if one of God's children totally abandons himself to trust the Lord alone. J. I. Packer wonders why most of us aren't willing to take that glorious plunge:

> *Why are we not free enough from fear to go full stretch in following Christ? One reason ... is that in our heart of hearts we are afraid of the consequences of going the whole way into the Christian life.... In other words, we are not persuaded of the adequacy of God to provide for all the needs of those who launch out wholeheartedly on the deep sea of unconventional living in obedience to the call of Christ.*[41]

Sam was not only willing to launch out into uncharted waters, he looked forward to each and every day on the high seas with God. He couldn't have lived any other way. He realized that life would hand him challenging problems; yet, he also was certain that he could commit all those problems to the Lord and be free of anxiety and worry:

> *God never calls a person to a work for Him without providing adequate resources for the job.... Our Heavenly Father gives His own unfailing presence (Heb. 13:5–6), the divine assistance of the Holy Spirit with and within you (John 14:26), the indwelling Christ (Eph. 3:16–17), needed nourishment from his Word (Matt. 4:4), and the power and privilege of prayer (John 16:24).*[42]

GOD'S REMARKABLE PROVISION

Over the years, the Lord used a plethora of uncommon, even bizarre, methods to provide for FCA's needs. Many times Sam had no idea God was setting up a divine appointment, such as the time he approached a businessman about funds for an FCA project.

Sam walked into the man's waiting room and saw an old gentleman in overalls reading a newspaper. The secretary told Sam that the owner was taking a break but would be back soon. As Sam waited, he read his Bible. Presently the old man turned to Sam. "You here to see somebody, son?"

Sam replied, "Yes, I run a school in French Camp, Mississippi, and I am wondering if this man can help us with a project."

The man responded, "Well, he's so busy that I don't know whether he'll be able to help you."

"If he can't," said Sam calmly, "we'll understand. The Lord will provide somehow."

Sam kept on reading his Bible and did not notice that the man left. After some time, the secretary indicated that the businessman would see Sam. Entering the man's office, Sam was flabbergasted to see it was the old man in the waiting room! The eccentric gentleman explained that sometimes he ate his lunch in the waiting room incognito just to see the kind of people who came to him for help.

The businessman got right to the point. "How much is it going to cost me?"

"I don't know," admitted Sam, "because the architect has not even finished the plans."

The man countered, "Here's $100,000. If it comes in under budget, bring the balance back."

Sam agreed and left. The project came in at $75,000. Over the objections of others who wanted to keep the rest of the money, Sam had the FCA treasurer cut a check for $25,000, then delivered it personally.

The man was astounded. "You're the first person who's brought my money back to me! I'm sure you could have used it, couldn't you?"

"Yes, we have only about two dollars left in the bank. Yet, you wanted it back, and I'm a man of my word."

"Look," yielded the man, "here's another $75,000. Add that to the $25,000 and see what you can do. I have some business in Mississippi. Why don't I stop in and see this French Camp Academy? I might want to do more."

From then on, Sam only had to pick up the phone and call the gentleman on his private line to get funds. If the project came in under budget, Sam sent the excess back, and the man added to it.

"If people had given anything in the past and were friends of the school, Daddy went to see them as a friend, not as a money-raiser," comments Becky Rogers. "He didn't ask anybody but the Lord for anything. He let people know the needs, and they decided before the Lord what they should do."

One of the most unique and interesting French Camp donors was A. S. Mitchell, head of a large lumber company in Mobile, Alabama. In his 80s and rather cantankerous in demeanor, Mitchell was retiring and liquidating some holdings by making substantial grants to educational institutions. He agreed to meet with Sam only to ask a few questions about French Camp, with no promises to donate any money.

Mitchell asked Sam abruptly, "What will you do with $10,000 at FCA?"

Sam never missed a beat. "We need a new sewage system."

"What would you do with $25,000?" Again Sam had a ready answer.

"What would you do with $50,000?" Sam told him.

"What would you do with $100,000?" Another lightning-fast response from Sam.

Later Sam admitted to friends, "The questions were easy to answer because FCA's needs were so great in those days that I carried them in the front of my mind and did not have to deliberate."

Sam noticed that Mitchell's secretary was taking notes. Mitchell ordered, "Go back and write me a letter telling me again what you would do with these gifts." When Sam left, he thought he could see Mitchell's strategy. The businessman wanted to see if the answers Sam had given him represented real needs. When Mitchell received Sam's letter, he'd surely compare it to his secretary's notes.

Sam wrote the letter, and shortly after that the school received a check for $10,000. Mitchell told Sam, "You can do anything you want with this money for FCA. You are not bound by anything you told me in our conversation." Once again Sam saw Mitchell's strategy and was careful to use the $10,000 exactly as he had promised he would—to improve the sewage system. After the work was done, Sam wrote Mitchell and thanked him for the money.

Sometime later, the eccentric businessman confided to Sam, "I want to explain to you why you are going to continue to get funds from me. The day before you were in to see me, the president of another institution was here, and I asked him those same questions. He wrote me a letter outlining what he would do with the money, and I sent him $10,000, telling him to use it any way he pleased. When I received his thank-you note, he informed me they were going to use it for something other than what he had told me originally. He'll never get another dime out of me."

"That certainly helped me see how faithful those of us in institutions must be with gifts," noted Sam. "If we make a commitment to use the money in a certain way, we need to honor that commitment." [43]

Another delightful and colorful contributor to the school was Horace Hull, introduced to FCA by the Graeber family. After meeting Sam, Hull participated in several pheasant hunts sponsored by the Academy, and eventually he and his wife visited the campus. According to Lewis Graeber, after Sam had showed them around, Hull observed, "Y'all need a dining room down here worse than anything; I'll donate $100,000 to build one. I'll give you $80,000 now, and I want you to borrow $20,000, which I will pay off." He did, and the dining hall was completed in 1959. [44]

Actually, Hull and Sam became close friends, even though at first Sam was a little put off by Hull's severe countenance—"It scared me!" [45] Yet, as Sam got to know Hull, he found him to be one of the most tenderhearted people he'd ever known, especially about the things of the Lord: [46]

> *What a dear Christian he was! Twice I found him in tears in his office. The first time he had heard a message on the necessity of being Spirit-filled. With tears running down his face, he said, 'I want to be spiritual so bad!' The other time I saw him in tears, he said, 'I'm frightened. I don't want to be like that rich young ruler. I want everything I've got to be used for Him, and nothing to stand in the way between me and Him.' He had been deeply touched because God had given him great resources. I comforted him, for we knew that he was faithful to pass his wealth on to God's glory.* [47]

Sometimes God tested Sam to see if greed might be taking hold. In 1955, the school desperately needed a building to accommodate larger meetings. A Christian mail carrier in Port Gibson, Mississippi, offered to introduce Sam to E. L. McGhee, an elderly bachelor on his route who was considering contributing to schools. Sam wasted no time in driving down to Port Gibson.

On the way to McGhee's house, the carrier informed Sam, "When you see where he lives, you're going to think that we ought to be raising money for him. He's from Kentucky with no kin down here or maybe anywhere. He's lived as a recluse, as if he hadn't a penny in the world. However, don't be fooled. He has bred horses across the years, and if he wrote you a check, it'd be good for whatever amount he wants."

Sam indeed found McGhee to be a crusty old gentleman living in rough circumstances. "He resided in a two-room, concrete block house. We sat at the kitchen table as we talked, with the screen door open. After a bit, a couple of chickens came into the kitchen, pecking around. McGhee didn't pay any attention to them, and I tried not to either. However, they eventually hopped up on the kitchen table, right between us. Although they didn't interrupt our conversation, I was right glad when he finally shewed them off!"

Sam confessed to McGhee that a $5,000 donation for a meeting hall would be one of the major ways he could help the school. After thinking about it a bit, McGhee went into another room and came back with a bundle of large bills wrapped in newspaper. He began to thumb out $5,000 in fifty-dollar bills, saying proudly, "Preacher, the government never got any of this money!"

Sam was dismayed. He knew he could not build a house of worship with untaxed money. Even though he could see his building flying away, he told McGhee, "Sir, I'm not judging you, but I can't take that money. You need to pay taxes on it first."

Sam thought he had surely lost the donation, but after a moment, McGhee responded, "Well, I don't agree with you, but if you want a check, I have a checkbook. You make it out, and I'll sign it." McGhee's next words helped Sam understand why the Academy hadn't lost the donation. "I'd like to have my name on that building. I never have done anything for anybody in all my life, and I'm doing it now." [48]

The result was McGhee Tabernacle. At Sam's request, its pulpit was inscribed with the words, "Sir, we would see Jesus." [49] Sam likely recalled this phrase from childhood; S. J. wrote these words on a card and tacked it on his pulpits throughout his ministry. [50]

Only God could have masterminded the varied ways support came to FCA. A wealthy planter might give Sam an envelope with a generous contribution after a service. One family, learning that the French Camp Presbyterian Church had no organ, donated their own personal electric organ. At the dinner table one evening, Sam mentioned to friends the difficulty of farming with only one tractor. Not many hours later, they were showing Sam the tractor and cultivator they would be sending to the school.[51]

Bill Whittington, an overweight Greenwood attorney, and Garrard Barrett, Bill's pharmacist friend who smoked too much, agreed that Bill would lose fifty pounds and Garrard would quit smoking over a six-month period. Whoever defaulted would give a thousand dollars to French Camp. Bill lost the weight, but Garrard lost his nerve during a strenuous night in Las Vegas! However, both sent a thousand dollars to the Academy. Each had silently intended to do so all along, while overtly encouraging the other to better health.[52]

One of the most surprising gifts came with no name attached. Arriving by ordinary mail, a box seemed to contain only a hodgepodge of costume jewelry. However, in the mixture was a diamond ring that sold for $15,000 and met an immediate and pressing need at the school.[53]

At times, gifts came to the school simply because Sam urged someone to visit FCA. Texas businessman David Dean and his wife were traveling home on the Natchez Trace when Dean said, "Honey, I promised Sam Patterson if ever I was close to French Camp, I'd stop and see the school." His wife didn't want to stop because she was anxious to get home that night. Yet, Dean prevailed on that Saturday morning, and, entering the campus, they saw a host of boys mowing lawns, waving, and grinning. The lads stole Mrs. Dean's heart, and she subsequently put FCA in her will for $25,000.

Some donations were so timely that only God could have orchestrated them. In 1957, Sam held services at Mt. Salus Presbyterian Church in Clinton, Mississippi, pastored by newly ordained Jim Baird. Sam shared with Jim and his congregation a serious prayer request. The federal government had recently required that all private schools inoculate their students with the new polio vaccine—a very expensive undertaking. The school certainly didn't have the funds. All week the little church prayed for God to provide the money.

One morning the two men were visiting a Mt. Salus member in the hospital. As they entered the elevator, a young doctor joined them and recognized Sam. "You don't remember me, but when I was a medical student you let me come up to French Camp and participate in a pheasant hunt even though I had no money. You told me that someday I would be able to repay French Camp. I want to do that right now." He wrote out a check, folded it, and gave it to Sam, who put it in his shirt pocket.

The doctor got off the elevator, and Sam made no move to take the check out and look at it. Jim finally coaxed, "Sam, aren't you going to open it and see how much it is?"

Sam replied nonchalantly, "No, it's all we need."

Unable to stand the suspense, Jim reached into Sam's pocket for the check and read the amount—five dollars more than was needed for the vaccinations!

When raising money, Sam wasn't joking when he told people, "I'll open my mailbox and see what's there!" Time and again people were astounded to see the heavens open, as it were, to fulfill a current need for which Sam had been praying.

Henry Watson tells of the time Sam and others had been praying for months for $3,500 to construct a new building on campus. Early one morning Henry's phone rang. "Henry," said Sam excitedly, "I've been traveling for two weeks, and I just opened all my mail this morning. Would you believe the first letter was from a woman in the Mississippi Delta donating $3,500 to use however we wanted!"

Through the years at FCA, Sam saw that kind of thing happen repeatedly. "I remember the volume of prayer and brash faith that characterized all those associated with the school and seeking its resurrection. We simply threw ourselves on the Lord, and the saying came true: 'A miracle a day at FCA.'"[54]

"He wouldn't give up on this school," exclaims Lewis Ward. "He kept praying and believing that the Lord was going to turn it around, and He did."

SOLVING FUNDING ROADBLOCKS

Sometimes God had to provide creative solutions to funding roadblocks at FCA. According to Ewing Carruthers, one such incident occurred in the early 1950s when the school was struggling to stay alive and the verdict was still out on its future. Sam came to Ewing for advice concerning a problem with a possible wealthy donor.

"This fellow was very interested in the work at French Camp but hesitated to give us a large sum of money. He felt that the school couldn't exist without Sam at that point; if he died and FCA had to close, the man feared his money would be wasted.

"I suggested that French Camp Academy take out a life insurance policy on Sam for $100,000, payable to the school. When Sam agreed to that, board members Bill Yandell, Sr., Hugh Potts, Sr., and I split the premium and sent in an application.

"You must understand how preposterous this request was. In those days, Sam made only $400 a month. The idea of someone with such a small income being insured for $100,000 was simply ludicrous. Yet, I was determined to try. I wrote a long letter to the underwriters, explaining Sam's ministry and French Camp's mission to children. Miraculously, they issued the policy! To this day, underwriters kid me about the preacher who made $400 a month getting $100,000 worth of life insurance."

The policy assured the donor that FCA could continue in the event of Sam's premature death, and he became a steady supporter. Moreover, the insurance company later issued another $25,000 policy to Sam personally, which the board funded.

"This story is evidence that people all over the country shared in Sam's determination to resurrect French Camp Academy," reflects Ewing. "Sam's dream of FCA being financially sound has indeed come true. Today, those early amounts seem like pennies, since the current endowment fund stands at approximately $31 million in securities and another $17 million in life insurance owned by French Camp."

Another interesting issue arose in 1955, again possibly over fears of a donor or donors. A routine title search, possibly ordered by a supporter who wanted to protect a large investment in the school, revealed that FCA did not own clear title to its property! In fact, further investigation showed that Central Mississippi Presbytery still owned it. The problem dated back to the early twentieth century when the Synod of Mississippi began acquiring schools to form a statewide "correlated" system.[55] On April 7, 1914, the Presbytery of Central Mississippi had voted to transfer the property and control of French Camp Academy to the Synod of Mississippi,[56] but the details of the transfer were never actually accomplished. This oversight made synod's subsequent control of FCA questionable.

On November 29, 1955, Sam personally appeared before a called meeting of Central Mississippi Presbytery at First Presbyterian Church in Jackson to ask the body to execute a quitclaim deed to FCA, conveying all property owned or claimed to be owned by the school. Presbytery did so,[57] and an hour later the Synod of Mississippi met at the church in a called meeting to do the same thing, thus finally perfecting FCA's title to its property and satisfying donors.[58]

THANK YOU, THANK YOU, THANK YOU

Sam took Dr. Robert Goode's early advice and never seemed to be able to thank people enough for their support of FCA. Tearfully, Henry Watson recalls the time Sam had been praying hard for needed funds, and Watson had helped. "Sam cried when I gave him $500 for that building. He was so appreciative."

Throughout the years, Sam never failed to begin his annual report to synod with praises and thanks to God for His abundant Endowment in Philippians 4:19. These doxologies to God, which read like dynamic sermons extolling the goodness and faithfulness of God, stand in stark contrast to the reports of other church organizations and institutions, who frequently asked synod for money or reported on capital fund drives to raise support.

In 1951, he was able to tell synod that FCA continued to operate in the black, and he gave all the credit to God:

> *Our report this year comes in the form of a testimony to the goodness of God and His faithfulness in answering prayer. We have day-by-day cast the whole weight of our needs upon Philippians 4:19, and we testify that not once has this promise failed.*[59]

Sam's reports were also unique in their overall tone of humble gratitude to all the friends of FCA:

> *Our report this year also comes as a direct expression of gratitude to the growing number of friends who have invested prayer, interest, and gifts in our mission. The support that has come to us from synod, presbyteries, local churches, and church classes and groups, plus a vast host of individual friends leaves us without adequate words to express our heartfelt thanks! While our work this year has been subjected at times to mistakes on our part, it has been all along the way a record of the miracles of God in these present days.*[60]

In 1952, as usual, he began his report:

> *Our report this year on the progress of the school becomes again a commentary on, and a confirmation of, Philippians 4:19. Our Lord has provided. We can see great areas open for improvement in our operation of the school from the human viewpoint, but we can see no room for improvement in our Lord's faithfulness. He has been completely dependable.... Our audit shows we closed the year with a net gain of $7,695.25.*[61]

The year 1953 saw more praise to God:

> *God did what Philippians 4:19 said He would ... the school had the largest boarding enrollment of its history ... and the operating cost per student was reduced this year by $66.60 per person.*[62]

In 1954, Sam reports triumphantly:

> *The board ... first of all desires to testify to the faithfulness of God in providing for our needs ... in keeping with Philippians 4:19. God's goodness and guidance made it possible for us to have the best year we have had since reorganization in 1950.... We are deeply grateful....*[63]

The year 1957 surpassed even 1954 in revenue and gifts. Sam's quiet certainty that God would provide in abundance was not lost on the watching world, as shown by these comments in 1959 from a Leland columnist:

> *With quite a number of church-related schools ... so poorly managed and under-financed, how does it happen that this little Piney Woods school seems to manage so well? ... There is but one answer for us— red-headed, hard-working, faithful Sam Patterson and those with whom he is associated....*
>
> *... Patterson has accomplished more in nine years there than many can claim in a lifetime. His deep and abiding faith in God's providence*

*already has marked him as a man who seldom falters because he is sure
of the ground on which he stands. Just as sure is Sam Patterson of God's
fulfillment of all His promises as is his certainty that the sun will rise
with each newborn day. I heard it said of him, 'Were any of you to travel
the length and breadth of Christendom, I doubt that anywhere you would
find one of greater faith ....' And this is true, for he communes with God
as a child of faith would with an earthly parent, fully confident that all
petitions will be heard and answered through grace and mercy.*[64]

By 1958, Sam told synod:

*I believe we at FCA say thank you more than any other people in the
state because we have so much to be thankful for, both to our Lord and
to our friends .... [the children have] kept us on our toes, sometimes on
our backs, always on our knees ... but the Lord has led us through our
problems and, by making the hands of His people His hands, He has
provided for our needs.*[65]

Also prominent in Sam's synod reports were requests for prayer, as in 1961:

*We have no requests or recommendations to make other than the
request for continued, fervent prayer of the synod that the Lord will, in
His various ways, supply support for the school's work and keep us true
to Him.*[66]

And in 1963:

*... The largest enrollment in the school's history, the largest
graduating class, and a year of much-needed physical improvement all
helped to make this past year one for which we thank God. We ask for
prayer in two areas: (1) That the needs of the school might be continually
supplied as they have in the past and (2) That the personnel of the school
might have the wisdom and courage of God in this day when the broken-
home area is increasing.*[67]

By 1965, the school had operated for fifteen years depending solely on God,
and Sam again gave credit where credit was due at synod:

*We all know that ' ... my God shall supply all you need' is in the
Bible, but to see God operate in our midst makes it even more wonderful
.... we invite all synod members to come see for yourselves what the
Lord is doing at FCA ...*[68]

In 1966, after sixteen years as president, Sam must have taken much joy in delivering the following tribute to His Lord:

> *God has so richly blessed us this year, as in years past, to faithfully honor the prayers and trust of the friends of the Academy in such a way as to meet the daily needs of this school. God supplies our needs in such a way as to keep us constantly recognizing that we cannot go another day without His blessing and help. Yet, He supplies in such a way as to make us confident that, month after month, year after year, He will and does meet the need. Our last audit showed that, again, we closed our fiscal year in the black. We praise God and thank all the friends He has given us for this.[69]*

The late Erskine Jackson was among many who admired Sam's testimony to God's faithfulness at every single synod meeting, even though others smiled indulgently at Sam's unusual method of financing and didn't take him too seriously. However, facts don't lie, and as the years went by, they could see Sam was right.

Erskine smiled as he relished the memory of the first time Sam spoke of FCA's Endowment at synod. "All the charitable institutions began to talk about how they were endowed and how they expected to be endowed in the future. Finally, the time came for the young, new president of French Camp to stand and share with the body the policy of French Camp. I can recall the ripple of smiles and amazement that came over the men when Sam declared, 'The Endowment of French Camp Academy is Philippians 4:19.' This faithful man, speaking almost in the ashes of the old French Camp and for every year thereafter, was God's prophet to us all—that our hope, faith, and trust should always be in God. French Camp was living on a shoestring, and God in His mercy was meeting every single need. What a testimony!"

FIND TEACHERS!

When Sam assumed his duties, one of the first critical matters was to find capable staff. After all, Sam loved to joke that he had barely made it out of school himself! The late Billy Thompson was coaching at Starkville High School and felt God was calling him when Sam asked him to be principal. In the very early years, these two men ran French Camp Academy. Actually, they became good friends and made a formidable team, complimenting each other beautifully in their styles of discipline. Sam acknowledged later:

> *Coach was a fine Christian man who had been reared in French Camp. For the next eight years, he was my right-hand man. I had to be out a lot raising money. We didn't have a large staff, and Coach*

really carried the load here on the grounds. He oversaw the discipline and the work program, in addition to being coach, choir director, and houseparent. Today, if you ask students whom they most remember from their FCA days, they will all say Coach Thompson. He was a tremendous asset.[70]

Says Thompson, "He wanted me to coach, and I told him I would if he'd let me be the principal! When he hired me he warned, 'We don't have any money in the bank. Our balance is exactly zero!' Yet, I never missed a payday. Mr. Pat pretty much let me run the school. I loved him because he never questioned my judgment. The first year I had to expel a good many kids. I'm sure the first time I expelled one, he didn't want to do it; a time or two we talked about it, but he never questioned me about it. Mr. Pat understood that we had to get control of the situation. We had inherited some tough kids who had been turned loose to do whatever they wanted; they were almost juvenile delinquents. We turned it around, thank goodness, with Mr. Pat praying and helping me with it.

"I made a lot of mistakes that he had a perfect right to get on me about. He would look to see that I had corrected them, but he never said anything to me. I worried that I had to be so tough that first year, but he assured me it was all right as long as I was sure I loved them. That's what they needed.

"How do I describe someone who I thought was almost perfect? If Mr. Pat had any faults, I didn't see them. He was completely honest and open with me; I always knew exactly what he was thinking. I never saw him lose his temper, and I never had an argument with him."

Lewis Ward agrees. "I'm sure Mr. Pat was like all the rest of us in that he wasn't perfect, but he came as near to being perfect as any human could be."

Sam provided discipline with grace, while Coach provided discipline with justice. Perhaps Sam's inherent infectious sense of humor simply won out over sternness much of the time; or, perhaps, he frequently harked back to similar unpleasant run-ins with teachers during his mischievous youth.

"All the kids loved Mr. Pat with a passion because he was good to them, even though he was firm," noted Coach. "He could be loving, but I had to be real tough."

Ben "Big 'Un" Hollis understood only too well the difference between the two men. One incident stands out in his memory. It was a tradition at FCA to give new students a playful "hard time." One day a young student arrived, and for a full week the kids scared him about Ben's huge size, warning, "Look out for Big 'Un; he goes crazy at the full moon!" The full moon did indeed come, and one night about nine o'clock, Ben chased the little fellow across campus. However, Ben didn't count on the child running pell-mell into Sam's house and hiding under the Pattersons' bed, where they lay sleeping. Startled, Sam jumped out of bed and coaxed the boy out. Then laughing heartily, Sam assured him that

Ben wasn't going to hurt him. He sent both of them back to the dorm and told Ben to cut out the pranks.

"Now, Coach Thompson," says Ben, "was a different animal altogether. He would've torn me up!"

Billy often led the singing for Sam's revival meetings. On one memorable occasion, he was leading "Leaning on the Everlasting Arms," and kept singing the chorus phrase "what a fellowship" as "water fellowship." When he sat down, Sam whispered to him, "What'd you sing that Baptist song for? You said 'water fellowship, water joy divine!'"

Billy delights in memories of marvelous Sunday night fellowship with Sam through the years. "Every Sunday night after we'd had the Sunday night service with the kids in the school auditorium, we'd go up to Mr. Pat's house and eat supper in the kitchen—nothing fancy, just whatever we found in the refrigerator. We didn't talk business much; we simply let our hair down and enjoyed talking." [71]

Some staff members were former FCA students rescued from dysfunctional homes. The late longtime FCA staffer Ralph Newman (FCA '57) grew up with an abusive, alcoholic father in a family of ten children. During his teen years, a Christian woman in his community took him under her wing and taught him scripture, catechism, and etiquette. Yet, Ralph never accepted Christ as his Savior. By high school, he was heading in the wrong direction, so she arranged for him to attend FCA. Getting off the bus in Weir, Mississippi, he began walking to French Camp and a new future.

"Mr. Pat was a huge influence on Ralph," relates wife Margie. "For three years after he came to French Camp, Ralph was a rebel at heart. Yet, that didn't stop Mr. Pat from showing Ralph deep love from a man who walked with God. Mr. Pat gave validity to Christianity."

Ralph accepted Christ just a few months before he graduated from high school. A guest evangelist was preaching at FCA, and Ralph was on the back row with other boys. They dared him to go forward after the service, and, completely unafraid, Ralph accepted the dare. Yet, as he stood before the evangelist, his heart was so convicted that he broke down and confessed, "I DO need God in my life." Subsequently, his life turned completely around, and he shed much of the anger he had stored for his family. He eventually forgave his father and led him to the Lord on his deathbed.

Margie watched Sam pour his life and heart into Ralph over the years. "While Ralph was in college, Mr. Pat called him regularly, and every year sent him a plane ticket to come home for Harvest Festival, even meeting him at the airport. When Ralph was a junior, Mr. Pat asked if he would pray about becoming a Bible teacher at FCA, and Ralph accepted. Beginning in August 1963, he became a houseparent to eighteen boys. We married that November. We never asked if or what we would be paid; this was simply where God wanted us."

Ralph wore many hats at FCA. In addition to teaching Bible and being a houseparent, he learned how to print the *FCA News* and helped tremendously on the farm. In 1968, Sam asked him to be Dean of Students, and Ralph entered Mississippi State University to get his masters degree in school administration.

Sam encouraged his staff to laugh, have fun, and not take themselves too seriously. He led by example, sometimes to the utter surprise of those around him. "We were dedicating the old swimming pool with a special ceremony and everyone was all dressed up," recalls Peggy Cockrell. "After the formal program, John Robert was standing by the pool, when suddenly Mr. Pat walked over and shoved him into the deep end. Everyone's mouth dropped open; many folks there didn't know Mr. Pat and were shocked. John was wearing a watch that his basketball boys had saved up to buy for him. Mr. Pat worried that his prank had hurt it, but it hadn't. We all had a good laugh!"

Andy Jones can vouch that good-natured kidding was also the order of the day under Sam's leadership. "Quite often at church we had sentence prayers. Mrs. James Atterbury, a veteran dorm mother, sat with her children on the front pew. One night the little redheaded Fitzgerald boy prayed, 'O Lord, help us to be good so that Mrs. Atterbury won't have to whup us so much!' For days, Mr. Pat kidded Mrs. Atterbury about being so cruel to the children that they came to church and prayed for deliverance! The next Wednesday night the same little boy prayed, 'O Lord, help Mr. Pat to preach better tonight than he did last Wednesday night!' As Mr. Pat headed for the door after the benediction, you could hear Mrs. Atterbury's heels clicking right behind him, catching up to kid him that a child had to pray for deliverance from his preaching!"

Sam was practical, and his staff benefited greatly from his ability to pinpoint trouble spots and address them simply and effectively. His wonderful little booklet "We Are Human," originally penned as a handbook for FCA staff in meeting the challenges of their jobs, gives advice on a number of common problems:

> *You are going to get tired.... Work and weariness often go together. You will enjoy your work for Christ at French Camp. But often the demand of hours and duty will cause you to feel depleted in nervous, physical, even spiritual energy. Then weariness sets in. Watch out for this.* [72]

"Mr. Pat told Ralph to buy a good mattress set," said Margie Newman, "because he would not do well as a staffer if he didn't get adequate rest. Before we married, Ralph saved his money and bought one. Mr. Pat was right!"

Sam also urged FCA staff to follow his lead in not being critical and judgmental. He tried to help them find "the lubricant that can cause us to work together without hot friction and grinding gears":[73]

Christians are human. Humans are imperfect ... you will be working closely, daily with colleagues as imperfect as you are. It is not enough to recognize this and 'make allowances.' To live with and be happy with colleagues who will make honest mistakes, and at times make what we might consider inexcusable errors ... we must do what the Lord has prescribed in Ephesians 4:1–3, [forbear one another in love]....[74]

In adding staff through the years, Sam was extremely careful whom he hired. He knew that the staff could become the most important human friends and influences in students' lives. These battered children were at a crossroads in life, and FCA staff could help turn their lives in the Lord's direction.

He wanted people who loved children and knew how to discipline properly. He understood that most of these children had never known love in their entire lives. Moreover, no one had cared enough about them to set firm boundaries. He taught his staff that these children needed loving discipline by a person who knew Jesus Christ well:

These boys and girls you serve, as do all youngsters, need the kind of love that makes them know they are important to someone; the kind of discipline that is fair, firm, and consistent; and the chance to know and live with a real man or woman of God who is not a spiritual fraud, but genuine.[75]

Ann Angle has always thought their first interview with Sam was rather odd. "Mr. Pat didn't ask us a lot of the questions we thought we'd be asked—doctrinal questions, such as our views on scripture. He simply visited with both of us and heard Stuart's testimony. He wanted to know where Stuart was with the Lord."

Sam also wanted people who had a missionary spirit and were willing to live on the edge with Christ. Sam was very honest with John and Peggy Cockrell when they came as dorm parents. "Mr. Pat told us that he could not promise us a salary. If the money came in, we'd get paid. If not, we wouldn't. He told us to look at the job as if we were going to Africa as missionaries. We were taken aback, but we decided to come."

Sam's viewpoint is evident in a story he liked to tell about an American businessman traveling in the Far East. He visited a mission leper colony and saw a young American woman treating repulsive sores.

"I wouldn't do that for a million dollars," he remarked.

"Neither would I," she countered.

"Well, why are you doing it?"

"I'm doing it for Christ."[76]

Sam took pains to instill in the staff a sense of responsibility before God in their high calling of bringing children to Christ and discipling them through the years. The job demanded their very best effort:

> *Perfection is not required in us for this Work, or else none of us*
> *would be here. What is required is a sincere recognition of the school's*
> *purpose and our own responsibility; a sincere personal commitment not*
> *only to live with these boys and girls, but to live for them; a quickness*
> *to note our own personal failures; a hastening on our part to bring our*
> *faults to the Lord in humble confession; and an immediate trust in Him*
> *to correct in us the wrongs.*[77]

Ironically, Sam accounted for the longevity of FCA staff by the low salaries they were paid. He felt that people worked at FCA for the sake of ministry, not money, and they found every bit of it and more there. Even though fine men have served as FCA presidents over one hundred years, Sam believed strongly that they were not the most important people to students:

> *The ones who have the most impact on the lives of the students are*
> *the staff. God has blessed and continues to bless this school with godly,*
> *consecrated staff people .... They are vital in communicating a sense*
> *of love and belonging, Christian convictions, and high ideals to boys*
> *and girls. Presidents will have places of honor, but the people who are*
> *having effective input in shaping the lives of people are the staff of the*
> *Academy.*[78]

Margie Newman greatly appreciated Sam's healthy relationship with the FCA staff. "I've been here since 1963, and I never saw him lose his temper, even though I have seen him upset. He led a very simple life and did not need much for himself; he seemed to be focused exclusively on others. He was a father figure on campus, always up early in the cafeteria before we got there with our children. As he drank his coffee, he smiled and talked to us about the upcoming day."

At times, some staff members needed to bank on that affirmation more than others. John Robert Cockrell and Ralph Newman often had more enthusiasm than common sense. One November morning they were sitting in the cafeteria, watching a flock of ducks land on the lagoon in front of the dining hall. Both had recently bought Remington 1100s. Itching to try out the guns, Ralph suggested, "John, let's go get our guns and shoot some of those ducks!"

"We stood on opposite sides of the lake and pounded those ducks!" remembered John Robert with considerable amusement. "Suddenly, we heard somebody whistling loudly, and we looked up to see Mr. Pat motioning to us furiously. We immediately went to his office and knew we were in serious trouble. Mr. Pat had a little scar on his face, and when you saw it turn red, which wasn't often, you better behave yourself because you're about to get a jacking up. Mr. Pat loved to hunt, but he was a firm believer in not killing anything unless you were going to eat it. He knew we were just practicing with our new guns. He dressed us down!

"However, as we left his office, we heard him tell a group of people visiting the school, 'If I get those two boys straightened out, they're going to be long-time staff members of French Camp Academy!' When he made those cute remarks, we knew he had forgiven us and wasn't really mad."

The two put Sam's good nature to the test again when the issue of expanding Lake Ann came up. The lake was bordered by inclining hills, and a field lay on the other side of the levee. All that was needed for expansion was a new levee to replace the current one. Sam and Ralph had discussed the idea, and both thought it workable. However, one didn't tell Ralph anything was a good idea unless one meant for it to happen. He and John Robert decided they'd go ahead and begin the project by breaking the levee. Sam was totally caught off guard, since he was still in the thinking stage. One minute the lake was very small, the next it was forty acres. Needless to say, the two boys were back in Sam's office immediately for another discussion!

FIND STUDENTS!

With school starting in just three months, FCA needed students. Sam began using every means to spread the word that the school was open and that it now had a program by which students could work to earn their tuition, room, and board. If a young person was in a situation of real need, Sam wanted everyone to know FCA would move heaven and earth to get that child in.

"The children that came to FCA in the '50s didn't have any money for tuition," explains Becky Rogers. "They had sponsors—people, churches, Sunday School classes. It wasn't 'Let's see if this will work for this kid.' French Camp was IT. More than once Daddy literally took children off the street and brought them back to French Camp with him."

The late Ladell "Dell" Flint (FCA '52) was one of those children. In 1950, Sam rolled into French Camp to start work with his furniture loaded in the back of the truck and Ladell in the front seat. "Mr. Pat and the good Lord were the only parents I ever had," wrote Ladell in undated comments written for FCA. "I was in jail over in the Mississippi Delta, and a kind man told the sheriff not to send me to Columbia Training School because Sam Patterson was coming to pick me up. Mr. Pat came and got me, and I helped him move in at French Camp his first day in June 1950. He raised me to believe that God and I together could make it through anything."

Ladell later became quite successful and every Thanksgiving and Christmas hosted FCA students at his home in New Mexico. He also sponsored other students, such as Jennifer Jones Meredith (FCA '88). "Mr. Flint so dearly loved and looked up to Mr. Pat," says Jennifer. "He often confessed he didn't know where he would be without Mr. Pat and his love for him."

As news of the school spread, students appeared out of nowhere. One young boy ran away from a cruel home and walked into Sam's office carrying his suitcase. "I have come to attend school," he announced. A friend had told him that if he were ever in trouble, he should go to French Camp for help.[79]

Sometimes Sam saved a child from himself. "I don't really know why Mr. Pat took a likin' to me," wonders Billy W. "Pete" Thrailkill (FCA '53). "I guess he saw I was headed for trouble. I was a district kid going to the grammar school, and in 1951 he brought me to the dormitory at FCA with my parents' blessing. I went to high school at FCA, and they were the best four years of my life. I joined the church at FCA, and even though I fell away when I left, I rejoined later and got serious with God."

By the time school started in the fall of 1950, FCA had sixty-seven boarding students, five of them the Jones boys. Sam told Erin Lail that he was determined to find the money to keep the boys at FCA:

> *I've written to the presidents of a number of young adult classes in the synod, suggesting that they each consider adopting one of our Jones boys for the school term as a class project. I believe we will receive a favorable answer .... If they do not put up all that is needed, I will find it somewhere. It can be gotten.[80]*

Six months later he wrote Mrs. Lail in deep gratitude, not only for her help with the Jones boys, but also for her support of the school:

> *You have meant so much, not only to these boys but also to the whole school. Your talk to synod was one of the primary contributing factors to our present existence. The tide of opinion seemed to turn from pessimism to optimism about the school as you talked to that group of laymen and preachers.[81]*

Steinreed Jones (FCA '58) was eleven when he and his brothers went to FCA that summer. "After getting accustomed to a full stomach, a comfortable bed, shoes, and clothes, I figured maybe French Camp was heaven. Before I went to FCA, I thought poverty was the way we were supposed to live. We didn't know we were poor. For the first time in our lives at FCA, we had shoes when we needed them and socks. Growing up, we went barefooted. Daddy could afford only one pair of shoes a year for us—at the beginning of school. I remember going to school barefooted in January because we'd worn our shoes out for that year. Our feet were so tough that we could run down a hill and slide on loose gravel without hurting them. Today, I can hardly walk across cement."

Fifty years later, Mary Ida Harper, dietician at French Camp in 1950, remembers little seven-year-old Lewis Jones (FCA '61) as if it were yesterday. "At that time, we ate family style; the food was dished up, put on the table, and passed around. It was a good old country dinner—plenty of vegetables, lots of food. Lewis probably had never seen that much food in his life. The faculty member assigned to his table pointed him out to me. 'That child isn't eating, Mrs. Harper, and he won't tell me why. Maybe he'll talk to you.'"

Mary Ida went over to the table and took Lewis by the hand. "I've got to go in the kitchen; why don't you come with me?" He followed her without a word. When they reached the kitchen, she said kindly, "I see that you're not eating. If you could have anything you wanted for supper, what would it be?" From his small, bowed head, she could barely hear him whisper, "Bread and milk."

"I knew immediately that bread and milk was all he had been accustomed to eating. We had cornbread muffins left from dinner that day, and we always had milk. I fixed him right up, telling him he could even crumble it in his glass if he wanted!"

"We were blessed by French Camp and Mr. Pat helping us," said Steinreed. "He took us in as a father would have. Before we came to French Camp, we had no idea about God. Our father wasn't religious. He always believed in God, but he didn't accept Christ until much later. Our mother was a Christian, but she didn't teach us. We never went to church—too many hardships. But God was taking care of us, even then. I became a Christian through Mr. Pat. He'd come by to check on us and witness to us all the time."

Often, students showed up at French Camp Academy quite unexpectedly. Very soon after Sam arrived at FCA that summer of 1950, he was sitting in his office when a young fellow knocked on the door. The boy looked to be about seventeen, with a shock of very blond, almost white hair sticking straight up on his head. Sam remembers:

> *He'd been downtown asking where my office was. He had a speech impediment, which he significantly overcame with time, but then it was very pronounced. He was dressed in a black suit that didn't fit him very well, with a black tie and a white shirt. He'd attracted quite a bit of attention because during the weekdays around here, nobody wears a suit except a preacher holding a funeral.*[82]

His name was Thomas McCaa (FCA '53), but French Campers would forever know him simply as "Cotton." He wanted to be a minister, but he didn't have any money. If FCA accepted him, he would have to work for tuition and board. He had hitchhiked from Greenville to Jackson because someone had told him that FCA was near Jackson. Upon getting there, he was told the school was near Winona. So he hitched to Winona. Night fell, and he got a room in a boarding house, where they told him how to get to French Camp.

"It was hot, hot, hot!" said Cotton. "I walked more than I hitched on a bumpy, gravel road. I finally found Mr. Pat. I had dressed up because I wanted to impress him, since I was asking him to let me work for an education. I wanted to go to school badly. I had a beautiful situation at home—a great mom and dad—but I could not make it in the public schools there. School officials didn't know then that I was deaf, and I didn't either. I just knew I couldn't understand what was going on around me. I still have trouble today, even with hearing aids."

Cotton stayed at French Camp for four years of high school, eventually becoming student director of the first summer camp program for children. "While he never fulfilled his dream of becoming a pastor," noted Sam, "he became a chaplain's assistant in the Air Force for twenty-eight years and has been a fine credit to the country and to the school ever since."[83]

Cotton was especially fond of Sam. "I would hate to think where I would be if Mr. Pat had not given me a chance. We had a very special relationship. Both of us were 100 per cent working and looking for every way to help FCA. I milked cows all year round. Since I was the oldest of nearly 100 kids at FCA, Mr. Pat had me tending the sick cattle.

"One morning as we were milking, Mr. Pat told me he had dreamed that the entire pasture was full of dormitories. Today, a half-century later, it is! Later, he dreamed that the administration building caught fire. That disturbed Mr. Pat so greatly that he immediately called an electrician to determine the cost of encasing all those old wires in aluminum pipes. The money came in to do it, of course, because of our Endowment."

At times, the communication between Sam and Cotton was mysterious and inexplicable. Cotton went to school year round, but one summer he wanted to go home for a week or two. He hadn't been home more than three or four days, when he had a strange compulsion to return to French Camp, even though he had no reason to do so. Arriving at the school, he walked up the hill and had almost made it to the dormitories when he met Sam.

"Cotton, how in the world did you get here so fast?" asked Sam.

Cotton replied, "Well, I got here in my normal time, about an hour and a half; I had to hitch, after all."

Sam was stunned. "Cotton, I just called your brother only thirty minutes ago to tell you to come back. Leon has the mumps, and you're going to have to do the milking today."

When Ben Hollis arrived in July 1950, his first impression of FCA was far from positive. "The campus looked rundown and shabby; all the buildings needed paint. We wandered around campus for a while, in and out of several buildings, and couldn't find anybody.

"Finally, this big, tall, red-haired gentleman came purposefully strolling across the lawn. As he drew near, I could see twinkling, friendly, blue eyes. When he introduced himself as the president, I couldn't believe it. He was in old, raunchy, khaki trousers and an undershirt, with sweat pouring off of him as if he were a manual laborer. He escorted us to his office, excused himself to freshen up and put on a clean shirt, and then returned to talk with us. I was so impressed with that man's confidence; he came straight at me and didn't mince words. When I left, I knew that FCA was where I wanted to be."

In the future, whenever Ben had a problem, he could always talk it over and pray with Mr. Pat, and the situation improved. Once he discovered a former FCA student was in Columbia Training School because of a problem with his stepfather. He told Sam about it, and they both agreed that his friend's problem was not sufficient reason for him to be at a reformatory. Sure enough, a few days later Sam came driving into FCA with the boy.

In later years, students came to French Camp from throughout the United States and as far away as Ecuador and Honduras. Many had no means to pay, but they were accepted, housed, fed, clothed, and educated along with the rest with no difference in treatment.

FIND FOOD!

After seeing the value of a good work program both at Glade Valley School and School of the Ozarks, Sam was convinced it was just the ticket to provide food for the school and teach solid work habits to students. Under the program, each student had to work at least an hour a day, with absolutely no exceptions. Sam made sure everyone had a job:

We farmed about 400 acres back in 1950. Care of the farm animals and cultivation of the crops made up much of the student work program. The boys milked the cows, baled the hay, slopped the hogs, fed the chickens, plowed the gardens, repaired the buildings, and maintained the grounds. The girls laundered the clothes, shelled and canned the produce, prepared the meals in the school kitchen, and baked the bread.[84]

Weecy Patterson (FCA '55) worked her way through FCA making bread. "Mrs. Pilcher came in one day and told the five of us that we were going to learn how to bake bread. I exclaimed, 'You've got to be kidding!' That was the first bread that French Camp had made. We made it with our hands—no mixers. It was so good we all gained weight."

Kenny Henderson (FCA '64) disagrees. "I love that bread now, but a lot of us hated homemade bread back then. We wanted real sliced bread!"

At different times the school had a dairy, beef cows, chicken houses, and pigs. The gardens produced almost any vegetable imaginable—beans, potatoes, peas, corn, and tomatoes. The dining hall had two big freezers, and by summer's end they were stuffed.

Sam loved to savor those days:

Fond are my thoughts of the meals in the old dining room in the basement of Sanderson Hall, now gone. We hoped for meat three times a

week and thanked God for biscuits, molasses, beans, and plenty of raw,
golden, Guernsey milk. [85]

"We ate food that kids today probably don't like, but it was good for us!" said
Billy Bishop (FCA '55). "It was straight out of the garden. Some kids might have
been better off than they were at home. I know I was."

Cotton McCaa didn't know how tight money was in those first years, and he
doesn't think his classmates did either. "Mr. Pat didn't let anyone know that. Yet,
we didn't feel poor, and we were never afraid of going hungry. We had plenty of
green beans, biscuits, and potatoes. None of us ate big helpings, but I never left
that chow hall hungry."

Bill Rogers agrees. "When I came to French Camp, the school was reportedly
in bad shape, but I never saw that. I can remember times we didn't have a lot, and
we ate biscuits and syrup. However, I felt loved and cared for while I worked and
learned; in addition, I had found adults I could trust."

Sam kept the harsh realities of life from the students, but Kenny Henderson
caught a glimpse one day. "I was with Mr. Pat when he was getting his shoes
shined. He took his shoe off, and his toe was sticking out of a hole in his sock. I
knew then that he didn't have any money for himself, either."

According to Ewing Carruthers, those running the work program had a
formidable job. "A staff member told me that getting students to do the work
was often harder than the work they did. Yet, they had a job to do, regardless of
how well they did it or how well they liked doing it."

Actually, most of the children didn't mind the work, often making a game of
it. It became a way of life, something not to be questioned. Besides, Sam found
so many ways to make it fun, often showing up to take pictures of the children
working. He also suggested that each year the boys who worked the cows name
a baby calf after one of the girls. Every female on campus vied for that honor!

One summer Sam issued this challenge: "I don't believe y'all can get 1,000
bales of hay." To prove him wrong, Billy Thompson and his student workers cut
people's hay all over the county and put a thousand bales in the barn.

Sam gained the love and respect of everyone because he never asked anyone
to do a job he wouldn't do. "Mr. Pat worked as hard as everyone else," noted
Coach. "One year we had a very cold spell. The temperature dropped to six
degrees with ten inches of snow. We sent all the kids somewhere, except some
of the boys who stayed with Mr. Pat and me. We patched broken water pipes and
fixed many other problems that can occur in cold weather."

That first Christmas, friends of FCA took the children into their homes to
give Sam and his miniscule staff a small break. The morning after they left,
dairy foreman Arlie McGlothin asked Sam, "Who's gonna milk these cows?"
Sam looked at him, thinking hard. "I guess it'll be you and me." The two milked
morning and evening through the entire Christmas break.

"The amazing part," admitted Sam later, "is that I had never milked a cow. I still remember how paralyzed my pinky finger was after that ordeal!"[86]

SPREAD THE WORD ABOUT FCA!

As the main ambassador for FCA, Sam wanted to make sure people understood the school's new mission; therefore, he came up with a new definition of the ministry:

> *FCA is not a school for delinquents, but a school/home for boys and girls who are faced with the loss of a normal home by parental death, divorce, or some other factor. The pupils are youngsters who are normal in every respect, worthy and financially limited, but are willing to work and to make a way for themselves. Our mission is to be Christ's hands in reaching and caring for these youngsters. Christian training, wholesome country life, sound schooling, and work are the diet of life here and are basic in the formula for building character and citizenship. Prayer, work, and a trust in God provide our basis for operation. God daily meets our needs.[87]*

Sam had already realized that people needed to see what French Camp was doing, not just hear about it from him. Taking the Jones boys with him had helped tremendously. Margaret Kimball declares that Sam never stopped thinking of ingenious ways to get the children in front of people and to challenge them to support FCA. "His head was like a manufacturing plant; he'd think of one thing, and before he got that going, he'd think of something else."

Sam loved music, and as the music program grew, he found a way to incorporate choirs and singing groups into his revivals. Some students even gave testimonies. Weecy Patterson sang in the girls' trio and her younger brother in the choir. "After we sang, Mr. Pat always wanted us to tell where we were from and something about ourselves. Yet, our mother and stepfather drifted, and every time we received a letter they were in a different town. As my brother's turn came one night, I heard his clear little voice pipe up in the stillness. 'Weecy, where do we live this week?'"

"I will always carry wonderful memories of Mr. Pat—such a kind, caring, godly man!" remembers Evie Clements Salter (FCA '55). "He drove the choir bus on many of our trips across the state and entertained us with his numerous tales. There was nothing he wouldn't do for us kids as our spiritual mentor and leader."

Students and staff back at the school always prayed for those sharing FCA's story. "During my years at FCA, we experienced some very difficult financial times," revealed Mike "Bird" Quayle ('FCA '64). "Mr. Pat always asked us to pray for the school's provisions. Whenever he prepared for a trip to a church or civic group, he'd ask us to pray for him and his message."

Jim Barnes (RTS '77) came to Christ after hearing a group of children from French Camp give testimonies at his church in Clarksdale, Mississippi. "One of the girls made an indelible impression on me when she shared the difference that Christ had made in her life. That very night I went home and accepted Jesus in my bedroom around 11:00 p.m." Later, Jim became a student at Reformed Theological Seminary, was received into the Presbyterian Church in America at French Camp Academy, and continued that close relationship with FCA during his pastorate at First Presbyterian Church in Kosciusko.

The music program became an even more valuable tool to communicate FCA's story when Mickey and Martha Parks began teaching in 1960. With Sam's complete support, they began a musical Gospel team with eight students called the Musical Messengers. Mickey had no idea whether the group would work out. "My wife and I were rank amateurs fresh out of seminary. Mr. Pat let the group sing four songs during one of his services. After we did a rousing version of 'Onward Christian Soldiers,' he sat in stunned disbelief and absolute pleasure. He rejoiced in anything uplifting for the FCA kids and honorable to the Lord. Over the years, he continued to encourage us in our efforts with such a kind spirit!"

Sam's prolific correspondence was another powerful vehicle to spread the word about FCA and keep the vision alive in people's hearts and minds. He never failed to share updates on the school's progress, news about the children, and a heartfelt invitation to visit, as exhibited in this letter to Bill Byrd in 1967:

> *I hope you will have the opportunity to visit French Camp. At least, I hope you'll be able to come for a day of good shooting during quail season…. This little school lives from day to day on just what God gives. It costs $650 a day to operate. Most of this has to come in the form of gifts. Every day the gift tally must show approximately $500, or we have gone in the hole that day. We live by prayer and hard work, and somehow God keeps enough coming to keep the school going and growing ….*[88]

As in Martinsville, Sam understood the vast power of radio, both to spread FCA's ministry and to share the Gospel. Upon his arrival at French Camp, he immediately began producing daily fifteen-minute broadcasts at seven a.m. on a Kosciusko radio station. People all over Central Mississippi began their day with "The Morning Message," a program of God's Word and music. Ann Angle first played the organ and Billy Thompson sang "Teach Me To Pray." Later, Mickey and Martha Parks added their signature "In Times Like These" as the show's theme song. Sam ended each message with the phrase thousands recognize even today: "I wish for you God's best; and, friends, God's best is Jesus Christ."

One of Sam's cleverest ideas to spread the word about FCA was the organized pheasant hunts in the early 1950s. Lewis Graeber, Jr. thought those hunts probably did more to spread the word about FCA's ministry than anything else the school ever did. Begun in December 1951, and continuing for many years, they attracted wealthy businessmen from far and near; even well known sports writer Walter Stewart of the *Memphis Commercial Appeal* participated and filed a glowing report. At $100 a person for a day's hunting, Stewart considered FCA's hunts a bargain. Hunting pheasant usually required an expensive trip (at least $500 total) to the Dakotas to bring back the same number of birds FCA promised.

The hunts were also the perfect vehicle to highlight the work of FCA. A group of students helped with each one, assisting the hunters, cooking, and working around the campsite. Their industrious spirit, ready smiles, and helpful attitudes conveyed it all—French Camp was making a positive difference in their lives.

"All we had to do was leave those kids with the hunters," says Ewing Carruthers. "They sold French Camp. The children were having so much fun they didn't know they were selling anybody anything. What impressed these businessmen most was that the kids helped do all the work; they had a ball going to get the fellows soft drinks! The guests could see in action the FCA work program; they learned that every one of those kids had a job back at French Camp and had to work five days a week. After the hunt, the deal was sealed when the children presented each man with a loaf of homemade FCA bread."

Sam gave credit to prominent planter William Yandell of Vance, Mississippi, for the idea of the pheasant hunts. Yandell was instrumental in sending a young boy to FCA, and one day out of curiosity he came to view the facility. From then on, he was hooked on the school. Some time went by, and Yandell called Sam, saying, "Y'all need to raise money for those kids. Let's put on a pheasant hunt." Yandell agreed to buy 300 chicks if French Camp would raise them. With help from local bird hunters, the pheasant hunt plans got underway.[89]

"I loved working with Mr. Pat on those hunts," reported the late Johnnie Pee. "I never saw him mad at anyone. He came to me first with the idea and asked me what I thought. Of course, I liked it because I love to hunt!"

The first hunts were at French Camp, but then supporters wanted longer hunts near Memphis. A landowner in Hernando, Mississippi, let the school use his land. The pheasants were raised at French Camp and transported to Hernando. In his element in the outdoors, Sam played host in an old house on the property, and students worked around the camp and on the hunt.

Sam roped Ewing Carruthers into the project very early. "After we graduated from Southwestern, the war came, and we all went our separate ways. Next thing I know, Sam called and told me about FCA's financial struggles and the possibility of raising money with pheasant hunts. My job was to try to get as many people as possible down to the hunts either at French Camp or at Hernando.

"However, I couldn't get enough wealthy people to do anything; so, we asked Bobby Lloyd, Chief Trust Officer at Union Planters Bank, to help us. He was the head of affairs for several wealthy men, from whom I hadn't been able to get a nickel to save a dying man. His passion was quail hunting and raising hunting dogs. Wealthy people paid him to put together hunting trips for them. He'd call up all his buddies, and say, 'Give me $100, and I'll do something different for you.' Then other passionate hunters called their friends who had means, too. That's when the hunts took off."

Sam always laughed when he thought about those hunts. The problem? They had guaranteed each person four birds for the $100 fee, but the birds tended to want to fly off before the hunters got there. Add to that the possible poor marksmanship of some of the hunters, and the dilemma increased. Not to be discouraged, Sam put his head together with French Camp natives Drew and Barney Thomas, Virgil Parkerson, Nathan Mitchell, and others to figure out how to make the birds stay put. Sam later acknowledged:

> It was a comedy of errors like you've never seen. I've hunted birds all my life, but I didn't know the first thing about pheasants because they're not native to this part of the country. The first method we tried was digging a hole, inserting a pheasant, and covering it with hardware cloth and grass. We attached a string to the hardware cloth and ran it out fifty to a hundred feet. We put a student behind a tree to pull the string and loose the bird when the hunters came along. It worked, but it took a lot of time.
>
> Our next scheme involved equilibrium. We discovered that if you spun the bird around, got him dizzy, tucked his head under his wing and put him under a bush that he'd cooperate for about thirty minutes. That plan worked better because after his thirty hung-over minutes, the poor fowl couldn't fly well enough to dodge a company of hunters.
>
> The interesting thing is that no one really caught on to that while we were doing it. We'd have to tell the hunters each time, and they were surprised. It was the most synthetic kind of hunting you can imagine.[90]

Students helped in every aspect of the hunt. Girls cooked, cleaned, and served coffee, while the boys tended camp and helped with the hunt. The pheasant hunts remain indelibly etched in Weecy Patterson's memory. "It was such fun. I was able to participate in two of them. Viola, the school cook, stayed with a local family and got up at three or four in the morning to cook breakfast on a huge gas oven. What a wonderful southern breakfast it was—eggs, bacon or sausage, biscuits! Three girls usually went on the hunt and stayed in a boarding house in town. Somebody picked us up about 4:30 a.m. to help her. After breakfast, two or three groups went in different directions. Halfway through the hunt, we served the hunters coffee. After hunting, everyone came back to the house for a round of grits, pork chops, applesauce, biscuits, butterbeans, and peaches. All but the grits and biscuits were raised at French Camp."

Johnnie Pee laughed. "I almost got killed several times on those pheasant hunts. People brought their sons along, wanting them to kill a bird. As the birds flew up, those kids followed them, swinging those guns around, and more than once, I found myself looking down a gun barrel. I hit the ground several times to keep from getting shot." Ironically, Pee did later die of a tragic gunshot wound in his own yard when he apparently fell in a hole, and the gun in his hands went off.

Billy Bishop also wonders why no one died during the hunts. "A woman with a 410 shotgun wheeled around trying to shoot a bird that had flown up. She succeeded in shooting holes in Coach Thompson's big cowboy hat. He relieved her of the gun, saying, 'Ma'am, I'll return this to you when we get back to camp!'"

The hunts were so successful that Sam made numerous contacts and gained the trust of quite a few wealthy executives. He reported to the 1952 Mississippi Synod that the hunts had netted the school $5,600 for farm improvement and made the school many, many friends.[91] The pheasant hunts were gradually phased out and replaced by annual quail shoots, which were also quite popular for a number of years.[92]

LET'S GET TOGETHER!

Sam brought the same vibrant community spirit to French Camp that had so endeared him to the people of Leland. Moreover, Sam understood that synod wanted the public to have a part in the planning and direction of the school, not only in the area of education, but also in economic, recreational, and spiritual interests.

"Daddy meshed the community and the Academy better than anyone before him," points out Becky Rogers, "because he interacted with people in the community. He was the common man's man; he hunted with folks, regularly had coffee with them downtown, and generally enjoyed being with them."

Indeed, all people were on level ground with Sam. Rich or poor, black or white, great or small, he was the same with everyone. "I'm just a sinner saved by grace," he'd say.

"He loved talking with farmers," disclosed the late Joe Mecklin. "If he was in conversation with wealthy executives who had a lot of money, and someone came up in work clothes, he'd acknowledge that person and make him feel important. A lot of farmers appreciated that recognition, and it opened many avenues of conversation."

High on Sam's priority list was improving education for the entire community. In the 1950s, school administrators in counties adjoining FCA did not want their children going to the Academy grammar school because it decreased attendance levels at county schools and subsequently lowered state government support. However, the line separating Montgomery and Attala counties was within three miles of FCA, making the Academy much closer for most people than the county schools. Also, parents were attracted to FCA's strong spiritual emphasis, solid music emphasis, and excellent sports program. Sam fought before a legislative committee for their right to go to FCA, and the legislation eventually passed.

In addition to education, Sam realized that healthy churches were essential. However, rural churches have a hard time keeping pastors, and French Camp was no exception. Over the years, Sam went to great lengths to keep the pulpit at French Camp Presbyterian Church filled and as early as 1951 began trying to help the church secure a pastor. The people of French Camp considered him the church's pastor and in 1952 wanted to call him formally, but the FCA board would allow him to be only supply pastor because of his extensive duties as FCA president. He gladly served as the church's supply, in addition to raising funds for FCA, preaching revivals, and eventually becoming a leader in church government. He served as treasurer of Central Mississippi Presbytery from 1948-1950, when he was elected presbytery moderator. In 1955 he was elected moderator of the Synod of Mississippi.

Understandably, in 1957 he asked to be relieved of the church duties because of his heavy schedule. The congregation reluctantly accepted his resignation and began looking for another pastor. Yet, by 1958, records show that the pulpit committee turned in their resignations because they could not find anyone who met with Sam's and the congregation's approval. After the session "...turned it all back into [Sam's] hands to settle," he finally agreed to remain the supply pastor. When he had to be absent, the church secured someone to fill the pulpit.[93]

He further endeared himself to the community, especially the rural folk, when he dedicated himself to reopening the Huntsville Presbyterian Church about six miles from French Camp. For lack of a preacher, the little church had long since abandoned services. Sam began preaching there, along with supplying French Camp Presbyterian Church. He got to know all the farmers in the area and spent many a Sunday meal sipping sweet tea with them.

As in Leland, Sam basically pastored the entire town. Locals note that he married, baptized, or buried ninety percent of the people in French Camp. Says Ruby Stevens, "He was out to save souls; it didn't matter if you were Presbyterian, Baptist, or whatever." Wade McGlothin (FCA '51) adds, "Mr. Pat wanted to be a peacemaker and keep unity among the community and the churches."

Mickey and Martha Parks could not agree more. "We watched a man live what he believed and love those around him. Though he was firm in his convictions, grace dominated his preaching. His non-polemic mentality in dealing with others of different doctrinal positions shaped our ability to let God move those of a different persuasion. In our years of pastoral ministry, that has served us well and kept as friends many who would otherwise probably be our foes, even in the faith."

Sam did have an amazing ability to stand up for his beliefs in a winsome, non-threatening way with all people, as evidenced by this entertaining story from Andy Jones. "When Sam came to French Camp, people wanted to introduce him to the community and invited him to go fox hunting. Basically, that meant sitting around a bonfire telling stories and listening to the dogs run. When a dog got hot on the trail of the fox, one of the hunters would say, "Listen at that sonofa____ talk to him!" He repeated this several times, and, finally, Sam observed, 'You know, I believe all of your dogs have the same name!'"

One of the community events Sam really got behind was Harvest Festival, a cross between a Thanksgiving dinner, a church bazaar, and a homecoming. In the early 1950s, FCA and the community had cause to give thanks since the school was getting back on its feet after a financial crisis. Enrollment was up, crops were good, and FCA had a new leader. Originally conceived by Superintendent of Schools Aubrey Gatlin, the first Harvest Festival was in October 28, 1952, put on by goodhearted neighbors and Academy staff calling themselves the French Camp Men and Women's Club.[94] Everything imaginable—goats, mules, pickles, baked goods—was auctioned off, with proceeds benefiting area churches and FCA.

However, the event soared to new heights when Sam formed the Community Club, which took over the administration of the Festival. More activities were added, such as the yearly auction of gorgeous homemade quilts by FCA staff, including French Camp's famous Scripture Quilt. People of note, including state and national leaders J. P. Coleman, Carroll Gartin, and John Stennis, stopped by to speak to the crowd. Of course, the sixty-yard picnic table, begun in 1953, continued to be laden with delicious food, inviting folk from all around to fellowship and eat. In fact, in later years, several sixty-yard tables had to be added![95] The event continues today on the second Saturday in October.

"Mr. Pat liked the idea because he never simply promoted the school and forgot about the community," explains Lynn Downing (FCA '60), who grew up in French Camp. "The Harvest Festival was designed not only to promote the school financially, but also to benefit churches in the area. People could designate proceeds to go to their church, French Camp Academy, or to another organization."

However, by far the greatest get-togethers were the annual Summer Chautauquas, begun by Sam in 1953. Sam felt the need for a concentrated time of Bible study, preaching, singing, and spiritual uplifting for the school and community. Usually held the third week in July, it was a seven-day saturation of Bible study and evangelistic preaching that drew people from far and near.[96] The first Chautauquas were in a large tent; later, they were held in McGhee Tabernacle. The old timers say it was an experience like no other, complete with sawdust on the floor, benches, a pump organ, and well-worn paperback songbooks. Sam brought in well known preachers and missionaries from everywhere, and the place was packed for a full week. Ruby Stevens is grateful to this day that Sam made sure anyone who wanted to come could do so. "Every day he sent a bus into the surrounding towns to pick us all up because back then many country people didn't have cars."

Years later, FCA Principal Sam Allen could recite the week's schedule in a heartbeat. "We had a meeting before breakfast called 'Morning Watch'; then we went to breakfast. About eleven, we came back for another Bible study. Everybody then went to dinner, and afterwards work and recreation. About 5:30, we'd go to the tabernacle again for missions service. Supper was next, then back for the evening meeting, which lasted a little over an hour."

Some of the most colorful, engaging speakers and musicians in the nation found their way to center stage at Chautauqua. One year the preacher might be the famous evangelist Jimmie Johnson, Billy Graham's roommate at Wheaton and Sam's longtime friend from Martinsville days. Or Red Harper, the well-known cowboy, might ride a chair across the stage. Clyde Taylor might lead songs, and the famous Merrill Dunlop was always at piano and organ.

Jimmie Johnson later revealed, "My family and I would rather come to French Camp Academy than any other place I preach. This school is one of the most unique in the country, and the work done by Sam Patterson and his staff is most outstanding." [97]

"We all looked forward to Merrill Dunlop's 'The Storm,'" said Becky Rogers, "because it seemed to be a believable storm, with thunder crashing and lightning flashing. The tent poles seemed to sway and the tent flaps snap with the rising crescendos of the music."

"Sometimes young children went down more than once to make a profession of faith," remembers Peggy Cockrell. "Once some of the faculty and staff told Sam he should put a stop to that. Sam quickly countered, 'No! You let them come because something is causing them to come. They may not have been quite sure the night before, and now they are.'" Former FCA camper Trish Minter is glad Mr. Pat held his ground, for her brother was saved at one of those Chautauquas.

BRINGING KIDS TO CHRIST

Chautauqua was by no means the only time Sam sought to bring God's message of salvation to the children at FCA. It was his top priority year-round. He once stated that FCA kids had to go to church more than anyone else in America. That might have been true, since they were in those pews six days a week listening to Sam preach. In 1985, Sam wrote:

For some one hundred years, FCA has provided the Gospel of Christ for the spirits and character of our students. We kept this Good News emphasis as bright, constant, and attractive as we could. We still do. The benefits were temporal as well as eternal. One staff member who was formerly in the public schools said to me, 'When I first came to FCA, I thought you folks overdid the religious emphasis. But I have noticed that we have fewer disciplinary problems than other schools, and I have concluded it's due to the emphasis on the Gospel here.'[98]

At times, Sam thought FCA might have overdone it, but Kenny Henderson disagrees. "Listening to Mr. Pat preach is one of my best memories from my years here. He never preached over anyone's head. His 'congregation' was very young—grammar school to high school—but everybody could understand his messages. Now I measure all preachers against Mr. Pat, and they all come up short."

From the very beginning, Sam geared all staff and programs to leading the children to Christ. Every student took a Bible course and went to daily chapel services; Sam also saw to it that every aspect of the school incorporated the basics of the Christian life. He was able to report to the 1951 Synod of Mississippi that 115 children had professed faith in Christ,[99] and by the 1952 Synod, the number had risen to 350, including district students and adults in the community.[100] By 1954, Sam was pleased to report to synod that a "number of our most promising students are seriously considering fulltime service in the ministry or mission field."[101] And by 1961, Sam could say joyfully, "I believe that there has been more spiritual growth in the lives of some of the Christian young people than I have ever seen in any one year since I have been here." In 1962, two FCA graduates were in seminary and one in college under care of presbytery, preparing for seminary.[102]

Says Dottie Trunzler, "One of the sweetest testimonies I ever heard about Sam was from a student who told my husband, 'No one can come to French Camp without becoming a Christian!'"

Often, the Gospel took hold in a student's heart simply by his or her exposure to the quiet intensity of Sam's faith. "When I first set foot on the campus in September 1961," notes Mike Quayle, "I met Mr. Pat and was in awe of him. I knew from that moment on that he was a man of God, and that he had a deep sense of my need to know the Lord as my Savior. He was a loving, God-fearing man who challenged us to put God first.

"I was always uncomfortable when I was with Mr. Pat because I knew he was in touch with God, and I wasn't. His life was such a powerful witness for Christ that I was struck by the presence of God. He was the first man I had ever been around who actually understood how lost I was and my internal struggle to come to grips with my personal need for Christ.

"Two weeks after graduation from FCA in 1964, I accepted Christ. The next day I called Mr. Pat and told him of my conversion. He urged me to keep Christ first, second, and last in my life and always seek to follow him in whatever I do. His words helped shape my life, and they continue to influence me today."

"I don't know anyone who more lived the scripture 'For me to live is Christ and to die is gain' than Sam Patterson," remarked Erin Lail. "One didn't have to be with him ten minutes (and he didn't have to say a word) for one to realize that he was filled with the Spirit of God. He was so close to God that I always felt he had one foot on earth and another in heaven. He must have influenced more lives than ten ordinary, dedicated Christians."

Sam certainly changed the direction of Wade McGlothin's life. "Being around Mr. Pat made me want to pattern my life after him and be more of a peacemaker than a trouble-maker! He stood up for his beliefs, but always in a peaceful way. I was past fifty years old when I was saved, and Mr. Pat wanted to help me. One day as we talked about the scriptures, he asked me if I had a commentary. When I said no, he gave me one by Wycliffe that I still use."

Much of the time God simply worked in children's hearts to bring them to Christ, but sometimes He let Sam take part, as in the amazing conversion of Ben Hollis. By 1952, Ben had listened to Sam preach about six times a week for two years; his physical ears had heard the Gospel over and over, but it had never penetrated.

One Sunday night after the service, Sam came out of the second floor auditorium to find Ben standing at the head of the stairs. Sam was shocked to see him; Ben had gone home that weekend, but he never got back in time to go to church if he could help it. Now Sam could see something was really troubling the child. With tears in his eyes and a distraught look on his face, Ben whispered, "Mr. Pat, I gotta talk to you right now." Sam led the boy into a classroom, where he began to blubber like a three-year-old. Sam had never seen the boy cry, even when he was hurt on the football field. Ben explained, "Mr. Pat, if I had slipped and fallen down those stairs and broken my neck, I wouldn't have stopped until I went straight to hell."

Sam was stunned. He had never heard Ben say "hell" without cursing. "You just don't know what I've done," he continued. Sam could tell the boy was under great conviction and that God was working in his heart. For the first time, Sam knew he had Ben's ear. He never asked and Ben never confessed what was bothering him that night. Sam simply told the boy, "I can't really do anything for you. I am just a poor sinner, too. Even if I could crawl down inside you, the two of us together couldn't straighten out what's wrong. Yet, I know another Person who can get down inside of you and begin to straighten it out. He'll do that tonight if you want him to."

Ben listened for about ten minutes while Sam shared what Jesus had done for him on the cross and how the Lord could come into Ben's heart and deal with his life. Ben indicated he wanted that, and he knelt down and prayed for the first time, saying, "Lord, I have made a mess of my life. I am asking you now to come in and straighten me up."

Sam was scared to tell anyone of Ben's conversion because he didn't know if it was genuine. Yet, Jesus did come into Ben's heart that night. The next Wednesday, he rose in chapel and confessed, "Everybody knows that I've been cheating my way through this school. I admit that and tell you now that those days are gone forever."

The evidence was there and continued to be there that Somebody had come down into Ben's life and given him the power to be different.[103]

AN UNCOMMON COMPASSION

Nobody gets too much heaven no more,
It's much harder to come by,
I'm waiting in line.
Nobody gets too much love any more,
It's as high as a mountain
And harder to climb.[104]

Sam probably never heard the Bee Gees sing those lyrics, but he knew without a doubt that they were engraved on the heart of virtually every child at French Camp. God gave him a deep connection with such desolation in the very young and an overflowing, never-ending wellspring of compassion for them. He knew that most of them had been kicked around since they were born, and life had been nothing but a vale of tears.

His mission was ever before him. On the wall in his office during those early years was a large painting on an old calendar. A young boy was at bat waiting for the pitch, tongue sticking out of the corner of his mouth, eyes gleaming as he prepares to smack the ball out of the park. Someone once asked Sam why he didn't throw that calendar out. He answered, "The kids here at French Camp came into this world wanting to hit a homerun. Some of them have a strike or two against them. That calendar reminds me that I am here by God's calling to help them hit a homerun and not strike out."

Knowing that a solid relationship with Christ was the only way to "hit a homerun," he vowed not only to preach Christ to FCA kids, but also to show Christ to them in every way.

Such missionary vision made a lasting impression on Ken and Lyn Utley, long-time house parents at the school. "We think of Mr. Pat every time we leave the tabernacle at FCA because we recall the words, 'Sir, we would see Jesus,' inscribed on the pulpit. That was the single vision of Mr. Pat's life, to know Christ and to make Him known to others."

Sam modeled Jesus for the kids—what it's like to trust Him and what it's like to trust an adult. Most FCA students had learned at a very young age that the world was indeed a dangerous place, and adults, especially parents, couldn't be trusted. "Many FCA students had to be convinced that they deserved love and that the motives of house parents and staff members were honorable," explains Shirley Rutland (FCA '64). "Nobody could inspire those beliefs in young people better than Mr. Pat."

Sam was probably the first adult most students had ever trusted, and he knew he had to be sincere. In his own personal life he worked ceaselessly to "put on" Christ, and when he was with others, he worked just as hard at erasing himself so others could see the character of Christ more clearly. He knew children were insightful:

> *Boys and girls intuitively, uncannily spot fakery, see inconsistency, sense insincerity, and recognize unfairness. You can't fool them. They will 'learn' you before you learn them.*[105]

"More than anything else in his life, Sam wanted to know and be like Jesus," comments longtime friend Charleton Hutton. "In 2 Corinthians 3:2-3, Paul says we are to be living epistles, billboards for Christ. Sam wanted to be a living signpost pointing to the Lord, always directing people to Christ. In word and deed, he always contrived to get himself out of the way so that people would not focus on him, but on Christ."

The unconditional tenderness and love of Christ radiated from Sam. What a joy it must have been for emotionally battered children to encounter such a person! Now adults, FCA students frequently cry at the mention of Sam's name or the very thought of him. Remembering one who loved and accepted so unconditionally does bring tears.

"I was a bad kid!" confessed Billy Bishop, crying quietly. "When I came to French Camp at sixteen, I had been expelled from my high school several months before. I grew up in a very legalistic environment, more do's and don'ts than the love of Jesus. I had totally rebelled and quit going to church at thirteen. Mr. Pat loved me—no, he loved everybody. Both he and Coach Thompson acted as the father I never had."

Most of us have not awakened to find someone kneeling over us, begging God to save our lives, but Ladell Flint did. "On a bright Monday morning in 1951, I wrecked the school truck and was lying in a ditch. When I regained consciousness, Mr. Pat was there beside me. With tears streaming down his upturned face and hands lifted above, he was praying, 'Father, please don't take him; he's so young. If one must go, then take me.' For two days and nights, he never left my bedside except to eat. Most of that time he spent in prayer."[106]

Such love inspires undying loyalty. "Anything that you write about him is going to be good," vows Pete Thrailkill. "You won't be able to write anything bad. If you do, it's going to be wrong!"

Sam knew how to begin where students were and encourage them to come around. He told them when they came to FCA they had a clean slate and could make what they wanted out of their French Camp experience. They never shared their backgrounds with each other, but they knew they could always talk with Coach or Mr. Pat.

One student's parents had given him an embarrassing name when he was born. Children had taunted him all his life. Sam picked him up at his home to bring him to French Camp and on the way tried to get the boy to talk to him. The youngster refused until they neared French Camp. He then told Sam what they called him in his hometown and begged Sam not to tell anyone his name. Sam told him that his name would be David at FCA. No one ever knew any different.

Coach Thompson kept secrets, too. "We had a little boy whose father regularly came home drunk and beat his mother. One day the boy shot him. We took the child on the condition that he'd never talk about it with the other children. Nobody ever knew he had shot his father except Mr. Pat and me. He pulled through fine, graduated from high school, and got a good job."

While some students wanted to come to French Camp, others definitely didn't. Their lives were going nowhere, and they knew they needed help, but they had given up on the world. However, they were no match for Mr. Pat's love. Coach remembers, "One new boy declared, 'I know nobody loves me, and I don't love nobody. I'm going to take care of myself.' Yet, after a couple of days he changed his tune, and Mr. Pat became a daddy to him."

Adeline Webb Ferguson (FCA '68) has a similar story. "I went to FCA in 1965, a very unhappy and resentful young woman. I was willing to use any means to get away from there and never return, even to the point of marrying a man more than twice my age. The letter of arrangements came in the mail. I told no one, but Mr. Pat knew. He called me to his office that Saturday afternoon and talked to me just like he would to one of his own. When the session was over, I knew that Mr. Pat had talked me out of running away and becoming a fifteen-year-old bride. I have never discovered how he knew of my plans. I'm just so thankful that he did."

With that perennial wide smile and twinkle in his eye, Sam always showed Christ's love selflessly to all people. Prince or pauper, adult or child, Sam treated everyone alike, giving each the same compassionate, unhurried attention and interest. Time meant nothing if someone needed him. Everyone loved to see this stocky, redheaded, good-natured man coming and wanted him to stay as long as he could.

Sam's glowing smile warmed Patsy Parkerson Burchfield (FCA '68) at FCA. "He was the happiest man at all times. As I grew older, I knew that his happiness came from his sincere and committed relationship with Jesus. He was truly a man of God who loved every day he spent living for Jesus."

A litany of praise comes from adults, too:

Irene Taylor—"He was always so jolly and had such a sweet smile on his face ALL the time. He showed by his fruit that he was a Christian."

Helen Branning—"I don't think you could find anyone, anywhere who could say anything against Sam Patterson."

Peggy Cockrell—"I've never heard of one person who didn't like him. Never."

Hugh Long—"Most people have some flaws or faults, but there wasn't anything offensive about Mr. Pat."

In a recent children's movie, a cartoon character walks through a barren field, and everywhere he steps a beautiful bouquet of flowers springs up. As he moves off into the distance, he leaves a trail of flowers in his path. Sam was like that; wherever he went, vibrant spiritual growth occurred. If a person did not know the Lord, there's a good chance he did after talking with Sam. If someone knew Jesus, his faith was likely strengthened. The grocery checker might simply count it a good day, basking in the memory of Sam's smile; another person might be left with the feeling that she was loved deeply. In Sam's wake at FCA, joyful children sprang up, ready to accept God's love, Christ's salvation, and personal responsibility to live a godly life. As Union classmate Ralph Buchanan noted, "Sam left a trail of blessing wherever he went."

People saw Sam as a great encourager and knew he was on their side, perhaps when no one had ever been before. "I can hardly put into words what Mr. Pat means to me," says Grace Presbyterian Church organist Carolyn Scoggins Rodgers (FCA '58) with deep emotion. "He helped me be who I am today. I owe him so much! He had more confidence in me than I did in myself. When I was twelve, he was convinced I could play for Sunday School at French Camp Presbyterian Church. The first time he asked me, I was mortified, but somehow Mr. Pat inspired people to do what they feared. Soon, I graduated to playing for the church service. Later, I played for him on his radio program and ended up a piano major. All because he believed in me!"

When Scott Boeving (FCA '64) came to FCA at age twelve, he had no confidence. "I had a tough childhood. My mom had been a very successful singer, but she had a nervous breakdown when I was five. I lived with my grandmother until she was too old to care for me. My father was a pilot who had been seriously wounded in World War II; he led a nomadic life, and I didn't even know him until I was twelve. I grew up with a lot of anger because Dad's family was quite wealthy (one of them had an air-conditioned doghouse), but they never helped my mother and my family.

"Mr. Pat meant stability and love to me. Crisis or no, he was always the same. He was ever quick to share hope and encouragement in a way that was not lofty or pious. He was instrumental in my coming to Christ, and he subsequently asked me to travel with him one summer to share my testimony. I felt I was in the presence of the Lord through what God was doing with Mr. Pat."

Sam wanted the very best for people and tried with all his might to see that it happened. He was sincerely interested in the lives of those around him, especially the students. No problem was too small to command his attention.

"His door was always open," recollected Sam Allen, "no matter how busy he was. No administrative quandary overshadowed someone with a problem. Kids came in and talked with him one on one; that's all some of them needed to be right as rain."

With tear-filled eyes, Billy Bishop says, "He touched my heart because he was always interested in me and cared whether I was getting my life straight and living right. He'd call me into his office at times to talk and share. When he found out I didn't have a Bible, he gave me his personal Scofield Bible with all his notes in it. He represented to me what Christianity ought to be. Recalling his love still makes me cry. Most of my friends at home ended up with really destructive lifestyles. By the grace of God and with Mr. Pat's love, I didn't; eventually I went into the Marines and later did mission work in Mobile."

"When I first came to FCA, we didn't have a lot of activities," recalls Kenny Henderson. "However, we did have sports, and we could count on Mr. Pat to make all the ballgames. That meant so much to us, because so many of us had not had a chance to win at anything in our lives. But we could win at sports!"

Trish Minter attended camp at FCA the summer her dad was in the hospital in the late '50s. Every week, Sam and an FCA board member went to visit her father to let her know how he was doing. "His concern made me feel so loved and important, even that I belonged to him!"

Whenever Sam saw a student with talent or interest in an area, he immediately set about to develop it. Absolutely nothing escaped his vigilant eye. Over the years, he paid not only for piano and voice lessons, but also for other extracurricular activities for numerous students and staff. Yet, Sam made a very modest salary at French Camp and would never accept raises. Therefore, it's a mystery how he managed to pay for all those extra opportunities.

Sometimes, however, the opportunity to bless cost Sam nothing. Joe Bowen (FCA '54) knew Sam cared for him, but he never realized how much until one summer day. Joe and others had just cut Sam's grass, and Joe had ventured into Sam's basement to explore. Suddenly, Sam appeared and wanted to know what Joe was doing in his basement. Thinking he was in huge trouble, Joe stammered politely, "I was looking at the short-wave radios you brought back from World War II, sir."

To Joe's utter amazement, Sam suggested, "Joe, if you're interested in short-wave radio, pick out two or three and take them with you to keep."

The gift delighted Joe beyond imagination. "If someone gave me a Rolls-Royce tomorrow, the thrill would not be any greater. Naturally, I rigged up the radios and began picking up stations five or six hundred miles away. I will never forget Mr. Pat's kindness to me."

Sam learned how far some kids will go to get any sort of attention when a little boy came to FCA from a difficult situation. About fourteen years old, he was one of those children who gets lost in a crowd—nothing outstanding about his appearance or personality. He wasn't very bad, nor was he exceptionally good at anything. For quite a long while, he drifted along at French Camp without anyone paying him any special attention.

Yet, one day the staff discovered that he was stealing. Quite a bit of pilfering had been going on in the boys' dorm, and after a room search they found almost all the items in the top drawer of his dresser. He'd made no attempt to hide them. They punished him, but before long, items were again disappearing. Three different times the dorm parent went straight to the little boy's dresser and found all the items in the top drawer in plain sight.

Sam and the dorm parent finally realized that the boy wanted to be caught. The only special attention he'd gotten since he'd been at FCA was when they had punished him for the theft. He'd rather have disciplinary attention than no attention at all. From that moment on, Sam and the dorm parent regularly let the boy accompany them on errands. Almost immediately they saw a distinct improvement.[107]

"Mr. Pat made a world of difference in the lives of so many kids," submits Shirley Rutland. "His dedication to the care and well-being of those of us who were not in control of our circumstances will live forever through us and our families. He was godly, honest, caring, and determined to provide the proper leadership so that good kids could become even better. Hundreds of thousands of youngsters in this world need a Mr. Pat in their lives and a home such as French Camp to be exposed to the power of Christian love and be nurtured for adulthood."

Sam also had a sense of humor with the children and gleefully told the following story on himself. One morning a boy came to see him very excited and upset, wailing, "Mr. Pat, I'm rooming with a girl."

Immediately Sam remembered the boy's roommate and realized that it might be true, though he couldn't believe it. The roommate had come recently, and many of his ways were effeminate. He was also a little withdrawn but had never given any trouble.

"What makes you think he is a girl?" Sam asked the boy.

"Well," offered the youngster, "for several weeks now, he's refused to take off his clothes when I'm in the room. He never takes a bath except at hours when no one else is in the shower. I kidded him about that this morning, and he said, 'There's a good reason I don't do that; I'm a girl.'"

Sam thought, "My land, could it be that we've had a girl living in the boys' dorm dressing like a boy, and we didn't know the difference?" He wondered how to resolve the situation without causing any disturbance. He decided to ask one of the coaches to go with him to the boys' dorm.

Sam told the coach, "We're going to let the school doctor examine this child to determine conclusively whether this is a girl or a boy." When they told the child they were taking him to the doctor, they were a little surprised he didn't raise any objection. Perhaps he knew that his roommate had come to Sam and reported that he was a girl.

When the student entered the examining room, Sam called the doctor over and told him the situation. "The only reason I brought this student here is because I want you to examine him and tell me whether this is a boy or a girl." The doctor was back in his exam room a little longer than Sam thought necessary, but after a while he came out and called Sam into his private office. Looking very serious and troubled, he asked Sam to sit down. Then he laughed heartily. "Well, I just want to tell you that you have a 100 percent boy there!" This young fellow had pulled his roommate's leg, and Sam's leg had been pulled in the pulling![108]

"JUST DO RIGHT"

Once people felt Christ's love and accepted Him as their Savior, Sam modeled how to walk the Christian life. Sam's mantra was simply, "Do right, do right, do right!" as he lived with integrity before both children and adults. He did right to please God, not because he was afraid of the consequences if he didn't (the reason most people stay on the straight and narrow). He could have chosen a more flowery phrase, but "Do Right" fit Sam's plainspoken ways.

"I guess in each child, deep below the surface for some of us, exists an inner sense of knowing right from wrong and good from bad, even when one is as rebellious as I was," reflects Shirley Rutland. "Mr. Pat knew this and worked hard every day in every way to make sure that the good prevailed through the actions of the young people at French Camp. We saw the gentle side of Jesus in him, which made us want to be as good as Mr. Pat wanted us to be."

Florida artist Evie Clements Salter is thankful for Sam's spiritual guidance. "I painted a Florida lighthouse that has become quite popular. When people tell me that my life shines like the light in that lighthouse, I know it comes largely from my impressionable years spent with Mr. Pat."

"He instilled in everyone the interest, desire, and determination to make a major contribution in life," remembers Suzanne Boykin Karam (FCA '62). "He was a great teacher, theologian, and counselor and taught me basic biblical principles to apply to daily responsibilities. He taught me to stay focused on the long-term goal of getting the best education possible while in a spiritual environment, and he tried to protect me from making life decisions based on worldly, transient factors."

Had Lewis Ward not known Sam, he believes he would have been in a lot of trouble. "Mr. Pat was the one who actually turned my life around and put me straight. He was a good man. There won't ever be another one like him around here in my book."

Kenny Henderson feels the same way. "Many of my friends at home ended up in some sort of trouble. "I laugh and say if it wasn't for French Camp, I'd probably be in jail, too! I want to think that I'm smart enough to have stayed out of that sort of trouble, but I don't know. I certainly wouldn't have learned to work and to take responsibility as I did at FCA. It changed my life."

Sam had to send some students home, but even some of them the Lord brought around in time. Robert Goff was one of those children. "Even though I was kicked out, French Camp still made a difference in my life. I was a problem child when I came and even when I left, but the religious training I received at FCA made all the difference in the world. Without Mr. Pat, I would never have had a chance. I failed to follow the Lord when I was at FCA, but I praise Him for giving me a second chance."

Students were not the only ones benefiting from Sam's spiritual leadership. FCA board member Ewing Carruthers counts Sam as one of the greatest influences on his life. After World War II, Sam's old Southwestern classmate came back to Memphis to pick his life back up in the insurance business. Money was tight as folks recovered from the war, and Ewing had no idea how long it would take to make a decent living. As he looked out the window of his tiny, stifling office on the fifth floor of the Sterrick building, he could hear the incessant grinding of the huge trucks as they labored up the hill. How he wished for a big sale to get him out of here, at least to an air-conditioned office with no noise!

Not long after that, a break appeared on the horizon. One day Ewing was preparing to call on a wealthy Memphis widow to try to sell her two very large insurance policies. He was beside himself with excitement; this could really get him going! As he was about to leave, who should open the door to his office but Sam Patterson. When Ewing explained his big opportunity to Sam, he was pleased when his friend exclaimed, "Well, we'd better pray about this!" Ewing thought, "Isn't that nice? Sam's going to pray that I sell this insurance!"

Sam began praying, but it wasn't at all the prayer Ewing expected. "Lord, Ewing's going out to sell this woman a policy. If it's really your will, if she really needs it, and if this will help him have a few more possessions, then let it happen." On and on Sam prayed, putting Ewing and his career in God's hands, not praying for Ewing to be a hotshot salesman. Ewing felt the heat of anger rise in his neck. Even though he felt like a heel for possibly using this woman to get ahead, he wanted to sell that insurance! He felt as he had in college when he argued with Sam—without a leg to stand on.

Ewing cries freely when he recalls Sam's challenge to be a godly man and put God's will for his life above money. "I want you to go out there," commanded Sam, "and if it is the Lord's will, you'll help her. As long as you live, every time you go into an interview, you better remember me!"

And Ewing has. "The woman did buy the insurance, but Sam made me see that I was responsible before God that she did. I don't know if I was a Christian or not, even though I grew up in the church. Yet, Sam made my faith a reality and challenged me. If I had not known him, there would be a tremendous void in my life. Business people are inclined to put more value on physical things, but he showed me how to value spiritual things. Sam's life was a living witness of Christ to me; he understood what was important."

To this day, Ewing keeps on his desk a treasured New Testament with this inscription from Sam, again undoubtedly influenced by C. T. Studd:

> *My favorite book—to a favorite friend!*
> *For your desk and briefcase—but especially for your pleasure.*
> *Setting forth a policy of insurance by a company (three members of the firm named on page 47, v. 19) with adequate resources to provide coverage for:*
> *All Men—John 3:16*
> *All Time and Eternity (eternal "life" coverage)—John 11:25–26*
> *All Events—Romans 8:28 and 37–39*
> *All Needs—Philippians 4:19*
> *This policy is not sold; it is offered—a gift by the "Company" (Romans 6:23, 5:15–16), complete payment having been made by the Second Person in the firm (Matthew 20:28, Hebrews 2:9, 1 Timothy 2:5–6, 1 Peter 2:18–19).*

A CONSTANT MENTOR

Work meant far more to Sam than simply getting a job done. He took every opportunity to use the jobs to mentor and teach others about the Lord and life. He likely learned this method from studying Jesus, whose training program was to allow the disciples to follow Him around, absorbing knowledge without even knowing they were being trained. Effective disciplers know this is the quickest way to success:

> *The world is full of people willing to explain how things should be done. But what people really want is a demonstration. The effective discipler is not the one with the most detailed training syllabus; [he] is the one who lives out his life in Christ in full view of the person(s) he is discipling. As the old saying goes, more is caught than taught.[109]*

From the beginning, Sam stayed in close contact with the students on campus, teaching and modeling, instead of sitting behind his desk. Ben Hollis understood Sam's strategy. "Mr. Pat wouldn't leave a kid alone long enough to feel sorry for himself. He always had some project in progress, and he'd find students to involve them. He stayed right there with us and helped—that made a big difference."

If the right job didn't happen to exist, Sam invented one. He was determined that students contribute and feel important. Bill Rogers is an excellent example.

Sam's heart must have broken for this well-behaved young man who never caused any trouble, but who had already endured so much pain. His mother had had polio and was in a wheelchair. When Bill was about six, his father ran off and left his mother with three children. Bill's grandfather helped his daughter, but when he died no one was left to care for the children. They were placed in foster homes, but by the time Bill was in first grade, his foster parents had become too old to care for him.

"By the grace of God, the welfare department sent me to French Camp. FCA was the only home I had. I couldn't get on the bus at Thanksgiving or Christmas and ride home to any family. I didn't see my mother for a long time, and she never wrote to me. When I found her after I graduated from high school, my father had come back to her. Their style of life was so very different from mine that I couldn't stay. I left and have never seen them again."

When Bill turned seventeen, Sam told him that he didn't like to drive (Sam loved to drive) and asked Bill if he wanted a job chauffeuring him to meetings and speaking engagements. Bill accepted with alacrity, giving Sam the opportunity to mentor and encourage him for three summers. "I really felt important because he thought enough of me to ask me to do that. While I was at FCA, I was the only student to chauffer him."

Sam not only bolstered Bill's fragile self-esteem but also gave him a chance to see how someone lives who is serious about a relationship with Jesus. "He read the Bible nonstop," Bill remarks incredulously. "In the car, we didn't talk much at all. He'd read the Bible for hours as we drove, as if it were a novel. At night, I never recall him staying up past nine o'clock. Then he'd be up at the crack of dawn, going for a long walk and stopping frequently to read his Bible. He said that morning was the only time he and God could have undisturbed conversation, and he was at total peace."

Sam was also a mentor to Ralph Newman. Even when Ralph was an unbeliever, Sam asked him to chauffer him all over the state to meetings. Later, Ralph took Sam's radio message to the Kosciusko station each morning for broadcast. Since Ralph loved to hunt, Sam tapped him to lead some of the pheasant hunts. "Sam was a real friend to Ralph," says wife Margie, "and he knew that Sam loved him even when Ralph was not responding to the Gospel."

Sam always looked for ways to help others get ahead and stand taller, even at his own expense. Such kindness lives today in the memory of Mickey Parks. "Mr. Pat allowed a person the freedom to pursue God-given gifts and abilities even when they overlapped his ministry domain. If one had something to offer the body of Christ or the world, Mr. Pat cheered that person on with all his being, but quietly so. In fact, sometimes we were not even aware of it until later.

"Martha and I were at FCA less than two months when Mr. Pat asked me to preach for him at First Presbyterian Church in Greenwood. He said he had another engagement and would not be able to make the trip. I spoke at the morning service and returned to French Camp with a check for $100, a fortune in those days! To my surprise, I found Mr. Pat at home that day. Only later did we realize that he had allowed us to take the job because he knew we needed help and that the church would give us a sizeable check. We have sought to emulate the big heart of a man who served God by serving people."

Stuart Angle was one of countless people (many of them FCA staff) who named Sam as a spiritual father. "Mr. Pat was like a father to Ann and me, spiritual and otherwise. I appreciated his belief in me when he hired me as a Bible teacher in 1956, since we were just out of college with no experience. I will always remember three things about Mr. Pat: he never forsook a friend, he put people before causes, and he was always with the children of French Camp. I tried to be just like him."

Without Sam's influence, Sam Allen felt he would not have become a commissioned Presbyterian lay preacher. "I also don't think I would have been as dedicated to the Lord as Mr. Pat inspired me to be by living his faith before me. A conversation with him always raised my spirit if it was flagging.

"I learned from Mr. Pat that these children are under much stress, since most of their parents want nothing to do with them. He taught me to have compassion for them. One boy in my dorm was afraid of being ridiculed by the other boys because of a bad burn scar on his back. Consequently, he didn't take a bath and began to stink. I thought of what Mr. Pat would do, and I allowed the boy to take a shower after everyone had gone to bed. Mr. Pat never sat us down and directed, 'Do it like this.' He taught by example and by the way he treated us. He had mercy on the staff because he knew we weren't perfect.

"Yet," Allen continued, "he surely could let you know when he was displeased. Once, I ventured my unsolicited opinion about what we should do in a certain situation involving students, and I saw him turn as red as a beet! He didn't say anything harsh to me or tell me it was none of my business, but I knew I shouldn't have said it! In the future, when things weren't going right, I simply stated, 'Mr. Pat, we've got a problem here. What do you think about…?' I came to understand that he pretty well had it all worked out. He was so close to the Lord that no problem was too big."

Hugh Long always felt anxious that he was taking up Sam's important time. "I knew that many people wanted to talk to him. Yet, he always set my mind at ease about that. What a blessing to work for such an encouraging and forgiving person! He expected top performance, but I knew he loved and cared about me and was not going to drop-kick me out of his life if I fell below his standard at times."

John Cockrell was impressed with the little notes Sam wrote to staff when he was away. "He'd be two or three hundred miles away and in the morning mail would be a note saying, 'Job well done' or 'Just thinking about you tonight.' I was coaching for him back in those days, and he'd write me a note saying 'Great job, Coach!'"

Sam mentored his family as well. "He never interfered in our marriage," remarked son-in-law Jimmy Rogers (FCA '61) gratefully. "He never offered advice that I didn't ask for. He helped us with decisions when we needed it. He had God-given insight into things that most of us didn't have. I miss my father as much as anyone would, but I miss Mr. Pat more."

LOVING DISCIPLINE

Coupled with tender compassion, sincere interest, and a call to integrity was Sam's ability to teach children how to be accountable for their behavior. He knew how to administer loving discipline, always seeking to break the sinful will but not the fragile spirit, already so battered in most of the children.

Said Sam, "As long as a student conducted himself or herself in such a way that it seemed that the school was doing him or her more good than that student was doing other students harm, we would not expel them."[110]

"I am amazed," notes Shirley Rutland, "that he knew so much about giving positive reinforcement to receive a positive response. He taught by example how to be a responsible person."

Some students learned easier than others. "He never had to spank me or talk rough," revealed Bill Rogers. "When he spoke to me, I listened."

Bill Mason (FCA '63) agreed. "He never had to spank me. They primarily removed privileges; paddling was not the major means of discipline."

Sam challenged some students' consciences, including that of Pete Thrailkill. "Mr. Sam taught my Bible class. He'd put the test questions on the board and walk out. The last question was always the same: 'On my trust, I did not cheat.' Now, it's hard to cheat and answer 'yes' to that question!"

Sam's reasoning appealed to Nan Cooper Hagerty (FCA '58). "When they decided that girls could not wear shorts anymore, all of us were upset. Mr. Pat mused, 'You know, most girls don't look as good in shorts as they think they do.' That has stayed with me to this day, and every time I put on a pair of shorts, I think about that statement!"

Nan and others took their medicine when they broke the rules. "Back in the 1950s at French Camp, we were not allowed to sit in cars with anyone. One time a friend whom I had met off campus came to see me right before dinner one night. I was so glad to see him that I ran and jumped in the car with him. We talked only a few minutes, but Mr. Pat was waiting for me when I got out of the car. That was the only time he ever had to punish me for breaking the rules."

Sam was always careful to set boundaries and force students to show respect to authority figures. Trying to be funny once, Steinreed Jones called Sam "Mr. Red." An ominous silence followed, as Sam spoke very slowly. "My name is Mr. Patterson to you. Always remember that, Steinreed."

"And I always have!" relates Steinreed. "I didn't know that I was a twelve-year-old getting out of hand. I knew he was in charge of us, and I respected that. He never once put himself on a pedestal, but he set boundaries."

"At times, however, Mr. Pat knew the only solution to a problem was to appeal to the 'Board of Education,'" said Rich Cannon. "Mr. Carter had a small patch of watermelons on the back side of Lake Ann, and two boys decided to help themselves to some. Mr. Carter caught them and reported it to Sam, who in turn asked me to be a witness in his office. The boys told us that they had survived in Jackson by stealing; therefore, they didn't consider their theft to be a crime. Sam replied, 'I'm here to tell you that stealing is wrong.' He promptly spanked both of them with the Board of Education, and I believe they learned a lesson."

Jimmy Rogers might be the only son-in-law in the country who was paddled by his father-in-law. "In the late 1950s, when I was about sixteen, a young man came to the school from Memphis. He was a tough street kid with an attitude. Since I was a staff student, I guess he assumed that I got special favors. I didn't care for him and thought he needed an attitude adjustment. Since I was once a fairly good scrapper, I went over to the dormitory one night and proceeded to work on his head, as the kids would say.

"Mr. Pat found out about it and called us into the office. He talked to us quite a bit about our error, then said, 'You know what comes next, don't you? I've got to paddle you.' He paddled me first, giving me five of the hardest licks I have ever had in my life. He did the same to the other boy. Finally, he prayed with us! From then on I had tremendous respect for him because I was afraid he'd do it again!"

On another occasion, Sam stepped outside about eleven o'clock one night to get some fresh air and heard children's voices down in the woods across the field beyond the hog pens. His house was on top of a hill, and at French Camp, when the atmosphere is just right, one can hear quite a long distance. Every now and then, he thought he could hear obscene words, so he decided to investigate.

It was a dark night with no moon. He started down to the woods but discovered that the voices were coming his way. The children were on the road, and as they drew closer, he could hear them trying out filthy words. He stood in the middle of the road, waiting for them to approach him. He'd encountered about everything in the Marine Corps, but this was the worst language he'd heard from a group of kids. In a few minutes, they walked right into him in the pitch-blackness.

They were very frightened. Sam began, "I want to know who's doing all that bad talk." He already knew that all four of them were guilty; yet, every single one of them denied it. He continued, "I have been standing right here. You didn't see me, but I heard every one of you using bad language." They all repeated, "No, Mr. Patterson, we weren't doing it." That irritated Sam; now they were lying in addition to cussing. He commanded, "Come on, we're going to go up to the office and straighten this out."

Arriving at the office, he quizzed them again and all of them once more absolutely denied using bad language. "Well," he said, "I'm going to give you a lesson now on how to talk, and I'm going to start on the other end from your talker." As he went in to get a paddle, one of the boys pled, "Mr. Patterson, would you pray for us first?" That touched Sam because he thought they were beginning to break. He almost relented, but he resisted the temptation and told them they'd pray after the paddling. He paddled them all soundly and forgot to pray. Yet, as they walked out of the office, every one of them stepped up to Sam and shook his hand.

That day Sam learned a truth about young human nature. "Children want to be disciplined even if they don't like it. They respect the source from which it comes. They knew they were getting what was right. I didn't abuse them, but I gave them a reminder that this kind of talk would not do at French Camp."[111]

A student named Albert from South Mississippi taught Sam a valuable lesson about the importance of being sensitive to young people's feelings:

> *One day I was walking across campus, and I heard the angry, loud voice of a staff member rebuking Albert. I could see that a number of students were within easy hearing of the reprimand. I hurried on with my business and forgot about the matter. However, later that day Albert came to me, saying, 'Mr. Patterson, I want to complain about Mr._____. He didn't treat me with respect today.' I'd never had a student put it exactly like that, but I knew what Albert meant. That faculty member could have called Albert aside and addressed the problem privately, especially since it wasn't a serious infraction. After that, I always admonished staff members to treat students with respect, consideration, and fairness. We made that a policy after Albert's complaint.*[112]

Although he had to administer discipline, Sam was the polar opposite of a legalist and was known for his forgiving and tolerant nature. "He believed that the Lord had such wonderful ways to bring different people to a point of repentance," explained Rich Cannon. "Therefore, he was never judgmental; he upheld the law but was merciful."

Those around Sam gained valuable insights into life, especially the fact that legalism didn't make one spiritual. On one occasion, Sam and Rich Cannon were on their way to a meeting. Sam was driving, while Rich read his Bible. "What are you doing, Rich?" Sam asked.

"Reading my Bible," responded Rich proudly. "My objective is to read through it at least once a year."

Sam countered, "You know what that'll do for you, don't you?"

Rich was delighted, thinking Sam was going to tell him what a mature Christian he was becoming. "No, what?"

"It'll make a legalist out of you. The question is not 'Have I gone through the Bible?' but 'Has the Bible gone through me?'"

"He was so right," says Rich today, "because I was thirty-five chapters behind and not getting anything out of my reading since I was trying so hard to catch up. I sincerely thanked him for the reality check; it was not a put-down but a lift-up!"

"Mr. Pat didn't let the pettiness of life spoil his joy in the Lord," points out Ann Angle," and he encouraged us not to either. One time a person used some words in front of me that I found most offensive. I was so very straight-laced! Infuriated, I went to see Mr. Pat about it, telling him the situation just got my goat. He looked at me a minute, then suggested, 'Well, Ann, if you don't put your goat out, nobody'll get it!' I have laughed a million times over that, and I always remember it when I need to lighten up a bit."

Scott Boeving has a similar tale. "One time I asked Mr. Pat his perspective on the controversy about the gifts of the Holy Spirit and praying in tongues. After a short discussion, he left, saying, 'Well, Scott, whatever language you pray in, pray for me!'"

A GOOD FRIEND—ALWAYS

Just because students graduated didn't mean they were out from under Sam's watchful eye. Nan Hagerty received a call from him the summer after her graduation. She was working for Horace Hull in Memphis, a job Sam had found for her. When he wanted to know where she was going to church, she admitted she didn't live close to one and didn't have any transportation.

"The next thing I know the pastor of a church in my area called, saying Mr. Pat had asked if someone could pick me up for church. Our spiritual well-being was very important to him."

A great number of FCA students have Sam to thank for the opportunity of a college education. Not only did he motivate Scott Boeving to get serious about academics, he also worked to get him a scholarship to Belhaven. Scott has now had a career in banking for thirty-five years. Through Sam's friendship with Lt. Governor Carroll Gartin, French Camp received ten junior college scholarships. One of those enabled Weecy Patterson to go to Itawamba Junior College, where she was an outstanding student.

Evie Clements Salter can also trace the path of her life from Sam's influence. "During my junior and senior years, as part of my FCA scholarship, Mr. Pat selected me as his secretary. I learned the administrative end of running an institution such as French Camp Academy and saw what marvelous business sense he had. That experience led to a business major at Montreat College, where I won a scholarship."

Bill Mason will always be grateful for Sam's support. Bill was eight years old when he came to French Camp in 1953, sponsored by a man in Glen Allen,

Mississippi. He and an older brother had been living with his mother in a small house with no running water; his mother hoed and picked cotton to hold the family together. He had no idea where his father was.

Bill came to know the Lord through Sam, and by the time he graduated, he knew he was called to the ministry. Sam vowed to back him fully. Campus jobs and loans, along with gifts from Sam, Lewis Graeber, and others put Bill through college and Reformed Theological Seminary. One summer, he also traveled with Mickey Parks' Musical Messengers over the Southeast, giving his testimony and telling the French Camp story. Sam took part in Bill's installation service to the three-church field he pastored for twenty years.

No matter how long they had been gone from French Camp, students always knew where to turn when bad times hit. Katie Taylor Landry (FCA '56), who came to know Christ through Sam, was a young wife in her 20s when her husband died tragically. "My pastor contacted Mr. Pat, who prayed with me, sent me literature, and comforted me at a time when I really needed to be reminded how much God loved me. He taught me that life would go on and that I would find happiness again while raising our baby boy. I did marry a very good man seven years later. I can easily close my eyes and see Mr. Pat smiling at me. I always saw Jesus in his eyes."

"In 1960, I did something that Mr. Pat had warned us over and over not to do," confessed Nan Hagerty regretfully. "I married a man who was not a Christian. He was also thirteen years older than I. I became very depressed because, among other things, he refused to go to church, and he didn't want me to go either. I wrote to Mr. Pat and told him all my troubles. He replied with a long letter, and I know he typed it with his own hands because of all the mistakes. How comforting to hear from him and to know that he cared enough to take the time to type the letter himself! I fully expected him to chastise me, but he did not. Instead, he gave me scriptural counsel, godly and wise advice that I could truly use."

Friends in French Camp also discovered that Sam was a loyal friend, just as people in Leland had. Whenever Pete Thrailkill was in the hospital, he'd look up and see Sam. "How did Mr. Pat find out? He stayed right behind me all the way and never gave up on me. One time I was hurt seriously when a big log hit me and busted my head open. I could see out of a little slit in one eye, and I spied Mr. Pat. They had called my family because I had to have surgery; I didn't think I would live. Mr. Pat prayed for me before they rolled me into the operating room. The next thing I knew, a woman in a white robe was shaking me, and a bright light blazed around me. Then I saw Mr. Pat and asked him where I was. 'Son,' he said, 'there ain't but three places you could have gone—heaven, hell, or back to earth!'"

Irene Taylor experienced Sam's compassion at a particular difficult time. "We lost our son in 1957, and years later, Mr. Pat was going through school pictures and sent me one of our son, saying he knew we did not want it thrown away. One of my friends counseled with Mr. Pat for hours. He was such a blessing to her that I believe he saved her life. He would do anything for people who needed him."

The late Helen Branning also knew how kind Sam could be. "When Talmage nearly died in 1973, Sam was preaching in Leland at special services. He immediately came back to be with me because he thought Talmage would not make it. In fact, doctors told Sam they had done all they could; they advised him to go back to French Camp and gather the congregation to pray fervently. God spared Talmage, even though he was on life support for a good while and in the hospital for a month. Sam was there with us the whole time."

A LOVER OF PEOPLE AND SOLITUDE

Sam loved to fellowship with others. Often, in the midst of his busy labors, he simply stopped and wanted to "hang out" with people. One afternoon he dropped in to visit the late Erline Crowder as she worked in her garden. "He had his overalls on and stood and talked as I worked. Since he loved fresh vegetables, one day I called and asked if he'd like to have lunch with us. He couldn't get there fast enough, and after lunch he walked over to our pond and spent time alone just wandering around."

Ann Angle recalls those impromptu visits, too. "Sometimes he'd drop by for no reason, saying, 'Y'all go on and do what you were doing. I just want to sit here a while.' He'd stay and talk for a bit, then he was gone."

Sam's informality taught Mary Jane Henley of Jackson a big lesson about hospitality. "One night he arrived an hour early to lead a Bible study at our house. We hadn't finished supper, and the table was a wreck with the children still in their high chairs. I was concerned for him to see the house in such a mess. He put me at ease when he urged, 'Don't worry about cleaning up, Mary Jane; I just want to sit here and enjoy your family.'"

To say that Sam loved people is not to say that he was a bon vivant, life-of-the-party type. In fact, he was just the opposite. While he always enjoyed congenial fellowship, he loved time alone. It's doubtful that those who knew Sam would peg him as a lover of solitude, since he constantly poured himself out for others and involved himself so deeply in their lives. Folks merely assumed he was a people-person.

"He and I were much alike in that way," observed Jimmy Rogers. "I'm not a people person, but I made my living surrounded by people, as did he. At times, I really wanted to pull away and be with my family or by myself."

Most of the time Sam wanted solitude in a woodsy, outdoor setting. His needs were very simple—a hot dog on the stove and a cup of coffee. Sam was never happier than when he was by himself, communing with God, staring at the stars, gazing into a campfire.

"During one winter break when I was in high school, Mr. Pat took about five of us camping," remarked Lynn Downing. "He wanted to teach us some survival techniques. All we were allowed to bring was some newspaper and a couple of blankets. We went over to Lake Ann in late afternoon, built a fire, and he showed us how to line those blankets with newspaper and put either our head or our feet toward the fire. The next morning we broke ice in the lake for cooking water, but we had not been cold at all during the night because of the techniques he showed us. I woke in the middle of the night, and everybody was asleep except him. He was standing by the fire in the dark, looking off, probably praying, with a cup of coffee."

"If Sam had a hobby, it was the outdoors," agrees Jimmy Rogers. "We loved bird hunting and fishing together, even deep-sea fishing. Every September we went dove hunting in the Mississippi Delta. When we camped, he'd carry a coffeepot and dip water out of the creek to make coffee right by the stream over a little fire. 'Aren't you afraid you're going to get sick?' I'd ask. 'No,' he replied, 'not if I boil the water long enough.' That was some of the best coffee I've ever had in my life.

"Sam and I traveled to many church meetings over the years. One of those trips stands out in my mind. We were staying at a campground in his little camper truck, and the weather was cool. One morning I woke up and could not find him anywhere. When I searched the surrounding area, I found him taking a bath in a frigid mountain stream flowing near our campsite. The temperature was thirty degrees, yet there he sat in his bathing suit, blissfully scrubbing away! I had trouble going from the camper to the shower house, but the weather didn't bother him a bit in the world!"

Jim Graeber and Sam became close camping friends after Sam came to FCA. "We both loved to hunt, fish, and camp out in the woods. Since he was so busy, he didn't get to go with me as much as he wanted. Yet, every once in a while he'd need to get away, and we'd spend several nights under the stars. Sam was so happy out there! He'd get his Bible and a chair and go outside to have his devotion."

Sam incorporated his love of the outdoors with his preaching and began buying small, economical cars, camper trucks, or travel trailers in which to camp or pull over and sleep. When he visited relatives in Arkansas, he rarely stayed in their homes, preferring to camp on Petit Jean Mountain near his childhood haunt, Nelson's Point. He came down to visit, but bedtime found him winding his way back up to the woods.

Sam's lifestyle and personality resulted in an exceptionally balanced individual, equally comfortable with himself or in fellowship with others. During his periods of solitude he learned much from the Lord and was able to communicate it in a winsome, non-threatening way.

"Mr. Pat was down to earth, but intellectual," observed Kay Johnson. "His intellect was tempered by his love for Christ and others; that's what made him so believable and personable. He balanced spiritual life and real life, which is rare in a theologian."

A HUMBLE, SIMPLE MAN

Sam held life loosely because he knew God held it so tightly. His reality was consumed with the knowledge that God controls all things in this world, and Sam did not fight God on this, as people often do.

"Sam believed only in real things," revealed Ewing Carruthers. "That's why he loved the outdoors; it was reality. He was an earthy, practical-minded person, and everything he experienced in this world was God's Word, ready to be interpreted to better conform us to Christ."

This utter assurance of God's goodness and control over his life manifested itself in many ways. Sam held short accounts with God and continually inspected his life for sins, confessing them to God and man quickly, then repenting and working to eradicate them from his life. Consequently, he was very comfortable with himself and could be transparent.

"Sam didn't have anything to hide," declares good friend M. B. Cooper. "Most people have a few secrets and erect walls to keep others from finding them out, but Sam didn't have any secrets. He was transparent; what you saw was what you got. I could say I sensed this because we were close friends, but I noticed he was that way with everyone. People felt very comfortable with him."

In the same practical, realistic way that Sam saw himself as a saved sinner, he viewed all men as sinners before the Lord; the ground is level at the cross, as it were. That's why he could treat a garbage collector with the same respect and dignity that he accorded a bank president. Both were potential heirs to the kingdom of God with him.

Because he knew Jesus was perfect and he was not, he could be honest about himself and not take himself too seriously. This made him unpretentious and humble, with nothing to prove to anyone. "One day after I was grown I was having a cup of coffee with Mr. Pat," said Kenny Henderson. "I told him he was probably the finest man I knew. He sat there a minute, then responded, 'You just don't know me well enough.'" Kenny pauses as he wipes tears from his eyes. "That really touched my heart. He admitted that he wasn't a perfect man. But in my eyes, he was a hero."

Although Sam was brutally honest with himself about his sin, he didn't continually put himself down so others could compliment him. C. S. Lewis describes Sam well:

Do not imagine that if you meet a really humble man he will be what most people call 'humble' nowadays: he will not be a sort of greasy, smarmy person, who is always telling you that, of course, he is nobody. Probably all you will think about him is that he seemed a cheerful, intelligent chap who took a real interest in what you said to him... He will not be thinking about humility: he will not be thinking about himself at all....[113]

Finally, knowing that God would take care of his every need allowed Sam to put absolutely no value on material possessions. "He was in the service of the Lord," explained Sam Allen. "Jesus told his disciples not to take anything with them except the clothes on their backs and the sandals on their feet. Their needs would be supplied, and they were. Sam saw himself as one of those disciples."

Sam also was constantly on the lookout for signs that he was becoming greedy. He took to heart one of God's commands in Luke: "Watch out! Be on your guard against all kinds of greed; a man's life does not consist in the abundance of his possessions" (Luke 12:15 NIV). He was scrupulous in the matter of FCA's finances. In the early hard years, the board offered him a $600 yearly raise, but he refused it, even though he was making only about $300 a month. He told them the school needed it more than he did.

"When he traveled for the school, he handled his expense account as if it were God's," marvels Hugh Long. "I saw him buy a hamburger when, as president of the school, he could have had a steak and thought nothing of it since FCA was paying for it."

Pat Posey (RTS '87) noticed the same integrity. "In the late 1950s I was principal of Falkner Attendance Center in Tippah County and asked Brother Patterson to have a chapel program. He did a splendid job, and I gave him twenty-five dollars, knowing that his salary at French Camp was somewhat limited. I intended for him to get a bit extra that month. However, when my bank statement came, the check was endorsed FRENCH CAMP TRAVEL FUND."

Sam's frugality knew no bounds. Erskine Jackson's wife, Eleanor, recalled that Erskine and Sam shared a black preacher's robe. "Erskine had a robe for weddings so he would not have to rent a tuxedo. Sam borrowed the robe occasionally because he told us he didn't use a robe enough to warrant buying one!"

"I believe Sam's determination to live on the edge with Jesus and eschew most things we think of as necessities had to do with his exceptional stewardship of the gifts God had given him," reflects Erin Lail. "He knew he had extraordinary abilities, and God needed him to use them. Other people might have been just as qualified, but they weren't as willing to do the hard things God asked, such as walk away from a cushy pastorate to a bankrupt school. Yet, Sam never, ever flinched. He trusted God's promises to the very end."

THE SACRIFICE

Sam was a missionary, pure and simple, and he never claimed to be anything else. He wore the blinders that give missionaries the courage to leave kith and kin and wander the earth to share God's redeeming love. It is a supernatural gift most people cannot fathom. No wonder scripture tells us, "How beautiful upon the mountains are the feet of him who brings good news…" (Isaiah 52:7 ESV).

Sam loved his family dearly, but he loved Jesus more. His focus was eternal. Everything in his life was put on the altar to Christ when he was converted. In commenting on Exodus 20:1, Matthew Henry says, "Whatever is esteemed or loved, feared or served, delighted in or depended on more than God, that (whatever it is) we do in effect make a god."[114] Sam came closer than most to knocking down the gods we keep after we are saved. In the crucible of survival at French Camp, God continued to pound to extinction any gods besides Himself in Sam's life. As long as he lived, Sam was sensitive to the temptation to put humans, even Stelle, before God:

> If a man has his wife as the center of his life, he will be unhappy and miserable because he knows that he is liable to lose his goddess; she may die or may cease to love him. If a woman's husband is god in her life, she can never be at peace because she may lose him, too. If children are the gods of parents the same holds true. Anytime people have a god that isn't the real God, they have to live nervous lives because they know deep down they are worshipping a god they will ultimately lose.[115]

"My parents were missionaries in South Korea, and Sam reminded me a lot of them," shared Kelly Unger, one of the first teachers Sam hired in 1951. "Missionaries work fervently and don't count the cost to themselves. He had that spirit of devotion."

"We were devoted to those kids, and both of us probably neglected our families," confessed Billy Thompson. "Nita raised our children, and I know Mr. Pat never did a lot with Becky. He was completely wrapped up in those FCA kids, loving them and helping them. Someone once asked if we had pastimes. I laughed. Our pastime was those children!"

Becky admits her family sacrificed, but she would not have had it any other way. "Daddy spent more time with FCA students than he did with me. Mom raised me because Daddy was gone all the time. I didn't have some things that I would have had if he hadn't been at FCA, but he was doing what God wanted him to do. How can I resent that? I would love to have had him around more when I was young, but God is good in that He gave him back to me in my later years. I traveled a lot with him in the last ten years of his life, and we had a wonderful time."

As adults, FCA students now know the vast sacrifice Sam made for them. "Mr. Pat was a very unselfish person, always giving of himself and his time," recalls Larry Hipp (FCA '65). "He gave up precious time with his family by staying on the road and raising money for the school. As I get older, I realize how important time is and how little of it we have. I am eternally grateful for the impact this godly man made on my life."

Stelle understood Sam's calling from the beginning because her focus was eternal as well. While his mission was to find out what Christ wanted him to do, Stelle saw hers as supporting him in that endeavor in whatever way she could. Sam considered her selfless adoption of his calling one of the greatest blessings of his life:

> From the beginning, she accepted the priority of God's claim on my life and the importance of His work. Never once in thirty years did she ever make me feel that my obligation to God and my calling as a minister were in conflict with her desires. Since I've been in evangelistic work in varying degrees all through my ministry, I was away from home far more than the average minister, perhaps more than I should have been. It is possible for a minister to neglect his family. I tried to follow what I felt was God's calling, and we had an understanding between us that His claims came first.
>
> However, she never did develop a poor attitude or pout, indicating that I was putting too much time into the Lord's work. I don't know all that she might have thought in her heart. She always hated to see me go, and she was always glad to see me come back. But she never said anything to put pressure on me to prefer her over what I sensed to be my responsibility to my calling.
>
> It was years down the road before I realized how blessed I was to be relieved of that conflict. She had a heart of wisdom. What a contribution she made to her own stature, to our love, and to the peace and tranquility of our household because she accepted that I was the one who was getting God's guidance regarding my responsibility to Him. I always tried to be fair to her, taking her with me whenever I could and being with her as much as I could when I was home. But I felt it more because she never put any pressure on me about it.[116]

"This melding of two hearts was truly beautiful," observed Becky. "Behind Daddy was Mother. He was always the spiritual head of our house, and she complemented him. They were literally Christian soul mates, studying and praying together, worshipping Christ together. I don't know where one started and the other ended."

Sam needed much help with the minutia of everyday life; happily, this is where Stelle excelled. Extremely focused and unbelievably organized, she became Sam's brain.

"She was an extension of Daddy," notes Becky. "Was she a good homemaker? No, she wasn't domestic. She rarely cooked because we ate in the school cafeteria, and she didn't sew. We had a housecleaner and a woman who did our laundry. She was a good wife. That was her calling."

It would be hard to fathom how any wife could have done more to support her husband in ministry. While Stelle's DCE training helped her teach Sunday School, chair church circles, lead Bible studies, and generally help with ministerial duties, she went far above the call of duty in making life easy for Sam. At her death, her bulging 3" x 4" black notebook held every facet of their daily lives. Among many other things, it listed:

—Every person they visited and every person who visited them
—Notations of who cooked what food, so Sam didn't thank Mrs. Jones for the superb pie, when actually she had made a casserole
—Hundreds of names and addresses of people with whom Sam corresponded
—Lists of thank-you notes to be written (checked off, of course, if done)
—Homemade calendar pages (why pay for them?)
—Over twenty pages of prayer lists containing nearly 1,000 names
—Notes for Bible studies and good scriptures
—Quotations worthy of meditation, such as, "The most dangerous Christian is one endowed with natural talent or good personality. He is tempted to draw men to himself instead of Christ"
—Recipes
—Endless To Do Lists
—Car mileage noted at the purchase of four new tires and how much pressure each should have

How many of these books could she possibly have gone through in nearly thirty years of marriage?

After one of Sam's evangelistic series that Stelle had attended, she typed up the names and addresses of every single host or hostess, organized by lunches and dinners. Beside each name was relevant information about the person or family so that Sam could make his thank-you note warm and personal. No detail was too small:

"Their furnace was out of order"
"Big boulders in front yard, plus many plants in the house"
"Harold was home for lunch—much talk about snakes"
"She had Sally Lunn bread for supper"

"Daddy was awful with names," recalls Becky. "He met so many people that he could never remember them all. Most of the time, he'd stick out his hand and say, 'Well, Law! Look'a here!' and shake the person's hand vigorously, not having any idea who it was and fervently hoping a clue would pop up soon to jog his memory. If Mother was anywhere around, she'd give him the name because she always knew."

Rich Cannon laughs. "That tickled me. Sam met more people named 'Look'a here' than I've ever seen!"

HEART ATTACK!

Yet, even Stelle could not protect Sam from himself. He never knew another speed other than full steam ahead, insisting on keeping an inhuman schedule of evangelistic preaching, running a school, and pastoring two churches. Rarely did he make time to exercise, mainly because he didn't like it. Appointment books show sporadic attempts to walk; one notation proves he bought a bike and rode it for a few weeks.

However, he did love a full refrigerator. To the end of his life, Sam battled the scale, and the latter usually won. "We called him a 'grazer,'" reveals Jimmy Rogers, "because he was always rummaging through the refrigerator. He loved food, mostly the unhealthy stuff, and ate anything he wanted. Hamburgers, seafood, fried food, gumbo, and sweets were all his favorites; he always had a horde of 'nibble food.'"

At times, however, Sam did give weight loss the good old college try, as Nan Hagerty discovered while waiting tables at FCA. "After each meal, we'd see Mr. Pat write something down on a small pad. For a long time we all wondered what in the world he was doing. Finally, someone asked and he replied, 'Counting calories.' He was very faithful to count his calories after every meal."

Yet, his lifestyle finally caught up with him, and friends began to notice symptoms of possible serious illness. "The last sermon I heard him preach was at Mt. Hermon Presbyterian Church (now First Presbyterian) in Madison, Mississippi," commented Charleton Hutton. "He seemed extremely tired that night and repeatedly paused in mid-sentence, only to begin a new sentence. This was most unusual because Mr. Pat was always quite eloquent. Fearing that he might be in danger of a stroke, at the end of the service, I begged him to see a doctor about his heart. At the very least, I wanted him to spend the night in Jackson, but he refused and returned to French Camp."

A week later, on October 4, 1961, Sam suffered a major heart attack.[117] *The FCA News* announced Sam's illness with concern in November 1961. The community and the Academy family were shocked and saddened; surely God would not take away their beloved leader! They all went to their knees in concerted prayer that God would bring Sam back to health. Warm letters went back and forth between Sam and the French Camp community, who loved him greatly and wanted him back. He, of course, also wished desperately to return:

How thankful I am for your constant prayers on my behalf. God has certainly heard all of them and is answering them... We miss you all and we look forward to the great day when we can return to French

Camp in January... All I can do just now is to pray God's blessing on you students, and this I am doing day and night ... I want the very best for all of you ... and God's best is Christ. John 14:6[118]

Erskine Jackson took over as acting president for two months, and it looked as if Sam's condition might be a detriment to the school's finances. Peggy Cockrell remembers the one time they weren't paid on time. "The money wasn't coming in because everybody was waiting to see what was going to happen to him. We just couldn't imagine losing him. We had to wait about half a month, as we prayed fervently. Looking back, it became a time of faith renewal on the campus."

Revival was exactly what Sam was praying for as he convalesced:

Day and night, Mrs. Patterson and I are praying that God will stir up a real spiritual awakening in the school and that His supply for the financial needs will be forthcoming ... I pray for the school but do not worry about it because I was never head of it, but am just the one who is in Christ, and He will see His work through.

Maybe He took me out of the work for this time to remind me and everyone that God's work is not dependent on a man. In these days He will prove Himself that He can and will bless and carry on His work regardless of any man present or absent.[119]

As he recovered, Sam couldn't help writing Ewing Carruthers to needle him playfully about the superior benefits of God's insurance policy over the earthly policy Carruthers had engineered for him many years before:

I seem to be making satisfactory progress, and will be out of the hospital right away. If all goes well, I will be back in circulation at and for French Camp sometime in January. The Lord has sure let me cash in on the 'benefits' of His policy as outlined in Psalm 103:2-4 and saved your company $100,000![120]

Actually, Sam was busy even while convalescing. Although chained to the house and bed, he kept up a lively correspondence. During December, Becky wrote him from Montreat Anderson College that she had met some unbelievers and wondered how she might defend her faith. On December 22, 1961, Sam answered her with a thirty-six page, handwritten letter outlining how to win others to Christ! (See Appendix E for full letter.)

By January 1962, Sam resumed the presidency on a limited basis but was soon back up to full speed. However, his doctors forced Sam to lessen his pace; the board hired Leonard T. Van Horn as Executive Vice President to relieve some of the workload.[121]

After the heart attack, Stelle redoubled her efforts (if that were possible) to protect Sam from stress. "From that time on, Daddy came first," recalls Becky. "She always put him before herself to some extent, but now even more so."

AN ETERNAL TRIBUTE

Sam's work at French Camp was indeed eternal, and his Christ-like ministry to the hurting, tear-stained children in that rural backwater of Mississippi ranks as, perhaps, the most lasting tribute to his stellar life. In this quiet country setting, he painted a picture of Jesus' love that no one could miss, especially those little ones. The ministry he began continues now, tracing joy on the faces of young people as they discover the love of God and a nurturing family for the first time. It's entirely possible that this very day you will encounter a French Camp graduate and not know it. Thousands of them are now scattered across the world in every conceivable profession, living full, productive lives with vibrant faith in a loving God.

Sam never took credit for FCA's success. Someone once asked him why God had blessed the school so mightily, and he replied:

> *Across its over one hundred years of existence, the school has never wavered in its commitment to sharing the Gospel of Christ. In addition, it reaches a group of people that God has a great interest in—young people whose chances are handicapped by a factor that they didn't contribute to or create. If French Camp Academy did not exist, someone would be obliged to create it, so great is the importance of its influence on the lives of young people to whom its unique ministry is directed. The ideals that we set out in the beginning have been greatly refined, and the faculty, staff, and administration have increasingly learned how to make the program work for the students. I believe the school is more effective now in communicating our objectives to the students than in the days when I was here. And I see it continuing to do so into the next century.* [122]

Anyone associated with French Camp Academy calls Sam the best friend the school ever had, a tremendous favor from God. Throughout the years, one sees clearly an outpouring of love for Sam and a deep appreciation for his leadership. Today, the school still operates on his principles. "Mr. Pat put us on the tracks that we still run on," says former FCA president Rich Cannon. "There's a ripple effect from people like Sam Patterson."

And Sam dearly loved FCA! Despite the overwhelming difficulties of his work there, he embraced every aspect of his job from the first moment:

Here and there I bump into fellows who are unhappy in their work. I can understand how that can be true, but I can't appreciate it with the sympathy born of being in the same boat. I like my work!

It is great to be associated with a gang of fine youngsters who face stiff problem situations with the stuff in them that makes them willing to work to make a way for themselves and to open a door on life that someone or something else has closed.

It is great being associated with a grand group of staff members who have sold out other interests to make these kids their mission in life.

It's great to be associated with the Lord in His work ... and this IS His work here! It is thrilling to watch God work the sustained miracle through which He converted this school into a mission for a special area of youth and has, without spoiling us with abundance, met our basic daily needs.[123]

Sam's love for French Camp Academy would remain until he drew his last breath. Yet, in the early 1960s he faced a dilemma. Even as he planned and prayed over the future of the Academy, hitting the road at every opportunity to raise money and keeping up a busy evangelical preaching ministry, God was calling his heart to another battlefield. Sam became alarmed at the liberal trends in his denomination, the Presbyterian Church in the United States. People no longer took God's Word or the precious doctrines of the church seriously.

In much the same way he had wrestled with the decision to come to French Camp many years before, he prayed earnestly now, wondering what he could do to bring revival back to the church. He could not know that he would soon become one of the prime igniters of a fire that ultimately changed the face of Southern Presbyterianism. And the roaring blaze would begin as a tiny spark right there in the little village of French Camp, Mississippi.

CHAPTER SIX

THE RTS YEARS
1962–1979

Attempt something so great for God that it's doomed to failure unless God be in it.

John Haggai

Ah, Sovereign Lord, you have made the heavens and the earth by your great power and outstretched arm. Nothing is too hard for you.

Jeremiah 32:17 (NIV)

The 1960s. Who can forget the seething cauldron of events boiling before our eyes in the United States for an entire decade? Death and dysfunction were everywhere, leaving a crimson stain on the history of a country not even two centuries old. Our children suffered physical death in riots on college campuses, and spiritual death as their professors taught them that God was dead. Thousands died in the far-off bloody jungles of Vietnam, while our leaders were systematically assassinated here at home. By the end of the decade, virtually no belief or institution was left intact, and that included religion.

Actually the church had been ailing, inching toward liberalism, for decades. Advances in science and a renewed emphasis on humanism in the late 19th and early 20th century had swallowed large chunks of traditional religious concepts. Especially in the United Presbyterian Church (the Northern Church), attacks on the authority of God's Word had become commonplace during the first third of the 20th century, and by the 1940s the trend had spread to the Presbyterian Church in the United States (the Southern Church).[1] Many in the PCUS were concerned as they watched a spiral downward to a lower view of the inspiration of scripture, a neglect of the biblical Reformed distinctives set forth in the original Westminster Confession, and a decreasing emphasis on the evangelistic mission of the church.

In the early 1940s, conservatives began to speak out. In May 1942, L. Nelson Bell, Billy Graham's father-in-law, founded *Presbyterian Journal* to call the Southern Presbyterian Church back to her historic loyalty to the Word of God and the church standards. With the integrity of scripture at stake, Bell and editor Henry Dendy wanted the *Journal* to provide a rallying ground, a place to look for leadership, and a medium through which people might find expression of common views.[2]

Conservative Presbyterians looked with increasing concern especially at their seminaries. All the schools seemed to be moving toward a position that questioned or denied outright the verbal inspiration by God of scripture and its inerrancy. Placing evangelical scholars on the faculties of liberal seminaries was impossible. Conservative leaders realized the key to the future of the church was the training of strong pastors, men of God dedicated to the preaching of the entire Word of God. The seminaries' weak view of scripture was producing weak pastors and was sure to prove devastating to the church if not stopped.

By 1948, the Continuing Church Committee, headed by Henry Dendy and Richardson Ayres, was calling for PCUS seminaries to reexamine the doctrines being taught.[3] Over the next ten years, several efforts were mounted to force the seminaries to uphold a higher view of scripture. The overtures helped for a time, but liberal teaching eventually crept back in.

EARLY EFFORTS FOR A NEW SEMINARY

Some felt that a new seminary would be a constructive and effective step toward recovery and renewal. While many had tried, it would take the unique blend of faith and charisma in Sam Patterson to galvanize people into action and overcome the myriad obstacles. As early as 1948, a very loosely organized group of southern conservatives, known as the Evangelical Fellowship, formed preliminary plans for a new seminary in Chattanooga. Rev. J. E. Flow of Concord, North Carolina, and Rev. John R. Richardson of Atlanta attempted to get financial support for the venture but were unsuccessful. Richardson recalled:

> *We contacted several men ... including Horace Hull of Memphis, to finance the new seminary. All expressed interest, but few were willing to provide the necessary funds to begin.... I think we sowed the seed that Sam Patterson developed, as [Hull] was the first major donor of the Reformed Theological Seminary.* [4]

Part of the reason for their failure could have been the group's belief that starting a seminary would take 1.5 million dollars. In a November letter to Richardson Ayres of Alexandria, Louisiana, Flow wrote:

> ... *If we bring in ... a million and a half from the outside, the local people I am sure will provide the land and the buildings that are necessary.*[5]

During the early 1950s, PCUS pastors Morton Smith and Jack Scott discussed the need for a new seminary while they were at Columbia Theological Seminary. Others wished a conservative seminary existed, but that's all it was—wishful thinking. At the same time, Dr. R. M. Crowe became president of Belhaven College, hoping to change it from a PCUS girls' school to a co-educational Reformed Bible college, and possibly even a seminary to train men for the ministry. At Crowe's urging, Morton Smith moved to Mississippi in 1954 to become professor of Bible at the school. While at Belhaven, Smith lobbied hard among First Presbyterian Church leaders and Belhaven board members for a new seminary to be connected to the college. However, his petitions gathered no support; the tremendous work needed to begin a seminary simply overwhelmed any sympathizers.

Meanwhile, Crowe's plans for Belhaven foundered on the rocks of administrative problems, and the move was abandoned.[6] Finally, in the spring of 1963, Smith gave up on gaining support for a new seminary and accepted a call to teach at Westminster Theological Seminary in Philadelphia. He could not know that very shortly his decade-old dream of a new seminary would begin to appear through the person of Sam Patterson.

Although very conservative, Sam was not calling loudly for a new seminary during the 1940s and '50s. His notes and diary during that time are silent on the issue. This puzzled more than one person. During Smith's first year in Mississippi, he heard that Sam was a very doctrinally sound Presbyterian evangelist. However, their initial meeting was rather chilly.

"I first met Sam at a Mississippi youth conference a few years after my arrival," disclosed Smith. "Our relationship was not estranged, but it was not openly cordial either. During those early years when we were trying to move Belhaven toward theological training, Sam didn't oppose us, but he didn't embrace the cause either. He saw himself primarily as an evangelist and said he didn't worry too much about the theological fine points. He seemed to stand off from us as a Presbyterian evangelist on his own, pretty much a loner."

Sam might not have been calling loudly for a new seminary, but he was certainly thinking about it. In 1953, late FCA Coach Billy Thompson recalled distinctly Sam's confession that he wanted to begin a new seminary. "It was Christmas, and the children were gone. We were riding horses out to Little Mountain south of campus. He told me he wanted to start a conservative seminary soon and wanted me to take his place at French Camp. However, that wasn't my cup of tea."

More than likely, with Thompson not wishing to take the FCA reins, Sam saw his first duty as putting the Academy on sound footing. Even though still concerned, he put ideas for a seminary on the back burner.[7]

With the hopes of Belhaven dashed, three PCUS pastors—Albert Freundt, Morton Smith, and John R. Miller—met informally in June 1958 to discuss the possibility of a new seminary. In early October 1959, Freundt spoke further with PCUS pastor Norman Harper and Jackson layman Robert Kennington. Both were favorably disposed, but Kennington was concerned about the large financial obligation. Later in October, Harper and PCUS pastor Julius Scott joined the original three pastors in presenting the idea for a new seminary to a group of laymen. The laymen were interested but were uncertain and somewhat hesitant about undertaking such a huge project at that time. Finally, on October 21, 1959, Freundt, Smith and Scott met in Brandon, Mississippi, to draft a proposal for a new seminary and share it with others. Yet, again the proposal lay dormant.[8]

The liberal-conservative conflict came forcefully to the surface at the Synod of Mississippi meeting on June 5, 1962, when several ministers brought a scathing memorial against Central Mississippi Presbytery. Among many other charges, they claimed the presbytery constantly criticized the PCUS, preferred men from non-PCUS background and seminary training for ordination, and generally promoted schism.[9]

Yet, it was not until the waning days of 1962 that an event occurred to grab Sam Patterson's attention and catapult him into the fray. His entry into the movement for a new seminary was certainly going to kick it up a notch. In this event, the controversy over the inspiration of scripture was magnified to such proportions that Sam could no longer ignore it. He knew beyond a shadow of a doubt that aggressive steps must be taken immediately to do something.

DO WE NEED AN INFALLIBLE BIBLE?

On December 24, 1962, the independent liberal *Presbyterian Outlook* published an article entitled, "Do We Need an Infallible Bible?" containing the viewpoints of professors from the four PCUS seminaries. The consensus of the four? It was evident that we do not need an infallible Bible because we do not have one. (See Appendix B for full article.)

Dr. Kenneth J. Foreman, Professor Emeritus of Doctrinal Theology at Louisville Seminary, wrote:

> *Is it necessary that all the numbers in the Bible shall be precise and accurate in order for me to find Christ there? Is it necessary that I shall know exactly what happened, to whom and in what order, when Peter denied Jesus, before I can be led to repentance?*[10]

Dr. John F. Jansen, Acting Dean and Professor of New Testament Interpretation at Austin Presbyterian Theological Seminary, wrote:

> *It seems pointless and futile to demand a Bible other than the Bible we actually have.... Have we a right to ask for some inerrant uniformity before we are ready to listen?[11]*

Dr. James H. Gailey, Jr., Professor of Old Testament at Columbia Theological Seminary, wrote:

> *There is no evidence that the infallibility of God has been communicated to those who preach the redemptive message....[12]*

And, finally, from Sam's beloved Union Seminary, Dr. James L. Mays, Professor of Biblical Interpretation, wrote:

> *When we examine the Bible, it appears that, whatever our opinion, God does not think we need an infallible book....[13]*

Sam was shocked and saddened at the articles but was uncertain what course of action to take:

> *I didn't know what to do. Actually I was glad that the articles were printed, and I felt that they put out on the table an issue that really needed attention.[14]*

Scarcely a week later, Sam opened his mailbox to find a letter addressed to all PCUS ministers from L. Nelson Bell. It was the first response Sam had seen. In it, Bell poured out his anguish and disappointment in his denomination's low view of scripture and spent two pages quoting biblical and confessional sources to remind them of their error. He ended with these words:

> *Brethren ... I appeal to you to consider the grave implications of the challenge now confronting our church. We are faced not merely with a low theory of inspiration, but a challenge to the truthfulness of the Word of God. History shows that when the Bible is trifled with or rejected, God turns to those who accept it in simple faith and makes them the instruments of His witnessing power.[15]*

Bell's sentiments echoed Sam's own convictions. No longer could Sam ignore the assault on the central issue of the inspiration of scripture. On January 8, 1963, he wrote and congratulated Bell for taking a stand, agreeing with him that the issue was not "Do we need an infallible Bible?" but rather "Do we have one?" And finally these strong words:

No doubt, this article in the Outlook *is a challenge. Perhaps it is actually a declaration of war. Perhaps it is all to the best. Perhaps the cold war we have been waging between the liberal and conservative elements in the Southern Presbyterian Church should come to an end. Controversy is not always bad. It is good when it involves refutation of alien attacks on either the Word of God or the Son of God.[16]*

At the stated meeting of St. Andrew Presbytery on January 15, 1963, Sam presented a motion seeking presbytery to commend the *Outlook* for bringing out into the open an issue that had been simmering beneath the surface for a long while. The motion also asked presbytery to petition the magazine's editors to select the same number of conservative scholars to present their views of scripture as soon as possible. According to Sam's notes, the motion was seconded, discussed mainly by opponents, and with practically no support, overwhelmingly defeated.[17] Presbytery minutes are terse, simply stating that it was tabled;[18] however, subsequent minutes show that it was never brought up again.

Actually, Sam admitted that the reason he had presented the motion was to see who in the presbytery would speak out concerning the attack on the infallibility of the Bible.[19] He was very disappointed that his conservative colleagues did not fight harder to rebut the article. In a letter to Dr. Bell on January 16, 1963, he said:

The wisdom of this approach to the Outlook *articles may be questioned, but it was disappointing that practically none of the brethren would, or did, speak up and out on the matter of this issue. Pardon me! The proponents of defeating my motion spoke out, but little or nothing was said by brethren who I believe have accepted the infallibility of the scriptures.[20]*

However, by the beginning of February, Sam understood and accepted the reason why the motion had received so little support:

The motion I put before presbytery was admittedly not a very good one …indicated by the fact that some of our brethren who certainly stand for the infallibility of the scripture apparently hesitated to say anything in support of the motion or to vote for it because … the Outlook *is a private paper, and it is not proper for presbytery to make requests of it.[21]*

Determined to fight the article's influence, however, he wrote Aubrey Brown, the *Outlook's* editor, on January 16, 1963, enclosing the presbytery motion and asking personally that the magazine allow the conservative side to be presented.[22] He never received a reply, but the lack of response did not seem to faze Sam. In a subsequent letter to Rev. James McNair, pastor of First Presbyterian Church in Shelby, Mississippi, Sam clearly decided to set his sights much higher than responding to a magazine:

> *The motion I made was not too good. I just felt some sort of stand should be taken by presbytery, and, knowing the 'climate,' I tried to word the motion in such a way as to give it a bare chance of getting through.*
>
> *I am sure there is a better way to meet the issue than yapping at the heels of an independent paper.... We have moved far away from the historic stand of Presbyterian and Reformed conviction. Integrity demands that the church define its position.... The faith of Christ will ultimately be that of the fate of the scriptures.[23]*

Morton Smith recalls an incident that propelled Sam to his next course of action, ultimately causing the genesis of RTS. "About that time, a former FCA student asked Sam where he should go to seminary.[24] After the *Outlook* article, Sam realized with alarm that he had severe misgivings about sending anybody to PCUS seminaries. He decided he needed to find out officially where they stood."

Sam was now a man with a divine mission. Disrespect for God's Word angered and saddened him, and he knew now that he had been far too slow to see the real danger of liberalism. On January 16, 1963, he wrote the presidents of all four PCUS seminaries, seeking their official positions on the matter of scriptural inerrancy. (See Appendix B for full text of letters.) Indeed, he told them he wanted to provide "... a guide to the thinking of a young man who may be considering entering seminary and would like to know ahead of time the seminary's position."[25] His letters were gracious, written with a humble deference and sincerity.

All four men responded courteously and straightforwardly within ten days, but not with the response Sam wanted. (See Appendix B for full text of responses.) He shared the responses confidentially with Dr. Bell and G. Aiken Taylor, editor of the *Presbyterian Journal*:

> *I expected to receive little or no reply, and if I did, I expected an evasive one. But a careful reading of these letters indicates that they are not, as a whole, evasive. As a matter of fact, the men seem to lay it on the line. The only trouble is the line they pick presents, I believe, a lower view of inspiration than our seminaries ought to be maintaining.[26]*

Sam faced the fact that encroaching liberalism had a life of its own and could not be stopped by existing institutions. In February 1963, he privately began trying to organize his thoughts on paper, developing ideas and writing position papers. In one labeled "Convictions That Gave Rise to RTS" and simply dated "April," he outlines the dangers of liberalism and his strategies to fight it:

Liberalism in the Christian faith is not revolutionary. It is an unrelenting tendency, always departing from spiritual truth, revelation, and redemption in infallible scripture and never returning to true orthodoxy. It creeps in slowly and is not recognizable until after it has infiltrated the whole. Until then, a strange integrity prevails that uses rubber words and coated terms.... Liberalism never gives ground to those of fundamental faith.

Hence, if orthodoxy is right and represents the faith we are to live for and, if necessary, die for, it is folly, weakness, and a sell-out of Christ's mission not to take constructive ... steps to maintain the life and growth of orthodoxy. Yet, Reformed evangelicalism can never make a good fight for the right as we know it without a conference program, a biblical training institution, and a seminary. No present institutions in our church are ever to be available for the conservative program.

The establishment of these ... would be a worthy cause for a test and even division. They could rally, nurture, and multiply conservatives. Time waited is time wasted. The longer constructive steps are put off, the harder they will be to take. Now we ought to seek God's guidance, count no cost too much when He leads, and start out in the courage of faith.[27]

In addition to the church's drift toward liberalism, Sam's early position papers show that he also saw the deadness of "churchianity" in America, among other things depending on the professional ministry to carry on the work of the church. He felt that the failure to feed, develop, and use the church's laity and youth (both high school and college) had resulted in:

1. *Vacant and spiritually hopeless, small churches*
2. *Pastored but hopeless, stunted churches*
3. *Millions of homes with no Sunday School or church relationship.*[28]

To combat this, Sam did NOT wake up one morning and decide, "I think I'll start a full-fledged seminary," especially one the size of RTS today. His spiritually fulfilling days at Ferncliff in his youth prompted him to think first of a Bible conference facility where all types of laity—men, women, high school, college, young adult, and families—could be trained to varying degrees of Christian vocational service. His emphases from the very beginning were teaching the Bible, instilling doctrine, and soul-winning. Youth figured prominently in his thoughts, since he had discovered at Kate Anderson that young people accept Christ far more easily than the elderly.

Sam's position papers highlight several targeted groups:

High school graduates and college students—grounding them in the faith and teaching them strategies for evangelism in college.

> *Young adults and older laity—training in Bible study, and service*
> *areas for Christ within the church and community.[29]*

If God blessed the institute and conference program, a seminary could be considered. Sam's love and concern for the local church and the spiritual welfare of the laity is one of the reasons that RTS today not only is governed by lay people, but has always had a rich lay-training program and puts great emphasis on the life of the local church.

Naturally, as Sam began exploring multiple ideas for such a center, he considered Petit Jean Mountain, where he had felt so close to God in his youth. In March 1963, while visiting Morrilton, he spent some time at Nelson's Point on Petit Jean. It was here that God gave Sam the noble vision that eventually resulted in Reformed Theological Seminary. As he sat on the pinnacle of the point, watching the Arkansas River flow lazily through the lush green fields, he claimed the point for Christ as a "cross-honoring crossroads Christian conference site."[30] His handwritten notes from that day overflow with scriptural doxologies of praise to God and divine promises to those who witness in His name:

> *By the grace of God, I consider this the first session of the French*
> *Camp Bible Conference or Petit Jean Bible Conference! Only the Lord*
> *and I are here. Yet, by His blessing and Providence, thousands will, in*
> *days to come, meet His Son here, hear His Word, and see the Cross....[31]*

The Episcopal Diocese of Arkansas owned the land; some weeks later, upon returning home, Sam wrote Bishop Robert Brown asking about the possibility of buying about eighteen acres at the Point with the help of a group of Presbyterian laypeople and clergy. Sam outlined in detail his plan for an evangelical training institute and conference ground for youth and laypeople "beyond sectarian lines to serve a five-synod area." He confessed that "the vision goes back some years with a history of much thought and prayer, and now I am convicted that overt steps must be taken."[32]

Yet, the Lord closed that door because the diocese had plans for the property and refused to sell.[33] The disappointment did not deter Sam in the least; in fact, he informed the bishop that he was thankful for the apparent difficulty in securing the land:

> *... If our project is not of God's leading, it will certainly not go*
> *through. Only if it is God's leading would or could it be blessed with*
> *success.... While I do have strong personal convictions in this matter*
> *... God does not favor Presbyterians with guidance withheld from His*
> *Episcopal servants. If He is leading, He will lead ALL parties in this*
> *matter to His will.[34]*

Thus, Sam willingly bowed to God's leading and began to move in another direction. Recalling the efforts to get a new conservative seminary going in the 1940s, he asked Aiken Taylor in April 1963, if any current moves in that direction were afoot. Sam now wanted to see a seminary that upheld scripture as an alternative for Presbyterian ministerial students. Notice below the letter's cryptic final line in which Sam again sanctions breaking away from the PCUS if necessary; obviously, however, he never felt that breaking point was reached in his lifetime:

> ... It appears that we can give up the idea of one of our seminaries turning back into a strong, evangelical, conservative position. The liberalizing will continue.
>
> Is there any thought regarding the establishment of another thoroughly Presbyterian seminary within the confines of the Southern Church that would be representative of orthodox Presbyterianism and conservative Christian faith?
>
> It would seem to me that (1) Fair play ... would recognize the right for at least one out of five or six seminaries to represent the faith and convictions of a small majority or a large minority, (2) Probably ONLY a seminary could really be effective in feeding virile faith into the church, and (3) This would be an issue worthy of conflict and even division, if such must come.[35]

Taylor replied quickly that "plans were in the formative stage for an evangelical college and possibly a seminary to be answerable to supporters of the *Presbyterian Journal*," but nothing concrete was currently in effect.[36]

Significant to remember here is that Sam's seminal ideas about moving the PCUS to more conservative views on the Bible, doctrine, and evangelism were always aimed at building up the church, not destroying it. Even when he spoke of division, he viewed it as a last resort, to be avoided if at all possible.

Meanwhile, an April 1963 letter to Erskine Jackson, pastor of First Presbyterian Church in Kosciusko, Mississippi, shows the seed of RTS had already been planted in Sam's heart, with French Camp as a possible greenhouse. In considering ways to avoid sure denominational opposition to the new venture, he thought the conservative Congregationalists in the 19th century had a good plan:

> A new seminary charter could not be secured because of liberal strength, so the Congregationalists developed Andover Academy (already chartered) into a seminary through its Bible department and for a hundred years ran a strong, orthodox seminary that served all evangelical denominations.
>
> I don't think a new seminary could be chartered under the Southern Church, but perhaps could be developed out of a chartered, church-related institution.

> *French Camp could be strategic. Independent of the court of*
> *the church but related officially as an independent subsidiary of the*
> *Academy, a Reformed conference and institute (possibly a seminary*
> *later) could be developed.*
>
> *... I'm dead serious in my conviction that God is ready for those*
> *of us who are fundamental to DO SOMETHING, AND SOMETHING*
> *AGGRESSIVE AND CONSTRUCTIVE. Spoutin' Sam*[37]

Until now, Sam had shared his concerns and ideas with only a trusted handful of people. Yet, in April 1963, he felt the time had arrived to gauge the feelings of fellow ministers about his ideas; therefore, he quietly began communicating his budding thoughts. On April 11, 1963, Sam sent personal letters to several carefully chosen PCUS ministers in Mississippi, proposing that the time was ripe for a seminary that presented the views of conservative Presbyterians regarding scripture, evangelism, and the Westminster Standards. Along with his own views, he included the seminary presidents' responses to his letter and a small treatise entitled "Inside Liberalism," chronicling Andover Seminary's unique history.[38]

Apparently the letter to John Reed Miller was the first one sent, since Sam later labeled it, "Initial letter that began seminary project rolling." In it, for the first time, he began to share how important this cause was to him:

> *The issue worthy of real contest and possible division should be*
> *that of the founding of a Presbyterian seminary ... in the Southern*
> *Church representative of the small majority or large minority of true*
> *conservatives and committed to orthodox ... evangelical truth, including*
> *... an infallible Bible....*[39]

Many years later, Sam reflected:

> *In a sense, RTS started underground in 1962 in a small shed behind*
> *my house on a country road called the Devil's Backbone near French*
> *Camp. For a number of months, in that small, no-name place off the*
> *Natchez Trace, a little mimeograph machine ground material out that*
> *was mailed hither and yon.*[40]

Indeed, Sam began a session with the typewriter and mimeograph that lasted two and a half years. In the process of researching this book, a copy machine was busy for two hours duplicating the correspondence and position papers generated during that period.

Sam had thrown down the gauntlet. It had come to a down and out fight, and Sam Patterson would be just the man to lead it. That redheaded, little scrapper on the playground would now be fighting not for marbles, but for the purity of His Savior's church. Nothing less than every ounce of strength would do. This time the fight would be different. This time a bold, yet lovable, warrior with incredible faith in God would lead the movement. According to Kenneth Gentry, it was a turning point:

> *The long struggle between conservative and liberal forces in the PCUS was now cast before the public in such a way that a more broadly based sentiment could be appealed to for help in establishing the long hoped-for seminary. With Patterson's entrance into the on-again, off-again effort, the forces desiring a conservative seminary began to be more organized and sustained.*[41]

Luder Whitlock, former RTS president, is among the many who agree with Gentry. "If there is any single human reason RTS is in existence, it is Sam Patterson. I don't know of anyone else who could have made it happen. Problems had been brewing for a long time, but the one missing ingredient was a person to step forward as a leader and spur the troops to decisive action. Sam stepped out very courageously and led an effort to make something happen."

GOING PUBLIC WITH THE VISION

The initial response to Sam's ideas from selected colleagues was extremely favorable, so he switched into high gear, inviting conservative Mississippi ministers who shared his concerns to French Camp for prayer sessions about a new seminary. Jack Scott remembers those sessions vividly, as men began to ask the Lord to change the church and to show them what to do in light of liberalism's devastating attack.

"That's really how I came to know Sam," said Scott. "At first our agenda was just prayer. Sam would say, 'I think it's time for another hour of fasting and prayer.' That amused me—an hour isn't very long to fast! We met about nine or ten in the morning, prayed until noon, then ate lunch and came home. This went on for at least a year; then it became more serious, as it was evident that matters were not getting better, but worse."

Sam and Leonard Van Horn, executive vice-president of FCA and professor of Bible, had already been praying about the issue for some time. "Sam and I had an overwhelming burden to provide solid Bible education for both ministerial students and laypeople," said Van Horn. "The subject came up in our discussions over and over."[42]

Finally ready to formalize the vision, Sam felt he had found four other ministers who would commit to working for a new seminary. He called a meeting of the group on Thursday, June 13, 1963, at the annual Mississippi Synod meeting in Memphis.[43] The meeting was highly confidential and the group purposely small. The ministers attending, besides Sam, were: William J. Stanway, pastor of First Presbyterian Church in Hattiesburg, MS; Erskine L. Jackson, pastor of First Presbyterian Church in Kosciusko, MS; John Reed Miller, pastor of

First Presbyterian Church in Jackson, MS; and James Spencer, pastor of First Presbyterian Church in Crystal Springs, MS.[44] Sam wrote:

> *A group of five ministers met in the dining hall of Southwestern College for a prayer breakfast to discuss and pray for the need of a new seminary committed to the inerrancy of scripture. We asked that God would lead so that we would not mis-step. We didn't want to make trouble for the church; we wanted to make a contribution.*[45]

Even before the prayer breakfast, Sam had already asked John Reed Miller to engage a hotel room in Jackson for the first week in July 1963, so that the group could meet again for prayer and discussion.[46] He also asked Leonard Van Horn to join the group. By mid-June, Sam had set up a July 5 meeting with Horace Hull, who had helped so much financially with French Camp Academy and had become Sam's dear friend.[47] Albert Freundt noted, "In June 1963, Dr. Miller told me that he and Sam Patterson were going to approach Horace Hull for financial support to open a new seminary, and he encouraged me to stay in Mississippi and teach in it."[48]

Like a general planning an intricate battle, Sam orchestrated the group's next meeting carefully, telling Miller in a June 17 letter that he didn't want it to be a "general bull session going around in circles."[49] He assigned topics to each man attending:

John Reed Miller—history of the theological conflict from Scotland to the present

Erskine Jackson—the basic issues being faced in the PCUS

James Spencer—measures that could perpetuate the orthodox Presbyterian faith

William Stanway—lessons to be learned from the Westminster experience

Sam Patterson—possible alternatives for peace in the church without sacrificing the purity of the faith[50]

The group had a productive meeting July 2, 1963, at the Robert E. Lee Hotel in Jackson, solidifying in the men's minds the need for some sort of conservative teaching vehicle, preferably an institute and eventually a seminary. It would provide a "worthy rallying point for conservatives" and challenge "the moderates to show their intolerance by raising opposition."[51] For the first time, a principle was voiced that Sam would repeat again and again in the coming tumultuous decade: "The liberals have not won the day. The moderates gave the church to the liberals."[52]

The group decided that a new seminary would have to be "quietly planned and suddenly presented, small and humble in origin." It must be dedicated to the verbal plenary inspiration of scripture and to the provision of ministers to tiny churches who could not get or keep a pastor.[53]

In a letter to Erskine Jackson on July 4, 1963, Sam praised the meeting and admitted that he had been slow to see the real danger of liberalism:

> *Perhaps [our meeting] will prove to be …a fuse.… Whether or not it is too late for remedy, only action and the test that action will bring, will tell. We all agree that moderation seems to always moderate in favor of the liberal dilution. I was so slow to really become convinced!* [54]

And to John Reed Miller he expressed slight incredulity:

> *It seems too good to be true on the one hand, and rather inducive to inordinate pride on the other, to believe that our Lord would honor us in this day, in this Church, to permit us to be a part of the vanguard to raise the banner anew and ring the changes on the easy progress of the liberals.* [55]

However, finally, in a letter that same day to William Stanway, Sam bared his heart. Lest you think Sam never faltered or had to struggle with his faith, listen:

> *The morning after our meeting, I must confess I roused up with this troubled thought: 'Why can't I just get back on the French Camp job and stay out of all this confusion and the conflict a continued effort will bring?' Then, in Psalm 69:7 during quiet time, God gave me His dose of curative medicine for the weak-knee ailment: 'Because for Thy sake I have borne reproach; dishonor has covered my face' [NASV]. I see more honor in that verse than all the approval and applause of churchmen.* [56]

One of the most important outcomes of that July 1963 meeting was the appointment of two committees—one to consider a plan for establishing a seminary and another, consisting of Sam and Van Horn, to investigate starting a theological institute, upgrading it to a seminary if they found adequate support from laypeople.[57]

"I don't know what happened to the other committee," said Sam, "but Leonard and I went to work immediately contacting laypeople." [58] They began with French Camp Academy personnel, then branched out to conservative elders, deacons, and laypeople in Mississippi and surrounding states. The huge positive response confirmed what they already had suspected: a drastic need existed for at least a layman's Bible institute to teach Bible and theology. Increasingly, Sam became convinced that the Andover approach would work. With such firm support, he and Van Horn simply took the ball and ran with it as God led. They spent the remainder of 1963 planning a school that would emphasize a doctrinal approach to the Bible based on the original Westminster Standards and would impart a knowledge of the Bible for use in witnessing to others.

Many years later Sam marveled at God's orchestration of events:

We never expected what happened at this point. The committee of ministers never had to meet again. Van and I began to consider that establishing an institute seemed an extremely wise and practical course of action, since we had French Camp Academy. The Lord led us to call on several Presbyterian ruling elders to gain their assistance. As we presented the project to each, it was as if God had prepared them for the moment. Each enthusiastically approved and joined the enterprise, becoming the founding board of directors.[59]

One of the first laymen Sam approached was a young Jackson attorney named Erskine Wells. The meeting has become legendary in the annals of RTS history. For years, Erskine had donated his time for French Camp Academy's legal business and had grown to love Sam. The moment he had met Sam years before he had been impressed with his spirituality. "When he rose before synod and begged them not to close French Camp, I knew he was an unusual man," said Erskine. "I felt compelled to help him."

Over forty years later, Erskine's eyes filled with tears as he recalled clearly that day when Sam stepped into his office and issued him the challenge of his young life. When Sam showed up that day, Erskine fully expected him to have some problem at FCA, but he was wrong. The two loved to jest, but that day Sam was not in a playful mood. He sat down and immediately became quite serious, telling Erskine that he had written all four PCUS seminary presidents and asked each his view of scripture. Not one of them thought the Bible was the infallible, inspired Word of God. They said that the Bible contained the Word of God, but it was not inerrant.

Sam let that sink in, then looked Erskine straight in the eye and said, "We need to start a new seminary, Erskine, and I want you to help me do it!"

Erskine recalled bursting into laughter and replying incredulously, "Sam, that's ridiculous! I've been glad to help you with French Camp, but, man, we can't start a seminary! We have no land, no buildings, no money, no library, no faculty, and no students. Sam, you're a great man of God, but you're a preacher. You live in an ivory tower, but I've got my feet on the ground and know the realities of life. It's completely out of the question. You'll just have to take my word for it."

His voice broke with emotion as memories flooded back, and he remembered how his life changed forever with Sam's next words. "I expected Sam to be taken aback, but he didn't back down or smile sheepishly. He held my eyes in a riveting gaze and shot back, 'Erskine, how big is your God?'"

The challenge took Erskine's breath away. Was it thirty minutes or thirty seconds before he recovered his senses? "When I finally got my breath back, I said the only thing one can say to a fellow like that: 'When do we start?' And Sam said, 'Now!'"

After Sam left, Erskine stared into space, wondering what in the world he had agreed to. Had he just signed his life away? Any logical person knew that the project was entirely impossible, but what could one do with someone as exasperating as Sam Patterson? There was no arguing with the man!

Erskine was glad he had agreed to Sam's crazy scheme only upon the condition that Sam recruit fellow attorney Robert Cannada and Jackson businessman Robert Kennington for the venture. He wasn't going into this alone! He and Cannada had been friends since Ole Miss law school; in fact, they were distant cousins. Robert Kennington was a successful retired businessman and an elder at First Presbyterian Church of Jackson.

True to his promise, Sam visited Cannada next. Robert recollected clearly the day Sam called for an appointment almost half a century ago. "It had been snowing heavily that day and the roads were dangerous, and I suggested we wait. Yet, Sam insisted on coming immediately from French Camp, so I decided to meet with him. I agreed wholeheartedly that we needed an institution teaching the inerrancy of scripture from a Reformed perspective. I told him I didn't know anything about starting a seminary, but I was open to it. I don't even know if I thought as far as to know if it was doable."

Cannada immediately called friend and fellow lawyer Frank Horton, who enthusiastically said yes. Erskine called friend Frank Tindall, who also agreed to be on the board.

Erskine knows without a doubt that Sam was crucial to RTS's beginning. "All the credit for the progress of RTS belongs to God, but those of us who were involved at the very beginning know that God greatly used Sam Patterson as the catalyst to bring about RTS. I don't believe we would have done anything like that, had it not been for his tremendous vision. I was skeptical at first; Robert, Frank, and I were young lawyers just beginning our careers and making only modest incomes. How could we volunteer thousands of hours to start a seminary and still feed our families? Yet, Sam inspired us to be dedicated. He had more faith than anyone I'd ever known, and it was infectious! As we saw the Lord blessing that seminary, all three of us became much more committed Christians because we began to see the power of God and what He could do working through Sam Patterson."

"Those men had to be persuaded," agreed Albert Freundt. "They have often said if they had known everything that was involved in starting a seminary, they might not have taken it on, even at the urging of such a persuasive person as Sam Patterson." [60]

In Sam, Morton Smith sees a fine example of a man with a burden who did something about it. "We all had his burden, but he laid it out to the brethren. He taught me that if a person sees wrong, he has to speak out about it and take a stand. Not that some of us hadn't taken a stand in other situations from time to time beforehand. Yet, none of us who wanted a new seminary was doing anything about it. Sam had the same desire, except that he was willing to share the burden. He believed the other founders were the only ones that could accomplish the task, and he wouldn't let them get up and walk out, saying, 'It's not our responsibility.' He figuratively put his foot in the door and told them they weren't leaving until they had committed themselves!"

Ministers, not laymen, usually founded seminaries. Yet, Sam deliberately chose to involve key laymen from the very beginning. Part of the reason was that he had a heart for building laymen up in the faith and watching God move through them. Sam was, after all, an evangelist at heart. It permeated everything he ever did while on this earth. Sam's emphasis on laymen is why RTS today has such a strong local church focus, providing excellent practical education for its students.

Another reason for involving laymen was purely practical. Dr. Robert Goode's advice had worked well at French Camp Academy; filling the board primarily with businessmen, not ministers, had put FCA right financially. Sam knew that he, and probably most ministers, were ill-quipped in business and legal matters. An ample number of ministerial advisors could keep the board on track doctrinally.

Yet, neither could the laymen do it alone. "The beginning of the seminary took both Patterson and the laymen," says Guy Richardson (RTS '77), president of RTS/Jackson. "Sam could not have put it together himself, but he was the one with the vision and faith. These men highly respected him, and his alarm over the serious state of affairs was what they needed to galvanize them into action."

As Sam and Leonard Van Horn planned and prayed over curriculum and organization through the fall of 1963, Sam continued to gauge support from fellow conservatives. In August 1963, he had finally met Henry Dendy, managing editor of the *Presbyterian Journal*, at *Journal* Day, an annual gathering of conservatives sponsored by the magazine. In a September letter, Sam speaks his mind and asks Dendy's opinion of the crisis:

> *... We might as well give up the ship unless we can have a seminary that stands consistently all across the board for the conservative position and for verbal plenary inspiration of the scriptures.*
>
> *I ... get the idea that a good number of conservatives believe that it will be possible for Columbia Theological Seminary to be slowly taken over for this position. I think this is wishful thinking and whistling in the dark. It just doesn't stack up with past experiences. Once a liberalizing tendency sets forth in any institution ... it seems to be an impossibility to turn it back to a conservative and fundamental position again.*
>
> *Do you really believe there can be any hope in our church apart from an educational institution for Christian leaders both among the laity and for ministers that does not try to mix the various views of the church and stands forthright for a solid fundamental Presbyterianism?* [61]

Sam was disappointed with Dendy's response:

> *I believe much progress is being made at Columbia … and I think you will continue to see some of the results of it this year and next … and in years to come. In the meantime we will be watching very carefully….*[62]

While Dendy and other conservatives were content to wait and see, Sam was ready for action. The PCUS seminaries had promised to teach more conservatively before and hadn't. Sam might have been slow to get on board for a new seminary, but now he was impatient with wasted time, especially since support for a conservative thrust seemed overwhelming. He said as much to John Reed Miller in November:

> *Great Guns! (spiritual, of course)…. If we could and would only discover the spiritual 'weapons of our warfare' and use them in a disciplined offensive, we could effect a revolution in the present set of things. The more conservatives I talk to, the more I find who can already see the dead end of the present conservative leadership in Weaverville [Journal headquarters], and that the status of their effort is more or less a tread-water affair.*
> *The time is going to be ripe, I believe, for our objective, and who knows, maybe we aren't fifteen years behind time. Maybe the stage is just getting set when a conservative thrust can be successful, even though success doesn't itself justify our faithfulness to God's leading in the plans.*[63]

Despite his disagreement in approach with Dendy, Sam considered him a strong ally and valued his wise counsel. Through the coming months, he kept Dendy apprised regularly of the Institute's progress.

Encouraged by the groundswell of support as 1963 drew to a close, Sam and Van Horn decided that God would have them move forward with the formal organization and announcement of the Institute by year's end. Sam told Dendy:

> *Van and I have sensed God's leading in this, and we have certainly been able to secure the support of some outstanding conservative Presbyterian laymen in this general area. At first, this is certainly a small project, but we will be as faithful to it as we can and see where God leads.*[64]

Sam had long ago appealed to the board of French Camp Academy for help in getting the Institute off the ground. While the FCA board, as well as French Camp Presbyterian Church, stood solidly behind him, they were concerned that he was taking on too much and wrecking his health. After all, he was still president of the Academy and had suffered a heart attack two years before. He was also supply pastor to French Camp Presbyterian Church and the small Huntsville Presbyterian Church near French Camp.

In November 1963, the FCA board insisted Sam take two weeks off to rest. While he did so and admitted that a recent "spell" had been a warning to slow down to a saner pace, he refused to cancel evangelistic services in Alexandria, Louisiana, "trusting God to cover me and He did."[65] Nothing but death was going to slow Sam down now.

AN INSTITUTE IS BORN

On December 20, 1963, French Camp became the birthplace of Reformed Biblical Institute, the forerunner of Reformed Theological Seminary.[66] On that date, the Board of Trustees of French Camp Academy formally agreed to allow the Institute to use its facilities and Bible Department personnel. Shortly thereafter, French Camp Presbyterian Church agreed to be the receiving agency for the Institute, and Sam Allen, the church's secretary-treasurer, became the Institute's treasurer.[67]

On Christmas Day 1963, hundreds of flyers went out announcing the birth of Reformed Biblical Institute. Studies included Reformed doctrine, as presented in the Westminster Standards; English Bible; and witnessing. Night classes would begin in January, followed by short-term courses during the summer for high school students who desired undergirding and grounding in Christian doctrine and biblical faith before entering college. Finally, a nine-month course was planned for the fall of 1964 for pre-college high school graduates and other young adults.[68]

"The beginning of the Reformed Biblical Institute will be small in all but faith and possibilities," claimed the announcement. It continued:

> *It comes as a result of God's leading and will survive and serve by His provision and protection. Basic in the founding convictions … is the fact that the Bible is the inerrant, verbally inspired Word of God … We covet your prayers, encouragement, and help.*
> *Leonard Van Horn and Sam Patterson.[69]*

The announcement stopped short of saying that RTI would be independent of synod control. Yet, as if anticipating the ire of the PCUS courts in using a synod-owned school to start an unsanctioned Bible institute, the announcement vowed that the new venture:

> *… will in no wise affect the program and operation of the Academy … and will not be organically related to the Academy, but would, through the Academy Bible Department personnel and library, be a projection of the ministry of this fine old historic Christian school.[70]*

Sam revealed some of his strategy to John Reed Miller on December 26, 1963:

> *This is a sort of 'Andover Academy' approach…. It will serve as a test-run to see what reaction may come from long-term conservatives….*[71]

On January 23, 1964, Van Horn began night classes entitled "A Summary of Christian Doctrine" at French Camp Academy with about fourteen laypeople in attendance. Positive response was immediate, as letters of encouragement and praise began coming in, along with donations.[72] Heartened by such support, Sam knew it was time to gather key supporters to put plans for incorporating the Institute into high gear.

The first unofficial meeting of the RTI planning committee met at Erskine Wells's office on Saturday, January 25, 1964. Present were Sam, Robert Cannada, Erskine Wells, Robert Kennington, Leonard Van Horn, and Horace Hull. The men shared ideas and made plans. Even at this early stage, they agreed not to be divisive or critical of other seminaries or denominations. Rather, they committed themselves to positive action in making the Institute's point of view known.[73]

Sam read his first important position paper to the group, in which he outlined the vision of an optional seminary representing a high view of the Bible and the original Westminster Standards, an emphasis on the evangelistic mission of the church, and a pastoral focus:

> *Our objective, as I see it, is not to initiate a head-on attack upon the liberal leadership and its institutions, but rather to offer to the people of our church an alternative to the present liberal leadership and education. Our objective is offensive in the sense that, by beginning in a small and unassuming way and trusting growing momentum to God, we may present the true case for and of Christianity, the Bible, and our Christian mission on earth.*
>
> *Since our Presbyterian people do not live under the heel of a dictatorship, but actually under the leadership that they have willingly elected to power … our task is to appeal to the people with a new presentation of the true Reformed faith. The people have elected to follow a leadership that has had no real opposition in terms of an aggressive institution…. All opposition has been that of papers such as the Journal and fights or skirmishes on the court floors.*
>
> *Our objective should be to offer to God an educational vehicle for His use in this fight. By developing a conference program of the highest order, drawing into it the finest of Reformed evangelistic personnel, we offer God a vehicle for the drawing of people who are inclined in our favor to a place and program of instruction and inspiration. By developing weekend laymen institutes to deal with Bible study, witnessing, and the Christian mission in the church, we offer to God*

vehicles for activating increasing numbers of laymen. By holding institute sessions for college students and seminary students, we press our way into the very institutions that are hurting the vitality of the true evangelical faith we promote.

If these objectives are faithfully and sacrificially carried through, we may expect:

1. *The church, by God's grace and using little nobodies such as men of our kind, may be swerved on its axis to a revival of true, evangelical, Reformed, mission-minded ministry.*

2. *The slow drawing together of folk of like mind, forming a larger instructed group to either operate as a minority party in the church or, in the expected event of actual dismissal or departure from the church of today, to form the basis of a continuing body of Presbyterian, fundamental believers.*

Should this latter course come true, the continuing group of conservatives would have an institution (institute or seminary), a conference program, or a program of lay-institutes to undergird the new body.[74]

Such an emphasis on peace echoed thoughts Dendy had shared with Sam not long before. Although the two differed in approach, they both had great hearts for the church and a deep desire to purify her without division:

Sam, let us always remember that there are many … who would like to do the right thing, but have not had the proper background or backing … to get them in the right paths. Let us continue to pray for that group which we do not want to lose, but which we want to help reclaim … for the Lord and His cause.[75]

Immediately after the meeting, Sam wrote follow-up letters to the other founders. He told Robert Cannada:

You made a major contribution by pointing out the necessity of operating on bare and true principle without feeling the need to yield to subterfuge or 'making appearances'….

In all the conflict ahead we cannot afford to sacrifice even a little honor. This is Christ's mission, and the Holy Spirit will leak out of any method not stamped with the dignity and purity of His own integrity. God knows we need the Holy Spirit in this!

In our work together in the days ahead, since we are ONLY seeking His good, we will have to trust each other as to intention but never fail to realize that any and all of us are subject to errors of many kinds. Hence, we will have to work together in a way that will permit us to bang heads, take issue, and object, yet never take opposition or personal affront.

> *I don't know whether we are big enough men to measure up to the stress we will have to keep on each other (aside from that of 'the outside' opposition), but we had better be!* [76]

In a letter the same day to Erskine Wells, Sam indicated faith that God would do great things with RTI, if they kept His Spirit about it:

> *I am convinced that the board of trustees that we are trying to incorporate will actually be much more than the control-factor of one institution. I believe, if we are wise, faithful, and Spirit-led, this group will be the nucleus of an effective conservative, general program that will finally secure the support of a large, conservative, Presbyterian segment. God can use that kind of 'army' as He sees fit in the days ahead.*
>
> *One thing is clear to me. We can't afford to be without fire in our hearts in this thing. But the fire must not be that of resentment at the opposition we will get. Some of it will come from the liberal men, some from our conservative friends. We have got to be big enough somehow to keep fired with the zeal of the Lord and keep out a root of bitterness. I hope we will be big enough…. If we fight God's war God's way, He will bless us!* [77]

Finally, in a letter to Robert Kennington Sam observed:

> *I am especially thankful for the gad-fly and cocklebur in you. It will mean protection in our movement. We must trust each other completely as to intent, but never fail to realize the errors of judgment that all of us will be prone to make. Hence, we will have to ride each other in strict fashion for Christ's glory. We don't count for anything in this but as a MEANS. Christ and His truth is the ONLY worthwhile thing about it.* [78]

After the meeting, attorneys Cannada and Wells began work on the charter of incorporation, while Sam, Van Horn, and Kennington started developing a long-range selection plan for board members. [79]

In all the group's deliberations, Sam endeared himself to his colleagues as a strong mentor and spiritual leader, as evidenced by this comment to Sam from Kennington:

> *I was taken by your idea that we should not only be praying about the Institute, but that we should be praying for each other, too … and I am doing so.* [80]

When Sam gave advice, he gave it humbly. Witness this comment to Erskine Wells:

*I'm great on telling the other fellow how to run his business, so give
me the knuckle if I get in your hair!*[81]

SMITH COMES ON BOARD

The committee knew they must immediately begin to acquire a competent
faculty, especially if a seminary was imminent. Again, Sam knew that he was an
evangelist, not a theologian. When he saw the depth of the theological morass
in which the church was mired, he knew he was in over his head. He and the
committee needed a consummate theologian to guide them. Dr. Morton Smith
was an obvious choice for the Institute's first professor. An ordained minister
and a guest lecturer at Westminster Theological Seminary, he had impeccable
theological credentials and a plethora of personal and influential contacts. He
also had been trying for years to build a new seminary from the ground up; surely
he would be sympathetic to this endeavor! On February 5, 1964, the committee
dispatched Van Horn to Philadelphia to talk with Smith.[82]

With faculty consideration underway, Sam began making plans in early
February to teach a six-week Bible course at First Presbyterian Church in Durant,
Mississippi, beginning in late March.[83] The night class had not been advertised
in the December announcement, so it is unclear when Sam or the planning
committee decided to include it. However, in a late February letter Sam labeled
this extension course a "pilot school of Reformed Theological Institute";[84]
therefore, the class could have been yet another effort to gauge interest in a full-
fledged seminary later.

On February 17, 1964, Cannada, Wells, Patterson, and Van Horn met at
Wells's law office. Under Sam's leadership, the group became more organized.
At his suggestion, they kept minutes for the first time, and the men present
(in addition to Kennington, who was absent for unknown reasons) composed
themselves into the Founding Committee of Reformed Theological Institute.
Sam knew that spiritual guidance was essential to the group, so he led them in
selecting Erskine Jackson and William Stanway as the first Ministerial Advisors.
The committee agreed that French Camp would be the founding site, unless God
led them to move it. They personally committed $17,000 to the work ($8,000 for
a library, $5,000 for a faculty member's salary, $1,000 moving expenses for him,
and $3,000 for other expenses).[85]

Interestingly, Sam's notes from that meeting indicate that the committee was
willing to work within the confines of the money God gave them. While faculty
salary and development expense was necessary, he felt the library amount could
be more limited at the beginning.[86] Again, this flexibility contrasts sharply with
earlier seminary startup efforts in which groups felt they needed a huge amount
of money to begin.

As the committee became more committed and organized, the founders realized they were charting a path from which they could not back down. As he had done in the past, Sam turned to the writings of beloved soldier-missionary C. T. Studd to encourage them:

> The committee I work for is convenient; a small committee, a very wealthy committee, a wonderfully generous committee and is always sitting in session—the committee of the Father, Son, and Holy Ghost. [87]

Emboldened, Sam knew that God was with the RTI founders, too. "We faced a scary future and didn't know what the outcome of all this would be, but we figured that we, too, had that Triune Committee, so we went ahead with the mission." [88]

During February and March of 1964, several pivotal concepts were fleshed out as work on the charter progressed. The Institute would be independent of any denominational control and would be wholly owned and governed by a self-perpetuating board consisting of a majority of Presbyterian laymen and a minority of ministers. [89] Sam wanted a "pan-Presbyterian seminary" (a phrase he coined himself), one that was "free to develop and serve as the trustees and faculty are led by the Word." [90] He saw the need for all Presbyterian churches to have a strong, evangelical seminary, not closely connected with any denomination. Bible-believing ministers could then be trained to return to any Presbyterian denomination and reform it from within.

Surely Sam's rationale for RTI's independence was based on his continual fight to free French Camp Academy from synod control. In 1964, FCA was still nearly ten years away from being completely independent. Sam explained the importance of independence to Dr. Cullen Story:

> It is almost impossible for a wholly church-owned-and-controlled institution not to eventually begin to reflect changing positions of the majority and of leadership in the denomination. This means that in such a context it is very difficult for an institution to maintain the position God raised it up to maintain. [91]

Sam also wanted to make sure the new institution upheld the purest form of the Westminster Standards, originally adopted by the PCUS founders, not the watered down version with liberal changes. He approved the new proposed charter written by Robert Cannada with the following suggested changes:

> I believe we need in the record the specific intent of the founders regarding the two factors that really brought the institution into being— first, the verbally inspired Bible, the Word of God written, and second, the Westminster Standards in the form subscribed to at the founding of the PCUS and in the historic interpretation of same. [92]

The firm stand by the board to subscribe to the original Westminster Standards later brought charges of unnecessary strictness, even among conservatives wanting to support the seminary.

Plans seemed to be moving smoothly until the committee hit a snag in persuading Morton Smith to teach. In a confidential letter to Robert Kennington after Van Horn's visit, Smith expressed intense interest in the project but refused to come, saying that he felt the present plan had two strikes against it—location and leadership:

> *I am very much interested in the idea of such a theological institute, especially in light of the possible future of its growing into something larger. Second, I am very impressed with the apparent support that it has among some of the leading conservatives....*
>
> *...But a more cosmopolitan location would be greatly preferable.... The same board could operate an institute in or around Jackson equally well, and with a great many advantages over French Camp.... First Church [Jackson]... could sponsor such an institute.... Students could rent housing in the area.... Three college libraries could supplement the institute's holdings.... The advantage of the ready-made faculty at French Camp is off-set by the availability of ministers in Jackson who could serve as temporary faculty.*
>
> *The second major drawback is the proposed administration of the institute.... Van Horn is very capable as an administrator in many ways, but ... he is not well-liked or respected by a great many of the people whose support would be needed to make such an institution go. I think it would be a serious mistake to name him, or for that matter anyone, as president of such a small organization.... If a president has to be named, I think Sam Patterson's name would add a great deal of prestige to the Institute. It would have a far greater opportunity of service and hope of survival than the present plan....I personally would be more inclined to come work under him than under Van.[93]*

Concerned that they might lose Smith, Sam went to Philadelphia himself in March 1964 to meet with the theologian, stopping along the way to visit Henry Dendy in Weaverville and John R. Richardson in Atlanta to apprise them of the Institute program. He was grateful for their lively support and appreciated their wise counsel.[94] His meeting on March 3 with Smith went well, even though this was their first contact since that chilly meeting back at the Mississippi youth conference.[95]

Now, however, Smith saw Sam much more interested in theology. "He had always cast himself as an evangelist; his messages were not deeply based in Reformed doctrine, nor did he feel they needed to be. He knew theology was necessary, but it was not his emphasis. He had always felt that people needed to hear a simple and straightforward presentation of the Gospel. Yet, with the discovery that all four denominational seminaries were casting off those 'old and outmoded views,' he began to see how important theology is."

Sam told Smith that his theological and educational gifts were desperately needed, since Smith had intimate knowledge of seminary education. The two spoke frankly about Smith's reservations concerning Van Horn, whom Smith and others felt had been behind the administrative problems at Belhaven that had caused Dr. Crowe's plan for a seminary to fail. Sam begged Smith to come back to Mississippi and at least meet the key leaders with whom he would work.

"Sam changed my mind, and I agreed to come take a look," said Morton. "He convinced me that Van Horn was not going to be president and run the seminary, as Van Horn had told me on his visit to Philadelphia."

Smith visited in Mississippi March 20–24, 1964, discussing plans for the Institute and a possible future seminary with laymen Robert Cannada, Robert Kennington, Erskine Wells, Frank Horton, and H. S. "Coot" Williford. According to Smith, all five of the men pledged $1,000 each to pay his salary because they trusted Sam's judgment implicitly.

"Sam was one of only three conservative men in the Synod of Mississippi who were so respected that they could carry anything they wanted to," Smith revealed. "Had he not come up and pled with me to come back to Mississippi and at least meet with those key laymen, I would probably have spent many years at Westminster Seminary. Meeting with those men whom I respected and in whom I had confidence, coupled with the knowledge that Sam would be leading the venture, persuaded me to come."

Sam wrote Morton and Lois Smith after their visit:

> *To my regret, you and I have not had the opportunity to be well-acquainted. I just want to share with you my feeling of tremendous respect for your spirit, attitude, and humility. As to your ability, I have for years had great respect for it. I do pray that God will give us the two of you!* [96]

Smith was happy to return and help the Southern Presbyterian Church. "I was very glad to find a soul-mate in Sam Patterson. I doubt that RTS would have gotten started without him. I was the only one pushing for a seminary at that time, and I had been called away from Jackson."

On March 25, 1964, the Founding Committee issued a call to Smith to serve as faculty member and associate of Van Horn, the administrative officer of the faculty.[97] French Camp Academy also issued Smith a call to serve as part-time chaplain at the school, counseling students and preaching. Smith and his family would live in the French Camp Presbyterian Church manse and have cafeteria dining privileges, both perks that compensated for the low salary.[98] On

March 28, Smith accepted both posts and agreed to start work on June 1, 1964.[99] Sam was overjoyed:

> *I praise God for your leading to come with us. God will make you, I believe, the key to the development of the seminary. I thrill to think of what you will mean to the Kingdom in the years ahead.*[100]

Early plans appear to have called for Smith to teach extension courses on doctrine and apologetics during the summer, but that was optimistic since he had his hands full with administrative duties to open the school. He spent the entire summer traveling, making contacts and building interest in the Institute, interviewing prospective professors, researching seminaries, and setting up various extension courses for the fall.

GOD FOUNDS A SEMINARY

With the addition of Smith, future plans took on much greater structure, detail, and urgency. Smith began pushing almost immediately for the board to move from institute to seminary status quickly, perhaps opening as a seminary as early as September 1965.

Today, Smith is thankful he was firm. "Pivotal to the development of the seminary was the decision to move forward from a simple Bible institute. If we had not pushed ahead, RTS might have remained merely an adult education institute or perhaps a Christian college."

Smith's eagerness and zeal took even Sam by surprise. He wanted a seminary as badly as Smith, but he and the other founders had planned to operate as an institute for several years to gain financial strength and respected stature in PCUS presbyteries before testing the waters for seminary status. They knew they were walking into a veritable hornet's nest of controversy, which gave pause to even one as fearless as Sam. He confided later:

> *I gathered that if we wanted [Smith] to stay we needed to get a seminary started; he had been called to start one and felt we were not serious about it. Frankly, I resented his position at the time, but I knew God was in it because it challenged us to move quickly.*[101]

As the group prayed and deliberated over the matter, Smith prevailed, since the group could see that God was obviously blessing their efforts. Sam cautiously conveyed as much to Dendy in May 1964:

> *We will operate at institute level this coming year, but we do feel God is giving evidence in our ability to take the venture to the seminary level earlier than we first thought. One thing is sure: if we get His blessings, we must stay on His beam.*[102]

Events were moving far faster than Sam had planned. What in the world had he started? Was Smith right? Could such a small group of "nobodies" pull off starting an independent seminary amidst the fierce opposition that was sure to come? Again, Sam revealed years later, he pulled out his ragged copy of *C. T. Studd: Cricketer and Pioneer* to gain courage from the old spiritual warrior for the fight. Some of Studd's words seemed to leap off the page, as if written especially for the founders. Sam made copies of a particularly rousing quotation for the board, titling it "Now Are We Led to Act!" Sam said later that "the words became our marching orders"[103] over the next tumultuous months:

> *Too long have we been waiting for another to begin! The time of waiting is past! The hour of God has struck!... In God's Holy name let us arise and build! The God of heaven, He will fight for us, as we for Him! We will not build on sand, but on the bed-rock of the sayings of Christ, and the gates of Hell shall not prevail against us. Should such men as we fear? Before the whole world, aye, before a lukewarm, sleepy, faithless, namby-pamby Christian world, we will dare to trust our God. We will venture our all for Him. We will live and die for Him, and do it with His joy unspeakable singing aloud in our hearts. We will a thousand times sooner die trusting in our God than live trusting in men. And when we come to this position, the battle is already won, and the end of the glorious campaign in sight.*
>
> *Believing that further delay would be sinful, some of God's nobodies and insignificants, trusting in our Omnipotent God, have decided on certain simple lines, according to the Book of God, to make a definite attempt ... an accomplished fact.*
>
> *Faith laughs at impossibilities and shouts, 'IT SHALL BE DONE!'*[104]

Sam ended the encouraging note with this scripture:

> *Therefore, my beloved brethren, be ye steadfast, unmovable, always abounding in the work of the Lord, forasmuch as ye know that your labor is not in vain in the Lord (1 Cor. 15:58 KJV).*

The decision to speed up the seminary opening put tremendous pressure on Sam. The RTI founders depended on his wisdom and knowledge in planning meetings, but he was also still chief administrator and fund-raiser at FCA, still a busy evangelist with a packed schedule, and still a supply pastor for two churches. While the FCA Board continued to support his involvement in RTI, juggling all those responsibilities was becoming a challenge. Handling both jobs might have been possible if RTI had remained an institute for several years as was planned, but Smith's insistence that they move quickly to upgrade to seminary status brought incessant activity to make it happen. The executive committee met twice a month, and Sam made countless trips to Jackson to attend each meeting and would continue to do so for several years.

Jack Scott feels Sam's presence was crucial during that time. "Sam was very much involved, very hands-on. The board met sometimes two or three times a month, and Sam was always there. He led all the meetings in the beginning and helped us formulate clearer ideas of our goals and how to accomplish them."

"You have to realize that Sam was the only one of us on the board who had ever seen the inside of a seminary," admits Frank Horton, chuckling softly. "We didn't know anything about running a school. It took a lot of faith and courage, and Sam had enough for all of us."

Time and again Sam set before the founders a high goal, worthy of all the loyalty, energy, and commitment they could muster:

> ... [The men on] this board are God-called history makers and shapers. We are, for Christ's sake, for God's sake, for the Gospel's sake dedicated to the mission of establishing in the deep South an institutional testimony for the highest view of scripture and the historic Reformed faith. Our proportions are small in exterior dimensions, but the cause we humbly seek to further and serve is tremendous, as is the Sovereign God we trust.[105]

Now that all were working toward the same goal, Smith, with his impeccable Reformed theological credentials, began to guide the founders in the many crucial decisions entailed in starting a seminary, not the least of which was how the school would be governed. Historically, schools were led either by a strong president or by a strong faculty chairman. The RTS board chose neither of these methods, opting instead for a very unique style of government. Under this system, RTI would have no president, but would be run by an executive committee of laymen acting as chief executive officer. Administration and faculty would all report to this committee, which would make all decisions.

"Our research showed that schools with strong presidents tended, over the years, to drift to that person's point of view," explained Robert Cannada. "We had seen formerly conservative schools become liberal in that way. We also decided that we would renew our professors' contracts yearly. In many cases, we saw that professors with tenure tended to run the seminaries and could teach whatever they wanted without fear of being fired. We didn't want that to happen at RTI."

Sam was in complete agreement with this system of governance. He was a visionary and an evangelist, with absolutely no desire for power; he saw a need, inspired others to catch the vision, and wanted to leave administration to those more gifted in that area. However, doing that at French Camp Academy had been far easier; Sam could leave the running of the school to the able Billy Thompson while he did what he loved best—preach and raise funds. Moreover, even though bankrupt, FCA had been an established school; at least some of the problems there Sam and his staff could anticipate. Yet, starting a new seminary was unknown territory both for him and everyone connected with the new venture. Whether Sam realized it at the seminary's outset or not, his guiding presence would be needed on and off all his years at RTS, a situation that would severely curtail his evangelistic endeavors.

While the Founding Board prayed over and completed the final organizational planning of the seminary, Sam's Monday evening classes on the nature and inspiration of scripture began on March 30, 1964, at First Presbyterian Church in Durant, Mississippi. Entitled "The Scriptures: Sceptre of God," the six-week certificate course (not for credit) cost only $2.50.[106] If you were in that class, Sam saved your registration form for the rest of his life in a folder marked "Durant Institute." Sam labeled his class as a "pilot school" of RTI, with an objective of twelve to twenty teens and adults. He actually ended up with thirty students.[107]

The organizational RTI Board of Trustees—Sam Patterson, Robert Cannada, Frank Horton, Robert Kennington, Frank Tindall, and Erskine Wells—signed the charter for Reformed Theological Institute on April 8, 1964, and the Mississippi Secretary of State's office set its seal upon it on April 13.[108] The charter set down officially the purpose of RTI:

> To establish, control, and develop an institute of theological studies established upon the authority of the Word of God standing written in the sixty-six books of the Holy Bible, all therein being verbally inspired by Almighty God and therefore without error, and committed to the Reformed Faith as set forth in the Westminster Confession of Faith and the Larger and Shorter Catechisms as originally adopted by the Presbyterian Church in the United States.[109]

The low-key, measured steps taken by the board during the Institute's genesis drew both praise from supporters and warnings of the opposition to come, such as this from Robert Strong:

> … There is nothing we need more than an orthodox seminary. And there is no graver problem than how to get one. Our denomination is under such tight control by its courts that an independent seminary would occasion prompt disciplinary action against ministers who would try to start one. And the door would in most places be slammed against students from such an institution who would apply for ordination. The charge would be schism, and I'm afraid it would be made to stick. Great is the pity.
>
> The cautious way in which you men are proceeding is altogether commendable. If you have patience and pursue a long-range plan, you will see how fast and far you can go.[110]

Sam was all too aware of the upheaval to come. In an April 1964 letter to Morton Smith, he was enthusiastic about the Institute's progress and sure of God's favor, but mindful that the founders were heading into stormy seas:

> No doubt difficult days are ahead of us, but every bit of encourage-
> ment that the good Lord permits us to have will be helpful to all of us in
> building up the right kind of fiber to face the certain discouragements
> that we will be running into along the way. Since God is in both the
> origin and the program of the Institute, we can count on victory.[111]

On April 30, 1964, the founders were jubilant as they met for the first time as a board of trustees at the organizational meeting of RTI, held in the Creole Room at the King Edward Hotel in Jackson at four p.m. They elected Sam as chairman of the board, Robert Kennington as vice president and, by unanimous consent, elected Van Horn as secretary-treasurer even though he was not a member of the corporation. Horace Hull and Charles Harmon were original board members, but Mississippi law forbade out-of-state individuals from being incorporators. Therefore, the two were voted onto the board at this meeting. The board also appointed Leonard Van Horn and Morton Smith as faculty members.[112]

In setting forth the Institute's purpose, the founders again reiterated for the record that, "Our endeavor ... is not ... an attack upon any of the church's institutions.... It is not divisive or schismatic ... but we believe our point of view ... has the right to be ... represented institutionally in the church." [113]

Although the balance on hand was only $753.64, the budget adopted on faith at this meeting was $22,700, much higher than in February 1964. Sam was appointed chairman of a committee to research sites for a permanent location.[114]

Location of the Institute continued to be discussed at subsequent board meetings. Morton Smith had made it clear he favored an urban location, while Sam was content to stay in French Camp. Possibly due to Sam's influence, the decision each time was to remain in French Camp until God moved the school elsewhere. Sam began asking others for counsel on the matter, including Henry Dendy:

> We will soon have to make some decision about a permanent location
> ...and will have to pit the advantages of the tranquility of a more remote
> location, such as French Camp, against those of an urban area.[115]

In May 1964, Sam told the French Camp Presbyterian Church Session that "being led by the Holy Spirit, he was sure God wanted the Institute to be located at French Camp...." [116] Providentially, however, events in the very near future would make that desire impossible.

OPPOSITION ARISES

Major opposition had not surfaced yet, since the school had been operating under the radar, so to speak. However, that changed the first week in May 1964, when the board issued the Institute's first press release. They minced no words about the school's purpose, announcing publicly that the Institute was "independent of ecclesiastical control." Sam further declared:

> *This project will work for the return of the day when evangelistic fervor, rooted in the biblical centrality of traditional Reformed theology, will put the strength of that Rock, the fire of the Spirit, and the passion of the Gospel, into the ministry of the Church.[117]*

In another 1964 news release, Sam made it clear the Institute was not looking for denominational support:

> *Believing that this institution has its genesis in God, it will look to Him alone for its support, recognizing that He will give this through His people who share like convictions of conservative, evangelical, Reformed faith. Its future is what HE makes it![118]*

While letters of encouragement continued to flood in, the publicity brought criticism, first from the laity. People primarily feared that RTI was a movement to lead a large group out of the PCUS. Others felt RTI had been formed to provide a segregated school for southern whites, while still others were sure RTI was an effort to foster an alliance with other denominations, such as the Orthodox Presbyterian Church. All of these fears were, of course, unfounded. In addition to his duties at French Camp and his preaching responsibilities, Sam answered each critical letter diplomatically and graciously, trying to explain the school's intentions. By July 1964, criticism was so widespread that the board prevailed upon him to write all PCUS sessions in Mississippi and surrounding states explaining the Institute's purpose and answering these objections.[119] Amidst the opposition, Sam kept his eyes on the Lord:

> *The response to the Institute has been very encouraging.... It goes without saying that opposition is also building up. This we knew would come. Every minister who associates himself with this work will be running risks. But what did we enter the ministry for? We are trying to maintain our testimony in this new school. It is as simple as that.... We can neither afford to permit our way, as God leads, to be blocked, nor can we afford the luxury of security....[120]*

However, he did realize that church courts might take action to prevent PCUS ministers from being involved with the Institute, as evidenced by this letter in June 1964 to Morton Smith:

> We may have some problems in the presbyteries.... Don't much think you and Van will be blocked, but I may be. It is all in God's hands. There is not any area of backing up ... and none desired. We can only trust Him and go forward. Second Chronicles 15–17 and Joshua 1:2–11 have been much on my heart.... At synod, many came to our defense. Praise God for the awakening that is going on.[121]

In light of the opposition, Sam "deemed it wise to be well-prepared for possible trouble" and asked Rev. W. A. Gamble to advise the RTI board of various possible actions that could be taken against the Institute, or against them as ministers and laymen.[122]

Strong objections to the Institute did indeed surface at the June 1964 meeting of synod. Sam could see that the battle lines were now clearly drawn:

> ... beneath the apparent personality conflicts across the church, there are important fundamental doctrinal differences. [One is] the nature of the inspiration and infallibility of scripture, and the other has to do with the nature and mission of the Church.
>
> One minister said to me, 'I don't deny that what you fellows stand for is the position of the Presbyterian Church in 1861, but today we have another church'....
>
> Some of us are afraid that the 'other church' is a far distance from the church of our origin, both in this country and in scripture.[123]

Thankfully, the opposition to RTI was met favorably by a number of Institute supporters, especially Rev. James Moore.[124] Sam was unstinting in his praise of Moore's impassioned speech at the 1964 synod meeting:

> The highlight of the synod meeting was the tremendous presentation you made for the verbal inspiration of scripture.... All in all, I think we came out very well. We had the chance to really present the heart of the difference between the church of today and the church of the Bible and had several hours to clearly set forth the distinctive factors regarding the historic Presbyterian concept of the Bible and mission of the church as against the new and alien 'church.'
>
> Keep your prayers going up for the infant institution. There will be no backing up or giving of ground. The seminary will be started. We are in God's hands, and He never backed up from Satan.[125]

While determined not to back down, Sam also saw clearly the tremendous controversy and ill-feeling such a stand would bring. Thus, he began preaching a Gospel of love and reconciliation that would not end until he drew his last breath in 1987:

> *... These are days when convictions will frequently be in conflict. I personally do not fear the conflict of uncompromising convictions in themselves, but I do fear the danger that we will fail of that love which alone can accept another's position without questioning the motive behind his position.... Only a spirit of love and fair play can cover the stresses of the day.*[126]

He continued the same counsel to Robert Cannada:

> *... In presenting a clear witness at synod, RTI rendered its first real service. We would not have gone into this if we had feared opposition, would we? If 'holding fast that which remains' is pleasing to God, as Revelation says, then while we displease many men, we please Him with whom we have to do.... If we can mix boldness with caution and refuse to compromise our conviction in this, while reacting in a spirit of love toward those who will try to scuttle us, God will give us the victory.*[127]

And to Robert Kennington:

> *Our convictions ... determine our conscience, which determines our course and conduct. There are points here that brook no compromise. What we are bound under Christ to do is to respond ... to our differing brethren in the spirit of LOVE. If we permit a 'root of bitterness' ... to spring up, we leak out the Spirit's power and we will wallow ... in the energy and disposition of the flesh.*[128]

Amazingly, the synod's only official action in 1964 was to request that the FCA Board of Trustees devote the facilities and personnel of synod-controlled French Camp Academy solely to the purposes specified in FCA's charter.[129] Although the outcome could have been much worse for RTI, this decision certainly threw a huge monkey wrench into Sam's "Andover Strategy." The fledgling Institute had to move, but where? Providentially, on June 23, 1964, the Session of First Presbyterian Church in Kosciusko, Mississippi, offered their church until a permanent location could be found, even volunteering to help the board find land for the school around their city.[130]

The synod ultimatum also forced both Van Horn and Sam to choose where they would labor—RTI or FCA? Leonard Van Horn acutely felt synod's intense pressure to be loyal to French Camp Academy. The conflict of interest between his FCA and RTI duties was unbearable, causing him to resign regretfully from the RTI board on July 1. In a letter to the board, he reflected:

> *It seems strange—and hard—to resign from the very Institute that the Lord laid on my heart. But it is not for me to figure out the ways of Him whose ways and thoughts are so much higher than mine. Thank you for your kind interest in this work of God, as you manifested from the beginning of Mr. Patterson's and my contact with you.*[131]

In a letter to RTS professor Albert Freundt nearly half a century later, Van Horn still recalled distinctly the pain of leaving RTI:

> *I hated to resign; it hurt down deep. I simply had to face it before Him, ask for His grace, and do it. I remember spending a night in prayer and tears. It had been a burden on my heart for years to be connected with a seminary that stood on the Word of God.*[132]

Sam, however, decided on a far more creative course of action, asking the FCA Board of Trustees in July if he could remain on the RTI Board but have no administrative or ·fund-raising responsibilities.[133] They granted his request immediately. It is a measure of the love and respect held for Sam Patterson by the board, faculty, and administration of French Camp Academy that they allowed so much of his time in those latter years at FCA to be taken by his new vision of RTI. Yet, such loyalty is not surprising. More than anywhere he had ever served or would ever serve, these faithful Mississippi folk latched on to his heavenly vision and were willing to do whatever it took to help him see it through. After all, just a few years earlier, they had watched him walk and pray with His God through the wreckage of their beloved school, and then seen it rise like a phoenix out of the ashes. They knew what Sam Patterson's God could and would do for His glory!

The synod action did far more, however, than change the school's location and leadership. It actually forced the founders to see what Smith had known all along: they needed a new seminary as quickly as possible. The RTI board meeting in July 1964 was momentous in several ways. Roused to urgent action, the founders decided to step out in sheer faith (with very little money) and open as a seminary in September 1965, only a year away. They accepted First Presbyterian Church of Kosciusko's generous offer of temporary offices and continued to agree the school should be on the Natchez Trace unless God led elsewhere. For the first time, a temporary executive committee was appointed (Sam, Robert Kennington, and Robert Cannada); it became a permanent committee on December 9, 1964.[134]

While the board tried to raise money for a seminary startup, Morton Smith, now registrar after Van Horn's departure, worked feverishly to lay the foundation for the future seminary. In the fall of 1964, crisp brochures outlined a new television Bible study and course offerings for the 1964–65 school year. On September 21, 1964, Smith began a twenty-minute Bible survey course on WLBT television in Jackson Monday through Friday at 6:30 a.m., with the time graciously donated by station manager Fred Beard.[135] The program lasted five years, and Smith believes it put RTI on the map in Mississippi. "People heard it all over the state, particularly in the Delta. Women told me that my program was more significant than *As the World Turns!*"

Also on September 21, Smith began extension courses on Christian doctrine in three southern cities—Jackson, Birmingham, and Kosciusko. After traveling by car over 6,200 miles for the Institute in October and November, Smith decided to take advantage of his World War II pilot training and his love for flying. Buying a small Cessna 150, he logged over 33,000 miles during the next year! The extension courses were quite popular, proving an even more urgent need for a seminary.[136]

Smith was unhappy that travel took up all his time, leaving none for critical foundational work on the future seminary. At the very least, the Institute needed a permanent location. Yet, by December 1964, the board was no closer to finding one, and with only about $1,000 on hand, they didn't have enough money to begin classes by the fall of 1965, their projected opening date. Therefore, a disappointed Smith saw the board postpone calling any professors; instead, they set September 1966 as the earliest target date for the seminary opening.[137]

WALKING BY FAITH

The founders might have been short on money, but they were long on faith, the operative word in those early days. Sam's unwavering conviction of God's goodness to provide carried everyone along. The young businessmen on the board were about to get the financial roller coaster ride of their lives as they lived with Sam on the raw edge of faith, probably for the first time ever. Sam had already operated for six years under God's Endowment Plan (Philippians 4:19) and had seen French Camp miraculously saved from bankruptcy.[138] He took the promises of God seriously, lived by them, and demanded that the RTI board do the same. He was determined not to ask men for money, but would depend on the Lord to provide.

Early *RTI Bulletins* were candid and sincere in their total dependence upon God, not man, for support:

> *This seminary is free to prosper or flounder financially as God moves the hearts of people of like mind. We are so freely, so helplessly dependent upon the mercy, protection and guidance of God alone that it drives us to prayer.[139]*

Under Sam's leadership, the board adopted a very strict financial policy on September 10, 1964:

1. *Complete confidence in the adequacy of Matthew 6:33 to cover the needs of God's work and workers. 'But seek ye first the kingdom of God and his righteousness, and all these things shall be added unto you.'*

2. *In the securing of funds for RTI, we observe and confine ourselves to the following as both the scriptural way of promotion and as the only truly God-honoring way:*

   a. *Faith and prayer will be our primary and constant approach to the supplying of our needs.*

   b. *We will witness only to the nature of our work, the nature of our needs, and ways support may be given for those.*

   c. *We will ask no man to give anything; but on the basis of the above, ask all to consider investing on the basis of the merit and the ministry of this work as God may lead them.*

3. *All individual and personal contacts for the school and all official and corporate effort for funds are to be kept in line with the above principles.* [140]

To this day, RTS still operates on these financial policies. The school takes no federal money and has never gone into debt to build or operate, even with a substantially higher current budget. The board continues to rely solely on the Lord for survival and expansion.

"I remember one time Sam and Mr. Kennington took on the whole world and said we should never ask for money," recalled the late George Gulley, later the seminary's executive secretary. "We were finally allowed to say, 'If you providentially feel led of the Lord, we would appreciate your consideration of a need we have at the seminary.' That passed muster with Sam. It didn't make all that much difference to me, but he was determined that no inch be given to the notion that man had anything to do with our blessings!"

Under Sam's influence, the early *RTI Bulletins* not only outlined the school's purpose and its utter dependency upon God, but also gave a warm invitation to readers to become a part of what God was doing. Sam obviously trusted that God would move a sufficient number to bring about His will:

So join with us as we work it out together with fear and trembling, vigor, sacrifice and joy with determination, secure in the knowledge that if we stand faithful to our calling, the Almighty One will supply our needs and send blessings until He Himself comes. [141]

"Sam and Robert Kennington had so much faith," remarks Frank Horton, with tears in his eyes remembering his own weak faith. "They insisted that the seminary not go into debt. If we needed a building, we had to have the funds on hand or in view before we started. As we talked with the many churches about the seminary in those early days, we could ask no one to do anything but pray to see if the Lord would have them be a part of it. And the Lord took care of it all. What a marvelous experience!"

"In those early days we were sustained by God, as Elijah was by the widow who gave up her bread," said Jack Scott. "Over fifty percent of the money came from donations of $25 or $50 a month. Most of the contributing churches were small to medium-sized congregations where Sam had preached."

Sam instituted the memorial gift system that had been so successful at French Camp, allowing supporters to donate in memory of the deceased or in honor of the living. The *RTI Bulletin* listed all names in each issue. George Gulley declared that as many as eighty checks a day for five or ten dollars each crossed his desk. "Most were from widows giving out of their small pensions. They were poor, but they knew and loved Sam. Most of them really didn't know why we needed a new seminary, but Sam said we did, and that was good enough for them! God took all those little bits and blessed them mightily."

However, a little later, the seminary did begin to receive large contributions, and Sam had to teach the board how to deal with God's bounty. "Either the second or third year, we received a donation of $25,000," recalled Frank Horton. "As businessmen who thought we knew 'the facts of life,' we felt we should put it aside and have an emergency fund. Yet, Sam said, 'The Lord brought it, and we need to use it! The Lord will bring more!'"

That large contribution likely came from David Dean, a Texas oilman who eventually gave millions to the seminary. Sam flew out to Houston specifically to thank Dean for the contribution. The businessman was stunned.

"Sam told me they didn't get many checks like that," said Dean, "and wanted me to know how much they appreciated it. I couldn't believe it. No one had ever made a special trip to thank me for anything. While he was here I suggested, 'Why don't we make it $100,000?'"

Frank Horton's eyes brim with tears at the thought of God's love and mercy. He is humbled to realize that God allowed him to be part of truly momentous events in the twentieth century. "Sam's faith was so contagious! He knew what God could do, even when we didn't. Back then, we were certainly not thinking in terms of multiple campuses. We were merely thinking of finding a small place to have classes, getting professors and students, and putting men in pulpits. How kind of God to bless our fumbling faith so greatly, when we would have settled for so much less!"

Sam would not take any credit for an abundance of faith, confessing that he was as weak spiritually as the rest:

> *God has honored this venture of faith—not as much as people give us credit for having. It was mostly grace. Every one of those original founding board and faculty members know that we never really believed for what we have today. We believed God would bless us and keep the little institution alive, but we never believed it could grow to this size. We praise God for His grace![142]*

With a seminary to build quickly, January 1965 found Smith continuing to search for faculty as he traveled to Grand Rapids, Michigan, to make contact with a number of men in the Christian Reformed Church. All were interested in the work of RTI, beginning a long and fruitful relationship with men of the CRC. Later, they would become some of the seminary's finest professors.

The issue of permanent location finally came to a head, and, after long months of research, Sam had to admit that an urban area was probably best. Location was critical, not only to the seminary's image and growth, but to its potential ministry to the church. After examination of several sites, including Memphis, the board concluded that Central Mississippi was the only presbytery in the PCUS that would agree to its members the privilege of teaching at an independent institution such as RTI. Since Jackson was the largest city in the presbytery, the board decided in February 1965 that RTI should be within a twenty-five mile radius of Jackson.[143]

H. S. "Coot" Williford of Jackson proved to be God's man of the hour when, in March 1965, he offered to volunteer without pay as part-time business administrator for RTI and share his offices in the Standard Life Building at no cost until the board could buy property in Jackson.[144] In later years, Sam named Coot as one of the greatest men he'd ever known. "He had remarkable integrity," said Sam. "To my knowledge, he never once said or did anything cheap or shabby."[145]

Albert Freundt, who would become one of Sam's closest friends, and James DeYoung were added to the faculty in June 1965, and Jack Scott was appointed in July. Says Scott, "To generate interest in RTI, they gave me a desk, a typewriter, and a secretary in Williford's office complex to write letters to laymen and churches." When the seminary opened in 1966, Scott added the posts of registrar and Old Testament professor to his already full day.

In June 1965, the board took a gigantic leap of faith and voted to change the school's name from an institute to a seminary.[146] Reformed Theological Seminary had officially been born; yet, as the saying goes, "Talk is cheap." The founders knew that God, and God alone, would have to keep the tiny school alive.

The search for a permanent location ended on August 30, 1965, when the board purchased the Howard Byrd property on Clinton Boulevard in West

Jackson at a cost of $75,000. It consisted of fourteen and a half acres of farmland, on which sat a lovely colonial two-story house (later dubbed the White House) and a dilapidated barn. Cows grazed on the gently rolling pastureland.[147]

Sam's old friend and RTS board member Horace Hull continued his gracious generosity by working out an ingenious arrangement in which RTS would eventually pay only pennies on the dollar for the site. Hull donated $25,000 to RTS and loaned the remaining $50,000, with the seminary paying only the interest on the loan until his death. Hull then put the seminary in his will; if, at the time of his death, RTS remained faithful to the inerrancy of scripture, the $50,000 would be forgiven.[148] On November 2, 1966, a little over a year later, this godly man died—just two months after RTS opened.

While at French Camp Academy, Sam had often called attention to God's bountiful blessings to the school and had vowed that FCA spent more time saying thank you than any institution he knew. It was no different at RTS. In his 1965 annual report as chairman of the board, Sam thanked God for a board of "uncommon dedication," for faculty who "are willing to risk their professional standing and future in coming to launch the seminary," and for the generosity of Horace Hull and H. S. Williford.[149]

However, in that same report he raised a cry of alarm over the seeming reluctance of the board to appoint ministerial advisors. He wanted them at once to initiate a committee of ministerial advisors to serve as counselors to the board and to carry RTS's cause in ecclesiastical battle. This would be the first of Sam's many attempts to be the watchdog of faculty interests before the board:

> Brethren, we cannot overestimate the risk being taken by the minis-
> ters on our faculty. They have put their ministries in jeopardy for life due
> to their participation in this endeavor. We owe it to them to at once draw
> to the seminary the open identification and support of selected ministers
> who will stand by our faculty … in the trials ahead.[150]

The board immediately complied, and a few months later, the Summer 1966 *RTS Bulletin* listed fifteen ministerial advisors.

The end of 1965 brought more signs that Sam needed to decide soon which school he would lead, French Camp Academy or RTS. Accelerated plans for a seminary meant more trips to Jackson, taking him away from French Camp and family. Moreover, his health simply couldn't take the strain of the schedule he had been keeping. He apologized to the RTS board at its November 1965 meeting because his report had to be read in his absence:

> A few days ago I was commissioned to a brief visit to the hospital
> and now am under house arrest at home for two weeks. I am in no real
> trouble and this falls in the category of 'prevention.'[151]

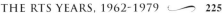

Although he had not intended to become a fund-raiser for both schools, wearing two hats had become unavoidable. Now, he was increasingly haunted by the fact that he was hurting FCA:

> *I faced a dilemma…. It was not a division of interest because I had 100 percent interest in both, but it seemed unfair to the Academy to have me now involved in raising funds for two institutions.*[152]

In the midst of deciding whether to relinquish the presidency of French Camp, Sam faced a plethora of other decisions in the early months of 1966. In his February chairman's report to the board, he detailed the challenges and obstacles before the RTS board as they worked to renovate the White House, to ready classrooms and professors' offices for school, to build and furnish a library, to find funds to operate and pay the salaries of the original five faculty members, to procure students, and to pray about placement in ministry for future graduates, all while facing strong opposition from the PCUS. Yet, characteristically, Sam told the board resolutely, "I don't know many things about the future, but I do know two things we can be sure of as we face the great opportunities before us: God is able and we are willing." [153]

GOD GIVES INCREASE

In the spring of 1966, Freundt and Smith developed the RTS catalog for the coming year, even though the school still had not one single student. By June 1966, the seminary had five full-time professors: Dr. Morton Smith, Rev. Albert Freundt, Dr. James C. DeYoung, Dr. Jack Scott, and Rev. Richard A. Bodey—and still no students.[154]

Sam later praised the original faculty for their courage:

> *In a way, the faculty ran the greatest risk. They were courageous, though no one thought about that. When we first started, a motion was made in the Synod of Mississippi (PCUS) to bring censure or some sort of punishment upon the ministers involved in it, but it was soundly defeated by the synod.*[155]

"Anyone associated with the seminary was under suspicion all the time," said Jack Scott. "All of the faculty knew that affiliating with the school meant returning to the PCUS would be difficult if the venture failed. Coming on board was an extraordinary step of faith, especially for the ordained ministers, because the church courts could put us on trial. Even though the seminary was in a conservative presbytery, we still had much opposition."

Yet, ostracism and career suicide were not the only matters for those first professors to consider. They also might not get paid. "Sam and the board told those first five men that the seminary had enough money in the bank to pay them a salary for one year," says RTS Professor Simon Kistemaker. "If the venture failed, they had burned their bridges and could not return. They all were willing to take the challenge."

Meanwhile, opposition to RTS continued to simmer on several fronts. Many people still failed to understand the need for a conservative seminary, and Sam took great pains to help them see the spiritual landscape with fresh eyes and to realize the critical need for church purification:

> If the new views of scripture and the mission of the church were producing a high rate of souls saved and a great revival of Christ-like living and great compassion for the spiritual welfare of others, we would be forced to recall that our Lord said, 'By their fruits shall you know them.' However, the record of professions of faith and the low ebb of real revival in our church, plus the decrease of men feeling called to the ministry, and the lessening of missionary interest all give evidence that the fruit of this new thought and current tendency is unproductive of the very things our faith calls us to.[156]

Some conservatives opposed RTS's insistence on abiding by the original Westminster Confession instead of the more modern, modified one. In a September 1965 letter to Erskine Wells, new board member Colonel Roy LeCraw asked if the RTS board would be willing to back off that strict stand (they were not) to gain more support:

> ... Conservatives feel they are obligated to support the current Confession. When you condemn it, you are condemning the very basis of the PCUS's current beliefs.
> Is there a way to temper our doctrinal stands sufficiently to enable many conservatives to support our seminary without being in the position of rejecting the church's Westminster Confession of Faith?[157]

Others, especially missionaries, were afraid that RTS's location in the Mississippi Synod would make it difficult for blacks to enter. Sam made it clear that discrimination was not the school's intention in the least:

> We take due notice of where we are. The only safe refuge we have for our ministers now is Central Mississippi Presbytery. We thank God for providing at least one presbytery where our faculty members can serve as Southern Presbyterians in an independent seminary. We do not intend to hang this work on a racial problem or any problem less important than the theological purpose which alone brought us into being. I believe those concerned about this will have less reason to be so as they watch the seminary move into its operation.[158]

The perception of RTS as a troublemaker was furthered when, in 1966, the Synod of Mississippi began an investigation into the teaching practices of Columbia Theological Seminary. Angry members of the PCUS thought RTS had instigated it. Sam was quick to deny any association with "this attack," calling it "a bad thing." He and two other RTS faculty were appointed to the investigation committee, and, alarmed, they immediately resigned.[159]

While disagreeing thoroughly with the synod's decision to investigate Columbia, Sam defended the Synod of Mississippi to seminary friends, feeling the synod was unfairly under the indictment of both the conservative and liberal groups:

> ...We don't want you to think we are radicals....First, not one church in the synod has made any effort to pull out of our beloved Southern Presbyterian Church. The spirit of the rebel is certainly in our state, but still these Mississippi conservatives, while perhaps more sensitive than other synods to the alarming state of affairs in the PCUS, are good church-loving people. Second, where else could a new seminary have started with its minister-faculty members protected from presbytery-level interference? With all its shortcomings, God has enabled this synod to give refuge to this institution He has raised up.[160]

Sam was grateful that seminary supporters understood RTS's position. Henry Dendy's response to the letter above is a good example:

> Your explanation about the synod of Mississippi is thoroughly satisfactory to me.... I am sorry they are making an investigation at this time because no matter how hard you try to allay fears along this line, someone is going to accuse the RTS group of being the instigators of this.
>
> I have always believed you when you said you were not attacking Columbia or any other seminary but were going out on your own on this.... I believe this work is of the Lord and that the Lord is going to bless it. You can count on my full support.[161]

The summer of 1966 was filled with hard work, excitement, and apprehension. In a 1972 paper chronicling the seminary's beginnings, Albert Freundt described the tense atmosphere as faculty and staff faced the unknown:

> We were on our knees in those days about many things. We wondered if we would receive financial support and how rapidly. We wondered if any students would come. We wondered if we would find faculty with courage to come. We wondered if students would be accepted in any presbyteries.[162]

As the board and faculty met and prayed, Sam wove four scriptures into the fabric of their discussions from which they derived great strength:

Genesis 1:1: "In the beginning God…" reminded them that all of history had its beginning in God, and God was the genesis of the seminary.

Isaiah 59:19b: "When the enemy shall come in like a flood, the Spirit of the Lord shall lift up a standard against him" reminded them that God was fighting for them.

Zechariah 4:6: "…'not by might nor by power, but by My Spirit,' says the LORD of hosts…" reminded them that God in His Spirit was their sufficiency.

Zechariah 4:10: "For who has despised the day of small things?" reminded them that God can use little men, since neither founders nor faculty were well-known. [163]

The faculty and board stayed on their knees all summer praying for students, and, through the grace of God, by the opening convocation on September 6, fifteen students were enrolled. During the course of that year God brought two more students.[164]

"I began at Westminster Seminary in 1965, and that year Morton Smith began calling me about Sam Patterson's vision for the seminary and encouraging me to come back south," relates Laurie Jones (RTS '69). "I had heard Sam preach many times at Belhaven and enjoyed his messages immensely. Therefore, I came back to be in the first class."

All the students took a significant risk. "I told prospective students that we may not be in existence three years from now," said Robert Cannada, "and even if they did graduate they could not be assured of a church in which to preach. We begged them not to come unless they felt the Lord calling them. We were operating on sheer faith with no funds and a great deal of denominational hostility. They had to come on faith."

Appropriately, the message of the first convocation in 1966 was missions-oriented, likely due to Sam's evangelistic influence. Dr. C. Darby Fulton, former executive secretary of the PCUS Board of World Missions, spoke on "The Relevancy of the Gospel." As time went on, Sam was pleased to see that a high percentage of RTS students went directly into the pastorate or missions; they carried with them, in Sam's words, "a responsible evangelism related to the doctrinal strength of the Reformed faith." [165]

A permanent facility now meant that Sam could spend several nights in Jackson before returning to French Camp. He carved out a small space for an office downstairs, with a couch that could double as a bed. Morton Smith's bedroom upstairs also served double duty as his office. Jack Scott remained at the Standard Life Building. Laurie Jones recollects he and other students pulled their mattresses out of the closet at bedtime.

The White House initially was the only campus building; students and faculty both lived and worked within its confines. Classes met in downstairs rooms, while daily chapel services, generally led by Sam, were held in its largest room. Sam wanted to instill in students as soon as possible the vision for church revival that beat in the hearts of the faculty and board. The side porch had been enclosed and served as a temporary library.[166]

When the White House was no longer adequate, a gift of four more acres adjoining the seminary made expansion possible. It contained an old home in poor shape, dubbed Tyrannus Hall (from Acts 19) by Academic Dean James DeYoung. Scott comments, "Many of the floors were giving way, and the walls were not certain.... Rainy or windy days were harrowing experiences. We had a running battle with mice, termites, cockroaches, and an occasional rat."[167] The structure was torn down in 1968 to make way for Grace Chapel.

Accommodations might have been cramped, but the Holy Spirit had obviously taken up residence in this small outpost of God's Kingdom. Students recall Smith frantically writing notes for that day's lectures, ripping them out of the typewriter and minutes later delivering them in class. Theology hot off the press!

"None of us had any experience starting a seminary," said Smith, laughing, "and our daily faculty meetings started at the end of class around four in the afternoon and lasted until ten or eleven o'clock at night for the entire first year. Imagine the myriad of decisions that had to be made in starting a seminary; new problems cropped up every day!"

The faculty and board worked closely those first two years. The executive committee met twice a month, and the faculty were invited to the board meetings to discuss matters. All felt an urgency, a call to dedicate time and money to the venture. Sam observed:

> *The early atmosphere at the seminary really stands out in my memory. In those days the student body was small but growing every year. A close prayer and fellowship relationship existed between the executive committee, the faculty, and the students; we were like a close-knit family.*[168]

Actually, Sam himself set the spiritual tone of the campus in those early days. "Basil Albert was the first man who arrived from outside of Mississippi," notes Smith. "Immediately upon introduction, Sam asked to have prayer with him to praise God for his coming, telling him that this was not going to happen to most men, but 'You're the first one to come from outside!' Such a simple thing, but it made a huge impact on the students."

Sam wrote each new student a warm letter of welcome on August 19, 1966, and gave each a copy of *C. T. Studd: Cricketer and Pioneer*, sharing with them how much it had meant to him:

> *During my college days, I was given a gift copy of this book. At that time, I did not personally know Jesus Christ as my Lord and Savior. I did not read the book, but I kept it in my possession. Later, when Christ had become my Savior, I read this book and have re-read it many times in the years that followed. I would assume that no other book has so affected my life as this one, except the Bible itself.[169]*

Sam set the pace in curriculum as well, especially evangelism. For Sam, to breathe was to share Christ. He felt winning people to Jesus Christ was integral to the strong Calvinism taught at RTS and considered it the first business of ministry. The seminary's first *RTS Bulletin* in April 1965 made clear the importance of evangelism: "Fundamental in the concept of theological training held by RTS is the dynamic union of the doctrinal strength of the Reformed faith with the warmth of evangelistic passion."

Yet, Sam knew he had his work cut out for him in an academic setting. Even as the seminary was opening, he told a supporter:

> *My great concern is that we keep the seminary hot and active in the area of evangelism. Every member of the faculty and all the board are of one mind in this; but having a mind in this direction and seeing that it comes true in the midst of a heavy academic schedule are two different things. However, thus far there is a very warm spirit in the young men in the seminary.[170]*

Another challenge was blending passionate evangelism with Reformed doctrine, which emphasized God's drawing man to Himself in sovereign grace over against man's independent decision to come to Christ. As Sam told Rev. Brister Ware, Calvinistic doctrine would affect both the message and the method, at times causing friction:

> *Calvinistic evangelism ...feels called to tell the whole truth regarding God's plan to save sinners, which does involve the distinctive doctrines of sovereign grace, always somewhat offensive to human thinking. Calvinistic evangelism also emphasizes the fact that evangelism should involve the biblical message ... along with the biblical methods of evangelism set forth and illustrated by the Savior and the Apostles. This means that there will be some differences between the message and method that Calvinistic evangelists use over against others, but it ought not to be interpreted as being a manifestation of a 'holier than thou' attitude. Nor should Reformed evangelists depreciate or discount the consecrated evangelistic effort of those with a different point of view.[171]*

Sam sought to make evangelism a centerpiece of seminary experience. Early students were required to participate in Coral Ridge's Evangelism Explosion in order to graduate. Over the years, Sam proposed several methods to encourage evangelistic spirit at RTS. While he never considered himself a faculty member, he saw to it that evangelism courses were offered from the day the seminary doors opened, teaching all but one of them himself for almost ten years until an evangelism professor was appointed.

That sacrifice meant cutting back drastically on his evangelistic preaching, but it paid huge dividends. Students gained a zeal and love for evangelism that would not have existed without Sam. "Classes of only five to ten people allowed brisk interchange and dialogue," notes Laurie Jones. "Sam loved that! He liked to share information, but he also tried to draw us into the instruction. It was a wonderful experience. Often the Holy Spirit's nearness in class brought me to tears."

Through the years, the evangelism classes also gave students a greater understanding of their need for Christ. Jim Barnes (RTS '77) remembers one such class. "Sam asked us, 'Has anyone in here ever done anything that was not from selfish motives?' That question made me realize what a sinner I really was."

Ron Bossom (RTS '75) took Sam's evangelism class during his first semester at RTS. One of their first assignments was to document how they had led someone to Christ. That should be easy, thought Ron. Although a Christian for merely a year, he had already led his best friend to Christ. A few days after Ron turned in his paper, Sam summoned him to his office. Ron went with a little trepidation— what in the world could he have done wrong?

Sam welcomed him with a broad smile and a friendly greeting. "Come on in, Ron! I'd like to get to know you a little better." Some of Ron's fear began to melt since he felt instantly at ease with this red-haired, friendly man with the Arkansas twang. When Ron told Sam that he'd been a Christian for only a year, Sam said with a huge smile, "Well, that explains a lot. I've read your paper, and, Ron, the Gospel's sure in there. Yet, you don't have the faintest idea how God used you to lead your friend to Christ, do you?"

"For the next thirty minutes," reminisced Ron, "he walked me through my paper and showed me where the Gospel was. I learned more in that short time than in all the months I had been at RTS. By the time I finished his evangelism class, I knew the Gospel. However, I also was stunned to realize something else. That day in his office, I realized I had been reprimanded—basically told that I didn't know what I was talking about. Yet, being offended never crossed my mind because of the kind way in which he treated me. On the contrary, I appreciated it!"

With the opening of the seminary in September 1966, Sam came to a prayerful decision. He would resign from the presidency of FCA. Urged on by the French Camp Board (particularly Lewis Graeber, Sr.), he had found an able successor for himself in FCA former staffer Stuart Angle. In October 1966, he turned in his resignation to become effective February 15, 1967. The board accepted it but asked that he think about the decision for two months. In December, he wrote a formal letter of resignation to the board, detailing his reasons for leaving and offering counsel to the board for the future:

> ...My action in resigning was not due to impulse or to dissatisfaction with the school or the board, but was the result of many, many months of prayer and careful consideration. This action is taken in the conviction that God has led in the matter and that the best interests of the Academy are primarily involved.... The best thing I could have done for the Academy was to come to it in 1950, and the best thing I can do now is to leave the presidency....
>
> I have not made this decision in order to take another work in a specific sense. I do not know what God has for me in the future, apart from evangelism, but I have no specific plans. Feeling that God has led in this matter of my resignation, I am convinced that He has definite plans both for the Academy on the one hand and for me on the other, and I am pleased to trust Him in this matter.
>
> ... If a change in the administrative leadership of the Academy is to be made, it is better for this to take place at a time when the school is facing no major problems, but rather seems to be making progress, possesses a fine staff, department heads, and vice-president, and is being encouraged by extensive facility improvements....
>
> It is probable that increasing controversy regarding the Reformed Theological Seminary will come, very likely immediately after the next General Assembly in June. The Academy will be hurt by my inescapable involvement in the controversy. This must not be....
>
> There is a need for administrative accomplishment here that I am not able to give. I have been used of God to win support for the school, increase its facilities, and cultivate an evangelistic, spiritual emphasis in the life of the school. However, our 'product,' in terms of young lives sent out from here, is far short of that which satisfies me.... The need is for a leader with the PRACTICAL and the SPIRITUAL qualifications to take the raw material of a good staff and a growing student body and develop a far more productive program....
>
> My life and love has been so entwined with French Camp Academy that it would be impossible to put words to my own feelings in this matter. Nevertheless, I do have a sense of rejoicing in the knowledge that this is God's special work and that under your supervision His man and plan will become evident. I further rejoice to know that He has plans for my further ministry and will make these known in His way and time....[172]

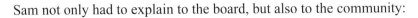

Sam not only had to explain to the board, but also to the community:

> *With the present and future growth of the Academy, its president must be a man who can give full-time-plus to the work. My health and other responsibilities prevent me from doing this. I am very optimistic about the Academy's future. Our last fiscal year was the best in our History; we have a strong faculty and staff, rapidly increasing enrollment, and a growing family of supporters and an excellent board. I feel the school's best years are just ahead.[173]*

"Mr. Pat was a loyal man, and he never wanted to do anything to detract from the ministry of French Camp," said Ann Angle, wife of the late Stuart Angle. "He also wanted to give the beginning of RTS his full attention; therefore, he needed someone he could trust to take over leadership at French Camp. One afternoon in 1966, Mr. Pat asked Stuart to meet him at Little Mountain. When Stuart returned he had the funniest look on his face. 'You're not going to believe this," he said, "but Mr. Pat wants me to take his place. Ann, I told him I was only thirty-four years old! He told me he was only thirty-three when he became president here in 1950!'"

With some measure of sadness in leaving his beloved French Camp, Sam also resigned as supply pastor for French Camp Presbyterian Church in February 1967.[174] Yet, in the years to come he never completely cut ties with the church, continuing to fill the pulpit at times and assist the session in finding pastors.

Sam's January 1967 report as chairman of the RTS board was again full of thanksgiving for God's unmerited favor:

> *Not just faith, but facts bear incontestable testimony that this work has been raised up by God and is being sustained by him. It is impossible to think of ways in which the Lord could more manifestly bless this seminary.[175]*

During the meeting, Sam urged the board to begin to take aggressive steps to attain accreditation, knowing that PCUS presbyteries could use this weakness to refuse RTS graduates. Sam noted that "unity of purpose and spirit has marked the board and the faculty of the seminary...." but warned, "Satan will not long let this area go unchallenged."[176]

Indeed, the board was already beginning to see the need for better communication with the faculty and a more centralized position of leadership on campus. In January 1967 they had named Jack Scott executive secretary of RTS to handle the ever-increasing administrative chores.[177] The ink was not dry on Sam's official retirement from French Camp Academy before the executive committee unanimously recommended that the RTS board issue Sam a call to the presidency of the seminary, even though originally the board had decided against having one. However, the position would not be a traditional presidency, but merely a "communicator-facilitator" between the faculty and the board.[178] The faculty, to a man, loved and respected Sam and thought he would be an effective communicator on their behalf to the executive committee. Board minutes show that Sam expressed a willingness to consider the call but said that he could not say definitely what his response might be. The matter was tabled and the executive committee decided to pursue the question of a CEO with the faculty and report back at the board meeting on September 5, 1967.[179] Apparently, after discussion with Sam, the matter was dropped, as it does not show up in board minutes during following months.

Perhaps one of Sam's reasons for refusing the RTS presidency was because he now saw another way to revive hearts in the PCUS by doing something he dearly loved. On October 1, 1967, he became a full time evangelist with Presbyterian Evangelistic Fellowship (PEF), a team of conservative evangelists also seeking to stem the liberal tide in the PCUS and bring biblical revival. Founded in 1958 by Rev. William Hill, the group set their own schedules and preached in churches with no guarantee of payment except travel and lodging. The church contributed whatever it wished (or nothing) to PEF, which in turn paid the evangelist. In Sam's case, RTS and PEF worked out an arrangement for both institutions to split Sam's salary.[180]

With talk of the presidency came pressure from supporters for Sam to appear more erudite with honorary degrees. One wrote:

> ... If Sam is going to be president, he should have an honorary degree.... I know he has already refused two, one because it was a liberal institution and the other because he felt it was hollow in that he had not earned it. However, he needs to see that it is not for his own sake but for the institution.... I think he should yield on this matter for the sake of a common cause.[181]

In 1963, Sam had, in fact, turned down Southwestern, his alma mater, "because I couldn't endorse their doctrinal position"[182] and in 1964 had said no to Bob Jones University because he felt he didn't deserve it:

> It has been my conviction for many years that a doctor's degree should be conferred only upon those who complete a specified academic or scientific work.... In the honorary field, any number of God's faithful servants would of necessity be passed over because institutions cannot possibly cover [those who] deserve such a degree.... Add to that the fact that the appetite of my own vanity is whetted in an inappropriate way by such a prospect....[183]

Sam didn't yield then, nor did he some years later. He was no sophisticated scholar, and he would not pretend to be. During his years on the Belhaven

College board, Lewis Graeber, Jr. recalled that the school tried twice to give Sam an honorary doctorate out of admiration, and he turned them down flat. Ed Williford also remembers when the School of the Ozarks wanted to accord Sam an honorary degree if RTS would award its president one. Sam couldn't say "Forget it" fast enough.

Word was continuing to spread about RTS, and in the fall of 1967, the student body doubled. Indeed, as time went on, Sam's integrity and commitment to Christ were unquestioned, and he had the faithful commitment of many. One supporter vowed, "I don't know much about RTS, but Sam Patterson is behind it, so it is bound to be OK."

Early *RTS Bulletins* overflowed with Sam's gracious spirit. Filled with scripture and catechism, they emphasized the lofty purpose of the seminary and its freedom from denominational control. Sprinkled with appeals for prayer and copious thanksgiving for blessings, they bore homey, personal touches that could have come only from Sam's kind heart. One even contained a handwritten invitation from Sam to the Winter Theological Institute.

On campus, Sam's personality seeped into every nook and cranny of early RTS life. The air must have fairly crackled with the Holy Spirit's energy. To those around him—students, faculty, board—Sam was like spiritual fertilizer; everywhere one could see blooming, growing Christians as he challenged them to give God their best. Sam's faith and close walk with God had so spilled over to the RTS board that its evidence fairly knocked Simon Kistemaker down when he was appointed in 1971.

"God's Spirit was moving strongly at the first board meeting I attended. How close they all were to the Lord! After a two and a half hour meeting, Mr. Kennington announced we would have a season of prayer. I thought someone would merely lead in prayer and thank the Lord for the meeting. Yet, the entire board knelt for thirty minutes, pleading with God to guide and direct them and to supply their needs. Then we all had lunch together. Only then did the meeting end. I was amazed and said to myself, 'These are men of faith.'"

George Gulley's life was turned on its end by Sam. Appointed as executive secretary in the summer of 1967, Gulley took Jack Scott's place when Scott began teaching Old Testament.[184] "I had become a Christian, and Sam strolled into my law office one day and asked me to come up to Jackson one day a week to handle some of the seminary's legal work. One day a week quickly turned to five or six days a week. I ended up letting my legal practice go and working at the seminary for fifteen years, commuting from Brookhaven."

Both George and Sam discovered that if they stayed three or four nights a week in the White House, they could work two more hours a day. Sam rose each morning around five, brewed a pot of coffee, and started breakfast, luring George out of bed.

"Those breakfasts during that first year were my times of closest fellowship with Sam," said George with a big smile. "We talked like two excited little boys about our relationship to God and about the challenges of the seminary. We had lively discussions, especially when visiting theologians such as Van Til were there. Sam often told me the backgrounds of the people that we were talking about. I was reading, studying, writing, and sitting in on classes as much as my time would allow."

In the fall of 1967, the FCA Board of Trustees bestowed on Sam one of the greatest blessings of his life in gratitude for his many years of service. Erskine Jackson wrote on behalf of the board:

> ... *I was asked to convey to you the profound appreciation and the boundless gratitude the board feels toward you for those years of faithful and fruitful service which you gave to French Camp Academy. Of course, we have tried in some way to do this before and simply could not find the words adequately to express it.*
>
> *We're not having any better success this time, either. But, anyway, our thanks continue to go up to God for the wonderful way in which he used you to build up the Academy and to bring real salvation into the lives of many boys and girls....*
>
> *At this past meeting of the board on October 10, a recommendation was adopted stating that the FCA Board of Trustees is assuming the entire obligation for the remaining indebtedness on your home at French Camp.... This is our gift of appreciation and love. May the Lord's blessings be for you and your loved ones!*[185]

Sam's handwritten reply to the board overflowed with emotion and thanks to God:

> *Words utterly fail me in this effort to give expression to the joy and gratitude that fills the hearts of Stelle and me in response to the gift of a home that the board has made to us. We surely never deserved such a bounty; the board certainly owed us nothing whatsoever. This all falls in the area of unmerited grace!*
>
> *I truly thank God for the privilege of serving so many years with such a cooperative, dedicated board. I rejoice at the support this board is now giving the Academy's new, devoted president. Without doubt, the greatest years of the school's ministry are just ahead. The patient, persistent work of the board will be manifestly rewarded.*
>
> *As I continue in my new calling with the Presbyterian Fellowship, which I am enjoying in the full, my constant prayers will be behind the Academy, and I will be pleased to render to Stuart and the school any possible assistance or service in winning and influencing friends for this great youth mission.*[186]

CHALLENGES AT HOME AND IN THE CHURCH

Student enrollment was up for the third straight year in 1968, and three graduates had been accepted for the pastorate in PCUS presbyteries. By July 1968, several presbyteries were taking neutral, instead of negative, stands against RTS. Yet, as the seminary's views spread because of greater promotional activity, so did adverse reactions by PCUS courts. Some conservatives were still suspicious that RTS had been founded for racial reasons, which was definitely not the case. A January 1969 faculty report showed several presbyteries opposing RTS strongly. One voted to drop from its roll candidates applying to RTS. Another voted not to allow any RTS personnel to preach in its pulpits, while yet another voted to refuse to put any RTS students under care.[187]

As expected, soon two presbyteries voted not to recognize the seminary as a standard (or accredited) seminary. These presbyteries were following the PCUS General Assembly's lead in interpreting the words "Standard Seminary" in the Book of Church Order as "accredited" in order to block RTS men from being approved.[188] The board had followed Sam's counsel and was aggressively seeking accreditation; during the years before the school was approved, Sam spent countless hours contacting conservatives in St. Andrew Presbytery, lobbying for the prior interpretation.

In other ways over these turbulent years, Sam became a very effective spokesman for RTS, and he loved the job. In February 1969, he invited members of his own St. Andrew Presbytery to RTS to gain a better understanding of the seminary's aims and program. Always he sought to maintain a kind and friendly attitude, answering criticisms graciously, emphasizing that the direction RTS had always taken was consistently positive, not destructive or divisive, and never racial. He answered every letter in detail, ever seeking to assure people that RTS was not in a fight with other seminaries but had a right to supply a seminary with a conservative position. His attitude went a long way to defusing hot tempers and adversarial action.

It is important to realize that Sam was not operating as a diplomatic public relations man for RTS, but honestly thought he was fighting the Lord's battle. While doing so, however, he never wanted to hurt the church or individuals. Goodness and kindness saturated his being; he truly wanted the best for everyone.

"Goodness oozed out of Sam Patterson's every pore," says Luder Whitlock. "Not many people are really good through and through, wanting the best for everybody, but Sam was."

In later years Sam was gracious about the early opposition in the PCUS:

Although the PCUS establishment didn't look with favor upon RTS, I must testify to the fairness with which the PCUS dealt with the rise of this school. Various presbyteries sent committees to investigate the school, and in nearly every instance, a good experience came out of it and more openness in the presbytery.

The General Assembly, on two occasions, ordered specially established committees to investigate RTS. Their reports in both instances were fair, and when given to the Assembly, did not bring any censure upon the seminary.

Those who graduated from RTS during the early years found acceptance in various presbyteries, making it possible for them to take up their work in their denomination. True, a few presbyteries refused entrance to RTS graduates, but they were few and never had any effect on the flow of our graduates into the PCUS.[189]

Starting a seminary from scratch and incurring the wrath of an entire denomination were minor compared to the next challenge the Lord placed before Sam. This one would ask Sam, like Abraham, to give up the person dearest to his heart in all the earth.

In 1969, Stelle found a lump in her breast but had told only her mother and made her promise not to tell Sam. While Stelle's life had always been about undergirding Sam, she now took it to a new level. Since Sam's heart attack in 1961, she had turned all her energies to keeping him healthy and protecting him from stressful distractions to his ministry.

Stelle knew Sam was under crushing pressure. Although he had divested himself of FCA duties, RTS was only in its third year, still taking baby steps financially and incurring deep opposition from both liberals and conservatives. Not only did he have to extinguish denominational fires, but he also felt compelled to join PEF in an all-out effort to bring revival. On top of all that, since the seminary had not been able to find an evangelism professor, Sam had been teaching evangelism courses each semester, juggling his preaching schedule in order to be in class. Finally, they were apart a great deal of the time, with Sam spending so much time in Jackson.

"Mother always put Daddy before herself," confessed Becky. "During my childhood, she'd say, 'Let's not upset your Daddy.' Since he didn't take care of himself, she had to. We can't know for sure, but had her condition been caught earlier, she very probably could have lived, at least a lot longer. Grandmother confided to me several years later that she blamed herself for agreeing to keep it from Daddy."

When Stelle thought the time was right and the pressure of work had lessened on Sam, she told him and went to the doctor. Unfortunately, the tumor was cancerous and had begun to spread. Doctors removed one breast at that time and began cobalt treatments. Yet, with methods available in the late 1960s, doctors could not promise Stelle and Sam much. However, the two were content to leave her condition in God's hands.

Some might argue that Stelle made a poor decision by not letting Sam know immediately, since getting treatment as early as possible would have prolonged her life for even more years of service to God and Sam on earth. While logical, the argument doesn't take into account both Stelle's and Sam's complete devotion to Jesus. The moment was what mattered; Sam needed his full attention on RTS and his evangelistic ministry now, not in some future circumstance. Eternal consequences were at stake now in the form of people's souls; they dared not give way to fear of the future.

Like Sam, Stelle trusted God completely. She would follow His leading now, giving Sam full attention and trusting that God would take care of her health down the road. Whatever came would be fine; either she would be healed or she would die and go to be with the Lord. This probably made perfect sense to Stelle, and to Sam when he found out, because here were two people who did not fear death in the least. Scrambling to the doctor to stay alive did not supersede other more immediate spiritual duties given to them directly by God.

The couple's commitment to Christ is at once beautiful and shocking. Their single-minded focus on the eternal leaves us in awe that each could so subjugate personal desires for the sake of Christ's will. Such selflessness is surely not often seen in our world today, even among dedicated Christians. Yet, their devotion should not surprise anyone. The situation had changed, but the bedrock determination from long ago to glorify Christ at all times still lived vibrantly in both of them, permeating their existence. It was the attitude that had sustained them as they lived for the Lord on the near side of hell in Martinsville; it was the courage to believe God could resurrect a dying school such as French Camp Academy; and most recently, it was the outrageous belief that the Lord would help "a bunch of nobodies" raise up a God-honoring seminary.

Believing God and enjoying seeing Him work beyond what we can understand was thrilling for the couple. It is, after all, what humans were created to do. For Sam and Stelle, it was the only life worth living. Therefore, they focused on the stunning increase God was providing RTS, while Sam sought to smooth the furrowed brows of seminary critics in the PCUS.

The summer of 1969 brought cause for rejoicing on several fronts. Sam reported in the *RTS Bulletin* that the seminary now had 1,300 individual donors and 140 church donors from thirty-two states and three foreign countries.[190] Moreover, increasing numbers of conservatives were becoming active in the fight to purify the PCUS. In August 1964, the seminary's doors had not even opened when a grassroots organization called Concerned Presbyterians formed with over 500 supporters. Their initial objective was to strengthen the conservative voice within the PCUS. In 1969, a group of 500 conservative ministers and missionaries formed Presbyterian Churchmen United and published a Declaration of Commitment in thirty leading newspapers across the South. Joining forces with Concerned Presbyterians, conservatives began holding rallies to inform PCUS members of the liberal agenda.

Initially, Sam was probably pleased to see these organizations, in addition to PEF, rally to the conservative cause so enthusiastically. Yet, he soon began to realize with dismay that more people were talking about leaving the PCUS to form a new denomination than staying to reform it. Forming another denomination was the farthest thing from Sam's mind. Three points of the liberal agenda seemed to be frightening conservative congregations and fueling the fires of division:

1. *Union with the very liberal United Presbyterian Church (the Northern Church from which the PCUS had withdrawn during the Civil War).*
2. *Proposed changes to the Westminster Confession, thus weakening the historic beliefs of the Presbyterian and Reformed denominations.*
3. *Presbyteries, not the local congregations, would now own local church property.[191]*

Essentially, southern Presbyterians began to feel that, if the liberals had their way, the church they had historically known would be gone forever, along with their church property if they chose to leave. They seemed to be fighting a losing battle. Even as conservative numbers increased, liberals were outvoting them by greater percentages each year at General Assembly. Division seemed to be the only answer.

In May 1969, Sam wrote the first of several papers urging unity over division by using weapons such as massive prayer and witnessing:

> *Until we can honestly say that we have really exhaustively tried a UNITED effort to use the 'weapons of our warfare,' which are not carnal (political) but powerful to the pulling down of strongholds, we are out of bounds to consider anything else. Among these weapons are:*
> 1. *Massive prayer.*
> 2. *Increased, aggressive, bold, alarming, evangelistic preaching of the Word.*
> 3. *Lay witnessing to the life-changing Christ. We have woefully neglected this, and it is probably the greatest offensive weapon we have.*
> 4. *United non-compliance regarding increasing denominational demands to conform and comply to that which conscience forbids.*
> 5. *Continue vocal opposition to error in the church.*
> *This course followed massively by our minority will probably force ultimate discipline and perhaps banishment from our church, but it will make the establishment the dividing aggressor, and then ...perhaps God will begin another reformation and revival.*
> *The above is my thinking. My mind is not shut.[192]*

In this paper, Sam had just begun to think and pray about church division; note the ending "My mind is not shut." During the next several years, he spent countless hours in prayer about it, growing more and more certain with each passing month that division was not the answer.

On top of all the denominational issues, so far God had not chosen to heal Stelle. She endured a second mastectomy and another round of cobalt, but all to no avail. The cancer then entered the bone, requiring two surgeries on her spine. Doctors now gave Stelle little hope of survival.

However, this news changed nothing in the couple's day to day life. They still prayed for Stelle's healing, trusting God to do His perfect will. Meanwhile, Sam and Stelle took their cue from old C. T. Studd, putting Christ before everything, even death. From the time she was diagnosed, Stelle was Sam's stalwart supporter in every way, never calling attention to herself or soliciting pity. She never let her health or her feelings get in the way of his ministry.

"After Mother got sick, Daddy was gone as much as ever," said Becky Rogers. "Yet, Mother never complained, never appeared sick, never acted as if anything was wrong until she went into the hospital for the last time. She went with him as much as possible, until she couldn't any longer."

A CONSUMMATE MEDIATOR

With the seminary up and running and a steadily increasing student body, Sam had enjoyed a little over three years as a fulltime PEF evangelist. God had blessed his preaching mightily, with many led to the Lord, and, in His providence, Sam's PEF ministry had benefited RTS enormously, with seminary support increasing significantly. Part of the reason was the persona of Sam Patterson himself. People trusted and respected him so much that his very presence generated funds. As he contacted churches and preached to their congregations, he gave continuous updates on the seminary, building goodwill. People heard his compelling preaching and realized that's what they wanted in a preacher. If Sam was training preachers at RTS, they wanted to get behind it. Finally, an alternative to liberal theology existed!

However, by the end of 1969, he could see that the seminary clearly needed his daily presence for more hands-on administrative duties, even though he loathed such work. Over the years, a good bit of friction had developed between the executive committee and the faculty. In the early days, communication between the two bodies had been greater, and Sam had been around more to run interference and interpret viewpoints. Tensions mounted as the faculty felt more and more that the executive committee tended to ignore their opinions and feelings, relegating them to mere onlookers in the running of the seminary. "We needed a facilitator between the faculty and executive committee," explained Robert Cannada, "to keep us informed of each other's viewpoints."

As usual, Sam was willing to sacrifice his evangelistic duties for the greater good. In January 1970, he agreed to become the executive committee's on-campus representative, while maintaining chairmanship of the board.[193] Since his new duties would require him to be on campus much more, he would have to move from fulltime to affiliate status with PEF—a major sacrifice for Sam. He could now hold services off campus only one week a month. Likely, he felt this sacrifice was temporary and saw himself soon getting back into the pulpit.

With his winsome, likable personality, Sam was indeed the perfect choice for this "on-campus" position. Because of his long experience in the ministry, he knew how to deal with people pastorally in solving problems. His infinite kindness, patience, and diplomacy were indispensable tools in mediating differences of opinion.

"While Sam was very sensitive to church and administrative issues, he was also protective of the faculty," said Luder Whitlock. "Some of the executive committee were much more concerned about the seminary being governed in the way they wanted. Sam's job was to bridge that gap."

"I probably wouldn't have gone to Reformed Seminary except for Sam," says Dr. Richard de Witt, former professor of systematic theology at RTS. "I don't know that I would have been asked! I spent seven and a half years there, and I wouldn't take anything for them. They were exciting, thrilling, rewarding years, and Sam was a large reason why. We all thought we were crusaders, but Sam kept us sane, sensible, and in touch with reality! We grew impatient at times that he wasn't more rigorous in his Calvinism, but he was right. We didn't need more of that; we needed what he had—godliness and a concern for the lost. He knew how to be in touch with ordinary folk as well as the high and the mighty, but was never impressed by them."

"I loved Sam Patterson," said Dr. Gerard Van Groningen. "I have taught in three theological educational institutions and under five presidents. Mr. Sam ranks with the top ones. He was a dear friend to me and my family. From the very beginning of our seven years at RTS, he reached out to us as 'folk from the north (Iowa).' In his very congenial manner, he did much to make us feel right at home in what to us was an unknown southern culture. I thoroughly enjoyed working under him at RTS. He expressed appreciation for our efforts and was constant in his encouragement to us.

"There were three L's in Mr. Sam's attitude and general demeanor," continued Van Groningen. "He was a man who LISTENED—at faculty morning coffee, at lunch time, at various faculty meetings, in advisory committee meetings, and in our personal visits. He had open ears, an open mind, and an appreciative heart. Mr. Sam was a LEARNER. He spoke often of how much he learned when he had opportunity to listen to discussions of theology and of academic matters. His ever-readiness to listen and learn endeared him to us and resulted in his being a wonderful LEADER. Understand this well—faculty and staff did not dictate to Mr. Sam. Rather, he was able to develop his own unique style of leading and being a capable and inspiring president."

Jack Scott also admired Sam's humble ability to learn from anyone. "If the seminary faced a hard decision, Sam wanted to 'lay out the fleece,' as Gideon did in Judges 6, or look for a sign that our decision was right. One day I reminded him that the practice was not biblical. The Lord himself said that the sign-seekers are an adulterous generation!"

Scott chuckles as he recollects Sam's mild-mannered response: "I never thought about it that way!" Later, Sam caught Scott and confessed, "I prayed over your comments, and you're right. That phrase doesn't belong in the Christian vocabulary." As far as Scott knows, Sam never used the term again.

Simon Kistemaker recalls Sam's gracious, encouraging manner at faculty reviews. Sam told him at his first review, "Simon, we are so happy and so thankful you have joined the faculty, and we hear nothing but good news about you."

"I couldn't believe my ears," states Kistemaker. "I was rather nervous, waiting for him to tell me where I had made mistakes. Yet, he said not a word of criticism. It was all appreciation, with a plea to continue my fine work. What a kind man!"

"Sam Patterson had his faults," said Albert Freundt, "but all things considered, he was the best man I ever knew. Everyone thought of him as his or her best friend, although Sam never set out to be that."

Faculty members were not the only ones who admired Sam; the staff held him in high regard, beginning with Cherry Ragland, Sam's secretary in 1969. "One of the highlights of my job was typing Mr. Pat's personal letters. It was like taking dictation from the Apostle Paul. In writing people, he always thanked them for either hospitality or donations to RTS. He asked about other friends and family, sometimes requesting that messages be passed on to them. He incorporated scripture and talked about the Lord as he dictated emotionally stirring messages to the bereaved, notes of encouragement to friends in crisis, and letters to ministerial colleagues, revealing his own troubled heart. I was continually blessed, as if I had read a passage of scripture or heard a sermon."

Cherry found Mr. Pat a comfortable man for whom to work. "He was quite focused on his job and required excellence; yet, I was very much loved. We didn't engage in small talk, but he wanted me to know he appreciated me without wasting time. As I left his office, he might say, 'You look nice today' or 'If you're busy this afternoon, it's not the end of the world if you don't get those done.' Those few words would ease the intensity of our serious work.

"Our conversations were about the beautiful day outside, the scripture he had read that morning, the book I was reading. We did not talk about people's lives, not because he didn't care, but because he had disciplined himself not to gossip. He could be blunt and very direct, but he didn't mean to hurt feelings. He simply did not want to waste time with anything he thought was sin or entanglement.

"After we graduated from RTS, Sam came to speak at our church. At the end of the service, he asked me to walk to his car so we could catch up. I begged him to come to the house for a longer visit, but he said, 'Cherry, if you and I get together for one more minute, we might gossip, and we can't have that.' His answer had come quickly—no apologies, no southern sweetness. At first, I was taken aback. Was this an excuse? But his meaning didn't take long to sink in. I said, 'You're right, but I surely do miss you.' He replied, 'I surely miss you, too.' We gave each other a hug, and he was gone."

Other student wives, such as Athena Davies, also loved Sam. "While Bill was a student, I worked at the seminary, and Mr. Pat was one of my bosses. What a patient man! The women on staff in the administration building appreciated his leadership so much that we decided to honor him with dinner in Vicksburg. At that time, Mr. Pat owned a large van that could seat us all. What a hilarious time we had! A highlight of the trip was when Mr. Pat entertained us with his CB radio. He had timed our trip so that, at a certain location, one of his friends called him and he replied with his handle, 'The Old Speckled Bird.'"

"He was a kind gentleman and so easy to work for," remarks Alicia Pittman, his secretary in the late 1970s. "He never made me redo typos; in fact, he was glad when I made them! He thought perfect letters looked inhuman, and making typos let people know he was real."

Finally, students found him to be the quintessential model for grace. Charles Chase (RTS '71) remembers Sam's Christ-like demeanor in the face of less than gracious treatment by some students, including himself. "Sam Patterson was one of God's giants. His grading in my missions class one year was ruthless; even the better students got less than stellar grades. We complained like the Israelites wandering in the wilderness, murmuring against the Lord. I am ashamed to say that I told *him* to his face that I thought that my final grade was wrong. As if that audacious insubordination was not enough, I learned later that Mrs. Patterson had been diagnosed with cancer and was fighting for her life. However, Sam was an anvil of graciousness, receiving blow after blow without retaliating in any way. Not once did he murmur about our murmuring. It was a beautiful imitation of our Lord not reviling those who reviled him!"

As at French Camp, Sam loved to have fun and simply refused to let the pettiness of life creep in. Problems that claimed Sam's attention were always critical, eternal matters of the heart and soul. At one point the executive committee became very concerned about James DeYoung's beard. They frowned on beards because so many seminary supporters did not like them. In a dither one day, committee members lamented, "How can we expect the students not to have beards if one of our professors has a beard?" Turning to Sam, they asked, "What do you think we ought to do about Dr. DeYoung's beard?" Sam looked at Robert Cannada and said, "What beard?" Later Sam was heard to say, "I'm not sure what prompts men to grow a beard, but by the same token, I don't know why it should bother us so much either!"

Sam didn't mind his leg being pulled, and he loved being in on pulling someone else's. Fascinated with wrestling, Sam talked late RTS Professor Norman Harper into going to a match with him one night. According to wife Mary Ida, Norman went for Sam's sake and against his better judgment; he'd die of embarrassment if anyone saw him there!

Entering the coliseum, Harper scanned the crowd. "Do you see that last row of people up there?" he asked Sam. "I'll bet somebody up there with binoculars is saying right now, 'Hey, look! There go Sam Patterson and Norman Harper!'"

Later, Sam and Hank Price, Norman's son-in-law, attached a picture of Norman to the body of a hulking wrestler, labeled it "Bruiser Harper," and hid it behind Norman's office door. Several weeks passed before Norman had to close the door for an interview with Art Toalston, *Clarion Ledger* religion editor. Norman was shocked when he saw the image and mortified when Toalston asked, "Your night job, Norman?"

Sam's favorite joke of all time was about three fellows who went fishing. While on the water, Jim fell out of the boat and drowned. The other two tried to decide how to tell his wife of the tragedy. John said, "Let me do it. I can handle things like that well, and I believe I can tell her in a way where she won't be too bothered about it." Yet, Bill said, "No, let me do it! I'm just o-o-o-o-o-zing with tact!"

They decided to let Bill do it. He knocked on the woman's door, and when she answered, he said, "Are you Jim's widow?"

She answered, "Well, I'm his wife, not his widow."

"The hell you say!" Bill shot back.

By February 1970, Sam had moved a trailer to Johnny Cleveland's Trailer Park in South Jackson so that Stelle and her mother could be with him in Jackson. He and Stelle had no idea how much more time God would allow them on this earth, and Sam could not bear being away from her as much as he had been in the last few years.

While Sam was gone, God providentially and mercifully provided Rita Riggins to help Stelle and her mother. A Louisiana native and the Pattersons' neighbor at the trailer park, Rita became acquainted with Sam as she dumped her garbage. Even though his green and white trailer sat next to the garbage bins, it was wooded, shady, and tranquil. In his few hours of free time, Sam sat out on the private side of his trailer under his awning with his Bible, gazing into the woods. At first, he and Rita merely exchanged pleasantries as she brought her garbage to the bin. As they began to know each other better, their families visited in each other's trailers.

"He had a peace that drew me to him," she remembers. "In addition to a lovely smile, incredible warmth radiated from those blue eyes. I had had such a poor childhood. My first memory was getting off the school bus and looking for my brother and my sister to see if my father had killed them. Mr. Sam was always very kind and gentle with me. I realized later on that he was the father I never had."

In 1970, denominational issues still occupied much of Sam's mind. As he heard the louder rumblings calling for division, Sam again affirmed he did not believe conservatives were ready to begin a new church:

> *The conservative thrust to this point has uncovered the enemy, exposed the error, and informed the people regarding true, evangelical, Reformed Christianity. I believe our next move should be more specifically God-ward with an avalanche of intercessory prayer that God will revive us, the conservatives, so that we will be spiritually qualified for the immediate future. I don't think we are. We are not spiritually ready to begin anything new ... such as a new phase of history-changing reformation. We need revival. We need to move into Acts 1:14, watch God move in and on us with a new power and unity as in Acts 2, and then participate in the Acts 3:28 of the 20th century.*[194]

To help speed revival in the PCUS, Sam worked night and day to help students overcome any opposition from PCUS presbyteries. Regularly he provided questions and answers for students, outlining what they should say when questioned on the floor of presbytery and how to conduct themselves to get accepted.

"When the first few classes of RTS graduates went out, most were received, but some were rejected," comments Robert Penny (RTS '70). "The latter could have happened to me without the leadership of Mr. Pat in St. Andrew Presbytery. He did everything he could to promote my acceptance. I made it through the two screening committees, but not without extensive questioning by the examiners. After the Commission had approved my candidacy, several key pastors expressed reservations. Mr. Pat traveled the northern one-third of Mississippi for a week seeking to allay fears and bring reassurance.

"The vote on the floor for my approval saw support from unexpected quarters and was successful with very few dissenting votes. That vote represented a milestone in the life of RTS and caused great praise and thanksgiving. It was the opening of the last door to service in Mississippi for RTS graduates. Mr. Pat was delighted. Our friendship was cemented for the rest of his life, and we worked side by side in the presbytery for several years."

Sam's spiritual guidance brought RTS many blessings during this time. As always, he preached patience, non-confrontation, and kindness in PCUS revival efforts. In 1971, a delegation of the Cherokee Presbytery (PCUS) in Georgia came to investigate RTS and its teachings, and Sam was spiritually ready for them. "Sam challenged the faculty to 'kill them with kindness,' recalled Simon Kistemaker, "and show them true southern hospitality and respect. He told us that, often, making and keeping a friend was harder than making an adversary."

The group gave the seminary a favorable report,[195] and, consequently, increasing numbers of students were accepted either under care of PCUS presbyteries or as pastors in churches.

Sam relished his job as mediator between board and faculty, but as time wore on, more administrative responsibilities cropped up than he had bargained for. Running the business affairs of the seminary had become too big a job for Sam and George Gulley.

"Sam handled the early executive affairs because that's what he'd had to do at French Camp, but he hated it," noted George Gulley with amusement. "He despised comparing this month's electric bill against last month's; therefore, everything of that nature found its way to my desk. And I was extremely busy, too."

In the spring of 1971, the Lord providentially provided Ed Williford, board member Coot Williford's son, to help in administration. Since high school, Ed had fallen in love with French Camp when Sam came to First Presbyterian Church in Jackson to preach or bring an update on FCA. He admired Mr. Pat greatly and had grown to love this humble servant of God. Ed believed in FCA's mission and over the years had prayed for the opportunity to work with Mr. Pat.

"Whenever I got a chance, I introduced myself and told him I was Coot Williford's son, hoping he might remember me and that it would lead someday to a closer association," recalled Ed. "Yet, every time I'd introduce myself, it seemed to be the first time we had ever met. I thought I wasn't making much progress!"

Other activities prevailed, and Ed did not work at French Camp during his youth. After college and military service, he ended up a businessman in Jackson for about fifteen years. For some time, he and his wife Sallie had wanted to be involved in missions, but no mission seemed to fit their family situation. They finally laid it aside and figured that the Lord was moving them in another direction.

In 1971, Ed asked his father if the seminary needed anyone with a business background. Coot referred him to Robert Cannada, who surprisingly said, "Ed, we've been praying for a good while for someone to help Sam Patterson and George Gulley with the business end of the seminary." Within a week Ed was appointed.

"Suddenly, I realized I'd be working closely with Sam Patterson," said Ed. "The Lord had answered my prayers! I worked with him hand-in-glove for ten years, and we hit it off extremely well. Never once did we have anything even close to an argument, difference, or conflict. It was a beautiful relationship—ten of the best years of my life."

Once, Ed reminded Sam that he had never seemed to remember Ed's name all those years ago. Sam replied, "Well, Ed, to tell you the truth, I still forget your name!" Both men laughed heartily.

Ed proved to be a marvelous gift from God to Sam, allowing him to be back where he was happiest—in a pulpit preaching salvation.

"Very soon after I came to work, Sam told me he didn't like fooling with personnel, finances, or administration problems," revealed Ed. "He saw himself as an evangelist first and foremost, but he also liked working with faculty and the board. He asked if I would tend to the accounting, administration, and personnel, and let him do what he liked. I thought it was a fine idea."

Thus they divided their responsibilities, even though there were no real job descriptions. Since both were early risers, they met every morning for coffee before office hours, thinking and praying through matters. Later, they started a prayer group with the staff from 8:00–8:15.

"The two men who, more than any others, personified the seminary in those early days were Sam and Ed Williford,' notes Richard de Witt. "They made an incomparable team. As long as I live, I shall treasure the experience of knowing and working with them."

"Sam let me know right off that he would be gone a great deal, since he was a PEF evangelist," said Ed. "Generally, he'd be somewhere in the South leading a weeklong revival at least once a month, and sometimes more. "He was so popular that he was usually booked up a year ahead.

"We could call Robert Cannada or Erskine Wells if we needed a decision. Or we could try to get Sam, although he was pretty hard to get, and he didn't work at letting you know how to get hold of him! He figured he wasn't that important to the seminary. He wasn't trying to be humble; he was humble. He wasn't trying to slip off to get out of something; it was just inborn in his heart to stay out of the limelight. That's one reason folks loved him so much."

Sam did, in fact, downplay his involvement in RTS's beginning and encouraged other people to do the same. When Erskine Wells told a group once that Sam was the reason for the seminary, Sam rebuked him, saying, "You're blowing me up too big."

YEA, THOUGH I WALK THROUGH THE VALLEY...

God gave Stelle and Sam only a year together after their move to Jackson. In May 1971, Sam was preaching revival services in Montreat, North Carolina, when Stelle entered the hospital for the last time. Mrs. Sellers knocked on Rita Riggin's door, asking if Rita could take Stelle to the hospital. Stelle was coughing very badly, but when they arrived at the hospital, she wouldn't let Rita call Sam; Stelle literally would die before she disturbed one of Sam's preaching engagements. Rita stayed at the hospital all night as Stelle suffered terribly. When Sam finally came home, Rita helped by ferrying Mrs. Sellers back and forth to the hospital and cooking meals.

Becky came and stayed with Stelle during the day, while Sam stayed at night when he was home. Sam's correspondence shows that he was still fulfilling revival engagements at the end of May, just weeks before Stelle's death. He wrote James Cantrell on May 24, 1971, "Stelle is in the hospital and won't be able to come, but indications are that I can." He did cancel a meeting the first week of June after she almost died. Yet, merely a week before she died he wrote Taylor Bird, "Until last week I still felt that there was some reasonably good chance that I would be able to come. Now I have very serious misgivings...."[196]

Sam later praised Stelle for such selflessness and devotion to the Lord in allowing him to continue to preach:

> *Even in those last three years when we knew that our time was rather limited, I still had freedom in doing God's work. The only time that she ever asked for preference was just before she died, when I was called to hold a funeral and was going to have to be away from her for a day. I think she was afraid she might go home when I was gone, and she asked me to stay with her. I don't think that was too much to ask.[197]*

Good friends, such as retired nurse Helen Branning from French Camp, stayed with Stelle at times. Sam looked forward to friend Jack Bushman's frequent encouraging calls. Elders from French Camp Presbyterian Church came to anoint, lay hands on, and pray for Stelle.

"I was so impressed that Mr. Pat did not beg that his wife would get well," said Sam Allen, "but merely that the Lord's will be done."

Near the end, doctors had to perform an emergency tracheotomy in order for Stelle to breathe. With a tube in her throat, she could not talk but communicated by writing on a pad. Bushman remembers that one day Stelle wrote, "Darling, would it be all right if we pray that the Lord please take me home now?" Sam replied gently, "No, honey, we must wait on the Lord because He is in control."

After six weeks in Baptist Hospital, Stelle went to glory in the early hours of the morning on June 29, 1971, just months short of their thirtieth wedding anniversary. She was only fifty-one. Sam was in such anguish the evening she died that he locked his keys in his car and left it running in the hospital parking lot. Security found it some five or six hours later around midnight.

Stelle was conscious right up to her death. A few hours before she died, Sam read Ephesians 1 to her. He later confessed:

> *Ephesians 1:11 says, 'He works all things after the council of his own will....' This is one of three verses in the Bible that I owe more to than any others. God only knows how many times I've read it.*
>
> *Stelle didn't understand why she needed to be taken so early, and she wanted God to deliver her. However, she was willing to accept what God brought because she knew there was meaning to it somehow, and so did I. This made less bitter what would have been a terrible tragedy otherwise. I thanked God that significance exists to events in this world because God is at work.[198]*

In the room after her death, Sam sat alone by Stelle's lifeless form, tears streaming down his face as he thanked his Lord that she was now in heaven with a brand new body. God had been so gracious; Sam had prayed to be with Stelle when she died, and the Lord had answered his prayer. He had left for just a minute to go for coffee, and God had waited to take her until he returned.

As he sat with Stelle, a nurse came in the room and asked sympathetically, "Mr. Patterson, isn't there somebody we can call? It's not good for you to be alone at a time like this." He turned to her and exclaimed emphatically, but not unkindly, "Lady, I'm not alone! I have my God right here with me."

Later, he took the time to pen the following words in his beloved, battered diary:

> *Tuesday, June 29, 1971—1:30 am:*
>
> *My beloved wife, Stelle, went to glory in heaven after three years of contest with cancer. God took her, but permitted me to be at her side as she breathed her last breath and enabled me to kiss her—but she was gone to Him. I knelt by her side and tried to sing 'The Doxology.' Broken of heart, I rejoiced in her faith and in her love and her now relief and glory with Christ.*
>
> *No man ever had such a wonderful, wonderful wife, surely! I loved—love—her with all my heart but know Jesus loved her more, and He took her. With what Christian dignity she faced illness and death! Eph. 1:10–13*
>
> *Am blessed with a wonderful daughter, Becky.*

In a letter to John Neville, pastor and RTS Ministerial Advisor from Hendersonville, North Carolina, Sam wrote, "I have never had to drink so deeply of grief and of grace. Thank God that grace is sufficient." [199]

When Rita Riggins discovered later that day that Stelle had died, she went down to Sam's trailer to check on him. "I'll never forget the loneliness in his eyes," she said softly. "He was already missing her. Yet, a calmness and tranquility hung over him like a mantle."

Sam first thanked Rita for all she had done in the past weeks. Then he said, "I would be remiss if I didn't ask you about your relationship with Jesus Christ."

Rita was stunned. Hours after losing the dearest person on earth to him, he was concerned about her salvation! Caught off guard, she wondered what to say to this kind man she had grown to love. She knew the Lord, but she also knew her Christian walk was not a deep one. His question, however, was disarming, not harsh and critical as she had always come to expect from others. So merciful was his manner that she decided to trust him and tell him everything.

Rita had been brought up a Roman Catholic but as a child had problems with Catholic beliefs. She had left the church and had been so ostracized by her family and so harshly criticized that she wasn't sure she was saved. Consequently, she had quit attending any church at all. As she spoke of her past humiliation for her beliefs, he simply listened, then told her he felt that little twelve-year-old girl had her doctrinal facts straight. She felt a tremendous burden lift.

A little later, Sam preached a series of sermons at First Presbyterian Church in Jackson. Rita attended those and never stopped going to church. "I grew up feeling I had to achieve to be accepted. Yet, I always felt an acceptance of a 'deeper me' from Mr. Pat. I didn't feel as if I had to perform. Mr. Pat understood that life was not wonderful because of his efforts; it was wonderful despite the adversities that had come his way. He knew he had to get out of the way because God was in control."

Tears well in M. B. Cooper's eyes as he recalls Sam's commitment to Christ even in Stelle's death. "Sam told me once, 'I keep praying that if there is some lesson to learn from her early death, I'll learn it. I surely don't want to miss it, because the cost was too great.'"

Obviously, Sam learned much wisdom from God in his grief, as evidenced by this excerpt from the Sovereignty of God sermon series:

> *You know what drives believers crazy? It's believing that a tragedy is simply a horrible accident that makes no sense and results in great waste. If the tragedy involves a loved one, that kind of thinking can tear one to pieces.*
>
> *As believers, we might not always know the reasons why things happen to us, but we can know that our lives are in His hands. Through Jesus Christ, we have His promise that He is at work in all things for good for them who love Him and are the called according to His purpose. What the world would call a tragic accident is not that to us who know Him. We don't understand, but there is sense to it. He will put reason and meaning to it, so it isn't a waste. God is at work.[200]*

There would certainly never be another woman to measure up to Stelle in Sam's eyes. He frequently said that Stelle was the greatest Christian he had ever known. Years after Stelle passed away, Ed Williford introduced Sam to a number of widows and encouraged him to ask them out. "However," noted Ed, "he always found a reason not to do it. As I leaned on him about it one time, he said, 'Ed, I better just level with you. When you've been married to the finest woman in the world, there's just no incentive to get interested in another one.' Therefore, I quit suggesting it or even kidding him about it because I could see that he would always think Stelle hung the moon. He probably thought that having a relationship with another woman would be an insult to her."

Jack Bushman concurs, laughing. "After Stelle died, widows in the churches where he preached wanted to cook for him and invited him to meals. However, he made sure he was always part of a group, no one-on-one situations. Sam was a great escape artist who had no intention of marrying again."

French Camp Academy records indicate that hundreds of people honored Stelle in memorials to FCA. In November after her death, the RTS Executive Committee approved a recommendation by the faculty to establish the Estelle Patterson Evangelism Fund, initially envisioned to fund lectures in evangelism.[201]

A HUMBLE GYPSY FOR THE LORD

From Stelle's death until his retirement from RTS in 1979, Sam chose not to have a home as such. He had given his French Camp home to Becky and her husband when they had moved back there in 1970, and he and Stelle had moved to Jackson. Two weeks after Stelle's death, Sam moved the large trailer back to French Camp and let Mrs. Sellers have it. From then on, he lived off and on in an apartment on the RTS campus or a small travel trailer on seminary grounds.

George Gulley always laughed merrily when he thought about his running battle with Sam to move that camper off campus. "His brother Hugh wanted to pay someone to burn it. I told Sam to get that trailer off campus because we didn't want RTS to look like a trailer park. However, Sam didn't pay a bit of attention to me and simply parked the trailer behind Grace Chapel out of the public eye."

Students, however, had no problem at all with Sam's humble abode. "While at RTS, my family lived in a tiny white house at the front of the RTS property," said Wilson Smith ('RTS 73). "We had a small backyard, and one day Mr. Pat asked us if he could park his small trailer there for a season. Can you imagine the famous Presbyterian evangelist and RTS founder asking a nobody like me if he could camp in our backyard? We were honored and thrilled for the company of such a great and humble man of God. Often we visited at his door, and he could be found praying or preparing evangelism lessons for the next day. He was never too busy for us.

"One day our daughter Debbie and Mr. Pat were walking in the yard. She tried to run and fell on a fire ant bed. Before Mr. Pat could rescue her, the ants had bitten her legs badly. As we carried her home, we all wept as Mr. Pat prayed for her. The Lord was gracious to give us a substitute grandfather and prayer partner right on campus in our backyard."

Robert Hayes (RTS '74) has a similar story. "Mr. Pat lived in a little travel trailer just yards from our house. We had a little dog we named after him. When my wife yelled 'Sam,' Mr. Pat confided to me that he didn't know whether she was hollering for the dog or for him; he thought he might be in trouble. He was such a wonderful inspiration, a WYSIWYG person—what you see is what you get."

Others remember Mr. Pat in prayer in his little camper. "Three things in particular stick in my mind about Sam Patterson—his humility, his deep spirituality, and his sincere love," said T. M. Moore (RTS '77). "I can still see the light in the rear window of the small Air Stream trailer under the fig tree behind the chapel where Mr. Patterson lived while I was a student at RTS. It was just a small travel trailer, but it was home to a spiritual giant. I recall how often the saints on Iona spoke of seeing a light glowing through the windows of their stone chapel when the great Colum Cille was inside praying. I can't help but wonder whether the light I often saw in that trailer was electric or otherwise. Mr. Patterson always carried himself with dignity and grace, greeting us by name whenever we saw him, retiring each evening to his humble abode where he dwelt in perfect solitude and joy with his beloved Lord. He aspired to nothing material in this world, only that he might be poured out as a living sacrifice to God in all he did."

"Mr. Pat was in his Toyota camper in the RTS parking lot late one afternoon," recalled Marshall D. "Mad Dog" Connor (RTS '81). "He was in deep thought as he read one of the many volumes shelved there. I thought then how remarkable that a man who had been so used of God would be studying in his twilight years. It was not difficult for me to cast in my mind's eye a picture of the Apostle Paul requesting 'the scrolls and especially the parchments' in his last letter to Timothy."

Living humbly and happily in a camper was merely one facet of Sam's unpretentious meekness. A whole new group of people had discovered his utter lack of concern for worldly goods. In April 1971, upon Sam's second visit to Trinity Presbyterian Church in Montgomery, his longtime friend Jack Bushman thought enough was enough. He suggested the congregation take up a collection to get Sam a new wardrobe. Mrs. Roberta "Berta" Holding organized the wives to buy clothes for Stelle that, sadly, she was never able to wear.

"After we gave them the clothes, both Stelle and Sam told me separately that they had been praying for almost a year that the Lord would do something to get Sam a new wardrobe," reveals Jack with a chuckle. "Sam told me his coats were getting so threadbare that he had to tell the church deacons to turn the lights down low at the altar when he preached. At the time, Sam had one pair of Hushpuppies and one pair of worn-out dress shoes. I warned him, 'Now that you have a new wardrobe and shoes, you're going to have to upgrade your preaching and preach up to your wardrobe.'"

The late George Gulley said one of the few times he saw Sam's temper flare was over extravagance. "Mr. Pat didn't get mad over pettiness, only for moral or spiritual reasons." Once, on behalf of the seminary, Sam and George visited a large church under construction. The pastor told them, "We want a huge organ in this church. We can get a Wanamaker for only $800,000, but we still need to raise some money for it. Sam, would you pray about it?"

Sam's face turned red, a sure sign he was riled. He said, "I will not pray for it! I think it's very extravagant, and you are going in debt for it just to show off."

"The pastor was dumbfounded," recalled George, laughing. "Sam stomped out of the church, leaving me to stammer some kind of apology."

Sometimes Mr. Pat's humble nature made it hard for Ed Williford to do his job. "We often had large functions to introduce people to the seminary. Many of them knew that Sam's vision had brought RTS into being, and they wanted to meet him and have a picture taken. Time and time again I'd try to find him, and he'd be gone! The first few times, I thought perhaps he had slipped out with somebody. I finally realized that when the time came for singling him out as a highly spiritual guy or the Big Leader of RTS, he went home to bed. I was left to explain why these people couldn't have a picture taken with Sam Patterson!"

PATIENCE, NOT DIVISION, IS THE KEY

In the autumn of 1972, RTS had over one hundred students. While very thankful, the board was concerned that the school was growing too fast, and they subsequently limited enrollment.

"I don't think any of us ever thought RTS would grow so large or even thought that desirable," said Jack Scott. "Sam wanted a reasonably small school where we could have a good relationship with all of our students. In those early years, my wife, Eleanor, and I were able to invite most of the student body, with their wives and families, to our home for supper. As we grew, we couldn't do that. We lost the great intimacy between students and the faculty. I began to feel as if I were on an assembly line—put a great deal into a student during a big classroom lecture and then not see him anymore. In the early years, I had all of them for a great many hours of teaching. It reached the point where I'd see students on campus and not know their names."

Perhaps all the founders underestimated the vast yearning for a conservative seminary dedicated to a high view of scripture. Yet, to Sam's dismay, events within the PCUS were causing conservatives to want more than a seminary. More and more conservatives were calling for a new denomination.

In 1972, the PCUS seemed to be inexorably moving closer to union with the Northern Church. Everyone anticipated the 1972 PCUS General Assembly would approve the final draft of the plan and send it to the presbyteries for a vote no later than January 1973. If the required number of presbyteries approved the plan, the 1973 Assembly would give its final approval and the denominations would unite immediately.

Richard de Witt outlined the situation well in a 1972 article in the *Standard Bearer*:

> … *As if our problems were not already sufficiently grave and the prospects for continuing a Reformed witness in the present situation with the PCUS dim enough, we are now confronted with another issue which vastly outweighs everything else that we have been called to face in the past…. A considerable number of ministers and congregations*

who find it possible to work in the Southern Church ... are convinced it will be impossible to have any part at all in the new denomination.... God can still reverse the present course of events ... but as responsible Christians ... we must make good use of the time God has given us to ensure the continuation of a Reformed and evangelical witness in the historic Southern Church.[202]

However, Sam was optimistic that the liberal cause was failing. He pointed to the conservative groups that had been formed—*Presbyterian Journal*, RTS, Concerned Presbyterians, Presbyterian Churchmen United, and PEF. Now PCUS churches kept thirteen PEF evangelists busy!

Wait, work, and watch is the formula.... God is permitting the liberal establishment ... to fall into a confusion of ineffectiveness, radical experimentation, and a desperate grasping for a way out. While still powerfully and deeply entrenched, liberal forces are increasingly suffering a growing disenchantment in the minds of people.... On the other hand, God is manifestly blessing with vitality, popular appeal, growth, and effectiveness the evangelical forces in the land, which are seeking to conserve and promote the biblical faith....Within our church, time and God are working in favor of evangelical forces seeking to honor His Word and to relate men directly to Jesus Christ. At this time, and for a long time, vote-power has belonged to the liberal forces. The vital life signs of these forces are declining, however.[203]

Sam urged conservatives to unite with moderates to defeat the destruction of the Confession and to block church union. If a great number of conservatives leave, Sam warned, the PCUS will be left wide open to liberal takeover. However, conservative groups were positioning themselves not to get caught if union took place. Plans for a new denomination continued to escalate, and RTS adopted a neutral position, saying the seminary was in full sympathy with those dedicated to the preservation of a Presbyterian church true to the principles on which the PCUS and the seminary were founded. RTS leadership was in a delicate position, since the seminary wanted to serve both denominations.

Yet, Sam himself was growing more and more sure he could not support division. By now, he had searched the Bible diligently, and God had showed him nothing to convince him to leave the PCUS. He believed God had providentially placed him in the PCUS and bound him with sacred bonds, as he told Billy Thompson:

It's our church. If something's wrong with it, I need to fight to correct it. Leaving it is not the answer. I decided I was going to read through the Bible, and if I found anywhere where God said I ought to split from the

> *church, I would leave.... After reading through the Bible, the Lord didn't show me that anywhere in there. So I'll stay and fight for the things that are right.*[204]

"Sam spent quite a bit of time in the chapel, praying that the rift might not occur," reveals Simon Kistemaker.

During 1972, Sam wrote his most detailed treatise outlining his views on the denominational issue. Entitled "A Paper Seeking a Biblical Basis for the Conduct of Believers Who Are In An Erring Church," it sought to show why he did not want to leave the PCUS:

> *The Sovereignty of God assures the church of His sufficient power, wisdom, and concern for the fulfillment of His purposes in the church of His Son.... He will guide, chasten, shape, shame, revive, withdraw power from, and otherwise deal with the church in the course of her periods of obedience and disobedience. It is for Him alone to dispose of her and to predestine her. It is for us to obey Him in her and set at doing it earnestly. Keeping constantly before us His sovereign power and purpose will contain our impatience so we can, with patience and obedience, look in the Bible for His way for us.*[205]

Sam then considered many Old and New Testament examples concerning God's dealing with erring followers, noting finally that the scriptures seem not to divide the urgency of seeking purity and unity in the church. Scripture calls for the rebuking of error and earnestly seeking to correct and restore the erring. It also calls for the vigorous search for unity. He ended with these stirring words:

> *Martin Luther said, 'Here I stand,' not 'Here I split.' To seek reform, revival, and even regeneration for the erring church may bring rejection and expelling. If so, then the erring ones are the 'dividers' as scripture has said they are. If we thus suffer at the hands of an erring church, let us be dead sure that we suffer the 'fiery trial' for behaving as Christians. Let us not go beyond scripture in dealing with God's church, but trust the Sovereign God to rule over, in, and through His church.*[206]

Imagine Sam's dismay when he opened the Jackson *Clarion Ledger* on October, 7, 1972, and saw himself labeled as a leader in plans for a Continuing Presbyterian Church, the group pushing for division. Sam was livid and immediately wrote a letter to the editor:

> *The implication is clear that I am identified with the conservative coalition's plans for a possible withdrawal from the PCUS. I am not in any way identified with this coalition and I am opposed ... to a division from or withdrawal from our denomination.... While I am in accord with*

the doctrinal concern of the Coalition Committee, my presence at that
meeting was due, in part, to my opposition to proposals for division.[207]

The specter of church division haunted Sam continuously, causing much
wear and tear on his emotions. In March 1973, he took a much-needed break
from preaching, teaching, and denominational concerns and joined a group led
by Dr. Robert Strong to the Holy Land. From March 1–22, Sam enjoyed sights,
not only of Israel, Lebanon, and Greece, but also several European countries.
Since he left no notes or memoirs of the trip, we don't know how he financed it.
Likely, it was a gift from a grateful friend or even congregation.

While the beginning of 1973 was pleasant and fulfilling, the year's end
brought excruciating emotional pain for Sam. Although union between the UPC
and the PCUS did not occur as thought in 1973, the opposition to it was so great
that conservatives went ahead with the division in the PCUS and in December
1973 formed the National Presbyterian Church (later changed to the Presbyterian
Church in America).

"Sam was heartbroken," revealed George Gulley. "The day all the pastors
officially signed the declaration, he went to Montreat to spend several days with
Nelson Bell."

"Sam regarded the formation of the PCA in 1973 as premature and utterly
unnecessary," explains Richard de Witt, "because it wasn't supposed to happen
until union between the PCUS and UPC denominations occurred; it would then
provide a continuing conservative Presbyterian church in the South. Everybody
was bracing for union, but it didn't happen until 1983. Sam would argue there
was no reason for the PCA in 1973."

Sam now had to face a grim reality. Even those closest to him, those who had
stood side by side with him in founding RTS, were giving up on revival in the
PCUS. In fact, several of the executive committee had been instrumental in the
formation of the PCA.

"Many people wanted a seminary such as Reformed for the same reason
they ended up wanting a denomination like the PCA," notes Ed Williford. "To
a man, anyone connected with RTS figured when the time came to sign up that
Sam Patterson would sign the PCA proclamation because his beliefs were so
similar to theirs. However, Sam let them know that he had never even seriously
considered leaving the PCUS. He wanted to found RTS to train ministers to
return to the PCUS and purify it. Then, lo and behold, many of the strongest lay
people and ministers ended up moving to the PCA, leaving him alone to fulfill
that commitment. His church vows were sacred, and even if he were the last one
standing, he would do all he could to make the denomination what he thought it
ought to be. He would not leave unless the Lord took him out of it."

Yet, friends and colleagues had finally said enough is enough. "We had tried
valiantly, but the liberals had taken over so much that it was absolutely hopeless,"
declared Erskine Wells.

Erskine Jackson agreed. "Sam wanted us to stay in there and fight. However, some of us had fought so long and so hard. We'd had it up to here and were ready to get out."

Sam, on the other hand, had no patience with such arguments:

> *If our primary compulsion to separate is described by phrases like 'I'm fed up' or 'I've taken all I can,' it is schismatic. To be led by these things can result in petulant disobedience to God. We were not called to the army of Jesus to be contented, at ease, or comfortable. His soldiers don't 'fade away'; they fight it out.*[208]

Instead Sam continued to preach patience:

> *In general, the most permanent accomplishments come by patient persistence. In some denominations, more liberal groups have won wars while conservatives have been winning a number of battles. We conservatives often are battle-oriented and seek to promote our causes by vigorous confrontations on particular issues, while holding somewhat aloof from loyal participation in the everyday operation in the machinery of the church courts. On the whole, the more liberal groups have practiced an amazing patient persistence in seeking their objectives while being very active in loyal participation at every level of denominational activity. This has enabled them to win the war while conservatives occasionally win some battles.*
>
> *Conservatives have a great asset in their sense of commitment to protecting the truth of the Gospel and propagating it. This commitment needs more to be harnessed to a patient persistence, a method of persuasion, and a deep involvement in every level of the denominational life. To be quickly encouraged and just as quickly discouraged can be a sign of immaturity.... The need today in the cause of Christ is a committed and mature statesmanship.... [This] always incorporates a patient persistence that tries to fulfill obligations toward both progress in purity and maintenance of unity.*[209]

Sam didn't give up on people, and he would not give up on his denomination. Again, Sam took his cue from Jesus:

> *It always helps me to remember how patient the Lord Jesus was in the days of His flesh with His disciples, who over and again failed to measure up. The church and its people today still fail to measure up, but we've got to manifest the same patience that the Lord Jesus did. He rebuked, but He stayed with His sheep.*[210]

Lane Stephenson believes Sam's patience grew out of a two-fold philosophy. "I have come to realize that Mr. Pat believed equally strongly in two truths—the inerrancy of scripture and the sovereignty of God, which gave his life stability and direction. His life and his preaching showed that he believed with all his heart that scripture was inerrant. He believed that God was sovereign over all things, especially over His church; that is why he believed we could wait and trust the Lord to see what He did in the midst of the circumstances. I think many have trusted the scriptures but do not have such a practical out-working of the sovereignty of God in their lives as did Mr. Pat."

However, Sam would never let his denominational views get in the way of personal relationships. He had too much respect for others. "He stood true to the PCUS in a humble way," observes Ed Williford, "and he didn't mince words in telling you what he believed. They weren't fightin' words, but they were clear and firm. He'd never hold it against me or anybody else for being a part of the PCA."

Sam said as much to William Smith in September 1973, just before the Presbyterian Church in America came into being:

> *These are trying times for all of us in the church, but I really believe that the new church is emerging in such a way as to make possible the continued fellowship of conservative men in both the old and the new churches. This is certainly illustrated by the unbroken fellowship between Morton Smith, Al Freundt, and myself here on campus.*[211]

In the same way, others could not fault Sam for his stand. They knew he was the soul of integrity. "While many people may have questioned some of his decisions, no one ever questioned his commitment to scripture or his love for the Lord," says Lane Stephenson.

Herb Bowsher (RTS '78) agrees. "No one questioned Mr. Pat's orthodoxy or commitment to Christ, and we all admired his calm and good-natured leadership. He was truly a unique leader and a gracious Christian gentleman."

PICKING UP THE PIECES

Sam must have been pleased to be able to partner again with long-time friend Russell Nunan in a unique plan to help rural Mississippi PCUS members in St. Andrew Presbytery who were victims of the division. In the fall of 1973, fourteen north Mississippi churches withdrew from the PCUS, but the congregational vote was not unanimous. Those members choosing to remain in the PCUS would now not have a place of worship. As a ministry to these committed few, the presbytery's Pastoral Commission, which Nunan chaired and of which Sam was a member, recommended that presbytery form a Church of the Pilgrims for these people to worship. Tiny Gillespie Memorial Church in Duck Hill offered its facility for worship. The church was active until 1982.[212]

The division threw many RTS students into a real spiritual battle. Sam refused to take sides and manipulate any of them in the throes of decision; he wanted them to make up their own minds before God. As usual, the Lord showed him an unusual, thoroughly unique way to deal with the problem and teach Ed Williford a deep spiritual lesson in the process.

"If a PCUS student asked Sam to help him/her win a denominational argument," explained Ed, "he'd send them to me, telling the student he could get an objective view since I was an elder in a PCA church. He never told me this was his plan; he just began doing it. I then realized that if someone came to me fighting the PCA battle, I shouldn't agree and team up with him against someone in the PCUS. Consequently, I began sending those students to Mr. Pat for an objective view. It was indicative of his purity that he would not strengthen another person's position against the PCA. I learned that we could both trust God to help students work out their differences and still hold to the faith without conflict with each other."

"Mr. Pat had a magnanimous spirit," said Ken Utley (RTS '81). "He demonstrated this to me in his reaction to my decision to part company with the PCUS. I had been under care of a PCUS presbytery and had been required to attend one of the denomination's seminaries following graduation from RTS. As a result of that experience, I came to realize that I could not remain in the PCUS. I knew how much he wanted conservatives to stay and try to bring change. He never expressed anything but support for me, though I knew he was disappointed. After all he had done for me, he could easily have asked me to reconsider, but not a word."

"The Lord used Sam Patterson at a crucial time in my ministry to verify a call to evangelical ministry in mainline Presbyterianism," recalled Don Elliott (RTS '73). "I responded to the vision of pumping faithful, biblical pastors into the PCUS to reform it from within. Yet, when I got to RTS, the vision slowly changed to hopelessness, to 'the gold has dimmed.'

"I was a senior in 1973, the year the PCA was formed. My class was split right down the middle. Sam Patterson, as president, probably had most of his faculty wanting to go PCA. However, he did not think that was being most faithful to the scripture. I still use his 'Behavior of Believers in an Erring Church' today in my ministry. He asked a question that has haunted me to this day: If all faithful pastors leave mainline Presbyterianism, who will give the faithful preaching of the Gospel to God's people that are still in the pews of those churches?

"Many said the vision had changed; now we need to start a new Reformed body," continued Elliott. "I asked a great number of friends, 'Are you going to strive for reformation in the new church?' They answered, 'Of course.' I countered, 'Why don't you stay where God's placed you, working, praying, and preaching for reform here?' The issues in the PC(USA) today are so black and white that it makes some of the battles being fought in the PCA rather trivial."

"Before I graduated," says Bill Young (RTS '76), "I decided that God was calling me to stay in the PCUS. I transferred my membership back to my home church in St. Andrew Presbytery. Throughout the whole process, Sam was very encouraging; he even attended the presbytery meeting when they voted on whether or not to accept my transfer of candidacy from the PCA back to the PCUS. The Candidate Committee recommended that I be required to go through all sorts of hoops before being accepted. Sam Patterson was one of several who worked to persuade the presbytery to accept me without all that, and they did!"

Sam not only counseled RTS students about church issues, but also their families. Cherry Ragland remembers when she and her husband were seniors and had received a call to a PCA church. John came home one day and to her complete shock said, "Cherry, I really believe God has called me to remain in the PCUS and be a testimony as long as I can." He had contacted the PCA church and refused the call. Cherry was six months pregnant, and they had very little money. How would they make it? She already couldn't buy hose, lipstick, and other toiletries, which really disturbed her. Yet, John had charged a book he needed for class at the bookstore. Cherry was furious. If he can buy a book, Lord, why can't I have the things I need to be a lady?

As she was complaining to the Lord one day, Sam walked by and she asked him about it. Without mincing any words, he said, "Cherry, I can't tell you anything except that your place is under John. Pray for your hose and your lipstick. If he's gotten a book, he really needs it. Pray that it will bless him. You can go without hose and lipstick and trust the Lord. But don't ever undermine John's position and place in your life."

Then he gave her a big hug and left. Cherry said not another word to John, but confessed her complaints to the Lord privately. As she kept dying to self, she realized it was summer and her legs weren't freezing. For a season she could bite her lips to make them red. Her small privations weren't the end of the world that she was making them out to be.

PCUS REVIVAL AT ALL COSTS

In 1973, Sam sacrificed again for the seminary, curtailing his preaching engagements to teach evangelism for three quarters, even handling two courses during the fall of 1973. However, in 1974, his priorities changed, and he began removing any obstacle that might hinder his evangelism in the PCUS. He felt the situation was critical. From now on, his main goal would be revival in the PCUS, a decision that would eventually put him on a collision course with the RTS board. But it was the call of God upon his heart:

> *Now that the National Presbyterian Church has drained so many*
> *evangelicals and conservatives out of our denomination, I feel that it is*

*all the more mandatory that those of us who are still in the PCUS should
try to have all the impact for biblical, evangelical Christianity that we
can.*[213]

In the spring of 1974, for the first time, he put PCUS revival above evangelism
classes at RTS. While he would teach two evangelism courses in the fall of 1974,
he was optimistic the board was finally closing in on a professor of evangelism
for the spring of 1975. For now, he asked the board to give him some freedom,
shown by this April letter to an RTS supporter:

> *During the past three or four years I have been so deeply involved
> in the life of the seminary that I have had to curtail in large measure
> my evangelistic work in the churches. The urge to move back into
> more evangelistic work has been so strong that I have requested a
> rearrangement of my work here in which the board will permit me to
> engage again much more fully in evangelism. While I continue to be
> associated with the work here as in the past, I will not be on campus as
> much as in the past and will be out in more meetings.*[214]

By June 1974, the board had granted his request, and Sam was extremely
happy to be back in church evangelism so intensely. By October 1974, his
preaching schedule was so busy that he was at the seminary only half the time.

In the fall of 1974, he even left PEF as an evangelist in order to safeguard his
work to revive the PCUS. Publicly, he said he didn't feel it wise to operate under
two boards any longer, but he told his friend Bud Jones the real reason:

> *I am still a supporter and contributor to PEF but not an evangelist....
> I am functioning as an evangelist for the seminary. Since PEF helped
> cause the separation in the Southern Presbyterian Church and the
> beginning of a new church, it does handicap me from being able to
> evangelize effectively in the Southern Church.*[215]

As RTS approached its tenth anniversary, Sam surely welcomed the Summer
1975 *RTS Bulletin* announcing the appointment of Dr. Luder Whitlock as
associate professor of evangelism and Christian education. In 1976, Sam must
have been ecstatic when the executive committee established a new Department
of Christian Missions and appointed Professor Guy Oliver as chairman.[216] With
two professors in the missions department, Sam would now be freer to preach, as
evidenced by the introduction of a new feature, "Traveling with the President,"
in the Summer 1976 *Bulletin*. It showed at a moment's glance where Sam would
be holding evangelistic meetings anywhere in the South.

Even as RTS strove to remain neutral in the denominational conflict, Sam
continued to work for revival and act as an able peacemaker on both sides, a
stance that angered some PCA supporters. They wanted RTS to align itself

more closely as a PCA seminary and accused the school of straddling the fence. Evangelicals maintained that RTS could not expect support from conservatives if it did not identify with the PCA.

In a kindly-worded reply to Bill Hill in February 1972, Sam said:

> *I do not feel you have aptly put the matter ... by saying we are sitting on the fence. We are standing and serving just where we believe God has put us, and we believe we are in the midst of His will in tending to our knitting as a seminary and not getting ... involved officially ... in the division matter.*[217]

On the other hand, PCUS supporters were alarmed and negative about the seminary; they didn't think RTS was neutral at all. Sam spent much time diplomatically answering letters such as the following, assuring people that RTS was not part of the PCA split:

> *I was interested in your remarks concerning RTS and the current withdrawal movement in our church. It would be my guess that ninety-nine percent of the folks who are doing any thinking about this proposed split believe your seminary is part and parcel of that movement.*[218]

Sam also built bridges with the PCUS by answering in detail questions about RTS and trying to quell suspicion about the PCA. In a 1974 reply to John Hendrick, executive presbyter of Brazos Presbytery (PCUS) in Texas, Sam wrote:

> *I believe that there is convincing evidence now that the leaders of the National Presbyterian Church are making genuine efforts to relieve this separation of as much bitterness and ill will as possible. I believe it will take its place as a growing force for Christ, but hope that it secures its growth through evangelistic efforts and outreach to the unchurched rather than by continued withdrawals from our denomination. I believe that men coming here out of congregations loyal to the PCUS from this point on will come with a desire to return to that denomination. This seminary and its faculty have declared they consider it seriously unethical to seek to alter the denominational loyalty of men who come here.*[219]

When invited, Sam also took every opportunity to hold evangelistic meetings in PCUS churches. His Christ-like behavior won numerous PCUS pastors over, giving Sam entrance into otherwise forbidden pulpits to build bridges of peace. In October 1974, George Kaulbach wrote the following to fellow ministers of Florida Presbytery (PCUS):

Sam Patterson is a Bible preacher. He is a very warm, loving Christian who preaches that way. He is not a wild-eyed fundamentalist who pounds the pulpit with a hellfire message, but rather one who rightly sets forth the electing love of God in Jesus Christ and the new birth. After one service I commented to an elder, 'Boy, I wish I could preach like that.' He said, 'No offense, George, but I wish you could, too.'

He is no longer associated with PEF. He is still chairman of the board at RTS. However, he will not embarrass you. He will lift up Christ. In a few short days, I have grown to love him as a brother in Christ. I commend him to you.[220]

A LIGHT TO STUDENTS

On campus, Sam's face seemed to light up whenever he greeted any of the students. His gentle and unpretentious nature made him very approachable. As at French Camp, his office door was always open; students, faculty, or staff could talk to him any time. In fact, much of the time one would not find Sam in his office, but out and about on the grounds, counseling and ministering to anybody within his reach.

Sam's faith was dynamic, full of zest and life. He had a vibrant relationship with the Lord and depended on it for every breath he took. Students and faculty knew instinctively what Erskine Wells had sensed many years earlier and termed "unusual." Sam's faith was not built on stale doctrine. It was living, breathing, exciting, dangerous. The Lord had taught Sam to relish His goodness, and Sam encouraged others to "taste and see that the Lord is good."

"Mr. Pat was a pastor's pastor; he loved us as green seminary students," noted Kirby Smith (RTS '79). "He was unselfish and lived a servant's life with a servant's heart. Talk is cheap, but a blind man could not mistake the real deal, and Mr. Pat was a Christ-like servant, kind and big-hearted to the little man, which we were as seminary students."

"Sam Patterson was foundational in my life," says RTS Chancellor Ric Cannada (RTS '73). "As a young boy I was taught to pray for Sam and French Camp, and I visited there several times with my father. When Sam began to discuss the dream of RTS with my father and others in 1962, I was fourteen. I watched as Sam, Dad, and the other founders prayed and worked for the establishment of RTS during my high school years. The week before I left home for college in the fall of 1966, I attended the first RTS convocation in which Sam presided. As a college student in the infamous 1960s, I often visited the RTS/Jackson campus for counsel and advice from Sam and the professors.

"When I became a student at RTS in the early 1970s, Sam was not only my seminary president, but also my professor of evangelism and a significant encourager and friend. I loved, admired, and respected Sam, seeing him as a mentor and a true father in the faith. I never dreamed I would have the enormous privilege to serve in Sam's position as the administrative and visionary leader of RTS. Like Sam, I seek to strengthen the foundation of the lives of future ministers of the Gospel, as Sam blessed and strengthened my own faith and life."

"Sam seemed to glow with his love for the Lord as he served others with his life," said Steve Merritt (RTS '83). "Soft-spoken and kind, he always seemed to have time for the person with him, although I know he was a very busy man with an intense love of spreading the Gospel of Jesus Christ."

"I complained to Mr. Sam one time that our students should be the 'cream of the crop' of Christians," confesses Cecil Brooks (RTS '75), "but I felt they acted very poorly at times, including me. Mr. Sam said, 'But, Cecil, they will act more like cream when they get back with the milk (the congregation).' How wise he was! I did better also when I got back with the milk!"

Guy Richardson will never forget one of Sam's profound theological reflections over lunch one day. "Sam told us that he once thought sin was a series of black spots and blotches at different points in the timeline of his life. He pictured God with a brush, dipped in His Son's blood, blotting out each one. 'Oh, here's one' and 'There's another one,' as He wiped each one out simply by a swish of His hand.

"However, Sam said he had come to realize that it's not that easy. Being the rebellious sinner he was, he had finally understood that Christ had to die for every breath he had ever drawn. The blood of Christ must cover his whole life, not just sins spotting his life here and there."

Other times, Sam talked with students about very practical matters. He devoted an entire chapel message once to handling finances. Realizing that ministers frequently have financial problems and gain reputations as bad credit risks, he wanted to insure that RTS students didn't fall into that trap. He encouraged students to pay any obligations on time so as not to bring discredit to the churches they served. If a student couldn't pay, Sam counseled, he should go to the one owed and explain the situation straight out, offering to pay something, even if the amount was small. He also admonished students not to ask for ministerial discounts; if merchants wished to give them, they could without being asked.

Numerous students recall learning valuable lessons from Sam. "He told us that he gave his problems to the Lord," said Ken Utley, "then asked if God wanted him to do anything to help solve the problem."

According to John Hutchinson (RTS '79), Sam told students that he opened the Word each morning saying, "Lord, I love you and want to keep your commandments. Please show me how I can obey you today."

"Mr. Pat's daily practice was to wait for the Lord to speak to him through His Word as he read it," continued John. "I have adopted the same practice, and it has been life-changing. I have also told others about it over the years. His memorable practice continues to bear fruit."

"Sam challenged us to memorize the Psalms," relates Henry Bishop (RTS '72). "I committed approximately sixty-seven to memory. Beyond a blessing, it's been very helpful to have them at hand in various pastoral situations. I have also challenged others several times to do the same."

Joe Hause (RTS '75) experienced a life-changing counseling session with Sam one evening. "I was emotionally stressed from the demands of study, while questioning my own presence in seminary training. Following dinner, my wife took the children for a walk while I talked with Sam. We ended up bowed in prayer on bended knee, seeking God's strengthening intervention. I rose up from that prayer meeting with thanks, renewed strength, and commitment to complete the task to which God had called me. Christ was in Sam trying to get through to countless others all the days of his Gospel ministry in the simplest of ways. He served the body of Christ tirelessly to the end of his days."

Sam taught the Hauses three vital truths that have enabled them to run the good race without wavering in ministry:

1. 2 Corinthians 5:11–19—we are ambassadors and ministers of reconciliation, not division.
2. Philippians 3:1–21—through the fellowship of Christ's sufferings, we press on toward the goal to win the prize for which God has called us heavenward in Christ Jesus.
3. Ephesians 3:20–21—God is doing immeasurably more than all we ask or imagine according to His power that is at work within us.

"One afternoon I had the opportunity to help Sam with a crisis situation," said Al Herrington (RTS '75, '77). "A woman in the subdivision close to the seminary was at home with her children, and she had a loaded pistol. After talking with Dr. Wallace Carr, professor of pastoral counseling, we went to her house and knocked on the door. The screen door was locked, but we could see her sitting in a chair with the pistol, the children around her. We continued to knock at the door and tried to reason with her. Finally, she opened the door and agreed to talk to Sam. Eventually, she gave him the pistol. We talked to her for a long time, ministering to her from scripture and leaving her a tract. Thank God no one was hurt. I saw that Sam was always ready to respond when a need arose and was always ready to share the Gospel."

During those early years Ed Williford and Sam handled numerous problems with students, who never seemed to have any money! "Frequently, students came to RTS sending up a trial balloon to see if the Lord was calling them," said Ed. "We learned to spot those who had a misfortune and didn't really seem to have a call. Sam taught me to see a red flag when a student said, 'I really feel called by the Lord to seminary, and if He'll find me a place to live, work out my support, and find a job for my wife, I'm going to come.' Before promising support, I learned from Sam to wait for a student to say, 'I feel led by the Lord to come. I don't know how I'm going to make it, but I'm not worried about that. I'll come in faith that the Lord is going to provide. My wife will have to find a job, and we'll have to find an affordable place, but we'll pray about it.' Sam thought that if students came with that sort of faith, we could stand with them on all of those things, turning them over to the Lord and trusting Him to work them out. Then we'd sit back and marvel at the countless ways that the Lord answered their prayers and provided support, often far above what any of us had hoped for."

Derek and Rosemary Thomas are a good example. Derek met Sam at a Banner of Truth Conference in England in 1976. He had left a liberal Presbyterian seminary in Wales after a year and a half of study to do an internship at a Reformed Baptist church in Oxford. He dreaded going back to the "soul-destroying" seminary in Wales. He had considered other conservative seminaries but knew he could not afford them, especially since he was engaged to Rosemary and looking toward marriage.

"I had lunch with Sam Patterson and asked him if I could possibly come to RTS," remembered Derek. "Sam said matter-of-factly, 'Write us; we'll look into it and let you know.'"

When Derek got home, that's exactly what he did, putting his case before the RTS administration but not really expecting to hear much. After all, Sam was a total stranger and his manner so understated. On the face of it, Derek reflected, the idea was probably crazy anyway. Rosemary had no idea where Mississippi was, and the only picture Derek had was from reading about Tom Sawyer and Huckleberry Finn.

Yet, the reply did come, in a record three weeks, with the seminary offering him virtually a full scholarship and housing! Did the offer include Rosemary? They had been dating for five years and did not want to put off marriage another three years while Derek attended RTS.

Sam said easily, "Why don't you marry her and bring her with you?"

"So that's what we did," recalled Derek in wonder. "We married in July and left for Mississippi in August. We had no idea how we would survive, but we knew that God did."

"In 1974," says John Hutchinson, "my fiancé, Cynthia, and I were involved in a youth retreat in Mississippi where Sam was the speaker. After one of his messages, we sought his counsel, telling him we were considering pastoral ministry. He didn't wait to hear the whole story, but immediately raised his gaze toward heaven and prayed, 'Lord, you've commanded us to pray to the Lord of the harvest to send forth laborers into the fields. I pray you'd send forth these two.' After that spontaneous supplication, we talked a little about RTS, and off he went to give the next message. After Sam Patterson prayed, there was usually little to talk about. The next year we married and entered RTS. Since then, Sam Patterson's prayer is still being prayed and answered as we serve the Lord of the Harvest in the Washington, D.C. area through the ministry of the McLean Presbyterian Church."

Sam's tranquil nature and loving spirit put new students at ease and gave them much-needed confidence. "I was, perhaps, one of the least qualified people to apply to RTS," said Gary Spooner (RTS '76). I suspect that I was accepted solely on Mr. Patterson's faith in my fledgling faith at the time. Almost a year to the day after I became a follower of Jesus Christ, I sat in his office wanting to become a student. All I could say was that I had grown up Presbyterian, joined the church at twelve, knew that I had come to know Jesus personally in the past year, and wanted to attend seminary simply out of a love for Christ and His Word. I could claim no significant current church relationship. As far as I knew, I was not called to the ministry; I intended to take my seminary degree back into journalism from which I had come. I knew very little Bible; therefore, I was a little nervous but filled with naïve enthusiasm.

"When Mr. Patterson walked into the room, I met Christian manhood in full bloom. He was one of the meekest men I have ever met. Welcoming me with a warm smile, he made me feel at home, listened to my story, and then we prayed together. I remember how his holiness and honesty during that interview became, for me, a living (and lasting) picture of the kind of Christian I wanted to be—vibrant, winsome, passionate for Christ and His truth, tender towards the weak and lowly."

Sam never allowed doctrine to take a higher place than scripture. Continually, he emphasized the supremacy of allowing God's Word to influence one's life. For at least one new student, God used that to confirm his calling. "When I went to RTS, I was more than a bit nervous," said Richard Wiman (RTS '77). "After all, I was coming to RTS as a Methodist. I knew next to nothing about Calvinism and the Reformed faith. Mr. Sam, then president, told us at orientation, 'Young men, whether you've grown up in the Presbyterian denomination or not, you may be wondering what it means to be Reformed. Simply put, it isn't being Calvinistic. It means to be daily reformed by the Word of God. If God's Word isn't daily reforming your thoughts and life, then you won't be able to preach the Gospel or rightly explain the Reformed faith.' After that, I knew I was where the Lord wanted me to be."

Sam also passed along to RTS students wisdom he had been imparting to French Camp Academy staff for years, warning would-be pastors of pitfalls, such as an out-of-control temper:

> *Temper means trouble. The only godly temper is a governed temper. Some Christians say, 'I get mad quickly, but I get over it quickly.' Perhaps quick murder is better than slow murder, but both are equally deadly. Your 'mad' may go quickly, but the wounds, folly, and damage are never quickly—and sometimes just plain never—gone.*[221]

He urged them to recognize weaknesses:

> *Thank God for your strong points ...but you have some weaknesses. This means danger ahead...! Your strong points can never make up for your weak points. Never forget this.*
>
> *Your personal, peculiar weaknesses can find their solution only as they throw you back constantly upon the grace of God, that His strength may fill them up. Thus, weaknesses in your life can become the greatest areas of strength in you as you let God do in you what you cannot do by yourself (2 Cor. 11:29, 12:9).[222]*

He warned them about being hyper-critical. Robert Hayes once told Sam disparagingly about a woman in his congregation who wore her skirts very short. "I was surprised when Mr. Patterson said, 'How short she wears her skirts is something for which she must answer to God, but how you respond to it is something for which you have to answer to God.' A light came on for me at that moment, and I learned not to be judgmental. I decided that I would try to do something about her inappropriate clothing, but I was not going to jump on her and dress her down about it."

Sometimes Sam even counseled students in matters of the heart. Every time a couple comes to John W. "Jay" Coker (RTS '79) for marriage counseling, Sam Patterson springs to his mind. While he was a student at RTS, the Lord brought a wonderful woman into his life and was obviously drawing them closer together. Yet, Jay wrestled with the relationship, asking himself, "Is this the one?" The struggle became especially intense one evening about ten o'clock, and he decided to call Sam for counsel. Even though the hour was late, Sam urged him to come immediately, so Jay made his way to Sam's very modest apartment upstairs in the White House.

"There he was," declared Jay, "in his pajamas, rocking and eating his supper—a bowl of cornflakes. I sat down to share my story, and after a lengthy explanation of feelings, thoughts, and fears, I asked him, 'Should I propose to Sharon?'"

Sam related some scripture about marriage and family, then shared the joy of his own marriage and love for his wife and the Lord. He finally asked Jay, "Do you love Sharon?"

John answered, "More than anything in the world."

Sam smiled widely and said, "Then you need to make a prayerful commitment."

"Should I propose to her?" Jay asked.

Sam responded, "If you love her as you say you do and believe this is God's will, then yes."

"After words of appreciation, I stood to leave," said Jay. "However, he wouldn't let me go without praying for us, placing us before the throne of grace. Sharon and I have been married over thirty years now. We give thanks to God for

Sam Patterson. God used him as a vital part of the foundation of our marriage, family, and ministry."

Finally, Sam was a stalwart friend and counselor in times of grief and pain. While at RTS, Bill Fox (RTS '76) lost his wife Judy to cancer in 1975, leaving him with four sons to raise. The pastor at his home church had come after Bill left for seminary, leaving him essentially "pastorless."

"Even though I was never one to stop by Sam's office and chat, I felt very comfortable asking him to hold Judy's funeral," said Bill. "As a seminarian, I felt he was my pastor. He went far beyond the call of duty, too, because he and Ed Williford had to fly to Greenville, Alabama, to do it. I so appreciated that ministry to me and my family."

No one knows better than Betsy Chestnut what a friend Sam could be in sorrowful times. Betsy and her late husband Carlos had been married only four years when they entered RTS in 1974 to prepare for the mission field. In October 1976, just before the two were to leave for a clinical year in Trinidad, Carlos was diagnosed with a very rare form of cancer. The couple was shocked, as was the entire student body. For two years the seminary family waited and prayed for healing as Carlos underwent grueling cancer treatments.

Sam felt their pain more than most, perhaps because he knew exactly what Betsy was going through as she watched Carlos suffer. Betsy remembers Sam's kindness and the wisdom he imparted throughout that time.

"He will always be precious to me because he was like God's arms around me at a very hard time in my life. I was confused about how to pray, and everyone was telling me something different about praying for healing. Mr. Pat told me that first, God is able to heal (Psalm 103). Second, it is our right as a child of God to ask for healing (John 5). Third, we trust the Lord to do what's very best for us (Romans 8:28). That clarified for me our position before the Lord and gave me great peace in all that confusion."

During Carlos's cancer treatments in Houston, Texas, Mr. Pat wrote to encourage them:

> *What a blessing you two are to me and to everybody who has contact with you. You will never know until heaven the impact on others of your unpretentious but genuine, confident commitment and trust in God through this difficult time. All of us here daily will be remembering you in prayer as you take further treatments in this current series. I have been thinking today a good deal about the statement in Psalm 105, declaring that among the blessings we never are to forget is the fact that 'He healeth all our diseases.' I take that to mean that God does not permit to come among men any malady or disease that He cannot heal. Further, I take that to mean that, on occasion, He is pleased to heal His people of any and every disease.*

That psalm goes on to say that these blessings are granted not on the basis of what we deserve, but on the basis of His immeasurable mercy and grace. Therefore, this psalm not only reminds us of blessings experienced, but blessings to expect, and encourages God's people to confidently come to Him in believing, submissive prayer to ask for such of these blessings as are needed. I find great delight in daily soliciting and expecting God's full healing force upon you, Carlos. Betsy, there is a burden and a testing in all of this that you carry that differs from what Carlos is experiencing. Hurting with someone you greatly love when you can't hurt for them is a very special kind of hurting. I truly praise God for the grace He is giving you. We never fail to strongly remember you in our prayers. Praise God.

You both are in such good Hands.

Devotedly,
Sam Patterson[223]

The Lord chose to take Carlos home in 1978, but only after he had witnessed to every single person he could—doctors, nurses, patients, hospital staff, and total strangers.

When Carlos died, Sam sat with Betsy, ministering to her with his love, concern, and care. Long after Carlos's death, Sam didn't forget Betsy. In fact, their bond grew stronger as each helped the other. Occasionally, they'd go for coffee and enjoy talking of heaven and how wonderful the day would be when they saw Stelle and Carlos again.

"Mr. Pat lovingly threw out a lifeline to me when I needed it," recollects Betsy. "I'll never forget the time I called him after the dog that Carlos had given me died of cancer, too. I hit my lowest point, thinking, 'Who's next?' I didn't even know dogs could get cancer! I told Mr. Pat I was about to throw what was left of my towel in and quit. I had about decided God didn't care and had forgotten about me. Mr. Pat said, 'Betsy, the God who knows you and loves you better than anyone else is in control of your life.'

"That's exactly what I needed. I realized then that I still had Jesus. I could make it another five minutes, or another hour, or another day. I could do this! My heavenly perspective returned, and I was back on track."

Sam loved to say, "Trouble is often an evangelist, drawing us nearer to God."[224] No one could agree with him more than Scottish theologian Andrew Murray, who provided Sam much solace in grief, especially after Stelle's death. One of Murray's quotations became so meaningful that Sam kept it in his Bible and counseled others with it frequently:

In times of trouble, God's trusting child may first say, 'He brought me here; it is by His will I am in this strait place; in that I will rest. Next, He will keep me here in His love and give me grace in this trial to

behave as His child. Then, He will make the trial a blessing, teaching me
lessons HE intends me to learn and working in me the grace He intends
to bestow. Last, in His good time He can bring me out again—how and
when He knows.' Say—I am here by God's appointment, in His keeping,
under His training, for His time.[225]

A RELUCTANT LEADER

In 1975, the seminary encountered a major roadblock with accreditation
officials, who absolutely refused to consider accreditation unless RTS appointed
a president. To get around this requirement, the board decided to appoint a
president in name only, whose duties would be assigned by the executive
committee.

Sam was in complete agreement with this tactic; he just didn't want them to
elect him! His increased evangelistic work had given him great fulfillment, and
he was optimistic about the future of the PCUS:

> *At the time of the division in the PCUS church, a large number of*
> *graduates in the seminary went with the movement forming the PCA*
> *church. This critical period has now passed. Now the PCUS students*
> *who come to the seminary come committed to that church and will be*
> *going back into it. This is reflected in the fact that in the past two years we*
> *have had no graduates that we know of who have gone into the PCA.*[226]

As cause for further optimism, in June Sam was invited to speak at the PCUS
General Assembly in Charlotte, a high honor and proof that he had an audience
in the PCUS.[227]

However, the board could find no one suitable for the job of president. In
characteristic selfless fashion, Sam finally accepted the post and was appointed
president March 10, 1975, giving up the chairmanship of the board to Robert
Cannada.[228] Actually, Sam's job description as president did not change his
duties in the least. He remained a facilitator/mediator between the faculty and the
board, between the board and the seminary supporters, and between the staff and
administration. He was as happy as a lark doing that and preaching the Gospel.
However, taking the post caused him to curtail his preaching again. He was
permitted to be off campus two meetings a month and was usually committed a
year in advance.[229]

Sam always saw his presidency as a temporary position. He hadn't wanted
it, had refused an inauguration, and wouldn't allow people to call him President
Patterson—"Sam" would do just fine. He was still, after all, just an evangelist.
"I truly loved Sam Patterson," said Jim Barnes. "He was a real Christian and a
reluctant leader whom God used to accomplish great things."

Sam was humble and didn't let the presidency inflate his ego. "Few men in my lifetime have I known that have been able to handle exaltation," said Ronald McKinney (RTS '74). "Sam Patterson was a humble man and remained humble to the end. He was not ashamed of his calling, but was profoundly moved by the fact that God had called him to be a minister of the Gospel."

Richard de Witt has said of Sam, "He was a refreshing example of a good, godly man, and it rested so lightly on him. He wasn't pompous or solemn, and he walked with God in an easy, comfortable way. Kind and thoughtful, he was just a benediction."

At no time was that more evident than in the exchange Guy Richardson had with Sam after he became president. "Just what do you really do as president of the seminary?" asked Guy playfully one day. Sam's eyes twinkled and without missing a beat, he said, "Well, I make the coffee and turn out the lights. I do the things that make people work together well."

"He showed a great deal of respect to others," said Alicia Pittman. "He didn't think of himself as a busy leader. Sometimes people of importance fake interest, turning it on for the moment. Yet, Mr. Pat met a person eye to eye and showed genuine, sincere interest in what he had to say, no matter his station in life. He was greater in spiritual stature than other, more prominent Christian leaders, but he was not impressed with himself at all. I realized his deep spirituality more when he was absent than when I was with him."

Simon Kistemaker remembers fondly how he discovered Sam's God-given skills in mediation. "I had a bit of a conflict with a student and told him, 'You're getting under my skin!' It was a fact! However, another student took me to task, telling me I should not have said that. I apologized sincerely and let the matter drop. Yet, it came to the ears of Sam Patterson, and he called me in."

Dr. K. is silent as he struggles to hold back tears. "I thought he was going to come down hard on me, but I saw him act with mercy as Jesus would have. He pointed me to the Lord and encouraged me so much! He assured me that together we could save my relationship with that student, and he wanted us to start working on it immediately. I said to myself, 'That's how it should be.' I can say joyfully that all was put straight, and my relationship with that student was better than ever."

Sam was so successful in facilitating relationships because of his positive attitude toward and deep love for people. He was the poster child for 1 Corinthians 13:4 ("Love suffers long and is kind") and was able to see each person in all the glory in which God had created them. In one sermon he taught:

> *You were different in the womb, and you are different even after He saved you, so that for all eternity Jesus is going to reflect His glory in a peculiar, personal and different way through you than anybody else. The same light that is coming through you is not going to be coming through anyone else.*[230]

"Sam was more Christ-like than any man I've ever known," confided Erskine Wells. "We had this maintenance man at the seminary who had a drinking problem. We put up with it for a long time, but finally we had had enough. Yet, Sam said, 'Give him another chance! Give him another chance!' Sam convinced us and we did, time and again. Sure enough, though, he'd slip off the wagon again. We finally had to let him go. Sam was always willing to go the extra mile to help the fellow, but, of course, we had to worry about what the grounds looked like."

Sam, on the other hand, probably never gave a thought to the grounds, especially when a human soul was at stake. This innate love radiated from him in a heavenly warmth, enfolding those around him in its soft, luxurious warmth. Men and women frequently weep at the mention of Sam's name or the very thought of him. Remembering one who loved and accepted so unconditionally does bring tears.

Ed Williford discovered Sam's proclivity for perseverance with people during his frequent problem-solving sessions with Sam. No matter the situation, Ed found that Sam always had the same answer: "I think you ought to go as far as you can in the right direction. Ed, you can't go wrong by doing right." Frustrated at first, Ed finally saw the wisdom and loving kindness in Sam's approach.

"To go as far as one can in the right direction," says Ed, "is often much further than anyone else would go!"

Ed also benefited personally from Sam's gentle mentoring. "I learned wisdom from him in so many ways. While we never had a cross word during my ten years under him at RTS, that surely doesn't mean that Sam didn't need to correct me. On the rare occasion when he did, I often didn't even realize that I was being corrected! He subtly taught me better ways to handle situations without my feeling as if I had been reprimanded. He also built my faith, especially when I accompanied him on hospital visitations. I loved hearing his words of comfort to the sick and his scripture readings. Before we left, he always asked me to pray, which built my spiritual confidence immensely. I was always so grateful for that privilege."

Because Sam thought each and every human had infinite potential, he viewed all people as valuable and treated everyone the same—from a street sweeper to a Fortune 500 executive. Such an attitude made him a marvelous encourager and helper.

"Even if you disagreed with him, you liked and trusted him," explains Luder Whitlock. "He could identify with you, want the best for you, and try his best to make sure it happened. You could look at his eyes and see he was a very kind man."

WORK TAKES ITS TOLL

With the frenetic pace Sam kept, it's not hard to see that his heart condition recurred. As early as 1971, fellow minister Brister Ware wrote to Sam:

> *From time to time I feel constrained to pray for your physical health, particularly that God will spare your heart in order that you might continue to provide the spiritual leadership for the seminary.*[231]

In March 1976, a letter to his brother Hugh shows that doctors had put Sam on a diet:

> *By skipping breakfast, which I never cared much for anyway, I find it is rather easy to stay satisfied on a 1500 calorie diet. I've backed up an additional notch on my belt and have recently worn a suit of clothes that I haven't worn in several years.*[232]

Apparently, though, changing his diet was not enough. By December 1976, he had to write several churches that had scheduled services and tell them "a significant change has developed regarding my heart condition, and my doctor has performed major surgery on my schedule."[233] Sam had to cancel all engagements for the next few months, cutting back on half of them for 1977.

By January 31, 1977, correspondence shows that the doctor had been able to see some improvement. Sam was optimistic. "We are trying to beat bypass surgery. As long as medicine and slowing down can achieve that, all will be well."[234]

By the end of March, in a letter to John Robertson ('74), Sam says,

> *I was stunned at the ultimatum by the doctor to cancel all series of meetings I now had scheduled ... and the general alarm he raised in connection with my present situation. He has called for intensified medication and a radical change in lifestyle to back off the present situation, avoiding both an attack and immediate surgery.*
>
> *What makes it all the worse for me is that I do not feel that condition and, in general, feel pretty well.*[235]

Correspondence in April 1977, revealed the condition was serious angina, but Sam was still able to carry on his work at RTS with frequent nitroglycerin tablets. Sam noted that he was responding well to his doctor's prescribed course, and "perhaps I'll be able to get him to lift the ban in a few months."[236] On April 14 he writes, "Being nailed down in one spot is indeed a new way of life for me. For almost thirty years I've been treading back and forth at regular intervals doing evangelistic meetings. However, I have plenty to do here."[237]

During the summer, however, his condition worsened, and on July 5, 1977, Sam entered Mississippi Baptist Medical Center to undergo heart catheterization. Results of the test showed that he needed open-heart surgery. Wilson Smith (RTS '73) prayed with Sam the day he discovered he needed surgery. "When is the surgery?" he asked Sam.

With a twinkle in his eye, Sam replied, "The doctor said I need it as soon as possible. I surprised him when I asked if we could do it tomorrow morning!"

Sam was a man of faith and action. Even though the surgery was not urgent, he wanted it done quickly. He always said, "If I'm anticipating a very bad experience, I want to hurry up and get it over with."

Doctors performed a triple bypass on July 7 with no complications. After two weeks in the hospital, Sam convalesced at Becky's home in French Camp for a month. By October, he was back in the pulpit doing one meeting a month. He was able to work in the mornings at RTS, with plans to be back fulltime in six weeks.

"Sam always had a good attitude," says Simon Kistemaker. "He had perfect trust in the Lord that his operation would turn out right, no question about it."

ARE WE CRITICS OR WITNESSES?

On July 28, 1977, RTS finally came of age and received full accreditation by the Association of Theological Schools. This status would certainly make it easier for graduates to gain entrance into PCUS presbyteries. But was it too little too late? With the formation of the PCA, numerous graduates were now planting churches in the new denomination, not trying to preach in the PCUS. The knowledge weighed heavily on Sam, and the stress could have been at least partially to blame for his recurring heart bouts.

The joy of accreditation was also tempered by the growing pains of a school only a little over ten years old. As early as 1975, Sam reported to the board that the seminary had been receiving some sobering criticisms of its graduates' unloving behavior:

> *During this past year the executive committee and faculty have sought to analyze the problem and see where we can more helpfully prepare our students for pastoral ministry.... At age ten, this institution must naturally be marked by some institutional immaturity. We are gaining wisdom with the experience of each additional year of operation. We are training students in the most dynamic, challenging doctrine in existence, the Reformed faith.... The very potency of this system of truth demands the wisest application and the most Christ-like spirit of zeal with gentleness. I predict that we in administration and faculty will be improving our job of preparing our students for service in the church.[238]*

Yet, by December 1977, the problem had escalated to the point that Sam was seriously concerned. On December 13, he outlined the issue to a special session of the executive committee:

> My basic concern has to do with an intolerant attitude that develops here in our students and jeopardizes their initial efforts at a pastoral ministry…. On the one hand, this attitude cultivates an inability to accommodate other persons, organizations, and churches without feeling guilty of compromise and thus cultivates inflexibility and rigidity. On the other hand, it cultivates premature suspicion and inclination to separatism that handicaps association, fellowship, and cooperation with the broad spectrum of Christian evangelical forces and people….
>
> Our doctrinal commitments (Reformed distinctives, verbal inerrancy) put us in a minority position in the Christian world, and in the immature this tends to cultivate a defensive attitude. Add to this the fact that newly becoming gripped by the great sovereignty doctrines of the Reformed faith often generates such enthusiasm that the student loses a sense of proportion … and becomes intolerant with all who desist or deviate.[239]

Sam then contrasted the existing attitude with that of the founders of RTS:

> [At the founding of RTS], we thought of ourselves as constructive conservatives.… We were not attempting to promote division or disruption and we said so…. We were prepared to be tolerant of others; we simply wanted to offer an option in theological education that would testify to our high view of scripture. We did not call names or bring accusations. And we were remarkably successful…. Conservatives rallied to our cause, but not all shared our moderation of spirit. They began to see an opportunity to begin a new and biblical denomination. A spirit of and call to division rapidly arose that gave birth to the PCA….[240]

Finally, Sam laid the reason for the current problem at the feet of church division:

> Such a division in the church gave birth to an atmosphere that includes much suspicion, accusation, and intolerance…. The acceptable world in the church is more and more the limited sphere of the few, small, separatist-oriented, highly doctrinaire denominations in the Reformed spectrum. It eliminates as valid spheres of hope, service, fellowship, and cooperation of the older and vastly larger Presbyterian communions. It even eliminates them as legitimate fields for 'missionary endeavor' by conservatives.[241]

Sam proposed several steps to remedy the situation, including cultivating broadness of spirit that seeks to find more common ground than those issues that divide. He also wished to see more pan-Presbyterian representatives in board membership and student enrollment. The executive committee purposed to implement helpful steps to correct the problem.

However, in April 1978, the problem still existed, as evidenced by this very frank excerpt from one of Sam's chapel messages on John 17:

> *This account by Jesus strikes terror to my heart. God knows the trembling I've done and still do. I know I must give an accounting of my ministry one day. For some He will say, 'Well done, thou good and faithful servant,' and I fear to miss that. I dread to miss that. I must hear it! I get so scared when I read this passage, even though I have preached the Gospel for forty years, and there are people in heaven because I preached the Gospel to them.... I am such a sinner that I don't have any room to judge anyone else. If you want mercy, don't be a judge. We are witnesses. You can say we need to be fruit inspectors and rebuke one another, but I don't understand it. I fear and tremble that God will stand me up one day and say, 'You produced judges and critics at that seminary, and I wanted witnesses to come out of there!'* [242]

A DIFFERENCE OF OPINION

Other tensions were mounting in Sam's relationship with the board, and he was in an awkward position. His decision to make PCUS revival a top priority had begun to conflict with seminary policy and with his position as RTS president. As he grew more and more vocal, RTS donors became increasingly upset. The seminary was trying to stay neutral in the denominational battle, and the board did not want to send mixed signals to its PCA constituency.

Sam never initiated visits or letters to churches encouraging them to stay in the PCUS; yet, when asked he always responded. The RTS board felt he was not authorized to do that and he should, as Robert Cannada put it, "tend to his knitting at the seminary." PCA supporters were confused when they heard the RTS president asking churches not to leave the PCUS.

In January 1978, the executive committee began requiring members of the RTS official family to notify them before accepting controversial speaking engagements. This request was "advisory in nature" but was to be "considered ... before making a final judgment in the matter." [243]

The faculty approved the measure with no changes; however, the measure was slightly more restrictive than the previous 1972 policy that allowed differing views without notice to the executive committee:

> *The seminary does not now and does not intend in the future to make any attempt to influence or control any member of its official family as to his personal views ... nor does it intend to limit the activities of any member of its official family ... as long as such activities do not hinder such individual's responsibilities to the seminary.[244]*

George Gulley had seen Sam disagree with the board before. "Sam was very cooperative with the board of trustees and the executive committee until they violated one of his basic beliefs, and then he'd come out of the lion's den roaring! I don't think many people ever saw that side of Sam, but it would usually occur when the executive committee had made a policy decision without what he considered proper thought."

Luder Whitlock agrees. "He was a courageous person of principle and integrity," said Luder. "If he really became convinced something was right or had to be done, it gave him tremendous backbone and motivation. His conflict with the executive committee during those last years made him very sad. He had convictions, and he simply could not do what they asked of him. I think he finally realized nothing would ever change, so he chose to leave."

Finally, Sam decided to step down as president, but still serve as trustee and member of the executive committee. Says Ed Williford, "He told me he retired two or three years early because he felt that his position concerning the PCUS put the seminary in an embarrassing position."

Sam was very frank publicly:

> *This move enables the right man to step into the presidency and enables me to give full time to the promotion of special seminary interests, especially as it serves a pan-Presbyterian role in training students from a number of Presbyterian and Reformed denominations.[245]*

And in later years he further elaborated on his move:

> *My retirement [was] motivated in part by a realization that while I served a useful purpose as the initial president of the seminary, the institution had now reached a broadening horizon of opportunity and service that demanded better qualified and more professional leadership, such as that which can be provided by a new president, particularly the one we have chosen for this office, Dr. Luder Whitlock.[246]*

While Luder was not Sam's first choice as a successor, he heartily endorsed him. According to Ed Williford, Sam had at first suggested Richard de Witt or Simon Kistemaker as ministerial possibilities, and had even proposed a lay possibility. Yet, the committee could not agree on any of those choices. However, when Robert Cannada suggested Luder Whitlock, Sam gave his full support. In his April letter of resignation to the board, Sam had high praise for Luder:

> *Supported by close observation of his personality, abilities, wisdom, insight, and rapport with faculty and students during the years of his service on our faculty, I believe that God has brought him to us for presidential service. He is a minister, scholar, committed Reformed theologian, and earnest evangelist. He is of such balance and graciousness as to make him accepted and respected by both the most 'reformed' and the most 'evangelical.' While he is a minister in the PCA, he did not leave the PCUS and was not involved in the division. No one on the faculty has consistently expressed more emphatically his confidence in the future of this institution than Dr. Whitlock. He has served on the boards of Westminster Seminary and Covenant College and has been sought for the presidency of another sister Reformed theological seminary.[247]*

"When Sam came to see me, I was actually wrestling with whether I wanted to stay at RTS, and I had just about decided to leave," confesses Luder. "I had received some invitations from other schools, and I wondered if I was cut out to be a professor. Sam helped shape my life, and I had great admiration for him and his amazing ministry. The tragedy is that RTS lost his influence because no door was ever closed to Sam Patterson. I wish the executive committee could have seen how much they needed him."

In April 1978, Sam asked for and the board granted him a leave of absence from the "full duties of President" from August 1, 1978, to August 1, 1979. During that time, Luder would serve as acting president and Sam would continue as seminary evangelist and special representative of the executive committee in several areas—alumni and funding contacts, active development of PCA, PCUS, ARP, and UPC interests and contacts, and attendance at various denominational courts. This would allow him to continue his pan-Presbyterian evangelistic and mediation work, with his duties to continue on a year-to-year basis at the executive committee's discretion. Sam asked to be granted president emeritus status when Luder officially took over as president on August 1, 1979.[248]

As in everything else he did, Sam left the office of president graciously. "I never heard him say anything against the seminary," revealed Richard de Witt, "and never saw the slightest hint of bitterness. He simply shrugged his shoulders. He had his eyes on eternal things and had no ambition for power. He was content to be the Lord's instrument and was willing to do what needed to be done."

During 1978–1979, Sam continued to work through roadblocks to RTS graduates in PCUS courts, humbly asking for moderation and grace in the denominational conflict:

> *... Far too often in the church we breach its peace by excessive positions, attitudes, and actions that [either] drive brethren away from*

*the church or ... pull brethren away from the church. God knows we
need the patience with one another that Christ had for His disciples.*

*I wish I could be at presbytery ... to ask forgiveness for strains that
I have put upon the presbytery and to appeal for great moderation ...
in dealing with earnest PCUS men who truly feel led by God to attend
some seminary which may [not] be a PCUS-owned institution.*[249]

At a dinner honoring Sam for his years of service on May 24, 1979, the
board announced its intention to establish a Samuel Coleman Patterson Chair of
Missions and Evangelism, since that was the subject closest to Sam's heart.[250]
While Sam would have thought the gesture cast too big a spotlight on him, the
chair was established in 1990 and newly-appointed Samuel Rowen was the first
to hold it. Rowen left in 1992 for the mission field, and the chair was vacant for
nine years until 2001, when Professor Sam Larsen was appointed to it.

A BLESSING TO THOUSANDS

Ironically, even though Sam never wanted the PCA to begin, the seminary he
founded actually provided the new denomination with what it needed to survive.
The PCA basically began with a seminary in hand.

"To start new churches, you've got to have trained ministers in the field,"
explains Scott, "and that takes years. RTS trained men for seven years before
the PCA came into existence. Sam meant for these students to go back into
the PCUS, but in actuality they became the nucleus out of which much of the
strength of the PCA came."

Morton Smith feels that RTS was instrumental in a rebirth of the Reformed
tradition in the Southern Presbyterian Church, but certainly not as Sam wanted it
to happen. "The Presbyterian Church in America would not have had anywhere
near its ministerial strength, had it not been for RTS. It did drain out of the PCUS
many of their strong evangelicals, especially in the ministry. Sam was saddened,
for he felt there was less likelihood that the PCUS could ever be reformed. If
the PCA had not been formed, it's hard to say if revival would have come to
the PCUS. Probably conservative ministers would have drifted out into other
existing conservative Presbyterian churches."

However, to the end of his days, Sam most likely found it difficult to focus on
the good brought by his actions so many years before, since he had instigated a
movement that had divided the very church he desperately wanted to save:

*Tragically, the formation of the PCA interrupted the course and
intention of RTS. This greatly divided the conservative sector originally
in the PCUS. While the seminary had no part in the plans for the new
denomination, ultimately a large portion of the ministers and even
trustees who had supported the seminary ended up in the PCA.*

The seminary became less concerned with providing constructive, conservative ministers for the PCUS, and became more and more an institution to train conservative ministers for a conservative denomination, now the PCA.

Across the years, the seminary has become exceptionally proficient in its calling to provide training for ministerial candidates. It has an outstanding faculty and a highly dedicated board of trustees. Nonetheless, I'm greatly disappointed that RTS was not able to hold more closely to its intention of providing constructive, conservative ministers for the PCUS and the United Presbyterian Church. It is my hope that in the future, God will have His own way of returning the seminary to a position more nearly in keeping with that which was, I believe, its God-given, original mission.[251]

In fact, even during the genesis of RTS in the 1960s, Sam was haunted by fear of God's judgment if he harmed the Church:

Some nights I lie awake dreading standing before God knowing I will be held accountable in starting the seminary. If it proved to be a hazard to the church of Christ, if it rent or hurt or harmed it, I would stand judgment for that. I'll tell you the truth, many times I almost backed out because I was scared to go on.[252]

As happens many times, we plan and plan, and then the Sovereign Lord brings about what He purposes. Why events played out as they did puzzled and dismayed Sam. It surely was one of the first questions he asked the Lord when he stepped through the gates of paradise. While RTS did not do what Sam had envisioned, in a larger sense, Sam was indeed an integral cog in the wheel of evangelical revival. Interestingly, what Sam wanted actually did happen, not in the PCUS, but in the denomination of his ancestors, the Associate Reformed Presbyterian Church.

"Hoping to stem the tide of liberalism in their own denomination," explains Jack Scott, "conservative ARP churches sent their best young men to RTS for several years. Those students graduated and went back to turn the ARP completely around, becoming strong pastors, professors, and college or seminary presidents."

Would Sam remain in the PC(USA) today? It's impossible to say, but it's entirely probable. While the church's impurity grieved him, he could live with it in infinite patience as he waited for God in His perfect timing to make things right. Sam's chosen path was a lonely one, but he felt called by God to it. He dared not shrink from it. Although being true to his heart hurt deeply, he was willing to be misunderstood by and estranged from almost everyone. On one hand, most PCA supporters, including Sam's closest friends and colleagues, could never fathom why he refused to leave the PCUS and why he continued to fight for her purity. On the other hand, PCUS supporters, in the denomination for which he was fighting, did not trust him because of his affiliation with RTS. Like many others in the PCUS, two of his Union classmates interviewed for this book had to be convinced that Sam had actually never left the PCUS. For decades, they had assumed he had left, based on his involvement with RTS.

As for RTS, in the end Sam may have had differences with the board, but his faith and vision in leading the founders of RTS have brought blessings to countless people and will continue to do that in the future. God has blessed the faith of those founders more abundantly than they could ever have conceived in their wildest dreams. Who would have believed it? In only forty years, from literally nothing, God has raised up a mighty work that is now impacting the entire world for His Kingdom.

Sam's greatest legacy to RTS will be that of a humble, Christ-like servant. He was God's servant as he responded to the call of faith to raise up a seminary true to God's Word. He was God's servant as he waited on Him to provide for the seminary's every need, and as he humbly and lovingly taught those around him how to trust God for all things. He was God's servant as, at every turn over the years, when the school needed his spiritual gifts, his communication and diplomatic skills, he sacrificed what he loved most—preaching the Gospel— for the need before him. He was God's servant because he was always about helping, giving, and uplifting, never about power or selfish ambition.

Richard de Witt penned a fitting epitaph to Sam's years at RTS. "Sam was one of Christ's noblest and choicest servants. His walk with the Lord was transparently devout and sincere. No one could question his integrity or the presence of God's grace in his heart. RTS can be grateful for such a founder."

Amazing what God can do with a servant who is willing to make the coffee and turn out the lights.

Baby Sammy Patterson

Sammy as a young boy

Sammy, a little older in knickers

The Patterson Family in 1932
Back row from left: Foster, Hugh, Jasper, and Grier
Front row: Lois, S. J., Lily, and Sam

The First Presbyterian Church manse in Morrilton

Sammy in high school

Scores of sketches, such as this one, grace Sam's diary

From left, Allan Merritt, Sam, and Tom Massey in high school

Sam and Allan Merritt with dates at Cedar Canyon on Petit Jean Mountain

BOY SCOUTS OF AMERICA

April 13, 1934.

Scout Sam Patterson,
Church St.,
Morrilton, Ark.

My dear Eagle Scout: Thru Ouachita Council #14.

It is with special pleasure and satisfaction that I approve the official certificate of the rank of Eagle Scout which you have achieved. On behalf of my associates here and of the National Council, I congratulate you. Your own desire, achievement and conduct have warranted the Local Scout Officials in recommending you for this, the highest rank in Scouting.

We sincerely hope that your Merit Badge work has given you a larger vision of the opportunities for earning a livelihood, and that you have fairly definitely determined what your life work will be. We trust that you will use every effort to make yourself proficient along that line. No country in the world offers greater opportunities to those who are ambitious, to make thorough preparation for their careers. I hope that you will consult your local Scout Leaders who may be in a position to advise you, and others in your school or your community who may help you in thinking your problem through. As you know, many of our most successful men have worked their way, in part or whole, through college.

As an Eagle Scout you are one of the outstanding Scouts of the country. In the year 1932, there were 9,225 Eagle Scout Awards out of a grand total membership of 1,262,735 men and boys on our records during the year. Our whole membership is interested in you future, and we hope that it may be one that will bring joy and satisfaction to you, to your home-folks, and to your Scout Leaders, and reflect credit upon the Boy Scout Movement.

You now have the privilege of continuing your service relationship to the Movement, exercising your leadership talent, and putting into practice the Scout Oath and Law, the Daily Good Turn, and the Motto, "Be Prepared."

Sincerely and cordially yours,
BOY SCOUTS OF AMERICA

James E. West

Chief Scout Executive.

JEW/BK
Enc.

"BE PREPARED"   ALL COMMUNICATIONS SHOULD BE ADDRESSED TO THE BOY SCOUTS OF AMERICA.   "DO A GOOD TURN DAILY"
2 PARK AVENUE, NEW YORK CITY.

Letter awarding Sam the coveted Eagle Scout Award in 1934

"Red" Patterson (second from right) watches Southwestern Lynx football with an injured ankle in 1935

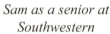

Sam as a senior at Southwestern

Sam (second from right) on kitchen duty at Ferncliff

*From left, Ralph Buchanan, Sam, and
John D. Smith with the Great Speckled Bird*

*Union Seminary
senior portrait*

*Sam and Stelle in front of
their Martinsville cotton mill
home in 1943*

*Sam and Sandy in front of
Martinsville cotton mill home*

Cotton mill home as it looks today

Kate Anderson Presbyterian Church in the 1940s

Interior of Kate Anderson Church in the 1940s

Sam as a Navy chaplain assigned to the Marines, circa 1941

Lt.jg. E.E. PHIFER   Lt.jg. R.E. POERSCHKE   Lt.jg. C.C. McPHEETERS   Lt.jg. G.W. MARQUETTE   Lt.jg. S.C. PATTERSON
Lt. J.J. CASSIDY   Lt. Cdr. S.W. RUSSELL   Lt. J.R. CRONIN   Lt.jg. E.R. ALLENDER
San Diego, California
March 1945

*Sam (far right, back row) taking up his first Marine duties
in San Diego, California*

Sam and Stelle having fun while stationed in San Diego during World War II

Sam (right) hard at work at French Camp Academy along with Billy Thompson, principal, (left) and Bob Bullard, business manager (center)

From right, Becky, Sam, and Stelle in French Camp's dining hall

The Jones Boys

Sam (far right, back row) gathers with French Camp staff at one of the famous pheasant hunts.

Back row from left, Billy Thompson, Student Billy Bishop, Student Alvin Reyer, Jimmie Henderson, Johnnie Pee, Student Doug Jones, Sam.

Front row from left, Drew Thomas, Student Sabra Slay, Barney Thomas

Sam with the RTS Board of Trustees and faculty during the seminary's early years

Sam (middle back row) at RTS's first convocation in 1966

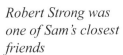
Robert Strong was one of Sam's closest friends

Sam at the dedication of the RTS Biblical Studies Building, named for L. Nelson Bell, Sam's mentor

Sam in his RTS office

Sam listens carefully to an RTS student's concerns

Sam and his successor as RTS president, Luder Whitlock

Sam and Stelle

Sam's daughter, Becky, and her
husband, Jimmy Rogers

Granddaughter Debbie Ivey (left), Sam, and daughter Becky Rogers

Sam dearly loved the outdoors his entire life

Sam with a huge catch

After retiring from RTS, Sam returned to his beloved French Camp

Sam's rustic cabin in French Camp during his retirement years

Sam studied, wrote sermons, and corresponded here right up until his death

Sam's cabin was sparsely furnished but had all he needed for comfortable living

Sam and Allan Merritt (left) chat during their
50th high school reunion in Morrilton in 1984

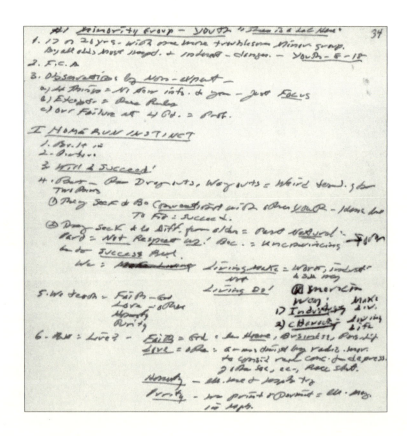

Sam's sermon notes in tiny scrawl on a 4 by 6 index card

CHAPTER SEVEN

THE EVANGELIST

Therefore, if anyone is in Christ he is a new creation, old things have passed away, behold, all things have become new.

2 Corinthians 5:17 (NKJV)

O, watchman, tell the message true,
Or if thou shirk thy holy task,
Their blood will I require of you
When I shall come with trumpet blast.

William Hill, Founder
Presbyterian Evangelistic Fellowship

Regardless of the numerous roles Sam played over the years, he never thought of himself as anything other than a simple evangelist, saying he'd been one from the time he got up off his knees at Union Seminary.

"I believe I enjoy preaching Jesus more than anything in the world," he often said. "Whether the crowd is big or small, I'm just grateful that someone will let me talk to them about Jesus for a while."[1]

"Sam did nothing with greater zest and enthusiasm than preach the Gospel," says Richard de Witt.

The picture of Sam in the pulpit is indelibly etched in countless minds—a stocky, smiling, red-head preaching straight from the heart in an endearing Arkansas twang. In one hand, held high, a soft-cover Bible lay open, ready to be read. For the longest time, little Maria Harper Price carried a red Bible simply because Sam preached from one.

"He was a watchman, a servant of the sacrificial kind, looking to others' needs and not his own," said Ron McKinney (RTS '74). "His heartbeat was to see men come to know Christ and be changed by the power of the Holy Spirit."

Sam's sermons held fire, but not like the blazing inferno below. They held the warmth and passion of God, a Father burning with love and reaching out to all of His lost children. Sam's one passion was to lead others to the Lord. Even as president of two schools, he always made sure he was given permission to preach, and preach he did.

Sermons came from his heart; his words were a part of him, the result of hours, days, and weeks in meditation. According to Bill Whitwer, Sam took notes during his daily devotions and developed sermons from them. He protected his time with the Lord, telling Mildred Coleman's pastor in Vicksburg that he would be unavailable for any counseling or visitation on a certain day. "We learned later," said Mildred, "that he had parked his van at the local RV campground and spent the day praying and fasting, a regular discipline for him. All of us knew that he had been with God. All who ever sat under his teaching or preaching or who had the privilege of conversing with him were forever blessed."

As a result, Sam's messages were easy to understand because he had already digested the scripture, taken the precepts to heart, and put them into practice, as the Apostle John did in Revelation 10:10–11 (NIV) when he "took the little scroll from the angel's hand and ate it" in order to prophesy to many nations, languages, and kings. In comments on this passage, RTS Professor Simon Kistemaker could easily be describing Sam:

> *Witnessing for the Lord calls for unflinching courage and gracious tact.... That person ought to have fully absorbed the Word so that it has become an inseparable part of his or her being. He or she must appropriate God's message by faith, obey it fully, be totally controlled by it, always remain true to its message, speak judiciously, and not become silent.*[2]

Sam never talked down to his listeners. He spoke as if to friends, imparting very important advice. In fact, he frequently addressed his audience as "friends." The hallmark of Sam's sermons was the simple, clear presentation of the Gospel. From first to last, God's truth had a chokehold on Sam's listeners. Young and old alike could understand his messages because he put the cookies on the lower shelf where all could reach them.

"Sam simply stood up and talked to people from the Bible, teaching them its truths," observed Lynn Downing (RTS '69). "The sermons had structure and prepared content, but they were personally communicated. I have tried to pattern my own preaching style after his because I saw how effective it was."

Frank Horton recalls, "From the moment I first heard Sam at First Presbyterian Church in Grenada in the late 1940s, my wife and I were always in the audience when Sam held a meeting within traveling distance."

"Sam was universally loved for his humble, straightforward, clear preaching," revealed colleague Morton Smith. "He was a great model for me in trying to reach all ages."

It is no wonder that many received Christ under Sam's preaching. The earnestness, care, and compassion communicated by Sam's voice were irresistibly appealing. Moreover, his urgency was compelling, so important that one must do it NOW! He winsomely painted for his listeners a God who is ever ready to accept us and is full of grace and mercy. Sam did not mince words about sin, but he was not damning. Always he held out the hope of Christ's everlasting love for mankind. According to Sam, when we confess and get right with God, He is waiting for us with open arms.

Other pastors learned much from Sam, such as the young Mississippi preacher bent on saving the world in his first pastorate. His sermons were fiery and full of damnation for sinners who did not come to Christ, but he wasn't seeing many accept the Lord. When he asked Sam to hold evangelistic meetings at his church, the novice pastor could see significant spiritual growth occurring in the congregation. One night as he and his wife drove home from the services, the young minister asked her, "Why do our members respond so much better to Sam's sermons than to mine?" She looked at him kindly and said, "The God of Sam Patterson, I love. Your God—well, I don't know."

Sam's informal, earthy style was humble and gentle, never intimidating or arrogant. His sermons always centered on the Gospel message and were never heavily theological, an emphasis Sam thought quite dangerous:

> *The most important thing we do in our preaching and teaching is to exalt Jesus. A heavy application of the law or a tedious, intricate development of various lines of biblical teaching, all will starve the poor sheep.*[3]

Part of the dynamic of Sam's sermons was his sincere and passionate delivery. One sensed the great love in his heart for his audience; he wanted so much for them to know what he knew and to possess a transforming relationship with Christ. Sam truly believed what he spoke. He had met wonderful, wonderful Jesus, and the desire for others to know the Lord flooded out of him, drenching all within the sound of his voice.

"I have always compared Sam's sermons to the low-level strategic bombing used by the United States to win World War II," noted Jack Bushman, who was saved under Sam's preaching. "Sam consistently came in low, and his spiritual 'bombs' were always right on target. If someone failed to get his message, that person plainly wasn't listening."

"I've always said if I knew when I was to die and could hear one last sermon, I'd want Sam Patterson to preach it," said Jim Baird, who considers Sam one of his spiritual fathers. "That man hit a homerun every time I heard him proclaim God's Word. He preached from the Bible and always raised up Christ in a wonderfully winsome manner."

At RTS, Sam's preaching influenced many. "Mr. Pat's life was the greatest lesson I learned in seminary," says Larry Wanaselja (RTS '78). "His simple, yet profound, ideas; his fervor and love for Christ; his heart filled with ardor and passion for the Savior were all a breath of fresh air in an academic setting. He loved the Lord Jesus Christ, and it oozed out of him every time he preached. It wasn't all in his head, but had worked its way down into his heart."

Dana Casey (RTS '80, '83, '86) agrees. "Of all the great preachers we were able to hear as seminary students, no one preached with more 'authority and not as the scribes' than did Mr. Pat. You knew he had unshakable faith in the Word he taught."

T. M. Moore (RTS '77) was also influenced by Sam. "His preaching was solidly biblical, wonderfully down-home and winsome, and passionate to the point of tears. He lit fires in our breasts. I wanted to be able to preach like Mr. Patterson, an aspiration I have since abandoned as beyond my grasp."

Sam always joked about keeping messages short, agreeing with George Burns's quip, "The secret of a good sermon is a good beginning and a good ending—and keeping the two as close together as possible." Apparently, Sam learned an important lesson about sermon length while living in Beaumont, Texas, for a year and a half during the early 1980s. Unknown in those parts, he didn't do any preaching, so he was able to react to sermons as one of the congregation:

> If a preacher can't say what he wants to say in twenty minutes, he ought to do something else! From now on, if I make one or two good points and people remember them, I've got it made.[4]

Sam's sermons were as appealing and compelling as Billy Graham's or Dwight L. Moody's, but he did not achieve their fame for several reasons. First, he cared nothing for recognition and, most likely, did not want to be in the spotlight. Second, he gravitated toward small churches. While he preached wherever he was called with the same urgency no matter the church's size, he always had special compassion for the small, rural church and its difficulty in getting and keeping good pastors. He went out of his way to grant requests from congregations such as the Poplarville, Mississippi church that asked him to hold communion services. The congregation could celebrate the sacrament only on the infrequent occasions when an ordained minister came. Fulfilling such requests gave Sam much pleasure.

Finally, although Sam's one desire was to preach, God kept placing other opportunities for ministry before him that he couldn't deny, most notably French Camp Academy and Reformed Theological Seminary. Whenever the Lord allowed, Sam was always in the pulpit, but history shows that he sacrificed his great love of preaching regularly for both schools. The picture that comes to mind is a racehorse straining to go in one direction, while his Master steadily pulls the reins in the other direction. Sam always obeyed his Lord's directives; but, when given his head, he always moved toward a pulpit.

Many people were amazed that Sam used no notes when preaching. Said Bill Rogers (FCA '65), "I've met only two preachers in my life who actually preached from their hearts and didn't read from a book or notes. Sam was one of them."

However, what looked so effortless and "from the heart" was the result of much work and meditation. In the early days of his ministry in Martinsville, Sam wrote out each sermon in an illegible scrawl that even *he* probably had trouble reading. A few years later he began outlining his sermons, but still writing them out in longhand. As he became more proficient in the pulpit, his outlines became very elaborate, some fifteen pages long.

By the time he reached Leland, he had learned how to condense his outline to a single note card with tiny printing. At that point, he likely used the outline only for the Herculean task of memorizing his many points. People who encountered this microscopic scribbling were flabbergasted. After Sam had preached a series of services in her church, hostess Lou Ann Webb returned some sermon notes he had left at her home:

> *I found this pink slip in your room.... As well as I can make out, it is notes on the first sermon you preached to us.... I don't want anyone to miss out on the Gospel of John as you preached it to us, but how this pink slip can help, I can't imagine. Did you study to be a doctor previously?[5]*

Sam replied humorously, "Thanks very much for sending the little pink slip with hieroglyphics on it. I know it looks like the written form of an unknown tongue!"[6]

A PICTURE IS WORTH A THOUSAND WORDS

Sam painted vivid pictures for his listeners; people recall his riveting illustrations over half a century later, even if they heard them as children in one of his legendary chalk talks. Until his death recently at age ninety-seven, Charlton Hutton remembered Sam's sermon on Zacchaeus in April 1951.

Sam saw all of life as grist for sermons. He wrote sermon illustrations, notes, outlines, quotations, and devotional thoughts on whatever was handy—bills, sales receipts, revival notices, and envelopes. He probably saved outlines from nearly every sermon he ever preached.

"He didn't tell other people's stories, nor did he use commercial illustration books for preachers," notes Jack Scott. "He told of his own personal experiences in the ministry."

Guy Richardson's (RTS '77) eyes still well with tears when he remembers Sam's story illustrating "Underneath are the Everlasting Arms."

"When Sam was young, he'd go rabbit hunting with his dog Speck. To get to the good rabbit-hunting land, they had to cross a railroad trestle over a deep chasm. Although Speck was thrilled to go hunting, he always grew terrified as they approached that trestle. He absolutely despised walking across those ties. The cracks were narrow, and he could never have fallen through; yet, he could see through them how far away the ground was. Sam would cross to the other side and call Speck, but the dog would refuse to come. Finally, Sam would walk off, and Speck would realize he'd have to follow or return home alone. Curling his tail between his legs, Speck would then tip-toe across the ties.

"Sam would then tell his listeners, 'That railroad trestle was built to hold a thousand-ton freight train, and this little dog—not thirty pounds soaking wet— was scared to death it was going to collapse, sending him to his death. Aren't we just like that? We can see all the possible threats and dangers in life, but we don't realize that God always has us in His mighty hands.'"

A French Camp youngster provided Sam with another memorable vehicle to help Christians understand that they don't need to fear death. A group was touring the school with Sam to observe the children on the work program. He was happy that they seemed favorably impressed. Suddenly, a mischievous eight-year-old boy approached Sam with closed hands, saying excitedly, "Mr. Patterson, guess what I've got?"

Dismayed, Sam instantly knew trouble was upon them, since he was fairly sure the boy had a mouse to display. Bravely, however, he played along and replied with trepidation, "I don't know." The little tyke then opened his hands and shoved them right in Sam's face, scaring him and forcing him to step back. In the boy's hands was an enormous red wasp—alive! Yet, the child said soothingly, "Don't be afraid. I've already pulled the stinger out! It can't hurt you."

Sam later told his listeners, "That wasp still looked bad, but I wasn't frightened any longer. That's the way we should feel about death."[7]

"Sam had a masterful way of making the scriptures applicable to life," said Richard Swayze, a retired PC(USA) pastor. "Early on, he challenged me to take seriously the importance of effective preaching, using appropriate humor and making the message relevant to the occasion."

Sam found illustrations for his sermons literally everywhere. Among his possessions is an ancient scrapbook, surely almost seventy-five years old, containing homilies, devotions, poems, and quotations. Its pages are brown and crumbling, as are many of its contents. The holes in the pages of the scrapbook, as well as the cover, have long since torn away from their string binder. Conceivably, Sam began collecting these in high school, college, or even in the early years of his ministry. Certainly these are thoughts on which he began meditating early in his Christian life. He did not become the Sam Patterson we knew overnight; it took a lifetime of contemplation on concepts such as these.

Even on vacation, Sam didn't cease looking for illustrations. Consider the following notes taken while on vacation in Arkansas:

> At midmorning, I was seated reading on the banks of a tiny stream which ran in front of our cottage. On the other side were a number of chickens and two ducks. A woman came out of a lunch house and scattered a basket of scraps. Immediately the birds were scratching, pecking, clucking, and grabbing in a frantic fury. One chicken, apparently by pluck and initiative, had secured a piece of bread for itself and began to run away with it so no one else could have it. Unfortunately, it was bigger than he could handle, and it kept falling from his beak. It was more than he needed, but, mind you, it was HIS, and he intended that NO other chicken should have any of it.
>
> Another chicken that had no bread saw the first chicken making off with the stolen booty. He was off after him, trying to get all or part of the bread for himself. The 'have all' had too much but did not intend to part with any. The 'have not' decided to take it from him by any means he could. As the bread fell from the first chicken's beak yet again, the second chicken grabbed it and took it far off. Now suddenly a 'have all,' he had no mercy for the 'have nots' and refused to share. The chicken sat eating the bread alone, while little chicks scurried around in hunger. I said to Stelle, 'Chickens offer a good study in human nature, don't they?'[8]

Tony Orlando and Dawn, in their hit "Tie a Yellow Ribbon 'Round the Ole Oak Tree," provided Sam with one of his favorite illustrations for the love of God in Christ Jesus. A prisoner is coming home after doing a three-year prison hitch and has written his girl that he is coming. If she wants him back, she should tie a yellow ribbon around a certain oak tree. If he doesn't see the ribbon, he'll stay on the bus and go away. He asks the bus driver to look for him because he can't bear the disappointment if the ribbon is missing. As they round the corner and the oak tree comes into view, the entire bus begins to cheer wildly. A hundred yellow ribbons festoon the tree![9]

Sam rarely joked in his sermons, but, according to friends, he loved to tell the following humorous story to wake people up. Three preachers—Baptist, Methodist, and Presbyterian—lived in a little town on the coast. They met for coffee frequently, and one morning all were complaining that they were worn out being pastors—counseling people, studying, visiting the sick.

The Presbyterian preacher suggested, "Let's get a boat and go fishing today." The others agreed, so they rented a boat and paddled out to fish. The Methodist preacher said, "Uh-oh, we forgot the fishing poles. I'll have to go get them." He stepped out on top of the water, walked across, got the fishing poles, came back, and got in the boat.

No sooner had he sat down than the Presbyterian preacher complained, "You didn't bring the bait. I'll go get it." He stepped out on top of the water, walked across, got the bait, came back, and got in the boat.

He'd barely sat down when the Baptist preacher reminded him, "You didn't bring our lunch! I'll go get it." He stepped out of the boat and sank like a stone. After he had tried three times to walk on the water and failed, the Presbyterian preacher looked at the Methodist preacher and chuckled. "You know, if we don't tell Joe where those rocks are, he's gonna drown!"

A MEEK AND HUMBLE MAN

Although Sam was a consummate preacher, much evidence shows that he often doubted he had anything worthwhile to say. Before speaking to the Christian Reformed Ministers Institute, he told Rev. Jacob Uitvlugt:

> *My only reluctance to speak arises out of my personal feeling of insufficiency. I am neither a scholar nor a theologian. I am an evangelist. However, I am greatly encouraged by the thought that God's Providence is in your invitation and God promises to enable His servants to do His will.[10]*

The only time Sam ever preached at the Pensacola Theological Institute was August 3–10, 1980, when he delivered one of his favorite sermon series, *Prominent Themes from the Gospel of Luke*. On the podium with the famous J. I. Packer, Sam admitted to his listeners more than once during the week that he was apprehensive:

> *It may be amazing that a person who has been preaching the Gospel for better than forty years would be filled with anxiety at a moment like this, but I have been. I know that the quality of these Institutes has been superior. I am embarrassed to add my own degree of mediocrity to them, but I am grateful for this privilege. And I believe in all of this that God has had something to do with my being here.[11]*

At another evangelistic meeting, he confessed to a congregation that even his grammar bothered him at times:

> *I preached for an RTS graduate recently, and a few days ago he sent me the transcript to proof in hopes of printing it. I know now that was just a nice way of getting me to read it. As I looked over it, I was absolutely horrified at my poor grammar. I'm still right shaken by it. I comforted myself as I corrected it by realizing that RTS students will never have this problem. Their errors will be caught and corrected before they become hardened out in the ministry![12]*

Apparently Stelle was a pillar of strength in building Sam's confidence. He later told congregations:

> *Stelle was a source of self-respect to me. More than any one factor in my whole ministry, she was responsible for my sense of confidence as a minister. She never put me down in my preaching. Never! A little later in the week she had subtle ways of telling me I had made a mistake, but she was tactful and kind. She always made me feel as if she'd rather hear me preach than anybody else. If she had a choice in conference speakers, she always chose to hear me. She made notes constantly and spoke so appreciatively afterward—not every time, but she did it enough. She never tired of hearing me preach, even if she'd heard the sermon five or six times. If you don't think that does something to a man's confidence, you just better think about that a little bit!* [13]

Yet, Sam's innate humility kept him from taking himself too seriously, as Andy Wells, son of RTS founder Erskine Wells, happily discovered. As a junior at Belhaven in 1971, he was in charge of securing chapel speakers. Although Andy didn't know Sam, he had heard about him from his father; therefore, he asked him to speak. However, the day before Sam was to preach, Andy learned that a friend of one of the college administrators had been accidentally scheduled in Sam's spot.

"I was horrified. What would I tell Sam? I could not get in touch with him, so I had to face him in the chapel parking lot when he arrived. With fear and trembling, I gave him the news and apologized profusely. I was fully ready for him to come down on me, saying, 'Son, I'm a busy man and you just wasted my valuable time. You need to get your act together!' Instead, he smiled this wonderful, gentle smile and said, 'That's okay, Andy. I understand. The preparation was very good for me.' I knew then that what my father had said all those years was true. Sam Patterson really was a spiritual giant with a meek and gentle spirit."

Sam sought always to point people to Christ in every way, both in the pulpit and in his life. He admired Luke and preached from his gospel frequently, dubbing him and the other gospel writers as the first members of "Authors Anonymous" because none of them revealed his own identity. He felt each was like the Holy Spirit, who bears testimony of Christ, not of Himself. This contrasted sharply with some churches and ministers, who made the focal point of ministry the personality, ability, and gifts of the messenger. Sam learned early that this attitude was not productive for God's Kingdom:

> *The summer before I went to seminary I was working at Ferncliff Conference Center [in Arkansas]. A denomination was bringing its session to a close and wanted us to help them hold a communion service*

on the lake. They asked the staff to erect a large cross across the lake from the congregation and arrange to set it aflame in the darkness when the group began singing 'When I Survey the Wondrous Cross.' They wanted the cross to continue burning until the song's end. Two other staff members and I began what we thought was an easy task. Yet, it wasn't. We didn't have any trouble erecting the cross, but it burned either too quickly or too slowly.

We finally noticed a row of rather dense bushes behind the cross. We realized that two of us could stand behind the bushes with kegs of kerosene and constantly slosh the fuel over the cross to keep it burning at a steady rate. Over a quarter of a century later, I can still remember how magnificent that cross looked! If we had not been obscured, we would have been a disturbing, distracting element. Yet, we were hidden, throwing the fuel on it unseen, and the cross shone in all its glory. I see that in Luke. He hides himself behind the wonderful portrait of Jesus, which he shows in undying color.[14]

J. I. Packer makes the same point in *Rediscovering Holiness:*

The Scottish scholar James Denney once said that it is impossible at the same time to leave the impression both that I am a great preacher and that Jesus Christ is a great Savior. In the same way, it is impossible at the same time to give the impression both that I am a great Christian and that Jesus Christ is a great Master.... The Christian will practice curling up small, as it were, so that in and through him or her the Savior may show himself great.[15]

"Humility was one of Sam's great strong points," observed Morton Smith. "He was teachable and never arrogant. That's why he could be so influential; people saw him as a humble, simple, straightforward preacher with boundless integrity."

Indeed, Sam had no qualms about admitting he had been wrong about issues. "I've had to change my preaching and my testimony a lot since I first became a Christian. When I first started preaching, I didn't know what I do now about scripture. If something in the Bible has showed me wrong, I have tried to change it, and I'll continue to do that."[16]

Much like the Apostle Paul, the more Sam grew in Christ the greater became his awareness of personal sin. He often wore a silver belt buckle with the letters CSA—"Converted Sinners Association"—and told congregations he was glad they didn't really know him well:

No one could know me and love me, but the Lord. I don't know anyone's life like I know my own. I used to tell Stelle that she loved me because she didn't really know me. I couldn't stand for her to really know me. Everybody would surrender their love for me if they knew what God knows about me. But God knows, and He loves me! None of us can stand too much inspection. If I entertain any kind of reputation, I know why it is. I move around a lot; I'm here four days and gone.[17]

The older he grew, the more Sam realized he had barely established a beach head on the vast continent of blessings and significance through Christ.[18] On February 28, 1962, the twenty-second anniversary of his conversion, he humbly wrote his siblings, "I'm still no prize for the Lord." An interesting assessment, since by then he had already brought hundreds to the Lord through his preaching, snatched a school from bankruptcy and put it on sound footing, become a beloved father figure to hundreds of young people, and endeared himself as a trustworthy friend in the Lord and mentor to countless people. In just two years, he would lead the way in the formation of Reformed Theological Seminary.

A HOST OF WITNESSES

While Sam was incredibly humble about his ability to preach, the record shows that God spoke mightily through him. Across the years, numerous people have revealed what Sam's preaching meant in their lives. Sam had to discover in glory the huge number of people who never told him.

Charlie Waggener was thirteen in the late 1960s when Sam preached a revival at First Presbyterian Church in Carthage, Mississippi. He'd been attending the revival all week and each night had heard Sam invite people to take Christ as their Savior. The night before the revival was over, he almost walked down the aisle but didn't.

"I didn't understand the Gospel and knew I needed to talk to Mr. Patterson, so I went up to the church. He drew a little diagram showing me a spiritual bridge I could walk over to receive life everlasting. He explained salvation so clearly! I thought the world was going to come to an end before that night, when I would be able to profess my faith before the church. There's no telling what would have happened to me in life if I hadn't talked with Mr. Patterson that day."

Others, such as Nancy Vincent, were silent Christians whom Sam encouraged to speak up. "I had earlier committed my life to Christ and considered it a private issue until Mr. Pat came to our church in Clarksdale, Mississippi, in 1970 for a week of spiritual emphasis," confessed Nancy. "I can still remember his sermon from John 21, when Jesus asked Peter if he loved Him. Mr. Pat gave an altar call each night, something I had never seen done in our church since I had joined as a young bride. I held back each time until the last night, when I *knew* that I had to make a public profession of my love for Jesus. It was the most wonderful and *freeing* experience I have ever had, and I have never been the same since."

"Mr. Pat was at FCA during my last years of high school," revealed Mary Howard Clark. "He was one of the finest Christians I have ever known. I enjoyed his devotions each morning in chapel; he made the Bible clearer in five minutes than most preachers can in thirty. I'm sorry I didn't abide by all he said, but when I really met the Master, all of Mr. Pat's teaching came back to me. For twenty-five years now, my Bible has been my most treasured possession."

In March 1975, Sam preached the series *The Revolutionary Aspects of the Lord's Prayer* in Vicksburg. "I still remember and think on things I learned that week," said Mildred Coleman gratefully. "He truly encouraged and edified us, and we were never the same after he left."

One summer, Sam preached a revival at a small mountain church in North Carolina. After one of the services, a mother approached him, saying, "My little girl has an abnormal fear of the dark. She won't sleep without a light on and won't go anywhere in the dark unless someone is with her, holding her hand. Last night after your sermon, I thought she'd be inside the church because she scarcely ever even gets out in the churchyard since the porch light doesn't reach that far. When I didn't find her, I was frightened. I began calling and finally heard her voice rise faintly from the darkness of the road way down the hill. I thought surely she had gone with someone down there. I hurried to her as fast as I could, but when I got there, she was standing in the middle of the road all by herself in the pitch-black darkness. I grabbed her and said, 'Honey, what in the world are you doing down here by yourself?' She said, 'I'm not by myself. The Lord is with me.'" During the revival, Sam had preached on the joy and freedom that come to each person who lives in the conscious awareness of the abiding presence of Jesus. That little girl had certainly gotten the point![19]

Sometimes Sam himself couldn't foresee God's life-changing work in souls as a result of his preaching. During his first series of evangelistic services after seminary, he preached on John 3:16. The only one responding to the invitation was a woman who was not only the president of the Women in the Church, but also the choir director. At first Sam thought such an active member merely wanted to rededicate her life to Christ. Yet, he could not have been more wrong.

"Mr. Patterson," she confessed, "as long as I can remember, I have believed *about* Jesus. The time has come when I must believe *in* him. I have accepted as fact what the Bible said about Jesus, but now I see a real need to put my life by faith in the care, control, and keeping of Christ, where it has never been."[20]

Sam also helped Maria J. Durham significantly in 1970 when he preached a revival in her small church in Petal, Mississippi. "After the service I asked Mr. Sam what to do about a close family member who was living in sin. He was very kind and didn't lecture or judge but told me to pray about it. That was truly a message from the Lord. Our relationship with that person has grown stronger over the years, and God was glorified. Mr. Sam also touched the heart of my friend, Mollie, with his love for children. She began a life of service to the primary Sunday School and has been there for forty years."

In another 1970 meeting in South Mississippi, a woman who had been converted two years before came into a new relationship with the Holy Spirit during one of Sam's revivals. Subsequently, she brought to the church quite a number of books on spiritism, magic, and the occult. In keeping with Acts 19:19, Sam led a book burning after the morning service.[21]

Over the years, many people wrote to express their heartfelt thanks to Sam for his ministry to them. Here are a few:

Alice McPherson, April 2, 1971

I believe with all my heart you were sent to lead my husband to Christ.... I was a Christian when I met you, but you have made it all so much more meaningful. Some things that were so very important before ...now have taken second place in my heart and life.... I thought I loved the Lord, but since hearing your sermons and having our talk ...I see I was not loving Him in the right way and putting Him first ahead of everything and everyone. I can do that now, thank God!

Joy Anne Fox, November 17, 1975

Your messages, with the underlying theme of the sovereignty of God, were such a blessing to me. No finer compliment can be paid to any man of God than to say that Christ became more precious and real through his ministry. I speak not only for myself but also for many of the folks at our church.

Erskine Jackson, February 8, 1970

... Those days went a long way in meeting some very pressing personal needs. I was speaking ...with deep sincerity when I said at our final service that a 'new beginning of obedience' had begun with ME.... Renewal in a quiet way has come for many, and we have had a 'session of refreshing from above.' Thank you!

Noni Mulheim, November 10, 1969

A couple of personal problems have been ironed out for me because of your clarification of God's Word. I just can't tell you how pointedly you spoke to our family and how much we all profited by it.

Nellie McPherson, November 24, 1970

You gave me a new understanding of the Christian walk, especially how to continue in the fullness of the Holy Spirit.... Before you came, one of my prayers was that God would bring revival to our church and to me personally. Until that first Saturday night, however, I had never stopped to consider what revival really is. God used that message to force me to decide whether or not I <u>really</u> wanted my life wholly surrendered to

Him. You know the confusion that followed, but thank God, that much has been set straight!

God used each of your messages to teach me something and/or answer prayers, one being that He would show me the things in my life which are displeasing to Him, since my sensibility to sin had grown quite dull. You hit home each day in one way or another, but your sermon on the crucifixion—the most powerful sermon I've ever heard—showed me in a new and very real way my worthlessness before Him and … my acceptance in His sight.… It has truly restored my joy in salvation.

Carole Crowell, April 9, 1972
… We needed the words you spoke from His living Word so badly. Our family will never be the same again.

Steve Irby, October 2, 1978
You will be glad to know you ministered to our church in a real way. Due to your preaching, several problems were exposed not a week later.… Members began to deal with them, which helped them advance in their Christian lives immensely. We thank God for the ministry you had!

Annie Fair Smith, February 19, 1977
I am a dedicated Christian and love the Lord with all my heart, but would you believe you made me love Him even more? You opened the scriptures in a way they had never been opened to me.

When Sam held a revival at Ebenezer Presbyterian Church (ARP) in Cotton Plant, Mississippi, in August 1969, he specifically prayed that God would bring at least one young man to sense a call to the Gospel ministry as He had in the life of Sam's father eighty years before. (See Appendix F.) Imagine Sam's joy when God answered that prayer in the form of young Marion Phagan, who planned to begin his witnessing ministry immediately in the military, then go to seminary.[22] Sam continued to counsel Marion while he was abroad:

I don't know of any part of your preparation for the ministry that will be more important than the part you are participating in right where you are now. While you are in the service, learning to maintain your own devotional time each day, learning to live faithfully for Christ in an alien atmosphere, and learning to witness for Him personally to fellow servicemen will be of utmost value.[23]

WITH PEN IN HAND

One cannot assess Sam's evangelistic ministry without taking a close look at his correspondence through the years, for it was a ministry in itself. He kept up with hundreds of people, both those to whom he preached and those he merely met, sharing the joys and troubles of their lives. His letters were always personal, warm, and gracious, leaving the recipient feeling special and certain beyond a doubt that Sam cared about him or her. He always extended a sincere invitation to "drop by for coffee and a visit." Since he typed most of them himself, the letters were filled with typos, misspellings, and grammatical errors, but Sam didn't care. He felt they made him seem more human. Surely they did just that for the many less educated people who corresponded with Sam:

> *We are praying for you at all time [sic] and I no [sic] the Lord will keep his hand over you. Thinks [sic] for saying something in your letter to Bro. Duke about me. It sure hup [sic] to no[sic] somebody else cares.[24]*

Sam had a great influence on this lady, according to her pastor:

> *Mrs. S____ was able to see Christ in you when you took the time to listen so patiently to her. This helped immensely.... A few days after you left, she got up and around and witnessed before many. She rejoiced, and we were blessed.[25]*

It has been said that Sam was one of the most thoughtful people on earth. It's true. He always wrote a warm letter of thanks to every person who did the smallest thing for him. Those who fed or kept him during revivals received individual notes; sometimes he wrote as many as eleven for one set of services. Sam did not do this to be mannerly, but because he was grateful. He always added a personal touch to make a simple thank-you note special.

To Blanche and John Kimbrough, March 18, 1971, he wrote:
> *Blanche, I did right well regarding my diet at mealtimes during the Lexington meeting, but those cookies and cakes you had sitting around in the kitchen almost ruined me between meals. They were delicious. I really enjoyed that can of cookies you gave me for the trip home.*

To Leon Webb and his wife, June 16, 1976, he wrote:
> *It would be impossible for me to tell you how much I enjoyed getting to be a part of your home.... You two people are truly my kind of people.... I intend to stop by from time to time to keep our friendship warm. Then, too, it is the same distance from there to here ... so I'll be counting on you folks coming by sometime.*

And he didn't leave the pets out:

> *Please drop Sissy a piece of bacon off the table and tell her you are giving it to her in my name! With a pat on the head, assure her of my affection and tell her she enhanced my sense of security and personal worth a great deal by making friends with me.*[26]

Sam endeared himself to many by recalling each item people asked for—bookmarks, a book on healing, information about a school. He made lists for himself and often sent things not requested.

> *I found out you can get a red Harper Study Bible, so I have ordered one for you.*[27]

Understandably, when Sam had to leave, people didn't want to see him go. Mary Alice made him a cake "just like Aunt Clara's" for Sam to take home, and Agnes made him "teacakes for the road." All felt a huge loss when Sam drove away:

> *We feel today that a member of the family has left us.... Even our two little boys have remembered to pray for you.*[28]
>
> *We started feeling lonely when you drove away.*[29]
>
> *... You must have more loving friends than anyone.... It was a privilege for me to be able to spend so much time with you.... I hope God's plan will allow me another opportunity to learn from you....Sharon and I hope you do drop by for that cup of coffee sometime and soon.... We will watch for that 'Speckled Bird' to come rolling in sometime.*[30]

OUT OF THE MOUTHS OF BABES

Sam's ministry to children and youth was every bit as powerful as his ministry to adults. From the beginning of his ministry, he realized that the young often respond to Christ far more easily than their elders. Whenever he had the opportunity, he spoke to both young children and youth—at camps, conferences, school chapels and classrooms, and church services.

"He had an open and unguarded relationship with students," remarked Ann Angle. "Yet, he was quite forthright about their need for Christ when he preached to them."

"I've shed many a tear in that old auditorium at French Camp when I saw some of my raunchiest boys go up and profess Christ under Sam's preaching," said Sam Allen emotionally. "I had almost given up hope on some of them."

As the daughter of Sam's good friend, the late Dr. Norman Harper, Becky Forester grew up seeing Sam as a frequent visitor in their home. Sam even baptized Becky and her sister, Maria. "Sam was one of the most gentle, patient men I've ever known. He was so down to earth and had time for everybody, whether one was five or fifty. Even when I was a small child, he'd stop and talk to me; I never felt I was too little or unimportant. He treated me no different than he treated any adult.

"He was a very powerful preacher. Usually children don't pay any attention to a sermon; they sit and color and wait for it to be over. Yet, even as a child, sitting still and listening to Sam was quite easy. I could understand exactly what he was talking about."

The last children's sermon Sam preached was in Leland on March 8, 1987, the week before he died. It stands as a classic example of Sam's ability to "put the cookies on the lower shelf." Sam could put together one of these talks in no time. Ann Aldridge reports that on the Sunday he gave this message, he had forgotten he had to give a children's sermon. He rushed off to a quiet room just minutes before the service to come up with some remarks. Notice how plainly and simply he lays out the Gospel:

> *People are a lot like pencils. You may not think so, but it's true. Pencils are about the same length and shape. They all have paint on the outside and wood on the inside, with lead down the middle. They all have little caps at the top. They are different, too. Pencils come in different colors, but the difference doesn't amount to much because it's just on the outside.*
>
> *In the same way, all people are made of the same materials and are shaped much the same. We have two eyes, two ears, two arms, and two legs. We have skin on the outside, muscle and bone on the inside, and way down inside of us is our spirit or soul. The pencil has lead and we have a spirit. People are different, too, but the differences are usually just skin deep. We've got black, white, red, and yellow people, don't we? But inside, we're all much alike.*
>
> *What is the most important part of a pencil? That's right—the lead! It represents the life of a pencil. A person's spirit or soul is the most important part of him.*
>
> *Who controls this pencil makes a great deal of difference. The pencil can't do anything by itself; somebody's got to use it. If you were to put this pencil and a piece of paper in the hands of your little brother or sister this afternoon, you'd probably have a mess, wouldn't you? A small child can't handle a pencil very well. Yet, if you put this pencil in the hands of an artist, she could draw a lovely picture. If you put it in the hands of a poet, he could write a beautiful poem.*
>
> *If we try to control our lives ourselves, the Bible tells us we'll do just what a small child would do with this pencil—make a mess. We can't run our lives alone in this world. The Bible teaches us to put our lives into*

the hands of Jesus, who did such a fine job of living His own life. He will take our lives and write a story that will be good and beautiful.

Now, another part of the pencil is quite important—the eraser. The company that made this pencil knew that the lead was going to misspell or use a wrong word. Therefore, the maker of this pencil wisely provided for those errors. When you make a mistake you don't have to scratch through it and make it look worse. That eraser can rub it out, and you can start all over again.

The Bible tells us that God knew when He created us that we would make many mistakes because we would try to run our own lives. He arranged for all the mistakes to be taken away with an Eraser—Jesus Christ, who died on the cross, shedding blood that can cleanse us from all sin. That's why the Bible tells us that if we confess our sins, God is faithful and just to forgive us our sins for Jesus' sake and erase them from our record.[31]

If a child or youth submitted a question on paper during one of Sam's talks, he might have saved it for the rest of his life. For example, at a Belhaven Summer Youth Conference in 1971, Lou Ann Miller asked:

Mr. Patterson, in one of your talks you said there were some people that the world would probably be better off without. If predestination is true, why did God put them here?

He also saved thank-you notes—all of them! After a 1971 talk to Willard Harrell's fifth grade class at First Presbyterian Church in Jackson, the class wrote him thank-you notes which he saved for the rest of his life. Here's a sampling:

John Travis
I love to hear you pray.

Nan Henley
Thank you for coming…. I taped one sermon for my mother…. How can you get up so early in the morning? I came to the early ones, and I was still sleepy.

Mimi Newman
I do thank you for the blessings you and God brought me through the chapel services. They have meant a lot to me, even though I have a test on it.

David Russell
I think I learned more than I ever have before. You taught me to really open my heart and let Jesus Christ in…. I have never really understood the Bible, but you helped me….

First-graders at another talk also wrote Sam thank-you notes. Susan, Leah, Toni, and Lou Ann said they had accepted Christ as their Savior. Others wrote:

Donna (no last name)
    … You made me feel so good that I think I will have a smile on my face every morning…. I love you.

Melissa Brown
    … You talked so good I went to sleep. I enjoyed it very much….

During a camp conference at which Sam spoke, God taught him that divine quickening power can regenerate even the youngest soul. One night, a six-year-old girl confessed, "Two nights ago I told my counselor that I wanted to be a Christian, and I knelt and asked the Lord Jesus to come into my heart. Oh, how He has changed my life!"

Sam laughed to himself, immensely tickled. What did a six-year-old have to confess? A sixteen-year-old would be different, he mused; anyone who goes sixteen years without Jesus would have to make plenty of changes. But a six-year-old? Immediately, however, he regretted his reaction:

> *I was ashamed of myself the moment I laughed because I knew it wasn't holy laughter. Later, I discovered how very wrong I was. A little heart opening up to Christ changes the whole course and destiny of a life. Because of her confession, I realized that little girl would one day be a different sixteen-year-old teenager, a different twenty-six-year-old mother, a different ninety-six-year-old woman. She was a little six-year-old sinner, and her heart needed the blood of Jesus and the quickening of the Spirit as much as any adult.[32]*

Sam never made that mistake again. After one of his sermons in 1972, little Melanie Underwood sent him a list of fourteen items she had decided to pray about and to work on in her life. Sam was touched by such commitment, saving her letter and a copy of his reply until his death:

> *Today I … came upon your confession prayer list, and it brought to my mind again the joy that was in my heart as I observed your faith in and love for Jesus Christ even though you are still a little girl. As I write this note to you, my earnest prayer goes up that the Lord Jesus Christ will keep His strong hand on your life and lead you finally and fully into His purpose for your life on earth.[33]*

When I was five years old," recalls Maria Price, "Sam came to my father's church, Wynndale Presbyterian in Jackson, Mississippi, to hold a revival. He did chalk talks for the children. He didn't talk down to us; we felt that he was explaining something very important. I have remembered one of them my entire life. It was centered around sin, and the 'i' in the middle of 'sin' stood for 'I am a sinner.' Sam made a cross out of that 'i,' saying that Jesus had died on the cross for me. I made a profession of faith that week, and he called me his 'daughter in the faith.' I had to talk to the session because they wanted to be sure I understood what I was doing. I knew *exactly* what I was doing. I was a sinner for whom Jesus had died, and I needed Him. The Gospel was so much a part of Sam's life that I knew his message wasn't fake—it was real!"

With sermons such as "God's Greatest Teenage Song Writer" (on David and the Psalms), Sam certainly had the attention of young people, too. His appeal to youth was nothing short of phenomenal.

"In our first pastorate at Water Valley, Mississippi," said William "Buck" Mosal, "Sam came for a week of revival services. Each night the church was packed as it had never been before, and on Youth Night over seventy young people came forward to profess Christ or recommit their lives to Him. Sam and I counseled those young people about their decisions until the wee hours of the morning."

As a teenager, Laurie Jones (RTS '69) attended the Pensacola Theological Institute at McIlwain Presbyterian Church when Sam was the youth crusade speaker. "I can still see him standing in the pulpit, saying in his wonderful Arkansas drawl, 'Today I'm going to talk to y'all about GWITS.' We all looked at each other, puzzled. He certainly had our attention! He continued, 'That stands for *People Who've Got What It Takes*.' He then began to explain that a personal relationship with Christ was what it would take to get us through life. I mark that as a turning point in my life, a catalyst to become a real disciple of Christ and to seek God's will for my life."

Says Jimmy Turner, "Under Sam's preaching, I was first convicted of my sin in college. He told us Bible study should be a regular discipline, giving God the opportunity each day to meet with us. Sometimes we won't even know what He's teaching us that day—only further down the road."

Marian Joseph has remembered the following illustration for nearly forty years from her days in the youth group at First Presbyterian Church in Jackson, Mississippi. Sam was teaching the concept of waiting on the Lord:

> *How do we wait on the Lord? Well, how do you tell a good waiter from a bad one? Remember how you fix your tea or coffee exactly as you like it, with the right amount of sugar, lemon, or cream? The bad waiter will come and, without asking you, fill that cup again. I have burned my hand several times by putting it over my cup to try and stop him. Now the taste is all messed up! I can't ever get it back to the way it was. But the good waiter will ask you if you would like additional tea or coffee. Waiting on the Lord is just like that. When we're not willing to wait for Him, we want it our way. We come in and mess it up. It doesn't thwart*

God's ability to accomplish what He wants to do. Yet, if we would ask Him if He wants our help, things would move along a lot smoother.[34]

"When I was a teen in the 1950s," relates Ann Angle, "Sam was my favorite speaker at youth conferences. Although his illustrations were incredibly simple, they invariably led me deeply into the truths of God's Word. One of his most memorable illustrations was in a sermon on forgiveness from Isaiah 1:18 ("... though your sins be as scarlet, they will be as white as snow..." KJV). He told us that a couple visiting London stayed in a hotel room across from Buckingham Palace. They could see the changing of the guard. However, the woman was puzzled. 'I thought the guards' coats were red, but they are white.' Her husband looked and agreed. Upon further investigation, they discovered the coats were indeed red, but the two were looking at them through a red stained glass window, making them appear white. Sam told us that, in the same way, Christ's blood covers our scarlet sins, making us appear as white as snow to God. That was a profound illustration in my young life, and I have never forgotten it. Not only has it encouraged me over the years, but I have also used it numerous times to encourage others."

Sam's relationship with young people did not end when the sermon was over. He maintained steady correspondence through the years with a number of young people. They wrote asking for advice and spiritual enlightenment, and he responded with warmth and interest, urging them to stay in touch. They interacted with Sam on an adult basis, telling him of their plans and voicing adult concerns about their faith and the world. He replied in kind, never treating them as children.

In this letter on May 12, 1970, Sam counseled student Gary Lane as the young man considered full time Christian service:

> *Gary ... there are three things that need not wait for graduation and ordination. Preparation and service come together at once as one committed to Christ engages in these three activities: daily Bible study, intercessory prayer, and personal witness through life and lips. Make these a part of your life regularly right now, and you're already in full preparation for God's purpose in your life. I praise God for your faith and for your commitment. Keep in touch with me.... I'm interested!*

Linda Provost needed help with her prayer life in this letter on February 14, 1971:

> *Mr. Pat ... thank you for your patience with me and your help when you were here in November.... I was in a spiritual slump and my prayer life had dwindled to almost nothing. The Lord really used you to show me this. I also thank you for your continued concern.... That meant a lot*

to me. If you have time, could you explain a little more about praying with thanksgiving? My follow-up prayers all sound alike....

Seventeen-year-old Dorothy Caulfield needed prayer about a boy she had just met, and Sam sent this kind reply on October 5, 1970:

Keep Jesus first, covering close relationships with prayer, and you will find that all human relationships will tend to work out God's way.

Judy Phagan rededicated her life to Christ under Sam's preaching at Ebenezer Presbyterian Church in Cotton Plant, Mississippi, his father's boyhood church. Sam kept up a steady correspondence with her and, as you can see in this letter on August 13, 1969, he was almost like a father to her:

I've read a chapter in Genesis every night since I rededicated my life to Christ that Wednesday.... I was hoping to talk with you about two small problems but did not get the chance. Someday ... I'll write you about those problems because I have faith in you.

As always, Sam was ever on the lookout for children needing French Camp Academy:

Everyone ... is greatly concerned that P____ can have release from the terrible pulls that are on her ... because of an amazingly mixed up, confused, and crossed up family situation.... This week she has come to know Christ as her Savior and is uniting with the ... church tonight. I truly believe she fits the very purpose for the raising up of French Camp ... and I earnestly hope that you will be able to find a place for her there.[35]

A GYPSY FOR THE LORD

Rarely did a host pastor meet Sam at the airport or take him there. Sam much preferred the economy of driving his small car, or later, his well-known Toyota camper truck. However, others who had to travel with him occasionally often had a different opinion.

"One year Claire and I caught a ride with Sam in his camper truck to a couple's retreat at my brother Jim's (RTS '77) church in Columbia, South Carolina," revealed Dudley Barnes. "It was a twelve-hour trip, and the seat was uncomfortably hard. I don't see how he took long trips in that truck. But that wasn't the worst part. The seat was not large enough for three people, so Claire and I took turns sitting on the driveshaft hump behind it, hunched over to keep from banging our heads on the roof.

"Yet, being with Sam was worth every bit of discomfort, and it turned out to be one of the best experiences of our lives. He kept us in stitches with his tales, and on more serious subjects, every word that came out of his mouth was like opening the Book of Proverbs."

Sam liked taking his own vehicle to preaching engagements for reasons other than economy. Cruising down the highway gave him ample time to meditate; in fact, some of his best illustrations came to him as he sped down the road:

> *Driving one day, I figured out how long the Bible would be if you stretched it out down the highway, line after line, and ran the speedometer on it. A regular-print Bible would be four and a half miles long. Out of that four and half miles of scripture, the most familiar and most significant verse is John 3:16.*[36]

Especially after he bought his Toyota camper, he combined preaching with camping and fishing trips, telling ministers, "I'll be sure to bring my casting rod"[37] and later reporting his successes:

> *Stopped by the reservoir on way back from Alabama and caught a nice mess of fish, which I cooked up for supper last night.*[38]

He also relished the freedom to come and go as he pleased. Rarely did he spend the night in a town after a sermon series because he wanted to get out of the limelight. "Generally, at the end of a series a church had a reception for the visiting pastor so people could get to know him better," said Ed Williford. "Mr. Pat might stick around for the first fifteen or twenty minutes, but before they knew it, he was gone!"

Hotels and motels didn't make much money off of Sam either. Since he was usually in a hurry both coming and going, he'd pull into a parking lot, sleep a couple of hours, and get back on the road. After returning in the wee hours, he often slept on the office couch and then put in a full day's work. He told Cherry Ragland:

> *I had a safe trip back, making only one stop of about two hours in the parking lot of a Holiday Inn for a little snooze. I got in here about six o'clock the next morning and have not felt the worse for it yet.*[39]

Finally, driving his own vehicle enabled Sam to indulge in one of his favorite pastimes—talking on his CB radio. He used it as an evangelistic tool, so it's not hard to see why his handle was "The Old Speckled Bird."

"At one or two in the morning," said M. B. Cooper, "those truck drivers were using bad language, and he'd interrupt, saying, 'This is the parson.'"

"He had a ball with those truck drivers," agreed Cherry Ragland. "He'd ask where they were stopping, and if he was tired, he'd stop and have a cup of coffee with them. He came to know them so well that they set up regular stops, and Sam had opportunities to share the Gospel over coffee or a meal."

PRESBYTERIAN EVANGELISTIC FELLOWSHIP

Sam's years as a full-time evangelist with PEF were likely some of the happiest of his life and certainly some of the most productive in terms of souls saved. When he came on board with PEF in 1967, he joined seven other evangelists seeking to promote biblical evangelism and real revival in churches through preparation, prayer, and preaching.

His spiritually mature presence was much appreciated by the younger evangelists. "I was fifteen years his junior and was blessed to serve with him because he taught me patience," recalls Ben Wilkinson, PEF's executive director upon William Hill's retirement. "Impatience is usually the mark of an evangelist. He wants everybody saved, and if that doesn't happen before dark, he wonders what he's doing wrong. Sam taught us that solutions come in the dark and after the dark—the next day and down the road. A man of prayer, he handled difficult situations in a calm and mature fashion; I never saw him angry. He was comfortable leaving matters in the Lord's hands."

Sam also brought valuable contacts to the young team, opening doors to churches that would otherwise have been closed. "Getting into new churches was difficult," continued Ben. "They usually called someone they knew, or they asked *Come* magazine for a recommendation. By the grace of God, my schedule stayed full, probably because the churches in which Sam preached really trusted him and were willing to try someone else on his team."

After each PEF revival, churches evaluated the evangelist, and Sam's reports were consistently glowing. At meeting after meeting, people of all ages made professions of faith and recommitted their lives to Christ. Even pastors gained new insights into their ministries. This was no accident; Sam followed the PEF manual carefully, requiring churches to begin extensive planning months ahead. A typical letter from Sam to a prospective pastor went like this:

> *Of course you realize that little can be accomplished in your church that will have lasting value unless adequate spiritual preparation is done beforehand. There is always the temptation to do as little as possible, but I believe that little work produces little results in God's economy, just as it does in the economy of the world. I am impressed by the extensive sales campaigns of the leading chain stores in order to inform the public of the benefits derived from the use of their products. Can we do less? I have seen God bring great and lasting blessing to churches (even quite small churches) when the people truly desired revival enough to work for it. He will do this in your church also. I urge you to put on the full*

program and let the people of your church and of your community know that you truly mean business.[40]

Prayer was a large part of the preparation for meetings. Sam told Jim Patterson (no relation) at Westminster Presbyterian Church in Atlanta that "... the two most important factors are getting prayer, prayer, prayer underway and devising methods to get spiritually needy people to the meetings."[41] Indeed, a report filed by Midway Presbyterian Church on one of Sam's meetings showed the huge emphasis on prayer:

> *The meeting ... was started by a Saturday night prayer vigil.... From early evening until the deep hours of the night, members of the church came to the Prayer Room for times of intercession..... As a result God led in some interesting and blessed ways during the week.*[42]

Sam actually went further than the PEF manual and suggested that the leadership of the church participate as faithfully and as fully as possible. He also recommended that the congregation "book" people to attend far in advance:

> *One of the weaknesses of evangelistic meetings is that so few people actually come who are completely out of touch with the Lord and the church. To remedy this, urge a large number of members to book half a dozen specific people to attend the services. Members should keep reminding visitors of the date far in advance. They will be much more likely to come.*[43]

Again, Sam's humility was evident in his dealings with churches. He asked for helpful suggestions both before and after meetings. Although he supplied publicity pictures of himself to churches if asked, he didn't like them used.[44] Keeping satisfactory snapshots was apparently at the bottom of his priority list.

Sam was also scrupulously honest. In one letter, he sent back $1.50 to the church in which he had just preached. A woman had paid Sam for a book from the PEF book table. Sam asked the pastor to send it in with the rest of the PEF donation.[45]

Sam's correspondence during his PEF days was legendary. For various reasons, he wrote hundreds of letters to people he met at revivals. Above all, he kept up with those saved under his preaching. He knew that only the miracle of God's grace would put people's lives back together, and he was ready to do as much as he could to be God's instrument in that miracle. The following encouraging letter to Jack Morrone is just one example of Sam's boundless concern for the lost:

Dear Jack,

You have been, are, and will be very much on my heart and in my prayers as God works within you against all the forces of sin and discouragement that are trying to destroy you.

Jesus Christ is 'able to save to the uttermost those who come to God through Him' (Hebrews 7:25). His blood provides the forgiveness you need, Jack, and His Spirit will be your strength....

As God shapes you into the man He meant you to be, there will be hurts and pain ... and opposition inside you and from the outside. Satan will not give up his long-time hold on you without using his bag of tricks. But if you humbly trust Jesus, feed on His Word, appeal to Him in prayer, and WAIT ON THE LORD (read Isaiah 40:31), He will keep you and finally bring you into a new day.

'If any man (Jack Morrone) be in Christ, he is a new creation; old things pass away, and behold, everything becomes new' (2 Corinthians 5:17). Jack, as regularly as a day dawns, let God speak to you through Bible reading. Then pray to Him in earnest. It will be strength to your soul.

I am claiming on your behalf Philippians 1:6: 'I AM CONFIDENT THAT HE WHO HAS BEGUN A GOOD WORK IN YOU WILL BRING IT TO COMPLETION AT THE DAY OF JESUS CHRIST.'

I'll be in touch![46]

According to Ben Wilkinson, Sam's continued interest in the lives of those saved under his watch and his steady correspondence with them was quite uncommon among PEF evangelists. "All of us on the team had busy schedules. Taking the time to write five to seven letters to somebody was not what we were about at that point. We were trying to get into as many churches as possible to share the Gospel. However, Sam saw the need of follow-up and nurturing."

Sam went far beyond simply keeping up with those saved through his preaching. He also wrote those to whom he had witnessed but who had not made a decision for Christ. His letters, such as this one to Carol Morrone, are virtually evangelistic sermons:

Dear Carol,

Thank you for letting me talk to you frankly about Jesus Christ.... Do not discount the significance of this letter. Rather, realize that this is a direct move of God through me to you on His behalf. If you throw up a road block to His love for and will for your life, you expose your young life to greater tragedy ahead than you may have known in the past.

God does love you, and He does have a plan for your life. Jesus Christ is offered to you as His gift, for He alone can bring you to be the woman God meant for you to be.... You need the forgiveness of your sins and the management of God in your life in order to live well now and to meet Him someday without utter and eternal loss. More is at stake than you can imagine.... I appeal to you to kneel before Christ and invite Him to come into your life and save you and guide you.... The Christ who prompted me to write to you at this moment stands at your heart-door.

'BEHOLD I STAND AT THE DOOR AND KNOCK. IF ANYONE HEARS MY VOICE AND OPENS THE DOOR, I WILL COME INTO THEM' (Rev. 3:20).[47]

Sam's responsibility could easily have stopped here, but he basically set up a counseling office through the mail. After he preached at a church, people wrote telling him what his sermons had meant in their lives, describing in detail their evangelistic contacts, and asking for prayer in certain situations. Often Sam's visit healed wounds, both among the congregation and the church staff, as people forgave one another and peace was restored. Here are a few examples:

Annie G. Hicks, November 29, 1976

Thank you again for taking time out of your busy day ... to let me pour out my problems to you.... I felt a need to talk with someone who would understand, and I thank God for sending you to me. You helped me to see things differently, and, I trust, through the presence of the Holy Spirit, my prayer life will be strengthened. Your visit in our community was a great blessing, and I feel sure we will all be better people for your having come our way.

M____ Cole, January 14, 1975

God has done wonders for me since I talked to you in September. He has given me the grace to overcome many temptations, and His grace has been working on K___. He has quit drinking and cursing, and he goes to church. We all read the Bible every night. [Others] meet with us to study Confessing Christ *every Monday night. When we complete the book ... we will join the church as a family.*

K___ and I talk about the Bible more than any other thing in our lives.... For the first time in my adult life, God is the most interesting topic of conversation. You brought me face to face with my guilt and helped me understand that only the Holy Spirit can give me the gift of grace.

Woody and Mallie Browder, December 28, 1976

[We] visited my parents.... After our initial statements to them as you suggested, the atmosphere immediately was cleared, and we all shared our regrets and our thankfulness to each other. I know this was necessary to fulfill God's will.... Thank you again, Brother Sam, from two who will never forget your love.

Sam even counseled his fellow pastors. Witness the following agony of soul from one minister:

> *Keep me high on your list before the Throne of His Grace. I'm just trying to hang on until you come…. This morning I am in tears…. My ineptness has kept me from even a shadow of a breakthrough in forming a love for Christ and the Bible message here. In all of my ministry … this field seems to have the poorest foundation in the Bible and the meaning of the Gospel. I have been unable to find a beginning place for teaching or for touching a single life.*[48]

Sam must have identified with this pastor as he recalled his own dark night of the soul in Martinsville when he felt he was getting nowhere in the pastorate. He encouraged this pastor to meditate on Romans 8:26–27.

Other pastors simply needed guidance into the pastorate:

> *… Many thanks for all your help, your listening ear, and guidance as I sought God's call back into the local pastorate…. The Lord has been gracious to me, confirming daily that I heard His calling here correctly. Please continue to pray for me and my family. Many thanks for being a part in God's working His will in my life….*[49]

And out of the pastorate:

> *…At the present time my wife and I are seriously considering leaving the pastoral ministry. Although there have been bright spots over the past 13 and one half years and God has used us to help a few people, we are not satisfied with what has transpired…. My family and I would deeply appreciate your careful, prayerful consideration of this matter and send us some counsel….*[50]

Finally, some pastors counted on Sam to help with difficult cases when he came for a meeting:

> *Sam, you are the only person I know of now that could have a conference with D. W. and get a hearing on spiritual matters … the truth of total surrender…. He turns everybody else off except you. See how God leads….*[51]

THREE NOTABLE CONVERSIONS

Although many people were saved under Sam's preaching during his PEF ministry, three conversions are noteworthy, for they evolved into lifelong friendships. These men were all quite different, yet Sam could relate deeply to all of them.

Jack Bushman

In 1969, Sam held a five-day revival at Trinity Presbyterian Church in Montgomery, Alabama. It was the greatest period of spiritual emphasis in the congregation's history. Over 4,300 people attended the twelve services, and great numbers made decisions for Christ.

Jack Bushman was the first person down the aisle on the final night. The only reason he attended the revival was because he had heard Sam before and been deeply moved. At the time, he was a very irregular churchgoer and didn't have a personal relationship with Christ. "Although the Lord had been working in my life for quite some time," he confessed, "I couldn't give Jesus the number one spot because I was so firmly entrenched in it."

Shortly after Jack was saved, Sam gave him his first Bible, writing on the inside cover: "To a friend from a friend, in the bonds of our mutual Friend— Proverbs 18:24, Sam Patterson." That was the beginning of a deep personal relationship that would last until Sam died. It was also the beginning of Jack's role as a Barnabas to Sam for many years. For reasons neither could fathom, Jack always seemed to show up when Sam needed help.

"Sam was such a sensitive and appreciative person," said Jack, "always thanking me for being such a good friend. I always felt that I should thank him for giving me the opportunity to help. What I was able to do for him was nothing compared to what he did for me. He provided me with such joy! One of his favorite phrases was 'Praise the Lord.' I'd give anything to hear him say that again!"[52]

William "Buck" Mosal

When Sam Patterson came to Canton, Mississippi, in 1954 to preach a week of revival services at First Presbyterian Church, seventeen-year-old Buck Mosal and his friends decided to check it out instead of partying. None of them had ever set foot inside a church and were curious.

"When Sam gave the invitation that Monday night," recalled Buck, "I went down front to make it known that I was lost and en route to hell. By God's grace, I left there saved! I still remember Sam's words that night: 'I never cease to be amazed how God can take an unholy man out of an unholy world, make him holy, then put him back in an unholy world and keep him holy in it.'"

After that service, the two men talked for several hours—a blessing for Buck since he knew nothing about Christianity. That night began a father-son relationship that lasted the rest of Sam's life.

"He basically adopted me," said Buck emotionally. "I told him I felt that God had not only saved me, but had called me to the ministry, even though I had always been so shy that I couldn't speak to a group for three minutes! He encouraged me and gave me Proverbs 3:5–6, which have become my life verses. He told me to study the Word and try to find a good college."

Buck had always planned on a career in the Navy, but from that point on he had no interest in the military. The Lord seemed to say to him, "I've got many people who can take care of the Navy. I want you to preach my Word."

"From that night on," Buck continued, "my friends thought I was a strange duck because I was different. I began studying the scriptures, as Sam had admonished me to do, and began attending First Presbyterian Church in Canton by myself."

In 1955, Buck entered Belhaven with his eyes toward the ministry. While in college, he preached for Sam at French Camp Presbyterian every other weekend for a couple of years when Sam was on the road preaching. Eventually, he graduated from Columbia Seminary and became an evangelist with Presbyterian Evangelistic Fellowship.

"I became an evangelist because Sam was one, and I came to Christ under his preaching. I also wanted to see others converted. God gave me the privilege to be a full-time PEF evangelist with Sam for several years. Today, I'm still preaching, and I praise God for Sam Patterson. I shudder to think where I might be now had the Lord not seen to it that I went to that revival service."

Alvarez Samuel "Bud" Jones

Sam believed he saw true revival only once in his lifetime, a revival so supernatural in its dimensions that it bore the marks of God.[53] It happened in the tiny mining town of Clifftop (population 1,000) in southeastern West Virginia. It was there in June 1968, that Sam met Alvarez "Bud" Jones, an uneducated, fifty-six-year-old coal miner who had just been laid off after forty years.

Until Bud's death in 1979, he and Sam kept up a lively correspondence. Sam had file folders on hundreds of churches and organizations, but only one bears a person's name—that of Bud Jones. It appears that Sam saved every letter he ever received from Bud and even some that he (Sam) wrote.

The obscure mountain village of Clifftop was so small it had only one church, used by the Methodists, Baptists, and Presbyterians, so everyone came to the revival. It started off much like any other ordinary series of meetings, but Sam continued to feel an unusual conviction that God was going to do a very special work during these ten days. One day he was walking past the church and had a very strong sense of divine urgency to visit whoever lived in the house on the hill behind the church.

A few hours later, the host preacher informed Sam they were going to visit a man and a woman who both needed the Lord desperately. Sam was shocked to discover they were walking toward the very house about which he had been convicted. He then was certain God was using him in a plan that had started before the foundations of the world.

When they arrived, the man was alone. He graciously invited them in and admitted quickly that he wasn't a Christian. "I was a lost ball in high grass," admitted Bud later to Buck Mosal. "My health was shot, and I was no longer any use to the coal company. To tell a man he's excess baggage and to take away his earning power is to break his spirit. I was really up a blind alley on a one way street. I had left the church at eighteen and never gone back. I believe as surely as God sent Moses to lead the children of Israel out of Egypt, he sent Sam to me. I don't believe anyone can have personal contact with Sam Patterson and walk away unscratched." [54]

Sam asked Bud for permission to explain from the Bible how one becomes a Christian, and Bud agreed. Yet, just as Sam began, a pickup truck drove up, and a buxom lady came in the back door. It was Bud's wife, Thelma. Seeing them in the living room, she turned angrily into another room. Sam thought she was probably mad because he and the pastor were there. He thought, "I'll just have to go ahead and talk to this man." As he did, though, he could hear her walk into the bedroom right next to them. So he lifted his voice because he wanted her to hear, too. He then began to hear her crying. Sam knew she was listening but didn't know if his words were the cause of her tears.

Bud freely admitted he needed the Lord. He knew he was a sinner, and he affirmed that the Bible told the truth about Jesus. Sam, however, urged him not to say this just to agree but to genuinely turn his life over to Jesus. Sam could not have known then how desperate Bud's situation was.

"Sam came into my life at a time when all hope seemed gone," Bud said later. "I had been fighting a battle with myself for two years but needed someone to invite me into the Kingdom of heaven. I'd lived my whole life here, and no one except my parents had ever asked me to be a Christian. Now they were gone. God knew I needed help, so He sent Sam. It wasn't a lack of knowledge of God's work; I needed a person whom I believed had received salvation to speak to me as one human being to another. Sam let me know that he wasn't born into this world a Christian but that he once had been where I was. He had made a move, and God had accepted him." [55]

Bud agreed solemnly to accept Jesus, and they knelt down together and prayed. Thelma was listening to all this. At that point, she came in the room and fell down in a chair at the other end of the room, still quietly weeping. Sam then began witnessing to her. She said nothing. She just looked at him, and he didn't know whether it was a mad look or a sad look. He plunged ahead and did the best he could to present the Gospel to her. He then told her that Bud had accepted Christ and urged her to do the same thing.

"No!" she shouted. "I can't do it.... I won't do it!" That's all Sam could get out of her. He knew he wasn't supposed to press her, but he did—hard. Bud began to plead with her, too, saying, "You know we need a Christian home. I've come to Christ! You do it!"

After a while she also professed Christ. Sam ruefully thought she might have done it to get him out of the house. They had a time of prayer, and he went home feeling bad because he had pressed her so hard. He believed her husband's profession had been real, but he had real doubts about hers. He walked out behind the preacher's house on the side of a mountain, remembering what Jesus had said, "... Whatever you ask in prayer, believe that you have received it, and it will be yours" (Mark 11:24, ESV). He quoted God's own words to Him and ended by praying, "Lord, I really desire that that woman's confession be an honest, earnest turning to Christ."

That night, they had the best revival crowd of the entire week, and Sam discovered why. Thelma had left the house five minutes after Sam and the pastor. She first went to her son-in-law down the road—with whom she'd had an altercation just before she had come into the house—and made peace with him. Then she remembered some other people with whom she was at odds, and she spent the next two hours going through the community getting right with people. Her actions set off a chain reaction in the little village, and others began doing the same, forgiving and reconciling. From that night on, people came to church and to the Lord! For the rest of his life, Sam felt reconciliation was the key to revival:

> *How do you get revival? If everyone who professes to be right with God began to get right with others—confessing and making restitution—people will listen. That's what 'Love God with all your heart and your neighbor as yourself' means. The only way our relationship with God will be effective evangelistically is for the world to see it impacting our dealings with other people. Although intense prayer and Bible reading are signs of conversion, those things alone will not impress the world and bring revival. If we want revival, Christians must let compassion and conscience prove to the world that when Jesus comes in, life comes! The flavor comes! The rising of the yeast comes, along with the sweet fragrance of Jesus Christ.*[56]

Bud, however, thought the revival's success also had much to do with Sam:

> *I speak the language of these mountain people, and I know their ways....They are on the defensive most of the time to outsiders, especially educated people, but you got to them as no one I've known.*[57]

Bud remained grateful to Sam for the rest of his life and followed his PEF ministry closely:

> *Christ went all the way to Calvary for me, and you came all the way from Mississippi to Clifftop to introduce Him to me....I watch your schedule and ...want you to know that each night you preach, I'm on my knees beside you in spirit....*[58]

Sam himself would look back on Clifftop for the rest of his days as a defining moment. Here, as in no other place, he had seen two souls reborn and begin to grow spiritually at an unbelievable rate. Sam would write to Bud later:

> *My mind returns in warm memory to no place I have held meetings as frequently as it does to Clifftop. Always you and Thelma fill the horizon of my thinking when I ponder those days. Not only did God give you a rather sudden birth, but I rejoice at the constant growth you have experienced in your love for and knowledge of Him and His Word.*[59]

So special was this couple in Sam's life that he kept up with their spiritual birthdays (June 21, 1968) for the rest of his life, always exchanging letters with Bud about this time. On their fifth birthday in the Lord, Sam even orchestrated a reunion in Atlanta of those saved at Clifftop and produced a birthday cake for them. Thelma couldn't come, so Sam sent five candles home with Bud for her.

Over the years following 1968, Sam watched in awe as God fashioned a church leader from this uneducated mountain man with no theological training. In March 1970, two years after Bud's conversion, the pastor serving Clifftop decided to move, thus threatening the very existence of the church in the small village. Sam counseled Bud and Thelma to allow the Holy Spirit to use them to encourage and strengthen His work there until another pastor came. Amazingly, Bud took Sam's advice and began teaching Sunday School and several Bible studies, plus leading prayer meeting. Sam was ecstatic:

> *It thrills me to see how you have grown in your Christian faith and how you have been willing to step out under God's leadership and assume responsibility early in your Christian life. God has given you a special gift of wisdom and discernment in your understanding of yourself, Christ and His work, and the people you work with. I have no doubt that he was preparing you for the time when there would be no resident minister. You are a shepherd of the flock there, and, though this poses you many problems, it is a great service for the Lord.*[60]

Several years went by, and still God didn't bring a pastor to the struggling church. Bud became discouraged as membership dropped off and people became spiritually listless. As usual, Sam was the voice of encouragement:

> *I don't think it is possible for anyone to serve as a representative of Jesus Christ ... without constant cause for discouragement to arise. However, discouragement cannot be countenanced, for it will surely dull the brightness of our witness. I know that the Holy Spirit is going to keep both of you encouraged just in proportion to the activity of the devil to try to keep you discouraged. Just keep the fire burning and the light shining....[61]*

By the end of 1974, however, the situation had grown worse. The liberal leaning of the PCUS distressed Bud and caused him to consider leaving the denomination. Sam found himself fighting the same battle he was waging in Mississippi when he counseled Bud to stay:

> *I deeply regret the discouraging aspects of the church situation there.... Bud, I just do not know what to advise.... If you move from Presbyterian membership to one of the other two denominations there, the situation might be worse. I do not believe in independent Christianity. We are Christ's flock of sheep, not lone wolves. My advice would be to stay where you are and trust God to change circumstances or hearts. While you are waiting, do the very best you can under the circumstances.[62]*

God only knows how valuable Sam's counsel to Bud was over those years. Surely there are souls in heaven who would not be there without Bud's witness. Taking the time to nurture a mentoring relationship with this lonely servant of God in a forgotten outpost was a labor of love that brought no accolades for Sam, except from Bud himself:

> *I sometimes feel low in spirit and wonder why I'm knocking myself out when it seems no one cares about their own souls. But then I remember a man God sent when I needed someone so much and that man cared about me and continues to care enough to keep track of me and is depending on me to keep the faith and even counts birthdays I have in Christ.[63]*

Perhaps corresponding with Bud increased Sam's faith in the omnipotent power of God to bring His Kingdom to fruition. In one of his last letters, Sam revealed how much Bud and Thelma's faith had encouraged him:

> *You cannot imagine what a joy it has been to me to watch God work in your lives. What sovereign grace! He surely set out to make the two of you His own, and God never fails. I rejoice at the leadership and the gifts in the Spirit he has given you to be his man and woman, His witnesses and testimonies in that community. I know there are great difficulties in*

such leadership and ministry. We'll keep writing and praying for each other and hope to be able to catch up—if not in this world, when we get to heaven![64]

SAM EXPERIENCES THE BRITISH ISLES

In the spring of 1976, Sam was honored to receive an invitation from the Banner of Truth to speak on evangelism at their 13th Annual Ministers' Conference at Leicester, England, March 29–April 1. Well-known theologian Iain Murray extended the invitation, feeling that Sam's practical approach to evangelism would add a valuable perspective for the men:

> *I can truthfully assure you that your presence would bring encourage-ment to the men. The fact that you combine your responsibilities at the seminary with an evangelistic ministry would in itself be a cause of considerable interest. Sometimes the image of the Reformed faith in America comes across as rather academic. I suppose onlookers in the British Isles would also say sometimes that our Reformed image in this country tends to be too much concerned with the intellectual side of the Christian life and not enough with compassionate and fervent outreach to a lost world.[65]*

Since numerous other organizations and churches in the British Isles wanted to hear Sam, the trip was extended to two weeks, with RTS graciously picking up the tab.[66]

Sam arrived in Belfast, Northern Ireland, on March 17 and the next day addressed the Evangelical Fellowship of Ireland. On March 19–21, he delivered three sermons on "The Bread of Life" at Castlewellan Castle to the Irish Reformed Fellowship, a group of ministers and laymen similar to the Pensacola Institute. Sam wrote friends:

> *For two days and nights, I lived and preached in a castle! It was bitter cold. The bedrooms were permitted heat only from 7:30–9:30 a.m. There was not much heat elsewhere. But we wore all we needed to keep fairly comfortable, and the great fellowship of the believers (mainly two or three brands of Presbyterians and Reformed Baptists) offset the climate.[67]*

After speaking twice more in Belfast, Sam left for Edinburgh on Monday, March 22. While there, he addressed members of the Reformed Fraternal of the Church, who wanted to be brought completely up to date on the controversy in the Southern Presbyterian Church, especially since the situation in the Church of Scotland was at that time remarkably similar to the crises being faced in the USA.[68]

While in Scotland, Sam was invited to eat in various homes. The meal included the Scottish delicacy haggis, a meat pudding made by mincing the heart, liver, and lungs of a lamb or calf, then combining it with suet, onions, oatmeal, and spicy seasonings and boiling it in the cleaned stomach of the animal for several hours. Sam simply couldn't eat it, but neither would he offend his Scottish friends, so he used a trick he had learned during his war years in China. He took a bite, brought his linen napkin to his lips, deposited his mouthful into the napkin, and dumped the contents into his coat pocket. His hostess was happy, and Sam smuggled the offensive food out, rejoicing that his pocket, not his stomach, was full of haggis.

According to Jim Baird, however, Sam's system backfired at times. "Sam and I were invited to preach a week of services at the Old Madison Church in Madison County, Mississippi, during the 1950s. They fed us each night until we were stuffed! However, at one meal the hostess had prepared a dish with eggplant, which neither of us liked. She hovered over us, wanting to heap more on the plate. As I was picking at mine, trying to hide it so I wouldn't hurt her feelings, I was amazed to see that Sam had finished his second helping. While I had to confess to the hostess that I couldn't eat any more, Sam went on and on about the delightful meal and the eggplant dish.

"When I saw him about a week later, he explained his trick but told me this time it hadn't worked so well. He had hung his coat up and forgotten all about the eggplant in the pocket until several days later. It had stained the coat so badly he had to throw it away. But it had been well worth it!"

While Sam was in Edinburgh, one beautiful spring day Murray treated him to a tour of several famous spots in Scottish evangelical history—among them, Thomas Chalmer's first pastorate and Robert Murray M'Cheyne's church and burial place. It was a memorable day for all.

Sam then moved on to Inverness, Scotland, where he preached at Greyfriars Free Church of Scotland, perhaps then the largest mainland congregation of the Free Church of Scotland. He loved the Scottish Highlands and, with the help of his hostess, was able to do a little shopping and sightseeing:

> *Thank you, Maurine, for taking me shopping and showing me Loch Ness. I will be able to give my grandchildren a full report on seeing the famous Loch, though I will have to disappoint them with my honest confession that I did not see the monster![69]*

Sam's messages at Leicester were two of his favorites, "Distinguishing Characteristics of Genuine Conversion" and "Christ's Evangelistic Use of the Love of God." They were well-received, and Sam seemed to feel comfortable, having overcome vague feelings of inferiority:

I do come from quite a distance away. But I don't feel any of that distance—I have been greatly blessed in this assembly. I don't see many faces I know, but I don't feel I'm among strangers. I have felt something of the mutual faith and love that binds us together as brothers.

Before I came down here tonight, I had a sense of disappointment that I would not bring you any new truth out of God's Word, not even a new interpretation or insight. But then I got a warm feeling in my heart that I <u>did</u> have the privilege to ask you to join me as we look at a bouquet of Gospel truths here in Colossians 1 that bless the hearts of those who love Christ. [70]

Sam may have felt inferior then, but all these years later Iain Murray is unstinting in his praise of Sam's messages at the conference. "Mr. Patterson's presence at the conference meant a great deal to the men. Professor John Murray, who had spoken there so often, had died the previous year, and Dr. Albert Martin, who was due to speak, was ill and could not come. Mr. Patterson arrived as a virtually unknown visitor, but his warm, engaging manner and the truth he spoke at once won the men and removed any sense of discouragement. It was clear from his splendid, winsome, and moving addresses that the Reformed faith is in no respect inimical to evangelism, and that it is only in the context of the Reformed faith that evangelism comes into its own.

"The note he struck was much needed on both sides of the Atlantic. We admire the wisdom of the founders of RTS that they did not look for a man with high academic credentials to be their first President, but a leader with the heart of a pastor and an evangelist. The first need is for schools of the prophets, not educational establishments."

Murray related that in June 1978, just a few months after the Leicester Conference, Sam helped him again when they both spoke to the Ministers' Institute of the Christian Reformed Church in Grand Rapids, Michigan.

"Mr. Patterson spoke to the hearts of the men there, as he had spoken to our own in Britain. His kind counsel to me on that occasion I have not forgotten. In one of my addresses he felt I was underestimating how God has so often worked by evangelists with little formal training, and he was right. We met too infrequently, but whenever we did, I came away refreshed and conscious that I had been with a true Christian."

After the conference, *St. George's News*, a publication of the United Reformed Church, printed a summary of Sam's sermon on Colossians and noted, "Mr. Patterson wanted to know if anyone was present who had not given themselves over to the Lordship of Christ—a question most would not think was needed in a company of ministers." [71]

On April 1, Murray drove Sam to London after the conference, stopping along the way to visit Olney, scene of the ministry of John Newton and once the home of William Cowper. Sam had been invited to preach both morning and evening services at Westminster Chapel on April 4.[72] He felt honored at the opportunity, but the very thought of preaching in the pulpit once occupied by the great Dr. D. Martin Lloyd-Jones began to unnerve him. During the two or three days before preaching, he tried to unwind by walking around London. He later admitted that he was so conscious of the responsibility of preaching at Westminster that he could barely pay attention to the sights.

However, something did catch his eye. One day he found himself strolling near Westminster Abbey on a lackluster street full of dilapidated buildings. High up on one of them was a sign that looked new and brilliant. In large, golden letters it proclaimed, TAKE COURAGE! Sam reasoned that a wealthy, public-spirited businessman had tried to encourage his fellow Londoners. He thought it a heartening message, especially given his fearfulness as he anticipated the coming Sabbath. He had sensed a certain bit of discouragement among the British, too; their prime minister had just that week resigned, and the pound was taking a beating. He was so impressed he took a picture of the sign.

At Westminster the next Sunday morning, he told the congregation about the sign and was quite perplexed when a ripple of laughter ran across the group. He hadn't meant it to be funny! Not until after lunch did he discover that he had made the biggest blunder he ever would in the pulpit. A member revealed that Courage was the most popular beer in London![73]

It might have been one of his greatest blunders, but that evening Sam received one of the greatest blessings of his preaching career. After the evening service, he was relaxing in the vestry with a piping hot cup of tea, but his faith was very low. After the morning fiasco, he didn't believe anyone would want to speak to him. However, he hadn't taken but a sip or two, when a deacon brought in a man who looked to be about fifty, introducing him as Mr. Pagan. Sam thought he heard Pagan, but he wasn't sure because he'd never heard anyone by that name. Sam asked, "Is that P-A-G-A-N?"

The man replied, "Yes, John Pagan," and he smiled. "But Mr. Patterson, I'm not a pagan now. I'm a Christian."

Interested, Sam asked kindly, "When were you saved?" expecting the man to recount a conversion experience in the distant past.

"Just a few minutes ago!" said the man excitedly. "I've been in the city two or three weeks at the Salvation Army. They've been trying to help me because I'm in deep trouble and have been in great distress. They told me that coming to services here might help, so I attended last Sunday and returned today. At the end of the service, you said Jesus was standing right in our midst, and anybody could have a relationship with him immediately by asking Him to enter his or her heart. That's what I did. Isn't it wonderful that we can do that?"[74]

SAM'S VIEWS ON EVANGELISM

Sam came to many of his views on evangelism over time, but one of his bedrock beliefs throughout his entire career as an evangelist concerned how God speaks to people. Sam felt that God's first thrust into the heart of a sinner was usually through proclamation, then explanation. He saw this in scripture, as the Gospels come first to proclaim, then the Epistles to explain:

> *Those who are very gifted at explaining the Gospel in detail are usually not as able to win people to Christ as those who proclaim the facts simply and clearly. Several years ago I read a missionary's account of his first five years on the mission field. He came home very discouraged—not worn out in body as much as in mind and heart. He had gone to the mission field with high expectations of evangelistic results, but he had had a very fruitless ministry in a field that could have been quite productive.*
>
> *He finally discovered his mistake. In his sermons, he had been trying to explain the Gospel very clearly, attempting to resolve all the questions about the doctrines of the Christian faith. When he returned to the field for a second term, he simply proclaimed what Jesus offered and quit trying to explain it as much. He then enjoyed a fruitful ministry.[75]*

Sam himself was able to accept and live with the tension of biblical truths that couldn't be explained, often saying, "I don't know why people worry so much about not having all the answers. They'll never be asked all the questions."

The Bible was his most important teacher. When Dottie Trunzler asked him what commentary he recommended, he told her he always tried to stick with scripture. He later told a congregation:

> *Watch out for all those extra books you read. The Bible is what you need to be reading. That's the real story of Jesus. If I wrote a book about Jesus, it would be full of errors, but God describes His Son perfectly in the Bible.[76]*

If Sam found his views ran counter to scripture, he changed them immediately. Often, deciding what God was telling him in the Bible took a good while:

> *… My problem isn't with the Bible being the inerrant, infallible Word of God. That was settled the day I came to know Christ. But I have had a good deal of difficulty in finding out really what Christ is telling me to do. I want to do what he tells me to do, not just what other people say He says I ought to do. I want to see it myself, and on some of those things I'm searching. I'm going to get my information from the Bible, and I'm going to follow what I believe it is.[77]*

God's Sovereignty

God's sovereignty in evangelism was a biblical truth Sam came to embrace only after many years as a Christian. When he first began preaching, his evangelistic approach centered more on man's free will. Yet, as he studied the scriptures, his ministry rapidly became more Reformed, with an emphasis on God's power:

> *From first to last salvation is of God. No man can take any credit for his salvation, and I used to do it for a long time. Over and over again when I gave my testimony, I said, 'The only really good thing I've ever done is believe in Jesus.' At that time I thought that God had done a lot of it, but I could take some credit. Then the Bible showed me the faith that beat in my heart came from the gracious work of that great God whose love had been working on me. Now I know I can't boast of anything except Jesus.*[78]

Sam also didn't realize for a long time that salvation had not been granted to him in time and space, but in eternity past, before the foundations of the world:

> *I used to say, 'As an old-fashioned sinner I knelt to pray, and God heard me and saved me. Then He wrote my name in the Lamb's Book of Life.' I don't say that anymore because that's not when it happened. It was not my faith that saved me; He wrote my name there before the foundations of the world. I don't understand it yet, but I preach many things I don't understand.*[79]

To illustrate this important truth, Sam liked to tell the story of Gallagher, a seventy-year-old man who came to Sam after a service in a small Chattanooga mission church. He told Sam that he had been there the night before and had vowed to his wife that he would never return. However, at supper the next night, she had asked him to go with her. Again he adamantly refused. Even so, she got dressed and asked once more.

"You know what I did?" he asked Sam incredulously. "I got up and came with her. And about halfway through the service, I became a Christian as God convicted me strongly. Mr. Patterson, I grew up in this community, and right where we're standing was a café where all the rowdies gathered to drink and fight. Every night I'd be down here with a gang getting drunk and fighting. Only God knows how many times I was beat up and left unconscious in that alley. I am so happy that it was right here that God reached out and dragged me to Jesus."[80]

To further drive the point home, in the same sermon Sam paraphrased the beautiful old Isaac Watts hymn, "How Sweet and Aweful is the Place":

> *Election is a word divine,*
> *For I can clearly see*

> *Had your choice not preceded mine*
> *I never would have chosen thee.*
> *'Twas the hand that spread the feast*
> *That reached out and drew me in,*
> *Else I too would have refused to come*
> *And perished in my sin.*[81]

Man's Goodness

Sam might not have understood some things, but of others he was firmly convinced. From the earliest days of his ministry until his death, Sam maintained that deep down everyone has a vein of goodness buried in him because man is made in God's image:

> *Much of the sin in the world ... is not because people are lowdown, mean, and naturally rotten.... Man isn't away from God because he is mean. He is mean because he is away from God. Sometimes people seem not to have a clean thought or a civil tongue in them. If we turned them upside down, we think we might find 'Made in Hell' rather than in heaven.*
>
> *Yet, on the whole, this isn't so! Jesus taught that God made us in His image, not the devil's. We left Him, but deep down in everyone is a streak of that good man that God put in us. Find me a place where Jesus says that man is naturally a rotten creature with no good in him. That's not the case. A terrible sinner is all mixed up; the rut is so deep he can't climb out, so he just gets worse and worse. Jesus said hard things about some men, but He always acted as though the sinner was worth saving. He had compassion on men, saying they were sheep without a shepherd. Jesus thought that most men really want the best, but they get so mixed up that they go to hell trying to find it.*
>
> *We Christians need to get Jesus' idea of the mean man. Then maybe we would love him rather than abuse him.*[82]

God's Mercy

Another of Sam's strongly-held beliefs was his deep conviction that God wants all people to be saved. He argued passionately for this often controversial position in the pulpit:

> *People who are trying to protect the sovereign dignity of God often say, 'God doesn't beg anybody to be saved.' Of course He does! God Almighty humbled Himself—came down to this earth and confined Himself to the womb of a woman. Through an unworthy disciple like me, the Creator is imploring and begging you to be reconciled to Him.*

If anyone asks me, 'Does God care for me?" should I say, 'Oh, I don't know if you're one of the elect so I can't answer that.' I'm glad that's not the truth! I love the God who humbled Himself and became my sin to save me. I'd be a handicapped preacher if I had to say, 'I can't see the Lamb's Book of Life, so I don't know whether you are one of the elect or not.'

If we are going to have God's faith, we'll have gaps because we don't have all the answers. I'm glad that there is an earnest and sincere love of God that makes Him desire everybody to be saved. I'm that way, and I'm far from being like God. I want everybody in the congregation to come to Christ because of a love that I believe the Holy Spirit has put in me. I'm glad that every time I preach I know that there's a God behind me who wants more than I for everybody in the room to know Jesus Christ! He's already declared it, saying, 'I have no pleasure in the death of the wicked' (Ezekiel 33:11). Rather, God delights in showing mercy. Do I love more than God? Oh, friends, it cannot be. Jesus wept over Jerusalem, the city whose leadership would kill Him. He tells us if we want to know God, we should look at Him. God has a compassionate, gracious, loving heart, and it never violates His sovereign electing grace. They stand as two columns holding up the structure of salvation; pull one out, and you have a warped salvation.[83]

Personal Testimony

Sam must have given the testimony of his conversion countless times in the course of his life, but in the writing of this book it was very hard to find. I searched high and low for years, listening to scores of sermons and asking the hundreds of people I interviewed. At first I wanted to hear it straight from Sam's mouth, but finally I would have settled for third or fourth hand from anyone. Always the response was the same: "No, I remember a lot of things Sam preached, but I don't ever remember his saying how he came to the Lord." Only a handful remembered hazy snatches of Sam's conversion. M. B. Cooper's response was typical: "I'm not sure that he would ever have told me his testimony; that just wasn't his style. He might have thought it egotistical, because he always stepped out of the spotlight." The account of Sam's conversion in Chapter Two was a gift of God, found only when Rich Cannon cleaned out his desk upon retirement from the FCA presidency.

Another reason for the scarcity of Sam's testimony could be that, over the course of his life, he began to cast a suspicious eye at personal testimony and urged caution in its use to keep from doing more harm than good:

As I began to hold meetings, I thought I should allocate one night to giving my personal testimony, which I did for a very short time. But

I began to discover that the night I gave my testimony was the sorriest night during the week of meetings—no real spiritual power there. I didn't understand it, but I backed off from it.

Then a great man of God, who had a tremendous testimony, came and held a series of meetings for me, and I had him give his testimony. I figured if anybody's testimony would be a major blessing in a meeting, this man's would. But the same thing happened. Every night was tremendously successful except the night he gave his testimony—it was a total bomb. The whole church noticed the difference.[84]

Finally, toward the end of his life, Sam apparently came to believe that personal testimony should be used very sparingly. During the first week of December 1977, he gave his testimony in an RTS chapel sermon (the tape is mysteriously missing), as he had done numerous times before. However, two weeks later on December 13, he preached a follow-up sermon entitled "Forming a Personal Testimony," confessing that in the days following that earlier chapel sermon, he had found himself reflecting on the validity, value, and dangers of personal testimony. Sam noted that in Acts 1:8 Jesus said, "You will be my witnesses" and such witness is carried on by testimony. Sam felt that testimony exists in three forms with differing values—objective, corporate, and personal.

The most important testimony is that of scripture, including the proclamation of the Word and the praise of Jesus Christ and God's works. Sam felt the objective testimony of the Bible and preaching of the truth with God and His Son as its focus should be central to sharing the Gospel.

Next in importance is corporate testimony, the praise of God's dealings first with Israel, then with His church. It is cast in the plural—how God saved, led, chastened, comforted, blessed, and disciplined Israel and then how He brings all kinds of people into the body of Christ. Sam felt conservatives had given this type of testimony short shrift:

Conservatives have gotten so discouraged with the visible church that we hardly ever give that kind of testimony any more. We're great on personal testimony—how God blesses you and me—but we don't think we have much to say about how God blesses the church. How unfaithful we have been on this point! He is blessing His New Testament church now more than Israel. We ought to watch for it and call the attention of the world to it. The New Testament has more to do with God's dealings with this corporate body than with people one-on-one.[85]

Finally, Sam came to believe that personal testimony is least important, and, while valid, must be used with care. The dangers of personal testimony include glorifying the sin instead of focusing on Christ's saving work; trying to make the testimony scintillating or funny; exaggerating one's testimony to impress (sanctified imagination); and leaving people with the idea that the only way God saves is the way He saved you.

However, if the testimony serves as a sample of God's saving work, as a demonstration of His grace, as an example of the great variety of ways God saves people, or as a vehicle for a person to see God's footprints over the course of life, Sam was in favor of its use:

> *It's helpful for a person to give his own personal testimony to trace God's working in his life. It does him more good than anyone else because it forces him to see that God has been working since before he was born to bring him to the place where he knows Jesus.*[86]

Evangelistic Invitations

Traditional evangelistic preaching focuses on the invitation, and Sam admitted that he embraced that concept when he first began his career in the early 1940s. By the 1960s, however, he had begun moving in a different direction in his meetings.

"While other evangelists worked toward an invitation and pushed for a response," said Lane Stephenson (RTS '76), "Mr. Pat simply gave an opportunity for people to come forward at the end. He never made the invitation the focal point, and he never used that response as a gauge to judge the effectiveness of the services."

As Sam began to study Reformed theology, he began to question the idea of invitations even more. He noticed that when he returned to places where people had responded to them, the churches weren't growing. Where, he wondered, were those who had supposedly been saved?

In the coming years, his different viewpoint became evident to friends. "His preaching changed after he left Reformed Seminary," commented Billy Thompson, who led the singing for Sam at countless meetings. "He didn't give an invitation anymore. I had 'Just As I Am' ready, but he didn't use it."

Reflecting on his own ministry, Sam came to believe that exhortation, not invitation, was the biblical way to win souls:

> *I have used practically every evangelistic invitation technique over my thirty-two-year ministry. However, I believe every evangelist, deep in his heart, entertains serious misgivings about techniques. We continue to use them because, in a sense, they work and can somewhat measure a man's ministry, but we sense that they can be manipulative. Using them engenders a type of pride that runs counter to the evangelist's desire for a pure spirit before the Lord. One begins to measure his ministry by how many professions he generates.*
>
> *We have not gone back to the Bible to measure these techniques against scripture. The word 'invitation' is used only three times in the*

Old Testament. The New Testament uses the word 'exhort,' meaning to urge or persuade by the preacher's use of the Word and God's use of the Holy Spirit to approach the souls, minds, and consciences of men. An exhortation does not ask for a response that the natural man can make—raising his hand or walking down an aisle—but one that only an awakened soul by grace can make—repentance toward God and faith in Jesus Christ.

I have come to believe that an open invitation has only one value: identifying people who are under conviction and to whom an evangelist might further apply the Word that he has preached.[87]

THE NEED TO EVANGELIZE

Sam took the Great Commission very seriously and expected everyone else to do so, too. His passion for souls was immense, his scope boundless, and his sense of urgency compelling. Maybe you'll recognize these sermon excerpts:

Perhaps the single most important statement Jesus ever made was John 14:6: 'I am the way, the truth, and the life. No one comes to the Father except by me.' Once you are convinced of that, it makes a difference how you look at people. If there's only one door, you want people to find it. Someone helped you find it.[88]

God thinks big. He never was going to be satisfied with just twelve apostles and a few disciples. He was going after nations—a planet full of people who love and honor Him.[89]

Jesus said, 'Come to me all you who thirst.' When you're a little thirsty, a Coke will do. But when you're dying of thirst, you want water, and that's what Christ offered.[90]

Sam took his cue from 19th century evangelist Henry Clay Trumbell, whom Sam thought was the greatest person the church had produced. Trumbell said, "Whenever I have the right to introduce a topic of conversation, I'm going to talk about Jesus." [91]

As far as Sam was concerned, no place was off limits to talk about Jesus. Bill Whitwer recalls Sam sharing a tract with a salesperson while shopping in Gadsden; as a student at RTS, Guy Richardson remembers Sam in lengthy conversation with the Coca Cola deliveryman, who received a tract as they parted.

"Sam, Ed, and I were having lunch one day," said M. B. Cooper, "and a fellow came in pretty tipsy. Sam looked at him for a while, and then rose and went over to have a conversation with the man about the Lord."

While Sam was at French Camp Academy, he went to see a businessman to raise money for the school. In the waiting room with him were two salesmen engaged in friendly conversation. The older gentleman was entertaining the younger man with tales of his early days on the road as a "drummer." After a while, the veteran salesman fell silent, then said abruptly, "Before I get off the road, I'd like to represent one product that everybody in the world needs."

Sam knew an opportunity when he saw it and asked, "How would you like to meet a man who's in that business? I represent Jesus Christ, whom *everybody* needs. Jesus said, 'I am the way, the truth, and the life, and no man—out of all these billions of people—comes to the Father but by me.'" [92]

Sam never traveled on a plane without sharing the Gospel with his seatmate. "Once Sam and I were on the same flight but seated far apart," commented Betty Edwards. "After we got off the plane, I expressed regret that we had not been able to talk, and he graciously agreed but was overjoyed that he had shared the plan of salvation with the woman beside him and that she had accepted Christ as her Savior."

Veteran missionary C. T. Studd once said, "True religion is like the smallpox. If you get it, you give it to others and it spreads." [93] Sam undoubtedly agreed and wanted every Christian—not just preachers and missionaries—to witness as they had opportunity. According to him, the early Christians didn't have evangelistic programs, yet evangelism permeated everything they did. He felt we should be doing a better job with the number of people and the amount of money we have today: [94]

> *I think we've been satisfied with less than what God had in mind. I read a statement recently about how we should get the Gospel out to the world by every means so Jesus will return. I don't think that's what the New Testament teaches. We are out to get people to Jesus, not just get Him back.* [95]

Sam felt that God has given the responsibility to the church—not the Rotary Club or United Nations—to see that every human being has the benefit of hearing the Gospel, making Christians the most responsible people on earth. [96] The responsibility is two-pronged; Christians must not only proclaim the Gospel, but we must also demonstrate its power in our lives:

> *We in the church say sin is the curse, and Christ is the cure. Do we really believe that? Why are we not pouring everything into this? Why aren't we obsessed with this?*
>
> *Suppose tomorrow you found a cure for cancer. If you were really convinced that you had, you'd have to tell somebody, wouldn't you? You'd be willing to be called crazy. If you really knew the answer, you would not quiet down. You'd pour all your money and your time into it.*
>
> *Yet, all that shouting will never convince anyone. You must also demonstrate that you have the answer. If you do, people will begin*

to take you seriously. Perhaps the church has failed to produce a satisfactory demonstration of our claim. The person who's dying of a disease, yet still proclaiming he has the cure for it, will never get people to pay much attention to him. Oh, the responsibility of those of us who are Christians to be demonstrations of Christ! We're not going to be in perfect spiritual health, but we should be in the process of getting better so Jesus' attributes can shine through.[97]

Moreover, Sam felt, we should be sanctified for others' sakes because they love, respect, and depend on us. He once heard a Baptist layman say, "Remember this: to someone you're the best Christian they've ever known." Sam never forgot it:

Keep your testimony right, your life straight. There's something sanctifying about knowing that I am responsible not just for myself, but for others who might be watching me and receiving strength from what God is doing in my life.[98]

Sam felt another aspect of demonstrating the Gospel in our lives is concern for others. He constantly exhorted Christians to serve and minister as Jesus did, reminding them that the church has many blessings and should also be a blessing to the world. Otherwise, our salvation becomes inverted and selfish:

With multitudes of Christians, the blessing of the church should be better than it has ever been. Even pagans should realize now that mankind's greatest asset is Christians. Jesus was a blessing to the world everywhere He went as He helped people and even gave His life. Taking up the cross means giving of ourselves.[99]

Sam had also learned that concern for others even helps a Christian fight off temptation. Constant Bible study, intercession for others, and regular evangelistic activity builds inner strength:

Very few things will make you stronger against temptation than always being alert to be used of God to introduce someone to Christ. Move the conversation in that direction whenever you can. Be careful to show to others that Christ is real in your life so they will give better attention to His claims.[100]

Sam constantly looked for opportunities to share Christ, waiting patiently for weeks, months, even years in order to earn a respectful hearing of the Gospel. He urged others to do the same:

We should do whatever we have to in order to get a hearing for Christ. I witnessed five years to a contractor who did some work for me.

He hated Christians and didn't want to be around them. At first I wanted to convert him quickly, but I saw that wasn't going to happen. Every time I tried to introduce a spiritual topic, he'd throw up a wall and start attacking Christians. As I saw it, my responsibility was to hang in there with him and let him test one Christian. He developed cancer and was on his deathbed before he would let me talk about spiritual matters. He finally indicated that he had put his trust in Christ. I don't know whether he really meant it because he didn't live to bear any fruit, but I had gone as far as I could in the right direction.[101]

"He wanted to get the Gospel to everybody," said Peggy Cockrell. "As a pastor and a friend, he kept talking to people and never gave up on them, even though some of them never changed their lives!"

Sam obviously went further than most in his passion and concern for men's souls, so it may surprise you to know that several times during his ministry Sam himself thought he fell far short of the mark in caring for others. At a Kate Anderson revival in 1941, Sam reported that the first few nights he sensed no warmth or movement of the Spirit. Only one person had accepted Christ. He knew something was wrong, and eventually he discovered what it was:

I was closing those meetings offering an invitation with no real passion for the lost in the audience. The next day I prayed for a heart with real burden for them. The next night I confessed to the congregation my hard heart of the night before, and I told them that God was answering my prayer for a heart of real concern. From then on, the meetings became visibly fruitful.[102]

Later in his ministry he admitted the same failing to a Banner of Truth Conference audience:

The biggest battle I've had to face in my ministry is an aspect of holiness that I long neglected and covered over with false piety. This aspect is a sincere concern for others. I felt that if I were honest and pure, I'd live a godly life, but I was wrong.

I'm careful about being overworked and letting people take advantage of me; I give excuses to get the rest I think I need. People constantly came to Jesus asking Him to do things they had no right to ask, and He had no obligation to do it. But He always gave of Himself. I know that I'd say, 'Come back tomorrow. I've got to get a little rest.' Thankfully, God is dealing with me on this issue.[103]

Sam openly admitted that he was lazy at times about sharing the Gospel while traveling. In the early 1970s he had just finished a seven-day revival in Baltimore at a United Presbyterian church and was more fatigued than he could ever remember. He had even asked the pastor to take him to the airport early so he could catch a nap before his 1 a.m. flight. As he fell asleep, he was ashamed to realize that a war raged within him. While one part of him prayed that God would seat him beside someone who needed to hear the Gospel, the fleshly side prayed that God would allow him to sleep.

When he boarded the plane, he was relieved to find the seat beside him empty, and it remained so until they reached Washington. People then began to flood onto the plane. He was slightly embarrassed because people looked at him and passed him by, leaving the seat vacant. That rebuked him—the Lord knew he wasn't fit to talk to! Finally, the seat beside him was the only vacancy left. The last person boarded, and Sam knew if the man sat down by him it was of God. The man made his way back to the tourist section and, indeed, took his seat next to Sam.

As they chatted, Sam realized quickly that he was talking to a man much sharper than he. Handsome, well-dressed, in his early thirties, the businessman was easy to talk to, but Sam grew uneasy. He did better when he felt superior to someone, but he was feeling quite inferior now. After conversing for a while, Sam finally asked, "What is your personal faith?"

"If you mean religion, none," the man said. "I was baptized a Catholic, but I never attended mass. I do have a philosophy of life, though."

He could express himself well, and for about ten minutes he outlined his beliefs. "I don't know whether there is a God or not, but it doesn't make any difference to me. I believe man is the closest thing to God that we know anything about."

Sam was impressed with his intellect and asked, "Have you ever read the New Testament?"

"Never," he replied.

"Well, you should," Sam replied, "because you'd be surprised to know that you're not the first one to believe some of this. A lot of what you say is in the New Testament. I can tell that you have thought carefully about life, and I appreciate your sharing it. Now can I share with you what I believe?"

A faint shadow passed over the man's features, and Sam knew he couldn't care less about Sam's beliefs. Yet, politely he extended Sam the floor. They had just passed over Richmond, Virginia, and Sam said, "About thirty years ago, some 25,000 feet below us, God came into my life through Jesus Christ."

At the mention of Christ's name, Sam knew he had lost the fellow. A nervous look appeared in his eyes, and he began to fidget. Sam gave him a ten-minute summary of what Christ had done in his life, but he knew the man wasn't listening—probably thinking what a nut he had for a seatmate.

Suddenly, however, the man demanded, "You're telling me that God was doing something in this Jesus Christ two thousand years ago. Well, I want to know what God is doing right now!"

Sam was stunned. No one had ever asked him that, nor had he ever thought about it. Yet, he heard himself say boldly, "I'll be glad to tell you what God is doing now," even though Sam had no idea what he would say next. However, the Lord gave him the words instantly. "It's no accident you're sitting in that seat, and I'm sitting here because thirty years ago God came into my life through Jesus Christ. Now God is in me trying to get across into your life."

That's when Sam really thought he'd lost him. The man tried to get up, but the seatbelt caught him. Then Sam saw he wasn't trying to leave, but was trying to twist around to look Sam square in the face. He said, "Man, that's good! Do you really believe that?"

"I really do," said Sam.

"Do you tell that to everyone you meet?"

"No, I've never said it before, but it's the truth," said Sam.

The man sat back and said, "If you'll go see a movie I have theological questions about, I'll give you my word that I'll get a New Testament and begin reading it." [104]

So intense was Sam about teaching others to share the Gospel that in December 1981, he wrote his daughter, Becky, a thirty-six-page handwritten letter on the subject—while recuperating from a heart attack! (See Appendix E.) Becky had encountered an agnostic roommate at Montreat Anderson College and had asked Sam how to deal with atheists and agnostics. Here is an excerpt:

> *The dis-believer (atheist or agnostic) is one who knows the Christian testimony, claims to have thoughtfully considered it, and has deliberately determined that it is false. The dis-believer will not be won by coaxing, chiding, or arguing because his problem is not lack of intellectual knowledge, but a true blindness of heart as real as eye-blindness. It is not that he will not see—he cannot... He needs to be given light and sight. This, God must do in his heart. Of course, your life and witness will and must give light ... but the Spirit must give the sight through the New Birth process.*
>
> *We are, therefore, to be ready at all times to witness to and for Christ.... We are witnesses to the dis-believer in two primary ways: by the testimony of a transformed life ... and by the testimony of our lips, backed by an informed mind. This 'lip' witness includes the testimony of 1) what Christ means to us, 2) what the scriptures say about Him, and 3) the testimony of Bible scholars....*
>
> *We are also to be ready to contend for the Christian faith. However, our contending must not be contentious, but in serious graciousness with courage. Our purpose is not to win an argument, but to win a soul—not to win a point, but a person. It is possible to win an argument but lose the soul because of a contentious, mean attitude. It is possible to lose an argument but win the soul because of a calm, gracious assurance of faith in Christ!*

We are not called to be 'wits' for Christ, but 'witnesses.' We are never to bluff or pretend when we are intellectually out-matched by the one with whom we contend. We are humbly, boldly, graciously to declare the truth of Christ in scripture and our experience, trusting the Holy Spirit to use these. We must pray for the dis-believer. Pray often and much for him. We can talk to God about him when we can't talk to him about God.

We must be careful to keep our own faith intact. A Christian is doomed to confusion, frustration, and non-effectiveness unless a fresh relationship is daily maintained with Christ through daily Bible study and prayer, shutting the world out. The result will be a consciousness of His blessed presence during the day and a daily life consistent with the high calling we have in Christ.

Remember, the thrill of living in Christ, witnessing to Christ, standing for Christ, contending for the faith of Christ, and thus winning others to Him is the Christian's privilege! The <u>consistent</u>, <u>uncompromising</u> life in Christ is an argument no dis-believer can answer.[105]

Though Sam constantly urged others to evangelize at every opportunity, he was a realist and knew how frightening sharing one's faith can be. He once heard the famous Dr. Manford George Gutzke admit to the same fear. The eminent Bible teacher's story of God's help for that fear impressed Sam mightily for the rest of his life.

It seems that Gutzke pastored a small church while he was in school in Texas. One day a woman in the church asked if he would talk to her nephew, who was coming to visit.

"I have raised this boy," she confessed, "and he is about to graduate from Harvard law school. Although I have tried to teach him the Christian faith, he doesn't seem to believe anything much. Would you promise to spend just an hour with him?"

Gutzke promised, but with misgivings. He didn't feel he could match wits with a Harvard graduate. The day came, however, and the fellow came over. Gutzke told the boy right off, "Look, I know why you're here, and I don't think it's because you want to be here. I think you merely promised your aunt you'd do it."

The fellow nodded sheepishly.

"Well," said Gutzke, "the only reason I'm here is because I promised her, too. I don't want to be here either, but let's make the best of it. There's a chair and a newspaper for you, and I've got some work to do, so we'll put the hour in."

They both laughed at the ridiculous situation and just fell to talking, not about religion but everything else. Very soon they could see that two more different people had never gotten together. They didn't agree on anything! So amusing was the situation that they began to see if they could find something they agreed on. They didn't find anything.

Finally Gutzke laughed and said, "I believe I know something we'd agree on. I think a full bucket has more in it than an empty bucket."

Surprised, the young man replied, "You know, I believe that."

Gutzke then countered, "My bucket is full. What about yours?"

The man looked at Gutzke for a long minute and replied sorrowfully, "Dr. Gutzke, my bucket is empty—so empty that I have considered self-destruction."

Gutzke then had the opportunity to tell the boy with what Gutzke's bucket was filled and from where it came.[106]

Perhaps Gutze's story resonated with Sam because he had a similar experience early in his ministry when he had to talk to a businessman who was obviously a pagan. Sam knew he needed to witness to the man but was intimidated because he thought the fellow was much smarter. He had graduated from one of the greatest institutions in the country.

After finishing their business, Sam summoned all his courage and asked, "What is your personal faith?"

The man replied, "I believe in a supreme being, but that's about as far as I've worked anything out."

The rest of his beliefs were centered on his worldly accomplishments. Sam discovered that he was a broken man—divorced, alienated from his children, discouraged, and a failure on the inside.

"Sam," he confessed, "your faith has made you a better and happier man, while mine has done nothing for me."

Upon leaving, Sam realized that only another Christian could match the witness God had given him. He prayed that God would never let him forget that pagans might have more wit, but not witness![107]

Sam admitted freely that witnessing was a struggle his entire life. While challenging RTS students to be bold in sharing their faith, Sam endeared himself to many by admitting how difficult that can be. Alan Carter (RTS '76, '80) remembers one of those confessional moments. During his first year at RTS, Sam and Jack Scott led a group of volunteer students in "cold turkey" evangelism in Clinton, a Jackson suburb near the seminary. The group met weekly to pray and then knock on doors in various subdivisions. Once, Sam and Alan were chatting in the car before their first visit, and Alan asked, "How long do I have to do this before I stop being nervous about it?"

Without hesitation, Sam replied, "I'm still nervous, Alan. You don't ever get over it."

"I've never forgotten that," reveals Alan today. "There he was, a middle-aged man and a well-known evangelist, and still a bit nervous doing evangelism. It both comforted and encouraged me to continue in and through the nervousness. The devil whispers to us that we could be better witnesses for Christ if we were more spiritually mature. That night Mr. Pat helped me grasp an eternal truth—the Christian life this side of glory is a constant struggle. Anything else is a lie."

GIVING TO EVANGELISM

Tithing to evangelistic causes was a top priority for Sam his entire life, even though his income was always modest and in retirement, meager. He believed evangelism should be high on everyone's gift list. From his small income, he gave to numerous organizations monthly, even if only five or ten dollars. He was fond of saying, "Jesus didn't talk much about saving; He talked about giving." Sam felt today's church had not accomplished nearly as much evangelistically as the early church, despite greater numbers and resources.

He pointed to the Macedonian Christians as role models for the modern church. Despite severe troubles, they were exuberantly happy and gave willingly, even lavishly, from the depths of their poverty:

> *The Macedonians gave themselves. Saving faith is not just receiving Christ as Savior, but also giving ourselves in service. Think about giving everything you own away; it would make you live by faith! That's what we as Christians are called to do.[108]*

According to Sam, the Macedonians gave to two causes that constitute the character of the ministry of Jesus Christ on this earth. They contributed to the fund to help poor Jews in Jerusalem, and they supported Paul's missionary efforts. Sam constantly pointed out that Jesus' primary concern was people's salvation, but He also tried to help those who were oppressed. Sam felt if the church began to meet temporal needs while preaching the Gospel—instead of being super-spiritual—Christians would get more of a hearing from the world than they do today. More than any generation, Sam noted, Christians today see the physical and spiritual needs of people in the world, and the church has more resources than ever with which to help.[109]

If anyone wondered how to free up more money for missions, Sam had a ready answer:

> *How can we give lavishly, even more than God requires? Look at your budget and decide how you could save money. Learn to live more simply and frugally, as the Lord Jesus did on earth. We Christians are luxury livers in America; we have finery of all kinds. Find cheaper ways to live. If we are willing to do this, Christians can provide not only the Gospel but also basic physical necessities for those in desperate need around the world.[110]*

Sam followed his own advice when, in 1979, he became convicted about two problems. The first was living too extravagantly, while most of the rest of the world lived in dire poverty. At the same time, the doctor had told Sam his heart condition couldn't survive the weight he was putting on.

About that time, he heard a news report saying that two thirds of the world's population ask, "How can we get enough to eat?" while one third of the population asks, "How can I keep overeating from killing me?" Sam instantly saw himself and knew he had to take action:

> *I figured if two-thirds of the world didn't have enough food for reasonable health, I ought to give these twenty-five pounds to somebody. I cut down on my eating, figured the cost of what I wasn't eating, and began giving about thirty-five dollars a month to the Lord to help starving people. I was giving my weight away!*
>
> *Sadly, a few months later I fell back into extravagant ways and began to put the pounds back on. But about two weeks ago I came to my senses and repented before God. I realized I liked the feeling I had when I gave myself away, and I am back on the program now!* [111]

A HEART FOR EVANGELISM AT RTS

"My first year at RTS, Sam drove down from French Camp to teach my evangelism class," said Laurie Jones. "God had equipped him as an evangelist, with a deep understanding of God's sovereignty on the one hand and a sincere passion for souls on the other. He put that balance in my life and helped me hone my evangelism skills. Remembering Sam's love for people has influenced my ministry throughout the years."

"I appreciated his zeal for evangelism," said Jim Stewart (RTS '72, '88). "To see the president of our seminary with a passion for lost souls was a great tribute to RTS and a tremendous encouragement to me in my evangelistic ministry there."

Students loved Sam's practical approach. "He didn't spend a lot of time telling us about the history of evangelism," revealed Richard Wiman (RTS '77). "Rather, we read John Stott's *Our Guilty Silence*, J. I. Packer's *Evangelism and the Sovereignty of God*, and Paul Little's *How to Give Away Your Faith*. Then he sent us out to share the Gospel with as many people as we could during the months we were together. Every week, Mr. Sam wanted to know how many we had witnessed to and how many had come to know the Lord. While most of us could report little progress, he always had numerous tales of his own evangelistic adventures. His passion for Jesus Christ, the lost, and his fledgling preachers was both humbling and motivating."

Dick Gates (RTS '76) recalls that Sam was frequently blunt in challenging students to share their faith. "Mr. Pat would ask, 'Are you ever alone with a man without telling him about Jesus? Silence isn't always golden; sometimes it's YELLOW!' He taught me that a confession with my mouth is a must. Living an upright, moral life without publicly professing Christ gives credit to man instead of to the grace of God. According to Mr. Pat, God is pleased with us even if the person to whom we are witnessing doesn't accept Christ. We are telling the truth about God."

Sam's tender heart for a student's personal walk with Christ was quite evident to John Ropp (RTS '74) immediately upon his arrival at RTS. "Mr. Pat was the first person ever to ask me about my remembrances of praying to receive Jesus Christ as my Savior when I was a child. I had to go far back in my memory to an event that I have used countless times since to help others see—and to remind myself—that receiving Christ can be a seemingly insignificant moment with eternal consequences."

Other students recall Sam's gentle sense of humor in class. "In Mr. Pat's personal evangelism class, we had to tape three different witnessing experiences," related Al Herrington (RTS '75,'77). "On the day of my report, I turned on the tape recorder, but there was only silence. We waited and waited, but the recorder had malfunctioned and not taped a word. I finally told Mr. Pat sheepishly, 'Mine was a silent witness!' After the laughter died down, he graciously asked me to record it again to be heard another day." Al has been in full-time ministry with Presbyterian Evangelistic Fellowship for seventeen years now.

Just as at French Camp, Sam never forgot RTS graduates, especially if trouble came upon them. Doug Murphy (RTS '78) found that out when a church planting ministry failed, devastating him.

"We had to leave the area and stay temporarily with my parents until a new direction and call came. My wife was pregnant with our first child, and I was without work. Sam learned of our situation and, on his way back to Mississippi, went out of his way to come for a time of prayer and encouragement with us. That was the kind of man he was. His visit meant so much and was one of the ways God helped me stay the course. Thank God for Sam Patterson."

Sam also liked nothing better than seeing RTS students establish churches and being asked to preach revivals for them, calling it the "grandest thing." One RTS graduate who seemed to appreciate Sam's visits the most was Lane Stephenson (RTS '76). Sam preached in the small mountain community of Tellico Plains in eastern Tennessee three times during Lane's twenty-year ministry there.

"The people greatly loved Mr. Pat," said Lane. "He was very much at home among them, and they with him. Mountain people are normally very shy around people from the outside, but they really opened up to him and held him in high regard, probably because of his humility. They were still quoting him years later."

However, the truth was that Lane benefited from Sam's visits even more than his congregation. "Since Lane was the only pastor living up on the mountain, he had his hands full with all the denominations," noted his wife, Carol. "He needed some encouragement. We had very few visiting ministers, and the church could not afford to send Lane to conferences—only presbytery. It was always very special when Lane could be with another pastor, especially Mr. Pat, and be fed spiritually."

Lane agreed. "Mr. Pat did more than anyone else to encourage and help us personally. I probably gained more from the services than anyone in being able to listen to his wisdom and watch how he interacted with people. I also had plenty of questions, and he was willing to sit down and talk with me. He was a simple, quiet person to whom I could talk as a friend. He had a great influence on me in those years of my pastorate when I knew that people paid more attention to who I was than to the fact that I had a seminary degree.

"I'd so much enjoy his visits, and I can remember feeling a real loneliness when he drove into the darkness after our last service. I'd almost cry when he left because his time with us had been such an encouragement to me."

A NEW CREATION

> Therefore, if anyone is in Christ, he is a new creation; old things have passed away; behold, all things have become new (2 Cor. 5:17, NKJV).

By Sam's own admission, he preached on 2 Corinthians 5:17 more than any other verse in the Bible.[112] He found the verse shortly after he was converted and never lost his fascination with it:

> If you looked over my shoulder as I preach to see my Bible, you'd see this verse is of tremendous importance to me. Your eye would immediately be drawn to it. I have highlighted in yellow the entire passage and drawn a circle around verse seventeen. I have underscored certain words in that verse and drawn two big arrows pointing to it, one from the bottom and one from the top. I have a date written out to the side of it. This verse ought to be a good friend stepping out of scripture to clasp your hand and remind you of who you are and what's being done for you.[113]

Sam wanted to be a New Man and understood the concept of being a new creation. He knew that with Christ in his life he could NOT continue in the old ways; change had to come. The focus of his life was to get others to see the need for that change and to submit to Christ.

He usually included verses five through seventeen in the series and expanded or contracted the message to fit the length of the revival. One of the most comprehensive treatments of the entire passage still in existence seems to be one entitled *A Time to Renew*, an eight-sermon series preached at First Presbyterian Church in Jackson, Mississippi, in October 1979.

No book on Sam's life would be complete without giving readers a glimpse of the powerful, winsome, dynamic presentation of the Gospel in these sermons. What follows is an edited compilation of the messages as they move through the text. During this series, Sam preached an entire sermon on the word "any"! The thoughts contained in these sermons are as fresh and compelling today as they were decades ago.

A Time To Renew
2 Corinthians 5:17

Second Corinthians 5:17 is a single sentence of about twenty-three words, seventeen of which are only one syllable. This verse presents the biggest, boldest, and broadest claim for Jesus Christ in scripture. Paul affirms here that the power of Jesus Christ is sufficient to transform the life of any human being—to make one right with God, right with others, and right within himself.

Paul speaks of this power as a Person (Jesus) set down in the very wreckage of humanity who can force lives back right again. That means that this verse presents the best and brightest hope for humanity. In Jesus Christ, any human being can see the possibility of a transformation that will alter the course and character, the direction and destiny of his life, beginning right now and never ending.

In verse seventeen, the Apostle Paul sends forth this mighty declaration: If any human being comes into direct relationship with Jesus Christ, the inevitable will take place. Old things will begin to pass away, and a brand new life will begin that will never end. Put anyone in direct contact with Christ, and the inevitable product is a new man. I can see the generosity of the Gospel here, the joy of Paul in the wideness of the free offer of the Gospel in Jesus Christ. Nothing limits the possibility of the free grace of Jesus Christ to transform lives, neither moral degradation nor moral achievement. The worst and the best will be transformed!

How does one become united to Jesus Christ? How can a person, and those around him or her, tell that the process is underway? In Luke 6:47–48, Jesus describes that person like this:

> *Everyone who comes to me and hears my words and acts upon them*
> *… is like a man building a house, who dug deep and laid a foundation*
> *upon the rock; and when a flood arose, the river burst against that house*
> *and could not shake it because it had been well-built (NASV).*

Here Jesus describes saving faith, yet doesn't even use the words! If we want to be united with Christ and receive a brand new life that will never end, we must come to Him, listen to what He has to say, and devote our lives to implementing what we learn from Him.

What do we receive when we come to Jesus? First, we receive His acceptance of us by virtue of His proven love for us. We come to Him to receive absolute forgiveness of all of our sins by virtue of the death He's already died for us. Next, we receive His living leadership over our lives by virtue of His resurrection from the dead. We receive the power to live after Him, for Him, with Him by virtue of the Holy Spirit that He gives to those who trust Him. You can do that sitting right where you are now. You need not move your body an inch because turning to Christ is an action of the heart. Finally, we render our allegiance to Him. Coming to Jesus is meaningless and will never change our lives unless we begin immediately to be a student or disciple of Christ. We must begin to learn from and about Him from His Word and His church. He tells us to implement what we learn for the rest of our lives.

I tell you, friends, you cannot do that in true faith and be the same kind of person! That's why a true Christian never fails to be a brand new creation! That day-by-day coming to Christ, looking to Him with a faith that is yielding up one's mind, heart, will, and body will make a new kind of living! You can begin today learning from Him by searching His Word and then earnestly seeking to live by His principles in your home, your business, your friendships. The best place to live is in the control of Christ. It is a place of safety.

If you could pull over Mississippi the climate of the tropics, you'd see a brand new kind of life issuing forth. You'd find new foliage and fruit in the yards and fields of our state. The New Testament teaches that this is just how it is when we accept Christ as our Savior. We immediately begin to live in a new climate, and it is so good! It blesses us, and we become a blessing. We have a constant life of relating to Him in faith and loving others. Imagine living every day just loving others! The person who has been renewed becomes a fountain of love! Such a life comes from God and envelopes our hearts and radiates out.

Christ's death on the cross provides our pardon and frees God up to let us enter into this new life in Christ. He is not our Savior because men killed him, though that was awful. God elected to sacrifice His son. Christ endured the wrath of God for us, was made to be sin for us, and was banished from God for me. Our Creator came and took our sins and paid for them. I can now share in the majesty of that new life, and I have His personal living presence with me. Jesus was our creator, and He came and took his creatures' sins. That I could share in that majesty and integrity is thrilling indeed. His Holy Spirit can come in and help conform me to His image.

Could it be that the God who can take smelly, dirty water from the cow trough in the barnyard, evaporate it into the heavens, and send it back for us to drink—could he have no design to save and transform creatures polluted and ruined in sin? Jesus displayed the type of life for which God is saving us. We need the application of His blood to the whole span of our lives. If we measure ourselves by one another, we are led to deception. We will be measured against Jesus. Someday we'll be just like Him. We are saved from sin to godliness—saved from being ruined caricatures of humans into people who bear clear evidence of the image of God increasingly in our lives. Salvation is not just to escape hell. We are all unique no matter what sin has done to us. In the second birth, God begins to bring a glory out of us that interprets the life of Jesus in a unique way. The more we gaze at Him, listen to Him, the more we become like Him.

I will give an interpretation of Jesus that no one will ever see unless it is given by me! God will never again make one like me! Think of a stained glass window with all those different colors coming together and sunlight flooding into different shapes and colors, new interpretations of the light.

When we are united with Christ, our lives are dominated by a new noble purpose—living for Him. Jesus died as our substitute, and we are to be Christ's substitute among men. Jesus' Spirit is not only in this world, but in you and me as believers. He'll live in all of my activities in ME. What a purpose we have for living now! In all my relationships I am to live Christ's character out—His integrity, purity, justice, faith, and love. His compassionate conduct and purpose must be present in me. I must be busy about doing what He did while he was here, using His body for the service of others.

When we are united with Christ, we have a new center in life. Most of our lives are fragmented and the different parts are in conflict. That's why we are in such a stew all the time. In Romans 1, Paul tells us that every human life gets off center; we put jobs, money, spouse, children ahead of God. Little wonder we are a disturbed people. Putting anything other than God at the center makes our lives unstable. God puts a worthy center in our lives; our multitudes of interests and activities become unified around our loyalty to Jesus. Peace comes when Christ is the center of our lives. He's the one who created everything and holds it all in His hands. Putting Christ at the center of our lives makes us better in every relationship.

Finally, when we are united with Christ, our lives are based on a new commitment. Saving faith is a confidence in Christ that causes one to commit oneself into His care and control for the rest of life. While one does not need to identify a time and place one was saved, the commitment needs to be specific, not general. It's real and up front and you identify with it. You have to know that it is there!

The Heidelberg Catechism is one of the best descriptions of the new life in Christ:

> *What is your only comfort in life and death? That I belong body and soul in life and in death not to myself but to my faithful Savior Jesus Christ, who at the cost of His own blood, has fully paid for all my sins and has completely freed me from the dominion of the devil; that He protects me so well that without the will of my Father in heaven not a hair can fall from my head; indeed, that everything must fit His purpose for my salvation. Therefore, by His Holy Spirit, He also assures me of*

eternal life, and makes me wholeheartedly willing and ready from now on to live for Him.

Jesus said a disciple must deny himself every day and take up his cross and follow Him. I don't know any other way to keep your commitment current than to come back to Him every day, fall on your knees, and recommit yourself. Every morning come to him as a sinner and cast yourself on His mercy, pleading for His grace and submitting your life to Christ, giving yourself up to be His man or woman that day. I learned this from a little group I was in six months after I was converted. I don't know how I would have made it as a Christian all these years without it. I know the initial commitment was genuine, but it's been easier to keep it current by every day coming to Him in that self-giving way, yielding my life to be filled by the Spirit.

Friends, it's embarrassing to be a preacher. I've spoken in His presence now, and once again I get so outdone with my inability to present to you the truth about him as I ought. I'm doing the best I can, but I've never done an adequate or worthy job. He's better than anything I've said. May He forgive me for that failure! I cannot present Him as wonderful as He is. I wish He'd just speak for Himself, but He is not going to do that. He uses sinners like me who've been saved by His grace to tell the story, and I've been trying to tell it.

You and He know the need of your own heart and what your response should be. If Christ is already at work transforming your life and you have become a new creature, even though you have a long way to go, thank Him! If you are not a Christian, Jesus Christ is here, right where you are, and He offers Himself. You can't see Him, but He stands at the very threshold of your heart. Tell God you are ready for your sins to be forgiven and start living God's way. Christ is the Savior of sinners, and He's made a promise. Those who come to Him, listen to him, and begin to learn how to live for Him as He gives grace, He immediately receives and *never* casts out.

I've gone as far as I can go. All I can do is talk about it, but Jesus Christ can *do* something about your life! And He stands right where you are—oh, if only you had eyes to see! He can step in and transform your life right now, and He *will do it!* Will you let Him?

CHAPTER EIGHT

THE PRAYER WARRIOR

God is a friend of silence. The more we engage in prayer, the more we can give in our active life. The essential thing is not what we say, but what God says to us and what He says through us.

Mother Teresa

Satan has no fear of prayerless studies, prayerless work, prayerless religion. He laughs at our toil, mocks our wisdom, but trembles when we pray.

F. B. Meyer

If evangelism was the driving force in Sam's life, surely rich and vibrant communion with God in prayer was his ever-present anchor. Yet, Sam never saw himself as a prayer warrior; on the contrary, he seemed to fear greatly that his actions might cause others to praise him as one:

> *If any of me 'leaks out' and I use prayer to lift myself up to create a reputation for myself as a great man of prayer—talking about how much I pray and how many of my prayers have been answered—I'm trying to get something from men, and that's an abomination to God.[1]*

Sam dealt with this problem in various ways, determined that he would give pride no berth in his life. One of the most notable strategies became his characteristic short prayers. Some people saw them as a sign of intimacy with His Savior, but others probably got closer to the real truth.

"Although Mr. Pat was deeply spiritual, I believe he didn't want to appear to be showing off by his eloquence in prayer," recalls Ed Williford. "You'd never know that he was a preacher by his prayers at mealtime. "They were always quite short: 'Lord, we thank you for this food, for this day, and for every blessing. Amen.' I learned that prayer from him and still use it today."

Paul admonishes us to "pray without ceasing" in 1 Thessalonians 5:17, and Robert Hayes (RTS '74) can testify to the fact that Sam took the command literally. While in seminary, Robert traveled with Sam to conduct a funeral in Carrollton, Mississippi, where Robert was the student pastor. On the way, they stopped for gas and coffee.

"After filling the car, I needed to use the restroom," relates Robert. "As I walked into the men's room, I heard someone praying. I stopped in amazement, wondering who it might be since the room seemed empty. Then I heard the word 'funeral,' and I suddenly realized that Mr. Pat was in the stall praying the Lord's blessing on the funeral and his sermon! Such dependence on prayer touched my heart deeply, and it has stuck with me all these years. I learned from him that day to pray *anywhere*. Today, if someone calls me for prayer, I ask if we can pray immediately, right there on the phone."

"I think about Sam Patterson's life of prayer every time I enter my office," says RTS Chief Operations Officer M. Steve Wallace (RTS '78). "It was initially Sam's office when he reluctantly became the first president of the seminary. I was a student at that time and remember thinking that much prayer was going on in there. Sam's prayers surely make this office a sanctified place, and his testimony continues to inspire and challenge me each day to make sure that prayer is an essential part of the life of RTS."

Prayer did indeed permeate the fabric of Sam's daily life. It was as important as any doctor's appointment or church function—often more important. Among Sam's personal papers are dozens of appointment books from the 1970s and 1980s, the pages of which are littered with people to pray for by name, right alongside the grocery and "to do" lists. One notation reminds Sam to "study, walk, buy cough drops, have devotions, and pray."

As Sam studied prayer throughout his life, he discovered a disturbing fact. When it comes to prayer, many religious leaders are like the shoe salesman who never wore shoes:

> We are guilty of a pious inconsistency by extolling prayer but not engaging in effective intercession. The two aren't necessarily the same. We believe in prayer; we preach messages on faith and prayer; we encourage our parishioners to believe in prayer and what it will produce. Yet, we're not all that faithful in practicing what we preach.[2]

He set out to remedy that problem in his own life. Later, he was grateful to God for showing him the real purpose of prayer:

> God works everything according to the counsel of His own will and purpose, which are eternal and were established before any creation ever came into being. He is working those eternal purposes out in individuals, nations, rulers, and the church in time and space. The Bible makes very

clear that God has many means to effect His will and purposes, and one of the most important and powerful is prayer. It activates God's work and will in the world. That's why Jesus taught his disciples to pray 'Your kingdom come, your will be done, your name be hallowed on the planet Earth.'[3]

Indeed, Sam's fervent prayers spread major ripples in the ocean of God's work on earth. James 5:16 tells us, "The prayer of a righteous man is powerful and effective" (NIV). Sam probably never knew how his emphasis on prayer impacted the life of Ron Bossom (RTS '75). When Ron came to RTS in 1971, he had been a Christian only a year, coming from a Roman Catholic and high Episcopalian background. One day while getting lunch in the convenience store on the edge of campus, he overheard one of the employees joking with an RTS upperclassman.

"Hey," the employee asked, "is it true that RTS wants to buy this store and turn it into a bookstore?"

"Yep, that's what we've heard," said the student.

"Well," the boy countered," this store is one of the better money-makers in this area. The owners will never sell it to the seminary."

The student turned, incredulous, and said, as if to a child, "No, you don't understand. At the top of that hill is Sam Patterson and a bunch of old men. They're praying right now about a bookstore. I've got some advice for you—either learn how to sell books or get another job because this building sure as shootin' is going to be owned by RTS."

"I had never heard anybody talk about the power of prayer like that," recalls Ron today. "I thought, 'Where in the world am I?' Not long after that, I did indeed watch that convenience store become the RTS Bookstore!"

Ron's next experience with Sam and prayer came during his first semester. One day Sam called Ron to his office, welcoming him with a big smile. "Ron," he said, "I've been looking at your record and see that you are a teacher. We've got an awful problem with our international students. They don't understand southern English and are lost in class. We've been praying about this and have decided that you're the man to work with them."

"It never occurred to me to say no," recalls Ron with a smile. "But my wife was floored."

"Ron," she said, "you're working night and day to catch up because you don't have the background of all these other students. How will you have the time?"

"But Sue," Ron said, "Mr. Pat and those guys were *praying*. I knew arguing was useless."

The money did help, though, since they were broke and did not know how they would pay for his second semester. Imagine Ron's surprise when he went to pay the bill, and the business office told him he didn't owe anything. "You're on staff now. Didn't Mr. Pat tell you?"

Ron was approaching his senior year when he next encountered Sam's singular brand of prayer. He had decided that most of the year-long internships encouraged by the seminary were unproductive; only one mildly interested him, but he thought it had been taken. In late May, he received a note in his mailbox to see Sam, who again welcomed him with a wide grin.

"Ron," Sam said kindly, "we have truly appreciated all that you have done with the international students. Yet, you came to RTS without having a background in Presbyterianism, didn't you?"

Ron had to agree. He wondered with some trepidation what was coming next.

"I can see from your grades that you are learning the Reformed faith well, but you don't have the seeee-soning (Ron can hear that twang now) that a man should get in seminary. So, Ron, we've been praying. We think you need to go to Prattville next year for an internship. Would you be interested?"

It was the very internship he had considered but thought was filled! Ron said yes. At home, Sue was excited at the news, but puzzled.

"I thought you were against year-long internships!"

Ron said, "I was. But they were *praying*. How could I fight it?"

Although Sam didn't live to see it, his prayers indeed furthered God's work dramatically. Upon graduation in 1976, Ron went to the Washington, D.C. area to plant one church and has been there ever since. Currently, he is planting his fifty-fourth!

DO YOU WANT PEACE THROUGH PRAYER?

From the moment RTS opened its doors in 1966, Sam began preaching one sermon to students every four years because he felt its message was so vital. He called it "Turning Over Problems: The Counsel of Psalm 37." Especially in verses 3–7, Sam felt David sets forth the attitudes that must be present when we approach God profitably. Move through these steps with a problem in prayer, Sam promised students, and God will give you peace. Following are highlights from that sermon.

Philippians 4:6–7 tells us, "Don't be anxious about anything, but in everything, by prayer and petition with thanksgiving, present your requests to God and the peace of God, which transcends all understanding, will guard your hearts and minds in Christ Jesus" (NIV). Here God is not promising what He'll do with the problem. He's promising peace to the one who has the problem. Regardless of what God does with the problem, He will equip that person to live with it so that he can keep functioning in his walk with the Lord.

All of us have prayed for such peace and not gotten it. That's probably because we haven't really prayed. Talking to God isn't necessarily prayer.

Certain attitudes must be present in the heart before talking becomes prayer. When we really pray, God says peace will always come—no exceptions! What are these attitudes? We find them in Psalm 37:3–7.

Trust in the Lord and do good (Psalm 37:3)

The first element that turns talking to God into prayer is trust. It means believing that He is who He shows Himself to be in the scriptures. It means relying on the Lord, believing not only that He is *able* to take care of our problems, but also that He is *willing* to do it. It means commitment to obey God, confident that He will reward those who diligently seek him.

When we look at God—infinite, eternal, and unchangeable—we see our problems in a different perspective. Measured by our ability to handle matters, problems will scare us to death because we don't know how to deal with them. Yet, the Christian should not be frightened or worried; we have the power of our gracious, omnipotent God to take care of any problem.

Once I received a phone call at RTS, and after I hung up, I realized I had a major problem on my hands. Immediately, I began to worry about it. I knew if I continued in this confused state I would lose my joy and not be able to function well. Therefore, I grabbed my Bible, even though I know these verses by heart, and headed for a secret place. I knelt, threw the Bible open, and filtered that prayer through this process that David sets out in Psalm 37. I got up a little while later with peace in my heart.[4]

Delight yourself also in the Lord (Psalm 37:4)

Even if we come to God in trust, we must guard against using Him as our servant in prayer. First, we must recognize with pleasure that He is such a great blessing to us. He is sufficient no matter what he does with our problems, even if we must keep them. Second, we must not only delight in doing His will, but also delight in His will always being done. We are free to tell the Lord how we want Him to answer the prayer, as long as we are willing to say in our hearts, "Nevertheless, not my will but thine be done."

Commit your way to the Lord (Psalm 37:5)

The Hebrew for "commit" is to "roll over onto the Lord." This doesn't mean to roll it onto the Lord just to get it off us so it won't hurt. It means to roll it off on the Lord so He'll be in control of it. Since we surely haven't been able to handle it, we should gladly give it up to Him.

"When I first heard this sermon," recalls Bill Everett (RTS '73), "Sam's wife had cancer, and he didn't know the outcome. He told us that he had done what the psalmist had exhorted and had committed his burden to the Lord. He reminded us that we don't need to keep asking God to help with a particular problem; once we've rolled it onto His back, we don't have to do it again and again. Rather, we can simply trust, thanking Him that it is in His blessed and sovereign hands and knowing that He will always do what is best.

"I have never forgotten that day in chapel. During almost thirty years of ministry, I have passed on Sam's sweet counsel, and I trust that it has been of help to others who have been weighed down with the burdens of this fallen world."

Rest in the Lord (Psalm 37:7)

After rolling a burden onto the Lord's shoulders, we must be still before Him and rest. If we are going to let God handle the problem, we've got to quit telling Him what to do about it. We've already had our chance, so we stand still until He activates us. Standing still in the face of a problem is difficult, even if we think God's got it. I recently had surgery and they put me to sleep—so it wouldn't hurt and so I wouldn't try to help! This was a problem the doctor had to work out without me because he had the expertise.

Wait patiently for Him (Psalm 37:7)

Finally, wait on the Lord. Waiting on the Lord doesn't mean that we are always standing still; sometimes we are very busy. It means we are always at attention. Consider professional waitpersons. The good ones wait, still and poised, by the table, giving attention to the will of the person who's going to order. Yet, the minute they get the orders, they are bundles of activity—taking the orders to be filled, bringing the food back, and refilling glasses. All through the meal, they are vigilant, watching carefully and checking back frequently to see if they can be of any assistance. If not, they busy themselves with other customers. However, if they receive a signal for help from the diner, they will immediately return and stand at attention, waiting to become active again at the will of the diner.

That's what it means to wait on the Lord. We recognize that we have put our problems in God's hands, and we return in prayer every day, thanking Him that He has them and waiting to see if God wants us to do anything. Instead of asking God to fix the problem, we ask if we can do something about the problem we gave Him. If He doesn't show us anything, we continue to wait.[5]

"I was going through an anxious time when Sam preached this sermon, and it gave me great peace," recalls Jim Stewart (RTS '72, '88). "Many times since then, when I have been anxious about something, I have turned to the notes I took on that sermon and have found peace through that psalm."

PRACTICAL STEPS TO EFFECTIVE PRAYER

As in every other aspect of his Christian walk, Sam sought to pattern his prayer life after that of Jesus. Over the years he counseled others in at least four practical areas to make their prayer lives more fruitful.

Rise Early Regularly

Sam noticed in scripture that an ordinary day for Jesus usually began in prayer in the pre-dawn quiet. Sam, therefore, did likewise. He understood that communion with God requires quietness and total concentration, best had before the cares and concerns of the day were upon him. The following quotation by Samuel D. Gordon must have resonated with him, since he cut it out and added it to his sermon scrapbook:

> *The faith that believes that God will do what you ask is not born in a hurry; it is not born in the dust of the street and the noise of the crowd. Such faith will have a birthplace and keep growing stronger in every heart that takes quiet time off habitually with God and listens to His voice in His Word.*[6]

Robert Hayes (RTS '74), the night switchboard operator during his years at RTS, says numerous people called Mr. Pat as early as five-thirty in the morning. "The first time it happened I said, 'I doubt he's in his office, but I'll try.' Sure enough, he answered! In time, I realized he was often in his office praying and having his devotions that early. I think many people knew that and were calling to ask him to pray with them."

"Early every morning, at 5:30 or 6:00 a.m., the light was on in his office," remembers Gary Spooner (RTS '76). "I knew he was meeting with God, like Moses in the Tent of Meeting. The light was glorious. I still think of it when I consider what it means to be intimate with Christ, my Savior."

"At RTS, I ran early in the morning before daylight," adds John Gess (RTS '74). "Practically every morning Mr. Pat was in the kitchen area in the back of the administration building reading the Bible and praying. Later, when he came to preach in my church, his only request was a place of quiet in the predawn hours for devotional time."

"While at RTS, finding a campus washer and dryer available when we needed it was a challenge," recalls Alan Carter (RTS '76,'80). "To beat the crowd we'd do the laundry very early. One morning I got up around 5:15 a.m. and groggily headed to the laundry room. I congratulated myself for being up and out so early, diligent to get the work done. However, my pride was short-lived. When I got there, Mr. Pat greeted me with a warm welcome—as he took his clothes out of the dryer! What time had this man gotten up? When I asked, he said he had come down shortly after 4:00 a.m. to start the clothes, then had returned before five to transfer them to the dryer. No doubt he'd been praying in between!"

Let God Talk

Over his lifetime, Sam studied the prayers of scripture, especially in the Old Testament, and asked practical questions. If prayer is communion with God, he wondered, how does the communion occur? Interestingly, he found in scripture that true prayer is not talking *at* God, as we normally do, but talking *with* God in conversation:

> *I was told very early in my Christian life that we've got one mouth and two ears, so we ought to listen twice as much as we speak. That made a lot of sense to me. A good way to begin your prayer time is to let God start the conversation. Open His Word and believe that He can speak to you. Read the Bible every morning as if God is speaking to your heart. Listen to Him carefully, then talk to Him. It's your time to offer your praise and petitions to Him. Then, once again listen to God, letting Him speak through His Spirit as He orders your thoughts and plans your day with you so that it will not be wasted. God's Holy Spirit is able to give you insights to wisely set the course for your day. As you think through the day, surrender your responsibilities and opportunities to God, making them count for Him.[7]*

Look to God for Guidance

Sam felt prayer was a tremendous gift from God and an invaluable tool for knowing Him, fellowshipping with Him, and gaining guidance for all of life:

> *Prayer is the most intimate means of communication and communion with God. Creation made provision for this because God created us to love Him, learn about Him, listen to Him, and live with Him. Salvation restored us so that we experience that union once more.[8]*

Among Sam's personal papers is a stained, much-used notebook page containing his own rules for seeking guidance from God:

1. *Be absolutely neutral, willing to do whatever God says.*
2. *Have no anxiety; otherwise, He cannot hear your voice.*
3. *Weigh pros and cons. Talk it over with a friend.*
4. *Ask God to make one Bible verse grip you.*
5. *When in doubt, don't act.*
6. *If the decision is according to God's will, peace will reign in your heart.*

Put People Before Prayer

Sam noticed very early that Jesus constantly gave Himself to the multitudes. His heart went out to them in compassion. Sam also noticed that Jesus had to withdraw from people frequently to pray in order to regain emotional and spiritual strength. Sam followed Jesus' example and spent much time in prayer. Thus, he became more like Christ and was better able to deal kindly, patiently, and wisely with the many people who came to him for counsel.

Sam observed that Jesus gave priority to people's needs and fit His prayer life to that calling. He either rose early in the morning or waited until the day was done and went up on a mountain to pray in the dark. Jesus sacrificed His convenience to get His prayer time in. Often, instead of resting or having a time of private devotion with God, He ministered to people. Sam cautioned fellow Christians to heed that:

> *While prayer is very important, it's never to be used to push people away. If we aren't careful, we will do that. I confess to judgment in my heart. The other day I made a long-distance call to a good friend who is the registrar of another institution. His secretary told me he didn't want to be disturbed. I knew what was going on; he was having his private devotions. In a way, I understood his thinking, so I just put in a call to the president of that institution and tended to my business with him. Yet, it did bring to my mind the fact that Jesus never let prayer dull His immediate response to people.*
>
> *Don't get sanctimonious and too strict as my friend did. By all means have your private devotions, but if they are interrupted, God will give you another time, perhaps later at night. Or maybe your prayer time should have been earlier in the morning to begin with!*[9]

THE LANDSCAPE OF SAM'S PRAYER LIFE

Sam's communion with God seems to have been a living, breathing entity, startling in its diversity and beautiful in its passion. The stories of both French Camp Academy and Reformed Theological Seminary would be greatly impoverished were Sam's prayers to be stripped from their histories. Just as the legendary George Mueller prayed down provisions from heaven for his orphans, there was Sam on his knees boldly before God's throne for over three decades, praying for these institutions. Sam never would have taken over the FCA presidency had he not listened carefully in prayer for God's voice in guidance. Once he got there, for what did he pray? In a word, everything.

"We'd come back from basketball games at midnight, and Mr. Pat would still be in his little office across the road from his house," said the late Billy "Coach" Thompson. "Many times I looked in the window and saw him on his knees in prayer."

RTS would not exist today without the thousands of prayers sent up on its behalf. Sam, of course, led that prayer brigade. While RTS president, he continued to place great emphasis on prayer, constantly urging supporters to lift up the struggling school:

> *The prayer-force of RTS is of inestimable value to this institution. Your intercessions secure for the seminary the prayer/promise blessings of God. To those who are not as actively employed ... please place high value on your opportunity to be even more fruitful through a ministry of intercession. How we value you and the contribution you make to RTS! Remember, too, that our daily staff prayer group delights in praying for your requests.[10]*

People and their needs were a huge part of Sam's prayer life. His devotion to prayer was truly stunning. If he ever told you he was praying for you, you could take that to the bank. He wrote your name on a list and in his heart, lifting you up *by name* daily before God's throne until he drew his last breath. In addition to appointment books, Sam's personal papers across the years brim with prayer lists totaling hundreds of names—on journal pages, scraps of paper, and backs of church bulletins. A Book of Common Prayer found in his small cottage has a prayer list with 253 names on it divided into categories. One grocery list reminds him to "get milk and pray for Mike."

"I had some financial difficulties in 1974," said M. B. Cooper, "and I shared them with Sam. He said, 'M. B., I'll make a covenant with you. I'll pray for you and Joyce every day, and y'all pray for me.' At Sam's death thirteen years later, his son-in-law, Jimmy Rogers, showed me a pocket calendar found with Sam when he died. In it were hundreds of names, scribbled in neat rows. There our names were, just as he had promised. He had indeed prayed for us by name for all those years!"

Sam admired the Apostle Paul's tenacity in fighting for people's souls and used him as a model for intercessory prayer:

> *Paul says in Colossians 2:1–3 that he is striving for Christians, both ones that he has seen and not seen. How could he do this while in prison? Paul turned prayer into a powerful means of spiritual warfare and used it mightily. He was strenuous in praying for people. I don't know how strenuous we are today; we have a much more relaxed attitude toward prayer, not as much a means of combat for souls.[11]*

A small poem by J. Danson Smith, found in Sam's personal papers, is evidence of prayer's importance to him:

> *If I forget to pray*
> *Will that withhold the blessing*
> *From someone far away?*
> *I do not understand it,*
> *How my prayers can avail.*
> *But if they should bring blessing,*
> *I'll pray—I will not fail![12]*

Sam's prayers were not generic affairs designed to cover a wide range of problems. They were very specific, aimed at placing before God the praises or petitions of particular people in all sorts of situations. Sam often addressed the issue of specific versus general prayer with RTS students:

> *A friend of the seminary told me recently that he was praying more generally for us now, not asking for specific things, and I was grieved to hear that. His problem? He had become paralyzed in his prayer life by predestination. Why pray for particular things if God already has ordained everything that's going to be?*
>
> *I'm sorry that my friend has fallen into this. I don't think he'll ever find his way out by resolving the puzzle of prayer and predestination because there is a great mystery in prayer. But the Bible has encouraged us to particular praying; the apostles practiced it, and Jesus taught it in the Lord's Prayer. God knows what we need before we do, but He tells us to pray for it. We pray for particular things—'ask and you shall receive'—in spite of the fact that we don't have all the answers. Doing so has brought me great joy over the years in my own prayer life.[13]*

The breadth and depth of Sam's intercessory prayer life is staggering, as you will see from the following excerpts from hundreds of letters either received by Sam or written by him. He saw prayer as an evangelistic tool and felt it was one of the most powerful agents for bringing the world to Christ and Christ to the world:

> *You can witness to a limited number of people, but you can pray for everyone. If I want to win people to God, I've got to talk to the person, but I've got to talk to God, too. When we pray for people for whom we have a burden, we are evangelizing![14]*

Therefore, he prayed for countless people to come to Christ:

> *I have certainly made Janie a matter of prayer, day by day, since I was with you.... I am just convinced that God is going to bring her right on to Christ.... Let's pray definitely that very quickly she'll come to really know Christ.[15]*
>
> *I will keep on adding my prayers to those of others to the end that Kenneth will soon come to the point when he will be free to open his life up to have Jesus Christ come in and give full forgiveness, to yield his life to follow Jesus as his Lord, and profess his faith.[16]*
>
> *Glad to catch up on Eddie's situation—will earnestly hold him up in prayer—hope to have an opportunity to talk with him. Romans 8:28 guarantees our prayers will not be fruitless.[17]*

Sam practiced what he liked to call "responsible evangelism," meaning that he felt bound before God to keep up with those who came to Christ under his watch:

> We can't simply bring someone to Christ. We have to go the whole way and disciple that person. Prayer is a large part of this.[18]

That's why Sam prayed constantly for (and corresponded with) every single person whom he led to Christ, often for years. Here's a letter from a newly saved young man just beginning college:

> I hope that you will continue to pray daily for me; it's so hard to keep going. Now that the newness has worn off, so to speak, I find it most trying to change my habits. Yet, I now have the peace that comes from knowing that Jesus Christ is with me and that he understands and loves me—no matter what![19]

Here's another letter encouraging a man who had just come to know the Lord:

> That day when we all knelt together in your living room and you called upon God to help you and to save you in Christ, I believe He heard your prayer and the work began.... In the days ahead I will certainly be remembering you before the throne of grace in prayer.[20]

Sam prayed constantly for those seeking guidance in tough situations:

> ... During prayer time, your name has often come to my mind and gone into my prayers as I have remembered our discussion during the meetings in the church there. May God make clear His way for you, give you patience as you wait upon Him and look to Him, and give you great joy in the outcome.[21]
>
> Since you were here and we talked, you have constantly been on my heart and in my prayers.... I want you to know that I have great joy in thinking of you and praying for you![22]

He was also quick to pray for anyone in spiritual or emotional difficulties:

> [Your spiritual difficulties] sound as if you have moved into the territory of Ephesians 6:10–20, a war zone that all of us have to contend in from time to time. Thank you for giving me the privilege of knowing how to pray with you and for you in this situation.[23]
>
> Thank you for calling to my attention the matter of praying for your son ...and his wife.... Please be assured that ever since I was with you, I have been interceding for them in prayer and will continue to do so.[24]

… Thank you for all your prayers that I know in my heart you have lifted up for our little family. We love and appreciate you so much for this.[25]

Sam's compassion for his suffering brothers and sisters would be difficult to match in any place or time. Over his lifetime he ministered in prayer to thousands in all types of grief, sadness, and trouble. In some cases, he saved lives.

"Thirty years ago, our three-year-old daughter died tragically," revealed one woman. "My life went to hell in a hand basket—alcohol, prescription drugs, an affair. After a few years, I became suicidal and felt it best to go be with the Lord. A failed attempt resulted in a six-week hospital stay and months of intense therapy.

"Mr. Pat visited me, and God spoke very clearly to me through him. It was a profound turning point in my life. He continued to counsel me for years, and God has blessed me beyond anything I could ever imagine!

"I remember so vividly when he said to me, 'I pray for you and your husband every day *by name.*' I knew he got up each morning at 4:00 a.m. to spend time with God. He probably prayed for hundreds of people every day, but to know that he was lifting us up by name every morning brought tears to my eyes. Such love made me want to be like him, or like Jesus, whom I saw in him.

"Later, Ed Williford opened the door for me to go back to work; I even returned to school and received a PhD. I will always be grateful to both of those godly men for the light I saw in their lives and for the help to get my life back on track."

"Sam was truly an inspiration to us and one of the dearest pastors we have ever known," recall Dorothy and Winston Dickey. "We first met him at a retreat in North Carolina during one of his seminars on prayer. A friend who came with us became a new person in his Christian life when he heard Sam say that it was not our actions, but our reactions, that cause our problems. Soon afterwards Sam came to speak at our church in Memphis and went with Winston to visit a dying friend. After Sam shared the Gospel and prayed with him, our friend received Christ and recovered!"

REVOLUTIONARY ASPECTS OF THE LORD'S PRAYER

You may be surprised to learn that Sam felt he did not really learn to pray until the mid–1950s. For years, he had been very dissatisfied with his prayer life and yearned for one with more substance and dimension. He lamented to one congregation:

I had read everything I could get my hands on about prayer and had listened carefully to innumerable messages on the subject. I put into practice a large number of prayer techniques I had collected. But

I didn't use any of them very long because none of them was any better than the ones I had worked out myself—and those weren't any good either.[26]

Sam's intense search for better communion with God surely caused him to choose the hymn "Teach Us to Pray" for his first radio broadcast at French Camp in the early 1950s. Its lyrics show clearly what was uppermost in Sam's heart and mind at the time:

> *Teach me to pray, Lord, teach me to pray.*
> *This is my heart-cry day unto day.*
> *I long to know Thy will and Thy way;*
> *Teach me to pray, Lord, teach me to pray.*[27]

On one scorching August day in the Mississippi Delta in 1953, Christ answered Sam's prayer and revolutionized his life. Around noon, he had been to see a man in Greenwood, hoping to elicit a gift for French Camp, but he had missed him. The man was to return about 1:30 p.m., and Sam wondered where he could go to stay cool on this stifling Delta day. One of the few air-conditioned buildings in Greenwood then was the public library, so Sam decided to spend an hour there reading his pocket New Testament.

The Bible fell open to Matthew 6, and Sam began reading Christ's instructions on prayer, really thinking about them for the first time in his Christian life. As he read, it was as if a lightning bolt struck him. He had been a fool, looking in every direction for help in prayer and neglecting to pay attention to his Savior's teaching. There it was in Matthew 6:9 as plain as day. Jesus said, "Pray then like this…." No longer did he need to cast about for a better method to pray:

> *That day I told the Lord that I would follow his instructions and pray as He wanted me to for the rest of my life. I have never wanted to change because Christ's principles have worked so magnificently! I don't think I've ever read another book on prayer.*[28]

Sam spent the next thirty years mining the Lord's Prayer for wisdom on how to pray. One of his most memorable sermon series is *Revolutionary Aspects of the Lord's Prayer,* in which he examines each part of the Lord's Prayer, revealing what God had taught him through years of simply praying and contemplating that prayer. Sam preached this series numerous times, sometimes under other titles, including *Christ's School of Prayer, The Lord's Instructions on Prayer,* and *A Series on Prayer* in RTS Chapel beginning in January 1977. So compelling was the series that the Banner of Truth invited him to deliver a message entitled "The School of Prayer" at its 1978 Ministers Conference in Atlanta. At one point, Reformed Seminary distilled excerpts of the material into a small booklet called "Christ's School of Prayer."

Over the years countless people, seeking to deepen their walks with Christ, asked Sam for tapes or transcripts of the *Lord's Prayer* series. No book on his life would be complete without allowing readers the privilege of digesting Sam's wisdom on prayer. What follows is a compilation and condensation of Sam's most important teachings on prayer in this series.

WHAT PRAYER IS NOT

After the Sermon on the Mount in Matthew 5, Jesus begins to teach the disciples about prayer in Matthew 6. He doesn't tell them to pray, because He assumes they are already praying. Every true Christian naturally reaches out to God in prayer. The problem was that they didn't pray satisfactorily. Most Christians today realize their prayer lives are not very satisfying to them or the Lord. But what to do?

Not to worry, because we simply have to listen to what Jesus has already told us. Through the Lord's Prayer, Jesus is teaching both the disciples and us to pray in such a way as to eliminate problems and make prayer the blessing it should be. His teaching on prayer in this chapter is not an option; it is a command. I have often wondered why I never paid attention to it. Jesus rebukes us, saying, "But why do you call Me 'Lord, Lord,' and do not do the things which I say? Whoever comes to Me, and hears My sayings and does them, ... is like a man building a house, who dug deep and laid the foundation on the rock" (Luke 6:46–48 NKJV).

Christ's course in prayer is not theoretical, but very practical. He isn't talking about why we should pray or what prayer is. Jesus is talking about *how we do it*. Jesus tells us not only the words to pray, but the territories in which to pray. The average person can say the Lord's Prayer in about thirteen seconds. However, if you *pray* the Lord's Prayer, you'll pray longer than you've ever prayed in your life. If you will do this, the dimensions of your prayer life will begin quickly to increase without your even trying. You're not even conscious of the clock in Christ's school of prayer.

Jesus opens up about five territories in the Lord's Prayer. We move through these, praying to God in connection with them and with our minds turned on, with our highest and best thinking. Praying the Lord's Prayer exercises one's mind, emotions, heart, imagination, and volition. I don't know of a better way for God, our blessed Father, to get a grip on our lives.

Interestingly enough, Christ begins by telling us how *not* to pray, giving three negatives. First, He says, "When you pray, you shall not be like the play-actors, for they love to stand and pray in the synagogues and on the street corners to be seen by men" (Matthew 6:5, NIV). "To be seen before men" means "to shine." Prayer is never an approach to men; it's an approach to God. It is never to be used to manipulate or impress people with your righteousness, piety, or the holiness of your cause.

Prayer is the way we move the hand of God, who has given us this access through Jesus Christ. We preach to impress people, but we pray to move God! Prayer is impressive and powerful with God, but it loses everything when it's used to impress, manipulate, or move people.

Not long ago I received a letter from a friend who needed money. He knew that, unbidden, I had helped him in the past and, more than likely, would help him now. He wrote, "Dear Sam, would you share a real burden in prayer with me? I need about seventy-five dollars; would you pray for this with me?" I almost wrote him back to say that the request would be a good thing to talk to God about, and that he should have simply written and asked me for the money. I would have sent it to him.

Jesus prayed in public but not to impress people. I've had problems here. In the past, when I ate in a restaurant I prayed over my food, not so much to thank God as to impress people that here was a man who believed in Jesus. I thought I was giving a good testimony. However, God doesn't need that to carry on His work. He does that by preaching. To put on a pious act in prayer to impress people isn't really a testimony. I still pray when I go into a restaurant, but I try to do it without anybody knowing I'm doing it.

Pastoral prayer is a difficult area for preachers. I've heard it said that a pastoral prayer is probably the least powerful prayer that preachers pray because we're so conscious of people. We're trying to turn an apt phrase, to make it rhyme if we can! I'd complete a sermon and call people to the closing prayer, then remember a very clever point I didn't make. In my closing prayer, I'd get that point over to the people. I once did this all the time, but I don't think I do it now. We don't preach to God; we pray to Him.

Many years ago a speaker at RTS advised students who were witnessing and failing to get the Gospel across to have a time of prayer with the person and share the plan of salvation. Yet, God doesn't need that to win people to Christ. Prayer is our approach to Him, not a witnessing tool.

Next, Jesus says, "And when you are praying don't use meaningless repetition, as the Gentiles do, for they suppose that they will be heard for their many words" (Matthew 6:7, NASV). Babblings would be the best translation for "meaningless repetitions"; they are not packed full of faith, thought, and earnest desires. Jesus taught that God will pay attention to the desires of our heart when we pray, but our hearts have to be in the prayer. Our conversations with God cannot be rote and trite, with no faith, feeling, or interest.

Repeat the same phrases in prayer only if they contain thought, faith, and interest. I've been praying the first prayer I ever learned all my life. Perhaps you have, too:

> *Now I lay me down to sleep, I pray the Lord my soul to keep.*
> *If I should die before I wake, I pray the Lord my soul to take.*

That's not all I pray, but I use those same words. However, they aren't empty words. I mean them with all my heart! I'd quit using them if they didn't mean something to me. They mean more to me now than they did when I learned them as a child.

That day in Greenwood, I realized for the first time that long prayers aren't necessarily more powerful. I always thought God would consider me more serious if I prayed a hundred-thousand-word prayer rather than a fifty-word prayer. I fell into that trap because all the great saints that I'd ever investigated—Paul, church saints, great missionaries—had gained their power by praying long and often. I decided I would do the same. Today, I thought, I'll watch the clock and try to pray for an hour instead of thirty minutes. That was tough! The clock moved so slowly.

Yet, that's not the secret! It is true that the saints prayed long and often, but it was because they had a deep relationship with God. Think of it this way. If you meet someone on the street whom you don't know well, the conversation is over in a few minutes because your relationship is shallow. How embarrassing if you had to stand there for a solid hour and talk to that person! You don't have friends, interests, or activities in common; you're in two different worlds.

However, perhaps next time you meet someone you know well but have not seen for a while. You talk excitedly, and after a while you look at your watch and realize you have been there an hour! You wish you could spend the entire day together. Since you have much in common with this person and your relationship is rich, you could easily spend a great deal of time talking.

This is one of the reasons why the saints prayed a long time. They had much in common with God. They were workers in His vineyard and very involved in its upkeep. They were not trying to mark time. The length of our prayers has to do with our business with God, not from a law or edict. God doesn't put a clock on our prayers. Begin with the relationship you have with God now, no matter how shallow, and take it to its limit. The good news is that continued prayer cultivates a deep fellowship with God. You will see your time in prayer increase without your even knowing it!

PRAYING IN THE PLURAL
"Our Father Who Art in Heaven"

In Matthew 6:9, Jesus begins to teach His disciples how to approach God in prayer. We are taught to pray in the plural (our, us, we). For the first time in my life, I wondered why. One might think that Jesus teaches this form of prayer because He primarily intends for it to be used in corporate or congregational worship, such as our Sunday services. However, the context makes it clear that this is not the case; even though in Matthew 6:6 Jesus instructs His disciples in their private, personal prayers to "go into your closet and … shut your door …," they are still to pray in the plural.

Pray With Christ

We see then that Jesus is asking us to pray in the context of our Christian relationships. First, we pray through Christ. We can approach God only in relationship to Christ. In a way, Christ is giving the disciples the authority to call His Father, Father. If He doesn't give us the authority, we don't have it! How can I ever say 'My Father'? By nature, I'm a child of disobedience. Jesus is God's only Son. I can become a son of God only by becoming part of Jesus. The work of the Holy Spirit ties my life with His life so that His blood washes into the sins of my life and His Spirit comes to live in me, and I'm dynamically united with Him. This is praying in His name.

I once thought praying in Jesus' name—saying "for Jesus' sake" or "in Jesus' name"—was like a little tag on the end of prayers. If I heard anybody pray and they didn't say the little magic words at the end of the prayer, I thought they were modernists or unbelievers. However, that isn't really praying in Jesus' name. Praying in Jesus' name means to be identified with Him. It's coming to God in the identity of His Son. Jesus has to usher me in. All of my relationship with God is based on Him.

The first thing I do now in prayer time is give thanks for Jesus. In the past, every now and then I would thank God for Jesus, but now I can't pray without doing that. I praise God that He chose me in Christ, that He created me through Christ, that He purchased me in Christ, and that He brought me into Jesus Christ. Now with Jesus Christ I can step into His presence any moment!

Our relationship with Christ is significant because, even as we pray, Christ is ever making intercession for us. His whole time is taken up with caring for His people. Jesus and I are praying together. Even if I'm in my closet praying all by myself, I'm not praying alone. I'm exercising this privilege along with my great High Priest, who is at the very right hand of His own Father.

However, I'd be scared to open my mouth when I got there if the Bible didn't tell me in Hebrews 4:16 to come boldly to the throne of grace, where I will receive mercy and grace to help in my need. What right have I got to go there? I don't, except by the gift of the grace and the mercy that's offered in the scepter of grace in Jesus. Grace rises afresh in your heart every day when you get before that throne of omnipotent holiness. Jesus never did, anywhere in His prayer, say anything about giving thanks, but He didn't have to. Jesus knew that if we prayed as He taught us, we'd be giving Him thanks all up and down the prayer, not in some special little section.

Pray With Other Believers

The relationship goes still further. We're a flock of people. God doesn't convert lone wolves. People are His sheep, and we belong to each other. The body is knit together with many members. Even though I'm in my closet praying all by myself, I'm not praying alone. I'm still related to a family so extensive that I don't even know how many brothers and sisters I have!

When I'm praying in the morning alone, I like to think that all across the entire planet millions of fellow Christians are praying to God just as I am. I think about the picture that rises out of the book of Revelation. Our prayers ascend from the earth, and the angel mixes incense with them, so that God receives all of them as a sweet-smelling savor, as if each were the only one.

I'm praying with my family. There's a real sense of church unity. I can pray without being concerned about which denomination others are in. I'm praying with brothers and sisters who have received Jesus Christ, and we're all interceding for this planet Earth and the people on it. Until I started praying the Lord's Prayer, I never really felt the sense of unity I possess with other believers in the Word—that great, wonderful family which is getting bigger every day. Praying the Lord's Prayer has cultivated a sense of appreciation for the communion of the saints. I'm praying with brothers and sisters with whom I disagree, many times seriously! Yet, we're in agreement now, as we go before the throne of grace and God receives all of our prayers. It's a sweet experience.

Pray With Those in Heaven

However, the communion is even deeper. A good portion of the church is in heaven. When my Christian brothers and sisters and I are praying down here, we know that much prayer and praise is going on in heaven. We realize that we pray to God and praise him together with all of the saints who are now in heaven. How encouraging, comforting, and stimulating to remember that, as we pray on earth, we are joining and participating with those who are in heaven, surrounding the throne with prayers and praises! When we are separated from dear loved ones through death, many of our corporate activities are interrupted, but not those related to prayer. We do not pray to believers who are in heaven, and we do not pray for them, but we do pray with them. Many of us have mothers, fathers, children, husbands, or wives in heaven, with whom we once bowed in a circle of prayer on earth. In a sense, we still pray with them each day as we on earth and they in heaven approach our father's throne. Therefore, saying "Our Father" is appropriate.

My father has been in heaven for decades and decades, but I still pray with him every morning. My wife and I had sweet and dear prayer times together on earth. Now, she's with the saints around the throne praying, but I am still praying with her down here. That's one time when even the difference of death is taken away, and we just belong to one another in the great communion of believers.

Truly, prayer is a family experience. Along with our great elder brother, Christ, and our other believing brothers and sisters in heaven and on earth, we are uniting in a special time of family worship before God. This very thought, and this united activity, makes us sense the unity and nearness of the church militant on earth and the church triumphant in heaven.

GIVING BEFORE GETTING: ADORATION
"Hallowed Be Thy Name"

Jesus teaches us not only to look to God in prayer, but also to look at and *recognize* him, hallowing His name and mentioning all that His name stands for. Christ teaches us to give God praise and adoration before we seek to get our requests.

I began to do something that I'd never really done, at least not at the beginning of my prayers. Most of my prayers were petitions to get things from God for myself. Now I saw that Jesus teaches me first to give to God what we owe Him—praise and adoration. Prayer ceases to be just a "gimme exercise" and begins to be a way to give to God. David was one of the great prayers of all time, and the psalms are wonderful examples of praise. Let David help you praise God as you begin the Lord's Prayer.

First, we praise God for who He is. Psalm 145 is a good example. In all of David's psalms, he can't help breaking into doxologies to the character of God:

> *I will extol you my God, O King,*
> *And I will bless your name forever and ever.*
> *Every day I will bless you,*
> *And I will praise your name forever and ever.*
> *Great is the Lord and greatly to be praised,*
> *And His greatness is unsearchable (Psalm 145:1–3, ESV).*

David goes on and on praising God in this psalm. Think about the One to whom you are praying and what He does for you, and you cannot help but be filled with praise and adoration.

Next, we praise God for what He does. In Psalm 103:1–2, David says:

> *Bless the Lord O my soul,*
> *And all that is within me bless his holy name.*
> *Bless the Lord O my soul,*
> *And forget not all His benefit (ESV).*

David continues to list all the things God does for us. No wonder we are filled with wonder and praise as we think of the awesome care God gives to us.

Finally, we praise God for where He is. It's important to remember that the one to whom we are praying is seated on the throne of God in heaven. This aspect of the Lord's Prayer bothered me for a long time. I always liked the fact that God was right here with me, not on a throne back up in heaven somewhere. However, Jesus teaches me that God is wonderfully omnipresent in His omnipotence. He can be both places simultaneously! Psalm 115:3 tells us that God's throne is established in the heavens, and He rules over everything. The omnipotence of God has now come to grip me. I still know that He's right here with me, but I like to realize now in prayer that I'm doing what science would love to do and isn't able to do—go to the center of the universe. Christians know where that is—at the throne of God in heaven. Every morning in prayer I go right to the center of the universe, without a missile, but just in the name of Jesus.

TWO PETITIONS: ASKING THE BIGGEST THINGS FIRST
"Thy Kingdom come, Thy will be done on earth as it is in heaven"

Jesus first asks us to pray for something so big that it takes every attribute He has to bring it to pass. We're asking God to bring the time when His Kingdom will be as manifest and His will as actively carried out on earth as it is in heaven. That's a huge petition! It's faith-stretching and mind-stretching. I once prayed for people to get to heaven, but until Jesus taught me to pray, I never seriously prayed for God's creation. I never really investigated in the Bible to see how important planet Earth is to God.

Creation has now taken on a brand new meaning. In the past, I depreciated the Creator's marvelous handiwork. I almost thought that His creation, particularly our planet, belonged to the devil. On the contrary, it's the Lord's! The certainty that God is going to someday bring His Kingdom to this earth causes my heart to rejoice every morning! In my prayer time, I immediately move into thanksgiving, thinking about what the future holds for our earth. God tells us how He's going to do it in at least three ways. Each day I move out into these three territories; that's why praying the Lord's Prayer takes longer than it once did.

First, God's Kingdom is already manifest on the earth in the church. As believers, we have been delivered by His sovereign grace from the dominion of darkness and transferred into the Kingdom of His dear Son. We need to pray for that part of the Kingdom. Don't just preach to the church or complain about the church. Instead, pray for the church!

In the past, I never did that. I was active in presbytery and fought liberalism, but until I began to see this concept, I never interceded much for the church. I never shed a tear over false doctrine! I never shed a tear for a liberal, until I started praying Jesus' way. Now I love the church much more, even with her faults and failures. Fountains of love have been opened up through intercession for the church. It's sanctifying for both the individual and the church.

Both Jesus and Paul prayed for the church—Paul in many of his letters and Jesus in John 17. They prayed for the purity of the church's faith and doctrine, for the holiness of the life of the church, for Christ's people to be true to His word. How we need to pray for those things! It's not enough to preach the truth and debate the liberals. We have to add strong intercession against their unbelief, earnest prayers that God would change their minds and that they be recovered. God blesses such prayer and brings fruit from it in His church.

When we pray for His Kingdom to come we are praying, "God, may your Kingdom come in your church." We pray for the church to show the unity of the

Kingdom. We pray for doing away with divisions, for the day when there will obviously be only one flock and one shepherd. We pray for the day we drop the human distinctions that divide us and our unity is altogether in our mutual faith in Christ and in one another.

The church doesn't represent that as perfectly as it should today. Therefore, people on the outside are puzzled. They can't see that the church offers anything better than the world because of our divisions, our defections from His truth, and the unholiness of our lives. So we need to pray for the unity of the church, for the day when we will all be blended into the whole body of Christ across the face of the earth. Jesus prayed for that in John 17.

If any people on earth should be seeking ecumenicity, Christians should be the ones. I hate to hear ecumenists put down. Most of the time in conservative circles, ecumenism is a slur. That's a tragedy! We're the very people who ought to be seeking what Christ wants for His church, an obvious, visible unity that the pagan world can recognize. We ought to seek it on our knees—pray for it, work for it, eagerly long for it! We should be grieved by differences that cause separations. We should never be willing to accept separation as the standard for the church. This opens up a vast territory for intercession. It's impossible to pray for a person without coming to love them, and it's impossible to pray for the church without coming to love the church of the Lord Jesus Christ.

Another way God is bringing His Kingdom to earth is through the conversion of sinners. Jesus told Nicodemus that no man can enter the Kingdom of God unless he's born again from above. It's through these generations that God adds citizens to the Kingdom. We pray for God to move in His Spirit and bring the peoples of the world to Christ, praying for both individuals and countries.

I pray for many individuals because I've been gathering them for a long time. If you pray for people by name, you're going to find that the longer you go, the list will increase. All Christians ought to be lifting up the names of certain people that God has put on their hearts or brought to their attention in a special way.

Since Jesus told us to go to all the nations, we also have a responsibility to pray for the nations of the world. About ten years ago, I began to wonder how many nations of the world I had specifically prayed for. As I began to jot them down, I wasn't troubled because I felt I had been doing a good job. However, I ended up with only five nations that I distinctly remembered interceding for on my knees. How meager the geography of my prayer life had been!

Recalling the book *Around the World in Eighty Days,* I resolved that I was going to become a world traveler, and every eighty days I'd go around the world. Now, I pray for two or three nations each morning. Many of them I don't know very much about, but I'm learning about them. The newspapers are more interesting now because often I see an article about a country for which I have just prayed. Being concerned for other countries in the world has certainly broadened my prayer life.

Jesus also told us to pray for laborers because they're few and the harvest is white! I've been tussling with that for a long time. I always had the idea that Jesus was telling us that many unsaved people are out there, so get out and go to work. However, now I think "white unto the harvest" means prepared people. I think God is bringing in an increasing number of the elect, and succeeding generations can expect more and more. If the fields were white in His day, they are even whiter today! Lift up your eyes and see what God is going to do! As we go out and bear witness, He's going to bring multitudes in. As we pray for laborers, we pray for ourselves: "God, lead me to someone today! Make me self-conscious of opportunities to be a faithful and effective witness."

Paul wanted churches to pray for him in five different areas. He asked for protection as he moved through the world as a witness (Romans 15:13); he asked for opportunities to witness (Colossians 4:2); he asked for boldness (Ephesians 6:18); he asked for opportunities for utterance (Colossians 4:4); and he asked that the Word would be fruitful (2 Thessalonians 3:1). We should pray those same things for our pastors, missionaries, and evangelists. Don't merely say "Lord, bless them," but *intercede* for them!

Finally, God will gloriously consummate His Kingdom in the Second Coming of Jesus Christ. In Mark 13:26, Jesus tells us that we will see "the Son of man coming in clouds with great power and glory" (ASV). Those are the two words that are put together. The glory comes from the power. And the power is going to be so productive! What will issue out of all of that is going to be so glorious! Little wonder that the two words belong together.

Paul expresses beautifully in Romans 8:18–22 the massive regeneration that will occur when Jesus comes back. He tells us that when Jesus, who is our life, shall appear, we will be with Him in glory. We will also see the glories in the universe as they were meant to be. When God brought the consequences of man's sin upon creation, He did it with the promise of salvation. The creation will be resurrected along with us, as the book of Revelation describes, in the new heavens and new earth. The last promise of the Bible is that of Jesus to that old apostle out on the Isle of Patmos: "Lo, I am coming." The last prayer in the Bible is John's response, "Even so, Lord Jesus, come." This is the final guarantee that *everything* is going to be made just right!

God is already at work making it right. Our prayers are behind the work of His church on earth. We want to see what He will do in our generation through His church. He's already at work in His converting work of the Holy Spirit, bringing increasing multitudes, generation after generation, into the Kingdom. And in His good time, our blessed Lord will come again.

GIVING BREAD AND FORGIVING SINS
"Give us this day our daily bread,
And forgive us our debts as we forgive our debtors."

Jesus first teaches us to seek the Kingdom of God and His righteousness. In our prayer life, we are to do what we should do in all of life—seek God's Kingdom first. Because God is interested in our needs, He's teaching us to ask for temporal needs while He brings His Kingdom to earth. Jesus uses the word "bread" to symbolize all of our temporal needs. Paul says in Philippians 4:6–7, "… In everything by prayer and supplication with thanksgiving, let your requests be made known unto God and the peace of God, which surpasses all understanding, will guard your hearts and minds in Christ Jesus" (ESV). In everything! Sometimes books on prayer make one feel guilty for praying about debts or health or crops. I'm grateful that Paul banishes that kind of super spirituality. We have a right to talk to God about anything that makes us anxious.

Pay close attention to the word "give" in this petition. It is a faith word to me, teaching us to live every day in pure faith that God will supply our needs. You've probably heard me talk about the supernatural acts of God that happened every day at French Camp and Reformed Seminary to supply our needs. The stories stagger the mind about how God, in answer to prayer, moves in and meets immediate physical needs. To support his orphans, George Mueller literally prayed in enough money and food each day to take care of several thousand orphans. He never had any program for raising money. He refused to tell people about his needs; he simply told God.

That style of life is not just for famous saints. Every Christian is supposed to live that way. If you trust your paycheck or your skill or your health or your employer rather than God, you are an idolater. Each morning we can stop being idolaters and say, "Father, you are the only one we really look to for our needs." In this prayer, Jesus commands His disciples every day to take their eyes off of everything on earth and direct them to the One in heaven who gives them everything they have. It's good to do this because you may lose your job or your health, but your heavenly Father is with you for eternity. He will provide other ways for your needs.

Notice that we are still praying in the plural for "our bread." We may have enough for a long while, but remember that we have Christian brothers and sisters who don't. We are praying for Christians all around the world, and some of them are in desperate situations. Believe it or not, Christians within a five to six mile radius of us may be facing great temporal need of some kind. We have fellow Christians around the world who have lost their families, homes, jobs, freedom, and almost lost their lives and their minds because of deprivation. These people are part of our spiritual family; if our fleshly family were in that kind of trouble, we'd be praying for them. We also pray for our human brothers and sisters who are not Christians. We need to pray for their salvation and for their needs because many are starving to death. We are to be like Jesus in loving our neighbors as we love ourselves. That means we are to pray for them.

After teaching us to pray for our daily bread, Jesus commands us to pray, "Forgive us our debts as we forgive our debtors." The order in which Jesus places this petition seems very appropriate. By this time, I've looked at God in prayer, really exercising my mind and heart to think about who He is in terms of His attributes. I've listed before God the things He's done for me in which my heart rejoices. I've looked at God in terms of His greatness and goodness, how He's infinite and eternal and unchangeable in all His being, wisdom, power, and glory. When I think of all of that, it's easy for me to realize that I don't love that great God as I should. The attitudes of my heart and the acts of my life scream that I'm a sinner before that great God! I rejoice at a God like that, and yet I am smitten in my heart to realize what a wicked person I am before Him. I've just been praying for my brethren in the world, and I'm conscious of the fact that I don't love them as much as I love myself. I'm prepared now to look at myself and realize that in relationship to God and others, I'm a wicked man. I'm a sinner who needs forgiveness before God. It's easy to confess sin here, and to be particular about it.

While God brings His Kingdom to earth, I also have spiritual needs. I need my sins forgiven, and I need to be forgiving. Jesus begins this sphere of spiritual need by teaching us to pray that God would forgive us our sins as we forgive those who have sinned against us. Implied in this is confession. Jesus doesn't say here "confess your sins," but when he teaches us to pray that God would forgive our debts, or our sin, he's dealing with the area of confession.

Jesus put the word "debts" in the plural here. The very fact that He said "debts" instead of "debt," and "sins" instead of "sin" means that when I come to confession, I need to be particular. That's why praying this way takes a little longer. If I begin listing my sins before God every morning, I'm going to put some time in! However, it's sanctifying! If every morning I seek to name before God the ruptures that I've had with Him, the things that I know displease him, I'll find myself saying, "Tomorrow morning I want to leave this one off my list." I'll be practical in sanctification by trying to wipe sins off my confession list.

The reason we're told in the Bible to confess our sins is that God wants *us* to be conscious of them because we're not always aware we have been sinning. He wants us to focus on them, to deal with them, to feel the horror of them, and to want to be done with them. Two or three besetting sins have bothered me over my years as a Christian. I've taken great joy in seeing how God can get me through a day without having to deal with them. I'm striving to be done with them because I don't want them in the list of my sins.

Then Jesus tells us how to ask for forgiveness: "Forgive us our sins as we forgive those who have sinned against us." That's the only way we've got a right to ask for forgiveness. We don't approach the Lord by saying, "Forgive us our sins *because* we forgive others." God can never forgive you because you forgive those who have sinned against you. The only cause for which God can forgive sins is Christ's atonement. Only because of the satisfaction that Jesus made in dying for his people can God find cause to forgive a sinner. We say, "Father, I'm pleading with you! Please treat my sins I've named before you the way I'm treating everybody else in connection with their sins against me."

This is the only part of the prayer that Jesus picks up after he finishes teaching the Lord's Prayer. He comes back to it in Matthew 6:14 when He says, "For if you forgive men their trespasses, your heavenly Father also will forgive you. But if you do not forgive men their trespasses, neither will your Father forgive your trespasses" (RSV).

In Matthew 18 Jesus tells a story about a man who owed another person over fifteen million dollars, more than he could ever repay. The man to whom he owes it is about to throw the fellow in prison, but the man begs for mercy. The heart of the man owed is deeply moved, and he decides to forgive the entire debt. Joy fills the debtor's heart! Yet, about a block down the street, he loses all his joy because he sees a fellow who has owed him fifteen dollars for quite a while. He's been forgiven fifteen million, but he doesn't enjoy that now because he's mad. He seizes the man and threatens to throw him into prison until he can collect the debt. The man falls down before him and vows to pay it back, and he could. Yet, the man owed wouldn't have mercy on him and threw him into prison.

Now the servants of the man who forgave the fifteen-million-dollar debt told their master what they had seen. The master called the debtor back and told him his debt was not forgiven either. Jesus concludes that passage with a strong statement: "And in anger, his lord delivered him up to the jailers until he should pay all his debt. You wicked servant! I forgave you all that debt because you besought me. Should not you have had mercy on your fellow servant?" (Matthew 18:34–35, RSV). Jesus said that's the way His heavenly Father will treat every one of you, if you do not forgive your brother from the heart.

A fellow who's been forgiven fifteen million dollars should not have a hard time forgiving a fellow for fifteen, should he? A person who has received the forgiveness of the Lord Jesus Christ for a life of sin ought not to find it impossible to forgive those who sin against him. Sincere Christians must do it. It is true that once a person is born again, he's never unborn. Yet, Jesus makes it clear that the way we can tell whether we're persevering is in part by our ability to forgive.

I have never in all my life had anybody seriously wrong me. I've never had a strong temptation not to be forgiving. Over the years, people's goodness to me has been amazing! Yet, some people have been treated very badly. Oh, I'd hate to have been treated as they were! Others might not have been sorely wronged, but they have a hard time forgiving. They're disturbed because they know it's a serious situation. There are several ways to help such people.

If someone tells me he can't forgive because he can't forget what a person did to him, I know I'm talking to somebody who doesn't know what forgiveness is. He thinks forgiveness is performing some sort of mental gymnastics in which one blocks a wrong from memory. However, forgiveness doesn't mean forgetting what somebody does. We may remember what someone has done to us every time we see him, yet still be forgiving. Twice in Hebrews we're told that God remembers our sins no more. I don't think He forgets them because God is omniscient. It's impossible for him to forget, in the way that we use the term. However, He doesn't use them against us, does he? He sets them aside so that His access to us is wider. We should do the same.

People also think they are unforgiving if they still feel hurt by a wrong done to them. What has that got to do with it? The Lord Jesus, when He arose from the dead, still had the scars of the cross in His hand, and He may—glorified in heaven right now—still have those scars in His hands and will through eternity. In a sense, they are a remembrance of sin, but not against us. God still knows that we're sinners and at times reminds His people of their sins so that they won't commit them again.

Forgiveness doesn't involve an emotional trick that wipes away the pain of a wrong done to us. All the rest of our lives we may carry a strong hurt because of what somebody did to us, but that doesn't mean we're not forgiving. Forgiveness and hurting are the same thing, in a way. God also hurts in His forgiveness. Jesus didn't become senseless to our sins when He saved us; He *suffered* for our sins! Forgiveness is all tied up in suffering!

Forgiveness certainly doesn't mean whitewashing either, saying, "What you did wasn't so bad," when it may be as black as hell itself. Forgiveness also doesn't mean lying to justify a person's wrongdoing, saying, "It was probably as much my fault as yours," when that is patently false. God never forgave me that way! He has always made my sins *exceedingly* black, but forgiven.

In Luke 6:27–28, Jesus explains what forgiveness is, saying, "… Love your enemies, do good to those who hate you, bless those who curse you, pray for those who abuse you" (ESV). Forgiving somebody means loving him and doing these things. In the Bible, love isn't a feeling, but a fact of goodwill that produces an act of blessing. Did God love the world so much that He felt a great throb of warmth for us? Maybe so, but the Bible doesn't talk about that. It says, "God so loved that He *gave* His only begotten Son."

We are to do good to people who wrong us. Pray to God to help you return good for evil. Pray and watch for the opportunity to be a real help and blessing to them. When God sees us doing good for others, speaking about good in others, even though we may always remember the hurtful action, this is forgiveness.

We are also to bless those who wrong us. In part, to bless one who has mistreated us means to speak well of them, to cease talking about what that person did to us. We may not forget it, but we quit talking about it and seek to speak what we can that's profitable, helpful, and good about him and to him.

Finally, we must pray for those who wrong us, even though we may think of what that person did every time we see him. For the rest of our lives we may bear some pain from that person's action, but we don't remember it *against* him! We're willing to set it aside and fellowship with him. We pray that God will give him a new heart, that God will close the gap, that God will be good to him, that God will bless him and meet his needs, even bringing him to repentance if necessary. When a person becomes our enemy, God calls upon us to make him one of our loved ones, placing that person in our prayers right beside our children, our wives, and all the people that we naturally love.

Jesus was tempted to sin at all points as we are, even hanging on that cross. The crowds were howling like dogs at him, blasting and humiliating him. I believe that Jesus was tempted to hate those people. However, He practiced what He preached and prayed for them, crying, "Father, forgive them." Surely he felt the tartness of the awful barbs those people yelled at him. Yet, He prayed for them. That's forgiveness!

Not only that, He blessed them, saying the only good thing he could say about them: "Father, they don't know what they're doing." He could have said, "Father, listen to what they're saying. Isn't it awful?" And that would have been true. But He didn't.

Finally, He did them a very good deed. By dying for their sins, He opened the door through which many of those very people would come.

When we pray as Jesus did, we see that we're not like Him because we must confess our sins, and He never had to. Yet, immediately we become more like Him when we pray "forgive us as we forgive others" and then forgive others for wrongs done to us.

Notice that "forgive us our sins as we forgive" is in the plural again. It's not enough to face our own sins as individuals before God; we're praying as part of the body of Christ, the church. In order to be concerned about the problems and needs of the church, we need to plead and pray for God's forgiving grace upon it. This is the time to be done with self-righteousness. How can we be self-righteous and look down our noses at others? While we're praying for the forgiveness of sins, let's confess the sins of our church and plead with God for His mercy and grace upon the church, for His power and deliverance.

LEADERSHIP AND DELIVERANCE
"Lead us not into temptation, but deliver us from evil."

Finally, I need for God to deal carefully with me, that I might not be led into temptation. I also need God to deliver me from evil. While He is bringing His Kingdom to fruition, evil and temptations are still rampant. I never did realize that this was the most difficult section of the Lord's Prayer for people to understand. Across the years of my ministry, I've had more questions asked me about that little fragment than any other part. I didn't think it was hard because

I had naturally decided what it meant. Yet, when people began to question me about it, I began to wonder if the Bible really supported the view that I had adopted without really thinking about it.

From the very beginning of the Lord's Prayer, Jesus seems to be leading us into a recognition of our weakness and frailty. After confessing our sins and the sins of the people of God, we've got good ground not to think more highly of ourselves than we ought. Except for God's grace, tomorrow we may fall into the same sins we commit today. In this regard, I often think of Psalm 69:5–6, where the psalmist cries (and I'm paraphrasing), "Don't let me scandalize your people, God, by my foolishness and sin." This comes from a confession of weakness, frailty, and our dependence upon God. I echo that prayer: "God, lead me this day that I won't scandalize the blessed Savior or bring shame upon his people or your name."

I've always thought that this petition is related to Jesus' prayer in Gethsemane, when he cried out, "My Father, if it be possible take this cup from me; nevertheless, not as I will, but as you will" (Matthew 26:39, ESV). Before this heartfelt prayer, James and John, with their mother, had come to Jesus and asked to be able to sit on His right and left side in His coming Kingdom. Jesus had said to them, "Can you drink the cup that I drink?" to which they had readily replied, "Of course we are able!"

How bold and self-confident they were! They felt their strength as godly disciples of Jesus Christ. But how did Jesus feel? Do you ever remember Jesus speaking of His death in a self-confident, boastful way? No. He dealt with it factually, but not boastfully. His disciples were very certain that they were able to drink that cup, but Jesus was going to have a hard time with it. He wasn't saying to anybody, "I'm able," even though He was.

However, Jesus' weakness is very different from human weakness. Hebrews 5:1–2 tells us, "For every high priest chosen from among men is appointed to act on behalf of men in relation to God, to offer gifts and sacrifices for sins. He can deal gently with the ignorant and wayward, since he himself is beset with weakness" (ESV). God is referring to Jewish priests here, but He is also talking about Jesus. A priest can be sympathetic with those he represents because he feels weakness himself.

Our weakness is related to our sin. His wasn't. The Bible teaches that Jesus experienced weakness and was tempted in every way as we are, which was part of his humiliation and incarnation, yet He did not sin! Hebrews 4:15 says, "For we have not a high priest who is unable to sympathize with our weaknesses" (ESV).

Hebrews 5:7–8 tells us, "In the days of his flesh … Jesus offered up prayers and supplication with loud cries and tears to him who was able to save him from death, and he was heard because of his reverence. Although He was a Son, He learned obedience through what He suffered …" (ESV). Jesus drank the cup and pulled through God's will. He never sinned at all. He maintained his sinlessness right to the end when He cried out, "It's finished!" and poured out His soul!

Our Lord Jesus Christ felt weakness and sensed temptation. If we pray Jesus' way, in no other place in the Lord's Prayer will we more earnestly call on God than at this point. "Lead us not into temptation" is our confession before God of our weakness. In effect, we are saying, "Lord, you know my limits, and you alone can give me strength. Don't lead me into temptation with the consequences that my evil heart will surely bring, but deliver me!"

PROBLEMS IN PRAYER

Sam's provocative thoughts on prayer proved to be life-changing for many. Some whose prayer lives had always been barren now found themselves in sweet communion with God. Even those who had enjoyed rich prayer lives found that Sam's insights helped them gain even greater spiritual depth. Both seminary students and fellow ministers have used Sam's principles to great advantage for almost half a century in their own ministries.

However, with characteristic humility, Sam adamantly refused any commendation for his ideas on prayer. As far as he was concerned, he had merely scratched the surface:

> After being associated for many years with two institutions and movements that were born in prayer and subsequently depended on it hourly for their existence, one would think that I could stand before you as an authority on prayer. Yet, I can't. I rejoice greatly in what I know but am painfully conscious of what I don't know. I'm a confessor in the school of prayer, not even a graduate, even though I've been attending for several decades. In fact, I feel as if I am still in elementary school. Jesus Christ is the teacher, and my life has been greatly blessed by praying the way Jesus says we're to pray.[29]

Part of the reason Sam felt this way was that, even after decades as a prayer warrior, he readily admitted that prayer at times raised great problems for him, in much the same way that election and predestination did:

> While I praise God for the problems that I've seen solved through prayer ..., I realize it introduces us to areas of impenetrable mystery. There are problems regarding prayer that I no more have the answer to now than I did the first year of my ministry. I really don't expect to ever get the answers here on earth. I used to think perhaps I would, but I've read almost everything that deals with the questions, and thought deeply about it all. However, God has not given me those answers. Actually, I think He means for it to be that way. We need to recognize that revelation hasn't given us all the answers to all the questions that can arise out of prayer.[30]

Sam encountered such a prayer conundrum in March 1942, shortly after his graduation from Union Seminary. He told RTS students about it in a sermon at the seminary's Day of Prayer on January 10, 1979. He had been invited to hold a five-day revival at Glade Valley School in North Carolina, where he had held a productive meeting once before. He was very excited about the opportunity to speak again to young people, especially high schoolers, and hoped for great blessings during the week.

However, after only two services, he was dismayed to find that the school had an atheist. A young man named Jack about Sam's age—in his mid-twenties— had dropped out of school in the eleventh grade and joined the armed forces. Now, after finishing his tour of duty, he had come to Glade Valley to graduate.

Jack was attractive, although sharp-tongued, and was a leader among the students. He came to the services only because attendance was compulsory; yet, for some reason, he kept his distance from Sam. Actually, Sam was glad and didn't try to close the gap because he was a little afraid. He had never worked with an atheist.

Yet, Sam knew he had to deal with the situation when some students came to him and said, "Mr. Patterson, you should hear what Jack's saying. He wants a little time during one of the services to challenge God, if He's there at all, to strike him dead sometime during the day."

"Well," recalls Sam, "I figured the time had come to talk to this young man! He was beginning to be competition now, and I'm sure all the students wanted me to do what he asked because Jack was talking about it all over campus."

Sam looked the boy up in the dormitory. Jack wasn't pleased to see Sam, nor was Sam pleased to be there. As they sat down to talk, Sam asked, "Do you believe in God?"

The lad answered, "No, I'm an atheist."

Quizzing him a bit, Sam found that Jack had been brought up in a Presbyterian church and had proper rearing. Yet, somewhere along the line, he'd become an atheist.

"Would you be willing to share with me what line of thought brought you to atheism?" Sam asked.

"I'd be glad to," Jack said. "I prayed for something, and I didn't get it."

Sam was stunned at such a silly and shallow reason for unbelief.

"I had expected him to say something profound!" confessed Sam to the RTS students. "Even so, the problem of unanswered prayer is a very real one; don't discount it and try to deal with it using clever illustrations or pious, pompous theological terms.

"I didn't know exactly how to handle Jack's prayer problem, but I knew one prayer that God would surely answer, and I went to bat with Jack on that, staying with him on it. One of the teachers had already told him he shouldn't be at the school. It seemed as if everything had been tried except kindness and interest. I found he hungered for understanding, so I worked with him. Christ helped him, and before the week was over, that young man got on his knees and prayed to receive Christ. It was a prayer of repentance asking Christ to take his life and save him, to make a new man out of him. I think God honored it, and a few years later he was teaching Sunday School at First Presbyterian Church in Winston-Salem."

Sam went on to admit to the seminary students that he had a difficult time understanding many things Jesus had to say about prayer. While he never doubted the veracity of Jesus' words, he confessed candidly to frustration when his prayer life often didn't match Jesus' words.

"For example," Sam told the students, "Jesus says in Matthew 21:18–22 that if one has faith and does not doubt, one can tell a mountain to throw itself into the sea, and it will be done. If we believe, we will receive whatever we ask for in prayer. Has your prayer experience always confirmed that? Mine hasn't.

"Or consider this statement that Jesus made in John 14:13: 'Whatever you ask for in my name I will do it, that the Father may be glorified in the Son' (RSV). I've always handled that by emphasizing that we should pray in His name, but I've always been conscious of the fact that this may not be the full answer, since experience doesn't always seem to happen this way.

"Two other Scriptures have been problems for me," he continued. "Jesus said, 'You did not choose me, but I chose you and appointed you that you should go and bear fruit and that your fruit should abide, so that whatever you ask the Father in my name, he may give it to you' (John 15:16, ESV). Later He said, '… Truly, truly, I say to you, whatever you ask of the Father in my name, he will give it to you. Until now you have asked nothing in my name. Ask, and you will receive, that your joy may be full' (John 16:23–24, ESV). Now, these are both tremendous statements that are absolutely true. Yet, often in our prayer experience we are puzzled because answers to our prayers don't seem to occur in that way. How do we handle these apparent contradictions? We must realize that, while we know much, we should be humbled by the fact that difficult questions exist. God has the answers, but He has not committed them all to us. However, He has given us places of refuge, such as 1 John 5:14: 'And this is the confidence which we have in him, that if we ask anything according to his will he hears us. And if we know that he hears us in whatever we ask, we know that we have obtained the requests made of him'" (RSV).[31]

GIVING AND GETTING WITH GOD IN PRAYER

Perhaps the clearest window to Sam's soul concerning his communion with God came in a sermon on prayer at RTS's Day of Prayer in 1979. In the following paragraphs, Sam lays the foundation for his dynamic approach to prayer, giving himself totally to God and expecting to tap into God's incalculable grace, omnipotence, and promises.

Prayer is one of the best ways to give to God. When we pray, we give Him attention and begin thinking about Him. We don't always do that, and we need to do it more. Most of the time we take Him for granted, even while living in His blessing.

By praying, we also give God a powerful means to work in this world. If God gives us material blessings and we reinvest it in His work, we help to continue His work here on earth. In the same way, God has given us a powerful instrument in prayer. When we give prayer back to God, we activate His attributes. God will turn Himself loose in this world through our prayers in a way that He would not if we didn't pray. Oh, we give a great gift to God when we pray! That's why Jesus said to pray for God's Kingdom to come and His will to be done. It's not simply a pious, nice act; it turns spiritual energy loose in this world! It brings to pass what God wills to do.

David was a man after God's own heart, and I think I know why. He gave himself to God. I guess that's the greatest gift we can give Him. David was so honest in his prayers, so childlike and frank with no pretensions. Everything in his heart spilled out to God in prayer. He praised God, thanked God, told God how he longed for Him and loved Him. He bragged on God. He also complained to God at times; he felt things should be different and couldn't understand why they weren't. Yet, he spoke out, baring his problems and difficulties. If he was afraid of anything, he talked to God about it. Over and over he assured God that he trusted in Him. Then David pled to Him in the wreckage of his life. He told God all about his sins, his folly, his foolishness. He wasn't a perfect man, simply a child with his Father.

We also get something from God in prayer. When I pray I reach into God's omnipotence and pull out great portions of it, activating it over the lives of the people for whom I pray. I reach into God's omniscience, His will and wisdom that are greater than mine or theirs and that can guard against the dangers of my praying amiss.

When I pray I reach into God's immeasurable grace in Christ Jesus. I reach into God's favor and grace and loving-kindness, turning it loose through prayer! I pull God's love, care, and favor down over people who are in dire circumstances.

When I pray I reach into God's promises because God's will is revealed in His promises and His commandments. I pull His will out of His promises right down on the people for whom I pray.[32]

Does this sound like your prayer life? Did you realize how far-reaching and powerful your prayers could be? Sam would say, "Oh, friends, don't waste another minute! Pray!"

CHAPTER NINE

THE RETIREMENT YEARS
1979–1987

The great use of a life is to spend it for something that outlasts it.
William James

But lay up for yourselves treasures in heaven, where neither moth
nor rust doth corrupt, and where thieves do not break through
nor steal.

Jesus Christ
Matthew 6:20 (KJV)

When Sam retired from the RTS presidency in April 1978, he was more than ready for a change. Undoubtedly, he meant it when he said publicly that RTS needed a "better qualified and more professional leader." After all, he had never wanted the position in the first place and did not like administrative work. However, other considerations probably also influenced his decision. His heart surgery in 1977 had slowed him down, and he knew he needed less stress in his life. Yet, the primary reason most likely was his desire for more freedom to work for revival in the PCUS in fulfilling his newly assigned duties as "Special Representative of RTS for Pan Presbyterian Relations."

Yet, Sam in no way planned to vanish immediately from the scene at RTS. On the contrary, he continued to live on campus for the next year in his small Airstream trailer. Although he had relinquished the day-to-day administration of the seminary to Acting President Luder Whitlock, he assured RTS supporters and students that he would still be very much involved in seminary leadership, retaining his seat on both the board and executive committee and staying active in faculty-executive committee relations.

As noted in *The First Forty Years*, a history of RTS compiled by the school for its fortieth anniversary in 2006, Whitlock's tenure commenced at the end of a painful controversy at the seminary:

> *In 1977 the seminary hired Greg L. Bahnsen as assistant professor of apologetics and ethics, succeeding Alan Killen. Bahnsen was a brilliant student of apologetics in the presuppositional tradition of Cornelius Van Til, but his theonomic approach to the application of Old Testament ethics for the contemporary church immediately placed him at the center of controversy.*
>
> *In the year prior to his appointment, his massive, 600–page book,* Theonomy in Christian Ethics, *was published. Faculty colleagues and Executive Committee members spent hours with Bahnsen in an unsuccessful effort to dissuade him of his theonomic convictions. Paul Fowler, professor of New Testament, wrote a lengthy critique, "God's Law Freed from Legalism."*
>
> *At the end of Bahnsen's first year, the executive committee was convinced that his theonomic convictions were incompatible with the seminary's confessional standards. Accordingly, the executive committee granted Bahnsen a leave of absence for a year, after which his contract was not renewed. Bahnsen's several friends and supporters within the student body were outraged at the executive committee's actions. Many of these students transferred to other schools, believing that the faculty was unwilling or unable to answer Bahnsen's arguments.*
>
> *Only slightly less controversial was an episode involving another faculty member at this time. Guy Oliver's instruction in missions took on a growing interest in evangelical social action that some thought entailed sympathy for elements of liberation theology (while critical of other features). Despite his denials, the executive committee believed it had evidence to support the charge, and his contract was also not renewed.*
>
> *Whitlock's first challenge as president was to shore up the seminary's weakened reputation. Although the school sought to terminate these professors quietly, both left publicly, stirring sentiments within the student body and filing grievances with the Association of Theological Schools that threatened the school's hard-won accreditation. When the ATS was satisfied that the seminary acted in accordance with its constitution and bylaws, the grievances were denied. Accreditation was not the worst of it. The defections of churches from the PCUS to the PCA created tensions between the PCUS and the seminary, even though several faculty members remained in the mainline church. While PCUS student enrollment maintained high levels for a time, it began to decline by the*

end of the decade. Fewer contributions came from PCUS churches, and by 1978 the total number of the seminary's supporting churches dropped significantly. The seminary experienced serious financial challenges, and this during a period of high inflation. In the midst of this struggle, the seminary suffered a key loss when Dr. John Richard de Witt (Sam Patterson's close colleague and kindred spirit) resigned and returned to pastoral ministry at Second Presbyterian Church in Memphis.

Whitlock later summarized his early years as president by evoking the title of Morton Smith's book on Southern Presbyterianism, How the Gold Has Become Dim. *The seminary was in danger of disappointing its hopeful and generous constituency. For some, the early progress of the school seemed to degenerate into disillusionment. The school needed to strengthen its faculty, rebuild its donor base, and develop new constituencies. Others might have shirked from the challenge. The seminary's board of trustees, now equipped with a youthful and energetic president, eagerly embraced it.[1]*

However, all of this controversy took its toll on Sam's spirit, especially the Bahnsen and Oliver incidents, as he had sought in vain to encourage the board to stand with both professors and prayerfully give the situations time to smooth out and improve. Finally, on June 1, 1979, he moved back to French Camp, two months before Whitlock was to take over officially as president on August 1, 1979. Apparently, FCA President Rich Cannon had made Sam an offer he couldn't refuse to entice him back to his beloved French Camp:

Mr. Cannon urged me to come back from Jackson and give oversight to the work of the church here, and anything else that I could do as a member of the FCA Board of Trustees.[2]

Back in his favorite place in the world, Sam lost no time in throwing his energies into improving French Camp Academy. On July 22, 1981, he helped Rich Cannon birth French Camp Radio, Inc. to provide a Christian witness for the community and win new friends for the Academy. With Stuart Irby, Jr., Sam became a board member and rejoiced when WFCA went on the air in October 1984 during Harvest Festival. Today the award-winning station broadcasts the Gospel in word and song all over the world.

Also during the 1980s, Sam was instrumental in persuading L. S. Hall to donate funds for the beautiful French Camp Lodge. Completed in 1987, the Lodge now serves as the headquarters for Camp of the Rising Son.

Although Sam officially retired from the pastoral ministry on July 8, 1979,[3] he had no intention either of stepping out of the pulpit or giving up his work in small churches. Not only did he return as supply pastor of French Camp Presbyterian Church, but he also revived tiny Huntsville Presbyterian Church, about five miles west of French Camp.[4] Is it any wonder the humble folk of this church loved him? When evangelistic preaching took Sam away, faithful stand-ins, such as RTS Professor Gerard Van Groningen and others, filled both pulpits.

As always, Sam's mind was on doing God's work. "He didn't come by the house much because he was so busy," recalled Erskine Jackson. "When he came to Kosciusko on business, he'd invite me for a cup of coffee. We'd talk for a while, and when I'd see his mind drift off to what he had come to town for, I'd simply say, 'Come again.'"

Writing to Brister Ware on August 13, 1979, Sam sounded supremely happy:

> *I am truly enjoying being 'home' again at French Camp! I am serving the church here with its Academy constituency, holding one or two half-week meetings a month, and doing some promotion for the seminary.*

The "seminary promotion" was Sam's gracious offer to help Luder Whitlock transition into the presidency by introducing him to Sam's personal contacts. In September 1979, Sam even traveled with Luder to the Dallas-Fort Worth area to meet RTS supporters Granville Dutton, David Dean, and others.[5]

In the midst of his many activities, Sam took time to reacquaint himself with the community. In French Camp, like no other place on earth, Sam seemed to be able to relax and enjoy those around him. He loved to drink coffee and made it a point each day to have a cup with friends.

"I left French Camp for a few years," said Wade McGlothin, "but when I returned I found Mr. Pat was still the same. Each morning, he'd stop by the little café in town for coffee with a few of us. He even started a men's breakfast at the Council House, and once a month he'd give a devotion."

Sam was friendly with all people and drew them together. "He always joined in the conversation but didn't dominate it," said Hugh Long. "People knew he was a Presbyterian minister, but he fit in so well with all the denominations that you'd never know it unless someone asked him about Presbyterian history. He didn't push his views on anyone."

Hugh's wife, Martha, appreciated how down-to-earth Sam was. "He was a working man and knew how country folks think. He gave the same attention and interest to someone in overalls, covered with mud, as he did to someone who donated hundreds of thousands of dollars to French Camp Academy."

"I'm just an ordinary guy," said Hugh, "but when I went to him for advice he showed as much interest in my problems as he would have to someone more wealthy or prestigious. During our four or five visits, I never once felt hurried to get down to business. He asked questions, and he knew how to listen. He'd then evaluate that one point, and listen again. That was special."

When Sam wasn't drinking coffee, he might be hunting or fishing with buddies—and dipping a little tobacco on the sly! Jack Ward was riding with Mr.

Pat one day in his old Chevrolet coupe when they had a wreck and the car turned over. Several tobacco cans tumbled out from under the car seats. Jack crawled out from his side of the car, and Mr. Pat from his side. Covered with dust and dirt, they looked at each other, and Jack said in surprise, "Sam, I didn't know you used tobacco!" Mr. Pat shot back, "Neither does anybody else!"

After Sam died one of his friends commented, "I don't know whether I loved him more for pointing to the Bible or pointing to that spittoon!"

A HUMBLE LIFE

Upon his return to French Camp, Becky and Jimmy thought Sam surely would live with them in the lovely home the school had built for him many years before.[6] Much to their chagrin, Sam had an altogether different plan.

"He found an old one-room cabin out in the country on Audrey Parkerson's place," said Kenny Henderson."Audrey gave it to him and even moved it over to Becky's and Jimmy's for him."

Becky and Jimmy worked hard to change Sam's mind about living in the rustic cabin, but to no avail. No doubt the legendary C. T. Studd influenced Sam's thinking once again. While in the depths of Africa, the great "Bwana Mukubwa" lived in utter simplicity (some would say privation). His one-room circular hut had a grass roof, walls of split bamboo, and a dried mud floor, cracked and endlessly patched. His bed consisted of goat hide strips acting as springs, with several khaki blankets, worn thin with age, serving as some sort of mattress. Close to his bed stood a homemade table with pigeon holes loaded with "gadgets" of every kind—scissors, papers, knives, milk tins full of pencils.[7]

Seeing Sam was never going to change his mind, Jimmy remodeled the inside thoroughly with paneling, carpet, recessed lighting, a ceiling fan, and a fine wood burning stove. "It looked like a Holiday Inn on the inside and a sharecropper's shack on the outside," said Jimmy, laughing. He begged Sam to let him put in a bathroom, but Sam wouldn't hear of it, allowing only a hydrant on the outside.

Rich Cannon tried, too. "Mr. Pat, come springtime I'm bringing my crew over here and putting you a bathroom in this place."

Sam replied, "I may take you up on that, Rich, but actually all outdoors is my bathroom for number one, and for real business and showers I just go to my mother-in-law's trailer."

A pan for shaving hung next to the front door, and a rocker sat ready on his porch. A simple man who needed no frills, Sam was as happy as a clam in his new home. In fact, his digs must have reminded him of "going over the hill" in childhood—some of the happiest times of his life. He could cook simple snacks on his stove, and eat normal meals any time he wished at Becky's and Jimmy's.

"He was in and out of our house constantly," revealed Becky, "but much of the time he just wanted to be alone." Actually, Sam often said he was never alone because the Lord was with him constantly. Time spent away from humans was likely time spent in sweet communion with Christ.

"During a freezing cold spell we'd gang up on him and order him into Mom's and Dad's house," recalled granddaughter Debbie Rogers Ivey. "But he was like a little kid, saying, 'I've got my woodstove and my sleeping bag. I'm perfectly fine. Goodnight.'"

Sam's humility did not go unnoticed by those who visited him. "I went down to see him several times in his little cabin to discuss some things that were troubling me," said fellow pastor Don Wilson. "I wondered how many former seminary presidents would be happy to live so humbly."

"At a time when we were working so hard to acquire a few material possessions," said Johnnie Henderson, "I went to his little one-room abode—you couldn't even call it a cottage. I remember thinking, 'This is really all anybody needs.' For the first time in my life, it occurred to me that there was another way to live that didn't involve trying to acquire things!"

Driving up to Sam's cabin in the evening, you might have found him rocking on his small porch, listening to the crickets. Or you might have seen him with his granddaughter Debbie.

"I visited him frequently in his little house. He was like a third parent. We spent most of the time outside, taking walks, making mud pies, or having picnics. In the winter, we'd sit by the stove. The cabin was warm and cozy even when the snow lay deep outside. Even though he was very busy, he made time for me. It was obvious that I was important, and he enjoyed my company. Every summer he took me on a little trip.

"We talked about spiritual things a great deal. If I didn't understand something at church, I always asked him. I'm sure I drove him crazy with my inquisitive mind, especially with questions about heaven. But he never said, 'Do we have to talk about that again?' or 'Why'd you ask a question like that?' He was always willing to go over the same ground. I got my share of spankings from him, but I never doubted that he loved me. Our youngest child is named for him."

Jimmy would have flown to the moon and back for Sam, so when Sam mentioned how nice a pier on the lake would be, Jimmy couldn't build it fast enough for "Granddaddy." He also put in a sink, a light, and running water.

"He loved to fish, so we stocked the lake with catfish. However, he didn't have the heart to keep them. He threw them back—sometimes he'd just come out and feed them! The only time we'd get to eat what we caught was when he wasn't there."

"Bill Whitwer was a champion crow shooter," recalls Ed Williford. "In Edwards, Mississippi, where he preached, the farmers loved for him to come shoot crows because they ate the crops. He could kill fifty crows in one day. He even taught some of us how to call them. When I got to French Camp, I invited Mr. Pat to go with us to shoot crows. He refused, saying he felt shooting crows for no reason disturbed the Lord's balance of nature. Soon after that I was over at his cabin and he said, 'Come here, I want to show you something.' He went out on his porch and a crow came down to eat corn out of his hand! We decided he didn't want us to kill his pet crow!"

Twenty years after his death, the small cabin looks exactly as Sam left it. Becky couldn't bear to go inside; therefore, it has remained frozen in time. His shaving kit lies open on a stool, and the small shelf above the stove still holds his salt and pepper shakers with a few bowls and glasses. His typewriter stands ready at the antique desk, along with his theological books.[8]

Twenty or thirty Bibles in numerous translations rest at various spots throughout the room, one with five bookmarks in it. Most of them have copious notations in the margin along with names of people for whom to pray. Sam may have followed C. T. Studd's lead and purchased a new Bible each year. Studd did so in order "[to avoid using] old notes and comments but to go fresh to the scripture itself."[9]

A two-drawer filing cabinet is the heartbeat of the room, holding correspondence from any person or organization with whom he worked, including folders on some three hundred churches. Stacks of sermon notes and handwritten sermons (Sam never typed a sermon) dating to the beginning of his ministry lie next to it in boxes. A Morris chair from the Patterson family graces one side of the room opposite an old radio on which Becky once listened to *Fibber McGee and Molly*. Prominently placed on one wall is a large sign proclaiming:

With the help of God and a few Marines,
MacArthur took back the Philippines.

On another wall, a second sign reads, "Sam Patterson, Evangelist." Scattered elsewhere are other keepsakes—a faded picture of French Camp pheasant hunters, a snapshot of Kate Anderson Church, and a small needlepoint of the RTS Chapel.

MORRILTON: FOREVER IN SAM'S HEART

Sam's ties to his old hometown remained strong throughout his life. As late as 1983, he was still subscribing to the *Petit Jean Country Headlight*. He loved going back to Morrilton to visit and was thankful to God for the opportunity to renew old acquaintances who had meant so much to him in years gone by. High on his list to visit each time were Victor and Louise Boren. If he didn't camp on Petit Jean, you could find him staying at their home. In a letter of thanks to them he said, "You two have meant far more to me than you will ever know!"[10]

At ninety-six, Louise's face lights up at the sound of Sam's name, and tears of joy come to her eyes as she remembers him with deep love. "He was the cutest, sweetest thing with such pretty red hair. Vic and I enjoyed his visits so much!"

Sam frequently visited Morrilton and the surrounding towns. When he preached, any honoraria he received went right back to Reformed Seminary. In April 1979, his diary records a visit to his father's old church, First Presbyterian Church of Morrilton, to preach at Holy Week services just prior to Easter. A particularly happy entry details a trip back to Morrilton on July 4, 1978, when he represented his family at the 125th anniversary of the Pottsville Associate Reformed Presbyterian Church, where his father served from 1904–1906. He fondly reminisced:

> *I camped one night on Petit Jean and hiked about six miles to Seven Hollows [on the southwestern side of the mountain]. At Morrilton I hiked boyhood paths over the hill, saw the dugout [now filled], the waterworks, Nimick Hill, Point Remove, and bridge road. Spent the weekend with Louise and Vic—grand family of mine. They are in the very first entry in this diary almost 50 years ago!*

He kept in close touch with many of his classmates, too. Typical of small town schools, classes loved having reunions, and a faithful few organized several over the years. Sam was always in great demand as master of ceremonies; he even gave invocations and devotions. He loved to plan surprises, such as giving the class tests on events of the 1930s. Correspondence shows that Sam was so popular that organizers of the reunions even planned the date around Sam's ability to get there! Many often wrote him afterwards, thanking him for his participation.

His thirtieth high school reunion was held in August 1964 on Petit Jean Mountain. Sam served as master of ceremonies and also gave invocations and devotions. He missed the forty-fifth reunion for some reason, and letters show that his classmates missed him dreadfully.

However, he made sure to attend the fiftieth gala celebration in June 1984. It seems that Sam and good friend Allan Merritt outdid themselves as co-masters of ceremonies. Classmate Emma Scroggins writes:

> *I can't believe you had all those 50-year-old clippings! We really appreciate you and Allan. Most of the credit for the reunion's success goes to you two. You make quite a team.[11]*

That reunion was probably the last time he got together with his lifelong buddy, for Allan died in October of that year. He had requested years before that Sam preach his funeral:

I have never been very comfortable around ministers, except for you, and it would be easier on my mind if you could find it possible to come here to preside at that occasion. You know very well that I am not a good Christian, but you also are aware, I hope, that I do have the right instincts and try at least most of the time to deal honestly and fairly with other people…. I cringe when I think of some strange minister trying to tell my friends and relatives, who know better, what a fine Christian I was.[12]

In June 1986, less than a year before he died, Sam attended his fifty-second high school reunion on his beloved Petit Jean Mountain. The occasion was bittersweet, since Allan was gone and the event was small. Apparently, Emma had to beg Sam to come:

I know it won't be the same without Allan. But I don't want to make any plans until I hear from you because I don't think we could have it without you as our master of ceremonies.[13]

AFRICAN BIBLE COLLEGES

In the summer of 1980, missionaries Jack and Nell Chinchen, founders of African Bible Colleges, needed someone to serve as acting president of their first campus in Liberia while they came home on furlough. Sam later revealed that he didn't want to go, but he knew he was needed. He didn't realize the adventure would become one of the highlights of his life.

Jack had discovered the measure of Sam Patterson several years before as he raised funds for the very first ABC campus in Liberia. Ed Williford, today director of development for ABC, had encouraged Jack to enlist Sam's help. Jack was reluctant, since he didn't know Sam well and felt sure he was extremely busy. However, to Jack's great surprise, Sam saw him immediately.

"What a unique person Sam was!" Jack recalls. "I was amazed at his willingness to set aside everything and give me his full attention. I had never encountered anyone like him—so Christ-like, so desiring to give of his time, energy, and knowledge to help somebody else out. We immediately hit it off as we began to talk about African missions. Of course our vision struck a chord with him, and he wanted to know everything about it. Sam really helped get ABC's feet on the ground, both in America and Africa. For that we will be eternally grateful."

During that visit, Sam didn't waste any time putting Jack in contact with potential supporters, saying, "I know a pastor in West Virginia with a real heart for missions. He ought to be involved in this." Without another word he picked up the phone, called the pastor, and secured Jack a slot in their missions conference. Subsequently, the church underwrote the construction of a building on campus.

"Sam was special to me because of his humility," explains Jack. "He was never one to put on airs. He was always the same, no matter where he was or what he was doing. I consider knowing him a privilege. He certainly showed me what it takes to be a real leader—caring for folks, loving the scriptures, loving the Lord, having a passion, not merely a concern, for lost souls. His great compassion enabled him to reach out and touch lives, drawing them to the Lord Jesus Christ.

"I don't know why I dared to ask him to stand in for me for a semester while we were gone in 1980, but I was short on folks who knew how to run a college. I forget whether he accepted immediately or whether the decision took some time, but he finally said yes!"

Sam left for Liberia on August 12, 1980. Northpark Presbyterian Church, under the leadership of Rev. Brister Ware, paid for Sam's plane ticket.[14] However, not everyone was excited about Sam's decision to go abroad.

"I did my dead-level best to talk Sam out of going to Africa," said Dr. Perrin Berry, Sam's doctor at the time. "I told him if his heart problem recurred he would have no quality medical help. He didn't listen to me for one second. I thought he was dead wrong, and I still do now that he is in heaven. I always thought of his physical good, and he always thought of his spiritual responsibilities—the most important thing on his mind."[15]

Ironically, however, Sam was healthier in Liberia than he had been in a long while. "While he was there, he ate healthy for the only time in his life," revealed the late Talmage Branning. "Greens, rice, and bananas were the staples of his diet, and he lost nearly forty pounds. Of course, once he came back to civilization he resumed one of his favorite pastimes—grazing!"

During the semester at ABC, Sam taught several Old and New Testament courses, in addition to personal evangelism. He told Jack later that he went to Africa thinking that he wouldn't need to do much preparation for his classes because the students would be educationally behind. However, he found them exceptionally bright and eager to learn, asking questions that the normal seminary student would never think to ask.

Sam later told the ABC Board:

> *I admit that I felt I would not have to do much preparation at all. I felt there was a wide gap between my background and the students I would face in Africa. But that attitude did not last long. By the end of the second day of classes, I was forced to retreat to my study and bone up just to keep ahead of the students. I had to stay there the balance of the semester.[16]*

Sam's humility made an indelible impression on the young theological students. They could hardly believe that a former seminary president would condescend to come teach at a college only in its second year. His selflessness for their sakes was remarkable.

In addition to teaching at ABC and preaching regularly at local churches, Sam filled knapsacks with Bibles and hiked the surrounding area distributing them, often venturing twelve miles away and showing up at immigration checkpoints on the border.

"One day," Irene Taylor relates, laughing, "he returned from giving out Bibles, and school officials told him he wasn't supposed to hand them out that day because it was a holy day in the local religion. Tickled, he told us, 'I don't understand why, but they took the Bibles anyway!'"

During Sam's walks along the riverside, the Lord began to lay the nearby primitive village of Old Yekepa on his heart. Although just across the river from the modern, beautiful ABC campus with its block housing and zinc roofs, the poverty-stricken people in Old Yekepa lived in thatched-roof, mud huts with no electricity or running water. Why not take his evangelism students there and share the Gospel? Jack was ecstatic when he heard Sam's idea. He had wanted to do just that but had not had time since the college was in its infancy. Sam could do the school a tremendous service by implementing an evangelism program there.

Delighted, Sam began teaching evangelism strategies in class, then putting them into practice in the village. Students did children's evangelism, sang and played guitars, and shared the Gospel with the elderly.

"He ignited a passion in us to share our faith with people who were different from us," said Augustine Davies. "I didn't understand his strategy then, but now I do. We should take every opportunity to talk to people, hoping that a way opens to speak of Christ."

That first year only one class of about twenty students and some staff were involved. Later, the program expanded to include forty to eighty students. Eventually, the students divided into several different Sunday afternoon outreach ministries, going to hospitals, prisons, low-income housing, and the train station. With the later acquisition of four vans to transport the students, they were able to expand the program to surrounding villages. The ministries continued to grow wonderfully for years after Sam left.

"In all my years in Africa, I've never seen someone fit in so well and so quickly in a cross-cultural experience," said Del Chinchen, Jack's son. "Usually people need much more time to acclimate themselves to the culture, especially as a leader. I think Sam's wisdom and spiritual maturity enabled him to transcend cultural differences to communicate and lead on a higher plane."

"I loved his leadership style," said Becky Chinchen, Jack's daughter-in-law. "He was a facilitator, a listener, a quiet leader with a humble spirit. He focused not merely on getting a job done, but always on mentoring others one-on-one in the process."

Sam was in his element among the African students and later told Jack that he would rather be in Liberia than anywhere in the world. It had to have been spiritual balm for his soul to leave denominational controversy and other disagreements to find peace and like-mindedness with Christians half a world away. In Liberia, he was surrounded by men who loved his leadership and were eager to learn how to share their faith. Had he not felt responsibilities calling him home, he likely would have stayed in Liberia for a very long time.

Sam returned from Liberia on December 4, 1980, and continued to help ABC raise funds. In February 1981, he helped the school receive a grant from the Maclellan Foundation by writing a glowing recommendation. He also wrote Rev. Paul McKaughn, encouraging Mission to the World (the PCA missions agency) to send missionary Paul Nasekos for a term of service at ABC.

School officials were unstinting in their praise of Sam's work:

> *What an impact you made in Yekepa and at ABC and in the hearts and lives of every student who had the privilege of sitting under your ministry! You are a hard man to follow, sir! You are loved and highly respected as only Africans can love ... completely uninhibited.... They speak of you almost reverently and love you dearly....[17]*

Talleyrand Saydee surely was one of those students:

> *Uncle Sam,*
>
> *Thank you for another letter of interest and encouragement. I'll repeat over and over again, I just love to hear from you and most especially to hear that you are praying for me always. To hear that alone gives me joyful strength in enduring. One thing I don't fail to do is to pray for you always. You are the 23rd person on my prayer list. I thought I need to pray for a man of God like you who had a great impact on my life during your short time with us at ABC. I praise God for you.[18]*

Cockerell also reported positively on the ministries Sam had instituted:

> *The ministries you started in the prison, the hospital, the schools, and the village of Old Yekepa are being carried on with zeal and enthusiasm. Each Monday night about 15 students meet for praise, prayer and planning for the ministries. Around 25 students are involved in the total ministry now. We are now going out many more miles than before—places hard to get to, but the Lord is enabling.[19]*

Sam had such a lasting effect on many of the students that they kept up a lively correspondence with him for years. As usual, he saved every letter, certainly adding these young men to his prayer lists. They wrote to him on every conceivable subject, as if to a parent. In fact, his influence had been so great that several called him their spiritual father.

For example, students kept Sam posted on the progress of the ministries he started, even writing to ask help with problems:

Peter Dabieh, n.d.
James Saydee and I have been witnessing at the [prison] cells on Sundays with fruitfulness. Borbor Gabriel continues with Old Yekepa Ministry, but he says that the people are stubborn (only a few are yielding.) Others join him to go there. We need your prayers, for there are problems with follow-up. Converts' addresses do not allow us to reach them, or we never have extra time to do follow-up with those whom we can reach.

James Blyee, September 16, 1981
The grace of God on our hospital ministry is growing Sunday by Sunday. The children's ward is more fruitful than last year.

Peter Siaway (ABC '83), now working with PEF international missionaries, September 4, 1981
I am an interpreter at the Old Yekepa Ministry that you started. The people are hard-hearted about the word of God, but the Lord's spirit is working in them.

Other students wrote to tell Sam how sorely he was missed and how much they appreciated his work:

Peter Dabieh, February 14, 1982
I personally miss you in the area of chapel sermons and classroom lectures! My desire is to sit under your lectures again either here or at RTS if God wills. It is my pleasure to request you please to be my Spiritual Father. I am sure of your great experiences and even your love toward us ABC students, unto me particularly.

Stephen Agyeman, Christmas 1980
I do not lie that the knowledge I personally acquired from you for the four months you were at ABC surpasses all the wisdom for almost all of my seven years of Christian experience. You are attaining that image of Jesus Christ.

Augustine Konneh, January 16, 1981
Do you remember the name we gave to you? 'Commentary.' Your presence was really a blessing to us, and we thank God for you.

Talleyrand Saydee, April 20, 1981

Hi Uncle Sam,

I love your truthfulness in the Lord's word. You were a challenge to me from your teaching. Your chapel messages were extraordinary and a special blessing to me. I am purposely writing to you for a scholarship to attend RTS when I graduate here.

Numerous students asked Sam for help; no request was too small. And he answered every one of them:

Augustine Konneh wrote on January 16, 1981

A rogue stole my sweat suit for jogging, and now I have none. Will you please send me one?

Edward Kiahuin, March 19, 1983

Will you please buy me one built-in flash camera? I would like to take some pictures at graduation.

And then on September 10, 1983

Will you please process my film for me? I would like two copies of each.

Although Sam had very limited means, he knew God owned the cattle on a thousand hills. His small tithe was always earmarked for one of the Lord's projects, and frequently it was a student at African Bible Colleges. On November 28, 1985, Edward Kiahuin wrote:

Through the grace of God you have played a very important part in my life both physically and spiritually. This I will never forget in my life. You have shown me such a love which is beyond my explanation. Your prayer and financial support carried me through college and your prayer support has found a job for me. How on earth can I forget such a godly man as you are? I am now in fulltime ministry with Campus Crusade.

Student after student asked for a Bible, and Sam fulfilled each request. Finally, seeing the need was so great, he sent $725 in August 1981 for the entire student body to get Thompson Chain Reference Bibles.[20] Where he got the money on his meager budget is anybody's guess. Perhaps this was one of those "projects" for which the Lord provided. Students were overjoyed:

Words are inadequate to express the appreciation and joy I felt when Mr. Chinchen handed me the Thompson Chain Reference Bible donated by you. I have long been wishing for a reference Bible.[21]

Sam helped several students gain entrance to colleges and graduate schools, even to RTS:

Stephen Agyeman, Christmas 1980
I do appreciate your concern for me for the very short time you were in this college and even for your personal initiative to intervene on my behalf with Tennessee Temple University.

Augustine Davies (RTS '88), October 17, 1986
I want to thank you for sparking the fire of RTS at ABC in 1980. During your time with us, our world and life view was broadened and widened. For me, it has never been the same. Being here at RTS is a reality of a vision conceived long ago during your time at ABC. We thank God for you.

Sam played a significant role in the life of James Saydee (RTS '87), the first African Bible Colleges student to enter RTS. James corresponded frequently with Sam about his financial problems. Sam worked to gain support for James and even contributed himself. Had it not been for Sam's help, James probably would not have graduated:

I got the wonderful gift you sent me two weeks ago. I appreciate every effort you are making toward my financial need. Only our Creator will reward you for what you have done and will continue to do while I am studying at RTS. You are 'God's Love Letter' to me and everything will be long remembered as long as life is within me.[22]

Sam also helped students get jobs after college and seminary:

Edward Kiahuin, February 4, 1981
I want to praise God for opening the door for me to work with ELWA [Eternal Love Winning Africa] as I shared my desire with you and it came to pass. I'm working in a village of my people. I thank God for you praying for me.

"I still quote Sam Patterson's teachings constantly today," says Augustine. "He always taught that we should not focus on the 'how' of evangelism, but the 'why.' Our passion and desire for God—to know who He is and His love for people—should always make us want to reach out to other people. We don't evangelize simply because we are commanded to do it. It has much more to do with our relationship with God. If we love God, it will come out. Mr. Sam challenged us to BE witnesses.

"He made such an impact in just one semester, not only because of the academic excellence he wanted us to pursue, but also because of the godly life he wanted us to lead. He urged us to make our Christian lives very relevant and practical in loving and serving people as we share our faith."

A CHANGE OF HEART

Upon his return from Africa, Sam continued to work tirelessly to keep churches from pulling out of the PCUS. The denomination was experiencing a hemorrhage of membership as they faced possible union with the United Presbyterian Church. Even in retirement he stayed active in presbytery and involved in the PCUS renewal movement. His efforts were rewarded when, in 1981, he was chosen as Mississippi's Man of the Year in Religion by the Total Living for Fifty Plus, Inc. in recognition of his professional, civic, and spiritual contributions in his state and community.

In April 1982, he partnered with Albert Freundt to write "A Call to PCUS Conservatives," a letter sent by Covenant Fellowship to over 200 PCUS ministers who were graduates of evangelical non-PCUS seminaries. (See Appendix C.) They called attention to the damage of separation/division to evangelical renewal in the PCUS and pled with their colleagues to remain in the PCUS.

Milton Winter, a longtime admirer of Sam and fellow St. Andrew presbyter, doesn't like to remember those sad days in the life of Mississippi Presbyterianism, but knows they are significant. "It is crucial to know who Sam Patterson was and what he stood for in a time when almost everyone with whom he was allied was going in a different direction. We had heartfelt talks about the state of affairs many, many times.

"In fact, he persuaded me to go to Union Seminary. He held out charity and good will both to those who agreed and disagreed with his position. He was one of those rare people who could differ with other people without becoming angry or making it a personal issue. I loved his emphasis on evangelism, that warm piety as opposed to just cold and harsh doctrinal correctness."

Although still as biblically conservative as ever, Sam himself had become convicted that church unity was all-important from his study of John 17 and other passages. In a letter to his brother Hugh on November 5, 1982, Sam revealed that he was tired of being an "aginer" and would be voting in favor of PCUS's union with the UPC:

> *This is the third time a definite plan of union with the sector in the 'north' has been before us since I have been a minister, 41 years. Twice I opposed the union. This time I will support it. I wonder if the change is in me or in the situation. Maybe it is some of both. I well understand the reasons advanced against the union, or reunion, and, the worse for me, find much merit there and cause for caution. Therefore, I am not (I think) dogmatic on the matter, nor am I crusading. But the issue is before*

us so that a vote-stand must be taken, and I intend to vote for it. I will summarize my reasons, not to persuade or debate, but because you have asked for my views. Weak or strong, right or wrong, this is the way I see it and feel about it. The order indicates no priority.

I've always been over on the extreme theological right—an 'aginer.' I'm tired of that now, as a basic disposition, and at least am open for other possibilities in the union. However, my vote will not just be a reaction to reaction. I have some positive convictions on the matter in the sense that I am more convinced of their probable rightness than wrongness.

I am for reunion in principle in that, since the church is Christ's, His ideal for its oneness (see His prayer in John 17 concerning this) is to be sought. The unity He states there is to be of such nature that the unbelieving world can recognize its reality. Organizational unity cannot be said to be the objective He puts forth, but it is the unity of one organism in which its parts are vitally coordinated and attached as in one body—the figure Paul uses in 1 Corinthians 12 and elsewhere. The many, massive, and multiplying divisions in the Christian church have caught the eye of the watching world (if it is watching), not its bent to unity and union. I see the reunion of the PCUS and the UPCUSA as one small effort to eliminate one separation which appears to me now to be useless.

I am for the reunion because of the prospect of hope I see for the future. By defeating union twice in my life, I do not see that either church has been any better off; rather, both have become more diluted in purpose and effective productivity. I think a third defeat will do nothing to change that. Perhaps reunion will offer the basis for a new sense of commitment to serve Christ and build up the church. I'm ready to try the other way now. Neither could be any worse off than they have been separated.

Then, the plan is a good one—the best yet, I think. It's a good statement of the church's purpose and mission with a priority structure that is exceptionally good. Its language regarding the faith is biblical and appealing to an evangelical conservative....

The conservative sector errs, it seems to me, by more narrowness regarding technical definitions and limitation regarding the Bible and other things than preservation of the truth and Gospel require. The liberals have erred more. In the accommodating provisions in the union, perhaps both will have beneficial effects on the other, and a better balance will be struck.

And a year later, in *This Week in the PCUS*, Sam remained convinced that union was the better way:

Twice over a 42-year ministry I have voted against the reunion of these two churches. I think fear prompted me because fear plays it safe and thinks in the negative. The scriptures propose faith and love. These discount self-protection, think in the positive, and will dare much to achieve our Savior's ideal for the evident unity of His church in the world ... faith and love move me to vote for reunion as a small, needed and important step toward my Savior's ideal for the unity of His church.[23]

In a called meeting on February 8, 1983, at Batesville, Mississippi, St. Andrew Presbytery approved the reunion of the two churches by a vote of seventy-two to forty. The required three-fourths of the PCUS presbyteries voted in favor of the reunion, formally signed in ceremonies at Philadelphia, Pennsylvania, in June 1983.

A RETURN TO ABC

Sam's lectern at ABC had barely grown cold in 1981 when Jack Chinchen began planning for his return. Not only were students imploring Jack to find out when Sam could return, but they were also writing Sam begging him to come—even students who had merely *heard* about Sam! All wanted him to return as a permanent professor; at the very least, they wanted him to attend the school's first graduation in 1983.

Jack began coaxing on May 21, 1981:

Nell and I praise God that He never allowed your commitment to come to evaporate. The college profited greatly. Missionary after missionary has expressed his appreciation for your presence, and, of course, the students are not going to be satisfied with just a one-semester stand from the 'walking commentary.'

He continued on May 11, 1982:

I have assured the students that you will be back with them for the second semester of the next school year. We are counting on your being with us. In fact, we are beginning to lay out the curriculum for 1983 and are slotting hours for Sam Patterson.

Then came the disastrous news from Sam on August 20, 1982:

All of you are constantly in my thoughts and my prayers. There is no way to estimate how greatly God enriched my life by those months spent at ABC. I have longed for the time when I might return and have prayed for guidance and provision for this. There is a difference this time. Last *time I was <u>needed</u> at ABC but really didn't want to go. This time I am not <u>needed</u> but just want to go.*

An urgent call has recently been put upon me by the relatively new president of Belhaven College to help them for the next year get out from under a $3,000,000 indebtedness that is killing the college ... It cannot survive without relief soon. Once again I have no desire to get involved in this kind of job, but there is the pervading sense that God is moving me into it. This, of course, would alter my hopeful plan to get back to Africa this school year.

Jack was devastated and knew he was going to face some heartbroken staff and students. He told Sam that he was puzzled and confused:

Your letter of August 20 has arrived, and as soon as I read it, I pulled out the copy of my May 11 letter to see where I had gone wrong ... to see what I said to cause you to write, 'Last time I was <u>needed</u> at ABC but really didn't want to go. This time I am not <u>needed</u> but just want to go.' Sam, not only are you needed, you are expected. All of us have been counting on you! If you fail to come, a whole student body is going to feel terribly let down, not to mention the staff. They have been anticipating this. They have taken you at your word.

Then also, we were counting on your being with us for the first graduation. We want this time to be special, and your presence would help in this direction. Finally, we are most concerned to keep a vital spiritual atmosphere on campus, and your presence certainly added that quality last time.

So Sam, please inform your friends at Belhaven that you must be in Liberia from mid-February to mid-June. Tell them that you will be worth much more to them after a spiritually stimulating experience in Africa....[24]

Yet, Sam's next letter to Jack was, if anything, even more discouraging than the former concerning his ability to return to Liberia.

Changes in my situation have developed, but none permit me to anticipate a return to ABC in 1983. The Belhaven Board has called off a million-plus drive for the present but four weeks ago my dependent mother-in-law, now 89, suffered a severe stroke.

She lived with Stelle and me for 30 years, and since Stelle's death I have cared for her. Her health was reasonably good in 1980, and she could make out in my absence. She has survived this stroke, surprisingly, but lost practically all sight and the use of her left arm and hand, and she is confused in mind. If she recovers enough to come home, I shall

bring her back and look after her…. For several years I knew that such
a development would likely occur and have had to deal with the Lord
concerning my responsibility. Out of that I have become committed to
her continuing care as best I can give it.

You cannot count on me. Were the above not a factor, finances
would be. I've never raised funds for myself, and I won't. I use only
what just appears from the Lord. My personal financial limitations and
obligations, especially now, are not encouraging regarding support for
a special mission.

To write negatively about a return to ABC is too painful. I'll just
have to close.[25]

During his retirement years, Sam did indeed live on a shoestring; at his death,
he had only eighty-seven dollars in his checking account. When he left the RTS
presidency in 1979 and scaled back his seminary responsibilities, his salary was
reduced. During his last years at French Camp, his only income was his Social
Security and his evangelistic work.

"I knew toward the end of his life that finances were tough," said Brister
Ware. "Everybody else may have thought he was preaching so much simply
because he liked it, but actually he needed it to make ends meet."

In the fall of 1982, Sam confessed as much while visiting with M. B. Cooper.

"Sam," said M. B., "I believe older people today are better off than they've
ever been, with Social Security and other aids."

Sam replied, "You may think so, but not necessarily. If I couldn't preach, I
could hardly make it."

Cooper was shocked. "We always thought of Sam as a giver, not a taker. He
just didn't spend any money on himself at all! One time I offered Sam a couple
of suits that were too big for me. He jumped right on that, saying, 'Let's go check
them out! I've just got one, and it's almost gone!' He'd done a lot for other
people but not much had been done for him."

Cooper immediately called close friends Victor Smith and the late John
McRae to work out a plan to help Sam on a continuing basis. All of them knew
that Sam would fight the idea, so they were stunned when he made no argument
at all in a letter to John and Victor:

Last week I had a lunch visit with M. B. in Kosciusko, and he shared
with me that you three had been considering a plan to provide financial
assistance to me.

At this point, I am wholly at a loss for words … as I was when
M. B. told me of this. I am at a loss for words because I am too filled with
emotion and wonder! The truth is told when I say that the wonder—awe—I
felt had nothing to do at that moment with any material benefit I might
receive, but with the fact that the three of you had such compassionate

concern for another. I was and am inwardly overwhelmed by this Christlike care for others—for me!

For the thought, the concern, the desire on the part of you three I am unspeakably grateful! What can I say?

God knows my heart in this, and I hope you do. The basic need-level for me is being met month by month. For many other people and causes this level is not attained. To God I have long looked and from God I have received enough (Psalm 23:1). I would not want to contravene any leading God may have given you three in this, but I do want you to know my situation for I would be loath to in any way take advantage of anyone, least of all you who have been moved by such a gracious concern for me.

God bless you all for your heart-intention toward me. My gratitude to God and to you is reverent and intense. Please believe me—I just can't say what I feel! Out of a full heart I am... Gratefully yours, Sam[26]

In God's economy, not only did Sam benefit, but those men grew spiritually. When John McRae discovered that Sam's tithe on the money he had given him was the exact amount Sam needed to send for a project, he exclaimed, "Man! To think God used me! That's strong!"

"Of all the people and organizations to whom I've given money, no one has been more appreciative than Sam," recalled Victor. "He always begged me to give it to someone else if that person needed it more."

To most people, Sam lived his life much like an acrobat working without a net. They could see themselves making that one mistake in judgment and plunging to their deaths—whether financial, emotional, spiritual or physical. Yet, Sam had 20/20 spiritual vision and could see that a substantial, heavy net lay beneath him—a net of God's unfailing love and His promise never to forsake His children. Sam believed this wholeheartedly.

Sam's views on the use of money are instructive to Christians today. Probably more than any other existing document, his sermon entitled "The Disciples and Possessions" paints Sam's views on material things. As you will see, Sam believed that he fell far short of any model of Christian giving:

Luke, in his development of discipleship, makes it very clear that the living out of one's discipleship will probably be most evident in our relationship to our possessions. Therefore, I will not preach on Luke 14:33 (NKJV): 'So likewise, whoever of you does not forsake all that he has cannot be my disciple.' I'm frightened by it! I don't understand the depth of it! What does Jesus want me to do? Whatever it means, I know I haven't done it, and I've never met a Christian who really tried.

In Matthew 20, Jesus identified himself as a Savior with a servant's mind. He came to serve, not to be served, to give His life a ransom for many. Jesus was constantly emptying himself out, giving himself—His energy, His time, His interest, His love, His power, His ministry, His grace. He was a dispenser, a giver! What a contrast to see his sheep going out and getting, getting, getting.

When Jesus first sent out the twelve in Luke 9, he told them to go out simply, not taking very much, and to use the powers He'd given them to bless the lives of people who have need of them. Later, in the Great Commission he sent them out with a full-orbed Gospel, but I believe that principle of self-imposed limitations on their possessions belongs as much to the Great Commission as the first commission. Christ has never removed the obligation of his people to give such as they have to meet people's needs. Jesus doesn't hold up prosperity as the goal of His servants, but instead tries to prepare them at every point to recognize the limitations that they must accept for their own lives, the generosity they've got to be willing to show toward everybody else.

In Luke 12 we see that Jesus was temporally as well as spiritually concerned and wants his disciples to care about people's earthly needs. The church can be too spiritual, I think. Our primary objective is to get people right with God, but that doesn't discount temporal needs. Jesus kept a better balance than the church does. In a way, we pay more attention to John 3:16 than we do to practical needs.

God's Word possesses wonderful balance. We need more to be soul-winners, to move people to a spiritual faith in Jesus Christ that will certainly bring them eternal life. However, the world will be more affected by that message when we demonstrate the teachings of Jesus Christ regarding our property. Jesus doesn't encourage saving or spending. He encourages giving and sharing.

A few months ago, I saw a television program on the starving people in Asia. One of the pictures was a pathetic little boy in Cambodia. The commentator said, 'By the time you see this picture, this boy will probably be dead.' I thought ,'There he is, right in front of me. How far is that TV set from where I'm sitting?' I mentally measured—seven feet. What would I do if that boy were sitting seven feet from me? Then I thought—he is.

Through television, God can put right in our living rooms the pictures of people who need a Savior and who also need help for their bodies! That ought to make Christians in this country start turning loose of their funds, start living on as <u>little</u> as they possibly can and putting <u>all</u> they possibly can into the bodies and souls of the people around the world.[27]

The new-found support from his friends allowed Sam to return to ABC as the commencement speaker for the first graduation ceremony on June 11, 1983, for which all were very grateful. Peter Dabieh, Talleyrand Saydee, James Saydee, and others with whom he had corresponded were in the graduating audience. Jack was elated:

> We are still singing praises that we received a YES from you concerning your being with us as our commencement speaker. We called the seniors aside this morning and shared the good news and there was whooping and rejoicing when they heard that you care enough to come!…
>
> Place the charges for the airfare to ABC. With the Lord in this, God will, in His own wonderful way, replenish. Even if the trip were to end up an expense, I can't think of a more vital investment of funds trusted to our care. You know how you sharpen a knife—when you are just about finished you give it those last few strokes right on the tip of the sharpened edge to make sure it is honed to perfection. That's what I see you doing with these fellows, and it is vital! This is to be no ordinary graduation![28]

The financial aid also allowed Sam to fulfill his heartfelt desire to help his grandson, Chris, who had been diagnosed at an early age with multiple learning disabilities. The famous Angie Nall School in Beaumont, Texas, thought they could help the boy, but they did not provide boarding facilities, requiring someone to act as caregiver. In June 1983, Sam put his life on hold and moved to Beaumont with Chris for a year and half. Using his own money, family funds, and financial help from friends, he rented an apartment and paid all the expenses. It was more than a monetary sacrifice, since Sam had to give up preaching. In a letter to Erskine Wells on September 28, 1983, Sam outlined life in Beaumont:

> I am charwoman, cook, housekeeper, and supervisor. I haven't preached since June 1, not being known in these parts. The school seems to be profitable for my grandson, and that continues to justify this abrupt life-style change for me.

"That he gave nearly two years of his life to bring his grandson along touched my heart deeply," said Jack Chinchen. "I've never forgotten that. But that's Sam. That's why he was so effective in dealing with young people."

Church trouble did not cease while Sam was in Beaumont, and being out of the fray was also a huge sacrifice for him. While he was gone, French Camp Presbyterian Church began considering whether to withdraw from St. Andrew Presbytery. Sam also was "greatly saddened" to hear that the officers wholly eliminated the presbytery from the church's benevolent gifts:

Having no opportunity for input at that time, I want to earnestly ask you now to reconsider this action and to reassume the responsibility that is rightly ours. I understand that a major concern in your decision has to do with the National Council of Christian Churches.... Even though a small amount proportionately of our denomination's funds go to the NCC, we have the right to be critical of that which we do not approve. But this does not, in my view, justify our hurting the overwhelming majority of good causes in service and mission our presbytery engages in....

Some of us, including myself, give regularly to the French Camp Church, believing that a due portion goes to its rightful obligation in support of presbytery causes. If withholding the funds continues, I will have to designate to the treasurer that part of my gifts are to go to Presbytery causes.[29]

In spite of Sam's letter, the deacons and elders voted unanimously to leave the budget as it was but decided to wait to withdraw from the church until Sam returned. [30]

After his return from Beaumont in April 1985, Sam resigned from the FCA Board and became president emeritus and director of deferred giving.[31] Again he was doing what he loved—raising scholarship money to help the children of French Camp.

In a fundraising letter on August 25, 1986, Sam says:

Dear Friends,
I am sort of a has-been who is still here and who is delighted to report that in my judgment, FCA is doing better right now than ever before.

However, Kay McNair Johnson knows that Sam was anything but a "has-been." "We needed his connections in the church to gain entrance to speak about French Camp, and he made himself available for that outreach. Yet, he was a consummate, unassuming servant, never trying to run the show. He was a silent worker because we didn't see him much. Yet, one could be certain that Mr. Pat, with his little schnauzer, Schnipps, was on the road speaking to groups about participating in the lives of children. His schedule was fairly amazing for a man who had 'retired.'"

SLOWING DOWN

In 1986, Sam's heart began acting up again, and his appointment books are full of reminders to pick up nitroglycerin prescriptions. Doctors suggested a second open heart surgery, but Sam adamantly refused. According to Ed

Williford, on more than one occasion Sam confided to him, "The doctors say that I must undergo another bi-pass operation if I want to live, but I'm just not going to go through the pain and expense of that again. I'm ready for God to take me to be with Him and Stelle if He wishes."

"Sam was a wonderful person, one of the finest men I ever knew," said his first heart doctor Perrin Berry, "but he was bull-headed as all get-out! He didn't argue a lot; he just did what he pleased. Through his adult life, he felt that when the Lord was ready to take him, he was ready to go."

Exercise and diet had been the bane of Sam's existence for years, and he was tired of being concerned about both. His appointment book shows he bought a bike at one point but rode it for only a short time. He noted, "I walk, but I do it like I'm taking medicine—because I have to."

"He'd come for Christmas Eve and get off his diet with the hors d'oeuvres," recalls Helen Branning with mirth. "One day just after he had passed his seventieth birthday he told us, 'I've been doing what everybody says to do about diet, but I've lived three-score and ten years, and that's all the Lord promised me. Now I'm going to start doing what Sam Patterson wants!'"

He had cut back his preaching engagements to once a quarter, and Lane Stephenson thinks the series Sam held at Epperson Presbyterian Church in November 1986 might have been his last. In Sam's cabin was an unused plane ticket for use in May to preach a series of meetings in Minco, Oklahoma.

"Our people loved him," said Lane. "When told of his death one of the Epperson ladies said it was like getting news of her own father's death."

During the summer of 1986 Sam decided to resign from the RTS Board of Trustees and apparently asked Jim Baird to present his request. In an August 8, 1986, letter to Sam, Baird relates:

> *I have talked with Bob Cannada concerning your desire to resign from the Board of RTS. Bob understood and said it would not be necessary for you to make any explanation. If you write …I am confident your request will be honored. Of course, you know that I and all others will do so with reluctance because of your great service to RTS and the personal love that individual board members have for you. I consider you one of my spiritual fathers. Therefore, anything I can ever do for you is yours for the asking.*

In an October 1, 1986, letter to Robert Cannada, Sam said he felt it was time for his slot to be filled by someone in a position to be actively involved in the board's work:

> *I well know that the love and respect I hold for all of you is that which you hold for me…. I rejoice at the fine faculty and new spirit at RTS and will continue to invest prayer and gifts in the work.*

The Executive Committee granted Sam's request,[32] and Cannada informed Sam of the action in a warm letter on November 10, 1986:

> *The executive committee met last week and, with great reluctance, agreed to accept your resignation as a trustee. While you have not given us clearance to do this, we took the liberty of electing you as director emeritus and we hope this meets with your approval. We simply do not want to ever completely sever our connections with Sam Patterson. You mean too much to us and to the seminary for this to ever happen....*
>
> *You will always have, in my mind, a very close connection with the seminary and will always be welcome at any meeting of the trustees or at any other meeting of any kind in any way pertaining to the seminary. In fact, you are invited and this invitation will remain open indefinitely.*

Sam might have been scaling back on many activities, but not efforts to help the young people at French Camp.

"The last time I saw him the week before he died," said Stuart Angle, "he came into my office inquiring about one of his students from the early 1950s. He had heard she was having some problems, and Mr. Pat was trying to find ways to help her."

Sam never tired of talking about French Camp and its mission. Two weeks before Sam's death, Richard de Witt discovered how true that was. At lunch with Sam and Ed Williford, de Witt naively thought that Sam wanted to visit as old friends, but he found out immediately that Sam wanted to talk business with him as well.

"It was like pulling teeth to get Sam to discuss old times and mutual acquaintances," said de Witt. "When I attempted diversionary tactics, he'd invariably pull the conversation back to the help he wanted from me in raising support for FCA. I confess that at the time I was disappointed. I coveted an hour or two with a man whose friendship I had prized for years.

"In retrospect, however, I find myself even more admiring of him because of his single-mindedness. Sam had turned seventy and soon would be seventy-one. In his view, little time remained for small talk. The Lord's business needed doing, and he meant to spend what time he had left in that service."

SAM'S GRADUATION

Sam was seventy years old when he met his Lord very early on Thursday morning, March 12, 1987, on a pristine beach near Fort Pickens, Alabama. It was fitting that he should enter heaven while camping and meditating so early in the morning. He always looked forward to camping with Becky and Jimmy and their children and this time had been no exception. He'd usually pitch his small tent beside their large camper. But this time, he wasn't feeling well.

"While we were fishing a couple of days before," said Jimmy, "he kept complaining of feeling bad and was taking nitroglycerin by the handful. He didn't look well. The afternoon before he died, we were out fishing on one of the piers. He went to the restroom and came back looking as white as a sheet. I knew then that something was wrong.

"The next morning about 7:30 or 8:00, I called him in for breakfast. As I walked outside, I noticed he was sitting, fully dressed, in the middle seat of his Toyota van, so I knew he had been up for hours. When he didn't respond, I walked over and realized he was gone. His face and body were cool, but some residual heat remained under his arms. He had no Bible or papers. His hand was over his heart, so it's obvious the heart attack had hurt. But it must have happened quickly."

Jimmy called the authorities and dozens of emergency personnel converged on the site. Since there was some residual heat in Sam's body, they tried to revive him for quite a while but never succeeded.

"Hindsight is always better than foresight, and I wish we had insisted that he go to the doctor earlier. He might have if I had asked him; anyone else, I don't know. He was pretty single-minded sometimes and didn't like to go to the doctor!"

Providentially, RTS grad Bill Fox ('76) was able to repay Sam's kindness to him years before when his wife Judy died at RTS. "My son Jim was a paramedic in Pensacola at that time. He was at home that day and heard the emergency call for Sam. I'm surprised he remembered Sam's name since Jim was only eight years old when Judy died. He called me with the news and went down to the emergency room himself to meet the Rogers when the helicopter arrived. I was so thankful that he could be there to minister to them in a strange city during such a stressful time."

The news spread quickly about Sam's sudden homegoing. One student called another, who called a teacher, who called a colleague, who called a friend. Sam's influence was far-reaching and his death a mighty jolt to hundreds.

Maria Price, Norman Harper's daughter, confessed, "When Sam died, Daddy just broke down and wept, saying the world would never be the same again."

"I argued with God when he died," said Erin Lail, "and I don't often say 'Why, God?' But it seemed such an inopportune moment for that mighty man to be taken from this world. I finally realized that Sam wouldn't want me to say that, so I repented of it!"

"One reason I was so sad when he died is that I knew I would never hear him preach again," said Jim Arnold. "But I'll see him in heaven, and I guess he's preaching there! I also felt I had lost a good friend and a man closer to his Lord than anyone I've ever known."

Over the next days and weeks, tributes to a great spiritual leader rolled in. The April issue of *French Camp Today* was dedicated to Mr. Pat. In that issue, Richard de Witt wrote:

> *Sam Patterson was one of the great men of the Presbyterian church. Those in positions of power and influence would regard such a statement with incomprehension. He was once moderator of the Synod of Mississippi (1956), but otherwise he never came near any post of consequence in the church. Sam's greatness lay elsewhere. But on that account it is likely to be far more enduring than is the case with movers and shakers in the denominational structure.*[33]

Donald Patterson, former pastor of First Presbyterian Church in Jackson, MS, wrote French Camp officials:

> *Few men have left an impact for good and for God on so many as he did. We did not agree on everything, but I never had a problem figuring out where Sam stood. We will miss him, but you all at FCA will REALLY miss him.*[34]

Rich Cannon told friends of French Camp Academy:

> *You can imagine what the homegoing of this good and godly man means to French Camp Academy. Our staff, students, alumni, and supporters all feel the same about him. We now have another personal reason for wanting to go to heaven. He was our dearest friend—so holy, so human, and so faithful!*[35]

Former Mississippi Governor J. P. Coleman, Sam's close friend, felt a stinging loss:

> *Probably the greatest difficulty continually confronting the human race is the necessity for giving up individuals such as Sam. I often think what the world would be like if we could only retain people like him for at least as long as Methuselah lived. Regrettably, the nature of our world is otherwise. We have to bow to it, but we can remedy it to a considerable extent by remembering men like Sam, in order that his contribution, guidance, and the light along life's pathway will not only be remembered, but will furnish a lamp to our path even when he is gone from us.*[36]

"When Sallie and I moved to French Camp in January 1987, we began going to his little church in Huntsville," said Ed Williford. "I thought it was too good to be true—living out my dream working at FCA with Mr. Pat and hearing him preach every week. As it turned out, it *was* too good to be true."

Sam was laid to rest on Sunday, March 15, 1987, at three o'clock in the afternoon. The crowd was so large that French Camp Presbyterian Church could not accommodate the hundreds in attendance, so they had Sam's funeral in King

Auditorium on the French Camp Academy campus. The hours surrounding the memorial service and funeral were filled with a lovely variety of remembrances by all. Smiles and laughter abounded as everyone recounted tale after tale about Mr. Pat or Brother Sam or Sam or Mr. Patterson.

"They brought the casket into the auditorium some time before the service," said Mary Ida Harper. "Ladell Flint (FCA '52), who dearly loved Sam, stood at the head of the casket like a sentinel and did not leave it until they removed it for the funeral. It was as if he were caring for Sam even in death."

The funeral, broadcast on WFCA, was a service of worship and praise, with hundreds of friends giving glory to God for Sam's life and ministry. After everyone sang "Onward Christian Soldiers," thanksgiving to God came in the form of majestic hymns, sermons, scripture, and personal testimonies about Sam's contribution to the church. Longtime friend and colleague Russell Nunan officiated at the service, with Mickey and Martha Parks singing "In Times Like These."

Norman Harper paid a moving tribute to the man who had been his mentor for over a quarter of a century:

> In 1564, at the death of John Calvin, Theodore Beza, his long-time friend and colleague in the ministry, said these words, 'The state has lost its wisest citizen. The church has lost its most faithful defender. The academy has lost its greatest teacher. Under God, all have lost their common pastor and comforter.' I do not think it would be too much to say this day that there is with us a sense of loss something akin to that.
>
> As I had privilege to observe the ministry of our brother who has gone to be with the Lord, certainly if anyone ever lived in the presence of God, it was this man. Through his faith in Christ, his love for God and for people, and his prayer life—his conversation of the soul with God—in every conceivable way, he dwelled in the presence of God, wherein is the fullness of joy. It has been said of the Apostle Paul that the will of God was the law of his life; the love of God was the power of his life; the glory of God was the end of his life. I think that same thing could be said about our brother in Christ.
>
> And God gave him an unusual gift to preach in such a winsome, loving, and wise way that the Gospel could be heard by the old and the young, the great and the small, the wise and the simple so that they could hear and respond....
>
> Second only to the Lord, Sam Patterson loved his family. They were always close to his heart wherever he was. All who knew him knew that to be true.
>
> He was also not a respecter of persons. It mattered not to him whether a person was rich or poor, black or white, great or small. He was the same with everyone.

And in a society in which we are tempted to play a role in order to sell ourselves or to sell our product, Sam Patterson was himself, not trying to impress someone else. In a very inauthentic culture, he indeed was an authentic Christian.

He never sought fame or material things for himself. Through the years, all of us who have known him in any way have heard him say many times, 'I'm just a sinner saved by grace.' Sam was for me a role model, a wise counselor, and a dear Christian friend.

Rich Cannon also had kind words:

I was in Denver when I received the word that Mr. Pat was in the presence of the Lord. I was there preaching and teaching students what Mr. Pat taught me. He taught us things like 'Never choose up sides' or 'Don't choose your enemy, let the Lord choose your enemies. Then you can love them.' He had conviction with compassion and commitment. Whether he was with you or away from you, you knew that this man cared about you. He cared about me. He cared about this place.

In these last days, as we have talked about different things that have happened at French Camp, we suddenly realized that we would put a matter on the back burner or forget about it altogether until Mr. Pat mentioned it. Suddenly, it became important. We see now that what he wanted to do here has been accomplished. By the grace of God, in the midst of his compassion and his convictions, he was committed to seeing the work of the Lord on to completion. Now, according to the scripture, he's waiting for you and me to remain faithful to finish the job. I am convinced, as you are, that God gave him to us for eternal purposes. It is my prayer, and our hope together here, that this work and the other works that he was so concerned about prayed for, and participated in will continue to remain faithful.

He was a simple man. He had a simple vision. He believed that God's people ought to love the Lord with all their heart and soul and mind. They ought to love their fellow human beings likewise, and they ought to participate in the church with all that God has granted to them until He comes.

He was so good! So human! So holy!

After the funeral, WFCA broadcast Sam's final sermon, "Burdens," preached at Leland Presbyterian Church the Sunday before his death. Ann Aldridge and other Leland Presbyterian members heard the broadcast as they drove home, and Ann later wrote poignantly about it:

It was one of those glorious sunsets for which the Mississippi Delta is famous. From the car radio came the words of Jesus, 'Come unto me, all who labor and are heavy laden, and I will give you rest.' The words were Sam's, in what was to be his last sermon, preached at our church only the week before.

We were on our way home from Sam's funeral, a carload of people who had reminisced and swapped stories all the way to French Camp that Sunday afternoon, March 15, to say last goodbyes to a friend who had shared his love of Jesus Christ with us over the years. It was a privilege for each of us to be in that car sharing these moments together. We remembered the events surrounding Sam that always brought forth smiles and hearty laughs.

At the funeral we had heard preachers and laymen praise Sam—for his faith in God, his love for the youth of French Camp, his work, his simple life, his wisdom, his appreciation for family and friends. There was nothing to be added. We felt truly blessed to have been even a tiny part of his life.[37]

Sam was laid to rest beside his beloved Stelle in the French Camp Cemetery at French Camp, Mississippi. If you go there, don't look for the grandest monuments. Both gravestones are meek and humble, as their owners were in life. Written on Sam's are two scriptures:

Psalm 1
Blessed is the man whose delight is in the law of the Lord.

Psalm 91
He who dwells in the shelter of the most high will rest in the shadow of the almighty.

REMEMBERING A GODLY MAN

RTS held a memorial service in the chapel for Sam on March 27, 1987, led by President Luder Whitlock. Whitlock thanked God for the remarkable way He had used Sam at RTS, throughout this state, and much of the world, in the name of the Lord Jesus Christ:

Above all, Sam Patterson was an evangelist. He was not an academician. He loved the Lord, and he loved the Gospel. More than anything else, he wanted to honor Christ and to make him known to the ends of the world.

RTS Executive Committee member Frank Horton echoed those thoughts:

He was a man that I loved. I would have wished that every one of you could have known him. But I would also want you to love his Christ, as he did. If there was ever a man that lived Christ, it was Sam. Eulogizing is the last thing that Sam would have wanted. He would want Christ to be exalted.

In its spring meeting, the French Camp Academy Board of Trustees approved a resolution honoring Sam and setting up the Sam C. Patterson Scholarship Fund in his name.[38] In the years since his death, many children have been able to share in the love and training at FCA as a result of Sam's dedication and this scholarship.

"That was such an appropriate memorial," said Becky Rogers. "While Dad's main effort during the early years at French Camp was building FCA's ministry, in later years his drive was to seek scholarship aid for young people who really needed French Camp Academy."

At the spring meeting of St. Andrew Presbytery, Milton Winter, fellow St. Andrew minister and longtime admirer of Sam, chronicled Sam's life in a moving tribute to his forty-six year career in the ministry.[39] Other than that, Sam's death didn't make headlines or magazine covers. Nor did it appear in the minutes of the Synod of the Mid-South PC(USA) at their meeting May 4, 1987. It seems that the 1973 session of the Synod of Mississippi (PCUS) was the last time memorials were written for ruling elders and pastors. In the past, beautiful testimonies in framed borders graced the pages of presbytery and synod minutes. Today, PC(USA) memorials are done at the synod level only for presbytery executives.

Perhaps the most lasting tribute and the one of which Sam would have approved most heartily was the renovation of the quaint French Camp Presbyterian Church. With the growing FCA student body and staff, the church was no longer adequate to accommodate the FCA family along with the local membership and frequent visitors. In addition, age had taken its toll on the church building, and the congregation could not afford the extensive repairs. The little church had a special place in the spiritual lives of so many FCA students, who over the past eighty years had come to know Jesus Christ personally through its ministry. Sam would have been pleased, since his heart was in keeping small churches vibrant and alive. Across the years, he had worked especially hard to provide this little church with godly leadership.

The project involved renovating and enlarging the sanctuary and annex with its thirteen classrooms. Jack Johnson was the general contractor for the project. Carpenters included Bobby McKnight, Billy McKnight, and Bill Barr. Also contributing to the construction were students, staff, former students, J. J. White Memorial Presbyterian in McComb, and First Presbyterian Church in Corinth.

The Sam Patterson Memorial Steering Committee set a fund goal of $250,000 for the project and an additional $100,000 as a perpetual maintenance fund. (See Appendix D.)

Buck and Betty Mosal refurbished the pulpit in memory of God's saving mercy to Buck through Sam's preaching. The beautiful stained glass window currently over the pulpit was discovered in the church attic during the renovation. It was originally over the door in the bell tower. In appreciation for the privilege of overseeing the church renovation, Jack Johnson funded the window's restoration, using materials from the old windows in the sanctuary.[40]

The newly renovated church was dedicated to Sam's memory on Sunday, November 19, 1989, at three o'clock in the afternoon, with a lovely reception following in the newly refurbished church annex. The church was packed and the service was broadcast over WFCA.

Russell Nunan presided over the service, with music by the French Camp Strings, French Camp Chorus, and organist Merrill Dunlop. The congregation joined in plenty of rousing hymns. Erskine Jackson and Gerard Van Groningen read scripture, interspersed among several moving tributes. Rich Cannon said:

> *I came to FCA in 1977 and had the rare privilege of serving under the tutelage of Sam when he came back to French Camp. He always seemed to show up out of nowhere when I needed answers to problems. He was the most simple fellow I've ever met in my life. I'd say, 'What do you think about this, Mr. Pat?' and all he might say was, 'I don't think I'd do that.' Other times he'd say, 'I like that.'* [41]

Jack Bushman said:

> *Sam was the most godly man I ever met. He led me and my children to the Lord. He gave me three Bibles, and I needed all of them. When he gave me the first one, he told me, 'If any man is in Christ he is a new creation.' I said, 'Sam, I can't tell that I'm much of a different creation. I seem about as sorry as the day you met me.' Sam said, 'No, because now you're worried about it!'* [42]

FCA Board Chairman Stuart Irby, Jr. presented to the church a bronze plaque of dedication with the inscription, "He was an evangelist at heart and showed it in everything he undertook." A lovely portrait of Sam was also unveiled.[43] Both the plaque and portrait hang together today in the sanctuary.

In the early 1990s, Lewis Graeber, Jr. commissioned the famous Leon Loard to paint Sam's portrait and donated it to RTS in recognition of Sam's outstanding ministry at the school.[44] At a special service in Grace Chapel on February 5, 1992, Luder Whitlock unveiled the beautiful portrait, which now hangs in the faculty lounge at the seminary. It is this portrait that graces the cover of this book.

Late in 2004, the RTS Board of Trustees voted to change the name of the small on-campus lunchroom from the Solid Rock to Patterson's Porch, in Sam's honor.

In 2006 the RTS Board of Trustees instituted The Sam Patterson Award in honor of Sam's deep concern for the health and future of the church. This award is given to individuals who have made a significant investment in the ministry of RTS over a period of years with their involvement, their prayers, and their resources. A candidate for this award is a person who not only has provided significant financial support to RTS, but also who has had an active and personal involvement over time with the seminary and who has shown themselves to be a model of godly stewardship. Robert Cannada and Elliot Belcher were the first recipients in May 2007 as part of RTS's fortieth anniversary celebration.

A BEAUTIFUL LIFE

J. I. Packer, in his thought-provoking work *Rediscovering Holiness,* points out that the godliness found in Jesus is simply human life lived as the Creator intended. It is a life in which the different elements of humanity are completely united in a totally God-honoring and nature-fulfilling way.[45] Christ alone can do this for us. Everyone who does not know Jesus Christ and is under the power of sin lives a "qualitatively subhuman" life.[46]

Packer goes on to describe the qualities found in an authentic human conformed to the image of Christ:

> *... Love in the service of God and others, humility and meekness under the divine hand, integrity of behavior expressing integration of character, wisdom with faithfulness, boldness with prayerfulness, sorrow at people's sins, joy at the Father's goodness, and single-mindedness in seeking to please the Father morning, noon, and night, were all qualities seen in Christ, the perfect man.[47]*

By those standards, Sam was a stunning example of true humanity. How he modeled for us the transformation that occurs when we place ourselves totally in God's keeping so that He can conform us to the image of His Son! Galatians 5:22–23 lists the fruits of the Spirit as love, joy, peace, patience, kindness, goodness, faithfulness, gentleness, and self-control. Rare is the man who exhibits all of the fruits in such fine fashion as Sam did. Usually a person has one or two in abundance but is deficient in others. How did he cultivate such a good crop? He once told Nellie McPherson to "Keep self-conscious about the filling of the Spirit through 'spiritual breathing,' and the fruit will naturally grow."[48]

Yet, these qualities weren't given to him on the proverbial silver platter. Throughout his entire Christian life, he worked tirelessly to make growth in Christ a priority. No doubt he echoed the words of this old hymn:

I'm pressing on the upward way,
New heights I'm gaining every day.
Still praying as I onward bound,
Lord, plant my feet on higher ground.[49]

The struggle for most people in life is to focus on what is really real; they find it difficult to sift through the pettiness, the urgent, the lure that constitutes our world. It is only time spent with the Lord that helps us filter all the fluff and live in the joyful freedom that is fellowship with God. After thirty years of putting Christ first, Sam didn't have to *try* to be like Christ. It had become who Sam *was*.

"I've never known a more committed Christian man than Sam Patterson," said Ed Williford, "although I've never known a Christian who did less to show it outwardly. As I came to know Mr. Pat well, I realized I was in the presence of a man of deep faith, a real man of God, but it was not because of outward religious trappings. He didn't use complicated spiritual terms to impress, he didn't pray long prayers, and he didn't even talk about the Christian faith overtly. But little things about him showed he was a spiritual giant."

"I never cease to be amazed at what God has done with this man who was willing to take God at His word and strike out in faith to do the job he felt led to do," said Becky Rogers. "His life is a testimony to the kind of God he worshiped."

Indeed, Sam's faith in what God could accomplish was legendary. Listen to his interpretation of Ephesians 3:20:

> *God can do what you ask; God can do all that you ask;*
> *God can do above all that you ask;*
> *God can do abundantly above all that you ask;*
> *God can do exceedingly, abundantly above all that you ask;*
> *God can do exceedingly, abundantly above all that you ask or even*
> *think.*

Like Christ, Sam was at peace with his God. "I never in my life met a man so in harmony with himself, His universe, and His God," Jane Montfort told Sam in a 1975 letter.[50] Rita Riggins agreed. "I knew that I didn't sense the presence of God as he did. He understood more than anyone I have ever known that 'still, small voice of God' every day of his life. I was always impressed with the stillness within him. For that to happen, a person must surrender everything to God. Then peace, tranquility, and serenity enter. Most of us want to hold on. He let go better than anyone I ever knew."

Also like Christ, Sam lived to do good—always the encourager, the helper, the one in your corner, ready to give every ounce of energy to help all succeed. He often said that he was a do-gooder and proud of it:

If you ever use the term 'do-gooders' derisively, I hope you'll quit. Jesus Christ has come to <u>make</u> us do-gooders! He's come to get the works of God done in us, and the works of God are to be concerned about all these people. Jesus has saved us not <u>by</u> our works, not <u>with</u> our works, not <u>through</u> our works, but <u>unto</u> good works that He has ordained.[51]

Sam imitated Christ so well that he did far more good than the average human during his nearly seven decades on earth. The good that he most wanted to do, of course, was to share Christ with others. That he did with almost every breath he took. "You are God's love letter to me," James Saydee once told Sam. How many hundreds could echo those words?

His was a beautiful life well-lived. He found God's light wonderfully and was a perfect channel for heavenly blessings and truth. He did it quietly, with no fanfare, no wide paper trail. He didn't write any books and authored very few papers. He certainly didn't write about himself, and, until now, no one else has either. He held no high offices in the church that would warrant recognition.

In the end, he would want you to remember him as a simple evangelist who lived to say, "Friends, I wish for you God's best. And God's best is Jesus Christ." If you've come to know that, Sam is smiling.

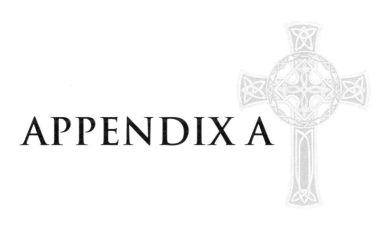

APPENDIX A

FRENCH CAMP
ACADEMY

*Sam stands outside Alexander Strange Hall
at French Camp Academy.*

French Camp Academy
and
Mississippi Synod's Grand Experiment
in Christian Education

Rebecca B. Hobbs

Historically, Presbyterians were at the forefront of education in the United States from the country's founding, but the turbulence and destruction of the Civil War halted emphasis on this vital endeavor for a number of years. Yet, as prosperity returned after the war, education-minded Presbyterians reaffirmed their traditional ideal of a college in every synod, an academy or high school in every presbytery.[1] In 1900, the Presbyterian Church in the United States (PCUS) renewed its zeal for Christian education and launched an ambitious plan to provide a thorough Christian education for its children, encouraging synods to take control of and regulate schools within their bounds. The PCUS General Assembly promised to help the synods with the organization, even vowing to raise a million dollars for the cause.[2]

However, the idealistic plan seemed doomed from the very beginning. Although each synod was eventually organized by 1926, the assembly's financial campaign failed. Much was pledged, but collection of actual cash just prior to the Great Depression was another story.[3] Theological giants such as James Thornwell and Robert Dabney argued that the church had no business entering the field of secular education.[4] Time would prove that the Assembly should probably have heeded their warnings.

Yet, many synods were excited about the plan. Following the Assembly's lead, the Synod of Mississippi began concerted efforts to form a statewide educational system. By 1913 it had acquired six schools, either by transfer from presbytery (Belhaven College, French Camp Academy, Central Mississippi Institute, Chamberlain-Hunt Academy, and Chickasaw College) or outright purchase (Mississippi Synodical College).[5] The synod had complete control of the schools—owning the property, trust funds, and investments, in addition to appointing all board members.[6]

The synod, though, did not anticipate how hard running the institutions would be. Gaining total control of the schools meant acquiring all their debts, which synod estimated at $100,000 in 1914. Raising the money became extremely difficult. The United States was on the verge of entering World War I, and the country was in a depression. Goods were scarce, and money even more scarce.[7] At times, synod had to take out new loans to pay just the interest—much less the principal—on existing loans.[8]

As early as 1914 tension was evident in synod minutes over the difficulty in school funding:

> *Your committee views with some alarm the apathy and indifference of ... our synod, who vote into existence such a committee as ours, charge them with the gravest responsibilities ... then forget their personal responsibility ... it takes the personal endorsement of executive committee members to keep our institutions in a solvent condition amid financial stress and storm.... Were it*

*not for the spirit of self-sacrifice and sense of responsibility of some of the
businessmen on our committee, we could not have borne up under burdens
imposed.[9]*

And in 1915 some alarm appeared:

*The banks have been good to us and have accepted this paper on their faith
in the Presbyterian Church and nothing else.... We will be wrecked as a church
for generations if we do not liquidate these loans.[10]*

This scenario would play out again and again during the next decades as synod watched
campaign after campaign fail, bonds mature with no funds to pay them off, and schools
beg for operating expenses. Synod leaders always looked hopefully, if not realistically,
to the future: "We are quite sure the proverbial 'silver lining' is coming even faintly
into view."[11] They forever expected a change in social and economic circumstances, as
well as better financial support for Christian education from Mississippi Presbyterians.
Neither ever came.

Synod leaders repeatedly asked Presbyterians to more solidly consecrate themselves
to Christian education, emphasizing the privilege of underwriting the support of
their schools:

*If we are asked why the synod owes so much, we reply that our obligations
practically all represent investments and not wasted money. For the first time in
the history of the Synod of Mississippi, the people as a whole are being called
upon to pay for their own property ... while our responsibilities are heavy, the
outlook was never better ... and the condition of our schools is improving since
the plan of correlation was adopted.[12]*

Records show that synod felt the main problem was a lack of communication;
members simply did not know how serious the problem was.[13] Leaders constantly urged
ministers to preach on Christian education to bring the financial needs of the schools
before the people:[14]

*Our people don't know the importance of Christian education ... because it
has not been presented to them. They will respond when the cause is presented
in its relationship to the whole kingdom of our Lord.[15]*

In reality, however, quite the opposite was true. Members understood the problem,
but they were financially strapped. Over the years, church school attendance and
financial support declined as PCUS members resented more and more paying taxes for
state schools, while also supporting church schools doing the same job, but not as well.[16]

Much of French Camp Academy's history is bound up in synod's ambitious project
and the efforts to make it work during the first half of the twentieth century. Most people
think that the FCA crisis into which Sam Patterson stepped in 1950 was the school's first.
It was, in fact, the fourth. By the mid-1930s, three major crises had already occurred at
FCA, any of which could have easily closed the school were it not for God's protecting
hand. Each crisis had a distinct influence on Sam Patterson's later presidency of FCA.

FCA'S FIRST MAJOR CRISIS

From the beginning, synod applauded French Camp Academy and Central Mississippi Institute as exemplary home mission projects.[17] Yet, they required almost total funding by synod. Since 1900 the public schools had been gaining strength in the South. With better equipment and low rates in board and tuition, they enticed more and more students away from the synod schools, especially FCA and CMI, both of which attracted rural families of low income.[18] Synod reported in 1914: "…with an agricultural high school in almost every county … there are more children in two or three of these schools than in all of our own, especially in rural communities." [19]

To make matters worse, from 1914–1916 the Mexican boll weevil caused widespread destruction of cotton crops around French Camp, turning the economy upside down and making it even harder for French Camp families to pay tuition.[20] To save money, synod consolidated FCA and CMI into The French Camp Schools with only one faculty.[21]

Yet, in 1916 synod belatedly realized it did not have the money to pay even one faculty at the schools. Synod had seriously miscalculated the debts of their newly acquired schools. The figure was not $100,000, but closer to $138,000 (and would rise to $147,000 by 1917).[22] Burdened with these debts and the operating expenses of the schools, synod announced it needed an extra $2,500 over board and tuition to pay the teachers at The French Camp Schools. They threatened to close the schools if some other organization did not help pay the teachers.[23]

The Board of Trustees of French Camp Schools called upon the women of the synod for the money, and the group began valiantly trying to raise the money.[24] The Women's Synodical was in its infancy as an organization when this challenge was placed before it. Moreover, war conditions and Red Cross work interfered. Therefore, the first two years they fell short of the $2,500 goal. However, by 1918 the synodical gathered its forces in earnest and for the next fifty years never failed to meet their expected donation to FCA.[25]

In fact, across the years God has used Presbyterian women more than any other group to keep FCA alive. In addition to helping pay the teachers each year, they have raised thousands of dollars to build several dorms, remodel buildings, and complete a number of other projects. At least twice they have reduced principal and interest on FCA loans, some at critical times. [26]

While Presbyterian women had brought The French Camp Schools a measure of peace, the existence of the institutions was still tenuous as synod realized what an enormous task it had set for itself. Church leaders recognized that they might be in over their heads:

> *The difficulty of maintaining church schools is increasing. Standards are being raised that are hard to reach. The growth of the sciences makes heavy demands upon the school for equipment. The cost of operating schools today is far beyond what it was even a decade ago.*[27]

FCA'S SECOND MAJOR CRISIS

While 1918 was the beginning of a time of renewed hope and peace for much of the world, the year was overshadowed by two events that posed the greatest threat yet to

FCA's survival. The first came in early 1918 when beloved FCA President Frank McCue left to become principal of Montgomery Agricultural High School.[28] It was a crushing blow to the school since McCue had made numerous improvements during his two terms as president.

In March, the FCA Board of Trustees announced that noted Hattiesburg minister and educator Rev. E. J. Currie would become president of FCA.[29] After founding First Presbyterian Church in Hattiesburg, Currie had remained as pastor for twenty-five years. Extremely interested in education, he had served as county superintendent of education for sixteen years even while pastoring. He had supervised the building of three high schools and many other schools in Forrest County and had been dubbed the county's "Father of Education."[30]

Apparently, Currie's selection as the new president was news to him also:

> Rev. Currie said he will accept [the presidency], although he had not sought it and had not been aware of his election until notified by the board of trustees.[31]

That he actually took the position is evidenced by a May 1918 *Choctaw Plain Dealer* story reporting that, "Rev. E. J. Currie, the new principal addressed a large crowd at French Camp Rally Day."[32]

Currie was just settling into his presidency when the unthinkable occurred on Wednesday, May 8, 1918. That evening, while everyone was at church, Central Mississippi Institute burned to the ground.[33] The school was thrown into chaos as the students were sent home, and synod leaders pondered what to do. Rebuilding would cost $20,000, money that synod didn't have. Concern mounted among French Camp supporters when Currie resigned as president, a move that precipitated talk of either closing The French Camp Schools or moving them to another location.[34]

One of the main contenders for the school was the town of Pontotoc, home to the now defunct Chickasaw College, acquired by synod in 1913. Synod had promised to open the school as soon as possible, but the thousands of dollars needed simply had not been available.[35] Pontotoc citizens likely saw this as a perfect time to force the issue.

Conscious that French Camp citizens would fight to keep the school and that the issue might become explosive, synod called a special session on June 20, 1918, in Jackson to decide the matter.[36] However, judging from Pontotoc newspaper accounts, the matter was being decided before the special session convened. On May 30, the *Pontotoc Sentinel* reported that the French Camp trustees were looking for a place to relocate:

> A committee is here today for the purpose of inspecting Chickasaw College and conferring with our citizens with a view to establishing the school here. This is a good opportunity to secure a live school with substantial backing and our people should lend every encouragement to the enterprise.[37]

A week later the *Sentinel* reported that French Camp Academy would locate in Pontotoc:

> This school is to be known as Chickasaw Agricultural High School and in addition to the regular preparatory work will include the full agricultural high school curriculum. The institution will have back of it the Synod of Mississippi

and Dr. E. J. Currie, one of the best known and most successful school men in the state, will be in charge.[38]

By June 13, another article stated that "Currie was to be president of Chickasaw Agricultural College assisted by French Camp faculty."[39]

Yet, the citizens of Pontotoc did not count on the tenacity and commitment of FCA supporters. Citizens of French Camp held a mass meeting on June 17, 1918, and decided to send as large a delegation as possible to the synod meeting on June 20. The group was empowered to assure the synod's Executive Committee of Education that all of the school buildings would be thoroughly overhauled and put in a comfortable and sanitary condition for the school opening in September.[40]

At the synod meeting on June 20, Pontotoc citizens offered $5,000 and 104 acres of land to remove the French Camp Schools to Chickasaw College, which would then be operated as synod's coeducational home mission school.[41]

Presbyterian women pled passionately for FCA to remain in French Camp. Twenty-six synodical leaders signed a petition stating:

Our hearts are burdened and troubled at any proposed change from French Camp. The long history of the past, the great work of the future is deeply impressed upon our minds and hearts. Are we to discontinue our work and our prayers?... Some have very uniquely described French Camp as The Hub of the Universe, one of its greatest assets being it remoteness—'far from the maddening crowd.' This asset, we fear, is now being called inaccessibility and is no longer considered an asset. We feel that we are voicing the sentiment of the majority of the women in our synod when we say that to us, French Camp is still The Hub of the Universe, Our Greatest Home Mission Asset.[42]

Synod decided that Chickasaw College should be reopened as a coed home mission school, with synod cooperating to make the school a success. The French Camp Schools would remain in French Camp.[43] French Camp citizens assured synod that FCA buildings would be repaired and made habitable, with the board supplying materials ($1,000) and citizens of the area doing the work ($1,000).[44]

Samuel McBride was subsequently elected president of The French Camp Schools, and E. J. Currie became president of Chickasaw College. Both schools opened in September.[45] McBride took a chaotic situation at French Camp and turned it around superbly. By 1919, he was able to report to synod that the school was out of debt for the first time in its history.[46] The years of McBride's presidency from 1918–1928 were years of growth and stability, even though the school was on a tight budget. By contrast, Chickasaw College was never supported adequately and fell deeper and deeper into debt, finally closing in 1930.[47]

FCA'S THIRD MAJOR CRISIS

The decade following World War I was generally a time of prosperity and recovery. During the 1920s, however, the Synod of Mississippi made some decisions that, coupled with worsening economic times toward the end of the decade, would spell near disaster for French Camp Academy. The Out-of-Debt Campaign, begun in 1918 to pay off the last $50,000 of the schools' loans, continued through 1924, but very little was collected despite strenuous efforts.[48]

Unbelievably, even though synod had not collected pledges on the old campaigns, in 1924 they began a Million Dollar Campaign to raise money for school endowments, with French Camp to receive $150,000.[49] In the coming years, providing its schools with endowments became an all-important mission for synod:

> The imperative need ... is for an education that is positively Christian. The church must supply this need or it will be unmet. There are only two sources of income for the church school, the one from tuition and the other from endowment. If the income from tuition is adequate it will be prohibitive to the child of moderate means. Hence, if the church is to do her full part, the endowment of schools becomes imperative.[50]

Yet, synod consistently failed to raise the money to make endowments to all the school possible. Even the schools that had small endowments, such as Chamberlain-Hunt, had to use them for operating expenses.[51] During his presidency at FCA, Sam Patterson would later reject synod endowments, instead looking to God exclusively for the heavenly endowment found in Philippians 4:19, "And my God shall supply all your needs, according to His riches in glory in Christ Jesus." (NASV)

By 1926, synod had collected only $138,000 out of over $500,000 pledged in the Million Dollar endowment campaign.[52] That same year, the PCUS General Assembly suggested that all synods should evaluate afresh their efforts in education. "Some," said the committee, "may be attempting too ambitious a program."[53]

Good advice, since one of the worst disasters in U.S. history was imminent—the Great Flood of 1927. Following several months of unusually heavy rain during late 1926 and early 1927, the Mississippi River flooded 27,000 square miles of land. Over 130,000 homes were lost and 700,000 people displaced. Property damage was estimated at 350 million dollars. Widespread depression ensued, and synod was forced to suspend the Million Dollar Campaign in December 1927, with some $458,000 to be collected.[54] As usual, however, synod was quite optimistic that the money would come in:

> Prayer and cooperation will complete the Campaign with a full Million Dollars subscribed. A few substantial gifts will assure Victory. The need is apparent. Presbyterians in Mississippi are financially able. The time is short. We hope those intending to support the Cause will not delay.[55]

Confident that pledges would soon be paid, in 1928 synod allowed French Camp Academy to borrow $25,000 against its promised endowment from the Million Dollar Campaign. Under Sam McBride's careful leadership, FCA had been operating without a deficit, and McBride felt the school desperately needed an administration building. The Executive Committee of Education endorsed the note, which was secured by a deed of trust on FCA.[56]

No one could know that just a few short months later the stock market would crash on Black Friday (October 25, 1929), plunging the United States into the Great Depression. Collecting pledges became nearly impossible, and synod begged people to contribute because schools, including French Camp, had borrowed against their endorsements and desperately needed the funds.[57]

Then, the unimaginable occurred. Between December 1930 and January 1931, the bank holding FCA's deposits failed, and Jackson National Bank called in the loan for the administration building.[58] Since the FCA deed secured the loan, the bank threatened foreclosure if it was not paid. Once again the women of the PCUS stepped forward to save FCA:

> *The Women's Synodical not only paid in full the amount for current expenses, but also … paid interest on all FCA notes and even reduced the indebtedness. They have raised the funds to pay the interest this fall and expect to make an effort to make a larger payment on the principal sum.*[59]

Even though saved from foreclosure, FCA was by no means out of the woods. Times were hard; in order to survive financially, the board cut salaries drastically, laid off teachers, and postponed much-needed building repairs. By 1935, teacher salaries had dropped to between twenty and thirty dollars a month. Despite low tuition, some parents had difficulty paying it. [60]

In 1932, synod began yet another campaign to raise $25,000 for school debts, admitting it was facing "unprecedented" financial difficulties.[61] In 1934, Central Mississippi Presbytery asked synod to consolidate FCA with financially beleaguered Palmer Home for Children in Columbus, Mississippi.[62] This overture apparently died, since no further record of it appears in synod minutes.

During the late 1930s, FCA operated without a deficit and began significantly reducing its debt for the administration building. In 1936 it recorded its highest attendance ever. Yet, other synod schools were not holding their own against the burgeoning public schools. Mississippi Synodical had such difficulty getting students that synod finally consolidated the school with Belhaven College in 1939.[63]

By the end of the decade the world was again at war. Goods were rationed, and experienced teachers left for the battlefield, putting pressure on schools to perform with less qualified faculties. In addition, the PCUS was taking a long, hard look at its role in education.[64] Perhaps Thornwell and Dabney were right; could the denomination's resources be redirected to better causes? The stage was set for the 1940s and the thrilling drama at FCA in which Sam Patterson had a starring role.

NOTES

1. Ernest Trice Thompson, *Presbyterians in the South, 1890–1972* (Richmond, Virginia: John Knox Press, 1963), 3:159.

2. Ibid., 163 and 166–167.

3. Ibid., 169.

4. Ibid., 185.

5. Minutes of Mississippi Synod (PCUS), November 18–21, 1913, 571.

6. Minutes of Mississippi Synod (PCUS), November 17–19, 1914, 627–628.

7. Minutes of Mississippi Synod (PCUS), November 17–19, 1914, 638 and Minutes of Mississippi Synod (PCUS), November 16–18, 1915, 706.

8. Minutes of Mississippi Synod (PCUS), November 16–18, 1915, 712.

9. Minutes of Mississippi Synod (PCUS), November 17–19, 1914, 646–647.

10. Minutes of Mississippi Synod (PCUS), November 16–18, 1915, 713.

11. Minutes of Mississippi Synod (PCUS), September 10–12, 1935, 376.

12. Minutes of Mississippi Synod (PCUS), November 21–23, 1916, 801.

13. Minutes of Mississippi Synod (PCUS), September 11–13, 1934, 302.

14. Minutes of Mississippi Synod (PCUS), September 15–17, 1931, 37.

15. Minutes of Mississippi Synod (PCUS), November 17–19, 1914, 644.

16. Thompson, 3:185.

17. Minutes of Mississippi Synod (PCUS), November 21–23, 1916, 790.

18. Minutes of Mississippi Synod (PCUS), November 17–19, 1914, 641 and Minutes of Mississippi Synod (PCUS), November 16–18, 1915, 707.

19. Minutes of Mississippi Synod (PCUS), November 17–19, 1914, 644.

20. Melinda Livingston and Charles Rich, *A Treasure on the Trace: The French Camp Story* (Baton Rouge, Louisiana: Franklin Press, 1996), 44–45.

21. Minutes of Mississippi Synod (PCUS), November 16–18, 1915, 707.

22. Minutes of Mississippi Synod (PCUS), November 21–23, 1916, 800 and Minutes of Mississippi Synod (PCUS), November 20–22, 1917, 10.

23. Minutes of Mississippi Synod (PCUS), November 21–23, 1916, 790.

24. Ibid.

25. Minutes of Mississippi Synod (PCUS), November 19–21, 1918, 104–105.

26. See Women's Work section in Mississippi Synod Minutes 1922, 1923, 1925, 1931, 1956, 1960, 1964.

27. Minutes of Mississippi Synod (PCUS), November 20–22, 1917, 26.

28. "Rev. F. L. McCue Head of Montgomery A.H.S.," *Winona Times*, May 3, 1918.

29. "Rev. E. J. Currie Will Leave City," *Hattiesburg American*, March 28, 1918, 8.

30. "Dr. E. J. Currie, Educator and Minister, Dies," *Hattiesburg American*, May 18, 1931, 1 and 7.

31. "Rev. E. J. Currie Will Leave City," *Hattiesburg American*, March 28, 1918, 8.

32. "Big Day at French Camp," *Choctaw Plain Dealer*, May 17, 1918.

33. Livingston and Rich, *A Treasure on the Trace*, 98 and "Fire at French Camp," *Choctaw Plain Dealer*, May 10, 1918.

34. Minutes of Mississippi Synod (PCUS), November 19–21, 1918, 123.

35. Minutes of Mississippi Synod (PCUS), November 21–23, 1916, 791.

36. Minutes of Mississippi Synod (PCUS), November 19–21, 1918, 101–102.

37. "Pontotoc May Get School," *Pontotoc Sentinel*, May 30, 1918, 4.

38. "French Camp Academy Will Locate in Pontotoc," *Pontotoc Sentinel*, June 6, 1918, 4.

39. "C. A. College," *Pontotoc Sentinel*, June 13, 1918, 5.

40. Minutes of Mississippi Synod (PCUS), November 19–21, 1918, 106.

41. Ibid.

42. Ibid., 104–105.

43. Ibid., 106.

44. Ibid., 124.

45. "Pontotoc Schools Open," *Pontotoc Sentinel*, September 12, 1918, and Minutes of Mississippi Synod (PCUS), November 18, 1919, 210.

46. Minutes of Mississippi Synod (PCUS), November 18, 1919, 210–211.

47. Synod pled with the Sunday Schools and youth to provide $3,000 a year to Chickasaw, a sum the groups never reached. Often they gave only a few hundred dollars (compare Mississippi Synod Minutes 1921–1929). This contrasted sharply with the Women's Synodical's constant care of French Camp over the years (see footnote 26). Currie asked numerous times for better support for the school, but to no avail (compare Mississippi Synod Minutes 1920, 1927, and 1929). Consequently, the school went deeper and deeper into debt and, by 1928, had a yearly deficit of $23,000 (Synod Minutes, November 20, 1928, 39). In 1929, the citizens of Pontotoc voted to give the school $5,000 for three years if synod matched the amount (Synod Minutes, September 17–19, 1929, 32). Neither body made good on its pledge, so in 1930 synod voted to close the school (Synod Minutes, September 16–18, 1930, 22–23). Chickasaw still had $40,000 in debts outstanding which was not paid until seven years later, thus draining the assets of synod for other schools (Synod Minutes, September 7–8, 1937, 535). Chickasaw was finally sold in 1939 for $5,200 (Synod Minutes, September 28–29, 1939, 705).

48. Minutes of Mississippi Synod (PCUS), October 3–5, 1922, 14; Synod Minutes, November 13–15, 1923, 27 and 30; and Synod Minutes, November 11–13, 1924, 29.

49. Minutes of Mississippi Synod (PCUS), November 11–13, 1924, 32.

50. Minutes of Mississippi Synod (PCUS), November 15, 1921, 18–19.

51. Minutes of Mississippi Synod (PCUS), September 15–17, 1931, 32.

52. Minutes of Mississippi Synod (PCUS), November 16–18, 1926, 9.

53. "Report of the Executive Committee on Christian Education and Ministerial Relief to the General Assembly," Minutes of Mississippi Synod (PCUS), November 16–18, 1926, 16.

54. Minutes of Mississippi Synod (PCUS), October 4–6, 1927, 31 and 34–35.

55. Minutes of Mississippi Synod (PCUS), October 4–6, 1927, 35.

56. Minutes of Mississippi Synod (PCUS), November 20, 1928, 4–5. Sam McBride died in a tragic accident while helping build the new administration building. (Ibid., 30.) The school had hardly recovered from the loss of McBride and his excellent leadership when the stock market crashed on Black Friday.

57. Minutes of Mississippi Synod (PCUS), September 17–19, 1929, 35.

58. Livingston and Rich, *A Treasure on the Trace*, 163.

59. Minutes of Mississippi Synod (PCUS), September 15–17, 1931, 33.

60. Livingston and Rich, *A Treasure on the Trace*, 163–164.

61. Minutes of Mississippi Synod (PCUS), September 13–15, 1932, 107.

62. Minutes of Mississippi Synod (PCUS), September 11–13, 1934, 216–217.

63. Minutes of Mississippi Synod (PCUS), April 14, 1939, 680.

64. Thompson, *Presbyterians in the South*, 3:185.

Minutes of the Synod of Mississippi
Called Meeting
Jackson, Mississippi
March 7, 1950

This is the original document with formatting and grammar left intact.

Report of Committee on French Camp Academy

At the last meeting of the Synod held in Memphis, Tenn. we learned of the financial crisis at French Camp Academy. After lengthy discussion the following action was taken and here we quote the minutes of Synod:

"That Synod authorize the Board of Trustees of French Camp Academy to borrow money to operate on this scholastic year, and that a committee be appointed to work with the Board of Trustees of French Camp Academy to study the entire matter of the school's present condition and future development and to report to a later meeting of Synod. The motion was duly seconded, discussed and carried.

It was then voted to instruct the Moderator to appoint a committee of fifteen to work with the Board of Trustees as indicated above.

The Moderator later on appointed the following committee:

Laymen: Major H. S. Johnson, Starkville; Messrs. W. J. Love, Columbus; W. A. Henry, Yazoo City; Hindman Doxey, Holly Springs; George McLean, Tupelo; J. A. Carpenter, Okolona; Hugh S. Potts, Kosciusko; C. H. Snell, Summit; C. C. Clark, West Point; and Ellis C. Woolfork, Tunica.

Ministers: R. S. Woodson, Yazoo City; R. A. Bolling, Cleveland; Sam Patterson, Leland; Erskine Jackson, Kosciusko; and T. Russell Nunan, Greenville, Convener.

The Committee met in joint session with the Board of Trustees of French Camp Academy on November 15, 1949 at French Camp, Miss.

Synod's Committee elected Rev. Sam Patterson as Secretary, and T. Russell Nunan as permanent chairman.

The School Officials, Rev. J. Hayden Laster, President, and Mrs. Margaret Kimball, Bookkeeper sat with the Trustees and Committee.

Our first course of inquiry was in reference to the financial standing of the School for the present year, which included the summer school.

The figures of the bookkeeper revealed first that the school was going into the red $152.09 a week or an average of $21.72 a day.

Secondly, the record of contributions revealed that gifts to the school had almost doubled over the previous year.

Gifts for the Church Year 1948 up to November 30th amounted to $2,717.14 while gifts up to November 15 for the present church year amounted to $4,328.89.

According to the latest report of the bookkeeper, receipts from students, the School District, Churches, and individuals equal necessary expenditures.

As you receive the rest of this report this fact must be kept in mind.

The school receives financial support from five sources: 1. Student fees. 2. School District at the rate of $8.00 per student—these students commute by bus. 3. Endowment which at present amounts to $25,300.00. 4. Church Benevolences. 5. The gifts of individuals—both of the Presbyterian Church and of other churches.

A survey of several years' audits reveals that the financial life of the school has fluctuated between the red column of financial death and the black column of financial health.

The audit of June 14th, 1940 through June 18th, 1941 reveals that the school made a net profit of $3,199.50.

The audit of June 19th, 1942, through May 27, 1943 reveals that the school made a profit of $778.94.

The audit of May 28, 1943, through June 23, 1944 reveals that the net loss before depreciation amounted to $2,005.07, and after the depreciation amounted to $4,881.79.

The audit of June 1, 1947 through May 31, 1948 reveals a net gain of $408.71.

The audit of June 1, 1948 through May 31, 1949 reveals a net loss of $3,222.09 before depreciation and $6,699.40 after depreciation.

Furthermore, we found that the Academy paid $5.75 per month per student to the grammar school for students of that age under our care.

In concluding this part of the report dealing with finances may we submit as information the findings of the sub-committee of Synod's Committee on French Camp, which was appointed to study the finances of the school.

"To Synod's Committee on the study of French Camp Academy:

Your sub-committee on Finance met at French Camp on December 20, 1949, at eleven o'clock in the morning. Present were C. C. Clark, C. H. Snell, W. A. Henry, and E. L. Jackson, who served as substitute chairman. Also present—T. Russell Nunan, and Mr. J. W. Cocke, who is the auditor for the Academy.

After full discussion and as careful considerations as time would permit, the sub-committee adopted the following:

We are amazed that our Academy at French Camp is getting along as well as it is! The patient is certainly getting along as well financially as can be expected.

In the light of the information before us we recommend:

1. That we try to work out a meeting between our Committee and the interested persons of the school districts served by the Academy for the purpose of discussing the cost of instruction at the Academy, with a view of asking them to assume a larger share of the per capita cost.
2. That the Academy be put on a definite operating budget.
3. That the Committee consider recommending to the Synod the raising of sufficient funds to put the physical plant in good and attractive condition.
4. That, in order for the Board of Trustees and the Administration of FCA to have time to work out the policies for the new F.C.A., we urge the churches to continue their present financial contributions, and increase them if possible.

5. That since the response to a special French Camp Day in Central Mississippi Presbytery was so fine, the other Presbyteries be asked to consider such a special day."

Respectfully submitted,
E. L. Jackson

Recommendations:

1. That the number of members of the Board of Trustees of French Camp Academy be set at eighteen instead of the number of sixteen; that three of these be men from three other Protestant denominations other than Presbyterian and the remainder be lay members and ministers of the Presbyterian Church, U.S.

SAM PATTERSON'S LETTER OF RESIGNATION
TO FCA BOARD OF TRUSTEES
December 27, 1966

This is the original document with formatting and grammar left intact.

TO THE BOARD OF TRUSTEES, French Camp Academy – Dec. 27, 1966

Last October I was led to give my resignation as president of French Camp Academy to the Executive Board, that this Board might determine the next steps in bringing this to the Board as a whole. It was decided that a) the matter rest for a period of two months, and b) that a meeting of the whole Board be called on this matter in later December or early January.

My action in resigning was not due to impulse or to dissatisfaction with the school or the Board, but was the result of many, many months of prayer and careful consideration. This action is taken in the conviction that God has led in the matter and that the best interests of the Academy are primarily involved.

I told the Executive Board that I felt the best thing I could have done for the Academy was to come to it in 1950, and that now I could see that the best thing I could do for this work in 1966 is to leave the presidency.

I would like here to present the reasons behind this action and would want the Board to understand that I have not made this decision in order to take another work in a specific sense. I do not know what God has for me in the future, apart from evangelism, but I have no specific plans. Feeling that God has led in this matter of my resignation, I am convinced that He has definite plans both for the Academy on the one hand and for me on the other, and I am pleased to trust Him in this matter.

1. First of all, if a change in the administrative leadership of the Academy is to be made, it is better for this to take place at a time when the school is facing no major problems, but rather seems to be making progress, possesses a fine staff, department heads, and vice-president, and is being encouraged by extensive facility improvements. Our last fiscal year was the best in the history of the school. The strain of the increased enrollment is telling financially, yet at this mid-year point the income and expense account are about even.

2. It is increasingly evident from the nature of the work we carry on, and the increasing growth of the school, that a full-time-plus president is needed. I am not able to be this now. Health and other God-given responsibilities prevent this.

3. It is probable that increasing controversy regarding the Reformed Theological Seminary will come, very likely immediately after the next General Assembly in June. The Academy will be hurt by my inescapable involvement in the controversy. This must not be. We have had a miraculous unanimity within our Board. The school enjoys a growing family of supporters. I feel that up to this point I have made a constructive contribution to the school. I fear that from this point on this will not be so.

4. The fact exists that there is a need for administrative accomplishment here that I am not able to give. I have been used of God to win support for the school, increase

its facilities, and cultivate an evangelistic, spiritual emphasis in the life of the school. However, our "product," in terms of young lives sent out from here, is far short of that which satisfies me. I believe that the tremendous need here now is for the development on the campus of a strong Christian Education program, including and going beyond the present program. The need is for a leadership with the PRACTICAL and the SPIRITUAL qualifications to take the raw material of a good staff and a growing student body and develop a far more productive program. I have done for French Camp what I believe my abilities can do. What needs now to be done, I am not gifted for.

My life and love has been so entwined with French Camp Academy that it would be impossible to put words to my own feelings in this matter. Nevertheless, I do have a sense of rejoicing in the knowledge that this is God's special work and that under your supervision His man and plan will become evident. I further rejoice to know that He has plans for my further ministry and will make these known in His way and time.

For the above stated reasons, and in the spirit of deepest affection and gratitude to all of you colleagues, I submit my resignation as president of French Camp Academy, asking that it become effective by February 15, 1966.

At this point I would desire to make the following observations.

1. I believe that you will find God's man by June 1, and I believe that he ought to come into a position that has been vacant for a few months. There are reasons why this will be of advantage to the new president, and to those who on the staff move from service under one administration to another.

2. The Academy now has a steady, dependable vice president, and three very able department heads who already have been carrying on the operation in able fashion, who can continue the operation without interruption between Feb. 15, and the arrival of a new president. I would suggest that Mr. Allen carry on under the supervision of a committee of the Executive Committee, such as Mr. Potts, Mr. Jackson, and Mr. Taylor, two of which could meet weekly with Mr. Allen to keep in touch with the work and give any counsel needed.

3. I would, if the Board felt this to be wise, spend the time available to visit widely over Miss., Tenn., and Ala., calling on our strong supporters and friends to acquaint them with the plans for advancement by the Academy and to encourage them in the continuance of support, giving assurance of my own continued support of the school and its work.

Respectfully submitted,

Sam C. Patterson

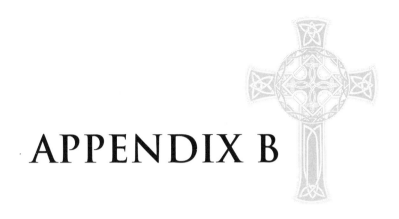

·APPENDIX B

REFORMED
THEOLOGICAL
SEMINARY

*All of the documents in this appendix are original
and have not been edited in any way.*

DO WE NEED AN INFALLIBLE BIBLE?

The Presbyterian Outlook

Volume 144   December 24, 1962   Number 47

Since in many Presbyterian situations questions underlying this inquiry are frequently encountered, several theological professors have been asked to give their respective comments in reply. Now that they have given their responses, *Outlook* readers are invited to make their comments on the question, keeping their replies brief and to the point.

EDITORS.

SOME QUESTIONS ABOUT THE QUESTION
Kenneth J. Foreman
Professor Emeritus Of Doctrinal Theology
Louisville Presbyterian Theological Seminary

1.   What is meant by an "infallible" Bible? What is usually meant by this expression is the meaning assumed here: a Bible without errors of any sort—grammatical, geographical, historical, scientific, numerical or moral. A genuine discrepancy of course involves an error, for of the two discrepant statements one or the other must not be true. Many believers in this theory about the Bible, when such discrepancies are pointed out as they cannot explain without arguments that sound suspiciously twisted, resort to the proposition that whatever errors may be found in our Bibles, there was none in the original manuscripts. This affirmation cannot be proved, it cannot be disproved. It will be worth discussing when we have the originals. But if this theory be true, it follows that we do not need an infallible Bible, for since the first copy wore out, the infallible Bible has been lost. In God's providence, this loss occurred. If we had needed it, isn't it likely that God would have seen to it that we had one?

2.   What is meant by "need"? I take it this means more than "would like to have …" It means there is some harm or danger that can be warded off only if we possess what we say we need. Whether we need an infallible Bible depends on the purpose of the Bible itself. Take a hammer for an illustration. If I use a hammer I need one with a solid head. I need that because I use the hammer to drive nails. It might as well be a dozen eggs if the head is light and loose. But do I need a hammer with a diamond-studded handle? I do not, because I don't want the hammer for decoration.

3.   So I ask: Why do we need the Bible? To make the way to God simple and the life in God real, someone has said. To introduce me to God, my fellowmen and myself. Do I need an infallible Bible to convict me of sin? To draw me to Christ? To guide me

on my earthly road? To lighten my death-bed? That is what the Bible is needed for. So we ask now in particular: Is it necessary that all the numbers in the Bible shall be precise and accurate in order for me to find Christ there? Is it necessary that I shall know exactly what happened, to whom and in what order, when Peter denied Jesus, before I can be led to repentance? Is it necessary for the Bible's geography to be above reproach before I can put my trust in the God of the Bible? If Saint Paul misquoted a passage in the Old Testament, does that make him a liar then and there, or does it make him a deluded man when he describes what Christ means to him? Must the Song of Solomon be without error (though what it means to have an errorless love song I don't know) if I am to believe with the Psalmist that God gives "songs in the night"? Here is a large library written by many authors, a number of them anonymous. If one of these writers make a slip, does that discredit all the rest?

The more such questions are asked, the more absurd it appears to affirm that we NEED an infallible Bible.

GOD IS INFALLIBLE
James H. Gailey, Jr.
Professor of Old Testament
Columbia Theological Seminary

The ordination vow taken by ministers, ruling elders and deacons of the Presbyterian Church, U.S., affirms belief in the Scriptures as the Word of God, "the only infallible rule of faith and practice." And the Confession of Faith, Chapter I, section 9, declares, "The infallible rule of interpretation of Scripture, is the Scripture itself ...." Do these intimations of infallibility in the Scripture indicate a hidden "vitamin" which is a necessity for the Christian life?

Though the Confession of Faith declares that the Lord Jesus Christ is the only Mediator of the covenant of grace, it is clear that the Scripture presents the word of life which is God's offer of salvation. Human agents also serve to proclaim the word of grace from the forgiving God to sin-cursed man. It is nevertheless clear that the need of man is met only through the redemptive work of Jesus Christ and through the work of the Holy Spirit within him.

Final Authority
God is infallible. Working in the persons of Christ and the Holy Spirit, he saves men from their sin. There is no evidence that the infallibility of God has been communicated to those who preach the redemptive message, and the uniqueness of the Bible consists principally in its special reliability in declaring "what man is to believe concerning God and what duty God requires of man." But this does not mean that every statement in the Scripture is complete or incapable of being misunderstood. Some parts of the Bible must be understood in the light of others. When the writers of the Confession of Faith used the word "infallible" they intended to assert that the Scripture is the final authority beyond which the church can make no appeal, since it is in Scripture that God has spoken.

The Bible is the authoritative and inspired written witness and instrument of God's redemptive work. In spite of difficulties of text and interpretation it speaks with the authority of direct experience with God; it reports honestly what has happened for man's salvation; it provides the confirmation of a variety of witnesses; most of all, since it is God's word, it is susceptible to use by the Spirit of God in the communication of the message of redemption to succeeding generations of men. The church has also been such a witness and instrument of God's redemptive work, but has lacked the special reliability of the Bible which comes partly through its written form in a closed canon and partly through the work of God's Spirit in inspiring its writing.

Human Limitations

It is God who is infallible. Because of the human limitations of readers and interpreters of the Bible the only meaningful sense in which the word "infallible" can be used for the Bible is to assert its authority. Why not then say that the Bible is the inspired and authoritative word provided by our infallible God? Why say "infallible" Bible?

THE BIBLE IS AUTHORITATIVE
James L. Mays
Professor of Biblical Interpretation
Union Theological Seminary

In the usual discussions of this question, the term "infallible" is taken to mean "completely without error of any kind" or "absolutely correct in every place and way." In this case, the answer to the question must be a clear "No" – and that for two reasons. Such a need would put us in an impossible situation as a believing church, because we do not have such an infallible book. And, if we did have one, we fallible men would not know what to do with it.

Presbyterians are supposed to build faith on the Bible, to get what is said in theology from Scriptures. And that includes belief about the Bible. We have to look at it and examine it to learn what is right to say in faith. It is presumptuous to refuse to look and to tell God what we need without considering what he has, in his grace and wisdom, given us.

When we examine the Bible, it appears that, whatever our opinion, God does not think we need an infallible book. Chapters one and two of Genesis put the order of creation differently. Facts about Israel's life in the wilderness are variously told in the Pentateuch. Kings and Chronicles report the history of Israel and Judah in different ways. There are predictions in the prophets which were not fulfilled literally in Israel's history as the prophets had expected them to be. Matthew, Mark, and Luke vary in their accounts of what our Lord said and did. What we see on reading the Bible carefully does not lead us to exclaim, "Ah! An infallible book." If I insist, then, that I "need an infallible Bible," I must be doing it because I am bound to some kind of theology which does not take the Bible as its authority.

What Interpreters?

Moreover, if we had a book whose value consisted of its infallibility, we could not use this value unless there were infallible men to go along with it. As soon as anyone reads and interprets the Bible, its words are qualified in the reader's thoughts and words by his fallibility. Do those who claim an infallible scripture presume that their interpretation is infallibly true? The Roman Church allows this prerogative only to the Pope speaking in very special circumstances, and it does so then because of a dependence on an infallible rule of faith which leads to the creation of an infallible voice to speak to the church. Pope Gregory VII used Jeremiah 48:10 to justify the terrible Inquisition. Protestants at times have used texts of which they thought they had infallible grasp to persecute other men. The illusion of men that they have in their possession an infallible truth brings on the delusion of absolute power which corrupts true faith. The truth of the Bible is God himself, and therefore it is a truth which binds us to God and keeps us in our position of sinful, finite men who must live humbly and trustingly—because we only see through a glass darkly and walk by faith, not by sight. Actually, "infallible" is not a very useful word; it raises the wrong issue in the wrong way as we speak about the Bible and our faith.

Its Right and Power

What we do have is an authoritative Bible which is the only rule to guide us in knowing what to believe as faith in God, and what to do as obedience to God. It is authoritative in that it has the right and power to rule our believing. The Bible has the right to define and shape Christian faith because it is the record of God's revelation of himself and his will to the men who are his witnesses, the prophets and apostles. The Bible has the power to create and sustain faith because God acts through and in the witness by his Holy Spirit to convince and to convert our hearts.

The authority of the Bible is best commended to the world, not by a fearful defense of its infallibility, but by lives which show the reality of that authority through strong trust and selfless obedience.

"SHOW US A SIGN!"
John F. Jansen
Acting Dean and Professor of
New Testament Interpretation
Austin Presbyterian Theological Seminary

All Christians believe that only through the Bible do we have access to the living Word of God. Some Christians go on to insist that this can happen only if we have a Bible without any errors or discrepancies. They insist that this is the only way to safeguard the Voice of God.

It seems to me that this demand for an inerrant Bible is not unlike the demand for signs that Jesus' contemporaries put to him so often. Show us a sign—then we will believe! This demand came not only from those who sought to discredit him. It came also from his friends and followers. But to both Jesus replies, "Unless you see signs and wonders you will not believe!" Always he makes it clear that the crucial sign is the sign of the Son of Man. To ask for other signs in advance, to demand other supports, to set conditions for believing—is not faith in him.

First, to Listen

Similarly, it seems pointless and futile to demand a Bible other than the Bible we actually have. If Mark's chronology of the temple cleansing is different from that of John, does that mean that Jesus Christ cannot speak to us through both accounts? Have we the right to ask for some inerrant uniformity before we are ready to listen? Can we set the terms? In plain fact, the church cannot guarantee or prove the foundation of her faith either to her own members or to the world. The church lives by listening, by trusting, by obeying.

Let us continue the analogy. Someone may object that, after all, Jesus Christ did give miracle signs. Indeed he did—and he does. But the signs he gave, and the signs he still gives, are not those that his followers try to set as preconditions. In the days of his flesh our Lord did not bypass human weakness or scorn imperfect disciples. Nor does he now obliterate or bypass the very human character of the biblical testimony. The sign he gives—the sign that matters—is the Lord himself. He meets us in the Bible—and that is enough. When we are content with that Sign, we find that the Bible is not less but more than what we expected. We find that the Lord does not need to talk at "long distance" in order to address us. "It is not with angels that he is concerned," says an epistle, but with men—real men.

"For our knowledge is imperfect and our prophecy is imperfect...." It wasn't a biblical "critic" who said that. It was an apostle of Jesus Christ.

SAM'S LETTERS TO
SEMINARY PRESIDENTS
AND THEIR RESPONSES

January 16, 1963

Dr. Frank H. Caldwell
Office of the President
Louisville Theological Seminary
109 E. Broadway
Louisville 2, Ky.

Dear Dr. Caldwell:

I believe this is the first time I have had occasion to write to you during my twenty some-odd years in the ministry of our church, and I write with a genuine sense of appreciation for a stirring address I heard you make many years ago when I was at a young people's conference.

Please believe me when I say that this letter is not written in any sense of antagonism. It is written in a deep sense of concern.

You have, no doubt, already read the enclosed articles published in the *Presbyterian Outlook*, one of which was written by Dr. Foreman, professor emeritus of Louisville Seminary.

I write to ask the following questions:

1)   Does Louisville Seminary have a clearly defined position regarding the nature of and the infallibility of the Scriptures, which would set forth the seminary's interpretation of the teaching of the Confession of Faith on these matters?

2)   Could a prospective student, applying for enrollment in Louisville Seminary, have from the seminary prior to enrollment a clear-cut statement regarding the position held by and taught by the Seminary relative to the nature and the infallibility of the Scriptures?

3)   If the answer to the above is affirmative, could I be provided statement such as would be given to prospective students making such an inquiry?

I feel that you would agree that an institution dedicated to our Lord Jesus Christ and the training of young lives in His name, will always be delighted to bear testimony to its convictions and position regarding these things.

Cordially yours,

Sam C. Patterson

January 21, 1963

Rev. Sam C. Patterson
French Camp Academy
French Camp, Mississippi

Dear Sam:

Your letter of January 16 has come to me today.

I appreciate the spirit in which you have written, but I must confess that I do not understand your great concern about these articles which appeared in the Dec. 24 issue of the *Outlook*.

The answer to the questions posed in your letter is that the seminary does not have such a faculty-approved, or Board-approved, statement of the institution's interpretation of these matters.

As you well know, almost any company of students of theology can argue almost indefinitely on an exactly satisfactory interpretation of practically any theological doctrine of significance. While, therefore, I would assume that various members of our faculty would prefer to change a word or a phrase here and there, I am fairly confident that our faculty would stand on the basically clear statements and implications which Dr. Foreman wrote as the first 31 pages of Volume I of *The Laymen's Commentary* as an "Introduction to the Bible."

In any case, if an inquiring student were to request something in writing which would represent our institutional position in approaching Biblical studies, I would refer him to that document.

With warm personal regards, I am

Cordially yours,

Frank H. Caldwell
President

January 16, 1963

Dr. James A. Jones
Office of the President
Union Theological Seminary
Richmond, Virginia

Dear Dr. Jones:

Please believe me when I say that this letter is not written in a spirit of antagonism.

It is written in a spirit of deep concern, as a graduate of Union Theological Seminary.

I have before me the article written by Dr. James L. Mays, professor at Union, appearing in the December 24, issue of the *Presbyterian Outlook*.

I am sure you have read the article, but in the event it has escaped you I am enclosing a copy of it.

This is written to ask two questions:

1)   Does the position taken by Dr. Mays in this article, which generally discounts the infallibility of the Scriptures, represent the position of Union Theological Seminary regarding the Scriptures?

2)   If his statement is not a presentation of the conviction held and taught at Union Seminary, do you have such a conviction or position, and if so what is it?

I feel that any institution that is dedicated to our Lord Jesus Christ and to the training of young lives in the doctrines of the church would be delighted to be called upon at any time to set forth its position regarding the Word of God, the Bible, and I am led to believe, from all I know of you, that this would earnestly be your sentiment in the matter.

Cordially yours,

Sam C. Patterson

January 25, 1963

The Reverend Samuel C. Patterson,
French Camp Academy,
French Camp, Mississippi

My dear Mr. Patterson:

Please let me thank you for your letter of January 16. I appreciate the candor with which you have written and the spirit in which the questions are posed with reference to the article by Professor Mays and the "conviction held and taught" at Union Seminary. I shall try to answer the issues you have raised as specifically and as quickly as I know how to do. Of course, there are limitations imposed by correspondence which may suggest to you a fragmentary dealing with the subject. This, I am sure, you will understand and appreciate.

The first question you posed affirms that the position taken by Professor Mays "discounts the infallibility of the Scriptures". The statement which he has written asserts that "infallibility is a fact". I cannot see, from the perspective determined by the four articles published in the *Outlook*, how any other position can be maintained. The question in the *Outlook*, as you will recall, was specifically "Do we need an infallible Bible?" The actualities of Biblical scholarship, proceeding from whatever theological positions, assert that "infallibility" is a non-tenable position simply from the evidence at hand, evidence that is in the Bible itself. And if the Church in our day is to maintain – as I for one believe it must maintain – the definitive nature of the Bible in determining the substance and consequences of the Christian Gospel, it must hold to that position in spite of, not because of, our possession of a book without evidences of "fallibility".

The whole matter turns, it appears to me, not on a doctrine of Biblical infallibility, but rather of "Biblical authority". The question is not "Do we have a volume without any contradictions, inconsistencies, or errors"; rather it is, "Do we have in the Bible a sufficient, determined, understandable, and communicable revelation of the work and word of God which declares the wonderfulness of the mysteries of His grace and the blessed consequences of sharing in the riches of His promises. The position of Union Theological Seminary is precisely that of the Standards of the Church – that the Bible principally teaches what man is to believe concerning God and what duty God requires of man; and that it is an infallible rule of faith and practice."

The "infallibility" in this instance appears to me to be precisely what the writers of the Confession were affirming – that in our knowledge of God and in our response to that knowledge, apprehended by faith, the Bible was to be the plumb line by which comprehension of truth and commitment of life must be measured. In such measures the wit of man's mind, the industry of man's labor, the energies of man's ideals are not to be left to their own devices. What God is, what He has done, what He proposes to do, and what He requires are matters which can be discerned definitively only by His revelation of Himself in the wondrous record of the Holy Bible.

Let me say that if this statement is not satisfactory, or if it raises questions which you would wish to discuss further, or if it poses problems with which you think we should wrestle here at the Seminary I shall appreciate your expressing such judgements in all frankness. We realize, as certainly you do, that we have a tremendous responsibility in preparing men who go out to preach the Gospel and to assume positions of responsibility in the life of the Church. They, as all people in our day, feel the acute pressures of the secular world, the deceits of wisdom which refuses to take God into account, the hazards of inadequate knowledge about the great truths of our faith, and the constant perils of claiming to know more about the Almighty than it is ever given to any man to know. As we share with them in the dilemmas created by the vocation upon which they enter, dilemmas which belong to the history of Christian witness in every generation, we are convinced that they need a pole star to keep them and us with the sense of direction which belongs to our following Christ and a sense of perspective with reference to their day by day routines. With every resource at our disposal we try to communicate the fact that the Holy Spirit, God's promised Guide into all truth, communicates to men individually and to all who await to hear the Eternal Will the substance and the implications of the Gospel through the Bible which still is kept "singularly pure" to accomplish the purposes our good Lord intended. We have other faults, I am sure, but I am convinced that the theological institutions of the Presbyterian Church in the United States are settled in this perspective – that what the Bible has affirmed as the fact and fruit of God's revelation of Himself is authoritative and must be proclaimed.

Once more I assure you of my gratitude for your letter. I wish we could find opportunity to discuss this whole affair which may, too easily and unexpectedly, and undeservedly, set brethren one against the other.

With most cordial good wishes, I am

Sincerely,

Jas. A. Jones
President
JAJ:m

January 16, 1963

Dr. David L. Stitt
Office of the President
Austin Theological Seminary
100 West 27th Street
Austin 5, Texas

Dear Dr. Stitt:

Please believe me when I say that this letter is not written in a spirit of antagonism. It is written in a spirit of deep concern.

You no doubt, have read the article written by Dr. Jansen, professor at Austin Seminary, and published in the Dec. 24, issue of the *Presbyterian Outlook*. The article is here enclosed.

I write to ask the following questions:

1) Does Austin Theological Seminary have a clear conviction and position regarding the infallibility of the Scriptures and the nature of the Scriptures which would set forth your (the seminary's) interpretation of the teaching of the Confession of Faith on these two matters?

2) Could a prospective student, applying for enrollment in Austin Seminary, have from the seminary in advance of enrollment a clear-cut statement regarding the position held and taught by the seminary relative to the nature of and the infallibility of the Scriptures?

3) If the answer to the above questions are in the affirmative, could I receive such a statement in view of the fact that this Academy from time to time has graduates attending college who plan to attend seminary, and with whom we will be giving counsel.

I believe that you would agree with me, that any institution dedicated to Jesus Christ and to the training of our youth, would be delighted to set forth for anyone its positive position and convictions regarding the nature and the infallibility of the Scriptures.

Cordially yours,

Sam C. Patterson

January 24, 1963

President Sam C. Patterson
French Camp Academy
French Camp, Mississippi

Dear Sam:

It is good to hear from you – our paths have not crossed in entirely too long a time. I hope that condition can be remedied one of these days.

Each professor at Austin Seminary, according to our constitution, is required to enter into the following engagements:

"I do sincerely believe the Scriptures of the Old and New Testaments to be the word of God, the only rule of faith and practice.

I do sincerely receive and adopt the Confession of Faith of the Presbyterian Church in the United States as faithfully exhibiting the doctrines taught in the Holy Scriptures.

I do sincerely approve of and adopt the form of government and discipline of the Presbyterian Church in the United States; and do solemnly engage not to teach anything that appears to me to contradict any doctrine contained in the Confession of Faith, not to oppose any of the fundamental principles of the Presbyterian Church government while I continue a professor in this Seminary."

Each member of our faculty subscribes to the above without question or demur.

Thank you for your letter and for copy of the articles which you included. We appreciate your inquiry – come out to see us.

Cordially,

David L. Stitt
President

January 16, 1963

Dr. J. McDowell Richards
Office of the President
Columbia Theological Seminary
Decatur, Georgia

Dear Dr. Richards,

Warm greetings to you and best wishes for this brand new year!

Please believe me when I say that this letter is not written in any spirit of antagonism. It is written in a spirit of deep concern.

No doubt, you have read the enclosed article written in the *Presbyterian Outlook* by Dr. Gailey, professor at Columbia.

I write to ask the following questions:

1)   Does Columbia Seminary have a clearly defined position or conviction regarding the nature of the Scriptures and regarding the infallibility of the Scriptures, which would set forth the Seminary's interpretation of the teaching of the Confession of Faith on these two matters?

2)   Could a prospective student, seeking to enroll at Columbia, receive from the seminary prior to enrollment a clear-cut statement regarding the position held and taught by the seminary relative to the nature and the infallibility of the Scriptures?

3)   If the answer to the above is in the affirmative, could I be provided with such a statement of position? While not a student seeking admission, I am in a responsible position in an academy which has sent students out, and will yet do so, into our church and seminaries.

I believe that you would agree with me that an institution dedicated to the Lord Jesus Christ and the teaching of His Word would be delighted for the opportunity to present its affirmation and clear-cut stand regarding the Word of God, the Bible.

Cordially yours,

Sam C. Patterson

January 25, 1963

Rev. Samuel C. Patterson, President
French Camp Academy
French Camp, Mississippi

Dear Mr. Patterson:

I am sorry that because of my absence from the office here for a number of days I have been delayed in answering your letter of January 16.

I appreciate the spirit of concern in which you have written and know full well that your letter would not be the result of any spirit of antagonism.

In answer to the question raised in your letter I would say that Columbia Theological Seminary has not undertaken to define its position regarding the nature of the Scriptures more exactly than does the ordination vow of our church which recognizes the Scriptures "as the Word of God, the only infallible rule of faith and practice."

It is my personal conviction that at the very least this statement indicates a belief in the "Doctrinal infallibility" of Scripture. To the best of my knowledge and belief there is no Professor of Columbia Seminary who holds a lower view of inspiration than this, and I am sure that Dr. Gailey did not intend to suggest a lower view. There are of course those who hold that the inspiration of Scripture involves "verbal inerrancy" but I do not understand that this view has ever been regarded by our Church as essential.

Indeed the late Dr. W. M. McPheeters, who believed in the "verbal inerrancy" of Scripture and was a strong defender of it, once told me that he thought those who framed our standards must have been divinely guided in the fact that they did not frame their statement in such a way as to require this view on the part of its ministry.

Because our Church does not require this view we have not felt that it should be required at Columbia Theological Seminary. At the same time it is our desire to emphasize the reality of inspiration and the full authority of Scriptures as our "Infallible rule of faith and practice." For this reason I regret very much the appearance of the article by Dr. Gailey in the context in which it appeared and have advised him as to my sentiments in the matter.

With personal esteem and every good wish, I am

Sincerely yours,

J. McDowell Richards
President

FIRST VISION OF RTS
Sam Patterson
3/1/63

*(Typed from hand-written notes made out on the "Saddle" of
pinnacle rock of the "Point", [Stout's or Nelson's Point],
Petit Jean Mountain, at 12:50 p.m., March 1, 1963)*

A PRACTICAL VISION WITH SPIRITUAL ENDS: Regarding the Providence of God that will, I believe, make this mountain "His mountain", and this "Point" a Cross-honoring cross-roads conference site, the power of which will encircle the Globe.

By the Grace of God, I consider this the first session of the French Camp Bible Conference, or Petit Jean Bible Conference!

Only the Lord and I are here. Yet, by His blessing and Providence, thousands will here, in days to come, meet His Son, hear His Word, and see the Cross!

From the human point of view, this Point is owned by the Episcopal Diocese of Arkansas, whose genial bishop, Bishop Robert R. Brown, Little Rock, told me that it would be useless to try to buy this property from them; that they had a grip on this land that they would never relinquish. I rejoiced!! Now only God, the true owner of this—and of all—could give this wonderful place for a holy ground where the Cross of Christ would tower, and His infallible Word be taught in all its beauty, power, and truth!

Hallelujah! As dear old C. T. Studd wrote, when all was humanly impossible, but the vision was in his eye: "Faith laughs at impossibilities, and cries: 'It shall be done'"!

I opened my Bible just now and it "fell" open upon 1 Cor. 2! What omen is this from God? Verse 2: "I am determined to know nothing among you save Jesus Christ, and Him crucified!" This will be the theme of this place and conference till Jesus comes! In my mind, for years, I have thought of the "Point" only with a Cross erected upon it.

Verses 4 & 5: Faith that is a demonstration of God's divine work, not man's enchanting arts! So 1) Shall this place be God's place of power demonstrated. 2) Shall this place be secured, provided, and given to us by God!

My Bible's pages just blew over to Romans 14 and my eyes fell upon: "For whatsoever is not of faith is sin." (v. 23). I cannot now sin against God by failing to, by faith, permit His power to give this place to Christ!

I claim for this—Psalm 121:1–2: "I will lift up mine eyes unto the hills (Petit Jean, this Point). From whence cometh my help? (Where can I get help to secure this place?) My help cometh from the Lord (is coming) which made (this place and) heaven and earth."

I claim Joshua's God for my God through Jehoshua Christ, and claim for Christ's people yet to be fed here that this place is (Joshua 1:1) "the land which I do give them…" I exult in the promise that "Every place that the sole of your foot shall tread upon, that have I given unto you" (Joshua 1:3). I will put my feet all over this place for Him!!! (Note: I did … in that I walked the length and breadth of the property that afternoon to survey and to claim for Christ.) I marvel in faith at verse 5: "There shall not any man be able to stand before thee…", and then "I will not fail thee nor forsake thee."

So will I (v. 6) be strong and of good courage, and divide this place and God's Book, as it shall be taught here, to this people!

I humbly accept the condition of loyalty to His Word (v. 8) as the condition of success and prosperity in this mission.

Back to 1 Cor. 2—verse 10 provides the blessing the Bible will be here at this place—where God will reveal His word unto us by His Spirit—"For the Spirit searcheth all things, yea, the deep things of God."

> SO—high on this Mountain,
> Deep in His Word,
> Thousands shall be blest,
> And Christ be adored!

For here God's Words, not man's (v. 13)—"the words…which the Holy Ghost teaches"—will bless, enliven, and send back to home, and out into the world's streams of life witnesses for the Saviour!

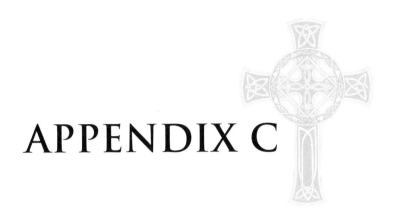

APPENDIX C

PCUS/PCA
CONTROVERSY

*All of the documents in this appendix are original
and have not been edited in any way.*

A Paper Seeking a Biblical Basis for the Conduct of Believers Who Are In An Erring Church

Sam Patterson
February 23, 1972

THE ISSUE

From Christ and the Apostles there comes to us in the New Testament warnings that in the course of time, and at the end of this present age, there will be grave departures within the church at the point of doctrine and conduct.

Matthew	7:15–20
	24:10–14
Acts	20:28–32
II Timothy	3:1–4
	4:1–4
II Peter	2:1–3
1 John	4:1

As we face today the tension caused by error and various approaches to apostasy in the church; as we face the possible or probable division within our own denomination, the ISSUE COULD BE STATED AS FOLLOWS:

What course does the true believer discover in Scripture for his course and conduct in the face of an erring, apostatizing, or even apostate church?

The purpose of this paper is not to attempt to prove or disprove various charges of apostasy in the church, and in our own denomination, but rather to address itself to the proper Biblical course for believers when their circumstances place them in a time of church apostasy.

PRESUPPOSITION PRINCIPLES

For folk of Reformed Faith our church, world, and life view is established and supported by two tremendous facts which must determine our outlook, attitude and conduct:

The Scriptures provide our only infallible guide.

The Sovereignty of God is the church's stay and support, forbidding our "playing God" with the church, but encouraging our obeying God in regard to the church.

1. The Scriptures are to be appealed to in this issue as "the only rule to direct us."

We may not appeal too much to church history but to the church's Book. We may not appeal too much to the Reformers, etc., as to their course, but directly to the Book they brought back to guide us.

As we contemplate a possible division, or separation within the denomination in which the Sovereign Providence of God has placed us, we may not appeal to our discomfort and unhappiness ("I'm fed up," "I'm tired of fighting," "I've taken all I can," etc.). To be led by these things can result in petulant disobedience to God. Our feelings must be, in themselves, set aside that we may appeal wholly and directly to the Scriptures for guidance.

In our appeal to Scriptures we must seek to:
- a. Avoid seeking to support a personal prejudice.
- b. Avoid using a "proof-text" approach, rather than seeking the full sweep of Biblical truth in the matter.
- c. Affirm our Reformed belief that the Church is one in the Old Testament and the New Testament and recognize that precept and example in both Testaments are applicable.

2. The Sovereignty of God assures the church of His sufficient power, wisdom and concern for the fulfillment of His purposes in the church of His Son. By His sovereign providence we have been placed as ministers in the Presbyterian Church U.S. When we took our ordination vows we bore clear evidence that: (a) we believed the Presbyterian Church U.S. to be a true part of the true Body of Christ on earth, (b) we believed He was placing us in this part of the Body of Christ, and (c) we were obligating ourselves to seek the purity and peace of this church with zeal.

We may not play god but rather obey God in our conduct of the affairs of His Church, or of our own ministry.

Our Sovereign God will guide, chasten, shape, shame, revive, withdraw power from, and otherwise deal with the church in the course of her periods of obedience and disobedience. It is for Him alone to dispose of her and to predestine her. It is for us to obey Him in her and set at doing it earnestly.

Keeping constantly before us His sovereign power and purpose will contain our impatience so we can, with patience and with obedience, look in the Bible for His way for us.

SOME SCRIPTURE CONSIDERED

In seeking to find our course in the face of apostasy and error within the church, the following Scriptures are suggested as having some bearing:

EXODUS 32

Perhaps we can call this the initial apostasy of the church. Delivered by God from Egyptian bondage under the leadership of Moses, in a temporary absence of Moses, Israel cried: "Up, make us gods who will go before us..." (32:1) They proceeded to make and worship a golden calf. God tested Moses with, "...let me alone... that I may consume them; but of you I will make a great nation." In other words, "Let me scrap these and start a new church with you." God was pleased with Moses' reply and did not consider it to be compromise with evil. (Exodus 32:11–14) He reminds God that they are His people, erring as they are, and appeals for God's covenant providence and blessing for them. No "new church" came of this but chastening did!

NUMBERS 14

Perhaps this could be called the second apostasy of the church. At Kadesh, promised success by God, the people of God are commanded to go in and take the promised land. They react in fear of the people to be encountered and rebel against God and Moses. Moses, Aaron, Caleb and Joshua appeal to Israel to obey God and trust Him. All is to no avail. God is disobeyed. Moses' leadership is rejected. The people almost stone the four faithful men. God again speaks of abandoning Israel and starting a new church with

Moses, "How long will they despise me … not believe me? I will strike them … and make of you a greater and mightier nation."

Again Moses evidently pleases God by mediating for Israel, appealing to the fact that God's honor and name are at stake in seeing Israel through; appealing to the power of God, and His promise of patience, "saying, 'The Lord is slow to anger and abounding in steadfast love, forgiving iniquity and transgression, but will no wise clear the guilty …'" He then says, "Pardon the iniquity of this people, I pray Thee, according to the greatness of Thy steadfast love, according as Thou has forgiven this people, from Egypt even until now." (Numbers 14:13–19)

God did not consider this a compromise by Moses. It pleased Him. No new church emerged. However, a wilderness journey for many years stretched ahead of this disobedient church. Moses, Aaron, Caleb and Joshua went right along with the erring ones in this wilderness way, though they did not go along with their rebellion. They were at once separated from disobedient Israel by their faithfulness, but in and among them in their ministry.

DANIEL 9

God's people, because of their deep and persistent disobedience to Him, were chastened in part with the Babylonian captivity. Daniel had been, we may be sure, a faithful servant of God, not sharing in the evil ways of the people … and yet he ended in Babylon as a captive because of the sins of the people. There, instead of renouncing the people of God in their sins, he prayed to God on their behalf and gave us one of the greatest prayers of pathos and passion in the Bible. Though not a party to their delinquency he identifies himself with them and their sins, appeals for mercy and concludes, "O my God incline Thine ear and hear; open Thine eyes and behold our desolations, and the city which is called by Thy name; for we do not present our supplications before Thee on the ground of our righteousness, but on the ground of Thy great mercy. O Lord, hear; O Lord, forgive; O Lord, give heed and act; delay not, for Thy own name's sake, O my God, because Thy city and Thy people are called by Thy name."!

What a prayer! Is this in contrast to how we express our concern for the erring church today? Do we love, intercede for, identify with, assume our share of guilt in, and seek to keep both ourselves and our God related to her?

The approach of Daniel in an apostate church seems to be the pattern of God's men in the Old Testament church.

JEREMIAH

Representative of the prophets of the Old Testament is Jeremiah. The heart-beat of his problem and purpose is found in the book by his name.

The prophets, to some degree, seem to be INDEPENDENT forces the Lord raised up to counter, in part, the erring and evil priesthood and kings. The priest and kings often disliked the prophets whom they could not control and who criticized them. Jeremiah was a prophet of a priestly family.

Though independent in mission, God never used the prophets to start new bodies, churches, etc.

Jeremiah is a sample. Faced with a situation in Israel comparable to our situation today in the church, he wanted to quit, or get out, even wished he had not been born. Yet God refused to let him have an exit, kept him IN that erring people until at last he was with them way down in Egypt as God's voice in their midst, though God, through Jeremiah, had forbidden the move to Egypt.

ZEPHANIAH 3

Last of the minor prophets before the captivity, Zephaniah was unsparing in his pronouncements regarding Judah, Jerusalem and other nations. Chapter 3 presents what is considered to be a "Woe" against Jerusalem. We might think of Jerusalem as the "headquarters" of the church of the Old Testament, the place of the church leaders. "Woe to you, rebellious and defiled, the oppressing city" (3:1) are his opening words. He mentions "her officials" (v.3), "her judges" (v3), "her prophets" (v.4), and "her priests" (v.4) charging great delinquency (perhaps apostasy would be appropriate). Yet he makes the amazing statement in v.5, "The Lord <u>within her</u> is righteous, he does no wrong ..." In v.8 God says, "Therefore wait for me." The Sovereign God then states His decision (v.8) and says (v.11–12) "... for then I will remove from your midst your proudly exultant ones, and you shall no longer be haughty in my Holy Mountain. For I will leave in the midst of you a people humble and lowly. They shall seek refuge in the name of the Lord..." Then, "The King of Israel is in your midst ..." (v.15) and "The LORD, your God, is in your midst" (v.17). <u>God IN THE MIDST of an erring people!</u>

The questions seem to be: Do we have a right to withdraw from our church until God withdraws from it ... if He does? Do we find in His word the counsel as to how to remain in an erring people who are called by His name, yet not follow their evil ways, but rather seek with zeal to intercede for, correct, denounce and witness to as needed the people among whom God has placed us?

MATTHEW 7:15–20

On moving through the New Testament, this is the first passage dealing with the prospect of false teachers in the church.

Christ's counsel is for the disciples to beware, watch for, and recognize false teachers as they arise. He declares that evil trees will be cut down and burned. Who is to cut them down and burn them? Are disciples to do it, or does God do it? The Epistles call for discipline by the church. The Scriptures below (Matthew 13) reveal how God at the end of the age cuts out the evil and burns it. At any rate here the issue is separation by elimination, not departure.

MATTHEW 13:24–30, 36–43

Our Lord's parable of the wheat and the tares relates to the co-existence of farmer's wheat and the enemy-sown tares. The comparison is to the "Kingdom of God." The counsel is, "No (reweeding out the weeds) lest in gathering the weeds you root up the wheat along with them. Let both grow together until the harvest." (13:29–30)

"Kingdom," "field," "world" are used. The Kingdom in this world would be the church. The point of the parable is to show a truth about the <u>Kingdom in the world</u>, not just the world outside the Kingdom. In fact, in verse 41 the tares are reported to be taken by the angel reapers "<u>out of his Kingdom.</u>"

The wheat are the "sons of the Kingdom" (the Elect). The tares are the children of Satan. <u>God</u> will make the separation at the end of the age.

Without carrying an interpretation to the extreme, it is clear that no encouragement is here given to division in the church.

MATTHEW 13:47–50

Again our Lord uses a parable to indicate that the Kingdom of Heaven in this age, on earth (the church) will catch into it good and bad fish (saved and unsaved, elect and non-elect). While the fishing was going on no division of the two kinds was forced. After the boat was ashore (the age ended) the separation was made by the angels.

One reflects at this point that when man enforces division in the church, divisions have resulted in which TRUE brethren are divided, and in each group are some who may not truly be brethren.

MATTHEW 23:37–39

Here our Lord announces that Jerusalem, earthly headquarters at that time of God's earthly church, will be a house "forsaken" and "desolate." This probably refers to the setting aside of the Israel-of-unbelief, which would reject Christ before and after His Resurrection, that Paul sets forth in Romans 11. Both Christ and Paul allow an "until" provision, indicating a time (at the Lord's return?) when Israel and Jerusalem will turn to faith.

The point here is possibly this: In the New Testament we do not have an instance of one group of people who profess faith in Christ separating from another group who profess faith in Him to set up another fellowship or church. Christ, in setting aside unbelieving Israel, is anticipating the separation which surfaces in the Book of Acts in which believers in Christ begin to part with those who never believed, or professed to, in Israel. (See Acts 19:8–9)

We do have instances of false disciples of Christ leaving Him and those who do truly believe in Him. (See John 6:66.)

ACTS 20:28–32

Paul counsels the elders of Ephesus regarding the sure rise of "wolves, who would mislead and seek to draw away the sheep." He urges the elders to "take heed" and to "be alert" and so guard the flock. There is no positive counsel to divide in the event that the "wolves" have partial success. The thrust is that they should keep false men exposed, and to try to keep them out.

ROMANS 16:17–18

Paul appeals to the "brethren" to "take note" of those in the fellowship "who create dissensions and difficulties in opposition to the doctrine which you have been taught." This could be both doctrine as to gospel truth and also doctrine as to proper godly conduct. At any rate the ones going against the apostolic teachings are branded the causers of division. In this sense those departing from the doctrine of the Apostles make themselves the causers of division. Nevertheless, to the true brethren, Paul indicates objection to dissension and division. Where there are present the troublesome folk referred to above, Paul tells the "brethren" not to follow, or go along with them, or to encourage them. Rather stay away from them. All this can be done without leaving the general fellowship of that church and starting another purer group across town. One need not read into this a command to divide the church. One dare not.

II CORINTHIANS 6:14–18

This was evidently not an attempt by Paul to start another or second Corinthian Church. The separation called for here evidently has in mind that with the pagan world which did not ever profess to belong to Jesus or to belong to His fellowship.

It would be evident, too, that IF one did believe that this passage refers to a situation involving unbelievers and believers <u>within</u> the Christian fellowship or church, the counsel to separation would require that we be able to accurately judge those in the church we will separate from as being "Belial" (or of him), "unbelievers," given to "idols," and "unclean."

I CORINTHIANS 5:1–2

Here Paul asks that the one who has sinned as he had just described "be removed from among you." True to Paul's consistent advice, church discipline ought to be exercised. This is not calling for church division.

I TIMOTHY 4:11

Having warned of departures from the faith in verse 1, Paul counsels Timothy to, "take heed to yourself." Timothy is counseled to keep his own doctrine and conduct right, though an influx of false teaching and teachers come.

II TIMOTHY 2:24–26

In the next sentence Paul will talk of coming evil days of the last days. Here he calls on Timothy, as the Lord's servant not to be "quarrelsome" about "senseless controversies" (those on unvital issues) but rather to be kind to all, forebearing, correcting opponents with gentleness. Thus, he says, "God may perhaps grant that they will repent and come to know the truth."

II TIMOTHY 3:1–16

In the face of the perilous time to come as the age lengthens, Paul counsels Timothy to attend to himself, "But as for <u>you</u> … continue in what you have learned, stay in and true to the Scriptures." Note Paul's steadfastness and example and expected persecution.

No counsel to draw out a "true witness" from the church.

II TIMOTHY 4:1–8

Part of the value of these passages by Paul, here and above, is to be seen in what he does <u>not</u> counsel Timothy to do. He does not counsel as to promote a "drawing away" type of division.

Here Paul tells Timothy, who he believes will face the rise of false teachers and false teaching, to "Preach the Word!" He urges him to be "unfailing in patience." Righteous anger at false teaching is proper, but a short fuse, untempered with "unfailing patience" can disrupt God's flock. Even though Paul says, "the time will come when folk will not endure sound teaching," keep giving it! Be steady! Suffer! Evangelize! These will "fulfill your ministry."

All of Paul's teaching regarding error in the church tends to be in the direction of exposing and resisting error at all costs, combating it with strong doctrine, pure living, great patience, trusting God to give repentance where needed, willing to suffer, seeking to discipline error, seeking to save those in the church who are in the snare of the devil. It does not seem to be bent toward division.

II PETER 2–3

Peter draws a vivid picture of error and apostasy in connection with the "false teachers (who will be) among you" (verse 1) in chapter 2. What description he uses of those "who have forsaken the right way," "accursed children" (verses 14 and 15)!

Reminding them of the Lord's coming and the sure judgment to come, he urges believers in the face of all, as they "wait for these things," to be "zealous," to be pure and "at peace," to remember the forebearance of the Lord, grow in grace and in the knowledge of the Lord, and thus not be carried away with the error."

II JOHN 8–11

John, warning of deceivers and anti-Christs in the midst who depart from the doctrine of Christ, commands the true believer not to "receive" such ones into the home (treat as a brother, as godly, etc.).

Here again the counsel is to recognize, expose, reject and not share in the ways or companionship of deceivers.

JUDE

Jude clearly identifies and vigorously characterizes the evil ones who "secretly gained admission" to the church and thus carry on their evil work of promoting bad doctrine and bad conduct.

What counsel will he give the true believers who face this in the church? It is to be found in verses 20–23. Scoffers and ungodly men will "set up divisions, worldly people, devoid of the Spirit." "BUT YOU" (true believers):

"keep yourselves in the love of God"
"build up yourselves in the most holy faith"
"pray in the Spirit"
"wait for the mercy of our Lord Jesus Christ unto eternal life"
"convince some, who doubt"
"save some, by snatching them out of the fire"
"on some have mercy with fear, hating the garment spotted with the flesh."
He then commits them to the keeping—Christ.
Again, we note what he did not encourage them to do. No dividing is mentioned.

REVELATION 2–3

There is special value here, perhaps. Here we have our Risen, Exalted, Enthroned Lord's last address to the seven churches of Asia. These seven probably represent the church and churches of the whole church era.

Our Lord rebukes and commends as the church deserves or needs in these letters.

Let us take for a sample one of the problem churches He addresses, the church at Sardis (3:1–6).

This church is described by Christ as having the name of being alive but really is dead (spiritually). He has not found its works perfect in His sight. However, there "are still a few names in Sardis, people who have not soiled their garments."

The picture is clear. The church is soiled and dead. The majority and the leadership belong to the erring party. Only a minority, and those not in leadership, remain. This would be the ideal situation for the Lord to call for a pull-out and the starting of a new church elsewhere in Sardis by the faithful few. However, to our surprise, He tells them to, along with all the church, awaken and "strengthen what remains" (v. 2).

"He who has an ear to hear, let him hear what the Spirit says to the churches" (v. 6).

OBSERVATIONS

The Scriptures seem not to divide the urgency of seeking <u>purity</u> and <u>unity</u> in the church. Neither is sacrificed. They:

1.   Call for vigorous promotion of true doctrine, evangelization, and godly living… PURITY! It calls for the rebuking of, contended with all error, and an earnest seeking to correct and restore the erring.

2.   Call for a vigorous seeking for unity (John 17, Ephesians 4:3). The separation that the Bible calls for does not foment division, but promotes unity. It is the separation that comes when (a) discipline is given (when possible), (b) believers avoid compromise with and companionship of false teachers and erring people, and (c) in which fervent efforts are made to recover the erring. UNITY is promoted among true believers in an erring church as they fellowship together, share and promote the "apostles' doctrine" (we believe this to be the Reformed faith), declare their faith, rebuke the erring, and seek to evangelize within and without the visible church, LOOKING TO GOD FOR SUCH DISPOSITION AND <u>HE</u> WILL MAKE OF OUR WITNESS AND OF HIS CHURCH.

Martin Luther said, "Here I stand," not "Here I split."

To seek reform, revival and even regeneration from God for the erring church may bring rejection and expelling. If so, then the erring ones are the "dividers" as Scripture has said they are.

If we thus suffer at the hands of an erring church, let us be dead sure that we suffer the "fiery trial" for behaving as a Christian.

Let us not go beyond Scripture in dealing with God's church, but trust the Sovereign God to rule over, in and through His church.

A View of the Infallibility and Inerrancy of Holy Scripture

Sam C. Patterson
Revised February 15, 1979

The following is an effort to share my own confidence in and convictions regarding God's written word, the Bible.

I do not accept as valid a dichotomy that:

1. Seeks to maintain a clear distinction between the original autographs and the present extant Scriptures, but rather I hold to a Holistic and organic view of Scripture which I believe is supported in Scripture itself and was the view of Jesus Christ and the apostles. That is, there is an organic continuity which prevails in Scripture, extending from the origin of Scripture to present extant manuscripts, so that what we have today has been by God's "singular care and providence kept pure in all ages, are therefore authentical." (COF, I, 8)

2. Seeks to maintain a clear and qualitative difference between infallibility and inerrancy. That is, to be "incapable of error" (infallible) and to be "without error" (inerrancy) are practically synonymous. The historic Westminster Confession consistently uses the word "infallible", which is indeed a sufficient and satisfactory term. In my view, that term is so organically related to the matter of inerrancy, that any problems that might be posed in connection with "inerrancy" would also need to be faced by any valid form of "infallibility".

A summary of the views maintained here regarding the inspiration, infallibility-inerrancy of Scripture is as follows:

1. Men who wrote the Scriptures spoke for God being inspired by the Holy Spirit, who "moved them." (II Peter 1:21), and thus the writings themselves are "God-breathed" (II Tim 3:16).

2. Without doing violence to, but rather using, the distinctive personalities and literary styles of the writers, the Holy Spirit graciously superintended the writings so that fallible men with their fallible modes and forms set forth in human words the truth that God intended to teach and affirm as the "whole counsel of God, concerning all things necessary for His own glory, man's salvation faith and life" (Ch 1, para. 6, Westminster Confession of Faith), all which is infallibly (so, inerrantly) set forth and preserved in Scripture which is therefore established in divine authority.

3. The original physical material of the original autographs are not existent today and no human hands ever held them in their totality, but the manuscripts that are extant today provide us, by God's good providence, in spite of transmission problems and difficulties, the infallible and inerrant teaching concerning all things necessary for God's own glory, man's salvation, faith and life. Thus, the divine intent in inspiration and revelation is infallibly and inerrantly achieved in the Bible we have today, being preserved in the extant manuscripts which God in His providence has given us as our authoritative and sufficient revelation of His will.

4. In no way do faults of grammar, occasional discrepancies in numbers, or order of events, etc. affect the inerrant and infallible achievement of the intent and purpose of Scripture as so clearly set forth in the Westminster Confession of Faith. Such textual problems are present, but they are minute, limited in number, and not one of them effects Christian doctrine set forth in Scripture from its origin till this day.

5. Thus, the infallibility and the authority of Holy Scriptures from their origin by divine inspiration to their present existence by divine preservation, remain unchanged, and the imperishable Scriptures are "the living and enduring Word of God" which stands forever." (I Peter 1:24–25).

A CALL TO PCUS CONSERVATIVES

Albert H. Freundt, Jr.
Sam C. *Patterson*
April 16, 1982

It is now quite clear that the proposed Chapter 6 on Church Property has received approval by a substantial majority of the presbyteries in the Presbyterian Church in the United States. It is most likely therefore that the 1982 General Assembly will enact this new chapter and thus make it a part of the Book of Church Order. The whole process has been duly and constitutionally conducted. This is the first time that the PCUS Constitution will have made it clear that the ownership of the properties of the local churches comes under the jurisdiction of higher church courts.

There are many aspects of this new chapter which involve no real change. It will not affect a church that is planning no defection. As long as a church remains in connection with the PCUS, it can buy, sell, and mortgage its property without reference to any higher church court (6–8). It is still within the power of the presbytery to receive and dismiss churches with their property (6–7). However, if a church seeks to leave the denomination without dismissal by the presbytery, any property that it may have is under the control of the presbytery (6–4). Also, if there is a schism within a particular congregation, the presbytery has the right to determine which faction is loyal to the denomination and therefore represents the true church in affiliation with the PCUS (6–5). The new chapter therefore simply places property among the other matters on the local level that come under the review and control of the presbytery. It is a Presbyterian principle that has been explicitly extended now to include church property. Some of us have opposed the chapter on the grounds that it was unnecessary, that it may be interpreted as an attempt to maintain unity on the basis of coercion rather than persuasion, or that for various other reasons it was not a practical or fair thing to do. None can complain, however, that the issues were not put before the church or that the amendment was unconstitutionally enacted.

Another matter that is a cause of great concern to some of our friends is that the reunion of the PCUS with the UPCUSA appears more probably now than at any time in the history of the separate existence of the Southern Church. A significant element in the PCUS is opposed to the union, and it remains to be seen whether the Plan for Reunion will receive the necessary three-fourths majority vote of the presbyteries required by the PCUS Constitution for organic union with other denominations.

The probable passage of the church property amendment and the possible passage of the Plan of Reunion have already caused several churches throughout the PCUS to seek withdrawal from the denomination. These churches are a minority of the evangelical or conservative wing of the PCUS. Some fear that they will never be able to leave their present denominational connection—with their property—if they do not leave prior to the enactment of the property chapter. The same fear was expressed by many conservative churches in the early 70s when they withdrew to form the Presbyterian Church in America. Some of the churches that are presently contemplating withdrawal are not dissatisfied with their present denominational identity, but they simply do not want to be part of a larger Church that brings them into an organic union with the Northern Presbyterians. No amount of reason is likely to allay their fears and suspicions.

It is our conviction however that no Biblical or theological principle is involved or violated in the passage of the property amendment or of a Plan of Reunion. We have failed to find a Biblical doctrine that clearly places the ownership of local church property either in the hands of local members exclusively or in the hands of the larger church. Likewise, unless one alleges that the UPCUSA is not truly a Christian Church—a position that few conservatives in the PCUS will take—then there is no violation of Presbyterian doctrine or practice to reunite two branches of the Presbyterian Church that have been separated since 1861.

Moreover, in the PCUS we have long lived under a constitution that allows amendments like the property chapter and union like that proposed in the Plan of Reunion to be approved, if and when these proposals receive the constitutional votes required in each case. One may believe that these proposals are good or bad for the PCUS, but he can hardly argue that they mark a denomination which has approved them or is likely to approve them as unworthy of fellowship.

For those churches in the PCUS which do not want to be in a permanent relationship with a reunited, mainline Presbyterianism in this country, Article 13 of the Plan of Reunion ("Procedures for Dismissal of a Congregation with Its Property") provides a gracious and generous opportunity for honorable realignment that has constitutional integrity, does not require any reasons to be offered for the causes of disaffection, and does not require a congregation to brand as apostate their sister churches and fellow Christians who choose to remain in the united Church.

Two things should be made very clear to conservative churches and ministers who are considering withdrawal at this time. Most of your sister churches and fellow ministers who are conservative will remain with the denomination into reunion and will not be alienated by change in the manner of holding church property. These are administrative matters—neither violation of some divine command or prohibition nor overthrow of some essential doctrine of the Reformed Faith.

Apparently there are some pastors who are encouraging their churches to request withdrawal, and some pastors whose friends, peers, and congregations are urging them to leave. The poorest of all reasons to leave a denomination, we believe, is concern about who owns the material goods of the congregation. That is certainly not taking the high ground of theological principle. Can this rationale take precedence over the Reformed doctrine of the unity of the visible church catholic? We urge a renewed study of the doctrine of the unity of the visible church to be found in the Scriptures, in the Westminster Confession of Faith, and in John Calvin's Institutes of the Christian Religion (Book IV, Chapter 1).

There continues to be a need for an evangelical witness within the mainline denominations. This is true of the PCUS now; and it will be true in the reunited Church, if the reunion is constitutionally approved. Those evangelicals who leave now over property will depart not only from the present denomination over a non-doctrinal disagreement, they will also leave the great majority of their evangelical friends who need and want their continued support and fellowship. There are many serious and scholarly studies that report an evangelical resurgence in our country and in the mainline denominations. This is no time to withdraw the evangelical witness from the PCUS or from a reunited Church that needs and may be ready in the near future to hear and receive it.

The reasons that have kept conservatives and evangelicals in the PCUS after 1973 are still valid. No essential article of Christian Faith or Reformed Theology has been officially or constitutionally denied. We need to stay within the fellowship in which God has providentially placed us to witness for the truth to which we are committed. This is what we intend to do and what we recommend to our friends.

The PCUS has its problems; and a reunited Church, should that come into being, will not be free of error. As our Confession of Faith says, "The purest churches under heaven are subject both to mixture and error" (XXVII, 5). We conceive it our duty to minister to an erring church, not to desert it; and we believe that God will be faithful to honor our witness, even if we should be expelled for bearing this witness—a prospect which all will grant it not very likely.

Why, then, the haste to withdraw at this time? Can it really be supported by Scripture or the doctrine of the Church? Let us make sure that our actions and conduct are guided by the Word of God and consistent with the church membership and ordination vows we have taken. Our obligations are to the Scripture and to those solemn commitments we have made, not to alienated friends and peers who are motivated by concern over who controls the physical properties of the church in case of an appeal to a higher ecclesiastical court.

What we have said is applicable, we believe, to ministers who have graduated from denominational or from independent evangelical seminaries. Now, we address a special word to those who have been trained in the non-denominational seminaries. None of those seminaries were founded to encourage or create division or schism in any denomination. The evangelical ones were founded to train and provide evangelical pastors for churches in denominations that were not necessarily controlled by conservative majorities. For the most part, the presbyteries of these denominations, such as the PCUS, have graciously been open to receive, ordain, and install graduates of these institutions on their own merit—not counting against them that they attended unofficial seminaries. These graduates have entered into the PCUS knowing that it was not a perfect Church, agreeing to seek its peace and purity. We do not know of any of these graduates who have like Luther been expelled for their witness to the truth. They are free to proclaim the Word of God and to uphold their testimony to the Reformed Faith. Some may feel that they represent a distinct minority position in their presbyteries or that the denomination has approved positions with which they cannot identify. But neither situation has historically been grounds for creating schism or justifying withdrawal. We ask ministers to consider the effect of this kind of action on their fellow graduates who do feel called and committed to minister in the PCUS or the united Church.

Mainline Presbyterianism, which is our PCUS heritage, has already suffered four major schisms (in 1741, in 1837, in 1861 and in 1973). When the first of these was healed in the 1758 reunion, the following principle was enunciated, which reappears on page 59 of the Plan of Reunion and to which we call our evangelical pastors and friends to follow at this time:

> *That when any matter is determined by a majority vote, every member shall either actively concur with or passively submit to such determination; or if his conscience permit him to do neither, he shall, after sufficient liberty modestly to reason and remonstrate, peaceably withdraw from our communion without attempting to make any schism. Provided always that this shall be understood*

to extend only to such determination as the body shall judge indispensable in doctrine or Presbyterian government.

Our present responsibility, then, is to that part of Christ's Church in which we find ourselves and to which our vows have committed us. To leave it now, without solid and profound justification, would be an act of unbelief—a lack of faith that God can or will yet bless, use, shape, and renew the Church. It would discount and disobey Christ's last counsel in the Book of Revelation to a small evangelical group in the problem church at Sardis, to "strengthen the things which remain" (Rev. 3:2). Separation at this time would weaken the evangelical truth that still exists. We have been called to suffer for the faith, perhaps, but never to divide the Church. It would discount the love that Christ has even for such a church as that at Laodicea, when he stood at the door, not to leave but to enter (Rev. 3:20). We are called to witness in and through the Church, not to depart from or reject any branch of what Christ calls "My Church" (Matt. 16:18).

Brothers in Christ, let us make every effort to maintain the true and faithful witness, without rending the Church of Christ through our activity or initiative. There are enough problems in the PCUS without our adding to them. Let us contribute to the healing of the Church, not to its demise or dismemberment.

APPENDIX D

DEATH

Note: The documents in this appendix are in their original form except the sermon "Burdens," which has been edited for print.

BURDENS
Matthew 11:28–30

Sam Patterson
Leland Presbyterian Church
March 8, 1987

Note: This is the last sermon Sam preached.

I have a little note in my Bible. I don't know where I got it or when I put it there, but sometime in the years gone by I jotted down something written by Oswald Chambers about Matthew 11:28–30. He said, "Here sin and sorrow have their end, and the song and the saint begin." What we do have here in Matthew, certainly, is a very gracious invitation to everyone who bears heavy burdens. As a matter of fact, when you hear or read these words, the invitation appears to be limited, in the sense that Christ is directing it to a subgroup of people: those who are burdened and troubled.

However, one can wonder: Where is the person who isn't constantly, all through life, bearing burdens, trials, tests, and troubles? Oh, I believe this invitation is as broad as mankind! Sin, death, suffering, and trials are all universal to the experience of men. When Christ calls for the burdened to come to him, he's not talking about a special group of people who have more burdens than others. He wants all the burden-bearing human beings in the world to come to him.

Eliphaz, one of the so-called friends of Job, said that man is as prone to have trouble as sparks are to fly upward. Job himself said man is of very few days, but of very many troubles. We can affirm that both of these are true. Trouble is our experience, and when Christ speaks the invitation, it ought to touch every heart, reach each one of us.

Peter tells us that Christians are no exception to this general rule, that everybody is going to bear burdens in this life. It's the universal calling and practice of humanity. First Peter 1:3–9 teaches that even though we have received new life in Christ here on earth, we will still be called upon to carry all kinds of burdens. Peter warns us not to be surprised when fiery trials come upon us, as if being Christians exempts us from any burdens.

In this passage, Peter twice says that we should also experience exceeding joy. Those things don't often go together. We don't often think of burdens and joy together. However, Peter says that in Christian experience, they can be put together. It is possible for those of us in Christ to have heavy burdens all through our lives, and yet not lose the joy of living.

We wonder how this can be, don't we? That's what Jesus is trying to teach us in Matthew 11:28–30 (paraphrased): "Come to me, and I'll teach you! Come unto me, all you who are laboring under burdens! Learn from me! I'll teach you how you can have rest." He doesn't promise release; I wish he did. Not now, not yet, now here. We won't get release from trials and troubles all through our lifetime. But Jesus does promise relief, in terms of rest, while we have them.

I don't think Americans have ever been as conscious of physical fitness as we are today. Everybody seems to be involved in a personal physical fitness program. One of the most popular, especially for men and athletes, is weightlifting. Everybody who has ever engaged in that sport discovers early that the ability to lift and hold up a large amount of weight does not depend only on strength. It depends just as much, and maybe more, on technique. There's a way to do it and succeed, and there's a way to do it that will lead to failure no matter how strong you are. Even the family doctor tells us that technique makes a difference. When we stoop to pick something off the floor, he will tell us there is a way to do it that will bring disability and a way to do it that will not break our backs.

That's what Jesus is telling us here. He says, "Come to me and learn. I'll teach you. I'll show you. I'll help you. Learn how to bear burdens." I always thought Jesus said, "Come to me, and I'll take your burdens away." But he doesn't. His slant is altogether different. He says, "Come to me, and I will show you how to carry whatever burden you're called upon to bear in life."

Peter and Paul learned principles of burden-bearing from Jesus. In Galatians 6:5, Paul gives us a principle that sounds as if it will only increase our burdens, not relieve them: "For each one shall bear his own load." Paul says that everyone must bear his own burden. Not much comfort in that, is it? What is Paul driving at here? Simply that everyone has to begin by assuming responsibility for carrying his share of the burdens of life, whether he or she likes the share or not.

Yet, in Christ, we'll never be over-burdened. Jesus said that the troubles and trials we have are common to men. God will not suffer you to be overloaded, but will, with the testing, provide a way of escape. He knows our load-limit. We're assured that whatever burdens do come, it's God's assurance that we'll not go under. But most of all, what Paul seems to be driving at is this: we are forbidden from casting our burden on everybody else. Everybody is to assume responsibility for going through life, carrying his own load of trouble and trials! We are to do this while being assured that God knows our limit. We can go on!

Most of us try to cast our burdens on others when we're troubled. We think there'll be some relief, and we've got wonderful techniques for doing that. Complaining is one. A lot of times we just keep spilling our own problems over on others. We make them share our burdens by complaining to them all the time! Or we use self-pity. We may not complain much, but it's that look, it's that air, it's that attitude that we have all the time that makes everybody sure that we're heavily burdened. Many times we simply shirk our duties or try to get others to do them because we are hurting. Christ forbids us to do that because it doesn't help anyway.

Nobody who carried a heavy burden ever found the burden lighter because he complained to everybody all the time. Nobody ever found the load lighter because he manifested self-pity all the time. Nobody ever saw the load get lighter because they shirked duty. The person's own conscience just adds to the load. Those people who try to cast their burdens over on others only increase the load they're carrying.

On the other hand, assuming responsibility for our lives and our troubles means surrendering to Christ. The good conscience of knowing that whatever burden I'm carrying, I'm doing the best I can to fulfill my responsibility in life as best I can really lightens the load.

Paul adds another principle to this, and once again it looks as if it would make the load heavier. In Galatians 6:2, he says, "Bear you one another's burdens...." Not only should you assume responsibility for carrying your own burdens, but you should also carry the burdens of others. That looks like it would just add to the load, doesn't it? Not only are we forbidden to cast our burdens on others, we're commanded to pick up a share of the burdens that other people bear. Not only are we assured that God will give us grace to bear whatever He brings upon our lives, He'll also give us grace to carry a portion of the burdens of others.

Here a strange mathematics begins to operate. We can illustrate it like this. Suppose you have a hundred pounds of personal problems. But you extend your hand and take over fifty pounds of somebody else's problems. Now, how many pounds of problems are you bearing? Ordinarily, when we say "add," we mean addition. If you add fifty to one hundred, you get one hundred and fifty. Yet, here addition turns into subtraction. If you have one hundred pounds of problems, and you take fifty pounds of somebody else's problems, you find that instead of being weighed down with one hundred fifty pounds of problems, you're only carrying fifty. The burden is lighter than it was when you just carried your own burdens! Everybody in this room has experienced that to some degree in his or her own life. There isn't a person here who hasn't given a helping hand to somebody and found that life's burdens were lighter, that his own clouds were not as severe.

Jesus makes a strange statement in Matthew 11:28–30 (paraphrased) when he says, "Come to me, you that are heavily laden. Learn of me. I'll give you rest. For my burden is light!" Why would Jesus say that his burden is light? He carried the heaviest responsibility and the most awesome burden that anyone ever carried—all the way to the cross. How in the world could he say 'my burden is light'?

The reason is partly because of what we have been talking about. He's saying, "I'll take your burdens, too. You who have burdens, come to me." People who take that attitude in life do have lighter burdens. Their hearts are lighter. It does make a difference when we are willing to be sensitive, to be thoughtful of others and their troubles, and we take note of them. When we have empathy, when we show sympathy, when we extend a helping hand or word, it never does anything but lighten our load. And our burdens are lighter. We can say the same thing that Jesus said.

Then Peter gives us the final principle in this Christian way of dealing with burdens. He says in 1 Peter 5:7, "Cast all your burdens on the Lord, for He cares for you." David is the one who first wrote that. He put it a little differently in Psalm 55:22: "Cast your burdens on the Lord, and He will sustain you." He'll hold you up! Both are good and are true. We're not to cast our burdens on others. Occasionally, we'll come upon others who will just naturally take a share in our burden, as we try to take the burdens of others. But we won't force our burdens on them. We've got another place to cast them.

But how do you cast your burdens on the Lord? How do you do that and find this relief?

Ordinarily, we think that means prayer. I think that is where we make a serious mistake. Prayer does have something to do with it, and we do pray about our troubles. But prayer itself won't cast a burden on the Lord. Simply by talking to God, you can't cast your burdens on him. You can talk about them to Him; you can complain about them to Him. You can appeal for help to Him. But you can't really put them on Him.

Jesus tells us how you do it. There's only one way to do it. He said, "Come unto me, all you who labor and are heavily burdened, and I'll give you rest. Take my yoke upon you!" Jesus says, take the burden of my Lordship on you, and all your burdens will belong to me. That's the transaction. That's the only way you can cast your burdens on the Lord. It's a transaction. Jesus said, "Take my yoke upon you. Give your life up to me. Unite your life to me. Let me be the Lord, the Savior in your life! Take my way as the way you will go. You take my yoke, my calling on you, and every trial you'll ever have will be mine."

Jesus was a carpenter and, no doubt, made these yokes that he spoke about. Two oxen yokes were what he was referring to here. If you put an immature, weak, young ox in the yoke with a mature, strong, veteran ox, the young animal will be able to carry a greater load because of the shared experience. All the strength, presence, and power of the veteran ox in the yoke with him becomes his! That strength, wisdom, and knowledge become his. He's able to pull along, just keeping pace with the old veteran. Together they can pull a tremendous load.

That's what Jesus is talking about. Link your life with Him. Give your loyalty, your love, your faith, your trust, and your life to Him. And every burden you've got will be His. You'll have a shared experience with His presence, with His Providence in your life, with His power and promise.

For Jesus does later promise full release, not just relief. There will come a time when we won't experience suffering and sin and sorrow. We have an inheritance that's incorruptible, that never fades away, and it's reserved in heaven. During this short time on earth, we'll bear all kind of trials. But we rejoice because we know someday we're going to have release into a kingdom of life that will last forever and be cursed by nothing. For heaven is real, and heaven is true, and heaven is there. For now, and for eternity, Christ offers a life to those of us who are heavily burdened.

As a matter of fact, Paul tells us in Romans 8:32 that Christ has already borne the heaviest burden we will ever have. He bore up, in His own body, our sins on the tree. That's our biggest problem. And if God has given us this blessing, why will He not give us everything we need? Will He not pick up and carry with us, we with Him, all the other burdens of our lives? Of course He will. If we believe this, we will really experience the joy of rest. We will have troubles, yet not lose the joy of living.

Bless, our heavenly Father, the call of Christ to our hearts. Give us the grace and wisdom to be willing to yoke our lives up with Jesus and to go with Him. We pray in His name, Amen.

Memorial
for
The Reverend Samuel C. Patterson
(1916–1987)

St. Andrew Presbytery
Milton Winter

Samuel Coleman Patterson was born July 8, 1916, a son of the Presbyterian manse. His father was the Rev'd Samuel Jasper Patterson, D.D., a Presbyterian schooled in the sturdy old Associate Reformed Presbyterian tradition. His mother, Lily Margaret Patterson, was the former Lily Margaret Davis of Monticello, Arkansas. The youngest of six children, Samuel was born during his father's ministry in Fort Morgan, Colorado, in the United Presbyterian Church there. He came as a child to West Point, Mississippi, in 1921, where his father served as Stated Supply of the Presbyterian Church, U.S. congregation there. The elder Rev'd Mr. Patterson came into the U.S. Church during his pastorate at Morrilton, Arkansas in 1924, and it was through this branch that Samuel Patterson entered the ministry.

Samuel Patterson attended Southwest at Memphis (B.A., 1938) and received his seminary training at Union Theological Seminary in Virginia (B.D., 1941). Upon graduation he was married to the former Estelle Sellers, who preceded him in death. To that union was born one daughter, Margaret Rebekah Patterson (Mrs. J. L. Rogers), who resides in French Camp, Mississippi.

Ordained by the Presbytery of Roanoke (Virginia) on June 8, 1941, Samuel Patterson served as Pastor of the Kate Anderson Memorial Church, Martinsville, Virginia (1941–44) and as a chaplain in the U.S. Naval Reserve (1944–46).

He returned to Mississippi in August, 1946, serving as Pastor at Leland until 1950, where he succeeded the Rev'd Charles E. S. Kraemer, who had left Leland to serve the prestigious First Presbyterian Church of Charlotte, North Carolina.

In 1950, Samuel Patterson went to serve the struggling academy at French Camp in the red clay hills of Mississippi. It was here that his most enduring work would be done. He was President of French Camp from 1950 to 1975.

Samuel Patterson was instrumental in the founding of Reformed Theological Seminary, which he served as President from 1975 to 1979. Throughout his tenure there he worked to preserve the unity of the Presbyterian Church, U.S. and to further its witness through the training of conservative ministers to serve within its bounds. He was personally opposed to and worked zealously against those movements which sought to divide the Presbyterian Church, U.S. severing his ties with those organizations which promoted division, finally leaving the seminary itself. He was granted the status of Honorably Retired by St. Andrew's Presbytery on April 30, 1979.

Mr. Patterson retired to French Camp, where he served as Stated Supply of the French Camp Presbyterian Church. He was instrumental in the reorganization of the Presbyterian Church at Huntsville, Mississippi, and was proud of the fact that this congregation provided a Presbyterian (U.S.A.) witness in Montgomery County—an area otherwise dominated by the Presbyterian Church of America.

Samuel Patterson's privately printed paper, "Seeking a Biblical Basis for the Conduct of Believers in an Erring Church (1971)," has been instrumental in persuading scores of conservative Presbyterian, U.S. and U.S.A. ministers and congregations to remain loyal to the denomination. Mr. Patterson readily acknowledged that his views on many issues had changed throughout the course of his ministry. He was instrumental in rallying conservative support across the denomination for such progressive ideas— racial desegregation, a contemporary declaration of faith, and reunion with the United Presbyterian Church in the U.S.A. He believed such stands were demanded by his commitment to Scripture and Reformed theology.

Samuel Patterson was the senior minister of St. Andrew's Presbytery and moderator of the Synod of Mississippi in 1956. He will be remembered as a Churchman and as a Preacher. He was supremely honored when he was chosen to preach before the General Assembly at Charlotte, North Carolina in 1975. His favorite pulpits, undoubtedly, were in the small churches across our denomination, and his final sermon was delivered at Leland, Mississippi, in the spring of 1987. He died at Pensacola, Florida on March 12, 1987. Funeral services were conducted at French Camp, The Rev'd Dr. T. Russell Nunan, presiding. "He being dead yet speaketh."

RESOLUTION HONORING
Samuel Coleman Patterson

FCA Board of Trustees
Spring Meeting, 1987

Whereas, our Heavenly Father in His matchless wisdom and grace took unto Himself our beloved brother and fellow laborer, Samuel Coleman Patterson, on March 12, 1987;

And whereas, his life among us was one of simple and humble Christian faith, giving us great encouragement and causing us to give thanksgiving to God;

And whereas, his service as President of French Camp Academy and President Emeritus was long and faithful, characterized by love both to his Lord and to his fellow Christians, and by sacrificial giving of himself;

And whereas, our Board of Trustees, French Camp Academy and the community have benefited greatly from the sound faith, consistent preaching of the Word of God, careful judgment, faithful praying, and vigorous life of our dear friend;

Therefore, be it resolved:

1.   That we give thanks to our Heavenly Father for the life and ministry of Samuel Coleman Patterson.

2.   That we express to his family our love and sympathy in their loss, which is ours also, and that we rejoice with them in the spiritual heritage that he has left them, assuring them of our love and prayers.

3.   That a copy of this resolution be sent to the family of our brother, and that a copy be displayed in a prominent place in the Academy with a picture of him accompanying it, and that they be recorded in our minutes, and that they be forwarded to the church and public press.

4.   That a memorial endowment scholarship fund be established in the name of Samuel Coleman Patterson that friends and loved ones may be able to give to, in order to enable many more young people to continue to be benefited by the grace of God and the goodness of the friends and loved ones of Samuel Coleman Patterson.

RESOLUTION HONORING
Samuel Coleman Patterson

French Camp Presbyterian Church
January 17, 1988

The following resolution was unanimously approved by the Session of the French Camp Presbyterian Church and is recommended to the congregation.

Whereas: Sam C. Patterson, our deceased brother and friend, was pastor or overseer of the French Camp Presbyterian Church from 1950–1983; and

Whereas: Sam C. Patterson, beginning in 1950, gave tireless leadership and personal effort, often to the detriment of his own physical health, to rebuilding French Camp Academy from a struggling institution with a small student body and meager facilities into a strong and effective institution with a large, growing student body and attractive, substantial facilities; and

Whereas: The students and staff of French Camp Academy comprise a substantial part of the membership of the French Camp Presbyterian Church with the entire French Camp Academy family meeting for worship at the church on Sundays; and

Whereas: The historic French Camp Presbyterian Church building, erected in 1904, is resting on unstable foundations, is deteriorating rapidly because of age, and no longer has adequate seating for its present members and the French Camp Academy family; and

Whereas: French Camp Academy and its alumni, the French Camp Presbyterian Church, the French Camp community and friends of Sam C. Patterson from around the world desire to establish a fitting memorial to Sam C. Patterson that will 1) Be permanent 2) benefit French Camp Academy 3) benefit the French Camp Presbyterian Church and Community and 4) be visible as a testimony to the glory of God and the life of Sam C. Patterson; therefore

Be It Resolved: That the Session of the French Camp Presbyterian Church requests that French Camp Academy, through its Board of Trustees and staff, coordinate the effort of raising funds for the purpose of renovating, restoring, and enlarging the French Camp Presbyterian Church (founded in 1849, present building erected in 1904) and Sunday School Annex (erected in 1946), thus enabling the Church to provide adequate worship and teaching facilities for the growing French Camp Academy family and community, and so that the historic building can be preserved for the next 100 years or more as a testimony to the glory of God and as a testimony to the life of Sam C. Patterson.

Sam C. Patterson Memorial Fund

Steering Committee
November 19, 1989

*T. Russell Nunan, DD, Chairman
Greenville, MS

Stuart B. Angle, Co-chairman
French Camp, MS (Deceased)

Rev. H. Richard Cannon, Co-chairman
French Camp, MS

Dr. James M. Baird
Jackson, MS

Dr. John Richard de Witt
Memphis, TN

Jack Bushman
Montgomery, AL

Ewing Carruthers, CLU
Memphis, TN

W. A. Taylor, Jr.
Louisville, MS

Robert C. Cannada
Jackson, MS

Rev. Dwyn M. Mounger
Bay St. Louis, MS

Mr. Ed Edens
Okolona, MS

**Mrs. George M. McLean
Tupelo, MS

**Mrs. John C. Stanley, III
Corinth, MS

Bobby D. Robinson
Vicksburg, MS

Dr. Norman E. Harper
Laurel, MS

*Stuart C. Irby
Jackson, MS

*Rev. Erskine L. Jackson
Kosciusko, MS

*Davis Fair
Louisville, MS

H. Talmage Branning
French Camp, MS

*FCA Board of Trustees
**Widow of Former Trustee

Sam Patterson Memorial Building Committee

*Talmage Branning, Chairman
*Jack Johnson, Vice-chairman
*Ed Williford, Secretary
Mrs. Mary Jasper
Harold Curtis

*Ralph Newman
Lewis Ward
Virginia Carlisle
Larry Littlejohn
Rev. Richard Cannon

*Executive Building Committee

APPENDIX E

OTHER WRITINGS

*All of the documents in this appendix are original
and have not been edited in any way.*

EVANGELISTIC ADVICE
TO BECKY

Sam handwrote the following thirty-six-page letter to his daughter,
Becky Rogers, while he recovered from a heart attack in 1961.

Dec. 22, 1961

Dear Becky,

Your comment that at college you had become acquainted with a few students who were atheistically inclined started in my mind a chain of thought that I would like to pass on to you. This is done with the hope that you might find, at least some of these ideas helpful to you in your future contacts with atheism, agnosticism, or dis-belief.

First of all let me point out a rather fine, but important distinction between the "unbeliever" and the "dis-believer" as these terms are used in this letter. The dis-believer is one who has heard or known the Christian testimony and faith, claims to have thoughtfully considered them, and has deliberately determined that they are false, or extremely doubtful. This includes a multitude of "shades" from the out-and-out atheist to the sincere and/or cynical doubter, who deny, claim to be untrue, or beyond proof the existence of a personal deity (God), the fact that the Bible is the Word of God and the "only infallible rule of faith and life", and the fact that Jesus is the Son of God, Christ, the only Saviour and Lord.

The unbeliever, in contrast, does not profess faith in Christ because he has not given the matter much attention, perhaps has never been challenged with a clear presentation of the Gospel, and while he has not accepted faith, he has not deliberately denied the truths of faith. We might say that the dis-believer is an un-believer who deliberately declares a position of denying or doubting the Christian faith and its basic truths. Both the "unbeliever" and the "disbeliever" are out of Christ and thus are out of salvation. However, in this writing I am considering the dis-believer and the atheist.

Let me outline what I believe the Christian's approach to the problem of the dis-believer and atheist should be. Consider first:

THE TEST

Since the atheist denies the truth of a deep and commonly held concept, the fact of the existence of God, and thus, also, denies that the Bible is the Word of God, and that Jesus Christ is the Son of God, etc., it is proper to tell him that the "burden of the proof" is on him. (The one who declares something to be a lie, or untrue, or a fraud must be able to prove this! Ask him to prove his position, not just declare it. Ask him to prove to you beyond doubt that there is no God, and so on.)

The usual procedure of the dis-believer is to demand that you do the proving. Do not permit this. Ask him to prove his denials with proven, undeniable facts that must certify to any intelligence that he is right. This, of course he cannot do. He usually follows the course of trying to embarrass the Christian by demanding "proofs" of him, and by assuming an air of "pitying toleration" of the Christian's stupidity by ridiculing his naïve position of faith.

You have the obligation of demanding of the disbeliever undeniable proof of his contentions.

This he may try to do particularly if he has read some literature or philosophy of atheistic slant (the great majority of the great philosophers of the world have either affirmed the existence of God or were unwilling to deny His existence), or if he has come under the influence and arguments of some atheistic parent or friend. He may site as facts some scientific theories such as a theory of creation that omits a Creator-God. Remember that science has proven nothing about this—that there are various theories and scientists are not in agreement. Remind your dis-believing friend that, as a matter of fact, "science" neither proves nor dis-proves the existence of God or the Christian faith. Science deals with creation, not the Creator. Some very great scientists have been and are believers. Some have not been.

He may ridicule the Bible and declare that certain things recorded in it just couldn't happen. Remind him that if there is a God such as is presented in the Bible, He could cause anything to happen. Be sure when he sites a problem or so-called contradictions in the Bible that he actually turns to the passage in a copy of the Bible. When a Scripture is the matter at hand do not trust the dis-believer's memory (or yours) of what the passage says. Ask him, then, if he has thoroughly studied with open mind what scholars, authoritative in Bible study, have said or written about this passage (commentaries, etc.). If he admits that he has not, remind him that he has not very "scientifically" or fairly faced up to the problem he himself has raised. Offer to furnish him with a book on "Answers to Bible Questions and Problems" for his consideration. If he says he has carefully considered the scholarly writings of Bible-believing students, to see their view point on this, ask him what he studied, and whose writings. Often dis-believers come to their conclusions without a full and fair consideration of all the facts, yet all the while pretending that they have scientifically and open-mindedly carefully examined the evidences. These ought to be "smoked out". I recall a young marine officer who had, as he said, given up his religious convictions. He made some very strong assertions regarding the character of "the God of the Old Testament", blaspheming assertions. I asked him if he were sure about this. He was. I told him that I regularly studied the Old Testament and never had found a God such as he described. He said, "Well, it is there." I suggested he site a passage that supported his view, mentioning, perhaps, that we could get a copy of the Bible so he could show me. He then admitted that he could not cite one example from Scripture and had read very little in the Bible. He said, "I just always thought this was true." He was an intelligent young lawyer before the war, but had taken a very unintelligent approach to his unbelief.

The dis-believer may argue that there are inconsistencies and hypocrisy in the lives of so many Christians. Remind him that there are fakers and pretenders in every group including atheists, communists, Rotarians, etc., but that while admittedly there is hypocrisy in the church often, still no one hit hypocrisy harder than Jesus Christ and the Bible. "They profess that they know God; but in works they deny him, being abominable, and disobedient, and unto every good work reprobate."—Titus 1:16 "Woe unto you, scribes, and Pharisees, hypocrites! For ye are like unto whited sepulchers ... outwardly ye appear righteous unto men, but within ye are full of hypocrisy!"—Matthew 23:27–28. We do not deny that there are hypocrites in the church. The Bible prophesied that such would rise up—and condemned them. This does not affect the fact that the truth of God, Christ, and the Bible stands! Nor does it alter the fact that there are, and have been, untold numbers of sincere, dedicated Christians.

The dis-believer may decry the divisions in the church resulting in so many denominations. Remind him that this is only in the visible or "organized" church, but that, as Christ prayed in John 17:20–23, all true believers in all denominations are one, united in the Spirit and faith. The fact that in one community there are Rotary Clubs, Lions Clubs, Kiwanis Clubs, Civitan Clubs, etc., does not mean that respective members are divided and opposed to each other. All of these are civic clubs, all having the same general objectives socially and civically in the community. All are united as citizens and Americans. This, generally speaking is true of the various Christian denominations.

The whole point being made here is that the dis-believer be put on the defense. You do this by insisting that he prove what he says is true—not just say it and then try to get you to prove that he is wrong. Force him to produce real proof of his denials and give evidence that, in a first-hand way, he has sincerely studied through thoroughly his position.

THE FACTS

You cannot prove to an atheist that there is a God, and the atheist cannot prove to you that there is not a God by human reasoning, talking, and arguments. The philosopher, Kant, illustrated this graphically in his "Antinomies." The true and final reasons for faith and for dis-belief lie beyond the sphere of mere "reasoning" and "arguments" and "debates."

At this point it is important that you, as a Christian know why you believe, and why the disbeliever doesn't, why you look at nature and creation and see clear evidence of a God-Creator, and the disbeliever, looking at the same creation sees no evidences of God, why the Bible to your heart is confirmed as the Word of God, yet to the disbeliever it is not and/or is nonsense; why you have realized a sin problem in your life, the need of a Saviour, and have recognized and received Jesus Christ as that Saviour, yet the disbeliever has no sense of "needing salvation" and holds no faith in Christ.

The "reason why" is to be found only in the Bible. There you will find the explanation regarding faith and dis-belief—the reason why some believe and some never believe. You will find that the reason is not based on differences of intelligence, learning, or personality. These factors are not involved directly, that is, primarily.

As a matter of fact the reason causing the difference between belief and dis-belief, cannot be accepted, understandably, by the dis-believer. You, however, as a Christian can know the reason and should. Again, the explanation is to be found only in the Word of God, the Bible. "The heart (of man) is deceitful above all things" Jeremiah says in Jer. 17:9. Man's own heart deceives him, fools him, and hides from him his true cause of unbelief. Jeremiah concludes that verse with a question "who can know it" (the human heart)? His answer is in the next verse: "I the Lord search the heart." Thus Hebrews 4:12 & 13 tell us: "For the Word God is quick (living), and powerful ... and is a discerner of the thoughts and intents of the heart. Neither is there any creature that is not manifest in His sight, but all things are naked and opened unto the eyes of Him with whom we have to do." God who alone knows the human heart and all its ways can explain the mystery of the believing heart, and the unbelieving, disbelieving heart, and He presents the reason in the Bible.

1. Why you believe:

It is not just because your parents did, and you have simply naturally accepted their position without thinking for yourself (many atheists suggest this, and the following as the explanation for your faith). Nor is the reason for your faith to be found in the fact that you have not been "scientific" (many great scientists have and do believe), or because you are naïve. When these reasons are given by the disbeliever to explain your "foolish faith" it will be disconcerting and embarrassing if you do not know the true reason. Isabel Kuhn tells ("By Searching") how her whole life was upset for a time when in college a brilliant professor, who had ridiculed the Bible, told those who professed to believe in the Bible: "Oh, you just believe that because your Papa and Mama told you so." She said, "There was no argument ... just the pitying sneer ... and the confident assumption that no persons nowadays who thought for themselves, who were scientific in their approach to life, believed the old story anymore." This attack led her for a time into what she called "The Misty Flats." "So I broke with my old religious habits and frankly went into the world." In her case, God used this challenge and experience to wake her up and later to bring her to a deep, true, understood faith.

The reason why the true Christian believer is suggested and presented in such passages as:

a. II Cor. 4:6—"For God, who commanded the light to shine out of darkness (Gen. 1:3), hath shined in our hearts, to give the light of the knowledge of the glory in the face of Jesus Christ."

b. 1 Cor. 2:10–12—"For God hath revealed them unto us ... for what man knoweth the things of a man, save by the spirit which is in him? Even so the things of God knoweth no man, but the Spirit of God. Now we have received not the spirit of the world, but the Spirit which is of God that we may know the things that are freely given to us of God."

c. 1 Cor. 1:26–30—"For ye see your calling (i.e. to salvation or saving faith), brethren, how that not many wise men, after the flesh (i.e. in their own wisdom and pride), not many mighty, not many noble are called (i.e. by God): But God hath chosen the foolish things (i.e. according to the world's view) of the world to confound the wise; and God hath chosen the weak things of the world to confound the things which are mighty; and the base things of the world, and things which are despised, hath God chosen, yea, and things which are not, to bring to naught things that are; that no flesh should glory in His presence. But of Him are ye (i.e. chosen, called) in Christ Jesus..."

This passage should be considered in the light of Christ's words in Matthew 11:25–27—"At that time Jesus answered and said, I thank Thee, O Father, Lord of heaven and earth, because thou hast hid these things from the wise and prudent, and hast revealed them unto babes. All things are delivered unto me of my Father: and no man knoweth the Son but the Father; neither knoweth any man the Father save the Son, and he to whomsoever the Son will reveal Him."

d. Colossians 1:12–13—"Giving thanks unto the Father ... who hath delivered us from the power of darkness, and hath translated us into the Kingdom of His dear Son."

e. John 6:44 (words of Christ)—"No man can come to me except the Father which hath sent me draw him …" Plus—"All that the Father giveth me shall come to me" (John 6:37).

All of these passages plus many more (Matt. 16:15–17, 1 Peter 2:9, II Peter 1:2–3, 1 John 5:20, II Tim. 1:9, I Thess. 1:4–6, Eph. 2:1–10, Eph. 1:4–9, Rom. 8:29–30, Acts 18:2–7, 2:47, 14:48, John 15:16, 10:26–27, Philippians 1:29, 2:13, Titus 3:4–7, 1 John 2:20–22, 27, etc.) reveal that all who believe in Christ and the Christian faith were brought to faith by the Work of God upon our hearts, taking away the natural sin—self blindness that is part of all human-nature, in its natural state, and giving to us that grace that brings faith in Christ. It is put like this in the Bible:

"Lydia … whose heart the Lord opened, that she attended unto the things which were spoken of Paul" (Acts 16:14). Thus she believed and became the first convert to Christ in Europe. So God does (and must) open our hearts to believe.

Also: "For we (Christians) are His workmanship, created in Christ Jesus" (Eph. 2:10), and, "For it is God that worketh in you both to will, and to do His good pleasure" (Philippians 2:13).

I have gone to this length to show why a person becomes a Christian. The person may be very intelligent or very dull of mind, very well educated, or without any formal education, very cultured and civilized or very heathen in background, highly scientific, or without any interest in science. These factors do not determine faith and disbelief. Both faith and disbelief can produce adherents from all these groups. Faith comes from a work of God upon the heart that enables that one being so dealt with to see—to see his sin—need, Christ the Saviour provision, and thus to entrust his life to Him! It appears that a person thinks and finds his own way to faith. Actually, however, behind the scenes, is the heart, the Holy Spirit is leading that one to sight and salvation.

2. Why do some disbelieve, that is hear and reject faith in God, or Christ, or the Bible?

Why is it that Psalm 19:1–3 makes sense to the Christian, but is nonsense to the disbeliever? Why is it that 1 Corinthians 1:18 is true: "For the preaching of the cross is to them that perish foolishness; but unto us which are saved it is the power of God?"

The answer is given only in Scripture and thus to the disbeliever cannot be accepted, but you, the Christian needs to know! The Bible declares that men dis-believe, reject the truth of God, because the "natural man," who has not been brought by the Holy Spirit into the "new birth," has his heart darkened to faith. He does not, and cannot, truly believe in heart until and unless God, by the "Spirit of truth" (Holy Spirit) works on and in that heart to remove the blindness. These verses are only a few that show this as the reason why some dis-believe:

a. John 3:3—"Jesus answered and said unto him, verily, verily, I say unto you, except a man be born again (literally "born from above") he cannot see the Kingdom of God."

b. Because of the truth above, 1 Cor. 2:14—"But the natural man (i.e. person born of the flesh but not yet "born of the Spirit"—Jn. 3:6) receiveth not the things of the Spirit of God: for they are foolishness unto him: neither can he know them, because they are spiritually discerned." Again, it is shown that discernment (knowledge personally) of God, Christ, the Bible, the "Christian faith" does not come by, nor is it rejected by purely intellectual means. It comes by "spiritual discernment" wrought in the heart by the Holy Spirit.

c. II Cor. 4:3–4—"But if our gospel is hid, it is hid to them that are lost: in whom the god of this world (Satan, John 12:31) hath blinded the minds of them which believe not, lest the light of the glorious gospel of Christ, who is the image of God, should shine unto them."

    d. Eph. 4:18—Here speaks of those out of Christ who "walk after the vanity of the mind: having the understanding darkened, being alienated from the life that (of) is in God through the ignorance that is in them, because of the blindness of their heart …"

    e. John 8:43–44a—Jesus says to His rejecters: "Why do ye not understand my speech? Even because ye cannot hear (with spiritual perception) my Word. Ye are of your father, the devil."

Again God's word reveals that dis-belief comes not because of intellectual and scientific pursuits or abilities—but from a "blindness of heart" that makes it impossible for a person "to see", "to understand" the things of God. This God calls, not intellectually, but "ignorance" (See Eph. 4:18 above). Thus the Psalmist says, "The fool saith in his heart, There is no God." Only the work of the Holy Spirit can bring the light of understanding and new life (See Gen. 1:2–3 plus II Cor. 4:6).

In Romans 1:19–32 is given the origin of this unbelief and disbelief—and the moral degeneration and spiritual disintegration of the human race. The moral and spiritual corruption and confusion of the human race did not come from the Christian faith—but from unbelief and disbelief, and professed "belief" which is not genuine. See II Cor. 5:17.

Thus the disbeliever will not be won by just arguments, refutations, etc., because the problem in him is not lack of intellectual knowledge, facts, etc., but a true blindness of heart as real as eye-blindness. Coaxing, chiding, arguing will not cause a person with blinded eyes to see. It is not that he just will not see—he cannot (see Jn. 3:3). He needs to be given light and sight. This God must do in his heart. Of course, your life and witness will and must be giving light (Matt. 5:14–16) but the Spirit must give the sight through the New Birth process. More along this line later, but for the moment remember that true faith will come to your dis-believing friend only as:

    1) Prayer is made continually that the Holy Spirit may open his heart to the truth.

    2) Your witness of life and lips is consistent, genuine, gracious and confident.

    3) He is willing to honestly seek the truth as stated in Jeremiah 29:13–14a: "And ye shall seek me, and find me, when ye search for me with all your heart. And I will be found of you saith the Lord."

Faith may come by 1) your intercession prayer and fruitful witness, 2) his (the disbeliever's) willingness to, from the heart, earnestly and honestly seek and search toward God, and 3) the Holy Spirit's renewing work in and upon his heart.

YOUR POSITION COMPARED TO THAT OF THE DIS-BELIEVER

It is good to compare (in your own mind, and share this with the dis-believer) your position as a person of faith with that of one who rejects the faith. Consider this:

1) If he is right—and there is no God, no Heaven, no hell, no Word from God, no Saviour, etc., you still have lost nothing in your holding and living by the Christian faith. It still is true that for this life, here on this confused planet, earth, this faith has produced and does produce the highest and most satisfying life, productive of the most

good both for the body and mind. It offers a compass for direction in life, a comfort for the ills of life, a strength for the tests of life, and a love for our fellow-sharers of life that disbelief cannot.

The Christian faith, even if false (which it isn't), produces the elements of life in a sincere, Christ-centered person, that 1) the world most needs, and 2) dis-belief cannot produce—such as the fruit of Galatians 5:22: "But the fruit of the Spirit is love, joy, peace, long-suffering (patient endurance), gentleness, goodness, faith, meekness (not weakness), temperance (the moderation of self-control)." These are the things that make life here and now worth living!

Atheism and dis-belief are not constituted to supply these. It is true that occasionally a dis-believer or unbeliever shows in his or her life the traits of graciousness and fine character—but these are not the results of dis-belief, but rather come from influences within and without that provide a conscience—arising from contact in life with the Christian or other religious—moral teachings in home or society, and the natural response of the "image of God" in which man was first created, and which sin has ruined but not totally obliterated. Left to its own results, the effect of dis-belief produces low standards and life as given in Galatians 5:19: "But the works of the flesh (unregenerate human nature) are manifest, which are these: adultery, fornication, uncleanness, lasciviousness (loose-living), idolatry, witchcraft, hatred, variance, emulations, wrath, strife, seditions, heresies, envying, murders, drunkenness, revellings, and such like." Also, Romans 1:25–32 present the natural results in the world of dis-belief and unbelief.

It is also true that many who "claim" to be Christians live by lower standards and then bring disgrace and ill-repute to the Faith and to Christ, giving the disbeliever a "talking point". "Not everyone that saith unto me, Lord, Lord, shall enter into the Kingdom of Heaven; but he that doeth the will of my Father which is in heaven"—Matthew 7:21. Just as the highly "moral" dis-believer is not representative of the true nature and general effects of dis-belief, so the low-living, so-called "Christian" is not representative of the true effects of the Christian faith.

In short—if atheism is right ("there is no God") you have lost nothing but rather profited by your position and faith

—BUT

2) If you are right (and you are) and the dis-believer is wrong, then he has lost all, including his own soul!

Thus, the Christian faith, sincerely held, not only produces a better life with far better Hope, but it has far better odds." "… He said unto them, Whosoever will come after me, let him deny himself, and take up his cross, and follow me. For whosoever will save his life shall lose it, but whosoever shall lose his life for my sake and the gospel's, the same shall save it. For what shall it profit a man if he gain the whole world and lose his own soul? Or what shall a man give in exchange for his soul."—Mark 8:34–37

Thank God, He has "opened our hearts" to know, and our eyes to see that:

Gen. 1:1

John 3:16

John 14:6

are true. As is the God who spoke these Words, and the Book in which He spoke them.

Thus we, with Peter can exult (1 Peter 1:3–4 and 8–9): "Blessed be the God and Father of our Lord Jesus Christ, which according to His abundant mercy hath begotten us again (caused us to be born again) unto a living hope by the resurrection of Jesus Christ from the dead, to an inheritance, incorruptible, and undefiled, and that fadeth not away, reserved in heaven for you—Jesus Christ: whom having not seen, ye love, in whom, though now ye see Him not, yet believing, ye rejoice with joy unspeakable and full of glory: Receiving the end of your faith, even the salvation of your souls."

So: "Cast not away your confidence, which hath great recompense of reward. For ye have need of patience that, after ye have done the will of God, ye might receive the promise. For yet a little while, and He that shall come will come, and will not tarry. Now the just (justified) shall live by faith: but if any man draw back, my soul shall have no pleasure in him. But we are not of them who draw back unto perdition, but of them that believe to the saving of the soul." Hebrews 10:35–39.

THE CHRISTIAN'S RELATIONSHIP WITH THE DIS-BELIEVER

The question now is: What can be the relationship, between the believing Christian and the dis-believer who repudiates the Christian faith on the basis of atheism or agnosticism (doubt)? The Christian here, as always, must be guided by the principles given in the Word of God. This will make for the safety of the Christian's steadfastness and be far more likely to bring the dis-believer to faith. Compromise at this point can injure the believer and greatly lessen the possible influence of that believer to be used of God to win dis-believers to Christ. To compromise here may win the approval of the dis-believer, but it will not win his respect for Christ or Christians.

First of all, the Christian should not have a relationship with the dis-believer that is based on an intimate, steady social companionship. Especially is this true for Christian young people regarding a disbeliever of the opposite sex. Dating, and such forms of intimate and regular association, between a Christian youth and a disbeliever is out!

II Corinthians 6:14–15 and 17: "Be not unequally yoked together with unbelievers: for what fellowship hath righteousness with unrighteousness? And what communion hath light with darkness? And what concord hath Christ with Belial (Satan)? Or what part hath he that believeth with an infidel (unbeliever, dis-believer)? Wherefore come out from among them, and be ye separate, saith the Lord, and touch not the unclean thing; and I will receive you."

II John, verses 9–11: "Whosoever transgresseth, and abideth not in the doctrine of Christ, hath not God. He that abideth in the doctrine of Christ, he hath both the Father and the Son. If any come unto you and bring not this doctrine, receive him not into your house, neither bid him God speed: For he that biddeth him God speed is partaken of his evil deeds."

Secondly, this does not mean that friendliness should be eliminated or cordial graciousness. On the contrary these, plus helpfulness, in the routine contacts with dis-believers are the order for a Christian who wants to see them finally brought to Christ. Col. 4:5—"Walk in wisdom toward them that are without, redeeming the time."

1 Tim. 3:7—"Moreover he must have a good report of them which are without (out of Christ)."

II Tim. 2:24–25—"And the servant of the Lord must not strive; but be gentle unto all men, apt to teach, patient, in meekness instructing those that oppose themselves, if peradventure God will give them repentance to the acknowledging of the truth."

A "holier than thou", "I'm too good to associate with you" attitude is taboo—out!

Jesus did associate with sinners! But not for social reasons or advantages, or any other reason than His desire and effort to win and save them. Associations based only and wholly on this desire and purpose are right between the believer and the unbeliever.

It is to be noted, however, that the dis-believer who blatantly, pridefully, rejected Him and would not hear Him, Christ scathingly rebuked and condemned. See John 8:42–45 and John 5:42–44 plus Matthew 23:1–36. This reminds us to mark the difference between:

a) The blatant, prideful, open rejecter of Christ, and the
b) Honest, sincere, humble doubter who wants the truth, but hasn't been able yet to find it.

Thirdly, it is necessary to remember that, having been saved by your faith in Christ, you are ambassador (representative and spokesman) for Him.

II Corinthians 5:19–20—"To wit, that God was in Christ reconciling the world unto Himself, not imputing their trespasses unto them; and hath committed to us the word of reconciliation. Now, then, we are ambassadors for Christ, as though God did beseech you by us, we pray you in Christ's stead, be ye reconciled to God."

We are, therefore, to be ready at all times to:

1) Witness to and for Christ—"Ye shall be witnesses unto me" Acts 1:8.

We are "witnesses" to the dis-believer in two primary ways:

a) By the testimony of a transformed life, a demonstration of Jesus Christ in our human lives. "Let no man despise thy youth; but be thou an example (sample, demonstration) of the believers, in Word, in conversation (daily walk), in love, in spirit, in faith, in purity." 1 Timothy 4:12.
b) By the testimony of your lips, backed by an informed mind. This "lip" witness includes the testimony of 1) what Christ means to you, 2) what the Scriptures say about Him, and 3) the testimony of scholars whose writings on behalf of the Bible and our faith you should become familiar with.

Splendid works by competent Biblical scholars can be secured at little cost in paperback editions such as those put out by Moody Press, and cover subjects ranging from the authenticity and inspiration of the Bible to evolution.

2) Contend for the Christian faith

"Beloved, when I gave diligence to write unto you of the common salvation, it was needful for me to write unto you that ye should earnestly contend for the faith which was once delivered unto the saints ... for there are certain men ... denying the only Lord God, and our Lord Jesus Christ." Jude, verses 3 and 4c.

In the face of disbelief and atheism the Christian part is not cowardly silence and acquiescence. As someone has said, "When it comes to witnessing, silence is not golden, it is yellow!" We are to stand for Christ, stand up for Him, and stand against attacks made upon Him. This is admittedly not easy, but is the part of honor—and part of our warfare here for Him. This is presented so clearly in Ephesians 6:10–18.

It is true that oft times we may be involved with those who by age, position, and intellect are our peers. None-the-less our call is to "contend for the faith" in what Paul calls "the defense of the gospel." Remember, God is for us and with us, and "greater is He that is in you, than he that is in the world" (1 Jn. 4:4). For instance Dr. Geo. Manford Gutzke, professor at Columbia Theological Seminary, when he was an agnostic young school teacher in Canada, was won to faith in Christ through the instrumentality of an uneducated farmer, who none-the-less, spoke and witnessed to Christ.

Again, as in witnessing, the three resources you have for contending are—use of 1) the Scriptures, 2) your testimony, 3) the material from Christian scholars in the field of Scriptures, science, etc.

BUT—our contending must not be "contentious", but in serious graciousness with courage. Our purpose is not to win an argument, but to win a soul, not to win a point, but a person. It is possible to win an argument but lose the soul because of a "contentious", mean attitude. It is possible to lose an argument but win the soul because of your calm, gracious, assurance of your faith and Christ!

We are not called to be "wits" for Christ, but "witnesses". We are never to bluff, pretend, etc. in our contending when we are intellectually out-matched by the one we contend with. We are humbly, boldly, graciously to declare the truth of Christ out of Scripture and our experience, and trust the Holy Spirit to use these.

"But foolish and unlearned questions avoid, knowing that they do gender strifes … be gentle to all men, apt to teach, patient"—II Tim. 2:23–24.

3) Pray for the dis-believer.

Pray often, pray much for him. You can talk to God about him when you can't talk to him about God. "The sincere fervent prayer of a righteous man availeth much" James 5:16b. Remember that the dis-believer's problem is spiritual blindness and only the Spirit of God can illuminate him to see and accept the truth. So—pray!

"And this is the confidence we have in Him, that if we ask any thing according to His will, he heareth us … if any man see his brother sin a sin not unto death, he shall ask, and he shall give him life for them that sin not unto death."—1 Jn. 5:14 & 16a.

"I exhort therefore that—intercessions—be made for all men—for this is good and acceptable in the sight of God our Saviour; who will (desires to) have all men to be saved, and to come unto the knowledge of the truth"—1 Timothy 2:1 and 3–4.

4) Be careful to keep your own faith intact.

"Beware lest any man spoil you through philosophy and vain deceit, after the tradition of men, after the rudiments of the world, and not after Christ."—Col. 2:8.

Remember that the disbeliever may be out to destroy your faith, just as you desire to bring him to faith.

A Christian is doomed to confusion, frustration, and non-effectiveness unless a fresh relationship is daily maintained with Christ through daily Bible study and prayer. If, during this time daily, the world is shut out, the result will be a consciousness of His blessed presence during the day, and will result in a daily life consistent with the high calling we have in Christ.

The consistent, uncompromising life in Christ is an argument no disbeliever can answer.

The thrill of living in Christ, witnessing to Christ, standing for Christ, contending for the faith of Christ—and thus winning others to Him is the Christian's privilege!

May God make you one of His answers to the unbelief and dis-belief of the world—to the "civilized", "cultured" pagan as well as to the savage, untaught heathen.

With you in the grip of Christ—

Love,
Your Dad

THE CHRISTIAN PREACHER

Sam Patterson

Excerpted from the brochure "Where Shall I Prepare for the Gospel Ministry?"
published by Reformed Theological Seminary (undated).

The best authority for what is adequate preparation for a preaching or teaching ministry is of course the Bible, particularly that portion which deals with this subject, namely, I Timothy, II Timothy and Titus. These Epistles, written by Paul, the great apostle missionary of the gospel, are an infallible guide to what a minister should be and do.

Paul states quite simply the basic purpose of the Christian minister in II Timothy 2:5–7, where he testifies that he himself is one appointed a preacher of Christ Jesus.

The Preacher Gives Attention to God's Word

To be a preacher of our Lord Jesus Christ involves many things. It requires, for one thing, giving attention to the Word of God—"Give heed to reading, to exhortation, to teaching" (I Timothy 4:13).

Reading God's Word and expounding that Word to the hearers—this is the very heart of the Christian minister's task. Nothing can be more important than your faithful handling of God's Truth. So again we read, "Give diligence to present thyself approved unto God, a workman that needeth not to be ashamed, handling aright the Word of Truth" (II Timothy 2:15).

Whether the Word of God is popular, or whether the hearers are favorable to it, is not a consideration. "Preach the Word, be urgent in season, out of season; reprove, rebuke, exhort, with all longsuffering and teaching" (II Timothy 4:2).

Furthermore, the Word must be proclaimed with authority, not your own authority, but God's. So Paul exhorts Titus, "These things speak and exhort and reprove with all authority, Let no man despise thee" (Titus 2:15).

You see then that the office of the Christian ministry is a noble calling and a heavy responsibility. To prepare for such a ministry, one must have the highest respect for God's Word. It is essential to all he will do and say.

Paul reveals that he so respected the Word of God, in commenting upon Timothy's background in the Scriptures. "But abide thou in the things which thou hast learned and hast been assured of, knowing of whom thou hast learned them and that from a babe thou hast known the Sacred Writings which are able to make thee wise unto salvation through faith which is in Christ Jesus" (II Timothy 3:14, 15).

It is impossible to fulfill the task of the Christian ministry without complete reliance upon an absolute and authoritative standard, God's Word, the Bible, is such a standard; and Paul would give every young minister-in-training the same directive he gave Timothy: "All Scripture is given by inspiration of God and is profitable for doctrine, for reproof, for correction, for instruction in righteousness, that the man of God may be complete, thoroughly furnished unto every good work" (II Timothy 3:16, 17).

The Preacher is Faithful to Sound Doctrine

"Thy Word is truth"—John 17:17.

A second thing involved in being a preacher of our Lord Jesus Christ is faithfulness to sound doctrine. Any reader of Paul's Pastoral Epistles can observe that this theme runs through his writings.

The Christian minister must be conservative in the sense that he is to conserve the sound doctrine coming from Scripture. That good thing committed unto thee guard through the Holy Spirit which dwelleth in us" (II Timothy 1:14).

Paul had no tolerance for doctrinal novelty and speculation. To be a loyal preacher of Christ, one simply has to be faithful to Christ's own teaching, of which Paul was a witness. Paul's words leave us no room for doubt as to his personal attitude. "If any man teacheth a different doctrine and consenteth not to sound words, even the words of our Lord Jesus Christ, and to the doctrine which is according to godliness; he is puffed up, knowing nothing" (I Timothy 6:3–4).

Taking just a few other brief statements from the Epistles, we find such exhortations as these: "Charge men not to teach a different doctrine" (I Timothy 1:3); "Reprove them sharply that they may be sound in the faith" (Titus 1:13); "Speak thou the things which befit the sound doctrine" (Titus 2:1). To these could be added many similar admonitions.

The Preacher Fights the Good Fight of Faith

A third thing involved in being a preacher of Jesus Christ is fighting the good fight of faith (I Timothy 6:12). To many, the conservative position is associated with strife and discord. But Paul exhorts Timothy, "Put them in remembrance charging them in the sight of the Lord, that they strive not about words, to no profit, to the subverting of them that hear" (II Timothy 2:14).

No less than seven times in his three Pastoral Epistles Paul uses words similar to these: "Shun foolish questionings, and genealogies, and strifes, and fighting about the law; for they are unprofitable and vain" (Titus 3:9).

Can anything be more positive than Paul's description of the Lord's servant? "The Lord's servant must not strive, but be gentle towards all, apt to teach, forebearing, in meekness correcting them that oppose themselves" (II Timothy 2:24–25).

To fight the good fight of faith, Timothy is challenged to use not the carnal weapons of the flesh, but rather to "war the good warfare; holding faith and a good conscience" (I Timothy 1:18–19).

The Preacher is a Leader

A fourth thing involved in being a preacher of Christ is leadership. By virtue of your office, you will be a leader when you are ordained to the Christian ministry.

The awesome task of the minister in regard to leadership can be seen in what Paul says to Timothy: "Against an elder receive not an accusation, except at the mouth of two or three witnesses. Them that sin reprove in the sight of all, that the rest also may be in fear … Observe these things without prejudice, doing nothing by partiality, lay hands hastily on no man, neither be partaker of other men's sins" (I Timothy 5:19–22).

Consider also these words to Titus, "For this cause I left thee in Crete that thou shouldest set in order the things that were wanting, and appoint elders in every city" (Titus 1:5).

For such responsibility God has granted to the Christian minister the help of the Holy Spirit. "That good thing which was committed unto thee guard through the Holy Spirit which dwelleth in us" (I Timothy 1:14). Again, "God hath not given us a spirit of fearfulness; but of power, and love, and discipline" (II Timothy 1:7).

The Preacher is an Evangelist

Finally, no preacher of Christ has fulfilled his task unless he is an evangelist. "Do the work of an evangelist, fulfill thy ministry" (II Timothy 4:5).

Evangelism, the work of proclaiming the gospel to the lost, is at the heart of the Christian ministry.

WE ARE HUMAN

Sam Patterson

*Sam wrote the following as a manual for
French Camp Academy staff members.*

Christians are human.

This fact faces us in every Christian enterprise.

We need to face this fact, now.

This fact explains the too frequent rise in Christian homes, churches, missions, organizations, and institutions of frictions and factions, of divisions and differences, of problems and petty peeves, of hurt feelings and hidden jealousies, of misunderstandings and plain meanness.

Such things are forbidden in Scripture, odious to all who observe them, damaging to the honor of the Saviour, damning to those we attempt to serve, and disheartening to those involved.

Such things are not uncommon.

Yet, such things need not be.

Christians are human. BUT Christians are also the children of God. In our salvation God has not only given us a place in His family, but also gives us the power to behave as a child of God.

The following pages are provided for the consideration of those of us who are called by God to serve Christ in the mission of youth at French Camp Academy. Attention is called to certain passages and principles in the Bible that have a very practical and a very spiritual application for our lives as we labor together with Christ in this school.

If these counsels of God are not honored in your life, it is certain that in time you will create problems and will yourself be a problem in this school. If these counsels of God are honored by you and find in you an humble yielding to the Lord who calls and counsels us, in spite of admitted limitations, your life and work here will be blessed ... and a blessing.

You and Your Lord

No work for God and no service in a Christian mission cause (such as French Camp Academy) can be fruitful, successful, or happy unless two relationships with Christ are a matter of fact in your experience.

In YOUR life—

1. Christ must be Saviour.

"For as many as received Him, to them gave He power to become the sons of God, even to them that believe on His name." (John 1:12)

That Christ, God's Son, died for sinners on the cross, and that He arose from the dead to be Lord of His people is a matter of history. That you have personally, definitely received Him in faith as your Saviour and Lord must also be a matter of your history.

He can only be served by lives He has saved.

2. Christ must be preeminent.

"...that in all things He might have the preeminence." (Col. 1:18)

It is not enough that Christ should be prominent in our lives. He must be preeminent. It is not enough that He should have a place in our lives. He must have the primary place.

Many (saved) people have Christ prominent in their lives, but not preeminent ... have Him in an important place but not in the first place. Because He is prominent, they will often seek to serve in a Christian mission. Because Christ is not preeminent, they usually become well-meaning problems and handicaps, being easily offended, prone to worry and suspicion, short of temper, irritable, self-concerned, critical ... and with all of this, often self-righteous. Thus the work suffers, frictions arise, and Christ is dishonored.

Our privilege of grace is to let the Lord be Lord, to give up wholly to Christ, and day by day live in the trust—life that may be ours as it was Paul's:

"I am crucified with Christ. Nevertheless, I live; yet not I, but Christ liveth in me, And the life I now live I live by the faith of the Son of God who loved me and gave himself for me." (Gal. 2:20)

You and Your Work

Your coming to serve in this Christian youth mission ought to be with the Inner Assurance! "Hitherto hath the Lord led me."

Your work here, then, is of Him, for Him, and unto Him. The quality of your fidelity, labor, and spirit must be approved by the One to whom account must be given.

The Lord's work is no place for laziness, listlessness, self-will, or excuses.

Our service is not to be guided by watching what, how much, or how little others do.

Rather, our work for Him is always to be determined by the principles He has given to us:

"And whatsoever ye do in word or deed, do all in the name of the Lord Jesus, giving thanks unto God and the Father by Him." (Col. 3:17)

"And whatsoever ye do, do it heartily, as unto the Lord, and not unto men; Knowing that of the Lord ye shall receive the reward of the inheritance: for ye serve the Lord Christ." (Col. 3:23–24)

"Therefore, my beloved brethren, be ye steadfast, unmovable, always abounding in the work of the Lord, forasmuch as ye know that your labour is not in vain in the Lord." (1 Cor. 15:58)

You and Your Resources

God never calls a person to a work for Him without providing adequate resources for the job. When you serve Him you are not left to your own strength, wisdom, and abilities.

IF you faithfully look to Him, your testimony will be, "He knoweth thy walking through this great wilderness: these forty years the Lord thy God hath been with thee; thou has lacked nothing." (Deut. 2:7)

Our unfailing promise is:

"But my God shall supply all your need according to His riches in glory, by Christ Jesus." (Philippians 4:19)

YOUR job CAN be done BY YOU because—

The Heavenly Father, through Jesus Christ, gives to you the following adequate resources:

His own unfailing presence—"For He hath said, I will never leave thee nor forsake thee. So we may boldly say, The Lord is my helper, and I will not fear what man shall do unto me." (Heb. 13:5–6)

The divine assistance of the Holy Spirit with and within you—"But the Comforter, which is the Holy Spirit, whom the Father will send in my name, he shall teach you all things, and bring all things to your remembrance, whatsoever I have said unto you." (John 14:26)

The indwelling Christ—"Strengthened with might by His Spirit in the inner man; that Christ may dwell in your hearts by faith." (Eph. 3:16–17)

The needed nourishment for the Word of God—

"Man shall not live by bread alone, but by every word that proceedeth out of the mouth of God." (Matt. 4:4)

The power, privilege, and provision of Prayer—

"Hitherto ye have asked nothing in my name: ask, and ye shall receive, that your joy may be full." (John 16:24)

Your Weaknesses and You

Thank God for your strong points. Your special abilities, gifts, and training have given you a place in the work of this school.

But you have some weaknesses. This means danger ahead! Your weaknesses may be in the area of health, spiritual life, nerves, disposition, or personality.

These weaknesses can mean failure in your work and problems to those who must work with you. They can mean serious problems to the boys and girls you want to serve.

YOUR strong points can never make up for your weak points. Never forget this.

Your personal, peculiar weaknesses can only find their solution as they throw you back constantly upon the grace of God, that His strength may fill them up. Thus, weaknesses in your life can become the greatest areas of strength in you ... as you let God do in you what you cannot do by yourself.

"Who is weak and I am not weak?" said Paul. And God said to him: "My grace is sufficient for thee: for my strength is made perfect in weakness." And Paul responded: "Most gladly therefore will I rather glory in my infirmities, that the POWER OF CHRIST may rest upon me." (II Cor. 11:20, 12:9)

"I can do all things through Christ which strengtheneth me." (Phil. 4:13)

You and Your Problems

You will have your problems.

During the course of your service here you will, as all men do, have certain personal problems arise. These may come from your family, your finances, your work, your colleagues, your health, etc.

These problems can give rise in you to worry, anxiety, fretting and nervousness. These can affect your disposition, work and effectiveness.

It is imperative that we all, for our own well-being and that of our work, learn to commit our problems to the Lord as they arise, and to learn to TRUST Him to the point of habitually resting ourselves and our problems in and on Him.

"Casting all your care upon Him; for He careth for you." (1 Pet. 5:7)

"Be careful (anxious) for nothing; but in everything by prayer and supplication with thanksgiving let your requests be made known unto God. And the peace of God, which passeth understanding, shall keep your hearts and minds through Christ Jesus." (Phil. 4:6–7)

"Fret not thyself...

"Trust in the Lord...

"Delight thyself also in the Lord...

"Commit thy way unto the Lord...

"Rest in the Lord...

"Wait patiently for Him...

"And the Lord shall keep them ... because they trust Him." (Ps. 37:1, 3–7, 40)

You and Your Weariness

You are going to get tired. Toil and tiredness go together. Work and weariness often go together.

You will enjoy your work for Christ at French Camp. But often the demand of hours and duty will cause you to feel depleted in nervous, physical, even spiritual energy.

Then weariness sets in. Watch out for this.

Weariness is not just being tired. It is being tired to the point of being discouraged and disheartened.

"No one knows how thin is the line between discouragement and failure," someone said.

Satan takes all kinds of advantages in weariness.

So the Scriptures urge: "And let us not be weary in well doing: for in due season we shall reap, if we faint not." (Gal. 6:9)

Our victory over weariness is promised in the Bible.

"But they that wait upon the Lord shall renew their strength; they shall mount up with wings as eagles; they shall run and not be weary and they shall walk and not faint." (Is. 40:31)

"Come unto me, all ye that labour and are heavy laden, and I will give you rest. Take my yoke upon you, and learn of me; for I am meek and lowly of heart; and ye shall fine rest unto your souls." (Matt. 11:28–29)

And thus—"We faint not; but though the outward man perish, yet the inward man is renewed day by day." (II Cor. 4:16)

You and Your Responsibility

Your work here gives you a place of responsibility in the two most important areas of life:

Young life—the boys and girls you work with,

Eternal life—the Christ you serve.

The primary aim of this school, and all who labor here, should be to bring these Young Lives into vital contact with Eternal Life through personal faith in Christ.

This demands the very best we have.

We must bring each youngster to faith in Christ. Then, on across the days and years of our work with him or her, we must secure growth in the Christian faith, the development of Christian character, a maturing in the Christian life, the adoption of Christian values, and so prepare them to leave the school ready for Christian citizenship for the years to come—on earth, and in heaven.

Fatal to this aim can be indifference, insincerity, inconsistency, a poor example, or a poor attitude on your part.

"And whosoever shall receive one such little child in my name receiveth me. But whoso shall offend (cause to stumble) one of these little ones which believe on me, it were better for him that a millstone were hanged about his neck, and that he were drowned in the depth of the sea." (Matt. 18:5–6) Thus spoke Jesus.

Perfection is not required in us for this work or else none of us would be here. But what is required is a sincere recognition of the school's purpose and our own responsibility, a sincere personal commitment not only to live with these boys and girls, but to live for them, and a quickness to note our own personal failures and a hastening on our part to bring our faults to the Lord in humble confession and trust Him at once to correct in us the wrongs.

"Not that we are sufficient of ourselves to think anything of ourselves; but our sufficiency is of God." (II Cor. 3:5)

You and Your Colleagues

Christians are human. Humans are imperfect.

Part of your problem is that you will be working closely, daily with colleagues as imperfect as you yourself are.

It is not enough to recognize this and "make allowances."

To live with and to be happy with colleagues who will be making honest mistakes, and at times manifesting what we might consider inexcusable errors; to protect ourselves and our colleagues from our taking a position of critic or judge for which position we have not been employed; to enable us to help instead of hurt when others seem to be letting down; we must do what the Lord has prescribed for just this situation:

"I therefore ... beseech you that ye walk worthy of the vocation wherewith ye are called, with all lowliness and meekness, with longsuffering, forbearing one another in love; endeavoring to keep the unity of the Spirit in the bond of peace." (Eph. 4:1–3)

"Let nothing be done through strife or vain glory; but in lowliness of mind let each esteem others better than themselves." (Phil. 2:3)

"Let us not be desirous of vain glory, provoking one another, envying one another. Brethren, if a man be overtaken in a fault, ye that are spiritual, restore such an one in the spirit of meekness; considering thyself, lest thou also be tempted." (Gal. 5:26, 6:1)

Only the love for each other that comes from our love for Christ can provide the lubricant that can cause us to work together without hot friction and grinding gears.

Never forget that the kids know it when you are at odds with or critical of another staff member. It always results in a degree of insecurity for them and a question mark regarding you.

You and Your Youthful Charges

These boys and girls you serve, as do all youngsters, need:

(1) The kind of love that makes them know they are important to someone.

(2) The kind of discipline that is fair, firm, and is consistent.

(3) The chance to know and live with a real man of God and a real woman of God who is not a spiritual fraud or fake, but genuine.

You must provide all three of these in YOU or rate an "F" for failure.

Boys and girls intuitively, uncannily—

Spot fakery

See inconsistency

Sense insincerity

Recognize unfairness

You can't fool them.

They will "learn" you before you "learn" them.

Thus, they will keep you on your toes, sometimes on your back, but always on your knees.

"And ye fathers, provoke not your children to wrath; but bring them up in the nurture and admonition of the Lord." (Eph. 6:4)

"And though I have all faith so that I could remove mountains and have not love, I am nothing." (1 Cor. 13:2)

"Train up a child in the way he should go, and when he is old he will not depart from it." (Prov. 22:6)

"The rod and reproof give wisdom; but a child left to himself bringeth his mother shame. Correct thy son, and he shall give thee rest; yea, he shall give delight to thy soul." (Prov. 29:15, 17)

You and Your Temper

Temper means trouble.

The only godly temper is a governed temper. Most tempers are ungoverned and ungodly.

Some Christians say, "I am hot tempered and get mad quickly, but I get over it quickly." Perhaps quick murder is better than slow murder, but both are equally deadly. Your "mad" may go quickly. The wounds, folly, and damage are never quickly, and sometimes just plain never, gone.

A fitful temper wags the tongue with the irresponsibility of a "drunk" waving a loaded, firing pistol. A fitful temper stirs the emotions without the restraint and reason of wisdom.

An adult temper tantrum is an immaturity that is intolerable.

Decisions and discipline regarding children, that come during a seizure of madness or temper, will probably be intemperate, unwise, and untimely. And if not, still the corrective value will be gone as you lose the respect and gain the resentment of the child you are dealing with.

Criticism and judgment regarding your colleagues made during a temper seizure will probably make an incision in the wrong place and irritate, not heal or help, the matter that made you mad.

"He that is slow to wrath is of great understanding; but he that is hasty of spirit exalteth folly." (Proverbs 14:29)

"A soft answer turneth away wrath; but grievous words stir up anger." (Proverbs 15:1)

"He that answereth a matter before he heareth it, it is folly and shame unto him." (Proverbs 18:13)

"He that hath no rule over his own spirit is like a city that is broken down, and without walls." (Proverbs 25:28)

"Let all bitterness, and wrath, and anger, and clamour, and evil speaking, be put away from you, with all malice." (Eph. 4:31)

You and Your Opportunity

This school offers you the opportunity of a lifetime.

It offers you the opportunity to make an eternal investment in a whole gang of young lives with needs, and problems, and eternal destinies.

To many of them you can become the most important human friend and influence of their lifetime.

They are just at the proverbial crossroads of life. You are entering their lives just in time to help them to take the right turn and to head in the right direction.

Think!

Could you have greater opportunity anywhere?

What if you loaf on the job? What if you fumble the ball?

But surely you won't.

God did not bring you here, and you did not come here, for, the crucifixion of such an opportunity.

You came to count for something.

You came to count for Someone.

"Every man's work shall be made manifest: for the day shall declare it, because it shall be revealed by fire; and the fire shall try every man's work of what sort it is." (1 Cor. 3:13)

You and Your Pay

A successful and gifted businessman in Canada determined to leave his position and go to India as a missionary.

A business house offered him four successive offers of employment with a generous increase in salary being made with each successive offer.

He replied in the negative to each offer.

The company was puzzled. Enough money ought to buy anything. "What's the matter? Isn't the pay big enough?"

He replied, "The pay is big enough but the job isn't."

He went to India. The job was bigger.

An American businessman visiting the Far East went out to observe a mission leper colony. He observed a young American lady treating and dressing the repulsive sores and the decaying limbs of the lepers.

He said, "I wouldn't do that for a million dollars."

She said, "Neither would I."

He said, "Well, what are you doing it for?"

She said, "I do it for Christ."

Your monthly check is a convincing evidence that you are not at French Camp for big pay. You are here for the big job. Christ is in your thinking.

But God has His own remuneration for faithful service.

"And whosoever shall give to drink unto one of the little ones a cup of cold water only in the name of a disciple, verily I say to you, he shall not lose his reward." (Matt. 10:42)

"Your Heavenly Father knoweth that ye have need of all these things. But seek ye first the kingdom of God, and His righteousness; and all these things shall be added unto you." (Matt. 6:32–33)

SOMETHING GOOD HAS HAPPENED TO DEATH
2 Timothy 1&4

Sam C. Patterson

A message delivered in 1974 by Sam Patterson, then president of Reformed Theological Seminary. RTS later reproduced his remarks as a brochure.

Paul seemed to talk as a madman. Everyone knows that death is sad news, bad news, not glad news. Yet the apostle called the death of the One he loved most "good news." He believed that Jesus' death did something good to death and filled the death of His people with good news.

Paul's last contribution to the canon of Scripture is his second letter to Timothy. In the opening sentences he speaks of the death of death accomplished by Christ*; in the closing sentences he speaks of his own death as a disciple of Christ.

The Death of Death

Not only is the sixth sentence in this epistle three verses long (II Timothy 1:8–10), it is also massive in the dimensions of its message. Here Paul makes one of the boldest affirmations concerning Jesus Christ ever made. In the same sentence, and in this connection, Paul pens a most devastating declaration about death. In verse 10, he gives death's obituary.

Who saved us and called us with a holy calling, not in virtue of our own works but in virtue of His own purpose and grace which He gave us in Christ Jesus ages ago, and now has manifested through the appearing of our Savior, Christ Jesus, who abolished death and brought life and immortality to light through the gospel (II Timothy 1:9–10).

Paul declares that the destruction of death has been accomplished. He proclaims that the death-blow to death has been dealt by Jesus Christ. He has "abolished" death! He has wrecked, ruined, and broken death. The phrase used may be translated thus: "He destroyed death." One commentator affirms that the thought can be rendered thus: "He has annihilated death."

Is Paul's statement true? Is he here carried away by his feelings into an inflated statement that is excessive and exaggerated? We answer these questions. Yes, the statement is true. No, the statement is not an exaggeration. Paul's statement is deliberate, factual, and substantive. It is not an expression of emotional extravagance. It is in keeping with the principle of integrity practiced by Paul in his writing and preaching, that is, to "refuse to practice cunning … But by open statement of the truth we could commend ourselves to every man's conscience in the sight of God" (II Corinthians 4:2).

Can we attend the funeral of a true believer in Jesus Christ today, see the evidences of death's reality—the lifeless body, the casket, the grave—and still claim that Christ has dealt the death-blow to death? The answer is yes. Paul speaks the truth. This truth is best declared in the very presence of death. It is in the letter announcing his own impending death that Paul declares that death has been fatally struck.

Elsewhere, the apostle explains what he means regarding death's death. He does this in such passages as I Corinthians 1. He shows that death received its fatal blow from the death, the resurrection, and the forthcoming return of Jesus Christ.

For I delivered unto you as of first importance what I also received, that Christ died for our sins in accordance with the Scriptures, that He was buried, that He was raised on the third day in accordance with the Scriptures ... then at His Coming ... comes the end, when He delivers the kingdom to God the Father after destroying every rule and every authority in power. The last enemy to be destroyed is death. Thanks be to God who gives us the victory through our Lord Jesus Christ (I Corinthians 15:3–4, 23–24, 26; Romans 7:25).

The sting of death is sin, Paul declares (I Corinthians 15:56). Sin brings death to man's relationship with God and enforces separation from God in this life and in the life to come. But Christ has taken sin's sting for His people. He has taken sin altogether out of the death of believers because He Himself has borne sin's condemnation, penalty, and judgment on their behalf in His own death on the cross.

He himself bore our sins on the tree, that we might die to sin and live to righteousness. By His wounds we are healed (I Peter 2:24).

That through death He might destroy him who has the power of death, that is the devil, and deliver those who through fear of death were subject to lifelong bondage (Hebrews 2:14c–15).

Christ having borne our sins has removed this separation and has reconciled and united us to God in total and eternal forgiveness both in this life and in the life to come. Now, even physical death cannot separate us from God.

For I am sure that neither death ... nor anything else in all creation can separate us from the love of God in Christ Jesus our Lord (Romans 8:38–39).

Christ has made death His handyman and has reduced death to a servant who can only open the door to heaven for Christ's people and so fulfill Christ's request:

"Father, I desire that they also, who thou hast given me, may be with me where I am, to behold my glory which thou hast given me in thy love for me before the foundation of the world" (John 17:24).

The redeeming death of Christ having removed sin from the account of those who belong to Him also removes sin's force so that death must usher their souls (self-conscious personalities) immediately into the glory of heaven.

The power of the grave has been broken in Christ's resurrection. He submitted to all that death and the grave could do for three days. Then, as Samson snapping the vines, He broke the bonds of death and stepped out of death and the grave and into the life of this world alive and risen! In so doing, He ripped the sinews, tore the tendons, cut the muscles, and broke the bones of the hand of the grave and so relieved its grip and grasp that it is not more than a temporary caretaker of the bodies of His people. The grave is, for them, no more than His depository in His good earth. It retains the bodies of His own, their souls being in heaven, until He comes in glory to raise them and endow them with bodies equipped for eternity.

We await a Savior, the Lord Jesus Christ, who will change our lowly body to be like His glorious body, by the power which enables Him even to subject all things to Himself (Philippians 3:20–21).

The Death of a Believer

In the fourth chapter of his second letter to Timothy, Paul speaks of his own expected death. He is in prison in Rome. He expects to be executed for his witness to Christ. He speaks words of confidence, comfort, and realism about his death. There is no fear. Though he will die, he will continue to live in the full benefits of Christ's triumph over death. Death is there, but does not darken the horizon of his future.

For I am already at the point of being sacrificed; the time of departure has come. I have fought the good fight, I have finished the race, I have kept the faith. Henceforth, there is laid up for me the crown of righteousness, which the Lord, the righteous judge, will award me at that Day, and not only to me but also to all who have loved His appearing (II Timothy 4:7–8).

In speaking of his impending death, Paul uses certain phrases that tell us some things about his own death, which we believe to be true as basic principles regarding the death of all who truly belong to Jesus Christ by grace through saving faith.

Note these three facts: A Believer's death is never untimely, never evil, and never fatal.

Paul's death was not untimely, nor is the death of any true believer. It is never premature or tardy. Paul says: "The time for my departure has come." The time is God's time. Paul speaks of his life as a "race," and he does not conceive of it as being interrupted and cut short by death. He has "finished" that race. Many at that time may have felt that Paul's life was being cut off at the zenith of its power and was being cut short prematurely before his work was completed. This was not Paul's viewpoint. His faith, and ours, affirms:

But I trust in thee, oh Lord, I say, thou art my God. My times are in thy hand (Psalm 31:14–15).

He works all things after the counsel of His own will (Ephesians 1:11b).

Your life is hid with Christ in God (Colossians 3:3).

Precious in the sight of the Lord is the death of His saints (Psalm 116:15).

Our good Shepherd is sovereign. His hand saves, keeps, cares for, guides, and protects His sheep. They are never "snatched" from His hand, not even by an untimely death. Rather, their "departure" as Paul calls the believer's death, is God's call to glory in His time.

My sheep hear my voice, and I know them and they follow me; and I give them eternal life, and they shall never perish, and no one shall snatch them out of my hand (John 10:28).

For some of God's people, the race of life seems to be a very short one, while for others it appears to be very long—measured by years. We are comforted by His Providence and know that, though we may not understand it, His purpose is fulfilled in what ever span of life He allots to us on earth. Consider our Savior. Prior to His death, He said, "My hour has not yet come." However, on the night before His death, He declared, "Father, the hour has come" (John 17:1). He was in the prime of His earthly life, 33 years of age. His public ministry was only three years old. From a natural point of view, it would appear that death at this point would be untimely and premature. This was not the case. He said, "And what shall I say? Father, save me from this hour? No, for this purpose I have come to this hour" (John 12:27). In terms of God's Plan, He fulfilled the full purpose for His coming, He secured our salvation. We believe that for those of us who are in Christ, God also accomplishes His purpose in the life span allotted us.

Paul's death is not "evil," nor is the death of any true believer in Jesus Christ. When Paul says in verse 18 of the fourth chapter of II Timothy, "The Lord will rescue me from every evil and save me for His heavenly kingdom, he is not saying that God will save him from death, but it will not be "evil!" It may be painful, awesome, but not evil. The concept is this: "To those who dwell in the shelter of the Most High, and abide in the shadow of the Almighty" it is said, "no evil shall befall you" (Psalm 91:1, 10). Paul knew that the sovereign grace of God so worked in and over His people that he could affirm: "We know that in everything God works for good for those who love him, who are called according to his purpose" (Romans 8:28). Everything includes the death of His people.

Is this not true of the death of our Savior? Though evil men designed to kill Him and planned to do this, and though it was their hands that nailed Him to the cross, still it was "according to the foreknowledge of God" (Acts 2:23). And the early Christians in Jerusalem affirmed that a Providence for good purpose presided over and overruled the evil intentions of the crucifiers, "to do whatever thy (God's) hand and thy plan has predestined to take place" (Acts 4:28). Though Christ's death seemed to be a victory for the Enemy and altogether evil, this was not the case. God's plan was prevailing and the greatest good the world knows came from this death, our salvation.

The death of Paul was not "fatal," nor is the death of any true believer. Death is never "the end." Rather, death punctuates the life of a believer with nothing more than a comma. The sentence of life goes right on through that comma into greater glory. Paul spoke of his death as a "departure." He was leaving here and going somewhere—to "His heavenly kingdom." Earlier Paul had written: "For me to live is Christ, to die is gain. My desire is to depart and be with Christ which is far better" (Philippians 1:21, 23). He said, "We are of good courage, and we would rather be away from the body and at home with the Lord" (II Corinthians 5:8). David spoke of going "through the valley of the shadow of death" (Psalm 23:4), that is through death from here to heaven. Thus at death, the soul (self-conscious personality) of the believer, goes immediately to heaven, while the body is kept, unite with Christ, in the grave until the further, final victory at Christ's return.

Paul declares in I Corinthians 15 and I Thessalonians 4, that when Christ returns He brings with Him His own who have died. He raises their bodies in their glorious eternal form as habitations for the everlasting glory of eternity. At that time, when He comes, His people then living in this world will not suffer physical death, but their bodies will be transformed in an instant with resurrection qualities and at that moment of His advent all the elect of the ages will together be caught up to meet and be with Christ in the Kingdom of eternal Glory. Christ returns with His heavenly people! The resurrection takes place! The final, never-ending reunion of God's total family occurs! His reign with us is without end, without sin, without death or sorrow! What a future!

Those who belong to Christ, therefore, may confidently face and answer two significant questions:

• Question 37, Shorter Catechism: "What do believers receive from Christ at death?"

Answer: "The souls of believers are at their death made perfect in holiness, and so immediately pass into glory; and their bodies being still unite to Christ, do rest in their graves until the resurrection."

• Question 1, Heidelberg Catechism: "What is your only comfort in life and in death?"

Answer: "That I belong body and soul, in life and in death—not to myself but to my faithful Savior Jesus Christ, who at the cost of his own blood has fully paid for all my sins and has completely freed me from the dominion of the devil; that He protects me so well that without the will of my Father in heaven not a hair can fall from my head; indeed, everything must fit His purpose for my salvation. Therefore, by His Holy Spirit, He also assures me of eternal life, and makes me wholeheartedly willing and ready from now on to live for him."

"Thanks be to God, who in Christ, always leads us in triumph, and through us spreads the fragrance of the knowledge of him everywhere" (II Corinthians 2:14).

* The terminology used in this message is suggested by the intriguing title of a definitive treatise on the atonement by John Owens, *The Death of Death in the Death of Christ*.

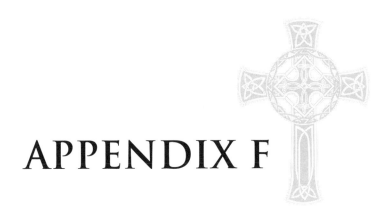

APPENDIX F

FAMILY

BEGINNINGS
Rebecca B. Hobbs

He shall be like a tree,
Planted by the rivers of water,
That brings forth its fruit in its season,
Whose leaf also shall not wither,
And whatever he does shall prosper.

Psalm 1:3 (NKJV)

... every man is a quotation from all his ancestors.
Ralph Waldo Emerson

Great men of God do not simply fall from heaven or spring up as weeds. They are planted by God (Psalm 1:3), many times in families where they are molded by experience and Providence into the servants they become. How Sam Patterson came to be the beloved man of God that he was is partly explained by the kind of people from whom he came. As Oliver Wendell Holmes so aptly put it, "This body in which we journey across the isthmus between the two oceans is not a private carriage, but an omnibus."

Reverence for the things of God did not begin with Sam, but was a strong trait on both his father's and mother's sides of the family for generations back. Both families are peppered with Presbyterian pastors and ruling elders, mostly ministering in the Associate Reformed Presbyterian denomination. If the men did not become pastors, they were usually instrumental in organizing churches or became ruling elders in existing churches. The women of the family were strong in faith and frequently married pastors or church leaders.

Sam grew up bathed constantly in a heritage of people who took God seriously and lived their lives according to His Word. Although pedigree does not save a person, Sam had a giant head start toward appreciating the things of God because of his heritage. Although in seminary he realized that heritage is not enough, one cannot overemphasize the role of his parents and ancestors in shaping Sam's spirituality.

Both sides of his family originated in Georgia, South Carolina, and North Carolina. His ancestors were all part of the great exodus from those states in the 1800s, settlers heading west looking for better farmlands and a stake in the new territories opening up. Some of his forebears stayed on the road for twenty years or more until they found the right spot to establish a home.

THE PATTERSONS

The story of Samuel Coleman Patterson actually began nearly three centuries ago with the birth in 1730 of his great-great grandfather John Patterson in County Antrim, Ireland. That's right, Sam's red hair was no genetic fluke! He was descended from several generations of sturdy Scotch-Irish stock, most of them Presbyterians. Apparently, John Patterson had connections with royalty, since he was granted land in the state of Georgia by the King of England and owned considerable property and several slaves. After fathering eleven children, he died in Elbert County, Georgia, in 1808. Historical papers indicate that he was an "intelligent, thrifty, well-to-do, and Christian man."[1]

John's eighth child was William Baskin Patterson, Sam's great-grandfather, for years a ruling elder in an Associate Reformed Presbyterian church near Anderson, South Carolina. Around 1853, he and his family became part of a large Scotch-Irish contingent looking for new land in the "west"; they appreciated the good climate and soil in the northern hills of Mississippi, and settled there. The area, which later became Tippah County, was located between the Pontotoc Ridge and the Flatwoods and was suitable for raising a variety of grains, vegetables, and fruits in the virgin soil without fertilizer. The climate was very comfortable, and wildlife was abundant.[2]

The period following the [Civil] war saw a great demand for cotton throughout the world, so the people settling in this region found a ready market for their cotton, no matter if it took a three-week trip to get the cotton to market, either in Memphis or Salisbury, Tennessee.[3] In fact, the popularity of cotton gave the new bustling town of Cotton Plant, four miles north of New Albany, its name. B. C. S. McAllister owned a cotton gin, and people began to speak of "going to the cotton plant," for no one said "gin" in those days. When the United States government started a post office there and asked for a name, McAllister suggested Cotton Plant.[4]

The community grew and prospered, becoming a distributing point for supplies to the farmers in the area. The Ebenezer Associate Reformed Presbyterian Church was organized July 16, 1842, in a log schoolhouse on the Cotton Plant Road, only a few hundred yards east of the site of the present church.[5] Today, the Ebenezer Cemetery is well kept, and many of the headstones bear the Patterson name. Sam's papers contain a letter concerning plans to restore some of the Patterson headstones.

William settled his family on "The Ridge," where the pasturage was excellent and the water overflowing near the surface. He became an elder at Ebenezer Church, and session records show he was a man of "godly and pious character."[6] However, he served in that capacity only a short time, for he died the year after arriving in Cotton Plant.

William and his wife, Jane (nee Henderson), had thirteen children, most of them married by the time they arrived in Tippah County; the next to youngest was Sam's grandfather, William Jasper, born in 1822. He was a thirty-one year-old widower, having married Margaret Carlisle who died before they had any children.

After the family arrived in Cotton Plant, William Jasper didn't waste any time finding a "bonny" bride in Isabella Catherine Foster, whom he married in 1855. She was a remarkably intelligent woman, with education above the times for a woman, having equipped herself to be a schoolteacher. Those who remember her speak of her jovial nature and witty mannerisms.[7] Her parents had moved from the Carolinas to Indiana, but she wanted to teach in the South, prompting her to move to Tippah County.

Isabella's family was notable. Her great-grandfather was James Couples Foster who was born in Ireland in 1753 and came to America in 1764, settling near Troy, South Carolina. A veteran of the Revolutionary War, he fathered eight children and was for many years a ruling elder in the Cedar Springs, South Carolina, ARP Church.

Sam's great-grandfather was Alexander Foster (1793–1853), who died shortly after coming to Cotton Plant about 1852. Church records show he was "… remarkable, not only for his piety, but for conscientiousness in the performance of whatever he believed to be his duty, irrespective of the opinions of others."[8] Alexander's first wife, Jane Crawford, died in 1832, after bearing him nine children. He then married Jane Adams, Sam's great-grandmother. From this union came six children. The oldest was Isabella Catherine, Sam's grandmother.

A TRAGIC BOYHOOD IN COTTON PLANT

William Jasper became a farmer, "quiet and unassuming but respected in community as an honest and able farmer."[9] He and Isabella had nine children, nearly half of whom died very young. The youngest, born January 2, 1875, was Sam's father, Samuel Jasper. Providence chose to bring some very difficult circumstances to him at a very young age. Such circumstances would be tragic even today, but in the nineteenth century, such problems frequently spelled catastrophe, especially for a family without financial means. Yet, they can also prove to be the cradle of the finest manhood, the birthplace of men of high determination and achievement.

Dedicated to the Confederacy, William Jasper served gallantly in the Civil War, but only for a short time. Foster Patterson writes, "… the strenuous military life proved too severe for a physical makeup that had never been rugged, and he was discharged after a few months service."[10] William Jasper died of pneumonia on January 7, 1878, at age 56.

After his death, daughter Margaret and her husband moved into the family home to help Isabella care for the family. Tragically, Isabella was dead within a year and a half of tuberculosis. She was only forty-five. Samuel Jasper was four when his mother died, and he often said later that the greatest vacant place ever torn in his heart was that left by the passing of his mother.[11] His older sisters recount how, after following the body of his mother to its last resting place in the old Ebenezer cemetery beside their father, Sam and brother Hugh were so grief-stricken that they wandered panic-stricken into the woods, unable to realize what had taken place. There they were found and comforted as much as possible, but the scars were never to leave them.[12]

After Isabella's death, Margaret took over the responsibility of the four young children and held the family together in the home place for a few years. Samuel Jasper wrote later:

> She did it under great difficulties, for the means were meager and the tasks many. By her devoted care, Christian instruction, and beautiful character she made a deep and abiding impression upon all of us…. She not only cared for my special needs, but she read the Bible to me and taught me to pray 'I lay me down to sleep.'[13]

Soon the burden of caring for her siblings grew too heavy, and homes had to be found for them with other people. Samuel Jasper went to live with Captain and Mrs. William

Spence, elderly people with no children. The loneliness soon became too great for a twelve-year-old boy; he missed his brother Hugh terribly. In *One Man's Family,* Samuel Jasper explains:

> As orphans, Hugh and I … passed through many tight places together. And in that 'school of hard knocks' our very souls were knitted together. He was always rugged and strong, while I was thin and frail; so he always fought my battles and hoed the long row and carried the heavy end of the load. He is as true a brother as any man ever had, and his devotion and fidelity have encouraged and inspired me all along life's way…. I have seen him tested by sorrow, misfortune, temptation, and sickness, but I have never yet heard him whimper or complain. He has as much grit and grace as any man I have ever known.[14]

So Samuel Jasper and Hugh went to live with cousins John and Martha Wiseman. Wiseman was an elder at Ebenezer Church. Two years later, Samuel Jasper moved to the home of Cousin John C. Newton, also an elder in the church, and began working on the farm for five dollars a month with board and laundry. Newton had married Samuel's first cousin Mattie. Samuel Jasper was happy here, as Mattie tried to be a mother to him, and her husband and her father, who lived with them, took a fatherly interest in the boy.

He grew up in that home reading the *Christian Observer*, the Associate Reformed newspaper, and books such as *A Life of Daniel Boone*, the Bible, and *Dr. Daniel Baker's Sermons*, the last of which he believes drew him to the ministry. Each evening, he gathered with the Newtons at the family altar.[15]

THE STRUGGLE FOR AN EDUCATION

One summer in his early teens, Samuel Jasper went to a revival at Ebenezer Church and gave his life to Christ. It was then that the call to Gospel ministry came to him, and he made up his mind to get an education and enter the ministry. From that determination he never wavered, even under difficulties and handicaps.

Bob, one of his older brothers, had become a successful businessman in New Albany and a ruling elder at Ebenezer Church. When Samuel Jasper decided to get a college education but didn't have any money, Bob paid his way through Robison High School in Salem, Tennessee, thus preparing him for college. His sister Esther also sent him a check to aid him in his struggle, although she did not have much money herself.

Samuel Jasper remembers that Bob was at first skeptical about his educational plans:

> When I told my older brother Bob of my ambition, he said … 'That is a worthy ambition, and I would love to see you achieve it, but it is simply beyond your reach. You have no money at all, and I know of no one who could finance your education, as it will require a good deal of money.' That struck me a hard blow. Recovering presently from the shock, I replied, 'I am going to graduate from Erskine College if it takes me until I am forty years old to do it!' At that, Bob said, 'I admire your determination, and if you are that serious, I will pay your way through Robison High School.'[16]

Through hard work, Samuel Jasper was ready for Erskine College in two years. Professor Robison, founder of the school, arranged for scholarship funds at Erskine; Samuel Jasper supplemented that with a part time janitor's job for two years. Since he had a taken a few freshman courses in high school, Erskine allowed him to enter as a trial sophomore; if he could do the work, he could remain. By burning the midnight oil, he succeeded and later led his class in grades. Other financial gifts and loans subsequently enabled him to give up the janitor's job and not have to drop out to earn money. He even set up a primitive barbershop in his room and gave many students and professors haircuts.

During his junior year, he began taking a couple of seminary courses, trying to finish early and save money. He continued to do that his senior year and remained one summer to do seminary work. As a result, he had completed the first year of a two-year seminary curriculum by the time he graduated from Erskine College. This allowed him to graduate early from Erskine Seminary in 1898.

Much like Sam, Samuel Jasper got far more than a theological education at seminary. During the summer of 1896, he began serving as supply pastor for Saline ARP Church near Wilmar, Arkansas. He had decided that it might not be wise to "keep company with the young ladies." He thought it would not be hard to do since "there would not be any young woman in Arkansas whom I would care about." The first Sunday, he was invited to have dinner with Mr. and Mrs. Calvin Grier Davis. Upon entering the dining room, he was introduced to their eldest daughter Lily and immediately changed his mind about girls in Arkansas. "I decided it would be my duty to give that member of my flock special attention. And from that time on, I employed all the persuasion and diplomacy, not to say deception, that I could command in the effort to win her hand and heart." [17]

They corresponded over the next year, and by the end of his second summer in the Saline church, he had her promise. From that point until they married, Lily painted a beautiful tri-fold screen for her trousseau, which Becky Patterson Rogers now owns. Samuel Jasper was twenty-four and Lily twenty-two when they married in 1899.

THE DAVISES

Lily and Samuel Jasper could not have come from more disparate backgrounds. While he grew up a poor orphan, Lily was raised in the relative comfort of an Arkansas plantation. His family was small and scattered, while the Davis clan was huge and close knit. Throughout Sam's life, they had grand family reunions at parks and retreat centers.

Anne Stephens, Lily's niece, says the Davises emphasized two things. "Religion and education were very important to them. If one family member wasn't able to get an education on his own, other members more able would help financially or in any other way they could."

Because of these emphases, many of Lily's ancestors were leaders in church, school, and community life. Her brother, Roy, and one of her cousins became pastors; one of her great uncles, Rev. Samuel Davis, became quite prominent in the ARP denomination. Nephew Grier Davis was also a pastor and became president of Montreat Anderson College.

Their families might have been different, but Lily and Samuel Jasper also had much in common. Lily's ancestors, too, had left the Carolinas and fought their way across the wilderness to carve out a home in new lands. Lily's paternal great-grandfather was

Israel Davis, born in Mecklinburg County, North Carolina, in 1784. His marriage to Sarah Nisbet in 1803 bore ten children, the fourth of whom was Robert, Sam's great-grandfather.

Robert married Margaret Nelson, and his sister, Sarah, wed Margaret's brother, William. Together the two couples left Mecklinburg County around 1837 and moved west through Tennessee and Mississippi to seek their fortune in unsettled lands. Determined to find just the right spot, the couples stayed on the trail for an incredible twenty years before arriving in Drew County, Arkansas, where they settled permanently around 1857. In fact, Calvin Grier Davis, Sam's grandfather and Robert Patterson's fifth child, was born in Lafayette County, Mississippi, in 1850 during their sojourn there. Upon their arrival in Drew County, Davis and Nelson immediately set about organizing the Saline Associate Reformed Presbyterian Church, where years later Sam's father, Samuel Jasper, would meet Lily, his true love and future bride.

And what a catch she was! Born January 4, 1877, on her parents' farm near Monticello, Arkansas, Lily was the oldest of nine children born to Calvin Grier Davis and Mary Allie Coleman Davis, who married in 1876. Traits that later endeared her to family, parishioners, and hundreds of friends, were evident early in the life of this gentle and kind lady. Her sister, Hattie Belle Davis Jackson, later in life penned a touching tribute to her older sister:

Sister

... It was spitting snow as Grier [Calvin Grier Davis] and Dr. Ragland dismounted. Next morning only tops of gateposts could be seen above the three-foot snow. 'Yes, a little girl, and as fair as a lily,' Dr. Ragland said to Grandfather Davis. And so it was at the Spring Communion Service that she was baptized and christened Margaret Lily Davis, for every first Davis granddaughter was a Margaret, and every first grandson a Robert.

... Lily early showed two marked tendencies, a tender and loving 'big sister' and a natural bent at homemaking tasks. Lily took care of the little children, always with such loving care. And when she was a very young girl it was said, 'Lily makes the best biscuits of any.' And so she developed these two wonderful traits that marked her life—mother and homemaker. At sewing, too, she was a real artist. When she was eight, the dress she cut out and stitched all by herself took first prize at the Drew County Fair in Monticello.

According to a tradition handed down from Coleman families, the oldest girl in the family was called Sister, the oldest boy Brother or Bubber, the next girl was Sissie (or Sis), the rest of them with Sis or Brother as a prefix. Thus in the [Calvin] Grier Davis family, Lily was Sister, Coleman was Bubber, Annie was Sissie, then Sis Ada, Brother Oma, Sis Irma, and Sha was Hattie Bell. Roy and Lois did not have to be respected. I thought every bonafide family did it this way until I was nine.

So you see there were nine [children], too many for one mother to mother. So there were assistants, the first of whom was Lily. And what a big Sister she was, always so gentle and loving and kind. When Irma and Hattie Belle were to stand in line with all the other children at Saline Sunday School and sing ... Sister saw to it that her two little sisters were dressed in new, lace-trimmed white dresses and had long, flaxen ringlets by way of the curling iron. With *much care and precision, she heated the long scissors-like iron down in the lamp chimney to just the right heat and, wrapping a small bit of the little girls' hair on it, made a lovely ringlet. There would be about a dozen long ringlets, and the bangs shorter. It required painstaking care, patience, and love.*

Then when schoolteacher Mr. McQuiston laid down rules on mischievous boys, she would coach Brother Oma all the one-mile walk to school on how he must behave. She said, 'I just can't stand to see you get a whipping at school.' And he didn't get one. And so it has been in this Davis family always. Sister was always about tops in creation. Once I said to Brother Sam [Lily's husband], 'We always thought Sister was the flower of the flock.' He quickly replied, 'She was the flower of any flock.'[18]

Lily's father, a ruling elder in the Saline Church, died January 31, 1898, at only forty-seven. His death came just one year before Lily's marriage to Samuel Jasper, who had the highest respect for his father-in-law:

He was a man of the highest Christian type—capable, conservative, upright, thrifty, and a leader and counselor whose assistance and opinion were often sought by his neighbors. He was an influential promoter of every worthwhile movement for the educational and religious welfare of the community ... he was one of God's noblemen.[19]

Lily's mother, Mary Allie, died in Morrilton on February 5, 1931. Again, Samuel Jasper had the highest praise for his mother-in-law:

[She] was a worthy mate for her worthy husband.... Left a widow with eight children at a time when times were hard, she never wavered but, with heroic faith and Christian optimism, she assumed her task and met the situation in a noble way. She made her home or headquarters with us during the last few years of her life and her presence in our home was always a delight to me. She was a benediction to us.[20]

NOTES

1. Dr. S. J. Patterson, *One Man's Family: A Brief Sketch of the Davis and Patterson Families and a Short Biography* (n.p., n.d.), 16.

2. Tippah County Historical and Genealogical Society, *The History of Tippah County, Mississippi* (Tulsa, Oklahoma: Heritage Publishing Company, 1981), 57–58.

3. Ibid., 57.

4. Ibid.

5. H. H. Robison and others, *Historical Sketch of the Associate Reformed Church of Ebenezer, Tippah County, Mississippi* (n.p., n.d.), 9.

6. Ibid., 13.

7. Patterson, *One Man's Family,* 12.

8. *The History of Tippah County, Mississippi*, 12.

9. Patterson, *One Man's Family*, 10.

10. R. F. Patterson, *The Best of Men* (Tarkio, Missouri: *The Tarkio Avalanche*, 1928), 11.

11. Ibid., 13.

12. Ibid., 12–13.

13. Patterson, *One Man's Family*, 27.

14. Ibid., 30.

15. Ibid., 54–55.

16. Ibid., 59–60.

17. Ibid., 40.

18. Patterson Papers, Private Collection.

19. Patterson, *One Man's Family*, 34.

20. Ibid., 35.

SAM'S SIBLINGS

SAMUEL JASPER "JAP" PATTERSON, JR.
1899–1972

Jap was the Secretary of Adult Education and Men's Work in the PCUS for many years and served as moderator of the denomination's General Assembly in 1965. Redheaded like his father and Sam, he had a rich vein of Irish wit. Passions included hunting, fishing, birddogs, and all sports, especially football. He was All State Halfback at Tarkio College and eventually became athletic coach at Arkansas College in Batesville, Arkansas, during Sam's childhood. Tarkio College conferred an honorary Doctor of Laws upon him in 1949, and Southwestern later awarded him the Doctor of Education.

GRIER DAVIS PATTERSON
1900–1971

Grier became a senior partner in a prestigious Chicago law firm. He was quiet, studious, and kind. Tarkio College awarded him an honorary Doctor of Laws degree.

JAMES KYLE PATTERSON
May 15, 1904–December 13, 1904

The family's first great sorrow, baby Kyle died of pneumonia in Steel Creek, North Carolina. He was seven months old.

ROBERT FOSTER PATTERSON
1905–1969

A member of Phi Beta Kappa, Foster earned a doctorate in philosophy and eventually became Dean of the College of Business at the University of South Dakota for twenty-two years. A studious leader, he was in great demand as an after dinner speaker. Active leader in several national business organizations and was mayor of Vermillion from 1956–1960. He was on several boards in the city.

His father commented in *One Man's Family*: "When he was just a boy, I thought he would be a preacher, for his favorite pastime was to climb upon the gatepost and with his youngest sister, Lois, as the choir and congregation, he would preach to her at great length and with great zest. He says that, not ever being able to reform his sister, he decided he would not be effective as a preacher."

Foster named his son Samuel Coleman Patterson.

MARGARET LOIS PATTERSON
1907–1995

"Sis" was the Pattersons' only daughter. She attended Arkansas College for two years before marrying Otis L. "Rip" Graham, a graduate of Union Seminary and a Presbyterian pastor. S. J. often said, "She is her mother made over." She and Rip had four children, who included former CBS legal correspondent Fred Graham and noted historians and authors Otis Graham, Jr. and Hugh Davis Graham. Between them, they have written over thirty books. According to Otis, Jr., "Her goal in life was to be a good mother and wife, and she richly achieved this."

HUGH MORRIS PATTERSON
1909–1983

Hugh shared Sam's interest in athletics and, like his brother Jap, was All State in college football. He coached high school football before teaching at Arkansas College. After serving in the Navy during World War II, he later attended law school, eventually becoming a senior partner at one of the largest law firms in Houston, Texas. He also served a term as president of the Houston Chamber of Commerce.

NOTES

CHAPTER ONE
The Early Years

1. Sam Patterson (chapel message on John 17, Reformed Theological Seminary, Jackson, MS, April 13, 1978).

2. His father's first two positions had been with Associate Reformed Presbyterian churches, first in Steel Creek, North Carolina, then in Pottsville, Arkansas. It was here that the family experienced its first sorrow. Little James Kyle, born May 15, 1904, lived only seven months before dying of double pneumonia. For a more detailed look at Sam's extended family history, see Appendix F.

3. R. F. Patterson, *The Best of Men* (Tarkio, Missouri: *The Tarkio Avalanche,* 1928), 36.

4. Dr. S. J. Patterson, *One Man's Family: A Brief Sketch of the Davis and Patterson Families and a Short Biography* (n.p., n.d.), 70.

5. Louise was S. J.'s sister Esther's child.

6. R. F. Patterson, *The Best of Men*, 46.

7. S. J. Patterson, *One Man's Family*, 49.

8. A. C. McGinnis, "A History of Independence County, Arkansas," *Independence County Chronicle 17*, April 1976, 8.

9. Ibid., 9.

10. For a more detailed look at the lives of Sam's siblings, see Appendix F.

11. S. J. Patterson, *One Man's Family,* 50.

12. Hattie Belle Davis Jackson, "Mama's Grandchildren," Patterson Papers, Private Collection.

13. A bag similar to a knapsack but worn over the shoulder.

14. Sam Patterson, "Order, Actions, and Results of Saving Faith" (sermon #3 in the series *Saving Faith*).

15. David F. Burg, *The Great Depression: An Eyewitness History* (New York: Facts on File, 1996), 51.

16. Letter from Sam to Bishop Robert Brown, April 6, 1963, Patterson Papers, Private Collection.

17. Dorothy McGuire, "Hardisons Settle on Rockfield," *Morrilton Democrat* (June 8, 1950).

18. Sam Patterson (chapel message on Phil. 4:10–13, Reformed Theological Seminary, Jackson, MS, February 26, 1975). In this sermon, Sam reveals that Speck was killed later by a German shepherd crossing their yard.

19. T. W. Hardison, "The Legend of Petit Jean," quoted in Petit Jean State Park promotional brochure, (n.d.). Hardison was a long-time resident of the mountain and founder of Petit Jean State Park and the Arkansas State Park System. Much later, in an undated diary entry, Sam wrote, "Dr. Hardison took a great deal of interest in me and encouraged my love for all the natural beauty and unusual aspects of the mountain."

20. Sam Patterson, "What Will You Do With Jesus?" (sermon, Kate Anderson Chapel, Martinsville, VA, October 3, 1941).

21.   Petit Jean was one of many parks built under Franklin D. Roosevelt's New Deal. The U.S. Army housed and fed the workers, all of whom were World War I veterans. After construction, the park was turned over to the state of Arkansas and today has more than 400,000 visitors a year.

22.   In a note at the bottom of this diary page, Sam later writes that Gordy was killed in an airplane accident in 1942 while in the Air Corps, and Ruby died of leukemia around 1936.

23.   Education in Arkansas had always been notoriously poor. The Great Depression limited public education even more. See Chapter One of Ebook *Bill Clinton: An American Journey* by Nigel Hamilton at www.ebooks.com/ebooks/book_display.asp?IID=192950, (accessed March 29, 2010). Hardcover copy also available (New York: Random House, 2003).

24.   Sam Patterson, "Ministers' Model and Evangelists' Example" (sermon on Luke 1:1–4, #1 in the series *Prominent Themes from the Gospel of Luke*).

25.   Sam Patterson, "Testimony of the World's Most Famous Teenager" (sermon on Psalm 23).

26.   Sam Patterson, "Praying in the Plural and Giving Before Getting" (sermon in the series *Revolutionary Aspects of the Lord's Prayer*).

27.   Sam Patterson, "The Master Is Come and Calleth for You" (sermon on John 11, Kate Anderson Chapel, Martinsville, VA, n.d.).

28.   Sam Patterson, "Praying in the Plural and Giving Before Getting" (sermon in the series *Revolutionary Aspects of the Lord's Prayer*).

29.   Ibid.

30.   S. J. Patterson, *One Man's Family*, 48.

CHAPTER TWO
College, The Call, and Conversion

1.   Sam loved Hugh and his wife Maggie. An able leader in church and community all his life, Hugh started at Ferncliff during the Depression as a custodian for twenty-five dollars a month, plus house, food, and utilities. Everyone knew him as Uncle Hugh and loved him. Today, a portrait of Hugh still hangs in Executive Director David Gill's office. Says Ferncliff historian Grainger Williams, "People still remember him. He was the finest kind of person ... and became a part of the community; people liked and trusted him."

2.   From a Bible study led by Sam at Rita Riggins's home, January 17, 1974.

3.   Sam Patterson, "New Man" (sermon on 2 Cor. 5:17).

4.   Martha Shepard, "Dr. Kelso," *Today* (October 31, 1993), 6. This entire section on Dr. Kelso was paraphrased from Shepard's excellent article.

5.   Minutes of Arkansas Presbytery (PCUS), August 25, 1938, 3.

6.   Sam Patterson (untitled address, French Camp Academy, French Camp, MS, May 24, 1983).

7.   Ibid.

8.   Sam Patterson (untitled sermon on the danger and tragedy of neglect, Kate Anderson Chapel, Martinsville, VA, October 26, 1941).

9.   Sam Patterson, "Stelle" (sermon, n.d.).

10.   Ibid.

11.   Sam Patterson, "Stelle" (sermon, n.d.) and Sam Patterson (untitled address, French Camp Academy, French Camp, MS, May 24, 1983).

12.   Sam Patterson (untitled address, French Camp Academy, French Camp, MS, May 24, 1983).

13.   Ibid.

14.   Sam Patterson, "Stelle" (sermon, n.d.).

15.   Charles H. Gabriel, "Calling the Prodigal," in *Great Revival Hymns*, ed. Homer Rodeheaver and B. D. Ackley (Chicago: The Rodeheaver Co., 1911), 66.

1. God is calling the prodigal, come without delay
Hear, O hear Him calling,
Calling now for thee.
Tho' you've wandered so far from His presence,
Come today.

Chorus
Hear His loving voice calling still
Calling now for thee.
O weary prodigal, come.

2. Patient, loving and tenderly, still the Father pleads.
Hear O hear Him calling,
Calling now for thee.
O return while the Spirit in mercy intercedes.

3. Come, there's bread in the house of thy Father, and to spare,
Hear, O hear Him calling,
Calling now for thee.
Lo! The table is spread and the feast is waiting there.

16. Sam Patterson (untitled address, French Camp Academy, French Camp, MS, May 24, 1983).

17. February 28, 1940, wasn't actually the last day of February, as he says here, since 1940 was a Leap Year, and the last day was the twenty-ninth. But who's quibbling?

18. Sam Patterson, "Reformation of Evangelism" (sermon, Christian Studies Center Summer Institute, 1973).

19. Sam Patterson, "Reformation of Evangelism" (sermon, Christian Studies Center Summer Institute, 1973) and Sam Patterson, "How to Preach" (chapel message, Reformed Theological Seminary, Jackson, MS, April 1977).

20. Sam Patterson, "How Do We Give to the Great Commission?" (sermon, Northpark Presbyterian Church in Jackson, MS, January 26, 1980).

21. Sam Patterson, "Ministers' Model and Evangelists' Example" (sermon #1 in the series *Prominent Themes from the Gospel of Luke*).

22. Sam Patterson, "Ambassadors for Christ" (sermon on 2 Cor. 5).

23. Sam Patterson, (chapel message on Phil. 4:10–13, Reformed Theological Seminary, Jackson, MS, February 26, 1975).

24. All of this material concerning the Bible passages Sam loved comes from his sermon "Ministers' Model and Evangelists' Example" (sermon #1 in the series *Prominent Themes from the Gospel of Luke*).

25. John T. Kneebone and others, ed., *Dictionary of Virginia Biography* (Richmond: The Library of Virginia, 1998), 1: 434–435.

"Belk soon became mired in a controversy arising from his outspoken participation in the Oxford Group Movement. He espoused Oxford Group teachings from the pulpit and in his popular radio sermons. Many members of his church preferred a more traditional ministry and criticized his advocacy of the movement. The controversy ignited intense emotion in the community. In 1937, the congregation split over his Oxford Group support. A faction supporting Belk started a new church, St. Giles, and installed him as pastor in 1938. By the time he retired in 1958, the church was the third largest in the presbytery." (Kneebone and others, 1: 435).

26. Walter A. Elwell, editor, *Evangelical Dictionary of Theology* (Grand Rapids: Baker Book House, 1984), 733–734. I relied heavily on this work for the entire discussion of the Oxford Group.

27. Sam Patterson, "Results of Rebirth in a Rich Man" (sermon #5 in the series *Prominent*

Themes from the Gospel of Luke). For a more detailed story about McDowell, see this sermon.

28. Sam Patterson, "Why We Become a New Creation" (sermon #2 in the series *Nature of the New Creation*). For a more detailed story about George's conversion, see this sermon.

Throughout his ministry, Sam always had a special heart for those with alcohol problems. Actually, Oxford Group principles became the basis for modern-day Alcoholics Anonymous since its founders were Oxford Group members. For more on this connection, see Bill Wilson's *Alcoholics Anonymous Comes of Age* (New York: Alcoholics Anonymous Publishing, 1957).

29. Elwell, *Evangelical Dictionary of Theology*, 734.

30. Ibid.

31. Sam Patterson, "Christian Womanhood" (sermon on Luke 8:1–3, Pensacola Theological Institute, Pensacola, FL, 1980).

32. Rev. Guy Smith, "The Great Speckled Bird," (n.p., 1936).

> What a beautiful thought I am thinking concerning the Great Speckled Bird,
> Remember her name is recorded on the pages of God's Holy Word.
> Desiring to lower her standard, they watch every move that she makes,
> For they long to find fault with her teaching,
> But really they find no mistake.
>
> In the presence of all her despisers, with a song never uttered before,
> She will rise and be gone in a moment, 'til the great tribulations are o'er.
> I am glad I have learned of her meekness; I am proud my name is in her book.
> For I want to be one never fearing, on the face of my Savior to look.
>
> Her wings shelter men of all nations, of earth's every color and race.
> She has gathered them all in her keeping to present to the Lord face to face.
> When Christ comes descending from heaven on the clouds as He writes in His Word,
> I'll be joyfully carried to meet Him on the wings of the Great Speckled Bird.

33. Sam Patterson, "Reformation of Evangelism" (sermon, Christian Studies Center Summer Institute, 1973).

34. Sam Patterson, "How Do We Give Ourselves to the Great Commission?" (sermon, Northpark Presbyterian Church in Jackson, MS, January 26, 1980).

35. Sam Patterson, "If Christ Were Tempted As We" (sermon #2 in the series *Sovereignty of God*).

36. Letter from Sam to each of the charter RTS students with a copy of Studd's biography, August 19, 1966, Patterson Papers, Private Collection.

37. Norman Grubb, *C.T. Studd: Cricketer and Pioneer* (Fort Washington, Pennsylvania: CLC Publications, 1933), 60–61.

38. Ibid., 89ff.

39. Ibid., 111ff.

40. Jacquelyn D. Hall and others, *Like a Family: The Making of a Southern Cotton Mill World* (Chapel Hill: The University of North Carolina Press, 1987), 354. Sam had no idea that he was making history along with the people he was shepherding. The southern mill village has come to be known as a distinctive form of working class community existing from about 1880 to the General Textile Strike in 1934, an event that improved working conditions greatly. After that, most mill villages became liabilities and disappeared. However, the Martinsville Mill was not unionized until the 1950s, so the mill village was still operating during Sam's tenure there.

41. Grubb, *C. T. Studd: Cricketer and Pioneer*, 145.

42. Sam Patterson, "A Major Problem in World Evangelism" (chapel message, Reformed Theological Seminary, Jackson, MS, April 14, 1982).

CHAPTER THREE
The War Years

1. Sam Patterson (address, Reformed Theological Seminary Senior Banquet, Jackson, MS, May 10, 1979.

2. Norman Grubb, *C. T. Studd: Cricketer and Pioneer* (Fort Washington, Pennsylvania: CLC Publications, 1933), 142.

3. Sam Patterson (address, Reformed Theological Seminary Senior Banquet, Jackson, MS, May 10, 1979.

4. Dorothy Cleal and Hiram H. Herbert, *Foresight, Founders, and Fortitude: The Story of Industry in Martinsville and Henry County, Virginia* (Bassett, Virginia: Bassett Printing Corporation, 1970), 154–155.

5. Jacquelyn D. Hall and others, *Like a Family: The Making of a Southern Cotton Mill World* (Chapel Hill: The University of North Carolina Press, 1987), xi. In addition to interviews with actual Martinsville cotton mill workers, the material in this chapter was augmented greatly by information from the in-depth study *Like a Family*. Based on hundreds of interviews with southern cotton mill workers, it gives a riveting account of life in the cotton mill village from its genesis to its subsequent disappearance.

6. Cleal and Herbert, *Foresight, Founders, and Fortitude*, 133–134.

7. Hall and others, *Like a Family*, 31.

8. Cleal and Herbert, *Foresight, Founders, and Fortitude*, 154–155.

9. Hall and others, *Like a Family*, 17.

10. Matt Chittum, "Draped in Prosperity," *Roanoke Times* (August 17, 2002).

11. Ibid.

12. Mrs. Harris was not converted under Sam's ministry at Kate Anderson, but in April 1947, when he returned to lead a revival. Three others also professed faith at that time.

13. Hall and others, *Like a Family*, 53.

14. Ibid., 354.

15. American Historical Association, "Mill Village and Factory," Jim Leloudis, http://www.historians.org/Tl/LessonPlans/nc/Leloudis/factory.html (accessed October 22, 2009).

16. Ibid.

17. Ibid.

18. Ibid.

19. Hall and others, *Like a Family,* 360. Doctors now know that brown lung disease results from prolonged exposure to cotton dust. Lack of research, as well as resistance by the textile industry, delayed any action on the disease in the United States until the 1970s. At that time, disabled workers, many breathing only with the help of portable oxygen tanks, packed OSHA hearings, where they testified to the human costs of millwork—air clouded with lint, management slow to acknowledge brown lung, and doctors who attributed workers' wheezing and coughing to something other than cotton dust. (Hall and others, *Like a Family,* 81, 360).

20. Ibid., 82.

21. Ibid., 179–180.

22. Anderson Memorial Church, "Twenty-Fifth Anniversary: Kate Anderson Presbyterian Church, 1941–1966," 1. Anderson Memorial was the first Presbyterian church in Henry County. It is now named First Presbyterian Church.

23. Jim Stegall, *Grace Upon Grace* (Franklin, Tennessee: Providence House Publishers, 2004), 56–57. Later, Miss Anderson's oil paintings caught the eye of art-lovers all over Virginia. Her talent brought much money into the Anderson household and sent all ten children to college.

24. Anderson Memorial Church, "Twenty-Fifth Anniversary: Kate Anderson Presbyterian Church, 1941–1966," 1.

25. The information in this paragraph is a compilation of material from Anderson Memorial, "Twenty-Fifth Anniversary: Kate Anderson Presbyterian Church, 1941–1966," 1 and a March 1945 report by Mrs. G.W. Ireson, church historian at the time.

26. Stegall, *Grace Upon Grace*, 72.

27. Ibid., 72–73.

28. The information in this paragraph is a compilation of material from a March 1945 report by Mrs. G.W. Ireson, church historian at the time, and *Grace Upon Grace*, 88.

29. Stegall, *Grace Upon Grace*, 87.

30. Margaret Frazier, "Your Woman of the Week," *Martinsville Daily Bulletin* (May 26, 1945).

31. Sam Patterson, "Journal of Kate Anderson Work," 40, Patterson Papers, Private Collection.

32. Minutes of Roanoke Presbytery (PCUS), April 22–23, 1941, 8.

33. Minutes of Roanoke Presbytery (PCUS), June 5, 1941, 21–22.

34. Minutes of Roanoke Presbytery (PCUS), September 30, 1941, 7.

35. Sam Patterson, "On Christ the Solid Rock" (inaugural sermon on 1 Cor. 3:11, Kate Anderson Chapel, Martinsville, VA, June 8, 1941).

36. Sam Patterson, "Journal of Kate Anderson Work," 28–29, Patterson Papers, Private Collection.

37. Sam Patterson (untitled sermon, June 15, 1941).

38. Sam Patterson, "Christ's Blueprint of Heaven" (sermon on John 14:1–6, Kate Anderson Chapel, Martinsville, VA, September 1941).

39. Sam Patterson (sermon on the danger and tragedy of neglect, Kate Anderson Chapel, Martinsville, VA, October 26, 1941).

40. Sam later told listeners, "I've preached on tithing only three times in my life, and I'm ashamed of that." Sam Patterson, "How Can We Give Ourselves to the Great Commission?" (sermon, Northpark Presbyterian Church in Jackson, MS, January 26, 1980).

41. Ibid.

42. Stegall, *Grace Upon Grace*, 88.

43. Sam Patterson, "Journal of Kate Anderson Work," 40–49, Patterson Papers, Private Collection.

44. Sam likely admired Fuller for his desire to spread the Gospel by radio to vast numbers of people right in their homes. Fuller had dived into radio in 1931 with *The Pilgrim's Hour*, but it was discontinued after a very short time. Later, his *Old-Fashioned Revival Hour* became widely popular, and by the early 1940s, it was broadcast a thousand hours a week in the United States and other countries. It subsequently expanded to almost every spot on the globe. For fifteen years, the program originated on Sunday afternoon from the Municipal Auditorium in Long Beach, California, where it drew huge audiences. In that hall numerous GIs, many to die in battle, found the Lord before being shipped out to theatres of war. (Believer's Web, "Charles E. Fuller, 1887–1968, Preacher, Broadcaster," author unknown, http://www.believersweb.org/view.cfm?ID=64, (accessed March 29, 2010). Stelle mentions in her letters going to hear Fuller and seeing "many souls saved."

45. Sam Patterson, "Journal of Kate Anderson Work," 34–36, Patterson Papers, Private Collection.

46. Ibid., 18.

47. Ibid.

48. Ibid., 41.

49. No doubt Stelle and Sam were influenced by C. T. Studd in their decision to wear only street clothes. Before his wedding, Studd said, "No smart wedding clothes for us—just our ordinary, native calico clothes, as plain as can be. I am for being registered at the Consul's, and then having a real hallelujah meeting, just something all for Jesus.... The [Chinese] people are ... horrified that we do not plan to get any wedding garments." *C. T. Studd: Cricketer and Pioneer*, (Fort Washington, Pennsylvania: CLC Publications, 1933), 77–80.

50. "Miss Sellers Bride of Rev. Mr. Patterson," *Martinsville Daily Bulletin* (November 17, 1941).

51. Sam Patterson, "Hope" (chapel message, Reformed Theological Seminary, Jackson, MS, August 31, 1976).

52. According to Buck Powell, the mill house is still there, although the windows are boarded up, and the front porch is sagging. This account chronicling Sam's indecision about the house and Stelle's subsequent introduction to it are drawn from the sermon "Stelle."

53. Sam Patterson, "Stelle" (sermon, n.d.).

54. Ibid. Sam and Stelle likely felt their home and neighborhood were fit for a king compared to the Studds' first home in China. Studd portrayed it graphically in a letter: "It had bare whitewashed walls, very uneven brick floors, a fireplace in the center of the room, and a brick bed. Our mattress was a cotton-wool quilt about an inch thick. That was our bed for the first three years until it became so infested with scorpions that we had to have it pulled down.

"For five years we never went outside our doors without a volley of curses from our neighbors. Everything that happened in that city the Chinese blamed on us. We had a year of drought, and our lives were at stake because they held us responsible. Gradually we got on familiar terms with the people by allowing them to come into our apartment and examine everything at will." *C. T. Studd: Cricketer and Pioneer* (Fort Washington, Pennsylvania: CLC Publications, 1933), 81–82.

The Studds lived in a remote village and would have to be gone five months for Priscilla to have a doctor deliver her babies. Thus, she had them all at home, with only a native male assistant. One of her babies died in childbirth, and Priscilla barely escaped with her life. (*Cricketer and Pioneer*, 84).

55. Ibid.

56. Sam Patterson, "Being Witnesses" (sermon, Kate Anderson Chapel, Martinsville, VA, June 18, 1941).

57. Sam Patterson, "Why Should We Pray?" (sermon #3 in a series on prayer).

58. Sam Patterson, "Any" (sermon # 2 in series *A Time To Renew*).

59. Sam Patterson, "On Christ the Solid Rock" (inaugural sermon on 1 Cor. 3:11, Kate Anderson Chapel, Martinsville, VA, June 8, 1941).

60. Sam Patterson, "A Major Problem in World Evangelism" (chapel message, Reformed Theological Seminary, Jackson, MS, April 14, 1982).

61. Sam Patterson, "Why Should We Pray?" (sermon # 3 in a series on prayer). The story of Alva Williams's prayer can also be found in an RTS chapel message on John 17 preached by Sam on April 12, 1978.

62. Minutes of Roanoke Presbytery (PCUS), October 13–14, 1942, 30–31.

63. Minutes of Roanoke Presbytery (PCUS), April 20, 1943, Home Missions Committee Report, 18–19. According to Buck Powell, the church bought the home from Martinsville resident John Stultz.

64. Ibid., 19–20.

65. News clipping from an unknown newspaper, November 25, 1942.

66. Minutes of Roanoke Presbytery (PCUS) September 8, 1943, 4–5.

67. Minutes of Roanoke Presbytery (PCUS), October 5, 1943, 9.

68. Sam Patterson, "Stelle" (sermon, n.d.).

69. Minutes of Roanoke Presbytery (PCUS), April 18, 1944, 4–5.

70. United States Military Records.

71. Sam Patterson, "Journal of Kate Anderson Work," 18–29, 60–63, Patterson Papers, Private Collection.

72. Anderson Memorial Church, "Twenty-Fifth Anniversary: Kate Anderson Presbyterian Church, 1941–1966," 5.

73. Buck Powell, interview by Rebecca Hobbs, November, 2008.

74. Stegall, *Grace Upon Grace*, 177.

75. Marine Corps History and Museum Division, "… And a Few Marines: Marines in the Liberation of the Philippines," Capt. John C. Chapin (USMCR (RET), http://www.nps.gov/archive/wapa/indepth/extContent/usmc/pcn–190–003140–01/sec5.htm (accessed October 22, 2009).

76. In a letter to Sam on June 5, 1945, Stelle mentions that their time together with Psalm 91 has changed to 10 p.m., likely because Sam still had duties at 8 p.m. They also begin trading verses.

77. About the same time, Stelle confided to Sam her dreams for life after the war. A letter on June 12, 1945, exuded: "Becky's a little doll! Sam, I'd like to have a lot of babies after the war. Would you? Let's get a country church and settle down and raise a big family! Plus chickens, cows, pigs (but no ducks and guineas)." Yet, a houseful of children was not in God's plans for the couple, and Becky would be their only child. After the war, Stelle suffered numerous miscarriages until she and Sam decided to accept God's will in the matter.

78. Sam Patterson, Annual Chaplain Report to Dr. Dan T. Caldwell, Defense Service Council in Richmond, Virginia, April 22, 1946. Patterson Papers. Private Collection.

79. John M. Elliott, "Back to the Philippines," *Naval Aviation News* (March-April 1995), 29.

80. More than likely, Sam had heard the ditty "The monkeys have no tails in Zamboanga" that dates back to 1890 and was on the lips of World War II GIs at the time. Most people don't realize it is a racial slur. Based on a famous anthropological hoax of the early 20th century, the song references photographs of Zamboangan natives with monkey tails attached to the base of their spines—the evolutionary missing link.

Zamboanga came to international prominence in June 2001, when terrorists kidnapped Philippine missionaries Martin and Gracia Burnham and held them in Basilan, an island some miles off Zamboanga Peninsula. Unfortunately, Martin Burnham died during the rescue attempt.

81. Marine Corps History and Museum Division, "… And a Few Marines: Marines in the Liberation of the Philippines," Capt. John C. Chapin (USMCR (RET), http://www.nps.gov/archive/wapa/indepth/extContent/usmc/pcn–190–003140–01/sec5.htm (accessed October 22, 2009).

82. Ibid.

83. Patterson, Chaplain Report, April 22, 1946, Patterson Papers, Private Collection.

84. Ibid.

85. Letter from Sam to Dr. Benjamin Lacey on July 2, 1945, Patterson Papers, Private Collection.

86. Angelfire, "China Page," http://www.angelfire.com/va2/worldwar2family/.html (accessed October 22, 2009).

87. Harold Stephens, *Take China: The Last of the China Marines* (Miranda, California: Wolfenden Publishers, 2002), 7.

88. Ibid., 21–22.

89. Sgt Grit Marine Specialties, "A History Lesson," Ed Fulwider, http://www.grunt.com/scuttlebutt/corps-stories/ww2/lesson.asp (accessed October 22, 2009). Fulwider, a Marine, served in North China after World War II.

90. Patterson, Chaplain Report, April 22, 1946, Patterson Papers, Private Collection.

91. Stephens, *Take China*, 32–36.

92. Navy Historical Center, "Extract on the Typhoon from Commander in Chief, Pacific Fleet and Pacific Ocean Area report on the Surrender and Occupation of Japan," Commander in Chief, U.S. Pacific Fleet and Pacific Ocean Areas Report, Serial 0395 of 11 February 1946, World War II Command File, Operational Archives Branch, Naval Historical Center, Washington, DC, http://www.history.navy.mil/faqs/faq102–6.htm (accessed October 22, 2009).

93. Stephens, *Take China*, 36–37.

94. Ferner Burkholder and others, ed., *Friends Made, Moments Shared, Memories for a Lifetime: An Oral History of VMSB343 United States Marine Corps in World War II* (Lemieux International Limited, 2000), 254.

95. Stephens, *Take China*, 39–40.

96. Ibid., 46.

97. Patterson, Chaplain Report, April 22, 1946, Patterson Papers, Private Collection.

98. Burkholder and others, *Friends Made*, 266, 279.

99. Ibid., 268–269.

100. Ibid., 247.

101. Stephens, *Take China*, 52.

102. Ibid., 142.

103. Henry I. Shaw, Jr., *The U.S. Marines in North China, 1945–1949* (U.S. Marine Corps, revised version, 1962), 8.

104. Burkholder and others, *Friends Made*, 251, 280–281.

105. Ibid., 250.

106. Stephens, *Take China*, 57–59.

107. Stephens, *Take China*, 90 and Burkholder and others, *Friends Made*, 268.

108. Stephens, *Take China*, 90.

109. Burkholder and others, *Friends Made*, 242.

110. Patterson, Chaplain Report, April 22, 1946, Patterson Papers, Private Collection.

111. Sam Patterson, "Relationship of Prayer to Evangelism" (sermon in a series on prayer).

112. Patterson, Chaplain Report, April 22, 1946, Patterson Papers, Private Collection.

113. Sam Patterson, "The Compassion of Christ" (sermon on Luke 7:36–50, #3 in the series *Prominent Themes from the Gospel of Luke*. Sam told this story many times, but this sermon has one of the fullest accounts.

114. Letter from Sam to daughter Becky on evangelism, December 22, 1961, Patterson Papers, Private Collection. See Appendix E for full document.

115. Sam Patterson, "What Salvation is Not" (sermon #8 in the series *A Time to Renew*).

116. Patterson, Chaplain Report, April 22, 1946, Patterson Papers, Private Collection.

117. Missionaries helped Sam more than once. In fact, he told Dan Caldwell in his annual chaplain's report on April 22, 1946, "The Protestant missionaries here have been a source of fine fellowship and inspiration to both the chaplains and the men. They have been tireless in their efforts to serve the men of the Armed Forces and to help make their stay here as entertaining and pleasant as possible."

118. Sam Patterson, "What Salvation is Not" (sermon #8 in the series *A Time to Renew*).

119. Burkholder and others, *Friends Made*, 271.

120. From a Bible study led by Sam at Rita Riggins's home, January 17, 1974.

121. United States Military Records.

122. Minutes of Central Mississippi Presbytery (PCUS), April 16–17, 1946, 475 and 487.

CHAPTER FOUR
The Leland Years

1. Sam Patterson, "The Master Is Come and Calleth for You" (sermon on John 11, Kate Anderson Chapel, Martinsville, VA, n.d.).

2. Louise A. Hester, *Inasmuch: The Life and Ministry of Thomas Russell Nunan* (Greenville, Mississippi: Burford Brothers Printing, 1993), 3, 4, 7, 9, 12, 13, 17, 18, 20, 69.

3. Sam Patterson, (children's sermon, Leland Presbyterian Church, Leland, MS, March 8, 1987, just four days before his death).

4. Louise Crump, "Delta Scene," *Leland Progress* (September 15, 1946).

5. Sam Patterson, (address, Reformed Theological Seminary Senior Banquet, Jackson, MS, May 10, 1979).

6. Jim Roberts, "Scouting Around," *Leland Progress* (n.d).

7. Ernest Trice Thompson, in his informative three-volume series *Presbyterians in the South* (Richmond, Virginia: John Knox Press, 1963), notes that English settlers in the South regarded education primarily as training for leadership, a privilege reserved for the well-to-do (1:235). However, the Scotch-Irish strongly disliked illiteracy. From John Knox they inherited the tradition of a school under the shadow of every parish church (1:80).

8. John F. Frierson, *Biographical Jottings of John F. Frierson* (n.p, n.d.), 19. For more on the fascinating history of French Camp, see *A Treasure on the Trace: The French Camp Story* by Melinda Livingston and Charles Rich (Franklin Press, Baton Rouge, Louisiana, 1996).

9. Ernest Trice Thompson, *Presbyterians in the South, 1890–1972* (Richmond, Virginia: John Knox Press, 1963), 3:163 and 166–167.

10. Minutes of Mississippi Synod (PCUS), November 20–22, 1917, 8–9. The schools acquired were: French Camp Academy, Central Mississippi Institute, Belhaven College, Mississippi Synodical College, Chamberlain-Hunt Academy, and Chickasaw College.

11. For a detailed look at Mississippi Synod's plan, see Appendix A, "French Camp Academy and Mississippi Synod's Grand Experiment in Christian Education."

12. Thompson, *Presbyterians in the South*, 3:185.

13. Ibid., 3:181. For more details on these schools, see Appendix A, "French Camp Academy and Mississippi Synod's Grand Experiment in Christian Education."

14. Minutes of Mississippi Synod (PCUS), September 24–26, 1940, 29.

15. Minutes of Mississippi Synod (PCUS), September 8–9, 1943, 302.

16. Minutes of Mississippi Synod (PCUS), September 6–7, 1944, 369.

17. Minutes of Mississippi Synod (PCUS), September 4–6, 1945, 459.

18. Minutes of Mississippi Synod (PCUS), September 3–5, 1946, 527.

19. Minutes of Mississippi Synod (PCUS), September 9–11, 1947, 615.

20. Ibid.

21. Melinda Livingston and Charles Rich, *A Treasure on the Trace: The French Camp Story* (Baton Rouge, Louisiana: Franklin Press, 1996), 197.

22. Margaret Kimball, videotaped interview by Denton Braswell, May 26, 2001.

23. Letter from J. H. Laster to former Mississippi Governor J. P. Coleman, November 29, 1984, quoted in Melinda Livingston and Charles Rich, *A Treasure on the Trace: The French Camp Story* (Baton Rouge, Louisiana: Franklin Press, 1996), 198.

24. Kimball, interview.

25. For more on the Lasters' extensive contribution to FCA, see *A Treasure on the Trace: The French Camp Story* (Baton Rouge, Louisiana: Franklin Press, 1996), 197–206.

26. Livingston and Rich, *A Treasure on the Trace: The French Camp Story*, 201.

27. Letter from J. H. Laster to former Mississippi Governor J. P. Coleman, November 29, 1984, quoted in Melinda Livingston and Charles Rich, *A Treasure on the Trace: The French Camp Story* (Baton Rouge, Louisiana: Franklin Press, 1996), 199–200.

28. Minutes of Mississippi Synod (PCUS), September 19–21, 1949, 36.

29. Ibid., 26. By 1953, Bolling would remind synod that women had given $111,000 for teacher salaries in thirty-seven years (Minutes of Mississippi Synod, September 8–10, 1953, 306). See Appendix A, "French Camp Academy and Mississippi Synod's Grand Experiment in Christian Education" for details of Presbyterian women's historic support of FCA.

30. W. Norton, "Sam Patterson," (Chapter 3 of untitled and unpublished manuscript on the history of French Camp Academy), 60, French Camp Academy Museum.

31. Sam Patterson, WFCA radio interview, 1985.

32. Ibid.

33. Minutes of Mississippi Synod (PCUS), September 19–21, 1949, 39–40.

34. Minutes of Mississippi Synod (PCUS), March 7, 1950, 88.

35. Sam Patterson, WFCA radio interview, 1985.

36. Minutes of Mississippi Synod (PCUS), March 7, 1950, 88–89.

37. Ibid., 90.

38. Livingston and Rich, *A Treasure on the Trace: The French Camp Story*, 201.

39. Sam Patterson, (untitled address, French Camp Academy, French Camp, MS, May 24, 1983).

40. Minutes of Mississippi Synod (PCUS), March 7, 1950, 91. See Appendix A for full "Report of Committee on French Camp Academy."

41. "Laster Writes," *French Camp Academy News* (May, 1950).

42. Minutes of Mississippi Synod (PCUS), March 7, 1950, 91.

43. Minutes of Mississippi Synod (PCUS), March 7, 1950, 92. After synod's approval of the committee's report, McAtee offered his resignation as a member and president of the FCA Board of Trustees. Synod voted to decline to accept the resignation.

44. Letter from Stuart Angle to FCA supporters, December 10, 1969, Patterson Papers, Private Collection.

45. Sam Patterson (untitled sermon, Kate Anderson Chapel, Martinsville, VA, September 1940).

46. Nunan could empathize with children in trouble, and the two men probably had countless prayer sessions concerning the plight of French Camp. Nunan had suffered severe psychological stress in elementary school when, as a "lefty," he was punished for not being able to write with his right hand. The stress caused a stutter that followed him into adulthood. Nunan, much like Sam, had also been a troublemaker in school. When he told his church session that he wanted to come under care of presbytery, they refused to endorse the idea until he took a year to get his priorities straight. [Louise Hester, *Inasmuch: The Life and Ministry of Thomas Russell Nunan* (Greenville, Mississippi: Burford Brothers Printing, 1993), 3, 6.]

47. Norton, "Sam Patterson," 3, French Camp Academy Museum.

48. Letter from R. S. McArthur, Chairman of the Nominating Committee for New President, to Sam on behalf of the FCA Board of Trustees, April 21, 1950, Patterson Papers, Private Collection.

49. Sam Patterson (untitled address, French Camp Academy, French Camp, MS, May 24, 1983).

CHAPTER FIVE
The French Camp Years

1. Minutes of Mississippi Synod (PCUS), November 15, 1921, 18–19. See also Appendix A, "French Camp Academy and Mississippi Synod's Grand Experiment in Christian Education" for more details.

2. See Appendix A, "French Camp Academy and Mississippi Synod's Grand Experiment in Christian Education."

3. Norman Grubb, *C. T. Studd: Cricketer and Pioneer* (Fort Washington, Pennsylvania: CLC Publications, 1933), 175–176.

4. Ibid., 125, 177. Studd later revealed the genesis of such faith. "We started our marriage with five dollars and some bedding. Our families knew only that we were in the heart of China. The last of our supplies were finished, and there was no hope of any more from human sources. The mail came once a fortnight, and the mailman had just come that day. If in two weeks the postman brought no relief, we would face starvation. We had a night of prayer. The postman returned in two weeks with a letter from a man neither I nor my wife had ever met. He said that God had commanded him to send us one hundred pounds; he had no idea why. We were different after that." (Grubb, *C. T. Studd: Cricketer and Pioneer*, 86–87.)

5. Letter from Sam to Jack Mitchell, August 23, 1974, Patterson Papers, Private Collection.

6. W. Norton, "Sam Patterson," (Chapter 3 of untitled and unpublished manuscript on the history of French Camp Academy), 2, French Camp Academy Museum.

7. Minutes of Mississippi Synod (PCUS), September 26–28, 1950, 102,104. See Appendix A, "Report of Board of Trustees of French Camp Academy."

8. Norton, "Sam Patterson," 2, French Camp Academy Museum.

9. Minutes of Mississippi Synod (PCUS), June 6–8, 1961, 22.

10. Norton, "Sam Patterson," 17, French Camp Academy Museum.

11. Ibid., 17–18.

12. Minutes of Mississippi Synod (PCUS), June 1–3, 1965, 22–23.

13. Minutes of Mississippi Synod (PCUS), June 5, 1973, 13.

14. Norton, "Sam Patterson," 18, French Camp Academy Museum.

15. Ibid., 7.

16. Ibid.

17. Kay McNair, "Mr. Patterson, Still Ministering to Us," *French Camp Today* (February 1985), 5.

18. Sam Patterson, WFCA radio interview, 1985.

19. Melinda Livingston and Charles Rich, *A Treasure on the Trace: The French Camp Story* (Baton Rouge, Louisiana: Franklin Press, 1996), 200. Also "Southern Bell Comes to French Camp," *French Camp News* (May 1950).

20. Minutes of Mississippi Synod (PCUS), September 26–28, 1950, 102.

21. The board promised to pay off the note, then give Sam the title if he never took a lien on the house, which he did not. Eventually, Sam deeded the house to Becky when she married.

22. Sam Patterson, "We Are Human," (French Camp Academy, n.d.), 15. See Appendix E.

23. Actually, the job never really got any easier. In a 1985 WFCA radio interview, Sam confessed that operating the school seemed like an impossible task during those first years, but the annual amount needed then was really very small—a few hundred thousand compared to substantially higher costs today.

24. Norton, "Sam Patterson," 3–4, French Camp Academy Museum.

25. Ibid., 4.

26. Ibid.

27. Ibid., 3.

28. Sam Patterson, "Mr. Pat Ponders," *French Camp Today* (December 1985), 4.

29. Norton, "Sam Patterson," 8–9, French Camp Academy Museum.

30. Margaret Kimball, videotaped interview by Denton Braswell, May 26, 2001.

31. Kay McNair, "A Pheasant Experience," *French Camp Today* (February 1985), 1–2.

32. "Good Things Happen on Campus; French Camp Alumni Come Home," *French Camp Today* (August 1985), 18.

33. Norton, "Sam Patterson," 23, French Camp Academy Museum.

34. Kimball, interview.

35. Sam Patterson, "Mr. Pat Ponders," *French Camp Today* (December 1985), 4.

36. Minutes of Mississippi Synod (PCUS) September 26–28, 1950, 103. See Appendix A, "Report of the Board of Trustees of French Camp Academy."

37. Ibid., 104.

38. Sam Patterson, Monthly President's Report to FCA Board of Trustees, August 4, 1965.

39. Brodie Crump, "French Camp Academy Was On TV and Old Stuff Hopes $$ Follow," *Kosciusko Star Herald* (August 14, 1964).

40. Patterson, "We Are Human," 9. See Appendix E.

41. J. I. Packer, *Knowing God* (Downers Grove, Illinois: InterVarsity Press, 1973), 245–246.

42. Patterson, "We Are Human," 6. See Appendix E.

43. Sam Patterson (untitled address, French Camp Academy, French Camp, MS, May 24, 1983) and Norton, "Sam Patterson," 21, French Camp Academy Museum.

44. Actually, there are several stories about why Mr. Hull gave that money. Sam revealed in a 1983 talk at FCA that Hull was taken with a young student named Rodney Trambell, who went along to carry the birds Mr. Hull shot. During one pheasant hunt, Mr. Hull asked Sam what he

needed at FCA. Since Hull was wealthy, Sam knew he could suggest a large need, so he mentioned a dining hall. Hull replied, "Well, maybe we can do something about that." A few weeks later, he contacted Sam, saying he'd give the money for the dining hall, with FCA raising a little more for classrooms.

Another story has Mr. Hull being taken with a big bulldog Sam brought with him when he came to work at French Camp; if boys got too close to the girls' dorm, the dog would jump the fence and chase them off. The story goes that Mr. Hull loved Sam's bulldog so much that he would come to pheasant hunts just to watch this "old dog go crazy like a young pup." He was so enthralled that he asked Sam what FCA needed. When Sam mentioned a dining hall, Hull replied, "Here's the money. Build it." Whatever the reason, the Holy Spirit ultimately caused Hull to help French Camp!

45. Sam Patterson, "The Disciples and Possessions" (sermon on Luke 12:14, 29, 31, 33, #4 in the series *Prominent Themes from the Gospel of Luke*).

46. Ibid.

47. Ibid.

48. Norton, "Sam Patterson," 23–25, French Camp Academy Museum.

49. Paul Culley, "Our God Provides," *French Camp Today* (August 1985), 8. The inscription is taken from John 12:20. Greeks had come to the feast and asked Philip, "Sir, we would like to see Jesus." The inscription urges the speaker to rely on God for the message, so that listeners will look beyond exciting oratory, clever construction, and personality to see Jesus.

When beautiful Grace Chapel at Reformed Theological Seminary was completed in May 1971, surely it was Sam who again wanted a plaque affixed to the pulpit with the words "Sir, we would see Jesus."

50. Dr. S. J. Patterson, *One Man's Family: A Brief Sketch of the Davis and Patterson Families and a Short Biography* (n.p., n.d.), 5–6.

51. Sam Patterson, "Ramblin' Round," *French Camp Academy News* (January 1956), 2.

52. Mary Jane Garrard Whittington, "Mission Not Impossible," quoted in a letter from Stuart Angle to FCA supporters on December 10, 1969.

53. Sam Patterson (untitled address, French Camp Academy, French Camp, MS, May 24, 1983).

54. Sam Patterson, "French Camp Yesterday," *French Camp Today* (August 1985), 10.

55. See Appendix A, "French Camp Academy and Mississippi Synod's Grand Experiment in Christian Education" for more details.

56. Minutes of Central Mississippi Presbytery (PCUS), April 7, 1914, 241.

57. Minutes of Central Mississippi Presbytery (PCUS), November 29, 1955, 110–111.

58. Minutes of Mississippi Synod (PCUS), November 29, 1955, 531–532.

59. Minutes of Mississippi Synod (PCUS), September 4–6, 1951, 193.

60. Ibid.

61. Minutes of Mississippi Synod (PCUS), September 4–5, 1952, 255–256.

62. Minutes of Mississippi Synod (PCUS), September 8–10, 1953, 318.

63. Minutes of Mississippi Synod (PCUS), September 2, 1954, 387–388.

64. Leroy B. Allen, "As the Twig Is Bent," *Leland Progress* (May 21, 1959).

65. Minutes of Mississippi Synod (PCUS), June 3–5, 1958, 36–37.

66. Minutes of Mississippi Synod (PCUS), June 6–8, 1961, 36.

67. Minutes of Mississippi Synod (PCUS), June 11–13, 1963, 37.

68. Minutes of Mississippi Synod (PCUS), June 1–3, 1965, 81, 84.

69. Minutes of Mississippi Synod (PCUS), June 7–8, 1966, 61.

70. Sam Patterson (untitled address, French Camp Academy, French Camp, MS, May 24, 1983). Coach Thompson had close ties with FCA since he had been raised in French Camp. One of his grandfathers had sold the school about 400 acres of land at only fifty cents an acre to begin FCA's farm. His other grandparents also gave some land to the school.

71. "Daddy loved eggs and made a mean omelet," said Becky Patterson Rogers. "One of my fondest childhood memories is enjoying one of Dad's famous omelets after church on Sunday nights."

72. Patterson, "We Are Human," 9. See Appendix E.

73. Ibid., 11.

74. Ibid.

75. Ibid., 12.

76. Ibid., 15.

77. Ibid., 10.

78. "Good Things Happen on Campus; French Camp Alumni Come Home," *French Camp Today* (August 1985), 18–19.

79. Paul Culley, "Our God Provides," *French Camp Today* (August 1985), 8.

80. Letter from Sam to Erin Lail, August 4, 1950, Patterson Papers, Private Collection.

81. Letter from Sam to Erin Lail, January 9, 1951, Patterson Papers, Private Collection.

82 Sam Patterson, WFCA radio interview, 1985.

83. Ibid.

84. Ibid.

85. Sam Patterson, "French Camp Yesterday," *French Camp Today* (August 1985), 10.

86. Sam Patterson, "Mr. Pat Ponders," *French Camp Today* (December 1985), 4.

87. Patterson Papers, Private Collection.

88. Letter from Sam to Bill Byrd, March 28, 1967. This letter is evidence that Sam's support for the school didn't wane after he officially retired as president of FCA in February 1967.

89. Kay McNair, "A Pheasant Experience," *French Camp Today* (February 1985), 1–2. Also, Mary Jane Garrard Whittington, "Mission Not Impossible," quoted in a letter from Stuart Angle to FCA supporters on December 10, 1969.

90. Kay McNair, "A Pheasant Experience," *French Camp Today* (February 1985), 2.

91. Minutes of Mississippi Synod (PCUS), September 4–5, 1952, 256.

92. Mary Jane Garrard Whittington, "Mission Not Impossible," quoted in a letter from Stuart Angle to FCA supporters on December 10, 1969.

93. Minutes of French Camp Presbyterian Church Session, April 8, 1951, July 3, 1952, November 27, 1957, December 22, 1957, and May 7, 1958.

94. Kay McNair, "Harvest Festivals Make History," *French Camp Today* (August 1985).

95. Ibid.

96. Chautauqua was an adult education movement in the United States, highly popular in the late 19th and early 20th centuries. People in rural areas benefited greatly from Chautauquas since they brought entertainment and culture with speakers, teachers, and musicians. Christian instruction, preaching, and worship were a strong part of the Chautauqua experience. The movement originated in the village of Chautauqua, New York, in 1874; in the 1920s, millions of Americans enjoyed them. However, their popularity died out with the advent of television.

Sam was probably quite familiar with this venue, given his association with Ferncliff and his interest in Christian conference centers. According to a letter from Sam to Horace Hull on July 13, 1963, Sam held a trial Chautauqua in 1953 to test the interest of rural Mississippians. He brought his old friend Jimmie Johnson and his team to conduct a crusade in the old gymnasium at French Camp. The entire surrounding area was invited. Soloist Clyde Taylor sang and directed the choir, while the famous Merrill Dunlop was at the piano and organ. The response was so overwhelming that Sam officially kicked off the summer Chautauquas the next year.

"He asked me when we should have it every year," said Billy Thompson, "and I told him all the old meetings were after farmers got their crops laid by and didn't have much to do. So we settled on the third week of July."

97. Sue Davidson, undated and untitled FCA news release, French Camp Academy Museum.

98. Sam Patterson, "French Camp Yesterday," *French Camp Today* (August 1985), 10.

99. Minutes of Mississippi Synod (PCUS), September 4–6, 1951, 194.

100. Minutes of Mississippi Synod (PCUS), September 4–5, 1952, 256.

101. Minutes of Mississippi Synod (PCUS), September 2, 1954, 388.

102. Minutes of Mississippi Synod (PCUS), June 5–7, 1962, 47.

103. Sam Patterson, "New Man" (sermon on 2 Cor. 5:5–17) in the *New Man* series).

104. "Too Much Heaven," words and music by Barry Gibb, Robin Gibb, and Maurice Gibb, copyright 1978 by Unicef Music, all rights administered by Unichappell Music, Inc., international copyright secured, all rights reserved, reprinted by permission of Hal Leonard Corporation.

105. Patterson, "We Are Human," 12. See Appendix E.

106. Undated comments by Ladell Flint written for FCA, French Camp Academy Museum.

107. Sam Patterson (untitled address, French Camp Academy, French Camp, MS, May 24, 1983).

108. Ibid.

109. New Christian Life Ministries, "Discipleship Ministry," http://www.newchristian.com/DiscipleshipMinistryPlan.pdf, (accessed March 1, 2010).

110. Sam Patterson, WFCA radio interview, 1985.

111. Sam Patterson (untitled address, French Camp Academy, French Camp, MS, May 24, 1983).

112. Sam Patterson (untitled address, French Camp Academy, French Camp, MS, May 24, 1983). Also Norton, "Sam Patterson," 14, French Camp Academy Museum.

113. C. S. Lewis, *Mere Christianity* (New York: Macmillan Press, 1943), 114.

114. Matthew Henry, *Commentary on the Whole Bible by Matthew Henry: Genesis to Revelation*, ed. Leslie F. Church (Grand Rapids: Zondervan, 1961), 93.

115. Sam Patterson, "Why We Become a New Creature" (sermon in the series *Nature of the New Creation*). Again, Sam was probably influenced by C. T. Studd. When the Studds married, they made this solemn promise to God: "We will never hinder one another from serving Thee." Studd told his wife, "It will be no life of ease which I offer you, but one of toil and hardship; in fact, if I did not know you to be a woman of God, I would not dream of asking you… It is to live a life of faith in God, a fighting life … I pray that we both make the same request every day to our Father, that we may give each other up to Jesus every single day of our lives to be separated or not, just as He pleases, that neither of us may ever make an idol of the other." (Grubb, *C. T. Studd: Cricketer and Pioneer*, 76, 80).

116. Sam Patterson, "Stelle" (sermon, n.d.).

117. Letter from Dr. Paul Mink at Attala Medical Clinic to Erskine Jackson, October 9, 1961, Patterson Papers, Private Collection. Mink said, "He has sustained a coronary thrombosis with myocardial infarction, and if all goes well, will remain in the hospital approximately three weeks."

118. Excerpts from Sam's letters to FCA staff and students, *FCA News* (January 1962).

119. Ibid.

120. Letter from Sam to Ewing Carruthers, October 30, 1961, Patterson Papers, Private Collection.

121. Letter from Dr. Paul Mink at Attala Medical Clinic to Erskine Jackson, October 9, 1961, Patterson Papers, Private Collection.

122. Sam Patterson, WFCA radio interview, 1985.

123. Sam Patterson, "Ramblin' Round," *French Camp Academy News* (January 1956), 2.

CHAPTER SIX
The RTS Years

1. In 1861, with the start of the Civil War, the Presbyterians in America split into what became the Southern Presbyterian Church (PCUS) and the Northern Presbyterian Church (UPC). The Northern Church became far more liberal over time; hence, the deep concern in later years that the two might reunite.

2. Henry B. Dendy, "Hath God Spoken? If So, Who Should Interpret His Word, Himself or Satan?," *Southern Presbyterian Journal*, May 1942, 4.

3. Kenneth Gentry, "RTS Ten Years Later" (Reformed Theological Seminary tenth anniversary history project, RTS/Jackson Archives, 1976), 12–13. While I always tried to use original documents as sources, I am indebted to Gentry's excellent research. I used it as a constant guide to help me navigate the history of RTS's beginnings.

4. Letter from John Richardson to Kenneth Gentry, September 30, 1976, RTS/Jackson Archives.

5. Letter dated November 30, 1948, RTS/Jackson Archives.

6. Gentry, "RTS Ten Years Later," 16, RTS/Jackson Archives.

7. For some time, Sam could have been toying with the idea of starting a seminary and following in the footsteps of well-known Bible teacher Charles Fuller. Stelle had written Sam on June 15, 1945, soon after he left for Zamboanga, "Fuller thinks he is going to be able to start a seminary next fall sponsored by the Fuller Evangelical Foundation to train evangelists for any church that will permit them to come in." Indeed, Sam saw Fuller carry through with his dream and become a co-founder in 1947 of Fuller Theological Seminary in Pasadena. In time, it became the largest multi-denominational seminary in the world.

8. Gentry, "RTS Ten Years Later," 17, RTS/Jackson Archives.

9. Minutes of Central Mississippi Presbytery (PCUS), July 19, 1962, 79–82.

10. Kenneth Foreman, "Do We Need an Infallible Bible? Some Questions About the Question," *Presbyterian Outlook,* December 24, 1962, 5.

11. John Jansen, "Do We Need An Infallible Bible? 'Show Us A Sign!,'" *Presbyterian Outlook,* December 24, 1962, 6.

12. James Gailey, " Do We Need An Infallible Bible? God is Infallible," *Presbyterian Outlook*, December 24, 1962, 5.

13. James Mays, "Do We Need An Infallible Bible? The Bible is Authoritative," *Presbyterian Outlook*, December 24, 1962, 6.

14. Sam Patterson, "Comments on the History of RTS" (undated speech at unknown location), Patterson Papers, Private Collection.

15. Letter dated December 31, 1962, "History of Origin of RTS in Letters and Documents" compiled by Sam Patterson, RTS/Jackson Archives. "History of Origin of RTS in Letters and Documents" is the only existing comprehensive collection of documents dealing with the genesis of RTS. A copy is now at the French Camp Academy Museum.

16. RTS/Jackson Archives.

17. Ibid.

18. Minutes of St. Andrew Presbytery (PCUS), January 15, 1963, 15.

19. Letter from Sam to Aiken Taylor, February 1, 1963, "History of Origin of RTS in Letters and Documents," RTS/Jackson Archives.

20. "History of Origin of RTS in Letters and Documents," RTS/Jackson Archives.

21. Letter from Sam to G. Aiken Taylor, February 1, 1963, "History of Origin of RTS in Letters and Document," RTS/Jackson Archives.

22. "History of Origin of RTS in Letters and Documents," RTS/Jackson Archives.

23. Letter dated January 21, 1963, "History of Origin of RTS in Letters and Documents," RTS/Jackson Archives.

24. This could very well have been French Camp Academy student Bill Mason (FCA '63), who graduated from RTS in 1970.

25. Letter from Sam to Aiken Taylor, February 1, 1963, "History of Origin of RTS in Letters and Documents," RTS/Jackson Archives.

26. Letter from Sam to Aiken Taylor, February 11, 1963, "History of Origin of RTS in Letters and Documents," RTS/Jackson Archives.

27. "History of Origin of RTS in Letters and Documents," RTS/Jackson Archives.

28. Sam Patterson, very early unpublished position paper concerning ideas for an institute, "History of Origin of RTS in Letters and Documents," RTS/Jackson Archives.

29. Ibid.

30. Sam Patterson, "A Practical Vision With Spiritual Ends," March 1, 1963, Patterson Papers, Private Collection. See Appendix B for full document.

31. Ibid.

32. Letter from Sam to Bishop Robert Brown, Arkansas Episcopal Diocese, April 6, 1963, Patterson Papers, Private Collection.

33. Letter from Bishop Brown to Sam, April 16, 1963, Patterson Papers, Private Collection.

34. Letter from Sam to Bishop Robert Brown, Arkansas Episcopal Diocese, April 6, 1963, Patterson Papers, Private Collection.

35. Letter from Sam to Aiken Taylor April 9, 1963, "History of Origin of RTS in Letters and Documents," RTS/Jackson Archives.

36. Letter from Aiken Taylor to Sam, April 12, 1963, "History of Origin of RTS in Letters and Documents," RTS/Jackson Archives.

37. Letter from Sam to Erskine Jackson, April 13, 1963, "History of Origin of RTS in Letters and Documents," RTS/Jackson Archives.

38. "History of Origin of RTS in Letters and Documents," RTS/Jackson Archives.

39. Letter from Sam to John Reed Miller, April 11, 1963, "History of Origin of RTS in Letters and Documents," RTS/Jackson Archives.

40. Sam Patterson (chapel introduction of Rich Cannon, Reformed Theological Seminary, Jackson, MS, April 4, 1986).

41. Gentry, "RTS Ten Years Later," 22, RTS/Jackson Archives.

42. Letter from Leonard Van Horn to Albert Freundt, March 30, 1972, Patterson Papers, Private Collection.

43. Albert Freundt, "Highlights in the History of Reformed Theological Seminary," *RTS Bulletin,* Fall 1976.

44. Sam Patterson, "Comments on the History of RTS," (undated speech at unknown location), Patterson Papers, Private Collection. Spencer, connected with the Evangelical Fellowship in 1948, was the only minister in the group who had actively sought a new seminary (Letter from James Spencer to Ken Gentry, March 28, 1977, Patterson Papers, Private Collection).

45. Ibid. Even while planning for a new seminary, Sam tried every avenue he could think of to move PCUS seminaries to a more conservative stance. In June 1963, he encouraged the session of French Camp Presbyterian Church to send Columbia Seminary a $540.00 contribution. He told them, "… If money withdrawn attracts the notice of a school (and it does), we are now in a better position to voice our convictions…. We have been willing to assume the position of an investor and can expect to be given consideration as such…. At least we have *done* something. Most never do." (Letter to French Camp Presbyterian Church Officers, July 1, 1963, Patterson Papers, Private Collection.)

46. Letter from Sam to John Reed Miller, June 4, 1963, "History of Origin of RTS in Letters and Documents," RTS/Jackson Archives.

47. Letter from Sam to John Reed Miller, June 24, 1963, "History of Origin of RTS in Letters and Documents," RTS/Jackson Archives.

48. Albert Freundt, "Journal (November 8, 1961–February 16, 1964)," entry on Thursday, June 6, 1963, Freundt Papers, property of Allene Freundt. Freundt was one of the original RTS faculty members and professor of church history for many years. He and Sam were quite close.

49. Letter from Sam to John Reed Miller, June 17, 1963, "History of Origin of RTS in Letters and Documents," RTS/Jackson Archives.

50. Letter from Sam to John Reed Miller, June 17, 1963, and letter from John Reed Miller to planning group, June 25, 1963, "History of Origin of RTS in Letters and Documents," RTS/Jackson Archives.

51. Sam Patterson, "Rather Random Report on Remarks," July 2, 1963, "History of Origin of RTS in Letters and Documents," RTS/Jackson Archives.

52. Ibid.

53. Ibid.

54. "History of Origin of RTS in Letters and Documents," RTS/Jackson Archives.

55. Letter dated July 4, 1963, "History of Origin of RTS in Letters and Documents," RTS/Jackson Archives.

56. Letter dated July 4, 1963, "History of Origin of RTS in Letters and Documents," RTS/Jackson Archives.

57. W. Norton, "Sam Patterson," (Chapter 3 of untitled and unpublished manuscript on the history of French Camp Academy), 28, French Camp Academy Museum.

58. Ibid.

59. Sam Patterson, "Comments on the History of RTS" (undated speech at unknown location), Patterson Papers, Private Collection.

60. Albert Freundt, "The History of RTS" (chapel address, Reformed Theological Seminary, Jackson, MS, November 21, 1985).

61. Letter from Sam to Henry Dendy, September 3, 1963, "History of Origin of RTS in Letters and Documents," RTS/Jackson Archives.

62. Letter from Henry Dendy to Sam, September 10, 1963, "History of Origin of RTS in Letters and Documents," RTS/Jackson Archives.

63. Letter from Sam to John Reed Miller, November 21, 1963, "History of Origin of RTS in Letters and Documents," RTS/Jackson Archives.

64. Letter from Sam to Henry Dendy, January 15, 1964, "History of Origin of RTS in Letters and Documents," RTS/Jackson Archives.

65. Letter from Sam to John Reed Miller, November 21, 1963, Patterson Papers, Private Collection.

66. Always central to Sam's desire to found a new seminary was concern to honor the truth of scripture. It remained his emphasis through all of his years at RTS. Yet, with plans to incorporate as an eventual seminary, the founders realized they must be just as concerned about theology. Hence, by January 1, the name had changed from "biblical" to "theological" institute. Sam, however, was a little slow to come around; in a February letter to the session of First Presbyterian Church in Durant, Mississippi, he refers to the school as Reformed Biblical and Theological Institute (Letter dated February 3, 1964, "History of Origin of RTS in Letters and Documents," RTS/Jackson Archives).

67. Minutes of French Camp Presbyterian Church Session, January 8, 1964, and January 26, 1964.

68. Announcement of Reformed Biblical Institute, December 25, 1963, Patterson Papers, Private Collection.

69. Ibid.

70. Ibid.

71. "History of Origin of RTS in Letters and Documents," RTS/Jackson Archives.

72. Letter from Sam to Mrs. Tom Hendrix, January 27, 1964, "History of Origin of RTS in Letters and Documents," RTS/Jackson Archives.

73. Letter from Sam to Robert Cannada, January 25, 1964, and letter from Robert Kennington to Sam, January 27, 1964, Patterson Papers, Private Collection.

74. Patterson Papers, Private Collection.

75. Letter from Henry Dendy to Sam, December 30, 1963, "History of Origin of RTS in Letters and Documents," RTS/Jackson Archives.

76. Letter from Sam to Robert Cannada, January 25, 1964, "History of Origin of RTS in Letters and Documents," RTS/Jackson Archives.

77. Letter from Sam to Erskine Wells, January 25, 1964, "History of Origin of RTS in Letters and Documents," RTS/Jackson Archives.

78. Letter from Sam to Robert Kennington, January 25, 1964, "History of Origin of RTS in Letters and Documents," RTS/Jackson Archives.

79. Ibid.

80. Letter from Robert Kennington to Sam, January 27, 1964, "History of Origin of RTS in Letters and Documents," RTS/Jackson Archives.

81. Letter dated June 8, 1964, "History of Origin of RTS in Letters and Documents," RTS/Jackson Archives.

82. Letter from Morton Smith to Robert Cannada, February 7, 1964, Patterson Papers, Private Collection.

83. Letter from Sam to First Presbyterian Church Session, Durant, Mississippi, February 3, 1964, "History of Origin of RTS in Letters and Documents," RTS/Jackson Archives.

84. Letter from Sam to Rev. William Rose, February 27, 1964, "History of Origin of RTS in Letters and Documents," RTS/Jackson Archives.

85. Minutes of RTS Founding Committee, February 17, 1964, "History of Origin of RTS in Letters and Documents," RTS/Jackson Archives.

86. Sam Patterson, "Proposed Reformed Theological Institute: Current Status, February 1964," rough notes in "History of Origin of RTS in Letters and Documents," RTS/Jackson Archives.

87. Norman Grubb, *C. T. Studd: Cricketer and Pioneer* (Fort Washington, Pennsylvania: CLC Publications, 1933), 125.

88. "History of Origin of RTS in Letters and Documents," RTS/Jackson Archives.

89. "In Conclusion," *RTI Bulletin,* April 1965. This was the first *Bulletin* published by Reformed Theological Institute.

90. Sam Patterson, "Proposed Reformed Theological Institute: Current Status, February 1964," rough notes in "History of Origin of RTS in Letters and Documents," RTS/Jackson Archives.

91. Letter from Sam to Dr. Cullen Story, February 14, 1966, Patterson Papers, Private Collection.

92. Letter from Sam to Robert Cannada, March 17, 1964, "History of Origin of RTS in Letters and Documents," RTS/Jackson Archives.

93. Letter dated February 7, 1964, Patterson Papers, Private Collection.

94. Letters from Sam to Henry Dendy and John Richardson, March 5, 1964, "History of Origin of RTS in Letters and Documents," RTS/Jackson Archives.

95. Letter from Morton Smith to Sam, March 4, 1964, "History of Origin of RTS in Letters and Documents," RTS/Jackson Archives.

96. Letter dated March 25, 1964, Patterson Papers, Private Collection.

97. Letter from Sam to Morton Smith, March 25, 1964, "History of Origin of RTS in Letters and Documents," RTS/Jackson Archives.

98. Letter from Sam and Leonard Van Horn to Morton Smith, March 25, 1964, "History of Origin of RTS in Letters and Documents," RTS/Jackson Archives.

99. Letter from Morton Smith to Sam, March 28, 1964, "History of Origin of RTS in Letters and Documents," RTS/Jackson Archives.

100. Letter from Sam to Morton Smith, June 10, 1964, "History of Origin of RTS in Letters and Documents," RTS/Jackson Archives.

101. Sam Patterson, "The History and Purpose of RTS" (message at Student Orientation, Reformed Theological Seminary, September 7, 1972).

102. Letter from Sam to Henry Dendy, May 1, 1964, Patterson Papers, Private Collection.

103. Sam Patterson, "Comments on the History of RTS" (undated speech at unknown location), Patterson Papers, Private Collection.

104. Grubb, *C. T. Studd: Cricketer and Pioneer*, 119–120, 223. Studd mocked the fearful and unbelieving, at one point writing a booklet entitled "The Laugh of Faith."

105. President's Report to the RTI Board of Trustees, January 25, 1965, Patterson Papers, Private Collection.

106. Durant Institute class registration form, Patterson Papers, Private Collection.

107. Letter from Sam to Rev. William Rose, February 27, 1964, "History of Origin of RTS in Letters and Documents," RTS/Jackson Archives.

108. Reformed Theological Institute Charter of Incorporation, "History of Origin of RTS in Letters and Documents," RTS/Jackson Archives.

109. Ibid.

110. Letter from Robert Strong to Robert Kennington, May 14, 1964, "History of Origin of RTS in Letters and Documents," RTS/Jackson Archives.

111. Letter dated April 7, 1964, "History of Origin of RTS in Letters and Documents," RTS/ Jackson Archives.

112. Minutes of Organizational Meeting of Reformed Theological Institute, April 30, 1964, RTS/Jackson Archives.

113. Ibid.

114. Ibid.

115. Letter from Sam to Henry Dendy, May 1, 1964, "History of Origin of RTS in Letters and Documents," RTS/Jackson Archives.

116. Minutes of French Camp Presbyterian Church Session, May 24, 1964, 39.

117. "Theological Institute Formed at French Camp," *Jackson Daily News* (May 5, 1964), 12.

118. Untitled 1964 RTI news release, Patterson Papers, Private Collection.

119. Letter from Sam on behalf of RTI Board of Trustees to PCUS Sessions, July 2, 1964, Patterson Papers, Private Collection.

120. Letter from Sam to Dr. Palmer Robertson, May 29, 1964, Patterson Papers, Private Collection.

121. Letter dated June 10, 1964, "History of Origin of RTS in Letters and Documents," RTS/ Jackson Archives.

122. Letter from Sam to Rev. W. A. Gamble, May 6, 1964, "History of Origin of RTS in Letters and Documents," RTS/Jackson Archives.

123. Letter from Sam to Rev. James Johnson, June 8, 1964, "History of Origin of RTS in Letters and Documents," RTS/Jackson Archives.

124. Minutes of Mississippi Synod (PCUS), June 2–4, 1964, 29.

125. Letter from Sam to Rev. James Moore, June 5, 1964, "History of Origin of RTS in Letters and Documents," RTS/Jackson Archives.

126. Letter from Sam to James Johnson, June 8, 1964, "History of Origin of RTS in Letters and Documents," RTS/Jackson Archives.

127. Letter from Sam to Robert Cannada, June 8, 1964, "History of Origin of RTS in Letters and Documents," RTS/Jackson Archives.

128. Letter dated June 9, 1964, "History of Origin of RTS in Letters and Documents," RTS/ Jackson Archives.

129. Minutes of Mississippi Synod (PCUS), June 2–4, 1964, 29, 49–50. The original resolution, which was much harsher and even called for censure of ministers involved, died in committee. Sam was very grateful to David Moore, who steered the resolution to the more sympathetic Judicial Committee rather than Bills and Overtures (Letter from Sam to David Moore, June 7, 1964, "History of Origin of RTS in Letters and Documents," RTS/Jackson Archives). Synod finally adopted only two sections of the original resolution.

130. Letter from Erskine Jackson to Sam, "History of Origin of RTS in Letters and Documents," RTS/Jackson Archives.

131. Letter from Leonard Van Horn to the RTI Board of Trustees, June 30, 1964, "History of Origin of RTS in Letters and Documents," RTS/Jackson Archives.

132. Letter dated March 30, 1972, Patterson Papers, Private Collection.

133. Letter from Sam to French Camp Academy Board of Trustees, July 16, 1964, "History of Origin of RTS in Letters and Documents," RTS/Jackson Archives.

134. Minutes of RTI Board of Trustees, July 1, 1964, and Minutes of RTI Executive Committee, December 9, 1964, Patterson Papers, Private Collection.

135. Morton Smith's Report to the RTI Board of Trustees, December 9, 1964, RTS/Jackson Archives.

136. Ibid.

137. Minutes of RTI Executive Committee, December 9, 1964, Patterson Papers, Private Collection.

138. Sam wrote several treatises on the subject of Philippians 4:19, including "God's Supply Program" and "His Method for Raising Money," Patterson Papers, Private Collection.

139. "In Conclusion," *RTI Bulletin,* April 1965.

140. Minutes of RTI Board of Trustees, September 10, 1964, Patterson Papers, Private Collection.

141. "In Conclusion," *RTI Bulletin*, April 1965.

142. Sam Patterson, "Comments on the History of RTS" (undated speech at unknown location), Patterson Papers, Private Collection.

143. Minutes of RTI Executive Committee, February 24, 1965, Patterson Papers, Private Collection.

144. Minutes of RTI Executive Committee, March 10, 1965. Williford would become a member of the executive committee on November 10, 1967.

145. Sam Patterson, "The Compassion of Christ" (sermon on Luke 7:36–50, #3 in the series *Prominent Themes from the Gospel of Luke*).

146. Minutes of RTS Board of Trustees, June 28, 1965. The name change became official on July 7.

147. Rebecca Hobbs, "Twenty Years Later—Remembering the Birth of RTS," *RTS Bulletin*, Fall 1985, 3.

148. Letter from Robert Cannada to Horace Hull July 15, 1965, outlining procedures to follow to secure donation and loan for the property, Patterson Papers, Private Collection.

149. President's Report to RTS Board of Trustees, November 15, 1965, Patterson Papers, Private Collection.

150. Ibid.

151. Ibid.

152. Norton, "Sam Patterson," 29, French Camp Academy Museum.

153. Minutes of RTS Board of Trustees, February 9, 1966, Patterson Papers, Private Collection.

154. "The First Ten Years," *RTS Bulletin*, Fall 1976.

155. Rebecca Hobbs, "Fellowship and Prayer Highlight RTS Early Years: An Interview with Morton Smith and Sam Patterson," *RTS Bulletin*, Fall 1985, 7.

156. Letter from Sam to J. Kelly Unger, Jr., June 24, 1965, "History of Origin of RTS in Letters and Documents," RTS/Jackson Archives.

157. Letter from Roy LeCraw to Erskine Wells, September 22, 1965, Patterson Papers, Private Collection.

158. Letter from Sam to Nelson Bell, August 9, 1966, Patterson Papers, Private Collection.

159. Letter from Sam to Henry Dendy, February 15, 1966, Patterson Papers, Private Collection.

160. Ibid.

161. Letter from Henry Dendy to Sam February 18, 1966, Patterson Papers, Private Collection.

162. Albert Freundt, "Historical Data on RTS Origin," 1972, 4–5.

163. Sam Patterson, unpublished notes on the beginning of RTS, Patterson Papers, Private Collection.

164. Gentry, "RTS Ten Years Later," 58–59, RTS/Jackson Archives and Albert Freundt, "Journal, April 15, 1965–October 8, 1966," entry on Wednesday, September 7, 1966, Freundt Papers.

165. Rebecca Hobbs, "Fellowship and Prayer Highlight RTS Early Years: An Interview with Morton Smith and Sam Patterson," *RTS Bulletin*, Fall 1985, 7.

166. Faculty Report to RTS Board of Trustees, June 27, 1966, RTS/Jackson Archives.

167. John R. Muether, *The First Forty Years: 1966–2006* (Jackson, MS: Reformed Theological Seminary, 2006), 33.

168. Rebecca Hobbs, "Fellowship and Prayer Highlight RTS Early Years: An Interview with Morton Smith and Sam Patterson," *RTS Bulletin*, Fall 1985, 7.

169. Patterson Papers, Private Collection.

170. Letter from Sam to Rev. E. P. Nichols, September 27, 1966, Patterson Papers, Private Collection.

171. Letter dated September 21, 1972, Patterson Papers, Private Collection.

172. Resignation letter from Sam to FCA Board of Trustees, December 27, 1966, French Camp Academy Museum. See Appendix A for full document. Sam very kindly offered in this letter to visit strong FCA supporters in Mississippi, Tennessee, and Alabama to acquaint them with the plans for Academy advancement and to assure them of his continued support of the school.

173. "Patterson Resigns," *French Camp Academy News* (January 1967), 1.

174. Minutes of French Camp Presbyterian Church Session, February 19, 1967, 75.

175. Chairman's Report to RTS Board of Trustees, January 31, 1967, Patterson Papers, Private Collection.

176. Ibid.

177. Minutes of RTS Board of Trustees, January 31, 1967, Patterson Papers, Private Collection.

178. Minutes of RTS Board of Trustees, June 27, 1967, Patterson Papers, Private Collection.

179. Ibid.

180. For more details on Sam's work with Presbyterian Evangelistic Fellowship, see Chapter Seven. Bill Hill was the only evangelist in the PCUS in 1958. For more on PEF, read Otto Whittaker's *Watchman Tell It True* (Reformed Educational Foundation, Manassas, VA, 1981).

181. Letter from Donald Graham to Robert Kennington, March 31, 1967, Patterson Papers, Private Collection.

182. Letter from Sam to Dr. Robert Jones, April 13, 1964, "History of Origin of RTS in Letters and Documents," RTS/Jackson Archives.

183. Ibid.

184. Minutes of RTS Executive Committee, May 30, 1967, Patterson Papers, Private Collection.

185. Letter from Erskine Jackson to Sam, October 12, 1967, French Camp Academy Museum.

186. Letter from Sam to Erskine Jackson, October 16, 1967, French Camp Academy Museum. With this letter, Sam enclosed a short message to Erskine and the board to be read at the FCA Board of Trustees meeting on April 25, 1967. It read, "No man ever worked for a finer board of trustees than I have. For all of you, and for you personally, I thank God."

187. Faculty Report to RTS Board of Trustees, January 21, 1969, RTS/Jackson Archives.

188. Ibid.

189. Norton, "Sam Patterson," 29–30, French Camp Academy Museum.

190. "Past Support," *RTS Bulletin*, Summer 1969.

191. Kenneth Keyes, "Meeting the Crisis in Our Church," position paper published by Concerned Presbyterians, Inc., February 1971.

192. Sam Patterson, "Statement of Sam C. Patterson," position paper on separation, May 16, 1969, Patterson Papers, Private Collection.

193. Letter from RTS Executive Committee to Sam, December 22, 1969, and RTS Executive Committee Minutes, January 11, 1970, Patterson Papers, Private Collection.

194. Letter from Sam to Joe Scharer, July 15, 1970, Patterson Papers, Private Collection.

195. Report on Committee Visit to Reformed Seminary, Minutes of Cherokee Presbytery (PCUS), October 19, 1971, 6, Patterson Papers, Private Collection. The Cherokee committee visited RTS October 5–7, 1971.

196. Letter dated June 22, 1971, Patterson Papers, Private Collection.

197. Sam Patterson, "Stelle" (sermon, n.d.). See this sermon for an in-depth look at Stelle's and Sam's deep spiritual relationship.

198. Sam Patterson, "The Sovereignty of God" (sermon #1 in the series *Sovereignty of God*).

199. Letter dated July 20, 1971, Patterson Papers, Private Collection.

200. Sam Patterson, "The Sovereignty of God" (sermon #1 in the series *Sovereignty of God*).

201. Minutes of RTS Executive Committee, November 30, 1971, Patterson Papers, Private Collection.

202. John R. de Witt, "Crisis in the Southern Presbyterian Church, Part 1," *The Standard Bearer,* January 15, 1972, 176–179.

203. Sam Patterson, "An Evangelical Alternative in the PCUS," June 30, 1972, Patterson Papers, Private Collection.

204. Undated letter from Sam to Billy Thompson, Patterson Papers, Private Collection.

205. Sam Patterson, "A Paper Seeking a Biblical Basis for the Conduct of Believers Who Are In An Erring Church," 1972, Patterson Papers, Private Collection. See Appendix C for full document.

206. Ibid.

207. "Patterson Says His Presence Did Not Indicate His Endorsement," *Clarion Ledger* (October 16, 1972), 12.

208. Sam Patterson, "Statement of Sam C. Patterson," position paper on separation, May 16, 1969, Patterson Papers, Private Collection.

209. Letter from Sam to Grady Oates, February 13, 1978, Patterson Papers, Private Collection.

210. Letter from Sam to Bud Jones (a West Virginia man Sam led to the Lord), December 17, 1974, Patterson Papers, Private Collection.

211. Letter from Sam to Rev. William Smith, September 13, 1973, Patterson Papers, Private Collection.

212. Minutes of St. Andrew Presbytery (PCUS), Adjourned Meeting, August 31, 1973, 35–37.

213. Letter from Sam to Leonard Bullock, February 14, 1974, Patterson Papers, Private Collection.

214. Letter from Sam to Mrs. Henry Grube, April 5, 1974, Patterson Papers, Private Collection.

215. Letter from Sam to Bud Jones, December 17, 1974, Patterson Papers, Private Collection.

216. "New Department of Christian Education," *RTS Bulletin,* Fall 1976.

217. Letter dated February 24, 1972, Patterson Papers, Private Collection.

218. Letter from Rev. John Newton to Sam, October 15, 1971, Patterson Papers, Private Collection.

219. Letter dated January 31, 1974, Patterson Papers, Private Collection.

220. Letter dated October 21, 1974, Patterson Papers, Private Collection.

221. Sam Patterson, "We Are Human" (French Camp, MS: French Camp Academy, n.d.), 13. See Appendix E.

222. Ibid., 7.

223. Letter from Sam to Carlos and Betsy Smith, October 1976, Patterson Papers, Private Collection.

224. Sam Patterson, "Why Do the Guilty Prosper?" (sermon #2 in the series *Sovereignty of God*).

225. Sam Patterson, "Passing It On," *RTS Bulletin*, Summer 1977. Michael Green, in his *1500 Illustrations for Biblical Preaching* (Baker, 1989, 388), offers the following story of this quotation's genesis: "… Murray was suffering terrible pain in his back one morning. While he was eating breakfast, his hostess told him of a lady downstairs who was in great trouble, and she asked his advice for her. Murray handed her a piece of paper on which he had been writing and said, 'Give her this advice I have written for myself; it may be that she will find it helpful.'"

226. Letter from Sam to Second Presbyterian Church elder Robert Metcalf, December 19, 1975, Patterson Papers, Private Collection.

227. The title of this message is lost to time. Montreat Presbyterian Historical Center located the tape containing the address, only to find it had accidentally been erased.

228. Minutes of RTS Board of Trustees, March 19, 1975, Patterson Papers, Private Collection.

229. Letter from Sam to Rev. John Gess, October 5, 1976, Patterson Papers, Private Collection.

230. Sam Patterson, "Christian Teachers and Spiritual Growth," (undated sermon).

231. Letter dated November 19, 1971, Patterson Papers, Private Collection.

232. Letter dated March 4, 1976, Patterson Papers, Private Collection.

233. Patterson Papers, Private Collection.

234. Letter from Sam to Rev. Thomas Patete, Patterson Papers, Private Collection.

235. Letter dated March 24, 1977, Patterson Papers, Private Collection.

236. Letter from Sam to J. W. Hassell, April 13, 1977, Patterson Papers, Private Collection.

237. Letter from Sam to Rev. Fred Zitzmann, April 14, 1977, Patterson Papers, Private Collection.

238. President's Report to RTS Board of Trustees, September 5, 1975, Patterson Papers, Private Collection.

239. Sam Patterson, "My Concerns Regarding Reformed Theological Seminary" (address to RTS Executive Committee, Jackson, MS, December 13, 1977), Patterson Papers, Private Collection.

240. Ibid.

241. Ibid.

242. Sam Patterson (chapel message on John 17 , Reformed Theological Seminary, Jackson, MS, April 13, 1978).

243. Minutes of RTS Faculty, May 22, 1978, RTS/Jackson Archives.

244. Denominational Involvement Policy Statement adopted by RTS Board of Trustees, September 15, 1972, Patterson Papers, Private Collection.

245. Art Toalston, "RTS President Resigns for New Job," *Jackson Daily News* (July 29, 1978), 1.

246. Sam Patterson, "Complaint, Concerns, Recommendations" (address to RTS Executive Committee, Jackson, MS, May 23, 1980), Patterson Papers, Private Collection.

247. Letter from Sam to RTS Executive Committee, April 11, 1978, contained in Minutes of RTS Executive Committee, April 13, 1978, Patterson Papers, Private Collection.

248. Ibid.

249. Letter from Sam to Christy Morgan, April 17, 1979, Patterson Papers, Private Collection.

250. Luder Whitlock, "Sam Patterson Honored," *RTS Bulletin,* Summer 1979.

251. Norton, "Sam Patterson," 30–31, French Camp Academy Museum.

252. Sam Patterson (chapel message on John 17, Reformed Theological Seminary, Jackson, MS, April 13, 1978).

CHAPTER SEVEN
The Evangelist

1. Sam Patterson, "Object of Saving Faith" (sermon on John 1, #1 in the series *Saving Faith*).

2. Simon Kistemaker, *Exposition of Revelation, New Testament Commentary* (Grand Rapids: Baker, 2001), 316–317.

3. Sam Patterson, "How to Preach" (chapel message on Galatians 2:15, Reformed Theological Seminary, Jackson, MS, April 26, 1977).

4. Sam Patterson, "New Purpose, Center, and Commitment in Christ" (sermon #3 in the series *A Time to Renew*).

5. Letter from Lou Ann Webb to Sam, October 5, 1976, Patterson Papers, Private Collection.

6. Letter from Sam to Lou Ann Webb, October 7, 1976, Patterson Papers, Private Collection.

7. Sam Patterson, "Death of a Believer" (sermon in a series on election).

8. "The Chicken Problem," notes made at Fountain Lake in Hot Springs, Arkansas, August 15, 1947, Patterson Papers, Private Collection.

9. Sam Patterson, "Source of Saving Faith" (sermon on John 6:37, 44, #4 in the series *Saving Faith*).

10. Letter from Sam to Rev. Jacob Uitvlugt, January 10, 1978, Patterson Papers, Private Collection.

11. Sam Patterson, "Ministers' Model and Evangelists' Example" (sermon #1 in the series *Prominent Themes from the Gospel of Luke*).

12. Sam Patterson, "Turning Over Problems" (sermon on Psalm 37).

13. Sam Patterson, "Stelle" (sermon, n.d.).

14. Sam Patterson, "Ministers' Model and Evangelists' Example" (sermon #1 in the series *Prominent Themes from the Gospel of Luke*).

15. J. I. Packer, *Rediscovering Holiness* (Ann Arbor, Michigan: Servant Publications, 1992), 121.

16. Sam Patterson, "The Gift of the Savior" (sermon on John 6:37, #2 in the series *Savior*).

17. Sam Patterson, "How to Preach" (chapel message on Galatians 2:15, Reformed Theological Seminary, Jackson, MS, April 26, 1977) and Sam Patterson, "Relationship of Prayer to Evangelism" (sermon #1 in a 3-part prayer series).

18. Sam Patterson, "Radically New, Right Now, Never Ending" (sermon on 2 Cor. 5:15–17, #1 in the series *A Time to Renew*).

19. Sam Patterson, "The Joy of the Disciples" (sermon on Luke 24:44–51, #7 in the series *Prominent Themes from the Gospel of Luke*).

20. Sam Patterson, "Characteristics of Genuine Conversion" (sermon on Colossians 1) and Sam Patterson, "Source of Saving Faith" (sermon on John 3:1–16, #3 in the series *Saving Faith*).

21. Letter from Sam to Bud Jones, November 3, 1970, Patterson Papers, Private Collection.

22. Letter from Sam to Judy Phagan, December 11, 1970, Patterson Papers, Private Collection.

23. Letter from Sam to Marion Phagan, March 26, 1970, Patterson Papers, Private Collection.

24. Letter from Mrs. Dewey Stinson to Sam, June 2, 1970, Patterson Papers, Private Collection.

25. Letter from Rev. George Duke to Sam, May 17, 1970, Patterson Papers, Private Collection.

26. Letter from Sam to Dick and Fran Harris, November 16, 1978, Patterson Papers, Private Collection.

27. Letter from Sam to Robert Newton, October 23, 1973, Patterson Papers, Private Collection.

28. Letter from Mr. and Mrs. F. M. Flewellen to Sam, February 4, 1969, Patterson Papers, Private Collection.

29. Letter from Kate and William Rogers to Sam, August 4, 1969, Patterson Papers, Private Collection.

30. Letter from Rev. Roy Flannagan, Jr. to Sam, June 23, 1976, Patterson Papers, Private Collection.

31. Sam Patterson, (children's sermon, Leland Presbyterian Church, Leland, MS, March 8, 1987).

32. Sam Patterson, "New Man" (sermon on 2 Cor. 5:5–17).

33. Letter from Sam to Melanie Underwood, June 21, 1972, Patterson Papers, Private Collection.

34. Sam Patterson (talk to youth group, First Presbyterian Church, Jackson, MS, n.d.).

35. Letter from Sam to Ralph Newman, August 8, 1974, Patterson Papers, Private Collection.

36. Sam Patterson, "The Gift of the Savior" (sermon on John 2 and 3, #1 in the series *Savior*).

37. Letter from Sam to William Robfogel, April 2, 1975, Patterson Papers, Private Collection.

38. Letter from Sam to Mr. and Mrs. Leon Webb, June 16, 1976, Patterson Papers, Private Collection.

39. Letter from Sam to Rev. and Mrs. John Ragland, December 10, 1975, Patterson Papers, Private Collection.

40. Letter from Sam to Rev. George Kirker, May 29, 1973, Patterson Papers, Private Collection.

41. Letter from Sam to Jim Patterson, November 29, 1968, Patterson Papers, Private Collection.

42. Presbyterian Evangelistic Fellowship evaluation report, September 25, 1970, Patterson Papers, Private Collection.

43. Letter from Sam to Jim Patterson, November 29, 1968, Patterson Papers, Private Collection.

44. Letter from Sam to Rev. Stephen Irby, May 17, 1973, Patterson Papers, Private Collection.

45. Letter from Sam to Jack Powell, May 20, 1970, Patterson Papers, Private Collection.

46. Letter from Sam to Jack Morrone, March 3, 1970, Patterson Papers, Private Collection.

47. Letter from Sam to Carol Morrone, March 3, 1970, Patterson Papers, Private Collection.

48. Letter from H. C. to Sam, March 23, 1970, Patterson Papers, Private Collection.

49. Letter from George Kessler to Sam, February 21, 1986, Patterson Papers, Private Collection.

50. Letter from Stephen Irby to Sam, November 17, 1982, Patterson Papers, Private Collection.

51. Letter from Bill Rose to Sam, December 17, 1970, Patterson Papers, Private Collection.

52. Letter from Jack Bushman to Sam, April 10, 1986, Patterson Papers, Private Collection.

53. Sam Patterson, "The Results of Rebirth in a Rich Man" (sermon #5 in the series *Prominent Themes from the Gospel of Luke*).

54. Letter from Bud Jones to Buck Mosal, April 5, 1973, Patterson Papers, Private Collection.

55. Letters from Bud Jones to Sam, May 29, 1974 and February 1, 1971, Patterson Papers, Private Collection.

56. This entire account of the Jones's conversions was compiled from information in Sam's sermon "The Results of Rebirth in a Rich Man" (sermon #5 in the series *Prominent Themes from the Gospel of Luke*), plus correspondence between Sam Patterson and Bud Jones from1969–1977.

57. Letter from Bud Jones to Sam, February 27, 1975, Patterson Papers, Private Collection.

58. Letters from Bud Jones to Sam, September 6, 1969, and March 8, 1970, Patterson Papers, Private Collection.

59. Letter from Sam to Bud Jones, June 22, 1972, Patterson Papers, Private Collection.

60. Letter from Sam to Bud Jones, June 25, 1973, Patterson Papers, Private Collection.

61. Letter from Sam to Bud Jones, October 21, 1974, Patterson Papers, Private Collection.

62. Letter from Sam to Bud Jones, December 17, 1974, Patterson Papers, Private Collection.

63. Letter from Bud Jones to Sam, July 17, 1975, Patterson Papers, Private Collection.

64. Letter from Sam to Bud Jones, August 16, 1977, Patterson Papers, Private Collection.

65. Letter from Iain Murray to Sam, October 21, 1975, Patterson Papers, Private Collection.

66. Minutes of RTS Executive Committee, October 31, 1975, Patterson Papers, Private Collection.

67. Letter from Sam to Ellen and Ed (no last name), March 22, 1976, Patterson Papers, Private Collection.

68. Letter from A. R. Dallison (Secretary of The Reformed Fraternal within the Church of Scotland) to Sam, March 15, 1976, Patterson Papers, Private Collection.

69. Letter from Sam to Dr. and Mrs. Murdoch Murchison, April 8, 1976, Patterson Papers, Private Collection.

70. Sam Patterson, "Distinguishing Characteristics of Genuine Conversion" (sermon on Colossians 1).

71. *St. George's News*, May/June, 1976, 5.

72. Letter from E. H. Paddon (Secretary of Westminster Chapel) to Sam, November 14, 1975, Patterson Papers, Private Collection.

73. Sam Patterson, "Discipleship Described" (sermon on Luke 6:46–47, #2 in the series *Prominent Themes from the Gospel of Luke*).

74. Sam Patterson, "It Is All of God" (sermon #4 in the series *Nature of the New Creation*).

75. Sam Patterson, "Ministers' Model and Evangelists' Example" (sermon #1 in the series *Prominent Themes from the Gospel of Luke*).

76. Sam Patterson, "God's Vehicles in Evangelism" (sermon #6 in the series *Evangelism*).

77. Sam Patterson, "The Disciples and Possessions" (sermon on Luke 12:14, 33, 29, 31, #4 in the series *Prominent Themes from the Gospel of Luke*).

78. Sam Patterson, "It Is All of God" (sermon #4 in the series *Nature of the New Creation*).

79. Sam Patterson, "The Gift of the Savior" (sermon on John 6:37, #2 in the series *Savior*) and Sam Patterson, "Sources of Saving Faith" (sermon on John 3:1–16, #3 in the series *Saving Faith*).

80. Sam Patterson, "The Gift of the Savior" (sermon on John 6:37, #2 in the series *Savior*).

81. Ibid.

82. Sam Patterson, "Ye Are My Witnesses" (sermon on Acts 1:8, #1 in a two-part series, Kate Anderson Chapel, Martinsville, VA, June 18, 1941).

83. Sam Patterson, "It Is All of God" (sermon #4 in the series *Nature of the New Creation*).

84. Sam Patterson, "Forming A Personal Testimony" (chapel message, Reformed Theological Seminary, Jackson, MS, December 13, 1977).

85. Ibid. While this is a direct quote from that sermon, this entire section on Sam's views of the three types of testimony was drawn from the same sermon, unless otherwise noted.

86. Sam Patterson, "The Source of Our Salvation" (sermon #4 in the series *A Time to Renew*).

87. Sam Patterson, "Reformation of Evangelism" (sermon, Christian Studies Center Summer Institute, 1973).

88. Sam Patterson, "Ambassadors for Christ" (sermon on 2 Cor. 5, #3 in the series *Evangelism*).

89. Sam Patterson, "The Command: Make Disciples" (sermon on Matthew 28:16–20).

90. Sam Patterson, (sermon on John 10:1, #5 in the series *Election*).

91. Sam Patterson, "God's Vehicles in Evangelism" (sermon #6 in the series *Evangelism*).

92. Sam Patterson, "The Command: Make Disciples" (sermon on Matthew 28:16–20).

93. Norman Grubb, *C. T. Studd: Cricketer and Pioneer* (Fort Washington, Pennsylvania: CLC Publications, 1933), 92.

94. Sam Patterson, "What is the Work of the Lord?" (sermon on 1 Cor. 15:58, #2 in the series *Evangelism*).

95. Sam Patterson, "Scope and Supplication of Salvation" (sermon #7 in the series *A Time to Renew*).

96. Sam Patterson, "The Command: Make Disciples" (sermon on Matthew 28:16–20).

97. Sam Patterson, "Radically New, Right Now, Never Ending" (sermon on 2 Cor. 5:15–17, #1 in the series *A Time to Renew*).

98. Sam Patterson, "The Command: Make Disciples" (sermon on Matthew 28:16–20).

99. Sam Patterson, "School of Prayer" (sermon on John 17:1–11).

100. Sam Patterson, "The Command: Make Disciples" (sermon on Matthew 28:16–20).

101. Sam Patterson, "Relationship of Prayer to Evangelism" (sermon #1 in a 3-part prayer series).

102. Sam Patterson, "How to Get a Revival" (sermon on 2 Kings 3:16, Kate Anderson Chapel, Martinsville, VA, October 10, 1941). Sam often used Old Testament passages for evangelistic services. In this passage, God told the Israelites they must dig ditches in dry soil to prove their faith before God would send them rain. Sam likened this to the modern church's digging ditches of genuine personal concern over the lost in the community; personal invitation; personal work; and personal prayer before seeing revival.

103. Sam Patterson, "School of Prayer" (sermon on John 17:1–11).

104. Sam Patterson, "Ambassadors for Christ" (sermon on 2 Cor. 5, #3 in the series *Evangelism*).

105. Letter from Sam to Becky Rogers, December 22, 1961, Patterson Papers, Private Collection. See Appendix E.

106. Sam Patterson, (sermon on John 10:1, #5 in the series *Election*).

107. Sam Patterson, "Ye Shall Be Witnesses" (sermon on Acts 1:8, #4 in the series *Evangelism*).

108. Sam Patterson, "Relationship of Prayer to Evangelism" (sermon #1 in a 3-part prayer series).

109. Ibid.

110. Sam Patterson, "How Do We Give to the Great Commission?" (sermon, Northpark Presbyterian Church, Jackson, MS, January 26, 1980).

111. Ibid.

112. Sam Patterson, (sermon on Colossians 1).

113. Sam Patterson, "New Man" (sermon on 2 Cor. 5:5–17).

CHAPTER EIGHT
The Prayer Warrior

1. Sam Patterson, (chapel message, RTS Day of Prayer, Reformed Theological Seminary, Jackson, MS, January 10, 1979).

2. Ibid.

3. Ibid.

4. Sam Patterson, "Turning Over Problems" (chapel message on Psalm 37, Reformed Theological Seminary, Jackson, MS, October 2, 1977). This entire section is a summary of the sermon.

5. Ibid.

6. Samuel Gordon, *Quiet Talks on Prayer* (Middlesex, England: Echo Library, 2007), 67.

7. Sam Patterson, (chapel message, RTS Day of Prayer, Reformed Theological Seminary, Jackson, MS, January 10, 1979).

8. Ibid.

9. Sam Patterson, "The Lord's Prayer (Part IV)" (chapel message, Reformed Theological Seminary, Jackson, MS, March 29, 1977).

10. Undated letter from Sam to RTS supporters, Patterson Papers, Private Collection.

11. Sam Patterson (address, Reformed Theological Seminary Senior Banquet, Jackson, MS, May 10, 1979).

12. Reproduced by permission of B. McCall Barbour, 28 George IV Bridge, Edinburgh, Scotland.

13. Sam Patterson, "The Lord's Prayer (Part VI)" (chapel message, Reformed Theological Seminary, Jackson, MS, April 22, 1977).

14. Sam Patterson, "Relationship of Prayer to Evangelism" (sermon on Matthew 28, #1 in a 1976 series on prayer).

15. Letter from Sam to Jane Allen, January 4, 1972, Patterson Papers, Private Collection.

16. Letter from Sam to Mrs. Kenneth Cole, February 6, 1975, Patterson Papers, Private Collection.

17. Letter from Sam to Mrs. Henry Grube, April 5, 1974, Patterson Papers, Private Collection.

18. Sam Patterson, "Relationship of Prayer to Evangelism" (sermon on Matthew 28, #1 in a 1976 series on prayer).

19. Letter from Sam to Gary Lane, January 12, 1970, Patterson Papers, Private Collection.

20. Letter from Sam to Arthur Worley, November 23, 1971, Patterson Papers, Private Collection.

21. Letter from Sam to Jim Atkins, November 8, 1978, Patterson Papers, Private Collection.

22. Letter from Sam to Sabra (no last name), March 4, 1983, Patterson Papers, Private Collection.

23. Letter from Sam to George Kaulbach, November 25, 1974, Patterson Papers, Private Collection.

24. Letter from Sam to Mrs. J. L. Hatcher, April 3, 1972, Patterson Papers, Private Collection.

25. Letter from Larry and Delores Sloan to Sam, July 27, 1979, Patterson Papers, Private Collection.

26. Sam Patterson, (sermon #1 in the series *The Lord's Instructions on Prayer*).

27. Albert Simpson Reitz (words and music), "Teach Me to Pray, Lord," *Broadman Hymnal* (Nashville: Broadman Press, 1940), 377.

28. Sam Patterson, (sermon #1 in the series *The Lord's Instructions on Prayer*).

29. Sam Patterson, (chapel message, RTS Day of Prayer, Reformed Theological Seminary, Jackson, MS, January 10, 1979).

30. Ibid.

31. Information in this section on Jack, the atheist, was taken from both Sam's chapel message at RTS/Jackson's Day of Prayer, January 10, 1979, and "The Master Is Come and Calleth for You" (sermon #2 in a series on John 11, Kate Anderson Chapel, Martinsville, VA, n.d.). Sam might not have known how to deal with an atheist early in his ministry, but the Lord certainly taught him how. In 1961, his daughter Becky asked how to respond to unbelievers whom she had met in college. While recuperating from a heart attack in Florida, Sam composed a thirty-six page handwritten letter answering her question and outlining in detail his thoughts on evangelism. See Appendix E for the entire document.

32. Sam Patterson, (chapel message, RTS Day of Prayer, Reformed Theological Seminary, Jackson, MS, January 10, 1979).

CHAPTER NINE
The Retirement Years

1. John R. Muether, *The First Forty Years: 1966–2006* (Jackson, MS: Reformed Theological Seminary, 2006), 45–46.

2. Sam Patterson, WFCA radio interview, 1985.

3. Minutes of St. Andrew Presbytery (PCUS), April 29–30, 1979, 9.

4. Minutes of St. Andrew Presbytery (PCUS), May 3–4, 1981, 41.

5. Letters from Sam to RTS supporters in the Dallas-Ft. Worth area, September 13, 1979, Patterson Papers, Private Collection.

6.   When Becky and Jimmy returned to French Camp while Sam and Stelle were in Jackson, Sam gave them the FCA home for their family. When Stelle died in 1971, Sam moved Stelle's mother, Mrs. Sellers, back to French Camp immediately and gave her the trailer that the three of them had used in Jackson. She lived there until her death.

7.   Norman Grubb, *C. T. Studd: Cricketer and Pioneer* (Fort Washington, Pennsylvania: CLC Publications, 1933), 189.

8.   When Sam retired from the RTS presidency, he gave Odell Fish (RTS '77) almost all of his theological library. Odell did not have a college degree and had received a Diploma Master of Divinity degree from RTS.

9.   Grubb, *C. T. Studd: Cricketer and Pioneer*, 189.

10.   Letter dated April 17, 1979, Patterson Papers, Private Collection.

11.   Combination of letters to Sam from Emma Scroggins, June 22, 1984, and December 9, 1984, Patterson Papers, Private Collection.

12.   Letter from Allan Merritt to Sam November 7, 1979, Patterson Papers, Private Collection. Merritt was then an editor with the *St. Louis Globe-Democrat*.

13.   Letter from Emma Scroggins to Sam, January 8, 1986, Patterson Papers, Private Collection.

14.   Sam Patterson, "The Command: Make Disciples" (sermon on Matt. 28:16–20).

15.   In his single-minded determination to go, Sam was likely influenced by veteran missionary C. T. Studd, whom he so admired. When Studd felt God calling him to Africa, he was fifty years old, penniless, and had been in ill health for fifteen years. Everyone advised against it, and Studd could not find any funding for the trip. Nevertheless, he decided to trust God, saying, "God has called me to go, and I will go. I will blaze the trail, though my grave may only become a stepping stone that younger men may follow." [Norman Grubb, *C. T. Studd: Cricketer and Pioneer* (Fort Washington, Pennsylvania: CLC Publications, 1933), 111–112.]

16.   Letter from Jack Chinchen to Sam, May 21, 1981, quoting an African Bible College prayer letter with highlights of Sam's comments to the board, Patterson Papers, Private Collection.

17.   Letter from Bob Cockerell to Sam, September 23, 1981, Patterson Papers, Private Collection.

18.   Letters from Talleyrand Saydee to Sam dated October 2, 1981, and August 29, 1986, Patterson Papers, Private Collection.

19.   Letter from Bob Cockerell to Sam, September 23, 1981, Patterson Papers, Private Collection.

20.   Letter from Jack Chinchen to Sam, August 21, 1981, Patterson Papers, Private Collection.

21.   Letter from Samuel Dennis to Sam, October 16, 1981, Patterson Papers, Private Collection.

22.   Letter from James Saydee to Sam, October 24, 1986, Patterson Papers, Private Collection.

23.   *This Week in the PCUS*, January 31, 1983, 2.

24.   Letter dated September 10, 1982, Patterson Papers, Private Collection.

25.   Letter dated October 11, 1982, Patterson Papers, Private Collection.

26.   Letter from Sam to John McRae and Victor Smith, September 21, 1982, Patterson Papers, Private Collection.

27.   Sam Patterson, "The Disciples and Possessions" (sermon on Luke 12:14, 29, 31, 33, # 4 in the series *Prominent Themes from the Gospel of Luke*).

28.   Letter from Jack Chinchen to Sam, March 16, 1983, Patterson Papers, Private Collection.

29.   Letter from Sam to French Camp Presbyterian Church Session and Diaconate, January 6, 1984.

30.   Minutes of French Camp Presbyterian Church Diaconate, February 7, 1984.

31.   Minutes of FCA Executive Committee, April 9, 1985.

32.   Minutes of RTS Executive Committee, November 6, 1986.

33.   Richard de Witt, "A Great Presbyterian Dies," *French Camp Today*, April 1987, 3.

34.   Letter from Donald Patterson to Ed Williford, March 17, 1987, Patterson Papers, Private Collection.

35. Memo from Rich Cannon to friends of French Camp Academy, March 25, 1987, Patterson Papers, Private Collection.

36. "Recollections of a Kind Man Continue to Be Shared," *French Camp Today,* April 1987, 7.

37. Ann Aldridge, "We Were Blessed to Have Been Part of His Life," *French Camp Today,* April 1987, 7.

38. See Appendix D for full resolution.

39. Minutes of St. Andrew Presbytery, Spring 1987, 93–94. See Appendix D for full tribute.

40. Nancy Green, "Church Dedication Set in Memory of 'Mr. Pat,'" *The Kosciusko Star-Herald* (November 16, 1989), Section B, 1.

41. French Camp Presbyterian Church Dedication Service, videotaped by Jack Johnson, November 19, 1989.

42. Ibid.

43. Ibid.

44. Leon Loard, who was eighty-three when he died in 2006, was a well-known portrait artist in Alabama. He was about sixty-nine when Lewis Graeber commissioned him to paint Sam. The son of a Montgomery grocer, Loard spent his childhood sacking and delivering groceries. In 1947 he began selling portraits door to door for $1.95 each. He didn't have a studio, so he developed his film in his bathtub. Soon he launched into oil painting, where he would ultimately become famous. The company he created has painted justices, governors, and business leaders.

45. J. I. Packer, *Rediscovering Holiness,* (Ann Arbor, Michigan: Servant Publications, 1992), 26.

46. Ibid., 27.

47. Ibid., 28.

48. Letter from Sam to Nellie McPherson, December 11, 1970, Patterson Papers, Private Collection.

49. Rev. Johnson Oatman, Jr. (words) and Charles H. Gabriel (music), "Higher Ground," in *Great Revival Hymns,* (Chicago: Rodeheaver Co. Publishers, 1911), 303.

50. Letter dated February 2, 1975.

51. Sam Patterson, "The Disciples and Possessions" (sermon on Luke 12:14, 29, 31, 33, #4 in the series *Prominent Themes from the Gospel of Luke*).

G

H

I

J

K

$\mathcal{T}$

$\mathcal{U}$